Books are to be returned on or before
the last date below.

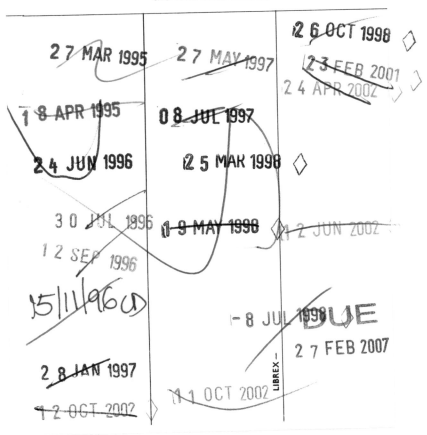

MODERN ENGINEERING ECONOMY

DONOVAN YOUNG

Georgia Institute of Technology

JOHN WILEY & SONS, INC.

New York • Chichester • Brisbane • Toronto • Singapore

ACQUISITIONS EDITOR   Charity Robey
MARKETING MANAGER   Susan Elbe
PRODUCTION SUPERVISOR   Sandra Russell
DESIGNER   David Levy
MANUFACTURING MANAGER   Andrea Price
COPY EDITING SUPERVISOR   Richard Blander
PHOTO RESEARCHER   Lisa Passmore
ILLUSTRATION COORDINATOR   Jaime Perea

PHOTO CREDITS

Chapter 1 Opener: Jerry Ohlinger's Movie Material Store
Chapter 2 Opener: Culver Pictures
Chapter 3 Opener: The Bettmann Archive
Chapter 4 Opener: C.V.S. Roosevelt Collection
Chapter 5 Opener: Photofest
Chapter 6 Opener: International Museum of Photography at George Eastman House
Chapter 7 Opener: H. J. K. Historical Library
Chapter 9 Opener: Peter Lerman
Chapter 10 Opener: FPG International
Chapter 11 Opener: UPI/Bettmann

This book was set in 10/12 Baskerville by York Graphic Services, Inc. and printed and bound by Hamilton Printing. The cover was printed by Phoenix.

Recognizing the importance of preserving what has been written, it is a policy of John Wiley & Sons, Inc. to have books of enduring value published in the United States printed on acid-free paper, and we exert our best efforts to that end.

Library of Congress Cataloging in Publication Data:

Young, D. (Donovan). 1936–
    Modern engineering economy / Donovan Young.
    Includes index.
    ISBN 0-471-54260-1
    1. Engineering economy. I. Title.
TA177.4.Y68   1992
658.15–dc20   92-27307
                                                 CIP

Printed in the United States of America

10 9 8 7 6 5 4 3 2 1

To my Becky

PREFACE

. . . .

MODERN ENGINEERING ECONOMY presents mathematical techniques and practical advice for evaluating decisions in the design and operation of engineering systems. Engineering economy calculations support both selection and justification of design alternatives, operating policies, and capital expenditures.

I assume that the reader, who is at least a junior-level engineering student comfortable with calculus, aims to acquire both an easy facility and a depth of insight in engineering economic analysis.

This book started when I first began teaching engineering economy to well-prepared students at the University of Texas at Austin and realized how hidebound the standard pedagogy had become. The students were brighter than the course. Students at Texas, and later at Georgia Tech, kept reinforcing my conviction that sounder, more compact, more elegant methods make learning easier and foster deeper understanding and sharper intuition for engineering decision making.

After years of building up course notes to enrich and clarify my engineering economy courses, I was given an opportunity to design a new course from the ground up for the fledgling Department of Systems Engineering at the United States Military Academy at West Point, New York. I prepared 40 sets of daily lesson materials, several design exercises, numerous homework assignments, exams, and short quizzes, all carefully coordinated to be taught by up to 20 instructors at the same time, and the result was the nucleus of this book.

One of my aims was to close the gap between what has traditionally been taught in school and what engineers ought to use on the job. This involves not only catching up with industry's best practices, but also unifying and simplifying. For instance, why teach present worth and annual worth as if they were distinct methods? Why not recognize that the annual-equivalent, common-life, and infinite-horizon ways of comparing alternatives with unequal lives are all the same? Why wade through a depreciation accounting procedure to make an after-tax decision instead of simply correcting capital expenditures for their depreciation efficiency? Why pretend, in school, that such simple measures as payback time are not useful, or fail to have a sound theoretical basis? Why ignore risk, inflation, continuous cash flows, and geometric trends? Why teach yourself (or grudgingly do without) what textbooks don't teach about risk, liquidity, inflation, and taxes?

Why not use hand calculators or spreadsheet programs or computer programs, rather than look up compound-interest factors from the back of an old-fashioned textbook? MODWORTH, a software diskette, is available from the publisher and is free to professors who adopt the book for use in their course. It is an interactive program that allows the user to specify or retrieve cash-flow sets and perform any of the calculations in this book on them.

Although the book is encyclopedic in most aspects of engineering economy, it retains all the teaching convenience of its daily-lesson precursor if the instructor uses or tailors a Course Calendar from the detailed course plans and variations given in the *Instructor Manual* (available to adopters from the publisher). For every class session, whether of 1-hour or 1½-hour nominal length, the plans give a detailed reading assignment, a list of the primary example problems to be covered by the instructor during the lesson, a list of secondary example problems on the same topic, and a list of end-of-chapter exercises pertaining to the lesson.

The wide variety of detailed course plans in the *Instructor Manual* is especially valuable for brisk-paced courses with broad coverage requirements. When there is no time to slow down for the full depth of each topic, the daily lesson plans guide the instructor quickly past the inessentials. The plans are also useful to ensure that inappropriate readings, examples, or exercises do not creep in for an instructor who has decided, for example, to omit continuous cash flows.

Where depth is more valued than breadth, the coverage can be more conventionally organized around whole chapters. Chapters 1, 2, 3, 4, and 5 constitute a core course, including some breakeven and sensitivity analysis and after-tax analysis. Chapter 6 (Leverage and Capital Budgeting) is optional in a first course. Chapter 7 (Public-Sector Decision Making) is also optional. Chapter 8 (Risk and Uncertainty) can be omitted, although its first section (Breakeven and Sensitivity Analysis) is highly recommended; this chapter does not assume any probability and statistics background. Chapter 9 (Probabilistic Decision Making) does assume a probability and statistics background; its material is somewhat advanced. Chapter 10 (Taxes, Depreciation, and Incentives) is a complete, modern treatment of its subject; some instructors may find the after-tax analysis at the end of Chapter 5 adequate, with perhaps some references to specific formulas or depreciation tables from Chapter 10. Chapter 11 (Design Exercises) provides integrated problems requiring at least three or four hours of student effort to solve and having some open-endedness.

In a junior-level three-credit semester course or a five-credit quarter course, appropriate coverage would be the first five chapters and two of the remaining chapters selected according to the emphasis desired by the instructor; for example, Chapters 6 and 10 provide a financial emphasis, Chapters 7 and 8 are appropriate for civil engineers, and Chapters 8 and 9 provide a probabilistic emphasis.

The book could also be used for a two-course sequence, with the second course at senior or beginning graduate level.

The chapters themselves have an innovative structure. Interspersed with the expository material are many solved illustrative example problems, at least one for every major concept. There are 78 of these, for example, in Chapters 4 and 5. They are stated in boldface type and solved in lightface type. Everything can be learned by logical argument and reinforced by example, or learned by example and clarified by logical argument, whichever suits the individual instructor or student best. Then there are exercises at the end of each chapter, at least two for every major concept. There are 71 exercises, for instance, at the end of Chapter 5. Bottom-line answers to half of them are given in the back of the book; full solutions to all of them are in the accompanying *Instructor Manual*.

Besides daily lesson plans, the *Instructor Manual* contains solutions to end-of-chapter exercises at the same level of detail and commentary as the in-chapter examples. It also has a 100-problem question pool, with solutions in the same style, arranged for convenient reproduction for homework problems or exams. It gives solutions and scoring plans for the Design Exercises of Chapter 11, and it contains transparency masters to support daily teaching from every chapter. Comments and notes are included at the end of many solutions to help the instructor anticipate in-depth questions from students about fine points and "ifs, ands, or buts."

DONOVAN YOUNG

August, 1992

ACKNOWLEDGMENTS

. . . .

I have been fortunate to serve on the same faculty with engineering economy giants John A. White, Gerald J. Thuesen, and Gunter P. Sharp-Bette and to enjoy their continual acts of kindness, encouragement, and inspiration. I have also worked with and been influenced by William G. Lesso, Leland T. Blank, Luis Eduardo Contreras, W. J. Kennedy, Jr., and Suleyman Tufekci.

John J. Jarvis and Michael E. Thomas gave me supportive leadership, and Col. James Kays of the U. S. Military Academy at West Point was responsible for the price-less opportunity to design a new engineering economy course from scratch. My most special gratitude goes to Richard A. Paradiso, who test-taught much of the material in this book and was absolutely unstinting in both support and criticism.

Manuscript preparation kudos goes (that's right, goes) to Sharon Bernard of the Hudson Valley, my daughter Virginia Catherine ("Ginny") Powell of Atlanta (who swears all the problem solutions are correct, because she redid them in her head as she typed them), and Ginny's mother Carolyn, who types so fast she wears out key-boards.

But if I could thank only one person, the choice would be easy: my wife, Becky Blankenship.

CONTENTS

Engineering design decisions affect not only the owners of an enterprise, but management workers and other constituencies as well.

ENGINEERING DECISION MAKING

. . . .

Engineering economy consists of techniques for assessing the *worth* of prospective projects, investment opportunities, or design choices. The reason for worth assessment is to support *decisions.*

1.1 ENGINEERING DECISIONS

This book covers techniques that are useful, when combined with technical knowledge and skills specific to engineering disciplines and application environments, for making engineering economic decisions. For example, at a factory where 200 electric motors were driving machinery, the inductive load on three-phase, 440-volt power circuits created a phase lag that lowered the power factor, causing the electricity bill to be high. An electrical engineer recognized the problem and realized a bank of capacitors could alleviate the lag. She sized the capacitors on a technical basis, estimated their installation costs, and estimated the resulting power savings. She compared the savings to the costs and decided that the project was worthwhile. She refined the decision by considering the effects of monetary inflation, risk, and taxes. She tried smaller and larger banks of capacitors and found that it was more economical to use a somewhat smaller bank than she had first considered. Her supervisor checked the technical and economic analysis, approved it, and asked her to prepare an appropriations request to justify the project to higher management.

Only part of the foregoing decision process is engineering economy per se: comparing the savings to the costs (discounted cash flow), refining the decision for inflation, risk, and taxes, and trying the various sizes (sensitivity analysis). The remainder, even the cost estimations and the preparation of an appropriations request, is engineering proper, although the philosophy of engineering economy should help with the whole decision process.

A set of steps in engineering economic decision making is listed below.

Steps in Engineering Economic Decision Making

0. Recognize the need for an economic analysis.
1. Formulate the decision problem: What are we trying to decide, what is given, and what is out of the question?
2. Establish criteria for estimating and evaluating consequences.
3. Generate alternatives.
4. Establish technical understanding of alternatives.
5. Estimate consequences of alternatives (costs and benefits).
6. Select the preferred alternative.
7. Perform sensitivity analysis; return to step 6 if necessary; prepare to obtain ratifications and seek approvals.
8. Document and communicate the decision and its justification; advocate or implement the decision.

E1. **Consider the question of replacing the furnace in a public school building. Refer to the listed steps in economic decision making. Suppose the school mechanic reported to the principal that the furnace was becoming unreliable, hard to maintain, and in need of replacement or major overhaul. If the principal agrees and commits himself to resolving this difficulty, a decision problem is born—step 0 of the process. Speculate how the remaining steps might unfold.**

  1. Formulation would consist of defining and describing the problem so it could be understood by everyone involved. The description would be documented, perhaps in a memorandum from the principal to faculty and staff.
  2. Criteria would be established. Suppose it was decided to choose, among ways of keeping the school warm enough, the solution that would minimize the sum of costs over the next five years. Someone trained in engineering economy would not use exactly that criterion, but it is similar to a more valid criterion: minimizing the present worth of costs or the equivalent annual cost (these quantities are defined in this book).
  3. Alternatives would be generated. Good work at this step would avoid prematurely ruling out possible solutions such as the do-nothing solution, an outside furnace maintenance contract, or a smaller furnace plus additional building insulation. One school saved hundreds of dollars by replacing the faulty closer on an outside door.
  4. To establish technical understanding of alternatives, the school mechanic might consult vendors and catalogs and perform heat-load calculations. Someone trained in HVAC (heating, ventilating, and air conditioning) or mechanical engineering should be involved.
  5. To estimate costs, the mechanic might obtain proposals and bids from heating firms and correct the projected fuel costs for the actual fuel prices in the area. Instead of estimating the benefits of comfort, it would be usual to adjust all alternatives to meet the same performance standard.

Examples of Decisions Supported by Engineering Economy Calculations:

1. An electronics engineer decides between two ways of achieving required reliability of a circuit: building it from more reliable components or providing a redundant standby circuit.

2. A chemical engineer determines the appropriate diameter of a pipeline, knowing that a greater diameter will decrease pumping costs throughout the life of the line but will increase purchase and installation costs.

3. A warehouse manager reviews stock levels of various stocked items, wanting to minimize the sum of "holding" costs (which increase when greater levels are stocked) and "stockout" costs (which correspondingly decrease).

4. A maintenance planner determines whether an extra $10,000 machine overhaul is worthwhile if it promises to extend the useful life of the machine.

5. A construction manager decides when to start an excavation, knowing that a late start will avoid some construction-loan interest payments but will risk delaying the entire project.

6. A mechanical engineer determines the appropriate balance between adding insulation to a building and increasing the capacity of its heating and cooling plant.

7. A civil engineer determines whether the prospective savings in driving time for motorists justify the cost of a new traffic access ramp.

8. A safety engineer compares the cost effectiveness of air bags for passenger cars versus improvements in seat belts.

9. A computer designer compares different ways of providing for speedy disk access.

10. A firm decides whether to open a new distribution facility to save delivery costs to customers far away from the nearest existing facility.

11. A software designer estimates how many extra sales of a product would justify the costly addition of an extra feature.

12. Given limited capital and a limited capacity to borrow money, a firm uses engineering estimates of benefits and costs to decide which capital investments to undertake.

13. A fleet operator decides whether to lease or buy the next group of trucks.

14. A military procurement official evaluates bids on a complex weapons system.

15. A laundry appliance manufacturer decides whether to keep its existing washing machine assembly or to redesign the assembly for automated manufacture.

16. A corrosion engineer estimates whether it is better to use stainless steel and replace a tank every five years or use carbon steel and replace it every three years.

17. On the basis of engineers' estimates of costs, a law firm decides what level of online legal reference service is most cost effective for its operations.

18. A process plant engineer compares three methods of abating air pollution, each with different capital investments and different operating costs.

19. A shipper balances speed versus fuel cost in selecting routes.

20. A large-scale row-crop farmer decides between 12-row equipment and more expensive but more efficient 18-row equipment.

6. Given steps 2 and 5, selection of the preferred alternative can be routine or difficult. Suppose the two solutions—the most elaborate gas furnace and one of the electric furnaces—gave about the same costs, so that sensitivity analysis would be required to clarify the choice.

7. Sensitivity analysis (Chapter 8) is the study of conditions under which a solution is valid. There may be side effects or subtle differences not reflected in the estimates of costs: the gas supply may be more or less reliable than the electricity supply, or one type of furnace may be more immune to student vandalism. The cost of one energy source may be more likely to escalate than that of the other. If a clear choice does not emerge, either the principal can make an arbitrary decision (having found it cannot cost significantly more than the rejected solution), or there can be a return to an earlier step.

8. Either the principal has the authority to expend the funds, or there is a procedure by which the choice is approved at a higher level. If there is a central contracting and purchasing authority for the school system, the principal and the mechanic may have little further to do with the project.

1.2 CONSTITUENCIES

In a democratic society, we expect decisions to be made on behalf of an explicit constituency, in such a way that it should not matter who makes the decision. Engineering decisions can be made in the private sector or in the public sector. The basic difference between the two is the special status of owners of an enterprise in the private sector. In both sectors, the interests of all constituencies are intended to be represented, but in the private sector the decisions are made, in principle, to maximize net benefits to the owners. This means that the interests of nonowners are seen as constraints (e.g., pay workers at least a decent wage) rather than as part of the objective.

E2. In return for a right-of-way condemnation, a county government offers to give to a light industrial plant one of two small surplus parcels of land adjoining the plant. Parcel A is more usable and is worth $45,000 as a parking area for equipment; parcel B would be seen by employees as worth $70,000 as a recreation area, but the plant management sees no particular value in additional employee benefits, viewing its employees as already coddled enough. Discuss the choice between parcels from a private-sector and a public-sector viewpoint.

Constituencies Affected by a Decision:

Owners (shareholders, partners)
Management
Employees
Customers
Suppliers
The public, future generations, mankind
Governments (surrogate for all nonowners)

As we will see in Chapter 7, the county would presumably consider the benefits "to whomsoever they accrue" and would choose to award parcel B as doing more total good to society. The plant management would presumably choose to receive parcel A as better for the owners.

1.3 COST AND BENEFIT CONCEPTS

In engineering economy, costs and benefits are seen in terms of *cash flows*. A monetary *receipt* is a positive cash flow; a monetary *disbursement* is a negative cash flow. A prospect or opportunity has a *worth* measured as the size (amount) of a monetary receipt to which it is considered equivalent. ("Equivalent" means desired to the same degree.)

Worth is a timed quantity. The worth now of a future beneficial event declines if the event's prospective timing gets later. A past ("sunk") event has zero worth. Worth has two times associated with it: the time of evaluation (e.g., now for "present worth") and the event time. Worth can be interpreted as how much one would be willing to pay at the time of evaluation to cause the event to occur at its event time. As the time of evaluation moves closer to the event, the event's worth increases to a maximum and suddenly becomes zero when the event is in the past.

As will be seen in Chapter 2, discounted cash flow methods, based on the simple geometric-series mathematics of compound interest, allow differently timed costs and benefits to be evaluated on the common scale of worth. When timing is not a consideration, worth of a cash flow is just the cash flow itself.

This section discusses several basic cost and benefit concepts from the standpoint of engineering economy studies. Since accounting deals with the past and engineering economy deals with the future, there are some distinctions in the treatment of costs and benefits between accounting and engineering economy. We will first illustrate the simplest concept of engineering economy—minimizing cost—and then deal with the concepts of *sunk costs, marginal costs, free resources, fixed costs, omitted benefits,* and *double counting.* These can all be treated here without the complication of timing considerations. Cost analysis where timing considerations are not important is sometimes called *present economy.*

The following example illustrates cost minimization. Here total annual costs are compared for alternative incandescent light bulbs. Since the benefits (light per bulb) are not equal for all alternatives, the costs are rendered comparable by *normalizing* for light output—that is, comparing costs per unit of light output.

E3. **Assume that electrical energy is purchased at a cost of $0.077 per kilowatt-hour and that a lamp that uses a nominal 60-watt incandescent light bulb is on for 1000 hours per year. The actual wattage the bulb draws and light output it emits depend on the bulb's efficiency and the voltage of the power supply. Consider the following data for a 120-volt supply:**

Product	Price	Actual Light Output, Lumens	Actual Power Drawn, Watts	Average Life in Hours
GE Softwhite	$0.77	855	65.27	1018
GE Miser	$0.89	855	61.51	984
Duro-Lite X2500	$1.70	780	74.28	4500

The GE Softwhite typifies the ordinary light bulb; the GE Miser typifies high-efficiency light bulbs designed to save energy; the Duro-Lite X2500 typifies long-life light bulbs. Until otherwise noted, we will ignore any differences in the quality of light.

(a) Which product is most energy efficient?

Since *lumens* is the output and *watts* is the input, lumens per watt is the relevant measure. (Efficiency has a general definition of output divided by input.)

1. GE Softwhite $855/65.27 = 13.1$
2. GE Miser $855/61.51 = \underline{13.9}$ most efficient
3. Duro-Lite X2500 $780/74.28 = 10.5$

(b) Which product has the lowest purchase cost per 1000 hour operating year?

Cost minimization is not valid unless benefits are equal; it is necessary to normalize for light output. Here the appropriate normalization is "for 855 lumens of output."

1. GE Softwhite $\dfrac{1000}{1018}(0.77) = \$0.7564/\text{yr}$

2. GE Miser $\dfrac{1000}{984}(0.89) = \$0.9045/\text{yr}$

3. Duro-Lite X2500 $\dfrac{855}{780}\dfrac{1000}{4500}(1.70) = \underline{\underline{\$0.4141/\text{yr}}}$ cheapest

Note that $855/780 = 1.096$ Duro-Lite bulbs are needed per ordinary bulb.

(c) Which product has the lowest energy cost per year?

Energy costs per year (for 855 lumens) are (note that 65.27 watts is 65.27 kilowatts per 1000-hr year):

1. GE Softwhite $65.27(0.077) = \$5.02579$
2. GE Miser $61.51(0.077) = \underline{\$4.73627}$ lowest cost
3. Duro-Lite X2500 $74.28\dfrac{855}{780}(0.077) = \$6.26952$

(d) Associated with each light bulb replacement is not only the purchase cost but several other costs: purchase effort, installation and disposal effort, and inconvenient loss of illumination. If these other costs are valued at $1.00 per replacement, which product has the lowest total cost?

1. GE Softwhite $\dfrac{1000}{1018}(0.77 + 1) + 5.02579 = \$6.76/\text{yr}$

2. GE Miser $\dfrac{1000}{984}(0.89 + 1) + 4.73627 = \underline{\underline{\$6.657/\text{yr}}}$

3. Duro-Lite X2500 $\dfrac{855}{780}\dfrac{1000}{4500}(1.70 + 1) + 6.26952 = \$6.927/\text{yr}$

(e) **In such applications as traffic lights or inaccessible lights, the additional costs associated with replacement may be higher than $1.00. How high must the additional costs be before the Duro-Lite X2500 has the lowest total cost?**

(This is an example of breakeven analysis, Chapter 8.)
Let R be the additional costs.

$Z_1 = 5.02579 + 0.982318(R + 0.77)$ total cost of GE Softwhite
$Z_2 = 4.73627 + 1.016260(R + 0.89)$ total cost of GE Miser
$Z_3 = 6.26952 + 0.2(R + 1.70)$ total cost of Duro-Lite X2500

If Duro-Lite X2500 has the lowest total cost, then $Z_3 < Z_1$ and $Z_3 < Z_2$. $Z_3 < Z_1 \Rightarrow R > 1.22$ and $Z_3 < Z_2 \Rightarrow R > 1.35$. So if the additional costs are more than $\underline{\$1.35}$, the Duro-Lite X2500 has the lowest total cost.

The decision criterion in the foregoing example was total annual cost. This is valid whenever timing of costs is not important, such as when cost-timing differences among alternatives are no more than about a year. However, one of the light bulbs in the example has a useful life of about 4.5 years. As the compound-interest methods to be introduced in Chapter 2 will show, there is a disadvantage associated with paying for something in advance, as compared to the alternative of deferring payments. Money has a time value. If the cheapest annual cost in the foregoing example had been that of the longest-lived light bulb, a decision based on that result could have been wrong. Methods that properly account for the time value of money will be introduced in Chapter 2 and used throughout the book.

The following example illustrates the treatment of sunk costs.

E4. Pete buys an inoperable lawn mower for $10, expecting to spend $16 to repair it and to sell it for $50. But after spending $20 on the repair, he finds it will take yet another $25 to complete the repair, and he also finds he will be able to get only $40 for it. What should he do?

He should complete the repair. The $10 purchase and $20 partial repair are sunk costs. There are two ways to treat sunk costs: ignore them, or include them in every alternative (there can be no alternative that undoes the past).

The alternatives are

1. Complete the repair.
2. Abandon.

Ignoring sunk costs, in alternative 1 Pete will now spend $25 to receive $40—a net gain of $15. In alternative 2, he will now spend nothing and receive nothing—a net gain of $0.

Including sunk costs in every alternative, in alternative 1 Pete will have spent $55 to receive $40—a net loss of $15. In Alternative 2, he will have spent $30 to receive nothing—a net loss of $30.

By either treatment of sunk costs, completing the repair is worth $15 more than not completing it.

> Sunk costs (past costs or irreversible committed costs) must be either ignored or included in every alternative.

The mistakes sometimes made with sunk costs are to accept an alternative that appears to avoid them (see Exercise 5 at the end of this chapter), or to consider them as an asset whose value must be protected. As an example of the asset view, in 1963 the Great Northern Oil Refinery began a $60,000 project to provide a facility to desulfurize JP-4 jet fuel. When the project was 95% complete, it turned out that there was no need for it. For several years, there arose no reason to spend the $3000 to complete the facility or to tear it down; it just sat there, looking to a casual observer like an operating part of the plant, and the final $3000 was never spent—that is, never wasted.

E5. A widget manufacturer has excess capacity. It must charge at least $40 per widget, because it sells 90,000 widgets per year for its only income, and its total annual expenses are $3,600,000. Yet it agrees to sell a special extra run of 60,000 widgets for $20 apiece. Can this be profitable?

Yes, if the marginal cost of producing widgets is less than $20 per widget. If total annual expenses to produce the extra widgets go up by less than $1,200,000, the special extra run is profitable. This may very well be the case, since with excess capacity the extra widgets will not cause a need for additional amounts of many of the manufacturer's costly resources. For example, making the extra widgets may require more labor and fuel but not more machines.

> Engineering economy studies generally involve marginal, not total, costs.

The concept of *fixed* and *variable costs* provides a simple model of marginal costs. Let there be some activity, such as producing widgets, where the amount of the activity, such as the number produced per year, is denoted x. Then the total cost for a given amount of activity is modeled as

$$T = F + Vx$$

where F is the fixed cost and V is the variable cost per unit of activity. Examples of fixed costs are management salaries, rent, replacement of large equipment, or expenses of the company yacht. Examples of variable costs are direct material and direct labor.

E6. The manufacturer in Example E5 has a cost accounting system in which at a production rate of 90,000 widgets per year the fixed and variable costs are considered to be $F = \$1,980,000$ and $V = \$18$ per widget. By this model, the assumed marginal cost per widget is $18 over any range in which the fixed costs do not change. Is the extra run contemplated in Example E5 profitable?

Yes, because $18 is less than the $20 additional revenue.

Note that the average cost (T/x in the fixed-cost model) is a poor estimator of marginal cost. Using the average cost is tantamount to assuming that for every extra widget there needs to be more secretarial service, more rent, more yacht expense, and so on. The next concept, closely related to marginal cost, is that of the *free resource*.

E7. At a storm-door finishing station, two workers place a cover and secure it with screws, while a third worker places warning labels on the rear face plate, waits until the cover is secured, and slides the door onto a conveyor. The third worker could perform the added task of placing preformed plastic packing on the door during the idle time spent waiting for the other workers to finish. Should any cost be attributed to this extra task?

This appears to be an inflexible situation. If so, the worker's time is truly a free resource and has no cost. Care must be taken, of course, to be sure that the idle time was producing no benefits.

E8. At the same plant, there is an inspector who often goes home early, but sometimes must stay late to accomplish the day's inspections. Under a plan to increase production, there will be more inspection work, but not enough to justify a second inspector. Should any cost be attributed to this extra inspection work?

Clearly yes, because the situation is a flexible one. Part of the new load is causing overtime and therefore will cause out-of-pocket costs in one way or another— employee dissatisfaction (which can translate into personnel turnover expenses) if nothing else.

> Idle resources are free only in inflexible situations.

E9. A lumber-cutting facility produces the by-product sawdust. The facility manufactures pressed-wood furniture as a sideline; this uses some of the sawdust, while the rest is sold at $0.30 per ton more than the direct costs of its packaging and delivery. Cost accounting records list sawdust at $0.14 per ton, based on a cost allocation to all products, one of which is this unavoidable by-product. For purposes of evaluating prospective projects that would use sawdust, how much is sawdust worth?

Every ton used by a new project would decrease the amount sold and would thus cost $0.30. The $0.14 figure does not represent any real "opportunity cost" and is irrelevant.

The foregoing example illustrates the concept of *opportunity cost*. A resource has an opportunity cost equal to the benefit forgone by using it. The cost of something scarce is what it takes to get more of it, whereas the cost of something plentiful is what it costs to divert it from its most profitable use. The opportunity cost of money—the idea that money always has an alternative use of being put to work by lending it at compound interest—is the basis for the discounted cash flow methods to be introduced in the next chapter.

There are many further cost and benefit concepts that are important to engineering economy but will be defined as they arise naturally in future chapters. Two more concepts deserve mention here: double-counting and benefit omission. These bugaboos can be avoided by using common sense, but they crop up in engineering economic analyses everywhere.

E10. An employee benefits package was said to yield $1.2 million of morale benefits measured in terms of additional worker productivity and also to yield $0.3 million of benefits due to its likelihood of preventing a strike. What is wrong with summing the two figures?

Workers don't work harder at the same time they are on strike; this is an example of double-counting that occurs when various costs and benefits are estimated assuming different background conditions. (Another kind of double-counting occurs when the same consequence is measured in two ways, as when fire prevention is credited both with reducing damage and with reducing insurance premiums for the same damage.)

E11. A "value engineering" consultant offers to find ways to cut unnecessary spending. An example is presented to prospective clients: "We looked at the garages for a tract of military houses. The function of a garage is to hold a car. By reducing floor space, eliminating utility connections and eliminating a door, we were able to save $1750 per house." What is wrong?

About 20 common useful functions of a garage can be listed. If the lost benefits were not balanced against the savings, inappropriate cuts were probably made.

1.4 DECISION CRITERIA

Money allows many things to be measured on a common scale. The financial model of a situation is far less complicated than the situation itself. If there were no such concept as money, making a decision would be difficult: Each alternative leads to a set of estimated future consequences, and one would have to compare one multidimensional description with another. With money and the techniques of engineering economy, each set of estimated future consequences has a *worth* expressed as a single real number, and the comparison is one-dimensional.

A paradigm for decision making is shown in Figure 1-1. There is a *system* that behaves, and its *behavior* is partly determined by *actions* that have been taken in accordance with *decisions* that were made. The decision maker holds a set of *values* that express the decision maker's preference for one set of *outcomes* over another. The *result* of a decision is the evaluated combination of the outcomes—that is, the result expresses how good or bad a given set of outcomes is.

Every decision process or decision support system supports at least three basic functions: *generation of alternatives, outcome estimation,* and *evaluation.* In engineering economy, the alternatives are different designs or investment opportunities; outcome estimation takes the form of estimating the economic outcomes of each alternative; and evaluation consists of determining the worth of each outcome—its economic result.

The most basic decision criterion in engineering economy is *cost.* We seek to minimize cost. If alternatives vary in the benefits they bring, we measure the benefits in money and seek to maximize *profit,* which is benefits less costs or receipts less disburse-

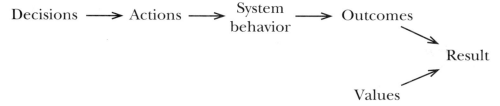

FIGURE 1-1. The Decision Paradigm.

ments. If alternatives vary in timing of their economic consequences, we define worth measures or efficiency measures that include the influence of time.

1.4.1 Worth Measures

Worth measures such as present worth, future worth, and annual worth will be defined in Chapter 2. If all relevant consequences of an alternative are expressed as a set of cash flows, a worth of the alternative can be computed. The worth can be interpreted as a measure of desirability; for example, to say that the present worth of an alternative is $1000 is to say that accepting the alternative is equivalent to being given $1000. Computations of worth depend on the opportunity cost of money as expressed by compound interest; for example, to say that the prospect of receiving $1000 two years from now has a present worth of $810 is to imply an opportunity to convert $810 now into $1000 two years from now, as by lending it out at compound interest.

1.4.2 Efficiency Measures

Efficiency measures such as rate of return, benefit/cost ratio, payback time, and net present value index will be defined in Chapter 4. Although worth measures depend on project size, efficiency measures are independent of size. Rate of return and payback time, for example, are measures of how fast the returns from an investment pay back the investment. Benefit/cost ratio and net present value index are measures of the size of returns from an investment, compared to the size of the investment. All these measures remain invariant if all the cash flows are multiplied by a constant.

   As will be shown in Chapter 5 ("Evaluation of Alternatives"), worth measures and efficiency measures each have different applicability in different situations, depending on such matters as whether the alternatives are contending for limited investment capital.

1.5 ACCOUNTING AND ENGINEERING ECONOMY

Accounting is the generation and analysis of the financial records of an enterprise. Not only are engineering decisions made in a microeconomic or financial environment that can be understood, expressed, and communicated only through the concepts and vocabulary of accounting, but accounting can directly influence engineering decisions: Taxes, incentives, and outside investment often depend not only on business results but on how they are described ("treated") by accounting. Also, the accounting records of an enterprise are a prime resource for estimating costs and other consequences of a proposed activity.

General accounting summarizes the overall financial health of an enterprise. The two most basic general accounting reports, introduced immediately below, are the *balance sheet* and the *income statement. Cost accounting* quantifies the costs of performing each of an enterprise's main activities; Section 5.1.3.4 in Chapter 5 presents a typical cost accounting structure for an enterprise and explains how properly to treat sunk costs, marginal costs, fixed costs, variable costs, overhead costs, and other costs that can be extracted from cost accounting records. *Depreciation and tax accounting*, and their subtle and arbitrary effects on engineering decisions, are the subject of Chapter 10.

1.5.1 The Balance Sheet

The balance sheet describes the financial condition of an enterprise as of a given reporting date, usually the last day of the fiscal year. The balance sheet is the chief record of an enterprise's economic size, debt, and ownership. A specimen balance sheet for the hypothetical enterprise Blandish Industries, Inc. is shown on the following page.

Note that the balance sheet shows *assets* on the left and *liabilities* and *owner equity* (also called *net worth*) on the right. Assets comprise all property of the enterprise; liabilities comprise all the claims of nonowners on the assets, and owner equity is the claims of owners. Thus the balance sheet equates *total assets* on the left with *total equities* (equities is the sum of liabilities and owner equity) on the right. Here Blandish Industries has $10,740,000 of total assets; since it has $5,520,000 of total liabilities, the total owner equity is the $5,220,000 difference.

1.5.1.1 Assets Assets are listed in decreasing-liquidity order: *Current assets* are cash and those that can be converted to cash within a year; *fixed assets* are relatively permanent and would not normally be converted into cash; and *other assets* might be difficult or impossible to convert into cash.

Within current assets, *cash* includes currency, checking accounts, and deposits requiring little or no withdrawal notice. *Marketable securities* are commercial paper, government securities, or other temporary investments of cash not immediately needed, which can be sold quickly at a fairly stable price; these are shown at cost, with their current market value given in parentheses.

Accounts receivable, the current amount for which customers have been billed but have not yet paid, is shown at the amount billed; separately shown is a reduction to provide for the predicted portion of accounts receivable that will not be received, based on audited experience or accepted accounting practice. *Inventories* consist of raw materials on hand, work in progress, and finished goods on hand; these are shown at cost or at market value, whichever is less.

Quick assets, not listed explicitly on the balance sheet, is *current assets* less *inventories*; this represents the current assets available to cover a quick emergency, on the assumption that inventories are less liquid than other current assets.

Fixed assets (also called *property, plant, and equipment*) includes property not intended for sale but used repeatedly in carrying out the enterprise's business. Various categories of fixed assets are often listed separately, such as buildings, equipment, office furniture, vehicles, and so on; in the illustrated balance sheet, Blandish Industries' land is listed as one item, and all other fixed assets are listed as another item (''plant and equipment'').

Blandish Industries, Inc.
Balance Sheet for December 31, 1992
($000)

ASSETS		*LIABILITIES*	
Current Assets		Current Liabilities	
Cash	520	Accounts payable	1,230
Marketable securities at cost (market value 940)	860	Short-term notes payable	740
		Accrued expenses	730
Accounts receivable	1,900		
		Total current liabilities	**2,700**
Less: provision for bad debt	(90)	Long-term liabilities	
Inventories	3,100	First mortgage bonds	1,800
Total current assets	**6,290**	Debentures	1,020
Fixed Assets		**Total long-term liabilities**	**2,820**
Land	540	**Total Liabilities**	**5,520**
Plant and equipment	5,030		
Less: Depreciation	(2,120)	*OWNER EQUITY*	
Total fixed assets	**3,450**	Preferred stock	320
Other Assets		Common stock	1,870
Prepayments and deferred charges	480	Capital surplus	480
Intangibles	520	Retained earnings	2,550
		Total Owner Equity	**5,220**
Total other assets	**1,000**	**Total Liabilities and Owner Equity**	**10,740**
Total Assets	**10,740**		

Fixed assets is shown at cost—the sum of purchase and installation costs for all items without regard to when acquired—then decremented by the accumulated *depreciation* charges. Depreciation works like this: say Blandish Industries acquired a $1000 machine in 1992. It is depreciated according to a depreciation schedule; under a typical schedule, say the standard MACRS 5-year schedule shown in Table 10-12 of Chapter 10, there would be a depreciation charge of $200 at the first fiscal-year anniversary after the acquisition, say six months after acquisition, and there would be annual depreciation charges of $320 at the second anniversary, $192 at the third anniversary, $115.20 at the fourth, $115.20 at the fifth, and finally $57.60 at the sixth fiscal-year anniversary after acquisition. Note that the depreciation charges sum to the acquisition cost. They form a set of fictitious delayed payments that replace the actual acquisition cost, as if Blandish had been able to acquire the machine by obtaining an interest-free loan. Acquisition of a $1000 machine adds $1000 to fixed assets; then each depreciation charge on the machine is subtracted from fixed assets as the machine ages.

Depreciation charges have three effects. Their *tax effect* is that Blandish would pay income taxes on profits calculated on the basis of the depreciation charges, which occur later than the actual acquisition cost and thus provide less relief. The *asset valuation effect* of depreciation charges is that assets are valued not according to market value, replacement cost, or earning power, but on an arbitrary basis. Both these effects distort engineering decisions. However, there is also the *smoothing effect* of depreciation charges: large, infrequent expenditures are treated as if they were spread out over the years. Without depreciation, an enterprise would appear unrealistically unsuccessful whenever it undertook large expenditures yielding long-term benefits, and correspondingly would appear unrealistically successful at other times.

In the Other Assets category, *prepayments* are the unused remaining value of such things as royalties, leases, or insurance premiums paid in advance. For example, if Blandish Industries had paid $30,000 for a three-year insurance policy a year ago, its unused portion could be treated as a $20,000 prepayment asset today. Similarly, if Blandish had spent $80,000 in addition to ordinary marketing expenditures to introduce a new product, it could defer "writing off" the expenditure and consider part of it as *deferred charges*.

Prepayments and deferred charges have tax effects, asset valuation effects, and smoothing effects similar to depreciation.

Intangibles are assets such as franchises, patents, and goodwill, which are valuable yet do not exist physically. Accepted conservative accounting practices tend to undervalue intangibles compared to their replacement cost or earning power.

1.5.1.2 Liabilities and Owner Equity

Just as assets were listed on the left side of the balance sheet in order from liquid to illiquid, liabilities are listed on the right side in order from short-term to long-term. *Current liabilities* are debts due within a year. The shortest-term current liabilities are *accounts payable*, where goods or services have been bought and must be paid for, usually within 30, 60, or 90 days. *Short-term notes payable* include money borrowed from banks or other lenders, to be repaid within a year.

Accrued expenses include such things as wages currently owed to employees and due to be paid in their next paycheck, interest coming due for the period up to the reporting date but not yet paid, and income tax expected to be owed for operations up to the reporting date (often listed separately as "income tax payable").

Long-term liabilities are debts due more than a year after the reporting date. In the United States, corporations borrow long-term money by issuing *bonds*. A bond is a promissory note that typically obligates the issuer to pay the lender its face amount at its due date, and meanwhile to pay semiannual face interest payments; for instance, a $10,000 bond due in 2010 and carrying a 10% face interest rate obligates the issuer to pay $10,000 in 2010 and meanwhile to pay $500 every half-year as interest payments (interest and interest rates are defined in Chapter 2). *First mortgage bonds* are secured by specific mortgaged assets. If the issuer cannot pay off bonds in cash when they come due, the lenders can cause the mortgaged assets to be sold to satisfy the debt. *Debentures* are bonds that are not secured; in case of trouble, the lenders who have purchased debentures are creditors with no special rights to assets.

Total liabilities is the sum of current and long-term liabilities. It represents the claims of creditors of all kinds against the enterprise's assets.

Owner equity is the enterprise's net worth after subtracting liabilities from assets. The owners are holders of *capital stock* that was issued (sold) in units of *shares*. A share has a *par value*, but when first issued it is sold for a usually higher market value. For example, when Blandish Industries was organized, say its first owners paid $370,000 for 3200 shares of $100 par-value preferred stock and $2,300,000 for 46,750 shares of $40 par-value common stock. *Preferred stock* and *common stock* are listed at par value. *Capital surplus* is the excess of market value at issue over par value: say the preferred stock brought in $370,000 for $320,000 par value, and the common stock brought in $2,300,000 for $1,870,000 par value, so that the capital surplus is $480,000. Blandish had initial capital equal to the sum of preferred stock, common stock, and capital surplus: $2,670,000.

Over the years, as the enterprise earns profit, it pays *dividends* to shareholders. Preferred stock earns a fixed amount of annual dividends per share; common stock earns dividends only after preferred-stock dividends have been paid, but common-stock dividends can be as great as profits justify. Earnings not distributed in dividends are *retained* in order to be invested in additional assets. The accumulated amount of these potential dividends forgone by shareholders over the years is listed as *retained earnings*.

To summarize Blandish's balance sheet, the enterprise has $10,740,000 of assets. Liabilities, which are creditors' claims against the assets, total $5,520,000. Owner equity or net worth, which is what shareholders have put into the enterprise both originally and by allowing part of earnings to be retained, is $5,220,000.

1.5.1.3 Financial Indicators from the Balance Sheet

Net working capital is total current assets less total current liabilities. This represents the amount available on which to operate in the coming year. If net working capital is near zero, then brief delays in collecting accounts receivable or in selling inventories may make it difficult to pay current liabilities. The *current ratio* is the ratio of total current assets to total current liabilities. To be safe from being forced to sell assets or to default on liabilities, enterprises in most sectors of the economy need to maintain a current ratio near 2.0.

Recall that *quick assets* is current assets less inventories. The *quick ratio* is the ratio of quick assets to total current liabilities. To be safe in a quick emergency, where there would be no time to obtain cash by selling down the current inventories, an enterprise should have a quick ratio no less than about 1.15.

E12. From the balance sheet for Blandish Industries, determine the enterprise's net working capital, current ratio, and quick ratio.

Given total current assets of $6,290,000 and total current liabilities of $2,700,000,

$$[\text{Net working capital}] = [\text{total current assets}] - [\text{total current liabilities}] = \underline{\$3,590,000}$$
$$[\text{Current ratio}] = [\text{total current assets}] \div [\text{total current liabilities}] \cong \underline{\underline{2.33}}$$

Given inventories of $3,100,000,

$$[\text{Quick assets}] = [\text{total current assets}] - [\text{inventories}] = \$3,190,000$$
$$[\text{Quick ratio}] = [\text{quick assets}] \div [\text{total current liabilities}] \cong \underline{1.18}$$

With a current ratio greater than 2.0 and a quick ratio greater than 1.15, Blandish Industries seems very safe from default in a bad year and safe from default in a quick emergency.

The balance sheet provides a snapshot of the enterprise's financial condition, but it does not indicate its profitability. We can imagine Blandish's staying in financial *stasis*, so that two successive balance sheets would be the same (except, of course, for the reporting date). This would require that Blandish operate at steady state: Accounts receivable and inventories would be generated at the same rate as they were drawn down, plant and equipment would be acquired at a rate just offsetting depreciation, and current and long-term debt would be incurred at the same rates as existing debts were paid off. Stasis would also require that all after-tax profits be distributed as dividends to shareholders, so that nothing would be added to retained earnings. But this says nothing about whether Blandish earns a billion dollars per year at steady state or a million—just that it operates at steady state and distributes all earnings to owners.

1.5.2 The Income Statement

The *income statement* subtracts *expenses* from *revenues* for a time span, usually from the last day of one fiscal year to the last day of the next, and reports the result as *net income* (or *loss*). The income statement is the chief record of an enterprise's profitability. A specimen income statement for the hypothetical enterprise Blandish Industries is shown on the following page.

1.5.2.1 Revenues *Operating revenues* is money received during the year in the enterprise's main business activity, *sales* is the total invoice price of goods shipped and services rendered during the year, and *returns and allowances* reflects refunds given to customers for returned goods or complaints. *Nonoperating revenues* is sideline earnings such as for renting out excess floor space or depositing temporarily excess cash in an interest-bearing account. Blandish Enterprises had $6,150,000 operating revenues and $1,460,000 nonoperating revenues during the year, and thus had $7,610,000 *total revenues.*

1.5.2.2 Expenses Nearly all *expenses* except interest payments on debt are considered to be *operating expenses*. For a manufacturing enterprise, *cost of goods sold* is separately listed and is subdivided into broad cost-accounting categories (labor, materials, overhead). *Overhead* includes those costs that are not easily attributed to a single product or process; an example is the costs for shipping, receiving, and storage in a warehouse. *Depreciation* is the accounting device that substitutes a smooth series of depreciation charges for actual capital expenses. For example, if Blandish acquired a $900,000 machine during the year, the $900,000 expenditure nowhere appears on the income statement. Instead, there is a depreciation charge of, say, $180,000; but the continuing depreciation charges for assets acquired before this year bring the total depreciation charges up to the $350,000 listed. Depreciation charges are more nearly constant from year to year than are actual capital expenditures, and in the long run they sum to the same amount.

Selling and administrative expense includes such things as salespeople's salaries and commissions, marketing costs (advertising, promotion, travel, market research, entertainment), executives' and office workers' salaries, accounting costs, nonmanufacturing computer expenses, and office expenses. *Lease payments* includes rental paid for any assets—land, buildings, equipment—that are leased rather than owned. Blandish

Blandish Industries, Inc.
Income Statement for Year Ended December 31, 1992
($000)

REVENUES

Operating Revenues

Sales	6,270
Less: returns and allowances	(120)
Total operating revenues	**6,150**

Nonoperating Revenues

Rents	1,340
Interest receipts	120
Total nonoperating revenues	**1,460**
Total Revenues	**7,610**

EXPENSES

Operating Expenses

Cost of goods sold

Labor	1,810
Materials	970
Overhead	450
Depreciation	350
Selling and administrative expense	360
Lease payments	1,600
Total operating expenses	**5,540**

Nonoperating Expenses

Interest payments	550
Total Expenses	**6,090**
Net Income Before Income Taxes	**1,520**
Income Taxes	610
Net Profit for the Year	**910**

Enterprises had total operating expenses of $5,540,000; its only nonoperating expense was $550,000 of interest on its bonds. The sum of both kinds of expense was $6,090,000 of *total expenses*. Subtracting expenses from revenues, we see Blandish had a $1,520,000 *net income before income taxes*.

All taxes except income taxes are already reflected in expenses or could have been listed separately or are "off the books." For example, Blandish's sales could have been subject to *sales taxes* at, say, 4%; a customer would pay $104 for a $100 Blandish widget, Blandish would transmit $4 to the tax authority, and the sale would contribute $100 to the *sales* line in the income statement. The $4 is "off the books." As a different example, Blandish's average warehouse inventory could have been subject to a property tax, and this "on the books" tax expense would be included in the *overhead* line.

Income taxes are listed separately. In the United States, income tax is wholly determined as a percentage of *net income before income taxes*; any structural change in the income tax laws requires a corresponding change in general accounting treatments or definitions, so that a single set of "books" serves in the multiple roles of keeping records in the tax "game" of enterprise versus tax authority and revealing the enterprise's financial condition and profitability to management, owners, and potential owners.

1.5.2.3 Financial Indicators from the Income Statement

The *net profit ratio* is the ratio of *net profit for the year* to *sales*; this ratio is useful in comparisons against other enterprises in the same business or against other years for the same enterprise. The *operating margin of profit* is the ratio of operating profit to sales, where *operating profit* is *total operating revenues* less *total operating expenses*; thus it is uninfluenced by results from nonoperating business sidelines or by interest on debt.

Total income is *total revenues* less all of *total expenses* except interest payments; it is thus what net income before income taxes would have been if there were no debt. *Interest coverage* is the ratio of total income to interest payments. This ratio should be at least about 3.0 for industrial enterprises; otherwise a drop in total income to one-third of its former value (not an unusual occurrence) renders the enterprise unable to pay the interest on its bonds without refinancing or selling off assets.

E13. From the income statement for Blandish Industries, determine the enterprise's operating margin of profit, net profit ratio, and interest coverage.

Given operating revenues of $6,150,000 and operating expenses of $5,540,000,

$$[\text{Operating profit}] = [\text{operating revenues}] - [\text{operating expenses}]$$
$$= \underline{\$610,000}$$

Given sales of $6,270,000,

$$[\text{Operating margin of profit}] = [\text{operating profit}] \div [\text{sales}] \cong \underline{9.73\%}$$

Given net profit for the year of $910,000,

$$[\text{Net profit ratio}] = [\text{net profit for the year}] \div [\text{sales}] \cong \underline{14.5\%}$$

Given total revenues of \$7,610,000, total expenses of \$6,090,000, and interest payments of \$550,000,

$$[\text{Total income}] = [\text{total revenues}] - [\text{total expenses}] + [\text{interest payments}]$$
$$= \underline{\$2,070,000}$$

$$[\text{Interest coverage}] = \overline{[\text{total income}]} \div [\text{interest payments}] \cong \underline{3.76}$$

Data from the income statement can be used to estimate the vulnerability of an enterprise to various risks, as the following examples show.

E14. What would be the percentage decrease in net income if Blandish Industries' total revenues were to decrease by 10% while expenses remained unchanged?

$[\text{Revised total income}] = [\text{total revenues}] \times (1 - 0.10) - [\text{total expenses}] + [\text{interest payments}] = \$1,309,000$. Compared to the previous total income of \$2,070,000, this is approximately a $\underline{37\% \text{ decrease}}$

E15. What would be the revised interest coverage if Blandish Industries' total revenues were to decrease by 10% while expenses remained unchanged?

$$[\text{Revised total income}] = \$1,309,000 \text{ as above}$$
$$[\text{Revised interest coverage}] = [\text{revised total income}] \div [\text{interest payments}]$$
$$= \underline{2.38}$$

Each year the net profit is distributed among the owners as dividends or plowed back into the enterprise (to acquire more assets) as retained earnings. A third general accounting report, the *statement of retained earnings*, accompanies the income statement and reveals how much of the net profit is distributed and how much is retained (it also shows how the dividends were allocated among various classes of owner such as holders of preferred stock and of common stock, and it usually reports earnings per share). Assume Blandish Industries' statement of retained earnings shows the following split of dividends versus retained earnings (amounts in \$1000):

Dividends	490
Retained earnings	420
	910

Now we can tell that Blandish Industries' previous year's total assets were \$10,670,000, because retained earnings added \$420,000 during the year while depreciation subtracted \$350,000, and the total assets at the end of the year were \$10,740,000.

1.5.3 Return on Investment and Cost of Capital

Ratios of annual data from the income statement to snapshot data from the balance sheet have units of dollars per year per dollar, the same as the *interest rates* to be defined in Chapter 2 and used throughout the book for determining worths of opportunities. Two of these ratios that are closely related to interest rates are the before-tax *return on investment* (ROI) and the *cost of capital* (COC).

The before-tax return on investment (more precisely, the "rate of return on assets before taxes") is defined as the ratio of income before taxes to the previous year's total assets:

$$\text{ROI} = \frac{[\text{net income before income taxes}]}{[\text{previous year's total assets}]} \qquad (1\text{-}1)$$

Blandish Industries has ROI = \$1,520,000/\$10,670,000 = 14.25%. The owners of Blandish Industries may be viewed as having invested \$10.67 million in the enterprise at the beginning of the year (by virtue of refraining from selling its assets for their book value), and this one-year investment has yielded a before-tax return of \$1.52 million. This before-tax situation is comparable to receiving \$1.52 million interest on a \$10.67 million one-year loan. A healthy enterprise in a typical year should have a before-tax rate of return (ROI) at least as great as the prevailing interest rate that could be earned by lending.

A maxim well illustrated by ROI is that *accounting concerns the past, whereas engineering economy concerns the future.* Obviously if you were actually contemplating dismantling an enterprise's assets in favor of lending out the proceeds, a more valid ratio to compare with lenders' interest rates would have as its numerator not this year's net income but next year's estimated net income, and as its denominator not last year's book value but the estimated proceeds if the assets were actually to be sold. Because assets are carried on the books at cost, not market value, it often happens that the balance sheet under-values the assets, and ROI consequently is an overestimate of the profitability of an enterprise for its owners.

Cost of capital (excluding the cost of retained earnings) is defined as the ratio of interest payments to liabilities:

$$\text{COC} = [\text{interest payments}] \div [\text{total liabilities}] \qquad (1\text{-}2)$$

Blandish Industries has COC = 550/5520 = 9.96%. COC is an overall average of the interest rates the enterprise is paying for current and long-term debt. A healthy enterprise generally has its ROI exceed its COC by at least 3 percentage points.

An after-tax return on investment cannot be defined in terms of general accounting data, because it depends specifically on equipment life, tax rates, and depreciation rules. However, it can be computed for individual cases by methods covered in Chapter 10. For enterprises in the United States in the early 1990s, the after-tax return on investment was frequently about 4 percentage points less than ROI. If an enterprise is in stasis, its assets will tend to grow at its after-tax rate of return on investment if profits are retained to offset depreciation, with the remainder distributed as dividends. In Chapter 2 we will define *net present worth,* which measures, at a given interest rate, the present equivalent of a set of related future receipts and expenditures. Suppose an enterprise in stasis suddenly identifies an opportunity to make a unique investment whose after-tax consequences have present worth P at an interest rate equal to the enterprise's after-tax rate of return on investment. Remarkably, the effect of accepting that investment opportunity will tend to be approximately the same as that of receiving a windfall of P dollars, which either brings future assets to P dollars more than they otherwise would be, or allows the owners to enjoy additional dividends worth P dollars.

1.6 INFLUENCES ON WORTH AND EFFICIENCY

Here is a brief preview of the issues that will be dealt with in the remainder of this book.

1.6.1 Cost and Benefit Estimation

Cost estimating is one of the most important skills practiced by nearly every engineer. Obviously it is important in engineering economy, since cost estimates appear in almost any economic study. Yet cost-estimating skills are so application-specific that they are not considered part of engineering economy. (It is even difficult to teach cost estimating within a discipline such as chemical, electrical, mechanical, or civil engineering, since each industry or activity has its own characteristics.) Costs depend too much on rapidly changing technologies to be covered in depth in this book.

1.6.2 Timing of Consequences

Chapter 2 gives a thorough treatment of discounted cash flow methods—the methods that allow comparison of differently timed cash flows.

A break from the past is that computed interest tables—the traditional tools for solving discounted cash flow formulas—do not appear in this book. They have gone the way of the slide rule. Section 2.3 (Compound Interest Computations) covers more convenient ways of cranking out answers, including hand calculators and spreadsheet programs.

Chapter 2 goes further than other textbooks in modern coverage of continuous cash flows (Section 2.7), geometric gradients (Sections 2.6.2 and 2.6.3), and timing conventions (Section 2.5.5). The treatment of such topics as effective and nominal interest rates (Sections 2.5.1 and 2.5.2) is particularly thorough, and no student should leave Chapter 2 without being easily able to compute such things as the monthly payments on a 30-year loan at 11.255% interest, to the penny.

1.6.3 Escalation and Inflation

Chapter 3 offers a unified treatment of the combined effects of monetary inflation and geometric escalation or deescalation. Readers will find the computation procedures both more flexible and easier than those in other textbooks.

1.6.4 Contention for Capital

When groups of investment opportunities are contending for limited capital, a new dimension is introduced. Capital budgeting procedures are presented in Chapter 6, including the hierarchical procedures that are used in practice.

1.6.5 Leverage

Leverage—the use of borrowed investment capital—is given a modern treatment in Chapter 6, where it is treated in conjunction with capital budgeting.

1.6.6 Public-Sector Considerations

Engineers working in the public sector find a special set of problems: Benefits are difficult to estimate, the constituencies affected by decisions are wider, and economy-based considerations, no matter how broad-based or well-intentioned, do not necessarily dominate the decision-making process. Chapter 7 introduces the subject of public decision making (not really making, but advising) from the perspective of welfare economics theory.

1.6.7 Risk and Uncertianty

Chapter 8, which can be understood without a probability and statistics background, covers breakeven and sensitivity analysis and introduces expected-value decision making, portfolio risk, and geometric risk. Chapter 9 ("Probabilistic Decision Making") introduces more advanced topics requiring some prior understanding of probability and statistics.

1.6.8 Taxes, Depreciation, and Incentives

Income taxes are cash flows that, because of depreciation rules and incentives, can make decisions vary from those that would be made if taxes are ignored. (A straight income taxation scheme with capital expenditures treated as current expenses—no depreciation and no incentives—would not distort decision making.) Chapter 10 covers after-tax analysis in a modern way, with emphasis on worth measures of depreciation schedules.

1.7 EXERCISES

1. For the capacitor decision described in Section 1.1:
   (a) From the list of Steps in Engineering Economic Decision Making, match each task the engineer performed with a specific step.
   (b) If the engineer failed to consider the noise to be made by the capacitors and the land they would occupy, what step was slighted?

2. In Example E1, a principal decided to solve a school's space-heating problem by doing whatever would minimize costs over the next five years.
   (a) If, instead, the adopted criterion had been to buy the most fuel-efficient new furnace that was adequate and within the budget, some possible solutions would be ignored or discriminated against. Name and discuss some of these.
   (b) Name specific groups of people in the school or connected with it who could be significantly affected by the space-heat decision. They should come from several of the categories in the list of constituencies at the end of Section 1.2.

3. In the numbered list of Examples of Decisions Supported by Engineering Economy Calculations at the beginning of the chapter, identify which decisions appear to be in the public sector.

4. In Example E3 the purchase price of the Duro-Lite X2500 bulb was relatively high. At what purchase price would this bulb have the lowest total costs of any bulb (assuming $1 as the replacement cost added to purchase price)?

5. The R&D (research and development) manager of a corporation conducted a project up to the ready-to-patent stage, at a cost of $417,420. Completing the patent would have cost $22,000 more, and the patent could have been sold for $300,000. Under the corporation's accounting policy as perceived by the manager, it would look worse to have a completed project showing a loss of $139,420 than to have spent $417,420 on unfruitful research, so the manager decided not to apply for the patent. How much did this decision gain or lose for the corporation?

6. Cost overruns on a "$10 million" project have increased the projected cost to $15 million. $10 million has already been spent. It would take $1 million of cleanup expenditures to abandon the project now. Assuming the benefits from the completed project are worth $10 million, is it worthwhile to continue?

7. A government that imposes income taxes is a silent partner with respect to non-capitalized expenses and profits; $1 of additional receipts adds $1 to profit and increases the tax bill by T dollars, where T is the tax rate; $1 of additional costs reduces profit by $1 and decreases the tax bill by T dollars. Thus the after-tax cash flows, either positive or negative, are $(1 - T)$ times the before-tax cash flows.

   A company pays $390,000 income tax on $1,500,000 of income. It paid 16% on the first $50,000, and so on, up to 40% on all income over $400,000 (thus it is said to be in the "40% tax bracket"). For purposes of analyzing a prospective project's after-tax cash flows, what is the proper value of T for this company, so that before-tax receipts and disbursements can be multiplied by $(1 - T)$ to obtain the after-tax receipts and disbursements?

8. At Blandish Industries, it is estimated that a prospective new sprinkler system would reduce expected fire losses by $20,000 per year, and it is known that it would reduce fire insurance premiums by $40,000 per year. Blandish will remain insured, and insurance will cover 80% of all fire losses. What are the prospective annual benefits, in dollars per year, of the system?

9. Ten cadets are planning to spend their seven-day spring break at Fort Polk, La. Assume Fort Polk is 1000 miles away. They have decided to share automobile expenses equally and are considering three alternative car rentals. One dealer has offered car A for $19.78 per day plus $0.10 per mile traveled. Car A has a capacity of four people. Another dealer has offered car B for $19.92 per day plus $0.08 per mile. Car B has the same capacity as car A. Still another dealer has offered car C for $27.50 per day plus $0.12 per mile. Car C has a capacity of six people. The cadets will do business with only one dealer and will respect the cars' stated capacity limitations. The group estimates that in-and-around mileage at Fort Polk will be about 385 miles.

   (a) What is the most economical choice for the group?
   (b) Given the above answer, what is the cost of travel per person?
   (c) How much money could be saved if the cadets allowed themselves to do business with more than one dealer?

10. Two pieces of heavy equipment have the same earth-moving capabilities, but one is built for fuel economy:

	Primo	*Uggle*
Lease cost, $/mo	560.00	640.00
Fuel, gallon/hr	4.1	3.3
Maintenance, $/hr	1.10	3.00

   (a) If fuel costs are $1.19 per gallon and the equipment is to operate 150 hr/mo, which alternative is cheaper?
   (b) Determine the greatest fuel price for which the Primo equipment is cheaper than the Uggle.
   (c) Given a fuel price of $1.19 per gallon, determine the greatest number of operating hours per month for which the Primo equipment is cheaper than the Uggle.

11. Aguapico, a mechanical engineering firm that performs heating, ventilation, and air conditioning (HVAC) work for architects, has $284,331.01 of assets and $110,011.10 of liabilities. Its owner originally put $55,000 into the firm to get it started. Since then, how much more money have the owners put into the firm?

12. Suppose that the balance sheet given for Blandish Industries is a draft, and in reviewing the draft it is decided that the provision for bad debt should properly be $100,000 instead of $90,000. Further suppose that because this change diminishes reported profit, the income tax obligation is diminished so that accrued expenses become $726,000 instead of $730,000. Dividends to shareholders (not shown on the balance sheet) remain unchanged. Given these changes, what other changes must be made to the balance sheet?

13. Let Blandish Industries have had an opportunity in 1992 to undertake a plant expansion that would have been very profitable in the long run. If the opportunity had been undertaken, $1,420,000 of long-term debt would have been incurred; $1,900,000 of fixed assets would have been acquired, but $380,000 of depreciation on the new fixed assets would have been charged during the year. Assume that there would be no effect on current assets and that the effect on current liabilities would be to increase them by $112,000 (mostly interest on new long-term debt). As measured by the current ratio or quick ratio, would it have been safe to undertake the plant expansion?

14. Suppose that the balance sheet given for Blandish Industries is a draft. Prepare a corrected draft incorporating the following changes, assuming that earlier balance sheets are also corrected and ignoring tax consequences or penalties.
   • It has been decided to increase the provision for bad debt to $150,000.
   • A widget-making machine has been discovered to be improperly "off the books." It was acquired in 1988 at a cost of $180,000, and a total of $150,000 of depreciation on it would have already been charged.
   • A promissory note secured by the above machine is also improperly "off the books." Most of the note has been paid off, but a balance of $40,000 is still owed to the lender.

15. In the balance sheet for Blandish Industries, what percentage of accounts is believed to be uncollectible? If the provision for bad debt were increased, what is the smallest percentage of uncollectible accounts that would correspond to reducing either the quick ratio or the current ratio to a level considered unsafe?

16. In the general accounting reports given for Blandish Industries, if costs for materials had been twice what they were, what would have been the percentage reduction in Net Income Before Income Taxes compared to what was reported?

17. With respect to the balance sheet and income statement for Blandish Industries, if the enterprise had never borrowed any money (no notes, bonds, or debentures) but instead had financed all activities with retained earnings and the proceeds from issuance of stock, while total assets remained as reported:

    (a) Determine the revised Total Liabilitites and the revised Total Owner Equity.
    (b) Identify an expense that would not exist, and determine the revised Net Income Before Income Taxes.

18. For Blandish Industries, if labor costs are 15% higher the next year after the year reported, and the enterprise is otherwise in stasis:

    (a) Determine the next year's prospective operating margin of profit, net profit ratio (assume that income taxes will be 40% of net income), and interest coverage.
    (b) Determine the next year's prospective Net Income Before Income Taxes and compare it to that of the reported year.

19. In the general accounting reports for Blandish Industries, if there had been a 20% increase in sales, a 20% increase in returns and allowances, a 20% increase in selling and administrative expense, and a 20% increase in cost of goods sold, while otherwise the data would have been as reported:

    (a) Determine the resulting percentage increase in Net Income Before Income Taxes.
    (b) Determine the resulting ROI and compare it to the reported ROI.

20. For Blandish Industries, determine a cost of capital that would be too high for financial health, and determine the corresponding interest payments, assuming that everything except the interest on borrowed money was as reported.

Money makes money.

COMPOUND INTEREST AND DISCOUNTED CASH FLOW

Recall that nearly every engineering decision discussed in Chapter 1 involved benefits and costs occurring at different times. There are exceptions—in Example E3 of Chapter 1 all costs were annual, and in example E4 of Chapter 1 all consequences were immediate—but normally there is a *time value of money* to consider. The usual engineering economy decision involves an *investment* undertaken now in hope of later *returns* on the investment. If you cannot say whether the benefits of receiving $275 per year for five years outweigh the cost of spending $1000 now, you cannot evaluate such an investment.

The accepted representation of the time value of money is *discounted cash flow*, in which costs and benefits are compared to loans and repayments at compound interest. Other evaluation methods such as *payback time* (Chapter 4) have advantages such as not requiring exponents, but since the 1950s discounted cash flow is the standard approach.

This chapter presents the mathematics of discounted cash flow. It introduces compound interest and cash flows; it develops compound-interest formulas for cash-flow patterns of practical importance; it discusses the various computational methods for compound-interest problems; it develops timing conventions and alternative measures of interest; and it develops and exercises the concept of *equivalence* to simplify and clarify complicated compound-interest problems.

Compound interest is important to engineering decision making because it provides a way of rendering differently timed money payments commensurable (*commen-*

surable, from the Latin roots for *together* and *measurable*, means able to be compared on a common basis). Spending money on a new facility or on an improved design is likened to lending, and the resulting benefits are valued only to the extent that they occur sooner or in greater amount than if the same money had been lent at an appropriate interest rate.

All compound interest formulas are based on the concept of repayment of the principal and interest of a loan at compound interest.

2.1 COMPOUND INTEREST

The concept of *compound interest* was known in European moneylending and insurance in the eleventh century or earlier. The basic concept of *interest rate* probably arose with the first cities, thousands of years ago, along with institutionalization of private property and money. The concept directly flows from the simple consideration that if you lend or borrow twice as much money, it is fair that you should receive or pay twice as much interest, but if you lend or borrow a given amount for twice as long a *time*, it is fair that you should receive or pay *more* than twice the interest. There should be interest on interest as well as on principal.

2.1.1 Lump-Sum Repayment of a Loan

Let the symbol i represent the *interest rate* for one compounding interval; the length of a compounding interval is one year if not otherwise noted.

Let a lender lend P dollars to a borrower for one interval, at an agreed interest rate i. The borrower is thereby obligated to repay the *principal P* and pay *interest iP* to the lender at the end of the interval.

A lump-sum repayment F occurs when, at the end of n intervals, the lender repays the loan. For $n = 1$, the agreed repayment is $P + iP = P(1 + i)$ dollars at time 1. What is the fair repayment for $n = 2$, $n = 3$, and so forth?

If, at the end of one interval, the borrower repaid $P(1 + i)$ dollars but immediately borrowed $P(1 + i)$ dollars at the same interest rate, the borrower would be obligated, at the end of a further interval (that is, at time $n = 2$) to repay the principal $P(1 + i)$ and the interest $iP(1 + i)$ of the second loan; this repayment totals $P(1 + i)^2$ dollars. The two successive loans are the same as a loan of P dollars for two intervals, since no net transfer of money occurs at time 1. Thus we see that if $P(1 + i)$ is the agreed repayment for $n = 1$, then $P(1 + i)^2$ is the fair repayment for $n = 2$.

Continuing, we see that if the $P(1 + i)^2$ repayment due at time 2 is borrowed for another interval, so that no net transfer of money occurs at time 2, then the borrower owes $P(1 + i)^2$ principal and $iP(1 + i)^2$ interest at time 3; this sums to $P(1 + i)^3$ dollars. In general, the lump-sum repayment F at the end of n intervals at interest rate i for a loan P is

$$F = P(1 + i)^n \qquad (2\text{-}1)$$

E1. At an annual interest rate of 15%, what is the lump-sum repayment of a $1000 loan for four years?

$P = 1000$, $i = 0.15$, $n = 4$. Hence $F = 1000(1.15)^4 = \underline{\$1749.01}$

Equation 2-1 can be inverted to determine any one of the four quantities F, P, i, n given the other three.

E2. If the borrower can repay $1000 after two years, what amount can be borrowed, given a monthly interest rate of 1%?

P is the quantity whose value is sought. $F = 1000$. There are 12 compounding intervals per year, because the length of the interval is given as a month; thus two years is $n = 24$ intervals. The interest rate (monthly) is $i = 0.01$.

$$1000 = P(1.01)^{24} \quad \text{implies} \quad P = \underline{\$787.57}$$

Equation 2-1 is consistent for noninteger n. At a compound interest rate i, a loan of P dollars due at an arbitrary time t_1 would have repayment amount $P(1 + i)^{t_1}$ if Eq. 2-1 holds for continuous time. If the borrower borrows this amount for a further time interval $n - t_1$, the repayment at time n would be $[P(1 + i)^{t_1}](1 + i)^{n-t_1} = P(1 + i)^n$, exactly as given by Eq. 2-1. Thus n need not be an integer.

E3. Determine the repayment for a $1000 loan at 10% annual interest if repaid at the end of 0.1 years, 0.5 years, 0.9 years, 1 year, and 1.5 years, assuming no penalty for arbitrary timing.

$F = 1000(1.10)^n$ for $n = 0.1$, 0.5, 0.9, 1, and 1.5:

n	F
0.1	1009.58
0.5	1048.81
0.9	1089.57
1	1100.00
1.5	1153.69

The various inversions of Eq. 2-1 are summarized in Table 2-1, which also gives the traditional names and symbols for the quantities associated with lump-sum loans.

TABLE 2-1. Lump-Sum Loan Quantities and Formulas

i = interest rate
n = interval

Formula	Remarks	Equation Number
$F = P(1 + i)^n$	$(1 + i)^n$ is the "single-payment compound-amount factor" denoted "$(F/P\ i,n)$"	(2-1)
$P = F/(1 + i)^n$ $= F\beta^n$ where $\beta = 1/(1 + i)$	β is the "single-payment present-worth factor" denoted "$(P/F\ i,n)$"	(2-1a)
$i = (F/P)^{1/n} - 1$	Interest rate given F, P, n.	(2-1b)
$n = \dfrac{\ln\ (F/P)}{\ln\ (1 + i)}$	"Term of loan" given F, P, i. The natural logarithms can be replaced by logarithms to any base.	(2-1c)
$F - P = P(1 + i)^n - P$ $= P\{(1 + i)^n - 1\}$	"Amount of interest" or "interest" (as opposed to "interest rate") for a lump-sum loan.	(2-1d)

$\beta = \dfrac{1}{(1+i)^n}$

E4. **Determine the loan that would be repaid by a \$201.14 single payment five years from now if the annual compound interest rate is 15%.**

From Eq. 2-1a, $P = 201.14\beta^5$ where $\beta = 1/1.15$. $\underline{P = \$100.00}$

E5. **Determine both the annual interest rate and the monthly interest rate for a four-month \$1054.41 loan that is repaid by a \$1111.78 payment.**

From Eq. 2-1b, with $n = 0.3333$ years, $i = (1111.78/1054.41)^3 - 1$

$$= \underline{17.227\%} \text{ (annual)}$$

With $n = 4$ months, $i = (111.78/1054.41)^{1/4} - 1 \cong \underline{1.33\%}$ (monthly)

E6. **How long does it take money to double at 8% interest?**

For money to double is for F to equal $2P$. From Eq. 2-1c, with $F/P = 2$ and $i = 0.08$, $n = (\ln 2)/(\ln 1.08) = \underline{9.006}$ intervals. (If the 8% is an annual rate, the answer is in years.)

E7. **What is the amount of interest for a \$1000.00 loan at 8% annual interest if it is repaid by a single payment after 17 years?**

From Eq. 2-1d, $F - P = 100(1.08^{17} - 1) = \underline{\$270.00}$. Or, from Eq. 2-1, $F = 100(1.08)^{17} = 370.00$, so $F - P = 370 - 100 = 270$. *Note:* Although the amount of interest is meaningful in tax accounting, it is a misleading quantity in engineering economy, since it compares two differently timed cash flows without placing them on a commensurate basis.

2.1.2 Compound Amount or Future Worth

The quantities F, P, i, and n in Eq. 2-1 have other interpretations in addition to those appropriate for moneylending. F has been interpreted above as the lump-sum repayment of a loan. Its usual name is *compound amount*: if P dollars is deposited in a savings account at interest rate i for n intervals, it grows at *compound* interest to the *amount F*. The name *compound amount* and the symbol F are standard engineering economy nomenclature for the quantity F in Eq. 2-1 and related formulas.

F is also called *future worth*, a term that is meaningful in an investment context. To someone who can freely lend money at interest rate i, having F dollars at time n is worth the same as having P dollars at time zero; thus F is called the future worth of P. For example, if \$1000 is a present amount and investments are evaluated using an interest rate of 12%, then the future worth of this present amount at time n is $F = 1000(1.12)^n$; at 12% annual interest the future worth of \$1000 after five years is \$1762.34.

If you were given \$1000 today and could lend it or invest it at 12% annual interest, doing so would convert it to \$1762.34 at time $n = 5$ years. Of course, if you lend or invest, you can't use the money for other purposes in the meantime. Thus, if money is worth 12% annual interest, you have a choice of enjoying either the use of \$1000 today or the use of \$1762.34 in the future. Thus, at $i = 12\%$, \$1762.34 at $n = 5$ and \$1000 at

$n = 0$ are *equivalent*, and $1762.34 is the future worth of the $1000. It is worth just as much to have $1762.34 in the future as to have $1000 now.

2.1.3 Present Worth

P in Eq. 2-1 is interpretable not only as the principal of a loan, but as the *present worth* at i of a future sum F. If you needed to use $1762.34 at time 5 and could invest at 12%, you could forgo the use of $1000 now and let it grow; conversely, if you promised to pay $1762.34 five years from now and could borrow at 12%, then $1000 is the amount you could borrow. Just as the future $1762.34 is the future worth of $1000 today, $1000 is the present worth of the future $1762.34—assuming money can be freely lent and freely borrowed at 12%.

If an investment were to yield a return of F dollars at time n, then from Eq. 2-1a we would determine that return to have a present worth of $F\beta^n$ where β is defined as the reciprocal of $1 + i$. Multiplying a future amount by β^n is called *discounting*, and $\beta = 1/(1 + i)$ is the present-worth one-interval *discount factor*.

E8. An investment is anticipated to return $1000 at time 1 (time in years) and also $2000 at time 2. If i = 10% is an annual interest rate at which money can be freely lent or borrowed, what are the present worths of each of the returns, and what is the present worth of both of them?

$\beta = 1/1.10$. The present worths are $1000\beta^1 = \$909.09$ and $2000\beta^2 = \$1652.89$, and their sum is $\$2561.98$.

E9. If the foregoing investment requires an expenditure of $2400 now, what is the net present worth of the investment? Interpret the answer.

$2561.98 - 2400 = \$161.98$. The returns are worth $2561.98 in the sense that they could be converted to this amount, which is the total amount that could be borrowed at 10% interest if the returns were the repayments. The expenditure is worth a negative $2400, since it occurs now and is a disbursement rather than a receipt. The net effect of the whole scheme, if the future returns are converted, is a net receipt of $161.98 at time zero. At 10% interest, without actually converting the returns, they are said to be "equivalent" to receiving $161.98 at time zero.

The above examples introduce some important concepts. First, two or more returns can have a combined present worth, just as two or more repayments could repay a single loan (because two or more loans made at the same time, each repaid by a distinct lump-sum repayment, are the same as a single loan having a set of repayments). Second, the present worth of a payment made at time zero is the payment itself. Third, receipts and disbursements have opposite algebraic signs.

2.2 CASH FLOWS

In engineering economy we consider a transfer of money to be characterized by its *direction*, its *amount*, and its *timing* after some arbitrary time zero. We express direction by making the amount a signed number, with a positive sign (+) denoting an inflow or receipt and a negative sign $(-)$ denoting an outflow or disbursement. A transfer of an amount A_t at time t *from entity* A to entity B is called a *cash flow* of amount A_t at time t *for an entity* A (it is also a cash flow of the negative amount $-A_t$ at time t *for entity* B).

2.2.1 Cash-Flow Sets and Cash-Flow Diagrams

A *cash-flow set* $\{A_t\}$ for a set of times $\{t\}$ represents a related set of receipts and disbursements. For example, if a lender lends $100 at time zero and receives a $115 repayment at time 1, from the lender's viewpoint there is a cash-flow set consisting of two cash flows: the negative cash flow -100 at time 0, and the positive cash flow 115 at time 1.

If two cash-flow sets are identical except that two cash flows that occur at the same time in one set are replaced by their algebraic sum in the other set, we consider them *indistinguishable*. Thus paying out $100 and receiving $90, both at time 1, is the same as—is indistinguishable from—having a cash flow of $-\$10$ at time 1.

A *cash-flow diagram* depicts a cash-flow set visually. Time is represented by a scale on a horizontal axis (abcissa). Cash flows are represented by vertical arrows; each arrow has a *horizontal location* that represents the timing of the cash flow, an orientation—up for positive, down for negative—that represents the sign of the cash flow, and a length that represents the absolute amount of cash flow to approximate scale. Numbers near the heads of arrows show the absolute amounts; numbers near or on the horizontal axis, where the arrow tails originate, show timings. Figure 2-1 shows two indistinguishable cash flow diagrams; although the two diagrams look different, they are called indistinguishable because the sets of cash flows they represent are indistinguishable.

In bookkeeping and accounting there are *net amounts* that do not necessarily validly substitute for their set of component amounts in all subsequent calculations and whose component amounts are not necessarily paid at the same time. In engineering economy, however, cash flows can be replaced by their net amounts *only* when they occur at indistinguishable times, and the net amounts *always* can substitute for their set of component amounts.

Figure 2-2 shows that coeval (effectively simultaneous) cash flows can be represented either by stacked arrows or by combined arrows that show their net; it also illustrates *splitting* of cash flows into an indistinguishable set for clarity or simplification. Note the convention of labeling only the leftmost amount when successive cash flows have a common amount. Note that arrow lengths are not necessarily to strict scale; a cash-flow diagram is merely a sketch.

Example E1 from the lender's viewpoint:

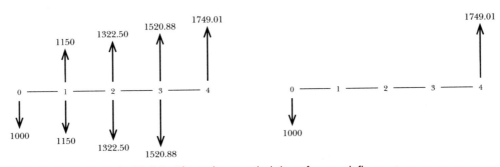

FIGURE 2-1. The indistinguishability of net-cash-flow sets.

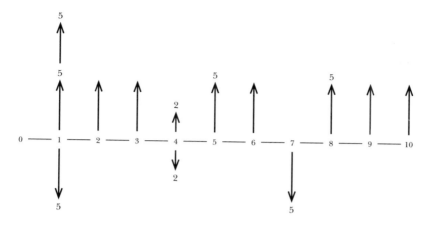

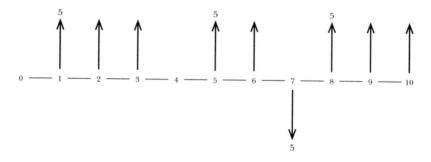

Combining of cash flows: The cash flow set represented by the above cash flow diagram is indistinguishable from the following one, in which net cash flows have been substituted for coeval sets of cash flows:

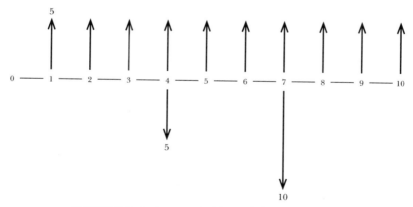

Splitting of cash flows: The cash flow set represented by the above two diagrams is indistinguishable from the following one, in which sets of coeval cash flows have been substituted for single ones where such splitting serves to reveal an overall pattern:

FIGURE 2-2. Indistinguishable cash-flow diagrams.

2.2.2 Compound Interest for Sets of Cash Flows

Let us now develop the definitions and tools needed for easy progress through the remainder of the book. We will define and use *worth*, *indistinguishability*, and *equivalence* for cash-flow sets and explore the basic properties of *geometric series*, *transaction sequences*, and *amortization schedules*.

2.2.2.1 Worth   If $\{A_t: t = 0,...,n\}$ is a cash-flow set, where we assume that for any particular time $t = m$ the amount A_m is the algebraic sum of all cash flows associated with that time, the *future worth of the cash-flow set* is defined as

$$F = \sum_{t=0}^{n} A_t(1 + i)^{n-t} \tag{2-2}$$

For example, if you deposit $100 today and $200 next year in a savings account that pays 8% annual interest, the balance at the end of the third year ($n = 3$) is the sum of the compound amounts of the first deposit, which will have been in the account for $n - t = 3 - 0 = 3$ years, and the second deposit, which will have been in the account for $n - t = 3 - 1 = 2$ years. Two separate applications of Eq. 2-1 would yield $100(1.08)^3 = \$125.97$ and $200(1.08)^2 = \$233.28$ as the compound amounts of the two respective deposits; Eq. 2-2 puts both calculations on the same time scale and sums the results to get $359.25.

The *present worth of a cash-flow set* $\{A_t: t = 0,...,n\}$ is defined as

$$P = \sum_{t=0}^{n} A_t\beta^t \tag{2-3}$$

where $\beta = 1/(1 + i)$. Equation 2-3 follows from the fact that since present worths have the timing $t = 0$, their sum is indistinguishable from the entire set of them. In the lending context, if A_t for each t is a repayment, then (from Eq. 2-1a) the loan repaid by A_t is $A_t\beta^t$; the loan repaid by the entire set of repayments $\{A_t\}$ is the sum of these loans.

Future worth and present worth are special cases of the more general quantity *worth*. At any time m, a discrete cash-flow set $\{A_t: t = 0,...,n\}$ has a worth F_m defined as

$$F_m = \sum_{t=0}^{n} A_t\beta^{t-m} \tag{2-4}$$

where $\beta = 1/(1 + i)$, and both the *worth evaluation time m* and the *payment times* $\{t\}$ are measured with respect to a starting time zero. Equation 2-4 is a generalization of Eqs. 2-2 and 2-3.

E10. Determine the worth, given a 10% interest rate, of the following cash-flow set at evaluation times $m = 0$, $m = 1$, $m = 2$, and $m = 3$:

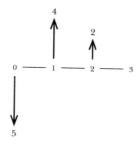

From Eq. 2-4, with $\{A_t: t = 0,1,2\} = \{-5, 4, 2\}$ and $= 1/1.1$:

$$\text{Worth at } m = 0 \text{ is } F_0 = -5 + 4\beta + 2\beta^2 = 0.2893$$
$$\text{Worth at } m = 1 \text{ is } F_1 = -5\beta^{-1} + 4 + 2\beta = 0.3182$$
$$\text{Worth at } m = 2 \text{ is } F_2 = -5\beta^{-2} + 4\beta^{-1} + 2 = 0.3500$$
$$\text{Worth at } m = 3 \text{ is } F_3 = -5\beta^{-3} + 4\beta^{-2} + 2\beta^{-1} = 0.3850$$

The worth at time zero, F_0, is the present worth; $F_0 = P$ in Eq. 2-3. The worth at time n, F_n, is the future worth; $F_n = F$ in Eq. 2-2. Worth can be interpreted in several different ways, allowing analogies between moneylending and other economic activities such as investing, insuring, betting, or comparison shopping. To understand the analogies and the various interpretations of worth, we need only to understand indistinguishability, equivalence, and transaction sequences.

2.2.2.2 Indistinguishability and Equivalence

From Eq. 2-4, since the set of discount factors $\{\beta^{t-m}\}$ is different for each distinct interest rate, the worth is equal at all interest rates for two sets of cash flows only if the sets have term-by-term identical amounts and timings. Thus *two cash-flow sets are indistinguishable iff their net cash flows at each time are equal to each other.*

Definition of Indistinguishability:
· ·

Two cash-flow sets are indistinguishable iff (if and only if) they have the same worths as each other regardless of interest rate.

From this it follows that paying off a one-interval loan and immediately borrowing, for the next interval, the amount just paid is indistinguishable from making a single repayment at the end of the second interval. Thus Eq. 2-1 follows from the concept of indistinguishability. Equations 2-2 and 2-3 also follow from indistinguishability; the total compound amount in a savings account is indistinguishable from the sum of the compound amounts of each deposit, and a total loan amount is indistinguishable from the sum of the loans that would individually be repaid by each one of the repayments.

One useful interpretation of present worth is that *the present worth of a cash-flow set is the loan that the cash flows repay.* Given this interpretation, if we augment the set of repayments by incorporating the loan itself, we see that at the interest rate of a loan, *the net present worth of the loan and its repayments is zero.*

E11. **A \$1000 loan at 15% annual interest is to be repaid by a set of two payments: X dollars at the end of one year and \$1000 at the end of two years. Determine X, and illustrate the two above interpretations of present worth in a moneylending context.**

The present worth of the set $\{X, 1000\}$ at times $\{1, 2\}$ equals the loan they repay. At $\beta = 1/1.15$, $P = X\beta + 1000\beta^2$ is the present worth of repayments. If this equals the \$1000 loan amount, then

$$X = \frac{1000 - 1000\beta^2}{\beta} = \underline{\underline{\$280.43}}$$

Alternatively, the present worth of the set $\{-1000, X, 1000\}$ at times $\{0, 1, 2\}$ must be zero at $i = 15\%$.

$$P = 0 = -1000 + X\beta + 1000\beta^2, \quad \text{giving the same result}$$

The two interpretations differ only in the trivial matter of whether the loan is part of the cash-flow set for which Eq. 2-4 is written; we can define the set of repayments and equate its present worth to the loan amount, or we can define the set of all payments including the loan and equate its present worth to zero.

Equivalence is the most important concept in engineering economy. It is what renders differently timed cash flows commensurable. See Section 2.8 for a full treatment.

Definition of Equivalence:
. . . .

Two cash-flow sets are equivalent at a given interest rate iff (if and only if) they have the same worths as each other at that interest rate.

A single cash flow at time zero whose amount equals P is equivalent to the cash-flow set for which Eq. 2-3 *at the fixed interest rate* yields P. Hence *two cash-flow sets that have the same present worth are equivalent at the interest rate at which the present worth is computed.*

E12. **Show that the following two cash-flow sets are not indistinguishable, but are equivalent at 10% interest.**

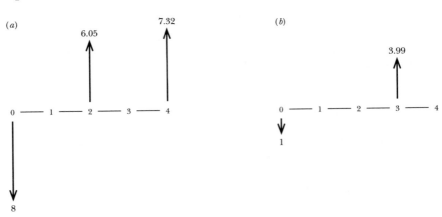

Let the two present worths be

$$P^{(a)} = -8 + 6.05\beta^2 + 7.32\beta^4$$

and

$$P^{(b)} = -1 + 3.99\beta^3$$

At various interest rates:

i	β	$P^{(a)}$	$P^{(b)}$
9.9%	1/1.099	2.03	2.01
10%	1/1.100	2.00	2.00
10.1%	1/1.101	1.97	1.99

The two sets are equivalent at 10% interest, since they have the same present worths at that interest rate. But to be indistinguishable they would need to have the same present worths at all interest rates; that would require identical net cash flows at identical times.

Two equivalent cash-flow sets not only have the same present worth; they have the *same worth at any time*. To see this, consider Eq. 2-4 at various values of m:

$$F_m = \sum_{t=0}^{n} A_t \beta^{t-m} = \sum_{t=0}^{n} A_t \beta^t (1+i)^m$$

$$= (1+i)^m \sum_{t=0}^{n} A_t \beta^t = (1+i)^m P \qquad (2\text{-}5)$$

Thus any cash-flow set having a present worth P at some interest rate i has a worth at time m of $(1+i)^m P$. Hence if any two cash flow sets both have the same present worths, they have the same worths at any time m.

The converse of Eq. 2-5 is

$$P = \beta^m F_m \qquad (2\text{-}6)$$

The concept of equivalence at an interest rate will be exploited further in Section 2.8.

E13. Determine the worths at time 4 at 10% interest for the two cash-flow sets of Example E12 by using Eq. 2-5 on the previous results; verify the answers by using Eq. 2-4.

At 10% interest, $P^{(a)} = P^{(b)} = 2.00$ from Example E12.
Equation 2-5 gives $F_4 = (1.10)^4 2.00 = \underline{2.93.}$

For (a), Eq. 2-4 gives

$$-8\beta^{-4} + 6.05\beta^{-2} + 7.32\beta^0$$

$$= -8(1.1)^4 + 6.05(1.1)^2 + 7.32 = \underline{2.93}$$

For (b), Eq. 2-4 gives

$$-1\beta^{-4} + 3.99\beta^{-1}$$
$$= -1(1.1)^4 + 3.99(1.1) = \underline{2.92} \text{ (round-off error)}$$

2.3 COMPOUND INTEREST COMPUTATIONS

Equation 2-4 for the worth of a discrete cash-flow set is the fundamental expression of the time value of money. Compound interest calculations of all sorts, from determining loan repayments to evaluating investments, can be solved using any one of three main computational approaches to manipulating Eq. 2-4: the *spreadsheet* approach, the *transaction sequence* approach, or the *formulaic* approach. Modern nonprocedural engineering economy software products, such as the MODWORTH program that accompanies this book, use all three approaches internally; externally, they merely require the user to specify or retrieve a cash-flow set, specify what result is required (present worth or worth at a specified evaluation time, rate of return, or any of many other functions to be defined later in this book), and specify an interest rate and any other applicable conditions (inflation rate, income tax rate, risk). Traditional manual procedures, involving looking up factors tabulated in interest tables, apply the formulaic approach. Financial hand calculators also apply the formulaic approach; they emulate the traditional manual procedures, but they evaluate factors on demand rather than retrieving them from tables.

2.3.1 Spreadsheet Approach

In modern computing environments the only significant costs of performing calculations are the human efforts of setup and data entry. Engineering economy problems often arise in a spreadsheet environment, where the data are available in matrix form. Typically there is a row for each cash-flow set, with time represented by column. The spreadsheet (term-by-term) approach is natural to use. For example, recall the cash-flow set in Figure 2-2. Suppose we want to determine its present worth at 10% compound interest, and suppose the data are available in the following form (from the upper version of the cash-flow diagram in Figure 2-2):

Time, t	0	1	2	3	4	5	6	7	8	9	10
Tax Savings	0	5	0	0	0	0	0	0	0	0	0
Receipts	0	5	5	5	2	5	5	0	5	5	5
Disbursements	0	−5	0	0	−2	0	0	−5	0	0	0

To determine the present worth of the cash-flow set, let $\beta = 1/1.10$ and form a row $\{\beta^t\}$ where t is the value in the time row:

Discount Factors	β^0	β^1	β^2	β^3	β^4	β^5	β^6	β^7	β^8	β^9	β^{10}

where β^0 is 1, β^1 is 0.90909, β^2 is 0.82644, and so on.

Also form a row that is the sum of the three cash-flow rows (the same as the middle version of the cash-flow diagram in Figure 2-2):

Net Cash Flows	0	5	5	5	0	5	5	−5	5	5	5

To determine the present worth, multiply term-by-term the elements of the Discount Factors row and the Net Cash Flows row, and sum the results. The result is about 23.18.

These manipulations may be performed not only by spreadsheet, but in any third-generation interactive language. Given the vector of cash-flow amounts $\{A_t: t = 1,...,n\}$ and a value of $\beta = 1/(1 + i)$, in the Basic language, if A is the vector, N is n, and B is β, the present worth is P as computed by the statements

```
10   P = 0                    initialize sum
20   FOR T = 1 TO N
30   P = P + A(T)*B^T          add A_t β^t to sum
40   NEXT T
```

In the APL language, if A is the vector and B is β, the present worth can be computed by the expression

$$+/A \times B*\iota\rho A$$

(ρA is the number of elements in A, which is n, and $\iota\rho A$ is $\{1,...,n\}$; $B*\iota\rho A$ is β raised to these powers; $A \times B*\iota\rho A$ is the vector of terms $A_t\beta^t$, and "$+/$" sums them.)

The worth at any other time m can then be determined by multiplying by $\beta^{-m} = (1 + i)^m$, as shown in Eq. 2-5.

Commercial spreadsheet programs (e.g., those trademarked Lotus 1-2-3 and Quat-troPro) and financial planning languages (e.g., IFPS by Execucom) usually have a present-worth function. Columns are often assumed to constitute an equal-increment time scale; the user identifies the row or rows containing cash-flow amounts and inputs an interest rate per time increment (see Section 2.5 for converting interest rates from one time scale to another); the function returns the present worth, which must be interpreted according to the timing convention adopted by the user or software designer: if the first column represents time zero, the worth is at that time; if the first column represents the first period or interval, the worth is as of one interval earlier. That is, if the payments are at times $\{1,...,n\}$, the present worth is at time zero, which is one time interval before time 1.

2.3.2 Transaction-Sequence Approach

Cash flows may be viewed as *transactions* that increase or decrease the balance of an account. Let the transactions be numbered $h = 1, 2,..., H$. Let the hth transaction have an amount X_h and occur at time t_h, bringing the balance to B_h.

The transaction-sequence approach to compound-interest computations consists of updating the balance at each transaction. Two things change the balance: the cash flow X_h, and growth of the previous balance B_{h-1} at compound interest in the time interval $t_h - t_{h-1}$:

Balance in an account after a transaction:

$$B_h = X_h + B_{h-1}(1 + i)^{t_h-t_{h-1}} \qquad [2\text{-}7]$$

E14. A depositor begins a savings account by depositing $1000. The account pays $i = 1\%$ monthly compound interest. Using Eq. 2-7, determine the balance after a $300 withdrawal that occurs three months later.

The first transaction is to add $1000 to an empty account, so $B_1 = 1000$. If the second transaction is to withdraw $300 at time 3, then $X_2 = -300$, $t_2 - t_1 = 3$, and Eq. 2-7 gives

$$B_2 = -300 + 1000(1 + 0.01)^3 = \underline{\underline{\$730.30}}$$

Actually many financial institutions regularly update their customers' accounts, and they round to the nearest cent at each step. If there are interest-crediting transactions at the ends of the first and second months, Eq. 2-7 gives the same final result:

At $t_2 = 1$: $B_2 = 0 + 1000(1 + 0.01)^{1-0}$ $= \$1010.00$
At $t_3 = 2$: $B_3 = 0 + B_2(1 + 0.01)^{2-1}$ $= \$1020.10$
At $t_4 = 3$: $B_4 = -300 + B_3(1 + 0.01)^{3-2} = \underline{\underline{\$730.30}}$

Note that, except for rounding, the addition of zero-amount transactions into the transaction sequence, such as for balance inquiries or for interest crediting, does not affect the final balance. Also note that with interest crediting performed at the end of each compounding interval, $1 + i$, is never raised to a power; before electronic computers, this was an important advantage of the transaction-sequence approach to financial bookkeeping.

Balance and compound amount are the same; the balance of an account at time t_h equals the worth of all the cash flows into and out of the account through time t_h. To see this, recall from Examples E8 and E9 the net present worth of a $2400 investment that yields returns of $1000 at time 1 and $2000 at time 2:

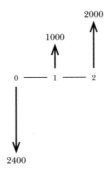

At $i = 10\%$ interest, the present worth of this cash flow set was asserted to be $161.98. Let us verify this using the transaction-sequence approach. The first transaction is -2400 at time 0; the next is 1000 at time 1; the last is 2000 at time 2:

At time 0: $B_1 = -2400$
At time 1: $B_2 = 1000 + 1.10B_1 = -1640.00$
At time 2: $B_3 = 2000 + 1.10B_2 =$ 196.00

Thus the transaction sequence gives a worth at time 2 of $196.00. From Eq. 2-1a, the present worth of this $196.00 is

$$P = 196(1/1.10)^2 = \$161.98$$

This verifies the earlier result and demonstrates how the compound amount of the cash flow set is the same as the balance of an account whose transactions are the cash flows.

It is usual to organize transaction-sequence computations in tabular form, with a row for each transaction. It is also usual to decompose Eq. 2-7 so that the interest J_h, which is the amount by which the previous balance grew at compound interest from time t_{h-1} to time t_h, is separately shown:

$$B_h = X_h + B_{h-1} + J_h \tag{2-7a}$$

where

$$J_h = B_{h-1}(1 + i)^{t_h - t_{h-1}} - B_{h-1} \tag{2-7b}$$

Usually there is a transaction at every compounding interval, so that $t_h - t_{h-1} = 1$, allowing Eq. 2-7b to simplify to $J_h = iB_{h-1}$. The following example shows the tabular form for both regular and irregular intervals:

E15. Bobby borrows $2000 from his employer and agrees to repay $500 out of each biweekly paycheck until the debt is retired. However, it is also agreed that he may make additional payments at any time or may receive wage advances at any time. The biweekly interest rate is 0.0057. Transactions proceed as follows:

h	Time in Two-Week Units	Interest	Payment	Balance
1	0	—	−2000	−2000
2	1	−11.40	500	−1511.40
3	2	−8.61	1000	−520.01
4	2.2	−0.59	−200	−720.60
5	3.5			0

(After borrowing at time 0, Bobby paid $500 at time 1, made a double payment of $1000 at time 2, borrowed an additional $200 at time 2.2, and paid off the account at time 3.5.) Verify the interest at time 2.2, determine the interest at time 3.5, and determine the closing payment.

The interest at time 2.2 is the interest on the balance −520.01 for the time interval 2.2 − 2 = 0.2:

$$-520.01(1.0057)^{0.2} + 520.01 = \underline{-\$0.59.}$$

The interest at time 3.5 is the interest on the balance −720.60 for the time interval 3.5 − 2.2 = 1.3:

$$-720.60(1.0057)^{1.3} + 720.60 = \underline{-\$5.34.}$$

The closing payment is X such that the closing balance is zero. The closing balance is the previous balance plus interest plus the payment:

$$0 = -720.60 - 5.34 + X_{3.5}$$

$$X_{3.5} = \underline{\$725.94.}$$

It should be noted that commercial loan accounts usually define the balance and interest amounts to have the opposite signs to those assumed here.

2.3.3 Formulaic Approach

Since most of engineering economy deals with estimates of future cash flows, we will deal mostly with simple patterns of cash flow: *equal-payment series* (Section 2.4), in which there are n equal cash flows at equal time intervals; *linear* and *geometric-gradient series* (Section 2.6), in which cash-flow amounts regularly increase or decrease with time; and a few simple *continuous-cash-flow profiles* (Section 2.7). For all simple patterns of cash flow, there are closed-form formulas that allow expressing worths compactly in terms of a few parameters. We use the formulaic approach throughout this book.

Standard interest tables for manual calculation typically have a page for each interest rate. On each page there is a row for each integer value of n. There is a column labeled *P/F* or *(P/F i,n)*, containing values of the "single-payment present-worth factor" for a payment of F dollars made at time n. Instead of solving Eq. 2-1a, the user looks up this factor and multiplies it by F to determine P. There is a column labeled *P/A* or *(P/A i,n)*, containing values of the "pain" factor (see Section 2.4 to follow) for a series of n equal payments of A dollars each, made at times 1, 2,..., n. There is a column labeled *F/P* or *(F/P i,n)*, whose values are the reciprocals of the values in the *P/F* column, so that to determine the future worth at time n of a present amount P, the user can multiply by this instead of divide by the *P/F* factor. Similarly there is a column labeled *A/P* or *(A/P i,n)*, whose values are the reciprocals of *P/A* (*A/P* is the factor that one can multiply by a loan amount to determine the amount of a series of equal payments that repay the loan; it is traditionally called the "capital recovery factor" because A can represent the periodic returns that pay off an investment P). Most tables also provide a column labeled *F/A* or *(F/A i,n)*, whose values are the product of *F/P* and *P/A* (if n equal payments of A dollars each are deposited into a savings account at the ends of periods 1, 2,..., n, then *F/A* is the factor that one can multiply by A to determine the final account balance). *A/F*, the reciprocal of *F/A*, is often provided also and is traditionally called the "sinking fund factor" because A can represent the periodic deposits that build up a sinking fund to amount F (a sinking fund is a savings account accumulated to pay off a debt or replace equipment).

Tables 2-2a and 2-2b illustrate standard interest tables for two interest rates: $i = 0.01$ or 1%, which is a typical interest rate when time is counted in one-month periods, and $i = 0.10$ or 10%, which is a typical interest rate when time is counted in years.

For rough estimation of the single-payment present-worth factor $(P/F\ i,n) = \beta^n$, the nomograph on the inside of the front cover can be used. A straight line through specific values of any two of the three quantities i, n, and $(P/F\ i,n)$ intersects the value of the third. For rough estimation of the "pain" factor to be defined in Section 2.4.1, the chart on the inside of the back cover can be used. There is a curve for each value of i; read up from n to the i curve, then over to the corresponding value of $(P/A\ i,n)$.

TABLE 2-2A. Standard Interest Table for 1% Interest

n	Single-payment compound-amount factor $(F/P\ 1\%,n)$	Single-payment present-worth factor $(P/F\ 1\%,n)$	Equal-payment series compound-amount factor $(F/A\ 1\%,n)$	Capital recovery factor $(A/P\ 1\%,n)$
1	1.0100	0.9901	1.0000	1.0100
2	1.0201	0.9803	2.0100	0.5075
3	1.0303	0.9706	3.0301	0.3400
4	1.0406	0.9610	4.0604	0.2563
5	1.0510	0.9515	5.1010	0.2060
6	1.0615	0.9420	6.1520	0.1725
7	1.0721	0.9327	7.2135	0.1486
8	1.0829	0.9235	8.2857	0.1307
9	1.0937	0.9143	9.3685	0.1167
10	1.1046	0.9053	10.4622	0.1056
11	1.1157	0.8963	11.5668	0.0965
12	1.1268	0.8874	12.6825	0.0888
13	1.1381	0.8787	13.8093	0.0824
14	1.1495	0.8700	14.9474	0.0769
15	1.1610	0.8613	16.0969	0.0721
16	1.1726	0.8528	17.2579	0.0679
17	1.1843	0.8444	18.4304	0.0643
18	1.1961	0.8360	19.6147	0.0610
19	1.2081	0.8277	20.8109	0.0581
20	1.2202	0.8195	22.0190	0.0554
21	1.2324	0.8114	23.2392	0.0530
22	1.2447	0.8034	24.4716	0.0509
23	1.2572	0.7954	25.7163	0.0489
24	1.2697	0.7876	26.9735	0.0471
25	1.2824	0.7798	28.2432	0.0454
26	1.2953	0.7720	29.5256	0.0439
27	1.3082	0.7644	30.8209	0.0424
28	1.3213	0.7568	32.1291	0.0411
29	1.3345	0.7493	33.4504	0.0399
30	1.3478	0.7419	34.7849	0.0387
31	1.3613	0.7346	36.1327	0.0377
32	1.3749	0.7273	37.4941	0.0367
33	1.3887	0.7201	38.8690	0.0357
34	1.4026	0.7130	40.2577	0.0348
35	1.4166	0.7059	41.6603	0.0340
36	1.4308	0.6989	43.0769	0.0332
37	1.4451	0.6920	44.5076	0.0325
38	1.4595	0.6852	45.9527	0.0318
39	1.4741	0.6784	47.4122	0.0311
40	1.4889	0.6717	48.8864	0.0305
41	1.5038	0.6650	50.3752	0.0299
42	1.5188	0.6584	51.8790	0.0293
43	1.5340	0.6519	53.3978	0.0287
44	1.5493	0.6454	54.9317	0.0282
45	1.5648	0.6391	56.4811	0.0277
46	1.5805	0.6327	58.0459	0.0272
47	1.5963	0.6265	59.6263	0.0268
48	1.6122	0.6203	61.2226	0.0263
49	1.6283	0.6141	62.8348	0.0259
50	1.6446	0.6080	64.4632	0.0255

TABLE 2-2B. Standard Interest Table for 10% Interest

n	Single-payment compound-amount factor (F/P 10%,n)	Single-payment present-worth factor (P/F 10%,n)	Equal-payment series compound-amount factor (F/A 10%,n)	Capital recovery factor (A/P 10%,n)
1	1.1000	0.9091	1.0000	1.1000
2	1.2100	0.8264	2.1000	0.5762
3	1.3310	0.7513	3.3100	0.4021
4	1.4641	0.6830	4.6410	0.3155
5	1.6105	0.6209	6.1051	0.2638
6	1.7716	0.5645	7.7156	0.2296
7	1.9487	0.5132	9.4872	0.2054
8	2.1436	0.4665	11.4359	0.1874
9	2.3579	0.4241	13.5795	0.1736
10	2.5937	0.3855	15.9374	0.1627
11	2.8531	0.3505	18.5312	0.1540
12	3.1384	0.3186	21.3843	0.1468
13	3.4523	0.2897	24.5227	0.1408
14	3.7975	0.2633	27.9750	0.1357
15	4.1772	0.2394	31.7725	0.1315
16	4.5950	0.2176	35.9497	0.1278
17	5.0545	0.1978	40.5447	0.1247
18	5.5599	0.1799	45.5992	0.1219
19	6.1159	0.1635	51.1591	0.1195
20	6.7275	0.1486	57.2750	0.1175
21	7.4003	0.1351	64.0025	0.1156
22	8.1403	0.1228	71.4028	0.1140
23	8.9543	0.1117	79.5431	0.1126
24	9.8497	0.1015	88.4974	0.1113
25	10.8347	0.0923	98.3471	0.1102
26	11.9182	0.0839	109.1818	0.1092
27	13.1100	0.0763	121.1000	0.1083
28	14.4210	0.0693	134.2100	0.1075
29	15.8631	0.0630	148.6310	0.1067
30	17.4494	0.0573	164.4941	0.1061
31	19.1944	0.0521	181.9435	0.1055
32	21.1138	0.0474	201.1379	0.1050
33	23.2252	0.0431	222.2517	0.1045
34	25.5477	0.0391	245.4768	0.1041
35	28.1025	0.0356	271.0245	0.1037
36	30.9127	0.0323	299.1270	0.1033
37	34.0040	0.0294	330.0397	0.1030
38	37.4044	0.0267	364.0437	0.1027
39	41.1448	0.0243	401.4480	0.1025
40	45.2593	0.0221	442.5928	0.1023
41	49.7852	0.0201	487.8521	0.1020
42	54.7637	0.0183	537.6373	0.1019
43	60.2401	0.0166	592.4011	0.1017
44	66.2641	0.0151	652.6411	0.1015
45	72.8905	0.0137	718.9053	0.1014
46	80.1796	0.0125	791.7958	0.1013
47	88.1975	0.0113	871.9754	0.1011
48	97.0173	0.0103	960.1731	0.1010
49	106.7190	0.0094	1057.1900	0.1009
50	117.3909	0.0085	1163.9090	0.1009

2.3.4 Search Computations for Rate of Return

In engineering economy we often invert the question: "What is the worth of this cash flow set at a given interest rate?" to ask questions whose answers are more difficult to compute:

"At what interest rate would the worth be a given amount?"
"How long must the cash flows continue for the worth to be positive?"
"How long could the cash flows be delayed for the worth to remain positive?"

Regardless of the computational approach—spreadsheet, transaction sequence, or formulaic—solving for an interest rate or a time can require a search technique, whereas solving for a worth or cash-flow amount does not. The quantity most commonly computed by search in engineering economy calculations is the rate of return.

Every cash-flow set that has both positive and negative cash flows has at least one *rate of return*, which is the interest rate at which the worth of the cash-flow set is zero.

Definition of Rate of Return:

A cash-flow set has a rate of return i^* if its worth is zero for an interest rate i equal to i^*.

Properties of rate of return and its use in decision making are dealt with extensively in Chapters 4 and 5. Here, let us give one trivial example:

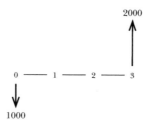

A \$1000 investment followed by a single \$2000 return after three years has a present worth $P = -1000 + 2000\beta^3$. For $P = 0$, we can solve for $\beta = (0.5)^{1/3} \cong 26\%$. Thus we say this cash-flow set has about a 26% rate of return. Recall Eq. 2-1b, with $F = 2000$, $P = 1000$, and $n = 3$, which gives the same result, $i \cong 26\%$. From that viewpoint, the interest rate on a \$1000 loan whose lump-sum repayment after three years is \$2000 would be about 26%. If a cash-flow set representing an investment and its returns has a rate of return i^*, then i^* can be considered as the interest rate at which the set's positive cash flows would repay loans constituting the set's negative cash flows.

For cash-flow sets more complicated than the above example, search computations are required to determine the rate of return. They can be accomplished using canned software routines (for example, most spreadsheet programs offer a rate-of-return routine) or by user-written logic. Here we will give the logic both for a user-controlled search and for an automated search.

2.3.4.1 User-Controlled Search Here is a program in Basic that determines the present worth of a cash-flow set for a range of interest rates IMM to IMX (entered as percentages, for example, 10 for 10% interest). Let N be the number of cash flows; let AMT be a vector of the N cash-flow amounts; let TIM be a vector of the N cash-flow times. Assign values to N, AMT, and TIM before line 50. Let INR be the interest rate that makes P = 0. The following set of statements obtains a minimum and maximum interest rate from the user, tries 100 interest rates in the range, and reports the worths and interest rates before and after the worth crosses zero. This gives a narrower range that the user can input in running the program again to refine the answer.

```
 50   INPUT "MIN, MAX % INTEREST"; IMM, IMX
 60   IMM = IMM/100
 70   IMX = IMX/100
 80   D = (IMX − IMM)/100
 90   POLD = 0
100   FOR INR = IMM TO IMX STEP D
110   BETA = 1/(1 + INR)
120   P = 0
130   FOR J = 1 to N
140   P = P + AMT(J)*BETA^TIM(J)
150   NEXT J
160   IF POLD*P > 0 THEN 200
170   IF POLD = 0 THEN 200
180   PRINT POLD, P
190   PRINT "ROR % BETWEEN "; 100*(INR − D); " AND "; 100*INR
200   POLD = P
210   NEXT INR
```

Consider the following cash-flow set:

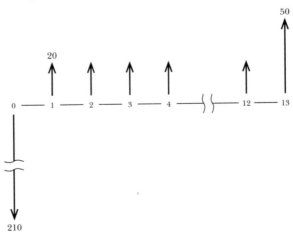

Running the above program for this cash-flow set gives the following result if the user first believes the rate of return must be between 0% and 20% and inputs "0, 20" in response to the "MIN, MAX % INTEREST?" prompt:

1.9862   −0.8230

ROR % BETWEEN 4.4 AND 4.6

Running again and inputting "4.4, 4.6" gives the result

$$7.0763\text{E-}04 \qquad -2.70176\text{E-}02$$
$$\text{ROR \% BETWEEN 4.542 and 4.544}$$

For a yet more accurate answer, the input "4.542, 4.544" yields

$$2.5177\text{E-}04 \qquad -724793\text{E-}05$$
$$\text{ROR \% BETWEEN 4.54204 AND 4.54206}$$

The process can continue up to the accuracy limit of the computer, increasing the accuracy two digits each time. To 7 digits, the rate of return is 4.542059%.

2.3.4.2 Automated Search

2.3.4.2 Automated Search The above user-controlled search has two disadvantages: It requires the user to participate, and it requires an unnecessarily large number of computations of P at various interest rates. Here is an automated search procedure that rarely requires as many as 10 computations of P and thus is practical for computing rates of return on a hand calculator without special software.

Consider the cash-flow set from the previous subsection. To follow the procedure conveniently using a hand calculator, use the following formula (the middle term will be derived in Section 2.4 and represents the worth of the series of $20 cash flows):

$$P = -210 + 20(1 - \beta^{13})/i + 30\beta^{13} \qquad \text{where } \beta = 1/(1 + i)$$

Solving this formula for 0% and 20% interest yields worths of 80 and -116.5424715. We will now begin a *bracketing interpolation* procedure for calculating rate of return.

Linear interpolation would give 8.1407341% as the interest rate for zero worth. This number can be computed as the y-intercept given by a linear regression routine where the **x** values are the worths and the **y** values are the interest rates. Alternatively, let i_1 and i_2 be two interest rates and let P_1 and P_2 be two corresponding present worths. By linear interpolation the next interest rate to try is

$$i_3 = i_1 - P_1 \frac{i_2 - i_1}{P_2 - P_1} = i_2 - P_2 \frac{i_2 - i_1}{P_2 - P_1} \tag{2-8}$$

For $i_1 = 0$, $i_2 = 0.20$, $P_1 = 80$, and $P_2 = -116.5424715$, this gives $i_3 = 8.1407341\%$ as before.

At this interest rate the worth P_3 is -42.295038. See Figure 2-3*a*. The new point (P_3, i_3) gives rise to a conjectured curve of i versus P, which is sketched in the figure. The curve passes through three known points, and if its curvature is coherent, its slope as it crosses the $P = 0$ vertical line should be between the old slope $(i_2 - i_1)/(P_2 - P_1)$ and the new slope $(i_3 - i_1)/(P_3 P_1)$ that is defined by a line between the new point and the point (P_1, i_1). See Figure 2-3*b*.
Thus i is bracketed:

$$i \text{ from old slope:} \qquad i_0 = i_3 - P_3 \frac{i_2 - i_1}{P_2 - P_1} \tag{2-9a}$$

$$i \text{ from new slope:} \qquad i_n = i_3 - P_3 \frac{i_3 - i_1}{P_3 - P_1} \tag{2-9b}$$

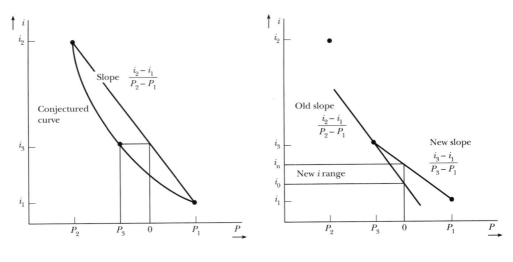

a. New rate i_3 and corresponding worth P_3 b. New i range from new and old slopes

FIGURE 2-3. Rate of return interpolation.

These equations give $i_0 = 0.038368259$ and $i_n = 0.053253079$ for our example. The corresponding worths are 10.1391678 and -10.4720139, but for greater efficiency it is best not to compute these but to compute P for interest rates inside the bracket, such as 4% and 5% (because the true slope was expected to be about halfway between the old and new slopes, so the interest rate is expected to be near the middle of the bracket, not near an endpoint).

Choosing these two interest rates suspected to bracket the rate of return completes one iteration of the bracketing interpolation procedure. The rate of return range was narrowed from the initial range of 0% to 20% to a range of 4% to 5%. To perform another iteration we would designate $i_1 = 0.04$ and $i_2 = 0.05$ and proceed as before. At each iteration the procedure requires three worth evaluations and three linear interpolations (or two-point linear regression computations). As is shown in exercises at the end of the chapter, the second iteration narrows the answer to four-figure accuracy: $i = 0.4542$ (then just the first interpolation of a further iteration would get the answer to seven digits: $i = 4.542059\%$).

2.4 EQUAL-PAYMENT (UNIFORM) SERIES

The cash-flow set $\{A_t = A : t = 1, 2, \dots, n\}$, consisting of n cash flows, each of the same amount A, at times $1, 2, \dots, n$, with no cash flow at time zero, is called the *equal-payment series*. An older name for it is the *uniform series*, and it has been called an *annuity*, since one of the meanings of "annuity" is a set of fixed payments for a specified number of years. The equal-payment series is the most important cash-flow set other than the lump sum, in that the vast majority of compound interest calculations in moneylending, finance, economics, and engineering economy are applied to cash-flow sets that consist of nothing but lump sums and equal-payment series.

2.4.1 The "Pain" Factor

The standard engineering economy symbol for the fixed payment size in an equal-payment series is A. The present worth of an equal-payment series, from Eq. 2-3, is

$$P = A\beta + A\beta^2 + A\beta^3 + \cdots + A\beta^n \tag{2-10}$$
$$= A\beta(1 + \beta + \beta^2 + \cdots + \beta^{n-1})$$

The sum in parentheses is that of a *finite geometric series*. The related *infinite geometric series* $\{1, \beta, \beta^2, \beta^3, \cdots\}$ has a finite sum $1/(1 - \beta)$ when $-1 < \beta < 1$, as can be verified by long division.

The sum in parentheses is then the difference between the infinite sum $1 + \beta + \beta^2 + \beta^3 + \cdots$ and the sum of the remaining terms beyond the β^{n-1} term, or $\beta^n + \beta^{n+1} + \beta^{n+2} + \cdots = {}^n(1 + \beta + \beta^2 + \beta^3 + \cdots)$. Thus

$$P = A\beta[(1 + \beta + \beta^2 + \beta^3 + \cdots) - \beta^n(1 + \beta + \beta^2 + \beta^3 + \cdots)]$$

$$= A\beta\left[\frac{1}{1 - \beta} - \beta^n\frac{1}{1 - \beta}\right] = A\beta\left(\frac{1 - \beta^n}{1 - \beta}\right)$$

But since $\beta = 1/(1 + i)$, it is true that $\beta/(1 - \beta) = 1/i$; also the limits $-1 < \beta < 1$ in terms of i are $0 < i < \infty$. Hence

$$P = A\frac{1 - \beta^n}{i} \qquad 0 < i < \infty \tag{2-11}$$

The quantity $(1 - \beta^n)/i$ in Eq. 2-11 is called the *equal-payment-series present-worth factor* and has the following symbol in standard engineering economy nomenclature:

$$(P/A \ i,n)$$

As an example of the nomenclature, $(P/A \ 10\%,5)$ is $(1 - \beta^5)/0.10$ where $\beta = 1/1.10$, or 3.79078677; at 10% interest, a set of five end-of-interval payments of A dollars each has a present worth of $3.79078677A$ dollars.

At zero interest ($i = 0$, $\beta = 1$), $(P/A \ i,n)$ is just n, so that the present worth is nA, the sum of the payments, as can be seen from the initial open form $P = A\beta + A\beta^2 + \cdots + A\beta^n$, or by applying L'Hospital's Rule to the closed form.

By multiplying numerator and denominator of Eq. 2-11 by $(1 + i)^n = \beta^{-n}$, the usually cited mathematical form of the equal-payment-series present worth factor is obtained:

$$(P/A \ i,n) = \frac{1 - \beta^n}{i} = \frac{(1 + i)^n - 1}{i(1 + i)^n} \tag{2-12}$$

Since "equal-payment-series present-worth factor" is too long a name and the standard nomenclature spells out a handy nickname, we will call $(P/A \ i,n)$ the "pain" factor. The nickname is consistent with its being the most complicated compound-interest formula in routine use; some students consider it a pain to compute $(P/A \ i,n)$.

Because computing values of $(P/A\ i,n)$ is very common, it is worthwhile to acquire skill in at least one routine way of determining $(P/A\ i,n)$ given i and n. Before the computer era the most practical method was to use interest tables like the ones illustrated in Section 2.3.3. Simon Stevin (1548–1620), who invented the decimal system of notating fractions and whose famous amphibious chariot/boat was celebrated in Laurence Sterne's novel *Tristam Shandy*, computed the first publicly available interest tables, beautifully printed by Christophe Plantin of Antwerp in 1582. Without significant alterations, these tables persisted until about 1990 as the chief tool for compound interest calculation, and this book is the first engineering economy textbook that does not contain at least 30 pages of them.

A subroutine for computing the "pain" factor is easy to write in any computer language:

Basic	APL
10 BETA = 1/(1 + I)	BETA ← 1 ÷ 1 + I
20 PAIN = (1 − BETA^N)/I	PAIN ← (1 − BETA*N) ÷ I

On a programmable hand calculator, it is worthwhile with the "pain" factor (but not with simpler factors such as β^n) to program it. With a $(P/A\ i,n)$ program, either on a financial calculator with built-in programs or with a user program, it requires four keystrokes and the two data values (PGM, program identifier, i, separator, n, RUN) to compute $(P/A\ i,n)$. Without a program, it requires 11 keystrokes and the two data values; for example, on a reverse-Polish-notation calculator (Hewlett-Packard), the actions are

Action	Value in Window	Values in Stack	
i value	i		
ENTER	i		
ENTER	i		i
1	1	i	i
+	$1 + i$		i
1/x	$\beta = 1/(1 + i)$		i
n value	n	β	i
y^x	β^n		i
CHS	$-\beta^n$		i
1	1	$-\beta^n$	i
+	$1 - \beta^n$		i
x⇄y	i		$1 - \beta^n$
÷	$(1 - \beta^n)/i = (P/A\ i,n)$		

E16. At 1.0125% monthly interest, a 30-year mortgage loan (360 monthly payments) has payments of \$560.11. Determine the amount of the loan.

From Eq. 2-11, with $A = 560.11$, $i = 0.010125$, $\beta = 1/1.010125$, $n = 360$,

$$P = A\frac{1 - \beta^{360}}{i} = 560.11(96.137816) = \underline{\$53,847.75}$$

E17. Under a licensing agreement, Buzz Products will receive a $10,000 royalty check at the end of every year for 18 years. What is the present worth of the series of payments at 9.5% annual interest?

From Eq. 2-11, with $A = 10,000$, $i = 0.095$, $\beta = 1/1.095$, $n = 18$,

$$P = 10000\frac{1 - \beta^{18}}{0.095} = \underline{\underline{\$84,712.66}}$$

The answer can be interpreted as the amount Buzz Products could borrow at 9.5% interest if it spent its royalty payments as loan repayments.

As $n \to \infty$, the infinite equal-payment series $\{A_t = A: t = 1,2,...\}$ has present worth $P = A/i$.

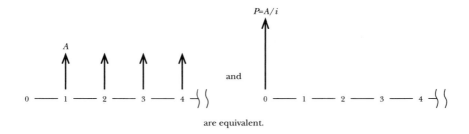

are equivalent.

The *equal-payment-series compound amount factor*, $(F/A\ i,n)$, follows directly from Eqs. 2-1 and 2-11:

$$F = P(1 + i)^n, \qquad \text{where} \qquad P = A\frac{1 - \beta^n}{i} \quad \text{for} \quad i \neq 0$$

$$= A(1 + i)^n\frac{1 - \beta^n}{i} = A\frac{(1 + i)^n - 1}{i} = A(F/A\ i,n) \tag{2-13}$$

Note that $(F/A\ i,n) = (F/P\ i,n)(P/A\ i,n)$, where $(F/P\ i,n)$ is the standard engineering economy symbol for the single-payment compound amount factor $(1 + i)^n$.

The family of Eqs. 2-11, 2-12, and 2-13 are transcendental in i or β and so cannot be solved for i or β. For integer n, the equations are polynomials in β or $1 + i$ and could be solved exactly for i in certain limited special cases (quadratic equation for $n = 2$, cubic for $n = 3$, etc.).

Given P, A, and i, we can solve for the number of payments n from Eq. 2-11:

$$P/A = \frac{1 - \beta^n}{i}$$

$$\beta^n = 1 - iP/A$$

$$n = \frac{\ln(1 - iP/A)}{\ln\beta} = \frac{-\ln(1 - iP/A)}{\ln(1 + i)} \tag{2-14}$$

For example, at 1% monthly interest, the number of monthly $100 payments needed to pay off a $1000 loan is (with $P = 1000$, $A = 100$, $i = 0.01$)

$$n = \frac{\ln[1 - 0.01(1000)/100]}{\ln\dfrac{1}{1.01}} = 10.5886 \text{ payments}$$

It would take 10 payments of $100 each and an eleventh payment of a smaller amount, or 10 payments with the tenth one being greater than $100, to retire the loan.

2.4.2 Periodic Equivalent (Annual Worth)

The formula for A given P is of course the inverse of the formula for P given A:

$$A = P\frac{i}{1 - \beta^n} \qquad \text{for } i \neq 0 \tag{2-15}$$

For a zero interest rate, $A = P/n$. The factor after P in Eq. 2-15 is called the *equal-payment-series capital-recovery factor*:

$$(A/P\ i,\ n) = \frac{i}{1 - \beta^n} = \frac{1}{(P/A\ i,\ n)} \tag{2-16}$$

As $n \to \infty$, the infinite equal-payment series $\{A_t = A:\ t = 1,2,...\}$ approaches an amount $A = iP$.

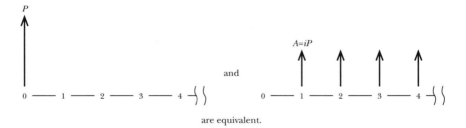

are equivalent.

E18. An auto loan is to have 36 equal end-of-month payments. The amount borrowed is $12,100. The interest rate is 0.91% per month. Determine the monthly payment amount.

From Eq. 2-15, with $P = 12100$, $i = 0.0091$, $\beta = 1/1.0091$, $n = 36$,

$$A = 12100\frac{0.0091}{1 - \beta^{36}} = 12100(0.0327008) = \underline{\$395.68}$$

Annual worth or *annual equivalent* is a worth measure sometimes used in decision making. It is called *periodic worth* or *periodic equivalent* if the compounding interval is other than a year. The periodic equivalent of an arbitrary cash-flow set $\{A_t:\ t = 0,...m\}$ is simply A for an "evaluating" cash-flow set $\{A,A,...,A\}$ at times $t = 1,2,...,n$, where this cash-flow set is equivalent at the interest rate to the arbitrary cash-flow set.

Associated with a periodic equivalent is its *horizon n*. Whereas present worth P is associated with time zero and future worth F is associated with the time of the final nonzero cash flow in a set, periodic worth has a designated horizon that is not necessarily the time of the final nonzero cash flow in the arbitrary set.

For example, we can ask for the annual equivalent with a five-year horizon of this cash-flow set:

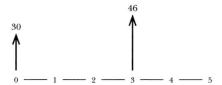

The annual equivalent is A in the evaluating set such that the evaluating set is equivalent, at a given interest rate, to the evaluated set:

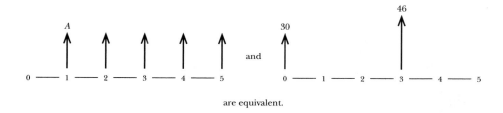

are equivalent.

E19. **Alma Soul has previously leased her song copyrights to publishers who would get the rights for five years and pay her an agreed fee at the end of each year. A publisher has made an offer to pay $30,000 now and $46,000 three years from now for a five-year package of copyrights. At 11% interest, express the offer in terms of her usual fee arrangement.**

We will find P equivalent to the offer, and then find A equivalent to P. For this offer, at $i = 11\%$, $\beta = 1/1.11$, $P = 30 + 46\beta^3$, in thousands of dollars. For the five-year evaluating cash-flow set, $A = Pi/(1 - \beta)^5$.

$$A = (30 + 46\beta^3)i/(1 - \beta)^5 = (63.6348035)(0.27057031)$$

$$= 17.21769 \quad or \quad \underline{\$17,217.69}$$

The annual equivalent or periodic equivalent when $n \to \infty$ in the evaluating set is called the *infinite-horizon annual* (or *periodic*) *equivalent*. It is iP where P is the present worth of the evaluated set. For example, if a cash-flow set has a present worth of $63,634.80 at 11% annual interest, its infinite-horizon annual equivalent is 11% of this, or $6999.83. Receiving $63,634.80 now is equivalent, at 11% annual interest, to receiving $6999.83 at the end of every year forever.

The *equal-payment-series sinking-fund factor* $(A/F\ i,n)$ is the reciprocal of the equal-payment-series compound amount factor:

$$A = F(A/F\ i,n) = F\frac{i}{(1 + i)^n - 1} = F\frac{1}{(F/A\ i,n)} \tag{2-17}$$

Note that

$$(A/F\ i,n) = (A/P\ i,n)(P/F\ i,n) = \frac{i}{1-\beta^n}\beta^n = \frac{\beta^n}{(P/A\ i,n)}$$

E20. A sinking fund is to be established to pay a known future obligation. At 8.5% annual interest, how much money must be deposited in the sinking fund at the ends of years 1, 2, and 3 to build up the sinking fund to $10,000?

From Equation 2-17, with $F = 10,000$, $i = 0.085$, $n = 3$:

$$A = 10,000\frac{0.085}{(1.085)^3 - 1} = 10,000(0.30653925) = \$3065.39\ /yr$$

Given F, A, and i, we can solve for n in Eq. 2-13 or 2-17:

$$iF/A = (1 + i)^n - 1$$
$$iF/A + 1 = (1 + i)^n$$
$$n = \frac{\ln(iF/A + 1)}{\ln(1 + i)} = \frac{\ln(iF/A + 1)}{-\ln\beta} \qquad (2\text{-}18)$$

E21. How many years would it take at a 10% interest rate for a series of year-end payments of $1000 to build up to $10,000?

From Eq. 2-18 with $F = 10000$, $A = 1000$, $i = 0.10$:

$$n = \frac{\ln(iF/A + 1)}{\ln(1 + i)} = \frac{\ln 2}{\ln 1.10} = 7.27254\ \text{years}$$

$F/A = 10$. From Eq. 2-13, $(F/A\ 10\%,7) = 9.487$, and $(F/A\ 10\%,8) = 11.43$; thus seven years is not enough, and eight years is more than enough.

2.5 TIME CONSIDERATIONS

Various measures of compound interest can be converted to one another by using the property

> A given interest rate, by any name, must give the same lump-sum repayment for a given loan.

In this book we use the compound interest rate per interval ("period" = "interval"), denoted i; the effective interest rate, which is i when the interval is one year, denoted i_{eff} (or i if a one-year compounding interval is understood in the context); the nominal interest rate r, which is the interest rate per interval times the number of intervals per year and which is also called "APR" (ANNUAL PERCENTAGE RATE) in transactions governed by the Federal Truth-in-Lending Act; the nominal continuous interest rate, also denoted r, which is the limit approached by the nominal interest rate as the number of intervals per year approaches infinity; the symbol $\beta = 1/(1 + i)$; and the expression $e^{-r} = \beta$, in which r always denotes the nominal continuous interest rate.

The following subsections develop the various measures of interest, the various measures of time, and the timing conventions by which unimportant timing distinctions can be ignored for conceptual or computational convenience.

2.5.1 Effective Interest Rate

In the familiar formula of Eq. 2-1, $F = P(1 + i)^n$, let there be m compounding intervals (periods) per year. Then n represents the number of intervals between the times of occurence of a loan P and its lump-sum repayment F. For an interest rate i per interval, the interest rate per year that gives the same repayment for the same loan is called the *effective interest rate* and is denoted i_{eff}.

Given $F = P(1 + i)^n$, which describes a loan in terms of time measured in intervals, we can describe the same loan in terms of time measured in years, where i_{eff} is the annual interest rate and n/m is the time span in years:

$$F = P(1 + i_{eff})^{n/m} \tag{2-19}$$

Equating the right-hand sides of Eqs. 2-19 and 2-1 and solving for i_{eff}, we have

$$(1 + i)^n = (1 + i_{eff})^{n/m}$$

Definition of effective interest rate:

$$i_{eff} = (1 + i)^m - 1 \tag{2-20}$$

Conversely,

$$i = (1 + i_{eff})^{1/m} - 1 \tag{2-21}$$

E22. A furniture loan has a finance charge (interest rate) of 1.5% monthly. What is its effective interest rate? Interpret the effective interest rate in this context.

From Equation 2-20, with $i = 0.015$ per interval and $m = 12$ intervals per year: $i_{\text{eff}} = (1 + i)^m - 1 = (1.015)^{12} - 1 = \underline{19.56\%}$.

Interpretation: If the customer purchased P dollars of furniture on credit and paid nothing at the ends of each of 11 months, so that the balance grew from P to $P(1.015)$ to $P(1.015)^2$, and so on, then the balance at the end of 12 months would be $P(1.015)^{12} = P(1.1956)$. Paying this balance would make the set of transactions indistinguishable from those of a one-year loan of P dollars at 19.56% interest.

E23. A five-year loan is to be made at 8% effective interest. Cite its interest rate per quarter if interest is to be compounded quarterly (four times per year).

Given $i_{eff} = 0.08$ and $m = 4$, from Eq. 2-21:

$$i = (1 + i_{eff})^{1/m} - 1 = (1.08)^{1/4} - 1 = \underline{\underline{1.94265\% \text{ per quarter}}}$$

We can define

$$\beta_{eff} = \frac{1}{1 + i_{eff}}$$

From the precursor to Eqs. 2-20 and 2-21, it immediately follows that

$$\beta_{eff} = \beta^m \tag{2-22a}$$

and

$$\beta = \beta_{eff}^{1/m} \tag{2-22b}$$

2.5.2 Nominal Interest Rate

Given interest rate i per interval, with m intervals per year, the *nominal interest rate r* is defined

$$r = mi \tag{2-23}$$

For example, 1% monthly interest is also called $r = 12\%$ nominal interest compounded monthly. Nominal rates are cited in informal language as per these examples:

"12% compounded monthly" = 1% per month
"18% compounded monthly" = 1.5% per month
"8% compounded daily" = 0.0219178% per day (assuming 365 days per year)

From Equations 2-20 and 2-23, the relationship between nominal and effective interest is

$$i_{eff} = (1 + r/m)^m - 1 \tag{2-24}$$

Nominal interest approximates effective interest, giving an underestimate that ignores "interest on the interest." In the United States, lenders in a wide variety of commercial lending situations are required to reveal the nominal interest rate and to label it prominently, cited as a percentage, as the ANNUAL PERCENTAGE RATE (APR).

E24. Determine the APR for the furniture loan of Example E21, which was made at a monthly interest rate of 1.5%. Compare the APR with the effective interest rate.

From Eq. 2-23 with $i = 0.015$ and $m = 12$:

$$r = mi = 12(0.015) = \underline{\underline{18\%}}$$

The effective interest rate was previously computed as 19.56%. The APR of 18% is an underestimate because its definition $r = mi$ ignores compounding within the year, whereas the definition of i_{eff} does not.

E25. A mortgage instrument quotes an APR of 12.231%. Determine i per month and i_{eff}.

From Eq. 2-23 with $r = 0.12231$ and $m = 12$:

$$i = r/m = \underline{1.01925\% \text{ monthly}}$$

From Eq. 2-20 with this i, or from Eq. 2-24:

$$i_{eff} = (1.0101925)^{12} - 1 = \underline{12.94\%}$$

2.5.3 Nominal Continuous Interest Rate

As the number of compounding intervals per year (m) increases without bound for a fixed nominal interest rate r, the rate per interval (i) will approach zero (Eq. 2-23), while the effective interest rate in Eq. 2-24 will increase toward a limit:

$$\lim_{\substack{r \text{ fixed,} \\ m \to \infty}} i_{eff} = \lim_{m \to \infty} 1 + r/m^m - 1 = e^r - 1 \qquad (2\text{-}25)$$

where $e \cong 2.718281828$ is the natural logarithm base, whose fundamental definition is as the limit of $(1 + r/m)^{m/r}$ as m increases without bound.

Equation 2-25 establishes the basis for *continuous compounding* of interest.

Continuous compounding is contrasted with *discrete compounding*, in which, strictly speaking, noninteger times are not defined. For example, if a payment is received before its due date, it may be credited as of the due date. All the formulas given in this chapter are valid for discrete compounding if times are restricted to be integers and are valid for continuous compounding if times are allowed to be noninteger.

2.5.4 Continuous Compounding of Interest

The compound-interest formulas developed thus far were shown to be valid for discrete compounding, in which all payment times are integer. The fact that the same formulas are valid for continuous compounding, where payment times are arbitrary, has been asserted and shown plausible, but not developed from first principles. We can now proceed to develop continuous-compounding formulas directly.

Let a lender lend P dollars to a borrower for one interval, where the duration of an interval is $1/m$ years (there are m intervals per year). The borrower is obligated to repay the principal P and pay interest iP to the lender at the end of the interval.

As in Section 2.1.1, if a lump-sum repayment F occurs at the end of n intervals, F repays the loan when $F = P(1 + i)^n$. This is Eq. 2-1. Now, given the definition of $i_{eff} = (1 + i)^m - 1$, which is Eq. 2-20, we can substitute $(1 + i_{eff})^{1/m}$ for $1 + i$ in Eq. 2-1:

$$F = P(1 + i_{eff})^{n/m} = P(1 + i_{eff})^\tau \qquad (2\text{-}26)$$

where τ is the number of years in the duration from loan to payment: $\tau = n/m$.

Note that by making m small enough and n large enough, we can express a given number of years (e.g., $\tau = 6.4183962$ years) to arbitrary accuracy. Thus Eq. 2-26 defines continuous compounding.

Since Eq. 2-20 or 2-21 is simply a definition, and since Eq. 2-1 was developed from first principles, Eq. 2-26 is from first principles. Using Eq. 2-1 with noninteger n is the same as using Eq. 2-26, as the following example demonstrates.

E26. At continuous compounding expressed as 14% nominal interest compounded quarterly, determine the repayment for a $1000 loan if repaid after 4.3172 quarters, using (a) Eq. 2-1 directly, and (b) Eq. 2-26.

The interest rate per quarter (Eq. 2-23) is $0.14/4 = 0.035$, or 3.5%.
(a) Equation 2-1 directly, with $i = 0.035$, $n = 4.3172$:

$$F = 1000(1.035)^{4.3172} = \underline{\$1160.11}$$

(b) Equation 2-26, with $i_{\text{eff}} = 1.035^4 - 1$ and $\tau = 4.3172/4 = 1.0793$ years:

$$F = 1000(1.035^4)^{1.0793} = 1000(1.035)^{4.3172} = \underline{\$1160.11}$$

In the limit, as m increases without bound, Eq. 2-26 expresses continuous compounding in terms of the nominal continuous interest rate r (called the "force" of interest in actuarial work). Inflections of Eq. 2-25 are

$$e^r = 1 + i_{\text{eff}} \tag{2-27a}$$

$$r = \ln\,(1 + i_{\text{eff}}) \tag{2-27b}$$

$$\beta_{\text{eff}} = \frac{1}{1 + i_{\text{eff}}} = e^{-r} \tag{2-27c}$$

Expressions in terms of r were traditionally used for routine computations in the days of slide rules, when it was more convenient to compute a fractional power of the natural logarithm base e than of an arbitrary quantity. Nowadays, it is easier simply to compute $(1 + i_{\text{eff}})^\tau$ than to determine r and compute $e^{r\tau}$.

E27. At continuous compounding expressed as 14% nominal interest compounded quarterly, determine the repayment for a $1000 loan if repaid after 4.3172 quarters, using the nominal continuous interest rate.

The interest rate per quarter is $i = 0.14/4 = 0.035$ or 3.5%. The effective rate is $i_{\text{eff}} = (1.035)^4 - 1 = 0.147523$.

From Eq. 2-27b:

$$r = \ln(1 + i_{\text{eff}}) = \ln\,1.147523 = 0.1376057$$

From Eqs. 2-27a and 2-26, with $\tau = 4.3172/4 = 1.0793$ years:

$$F = P(1 + i_{\text{eff}})^\tau = Pe^{r\tau} = 1000e^{(0.1376057)(1.0793)}$$

$$= \underline{\$1160.11}$$

Compared to computing $1000(1.035)^{4.3172} = \$1160.11$ directly, it is inconvenient to add the intermediate step of determining r so as to use $e^{r\tau}$ instead of $(1 + i_{\text{eff}})^{\tau}$.

The nominal continuous interest rate r is used in continuous cash flow formulas (Section 2.7), where e^{-rt} is a more natural quantity than $\beta^t_{\text{eff}} = 1/(1 + i_{\text{eff}})^t$ to use in formulas that involve integration of functions.

A distinction must be drawn between discrete compounding as a *means of expressing an interest rate* and discrete compounding as a *rule in monetary transactions*. If a citation such as "14% compounded quarterly" is meant as a rule governing transactions, it literally forbids transactions between intervals. Carried over into engineering economy applications, this interpretation would imply, for example, that a $10,000 cost incurred in the middle of a quarter would have to be treated as if it occurred at the beginning or end of the quarter. Continuous compounding is assumed throughout this text where cash flows such as savings, operating costs, and capital expenditures are involved, except that discrete formulas can be used for simplicity.

2.5.5 Timing Conventions

It has been conventional in engineering economy to treat most expenditures in a time interval as if they occurred at the end of the interval. There are three reasons for this:

1. An end-of-interval convention is simple.
2. Money is less useful for short arbitrary time intervals than continuous compounding implies.
3. Errors introduced by an end-of-interval convention are small.

The mathematics of discrete formulas is simpler than that of continuous ones, and a coarse time scale discourages unneeded estimation of precise timings. Some engineers object to continuous compounding on the practical grounds that a windfall could not be invested at once (unlike depositing money in a bank, investing in productive assets requires time to plan, design, procure, construct, etc.), and that an end-of-interval convention models such delays—if not well, at least better than continuous compounding models them. This second argument echoes moneylenders who view early payment of a loan as a loss of interest that they would otherwise have kept earning. Lenders are also inconvenienced by expenditures at arbitrary times ("substantial penalty for early withdrawal"). Compound interest is an imperfect pricing structure for either moneylenders or investors (it ignores such costs as those of identifying borrowers or investments, and the facts that money not lent or invested earns nothing and that money quickly needed is more expensive to borrow). The third argument, that errors are small, is valid for time intervals up to about a year for most situations, as we shall explore below.

The specific convention most often used is the *end-of-year convention*. This is the coarsest form of the end-of-interval convention; some analysts prefer using half-years or quarters.

A rough estimate of the end-of-year convention's effect on engineering-economy decision making follows from noting that it tends to treat in-between cash flows as if they occurred about a half-year late. (A more rigorous treatment of accuracy is given in Chapter 8, Section 8.2.). The effect on decision making can be very small if all alternatives are similarly affected; that is, if the end-of-year convention reduces the present worths of two alternatives by about the same amount, the one with greater worth under the end-of-year convention is probably the one that would have had greater worth under more accurate timing estimates.

E28. **At 20% effective interest, compare the present worths of the cash-flow set A and its end-of-year representation B.**

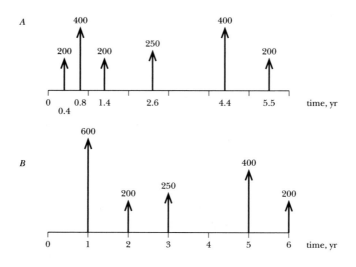

Where $\beta = 1/1.20$,

$$P_A = 200\beta^{0.4} + 400\beta^{0.8} + 200\beta^{1.4}$$
$$+250\beta^{2.6} + 400\beta^{4.4} + 200\beta^{5.5}$$

$$= \underline{\$1094.92}$$

$$P_B = 600\beta + 200\beta^2 + 250\beta^3 + 400\beta^5 + 200\beta^6$$

$$= \underline{\$1011.30}$$

Comparison in terms of the reasons given for end-of-interval conventions: (1) The computations for B are slightly simpler (63 keystrokes for A and 41 for B to compute P_A and P_B by hand calculator); also, if cash-flow timings are estimated, less estimation effort would be required for B than for A. (2) If there were an annual budget cycle or other reasons for holding midyear receipts to year-end, B might represent reality as well as or better than A. (3) P_B underestimates P_A by about 7.6%.

In Section 2.7 we will show that the end-of-year convention should tend to underestimate present worth by a factor r/i_{eff} where $r = \ln(1 + i_{\text{eff}})$ is the nominal continuous interest rate. For 20% interest, r/i_{eff} is about 0.912, so the convention would tend to underestimate by about 8.8%. In the example above, the convention gave a 7.6% underestimate. In an engineering economy decision problem comparing the example cash-flow set with an alternative one, which would probably be underestimated by an amount roughly near 8.8%, the discrepancy would be on the order of 2% to 4%; errors in estimations of cash-flow amounts are generally considered to cause present-worth inaccuracies in the neighborhood of 5%, so the end-of-year convention is not likely to add unacceptable errors to the analysis.

Consistent with the end-of-interval convention is the convention that *small time differences are ignored.* Differences of more than a year are never considered small. For most engineering economy studies, differences of a few weeks are always considered small.

E29. When Hagerty Furniture holds a sale, there is a spike in the sales statistics. Consider a five-day sale that is expected to increase revenues by $4000 per day for five days and by $2000 on the sixth day.

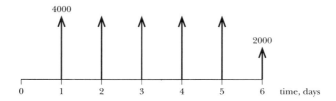

Assume a daily interest rate of $i = 0.0002$, which is $r = 365(0.0002) = 7.3\%$ nominal compounded daily (365 days/yr) and is $(1.0002)^{365} - 1 = 7.5722685\%$ effective.

Determine the present worth of the additional revenues (as of the beginning of the first day).

$$P = 400\frac{(1 - \beta^5)}{0.0002} + 2000\beta^6 = \underline{\$21,985.60}$$

Compare the results with the simple total of increased revenues.

$$\text{Total} = 4000(5) + 2000 = \underline{\$22,000}$$

a negligible overestimate. In an engineering economy study, the additional sales revenues would be treated as a single cash flow of amount $22,000. Its time, depending on the enterprise's adopted timing conventions, would be either the date associated in the database with the sale (typically its start date) or the end of the interval in which the sale occurs.

The end-of-year convention tends, approximately, to shift all cash flows approximately $\tau = 0.5$ years to the right. Thus, approximately, it has no effect on a choice: The alternative with greater worth tends to be the same one with or without the convention.

It is sometimes misleadingly stated that the end-of-year convention treats revenues as occurring at year ends and investments as occurring at year beginnings. That would seem to be excessively conservative, shifting negative cash flows to the left while shifting others to the right. However, the usual capital investment involves early costs (engineering, purchasing, constructing, etc.) that finally culminate in a facility. The facility's startup date is conventionally designated as time zero. Thus the convention really treats investments just like other costs and disbursements; just as year 1 started at time 0, year 0 started at time -1, and all the disbursements in that zeroth year are treated as if they occured at year-end, which is time zero.

Computations sometimes involve converting from one time scale to another. Time conversions follow various conventions. In the United States, the most usual system is a somewhat inconsistent one:

Traditional Time Conversions:

    24 hours per day
     7 days per week
    52 weeks per year (implies 364 days/yr)
    30 days per month
    12 months per year (implies 360 days/yr)
    13 weeks per quarter
   365 days per year (not 364 or 360 implied above)
  8760 hours per year

Discrepancies are ignored, and in case of conflict a lender chooses the more traditional or the lender-favorable interpretation. Usually very small amounts of money are involved in distinctions such as whether a year has 364, 365, or 366 days.

A consistent conversion system, adopted by a few international banks in recent software for money administration, is as follows:

Consistent Time Conversions:

    24 hours per day
     7 days per week
   365.25 days per year
    12 months per year

Hence:

  8766 hours per year
  $365.25/7 = 52.17857143$ weeks per year
  $365.25/12 = 30.4375$ days per month
  $365.25/4/7 = 13.04464286$ weeks per quarter

Accounting software packages with built-in calendars have tended to use a system similar to this but with 365 days per nonleap year and 366 days per leap year.

2.6 GRADIENT CASH FLOWS

This section develops worth formulas for *gradient* cash-flow sets: the *uniform* or *linear gradient*, in which the payment at time t is G dollars more than the one at time $t-1$ (Section 2.6.1); the *geometric gradient*, in which the payment at time t is $1+g$ times the one at time $t - 1$ (Section 2.6.2); and the *general geometric gradient*, in which a geometric trend is superimposed on an arbitrary cash-flow set (Section 2.6.3).

The uniform or linear gradient is tedious mathematically and fits few actual situations that the geometric gradient would not fit better. Nevertheless it has been widely taught in engineering economy. The geometric gradient is simple and fits many situations well. The general geometric gradient forms the basis for modern treatments of monetary inflation and escalation (Chapter 3).

2.6.1 Linear Gradient Series

When a series of cash flows $\{A_t: t = 1,...,n\}$ changes by the same amount G (called the "gradient") during each interval, it is a uniform or *linear gradient series*. The series of amounts is

$$\{A_1 + (t - 1)G: t = 1,...,n\}$$

For example, the cash-flow set $\{1200, 1100, 1000, 900, 800\}$ has $A_1 = 1200$, $G = -100$, and $n = 5$; it might represent, for example, linearly declining annual revenues from an asset held for five years. Term by term, this series has present worth $1200\beta + 1100\beta^2 + 1000\beta^3 + 900\beta^4 + 800\beta^5$, which for $i = 0.15$, $\beta = 1/1.15$, is 3445.07. We will derive a closed-form formula for the present worth of a linear gradient series.

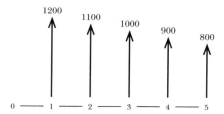

Figure 2-4 depicts a linear gradient series broken into two parts and the residual infinite series that would continue the linear trend forever.

Let P denote the present worth of the gradient series. Let P_∞ denote the present worth of the infinite gradient series $\{A_1 + (t - 1)G: t = 1,...,\infty\}$. Let P_G denote the present worth of the infinite gradient series $\{0, G, 2G,...\}$ at times $1,2,...$, which is the previous series without $\{A_1, A_1, A_1,...\}$. Finally, note that (from Eq. 2-11 with $n \to \infty$) the present worth of the infinite series $\{A_1, A_1, A_1,...\}$ is A_1/i and the present worth of the infinite series $\{nG, nG, nG,...\}$ is nG/i. This gives us names or values for everything in Figure 2-4.

First note that $P_\infty = A_1/i + P_G$, since the infinite gradient series $\{A_1, A_1+G, A_1+2G,...\}$ is indistinguishable from the combination of the series $\{A_1, A_1, A_1,...\}$, which has present worth A_1/i, and the series $\{0, G, 2G,...\}$, which has present worth P_G. But $P_G = 0 + G\beta^2 + 2G\beta^3 + 3G\beta^4 + \cdots = G\beta^2(1 + 2\beta + 3\beta^2 + \cdots)$.

The sum in parentheses is the term-by-term derivative of an infinite geometric series sum. Recall from Section 2.4.1 that $(1 + \beta + \beta^2 + \cdots) = 1/(1 - \beta)$, so that (multiplying both sides by β) we have

$$\beta + \beta^2 + \beta^3 + \cdots = \frac{\beta}{1 - \beta}$$

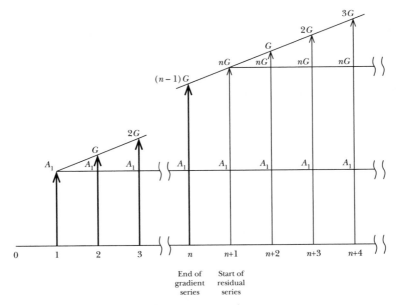

FIGURE 2-4. Linear gradient series.

Taking the derivative of both sides with respect to β, we have

$$1 + 2\beta + 3\beta^2 + \cdots = \frac{1}{(1-\beta)^2}$$

Thus

$$P_\infty = \frac{A_1}{i} + G\frac{\beta^2}{(1-\beta)^2} \tag{2-28}$$

Now consider the residue series of cash flows starting at time $n + 1$. This infinite series is broken into three parts: $\{A_1, A_1, A_1,...\}$ at times $n + 1$, $n + 2$,... is one part; $\{nG, nG, nG,...\}$ at times $n + 1$, $n + 2$,... is another part; and $\{0, G, 2G,...\}$ at times $n + 1$, $n + 2$,... is the third part. Consider the worths of these infinite series evaluated at time n. The $\{A_1, A_1, A_1,...\}$ part has a worth at time n of A_1/i (from Eq. 2-11 with $n \to \infty$, with time counted from n as time zero), and hence its *present* worth (from Eq. 2-6) is $(A_1/i)\beta^n$. The $\{nG, nG, nG,...\}$ part similarly has present worth $(nG/i)\beta^n$. Finally, the $\{0, G, 2G,...\}$ part has a worth at time n already derived as the second term in Eq. 2-28, so its *present* worth is

$$\frac{G\beta^2}{(1-\beta)^2}\beta^n$$

All that remains is to collect quantities. P, the present worth of the finite linear gradient series, is P_∞ less the present worth of the residue series:

$$P = \frac{A_1}{i} + G\frac{\beta^2}{1-\beta^2} - \left[\frac{A_1}{i}\beta^n + \frac{nG}{i}\beta^n + \frac{G\beta^2}{1-\beta^2}\beta^n\right]$$

Recall that $\beta/(1 - \beta) = 1/i$; hence $\beta^2/(1 - \beta^2) = 1/i^2$. Making this substitution, and factoring β^n out from the residue present worth in brackets, we have the *linear gradient present-worth formula*:

$$P = \frac{A_1}{i} + \frac{G}{i^2} - \beta^n \left[\frac{A_1}{i} + \frac{nG}{i} + \frac{G}{i^2} \right] \tag{2-29}$$

E30. Sales revenues for a lift-truck product line are estimated to be $500,000 in the coming year and to decline by $40,000 each year. Using the end-of-year convention, determine the estimated present worth of the coming five years of sales revenues, at 15% interest.

$$i = 0.15, \qquad \beta = 1/1.15, \qquad A_1 = 500000, \qquad G = -40000, \qquad n = 5$$

From Eq. 2-29:

$$P = \frac{A_1}{i} + \frac{G}{i^2} - \beta^n \left[\frac{A_1}{i} + \frac{nG}{i} + \frac{G}{i^2} \right]$$

$$= \frac{500000}{0.15} - \frac{40000}{(0.15)^2} - \beta^5 \left[\frac{500000}{0.15} - \frac{5(40000)}{0.15} - \frac{40000}{(0.15)^2} \right]$$

$$= 1{,}555{,}555.56 - \beta^5 \, [222{,}222.22]$$

$$= \$1{,}445{,}071.84$$

$$\approx \underline{\$1.4 \ \textit{million}}$$

When A_1 is positive and G is negative, the final nonnegative cash flow occurs at the integer time between L and $L + 1$, where

$$L = \frac{A_1}{-G} \tag{2-30}$$

is the positive life of the linear gradient series.

For example, a series with $A_1 = 500$ and $G = -39$ has $L = 500/39 = 12.82$ years of positive life, and its final nonnegative cash flow occurs at time 13. P in Eq. 2-29 is maximized by setting n equal to the worth-maximizing life n^*:

$$n^* = \text{int}(L + 1) \tag{2-31}$$

[where the operator int(x) rounds down its argument to an integer]. For example, with $A_1 = 500$ and $G = -39$, the worth-maximizing life is 13 years, and the present worth for this life at 15% interest is $1889.30.

The most common use of the linear gradient in engineering economy is to represent increasing operating or maintenance costs as equipment or facilities age. Another use is to represent declining revenues when productivity or market share is shrinking linearly.

2.6.2 Geometric Gradient Series

When a series of cash flows $\{A_t:\ t=1,...,n\}$ changes by a constant multiplicative factor $1+g$ from interval to interval, it is a *geometric gradient series*. The series of amounts is $\{A_1,\ A_2,\ ...,A_n\}$ where $A_t = A_1(1+g)^{t-1}$:

$$\{A_1(1+g)^{t-1}:\ t=1,...,n\}$$

Figure 2-5 illustrates an increasing geometric gradient series having $A_1 = 990$, $g = 0.10$, $n = 6$; and a decreasing geometric gradient series having $A_1 = 810$, $g = -0.10$,

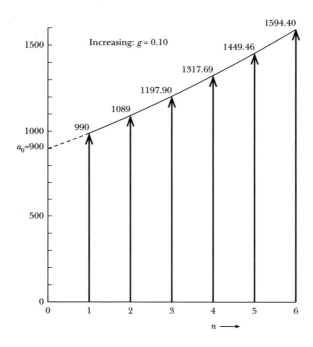

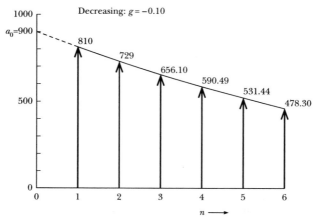

FIGURE 2-5. Geometric gradient series.

$n = 6$. Such series are useful in modeling growth or decay in many kinds of costs and revenues and are the series that represent the effects of monetary inflation (Chapter 3) and the most-used depreciation schedule—declining balance depreciation—in tax accounting (Chapter 10).

The present worth of a geometric gradient series is easily computed by using the "pain" formula at a substitute interest rate that reflects both compound interest and geometric growth $(g > 0)$ or decline $(g < 0)$.

We define a_0 as the *zero projection* of the series $\{A_1, A_2, ..., A_n\}$, so that $A_1 = a_0(1 + g)$, $A_2 = a_0(1 + g)^2, ..., A_n = a_0(1 + g)^n$. Thus we reexpress the series $\{A_1(1 + g)^{t-1}:$ $t = 1, ..., n\}$ as

$$\{a_0(1 + g)^t: t = 1, ..., n\}$$

For example, if $a_0 = 900$ and $g = 0.10$, the series starts with $A_1 = 990$, $A_2 = 1089, ...,$ as in the increasing series in Figure 2-5; or if $a_0 = 900$ and $g = -0.10$, the series starts with $A_1 = 810$, $A_2 = 729, ...,$ as in the decreasing series in Figure 2-5.

The present worth of a geometric gradient series is

$$P = A_1\beta + A_2\beta^2 + \cdots + A_n\beta^n$$

$$= a_0(1 + g)\beta + a_0(1 + g)^2\beta^2 + \cdots + a_0(1 + g)^n\beta^n$$

Note that this is just a geometric series sum. We define a *substitute discount factor*

$$\alpha = (1 + g)\beta \tag{2-32}$$

so that

$$P = a_0(\alpha + \alpha^2 + \cdots + \alpha^n) \tag{2-33}$$

Recall the development of Eq. 2-11, Section 2.4.1. Just as $(\beta + \beta^2 + \cdots + \beta^n)$ is the "pain" factor for an interest rate $i = 1/\beta - 1$, $(\alpha + \alpha^2 + \cdots + \alpha^n)$ is a factor of the same form for a substitute interest rate

$$s = \frac{1}{\alpha} - 1 = \frac{1 + i}{1 + g} - 1 \tag{2-34}$$

Unless $\alpha = 1 \Leftrightarrow s = 0$, we have the closed form, analogous to Eq. 2-11, of the *geometric-gradient-series present worth*:

$$P = a_0\left[\frac{\alpha}{1 - \alpha}(1 - \alpha^n)\right] = a_0\left[\frac{1 - \alpha^n}{s}\right] \tag{2-35}$$

The quantity in brackets is just the "pain" factor for the substitute interest rate. Thus, to compute the present worth of a geometric gradient series, simply multiply the zero projection of the series amounts by the "pain" factor for the substitute interest rate.

For the case $\alpha = 1 \Leftrightarrow s = 0$, which occurs when growth just offsets discounting, the formula becomes

$$P = a_0 + a_0 + \cdots + a_0 = na_0 \tag{2-36}$$

E31. Determine the present worths of the two geometric gradient series cash-flow sets illustrated in Figure 2-5, at $i = 15\%$ and at $i = 10\%$.

The *increasing series* has $a_0 = 900$, $g = 0.10$, $n = 6$.

For $i = 15\%$, the substitute discount factor is $\alpha = (1 + g)\beta = 1.10/1.15$, and the substitute interest rate is $s = 1.15/1.10 - 1$. Hence

$$P = a_0[P/A\ s,n] = a_0\left[\frac{1 - \alpha^n}{s}\right] = 900[5.150316476] = \underline{4635.28}$$

For $i = 10\%$, the substitute discount factor is $\alpha = (1 + g)\beta = 1.10/1.10 = 1$, and the substitute interest rate is $s = 1.10/1.10 - 1 = 0$. This is the case where growth just offsets discounting:

$$P = a_0 n = 900(6) = \underline{5400}$$

The *decreasing series* has $a_0 = 900$, $g = -0.10$, $n = 6$.

For $i = 15\%$, the substitute discount factor is $\alpha = (1 + g)\beta = 0.90/1.15$, and the substitute interest rate is $s = 1.15/0.90 - 1$. Hence

$$P = a_0\left[\frac{1 - \alpha^n}{s}\right] = 900[2.772876202] = \underline{2495.59}$$

For $i = 10\%$, the substitute discount factor is $\alpha = (1 + g)\beta = 0.90/1.10$, and the substitute interest rate is $s = 1.10/0.90 - 1$. Hence

$$P = a_0\left[\frac{1 - \alpha^n}{s}\right] = 900[3.15006935] = \underline{2835.06}$$

A_1 is frequently the most convenient cash flow to estimate in a geometric gradient series. For example, maintenance costs for a facility might be estimated as \$4200 for the first year and be estimated to increase 7% per year ($g = 0.07$); from the definition of a_0, we have $a_0 = A_1/(1 + g)$, so this series would have $a_0 = 4200/1.07 = 3925.23$. In other cases, one may estimate a_0 directly as what the cash flow would have been in the interval just ended. In general, if the cash flow at time k is the one considered to be known or estimated, we compute

$$a_0 = A_k(1 + g)^{-k} \tag{2-37}$$

where A_k is the known or estimated cash flow in a geometric gradient series.

E32. Determine the present worth at 15% interest of 10 years of royalty payments that are expected to reach \$10,000 annually by the fifth year and are expected to increase 5% per year.

$\beta = 1/1.15$, $n = 10$, $g = 0.05$. The estimated cash flow at time $k = 5$ is $A_5 = 10{,}000$. The zero projection is $a_0 = A_5(1 + g)^{-5} = 7835.261665$.

The substitute discount factor is $\alpha = (1 + g)\beta = 1.05/1.15$, and the substitute interest rate is $s = 1.15/1.05 - 1$. Hence

$$P = a_0\left[\frac{1 - \alpha^n}{s}\right] = 7835.261665[6.2723027] = \underline{\$49,145.13}$$

Equation 2-35 is valid except when growth and interest discounting just offset each other. In particular, it is valid when growth exceeds interest discounting, so that each successive term in the series makes a greater contribution to worth, and the substitute interest rate is negative.

E33. **A product's sales revenues were $21,000 in the year just ended and have been growing at 20% per year. At $i = 12\%$, what is the present worth of the next six years of sales revenues if the same growth rate is maintained?**

$a_0 = 21,000$, $g = 0.20$, $\beta = 1/1.12$, $n = 6$. $\alpha = (1 + g)\beta = 1.071428571$, which exceeds 1. $s = 1.12/1.20 - 1 = -0.0666$, which is a negative substitute interest rate.

$$P = a_0\left[\frac{1 - \alpha^n}{s}\right] = 21,000\left[\frac{-0.512792418}{-0.066666667}\right] = 21,000[7.691886266]$$

$$= \underline{\$161,529.61}$$

2.6.3 General Geometric Gradient

Geometric growth or decay can be superimposed on *any* cash flow series by using the substitute interest rate s and the substitute discount factor α. The geometric gradient series formula developed in Section 2.6.2 is just the special case in which growth or decay is superimposed on an equal-payment series; every payment would be a_0 except for the geometric growth, so the present worth is a_0 times the "pain" factor with the substitute interest rate. In general, we can estimate a set of payments $\{A_t\}$ ignoring geometric factors such as monetary inflation, deterioration, growth, price escalation, market expansion, and the like, and then compute the present worth at a substitute interest rate s using the uncorrected amounts $\{A_t\}$. The result will be the same as if we had (more tediously) computed all the corrected cash flows $\{G_t\}$ and then computed the present worth at the usual "market" interest rate i.

Let there be a *gradient set* of cash flows $\{G_t\}$ for which we wish to determine the present worth. However, our estimates are in the form of a set of cash flows $\{A_t\}$ obtained in a manner that ignores the gradient. That is, we know $\{A_t\}$ and wish to determine the present worth of $\{G_t\}$ where each cash flow in $\{G_t\}$ is related to the corresponding cash flow in $\{A_t\}$ by

$$G_t = (1 + g)^t A_t \tag{2-38}$$

At interest rate i, with $\beta = 1/(1 + i)$, the present worth of $\{G_t\}$ is, from Eq. 2-3 and 2-38,

$$P = \sum_{t=0}^{n} G_t\beta^t = \sum_{t=0}^{n} (1 + g)^t\beta^t A_t = \sum_{t=0}^{n} A_t\alpha^t \tag{2-39}$$

where $\alpha = (1 + g)\beta$ is the substitute discount factor defined in Eq. 2-32. Equation 2-39 defines the *general geometric gradient* method: To determine the present worth of a gradient cash-flow set $\{G_t\}$ that is the result of superimposing geometric growth or decay at rate g on a cash-flow set $\{A_t\}$, compute the present worth of $\{A_t\}$ at the substitute interest rate $s = (1 + i)/(1 + g) - 1$ and substitute discount factor $\alpha = (1 + g)/(1 + i)$. *The present worth of $\{G_t\}$ is the present worth of $\{a_t\}$ with $i \rightarrow s$ and $\rightarrow \alpha$.*

E34. **Based on today's market share, the prospective annual cash flows of a project are as follows:**

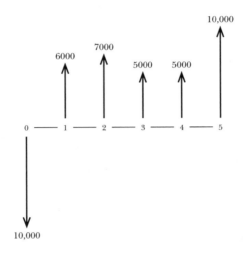

Actually, the market share is expected to decrease 4% per year, and the cash flows are proportional to market share. Determine the present worth of the project at 20% interest.

$i = 0.20$, $\beta = 1/1.20$. P is of $\{G_t = A_t(1 + g): t = 0,1,...,5\}$ where $g = -0.04$. $\alpha = (1 + g)\beta = 0.96/1.20 = 0.8$. From Eq. 2-39,

$$P = -10,000\alpha^0 + 6000\alpha^1 + 7000\alpha^2 + 5000\alpha^3 + 5000\alpha^4 + 10,000\alpha^5$$
$$= \underline{\$7164.80}$$

The next example demonstrates how the geometric gradient series of Section 2.6.2 is a special case of the general geometric gradient.

E35. **Ignoring the prospect of 10% annual growth, a maintenance contract is earning annual revenues of $900. If the growth materializes, what is the present worth of the next six years of revenue at 15% interest?**

From the viewpoint of the general geometric gradient method, we have a cash flow set $\{A_t\} - \{900, 900, 900, 900, 900, 900\}$ whose present worth we can calculate at the substitute discount factor $\alpha = (1 + g)\beta = 1.10/1.15$ in order to determine the present worth at $\beta = 1/1.15$ of the actual gradient set $\{900(1.10)^t: t = 1,...,6\}$.

$$P = 900(P/A \; i,6) \text{ with } i \rightarrow s = \frac{1}{\alpha} - 1$$

$$= 900\left(\frac{1 - \alpha^6}{s}\right) = 900(5.150316476) = \underline{\underline{4635.28}}$$

There is no real distinction between this approach and that of Eq. 2-35 (for the geometric gradient series).

The general geometric gradient will be used extensively in Chapter 3 for handling monetary inflation and escalation. The technique is especially valuable for advanced engineering economy work. For example, a large energy-management-design software package was developed for office-building design. Key parts of the design calculations involved determining the worths of alternatives. Inputs included fuel prices and an interest rate, but no fuel-price escalation factors. Reprogramming effort to remedy the deficiency was budgeted at several hundred programmer-hours. But it ended up requiring only seven new functional lines of computer code: It was necessary only to input an escalation factor g for each fuel, compute s, and replace i with s in the worth computations for the cash flows proportional to that fuel's cost.

2.7 CONTINUOUS-CASH-FLOW PROFILES

In situations where continuous compounding is considered appropriate as a timing convention, as opposed to treating cash flows as if they occurred at the ends of time intervals, the concept of *continuous cash flow* is useful. Continuous functions sometimes have a compactness highly desirable for cash-flow modeling. For example, two or three parameters can define a sinusoidal description of seasonal energy savings or costs; the same is true of asymptotic or s-shaped growth of revenues or costs to a steady level, or of revenues or costs that grow to a peak and decline.

It is sometimes easier to visualize, estimate, and compute the worth of a cash flow pattern if it is descibed as a continuous-cash-flow profile rather than as a set of discrete cash flows; a profile formula and its parameters express the essence of the pattern, which would otherwise be hidden when expressed indirectly as amounts in a discrete-cash-flow series.

Interest in continuous-cash-flow profiles can be traced in actuarial science back to the mortality laws of De Moivre (1724), Gompertz (1825), and Makeham (1860), all of whom sought to evaluate worth of life insurance or life annuity contracts by integration of a continuous formula.

2.7.1 Continuous-Cash-Flow Present Worth

Define $F(t)$ for continuous time t as an *instantaneous rate of cash flow* expressed in dollars per year. Let time be measured in years, and let $\beta = e^{-r} = 1/(1 + i_{\text{eff}})$ represent interest. Recall $r = \ln(1 + i_{\text{eff}}) = -\ln \beta$ is the nominal compound interest rate.

An infinitesimal payment $F(t) \, dt$ occurs at time t, and its contribution to present worth is $F(t)\beta^t \, dt = F(t)e^{-rt} \, dt$. The sum of these contributions, if $F(t)$ is defined for $0 \le t \le n$, is

$$P = \int_0^n F(t) e^{-rt} \, dt \tag{2-40}$$

Equation 2-40 defines the *present worth of a cash-flow profile.* We should note here that one is free to define $F(t)$ for all nonnegative t, that is for $n \rightarrow \infty$, by changing the form of $F(t)$ or expressing it as a difference of two functions. Thus Eq. 2-40, with $n \rightarrow \infty$, defines the familiar *Laplace transform* of $F(t)$, with r as the transform variable. Laplace transforms are exhaustively tabulated, so that Laplace transform tables give the present-worth formulas for almost any conceivably useful cash-flow profile.

Since $F(t)$ can be a sum of functions, Eq. 2-40 can express a composite pattern consisting of many parts whose cash-flow rates are additive. Lump sums can also be included, as will be shown below.

Perhaps the simplest cash-flow profile is the constant-rate profile or *uniform continuous series,* where the rate is $F(t) = \bar{A}$ dollars per year from time zero to time n. This profile is used to express revenues or savings that flow throughout a time interval at a level rate. From Eq. 2-40, the present worth of $\bar{A}$ dollars per year for n years is

$$P = \int_0^n \bar{A} e^{-rt}\, dt = \bar{A}\, \frac{1 - e^{-rn}}{r} = \bar{A}\, \frac{1 - \beta^n}{r} \tag{2-41}$$

The "parn" factor $(1 - \beta^n)/r$ is denoted the "continuous compounding present worth factor" in the literature, usually expressed in the rightmost form shown here:

$$(P/\bar{A}\ r,n) = \frac{1 - e^{-rn}}{r} = \frac{1 - \beta^n}{-\ln \beta} = \frac{e^{rn} - 1}{re^{rn}} \tag{2-41a}$$

E36. A contractor will receive weekly payments of \$450 each for 90 weeks. At $i_{eff} =$ 15%, compare the present worth of the cash-flow set when computed (a) as a continuous profile, (b) exactly (weekly), and (c) by the end-of-year convention.

(a) Assuming 52 weeks per year, $\bar{A} = 450(52) = \$23{,}400$ per year, paid for $n = 90/52 = 1.73076923$ years. From Eq. 2-41, with $\beta = 1/1.15$, $r = \ln\ 1.15 = 13.976194\%$:

$$P_{continuous} = 23{,}400 \frac{1 - \beta^{90/52}}{r} = 23{,}400[1.53734206] = \$35{,}973.80 \cong \underline{\$35{,}970}$$

(b) Assuming 52 weeks per year, with time measured in weeks, $A = 450$, $n = 90$, $i = (1.15)^{1/52} - 1 = 0.2691345\%$ *weekly,* $\beta = 1/(1 + i) = 0.997315879$. From Eq. 2-11:

$$P_{weekly} = 450 \frac{1 - \beta^{90}}{i} = \$35{,}925.48 \cong \underline{\$35{,}930}$$

(c) Assuming 52 weeks per year, the contractor receives $A_1 = 450(52) = \$23{,}400$ the first year and $A_2 = 450(90 - 52) = \$17{,}100$ the second year. From Eq. 2-3 with $i = 15\%$, $\beta = 1/1.15$:

$$P_{end\text{-}of\text{-}year} = 23{,}400\beta + 17{,}100\beta^2 = \$33{,}277.88 \cong \underline{\$33{,}280}$$

With the weekly computation as standard, the end-of-year convention gives about a 7.4% underestimate, whereas the continuous approximation gives a negligible overestimate.

To see how continuous cash-flow modeling can handle lump sums, let us approximate a lump sum A_t at time t with a uniform rate $\bar{A}$ for a small duration of m years starting at time t. Now by the definition of $F(t)$ the total amount paid in an interval t to $t + m$ is

$$T_{t,t+m} = \int_t^{t+m} F(\tau) \, d\tau \tag{2-42}$$

Thus if $F(\tau) = \bar{A}$ for a duration m is to have a sum A_t, then $\bar{A} = A_t/m$. For example, a lump sum of \$100 could be approximated as $\bar{A} = 5000(100) = 500{,}000$ dollars per year for $m = 1/5000$ of a year, with its discount factor varying from β^t to $\beta^{t+0.0002}$, or very close to β^t.

Carrying this approximation to vanishingly small m, with $F(\tau) = A_t/m$ for $t < \tau < t + m$ and zero otherwise, Eq. 2-40 gives

$$P = \int_t^{t+m} \frac{A_t}{m} e^{-r\tau} \, d\tau = \frac{A_t}{rm} \left(e^{-rt} - e^{-r(t+m)} \right)$$

$$= \frac{A_t e^{-rt}}{r} \left(\frac{1 - e^{-rm}}{m} \right)$$

Now the limit of the quantity in parentheses as $m \to 0$, from applying L'Hospital's rule, is r. Hence

$$\lim_{m \to 0} P = A_t e^{-rt} = A_t \beta^t$$

Thus the continuous-cash-flow method gives the familiar formula for the present worth of a lump sum.

Given a lump sum of A_t dollars as part of a cash-flow profile, it is convenient to have a quantity with units of dollars per year, so that it may be mathematically manipulated and integrated along with other profile components. Dirac invented the Dirac delta, δ_t, for just this purpose: $A_t \delta_t$ is a psuedofunction defined such that its integral over any interval including t is A_t; and the integral of $A_t \delta_t e^{-r\tau}$ is $A_t e^{-rt}$.

E37. Determine the present worth, at $r = 0.09$, of two years of continuous savings of \$2000 per year along with a loss of \$3000 at time zero and a gain of \$1000 at time 2.

$\beta = e^{-r} = e^{-0.09}$. From the obvious treatment of lump sums and with Eq. 2-41 for the uniform continuous series, we have

$$P = -3000 + 1000\beta^2 + 2000 \left[\frac{1 - \beta^2}{r} \right] = \underline{\underline{\$1495.93}}$$

Formally, one could use Dirac deltas to put into the basic Eq. 2-40 the profile

$$F(t) = -3000\delta_0 + 1000\delta_2 + 2000$$

$$P = \int_0^2 (-3000\delta_0 + 1000\delta_2 + 2000) e^{-rt} \, dt$$

$$= -3000e^{-r0} + 1000^{-r2} + 2000 \left[\frac{1 - e^{-r2}}{r} \right] = \underline{\underline{\$1495.93}}$$

2.7.2 Worths for Common Profiles

Figure 2-6 gives present worth formulas for several continuous-cash-flow profiles. The "profile" column gives a graph of $F(t)$, and the "present worth" column gives the corresponding present worth.

The second profile, for continuous exponential increase or decrease, is more convenient than the analogous discrete geometric gradient series in some ways. One advantage is that the continuous rate of increase $\bar{g}$ appears only in the sum $r + \bar{g}$. In superimposing exponential growth at exponential rate $\bar{g}$ on a cash-flow set, the substitute *nominal continuous* interest rate is $r + \bar{g}$, where $\bar{g}$ is such that

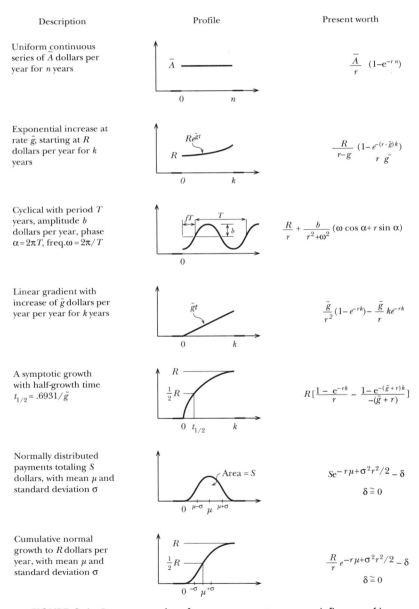

Description	Profile	Present worth
Uniform continuous series of $\bar{A}$ dollars per year for n years		$\dfrac{\bar{A}}{r}\,(1-e^{-rn})$
Exponential increase at rate $\bar{g}$, starting at R dollars per year for k years	$Re^{\bar{g}t}$	$\dfrac{R}{r-g}\,(1-e^{-(r-\bar{g})k})\quad\dfrac{1}{r\ \bar{g}}$
Cyclical with period T years, amplitude b dollars per year, phase $\alpha=2\pi T$, freq.$\omega=2\pi/T$		$\dfrac{R}{r}+\dfrac{b}{r^2+\omega^2}\,(\omega\cos\alpha+r\sin\alpha)$
Linear gradient with increase of $\bar{g}$ dollars per year per year for k years	$\bar{g}t$	$\dfrac{\bar{g}}{r^2}(1-e^{-rk})-\dfrac{\bar{g}}{r}\,ke^{-rk}$
A symptotic growth with half-growth time $t_{1/2}=.6931/\bar{g}$		$R\left[\dfrac{1-e^{-rk}}{r}-\dfrac{1-e^{-(\bar{g}+r)k}}{-(\bar{g}+r)}\right]$
Normally distributed payments totaling S dollars, with mean μ and standard deviation σ	Area = S	$Se^{-r\mu+\sigma^2r^2/2}-\delta$ $\delta\cong0$
Cumulative normal growth to R dollars per year, with mean μ and standard deviation σ		$\dfrac{R}{r}\,e^{-r\mu+\sigma^2r^2/2}-\delta$ $\delta\cong0$

FIGURE 2-6. Present worths of common continuous cash-flow profiles.

$$1 + g = e^{\bar{g}} \tag{2-43}$$

$$\bar{g} = ln(1 + g) \tag{2-43a}$$

The substitute discount factor is $\alpha = (1 + g)\beta = e^{\bar{g}}\beta$, the same as for discrete cash flows.

To relate exponential increase to discrete geometric increase, where parameters R and $\bar{g}$ define the exponentially increasing continuous profile while a_0 and g define the geometric gradient series, the appropriate conversions are (as will be developed in Section 3.4) as follows

Discrete to continuous:

$$\bar{g} = ln(1 + g) \qquad \text{and} \qquad R = a_0(1 + g)(\bar{g}/g) \tag{2-44}$$

Continuous to discrete:

$$g = e^{\bar{g}} - 1 \qquad \text{and} \qquad a_0 = R\frac{g/\bar{g}}{1 + g} \tag{2-45}$$

For example, the discrete increasing geometric gradient series illustrated in Figure 2-5 had $a_0 = 990$ and $g = 0.10$. The corresponding continuous profile has $\bar{g} = 0.09531018$ and $R = 943.57078$. This R is the instantaneous cash flow rate at time zero such that the total cash flows in the successive years are 990, 1089, and so on as given. At any given interest rate i_{eff}, the profile will yield a greater present worth, because the discrete model treats money received during the year as if received at the end of the year. The ratio of the continuous present worth to the analogous discrete present worth is

$$\frac{P_{exponential}}{P_{Eq2-35}} = \frac{\bar{g}}{g}\left(\frac{i - g}{r - \bar{g}}\right) \tag{2-46}$$

For example, the discrete increasing geometric gradient series illustrated in Figure 2-5 has a present worth of 4635.28 from Eq. 2-35; the corresponding continuous profile, with the $\bar{g}$ and R mentioned above and $r = ln(1 + i)$ where $i = 15\%$, has a present worth of 4969.32 from the exponential-increase profile formula. This is 7.206% more, as could have been calculated by Eq. 2-46.

The formulas given in Figure 2-6 will be exploited throughout the book wherever continuous models can offer more insight or convenience than discrete models. Here is an example that illustrates the general nature of continuous models in engineering economic decision making:

E38. An oilfield contains T barrels of oil, earning revenues of Ve^{ht} dollars per barrel at time t in years (prices are assumed to rise at exponential rate h). The initial development cost is YB dollars, where B is the initial pumping rate (barrels per year); this is the cost of wells and equipment to pump the oil and get it to market. The pumping rate declines exponentially at exponential rate a, so that the pumping rate at time t is Be^{-at} barrels per year (production declines as the oilfield ages). The total oil recovered will be T barrels:

$$\int_0^\infty Be^{-at}\, dt = T$$

whence

$$\frac{B}{a} = T$$

$$a = \frac{B}{T}$$

In terms of the nonnegative quantities Y, B, V, h, and T and the nonnegative nominal continuous interest rate r, derive an expression for the present worth of the project of developing the oilfield.

Be^{-at} barrels per year multiplied by Ve^{ht} dollars per barrel is $BVe^{-at}e^{ht}$ dollars per year instantaneous rate of cash flow; multiply by dt to get an infinitesimal payment, multiply by e^{-rt} to get an infinitesimal contribution to present worth, and integrate from $t = 0$ to $t = \infty$ to get the present worth of revenues. Subtract the investment at time zero. Thus

$$P = -YB + \int_0^\infty BVe^{-at}e^{ht}e^{-rt}\, dt, \qquad \text{with } a = \frac{B}{T}$$

$$= -YB + BV\int_0^\infty e^{-(B/T - h + r)t}\, dt$$

$$= -YB + \frac{BV}{\dfrac{B}{T} - h + r}$$

This formula implies an optimal initial pumping rate B, which can be shown by setting $dP/dB = 0$. It also lays bare some economic insights, one of which is that if $h \geq r$ the best B is zero (it is unwise to sell oil if its value is growing faster in the ground—at rate h—than the monetary proceeds would grow above ground—at rate r).

2.8 EQUIVALENCE

We have stayed mostly within a moneylending context in developing compound-interest formulas, but moneylending is not the essence of engineering economy. As engineers we are chiefly interested in evaluating technological opportunities. After we estimate costs and benefits, each opportunity has an associated cash-flow set. With the help of the concept of equivalence, we can determine which cash-flow set we prefer; this determines, or helps to determine, which opportunity we prefer.

2.8.1 Equivalence as a Basis for Evaluation

To evaluate a cash-flow set, we rely on a metaphor of equivalence that is an extension of the more basic metaphor of indistinguishability. The metaphor of indistinguishability merely asserts that acceptance of a prospective cash-flow set is indistinguishable from undertaking a series of lending or borrowing transactions that would give rise to the identical cash-flow set. For example, spending $10,000 on an improvement that will save $4000 per year for eight years is *indistinguishable* from lending $10,000 and receiving $4000 per year for eight years as repayment. But with the added concept of a *surrogate banker*, defined as willing to lend or borrow any required amount at any time at a given interest rate i, we can use the concept of *equivalence* (defined in Section 2.2.2.2) to extend the metaphor to the metaphor of equivalence:

Metaphor of Equivalence:

. . . .

At an interest rate i, accepting a cash-flow set is equally preferred to accepting any cash-flow set equivalent to it at i.

Recall the definition of equivalence: Two cash-flow sets are equivalent at i iff they have equal worths at i. Recall that equal worths evaluated at one time implies equal worths evaluated at any time (two cash-flow sets with equal present worths also have equal future worths at arbitrary n, and vice versa). But cash-flow sets equivalent at one interest rate are not, in general, equivalent at another interest rate.

By the metaphor of equivalence asserted above, spending $10,000 to save $4000 per year for eight years is equivalent at 10% interest (with the end-of-year convention) to receiving $11,339.70 at time zero, because $11,339.70 is the present worth of the cash-flow set at 10% interest.

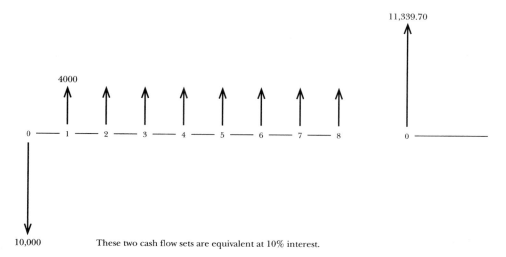

These two cash flow sets are equivalent at 10% interest.

The metaphor asserts that for a decision maker for whom $i = 10\%$ is appropriate, accepting the opportunity to spend $10,000 and receive $4000 per year for eight years is, in some sense, like picking up $11,339.70 off the ground!

An investment opportunity is equivalent to a windfall equal to its present worth, in this sense: A series of lending or borrowing transactions with the surrogate banker can convert the opportunity to the windfall, and vice versa. For example, imagine borrowing $21,339.70, pocketing $11,339.70 of it, spending the remaining $10,000 on the improvement, and receiving each annual $4000 savings from the improvement but immediately paying it to the surrogate banker as a loan repayment; since this tedious set of transactions is indistinguishable from just receiving $11,339.70 at time zero, we have illustrated the sense in which an investment opportunity is equivalent to a windfall equal to the investment's present worth.

In general, the metaphor of equivalence says that if there effectively existed a surrogate banker at interest rate i, transactions with the surrogate banker could be arranged to convert any cash flow set to one indistinguishable from any other cash-flow set that is equivalent to the first one. But if we accept the effective existence of the surrogate banker, there is never any need to construct the elaborate set of transactions necessary to convert a cash-flow set to an equivalent one. We can simply compute present worth, or any other worth such as future worth or annual equivalent, and use the worth as a measure of the desirability of an opportunity.

E39. **A bulldozer can be leased from vendor A according to a contract having many confusing provisions. The customer reduces the confusion by doing some estimating and prepares a cash-flow diagram showing the net outlay each month for everything, including fuel, maintenance, lease payments, and so on. The final month has a positive cash flow $A_n = \$6120$; all the preceding cash flows are negative. No estimate is made of the value of the benefits to be gained by using the bulldozer. Built into the contract is an interest rate of 11.8% APR.**

Vendor B can offer an identical bulldozer. This vendor prepares a similar cash-flow diagram in an effort to simplify the customer's decision, but the cash flows are more than those for Vendor A for certain months while being less for other months. The customer is unable to decide.

Vendor B considers two possible ways to close the sale. By path $B1$ the vendor could offer to lend and borrow at 11.8% APR on a complicated schedule such that every month's cash flow except the last one will match that of the other vendor. Alternatively, by path $B2$ the vendor could compute the present worths at 11.8% APR of both cash-flow sets. Assume that by path $B1$ the vendor would show the only difference between the two plans is that the B plan gives $A_n = \$7240$, which is \$1120 more paid to the customer than under the other vendor's plan; assume that by path $B2$ the vendor would show that the large negative present worth of the B plan is \$787.46, less negative than the large negative present worth of the A plan.

Assuming the customer effectively has a surrogate banker at 11.8% APR, which analysis—the one by path $B1$ or the one by path $B2$—is more valid? more difficult to compute? more impressive to the customer?

Both are valid. Path $B1$ is more difficult to compute. Path $B1$ might be more impressive, especially to a customer not competent in engineering economy.

What constitutes effectively having a surrogate banker? In practice, the *ordinary course of business* serves as a surrogate banker well enough for most enterprises so that they perceive, more or less accurately, an appropriate interest rate to use in financial decision making. There are techniques for estimating and fine-tuning this rate, which is called the *minimal attractive rate of return (MARR)*; these are treated in Sections 5.1.4 and 6.2. Here we merely remark that being either a chronic creditor or a chronic borrower serves approximately as a basis for equivalence calculations:

Chronic creditor: Maria has a substantial savings account that pays interest at rate i. By a series of well-timed withdrawals and deposits, she can convert a cash-flow set to another one equivalent at i.

Chronic debtor: Ahmad runs substantial balances on his credit cards, which charge interest on the balances at rate i. By adjusting his usual schedule of payments and charges, he can convert a cash-flow set to another one equivalent at i.

The following example will illustrate how equivalence calculations and surrogate-banker transactions have the same effect.

E40. Maria, whose savings account pays 9% annual compound interest, has an opportunity to spend $1000 now in order to receive $1400 three years from now. Devise a set of transactions with her savings account (her "surrogate banker") that will convert the opportunity to a single cash flow of P dollars at time zero; then show that the computations are exactly those of the equivalence calculation of computing the present worth of the opportunity's cash-flow set.

The opportunity's cash-flow set:

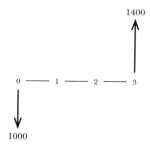

From the savings account (surrogate banker), withdraw $1000 + P$ dollars at time zero; deposit $1400 at time 3. This converts the cash-flow set to an equivalent single cash flow at time zero:

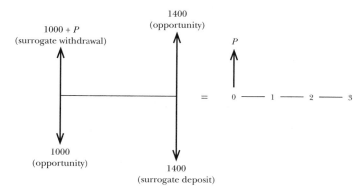

For the surrogate account to be unaffected, the $1400 deposited at time 3 must equal $(1000 + P)(1.09)^3$, which is the amount to which the withdrawn $1000 + P$ dollars would have accrued otherwise.

$$(1000 + P)(1.09)^3 = 1400$$

$$P = 1400(1/1.09)^3 - 1000$$

$$= \underline{\$81.06}$$

But the equation for P resulting from these tedious surrogate transactions is the same as that for computing the present worth at 9% interest of the opportunity's cash-flow set:

$$P = -1000 + 1400\beta^3 \quad \text{where} \quad \beta = 1/1.09$$

$$= \underline{\$81.06}$$

An *equivalence calculation* is a calculation that determines the amount in a cash-flow set that is equivalent at i to a given cash-flow set. Of all equivalence calculations, the calculation of *present worth* is conceptually the simplest. Given a cash-flow set and an interest rate, Eq. 2-3 gives the single cash flow at time zero that is equivalent to the cash-flow set. By the metaphor of equivalence (equivalent cash-flow sets are equally preferred), if we compute P as the present worth of a cash-flow set, we equally prefer either the cash-flow set or a time-zero cash flow equal to its present worth.

The surrogate-banker transactions are never computed explicitly. They simply serve to justify the metaphor of equivalence. This metaphor, which is sometimes called the *principle of indifference*, is justified thus: If a surrogate banker effectively exists at interest rate i, it is possible through surrogate transactions to convert a cash-flow set to any other cash-flow set to which it is equivalent at i; the two sets must be equally preferred if they are freely convertible.

In particular, a cash-flow set can be converted to its present worth, in which case the metaphor of equivalence asserts that a cash-flow set and its present worth are equally preferred.

To compare two different cash-flow sets, it is obvious that the cash-flow set with greater present worth is preferred. Let opportunities A and B have present worths $P^{(A)}$ and $P^{(B)}$. Choosing A or B is equivalent to being given $P^{(A)}$ or $P^{(B)}$ dollars at time zero. Since one prefers being given more to being given less, $P^{(A)} > P^{(B)}$ means that A is preferred.

More generally, *the cash-flow set with greater worth at any fixed time is preferred*. This follows from Eq. 2-5: If $F_m^{(A)} = (1 + i)^m P^{(A)}$ and $F_m^{(B)} = (1 + i)^m P^{(B)}$, then $P^{(A)} > P^{(B)} \Leftrightarrow F_m^{(A)} > F_m^{(B)}$. It is also obvious, since one prefers being given more at time m to being given less at time m. Cash-flow sets can be compared using any worth measure (such as future worth or annual equivalent), and the comparison is valid to whatever extent the surrogate banker effectively exists.

2.8.2 Equivalence Insights and Discounted Cash Flow

Much of engineering economic analysis boils down to comparing the worths of cash-flow sets. We close this chapter with some simplifying insights and concepts that provide short-cuts and accuracy checks: discounting, time-shifting, and time-scaling.

2.8.2.1 Discounting To multiply a cash flow A_t by the *discount factor* β^t is called "discounting" it, and the product $A_t\beta^t$ is a *discounted cash flow*, which is this cash flow's contribution to the present worth of the cash-flow set $\{A_t\}$. The present worth of the cash-flow set is, of course, the sum of its discounted cash flows.

Now if compound interest were not a relevant consideration, you could evaluate and compare cash-flow sets simply by algebraically adding their cash flows: for example, a copier that costs $4000 to buy, $5000 to maintain, and $6000 to operate, and produces $22,000 worth of copies and could be sold for $1000 at the end of its life would have a net value—ignoring the time value of money—of $-\$4000 - \$5000 - \$6000 + \$22,000 + \$1000 = \$8000$. A different copier with different costs and benefits would be judged better or worse—ignoring the time value of money—according to whether its net value was greater or smaller than $8000. To correct this obvious comparison procedure to take into account the time value of money, it is only necessary to discount each cash flow: The sum of discounted costs and benefits is the copier's "discounted value" or "discounted-to-present value" or "present value"—a sum we have identified as the present worth of the cash-flow set associated with the opportunity of acquiring the copier. Thus the effects of compound interest can be expressed simply by discounting each cash flow; this is the discounted cash flow (DCF) viewpoint.

E41. **Assuming 12% interest, a five-year copier life, and a distribution of maintenance and operation costs and production revenues over the life using the end-of-year timing convention, "correct" the $8000 value of the copier mentioned above to account for the time value of money.**

The $4000 purchase cost occurs at time zero, and the $1000 salvage at time 5. The $5000 maintenance cost is $1000 per year, the $6000 operation cost is $1200 per year, and the $22,000 benefit is $4400 per year.

$i = 0.12$, $\beta = 1/1.12$

$$P = -4000 + 2200\left(\frac{1 - \beta^4}{i}\right) + 3200\beta^5 = \underline{\$4497.93}$$

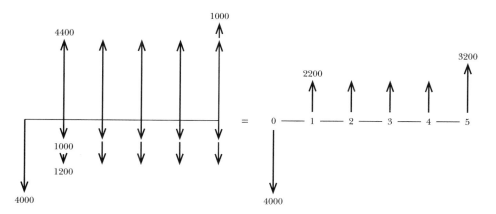

There is really no distinction between present-worth analysis and DCF analysis. If every cash flow were individually discounted ($P = -4000 + 4400\beta - 1000\beta - 1200\beta + 4400\beta^2 - 1000\beta^2 - 1200\beta^2$, etc.), terms would be collected to get the preceding equation; after collecting terms multiplied by like powers of β, the expression would be

$$P = -4000 + 2200\beta + 2200\beta^2 + 2200\beta^3 + 2200\beta^4 + 3200\beta^5$$

and invoking $\beta + \beta^2 + \cdots + \beta^4 = (1 - \beta^4)/i$ would give the equation solved above.

2.8.2.2 Time Shifting To determine the present worth of a cash-flow set such as this

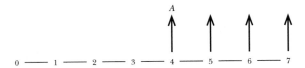

one, there is really no need to make a change of index variable in Eq. 2-4 or 2-6 nor to invoke the principle of indistinguishability to compute P as the difference between the present worth of seven payments and the present worth of three payments. Rather, we can first invoke the equivalence of the four payments of A dollars each to a payment of $A(1 - \beta^4)/i$ dollars at time 3 and then invoke the equivalence of that payment to one at time zero that is β^3 as large:
This cash-flow set

is equivalent to its worth at time 3

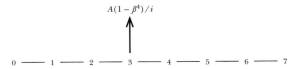

which in turn is equivalent to the present worth

In terms of the concept of discounting, we can "discount the series back to time 3" and then "discount the result back to time 0." In terms of the "pain" factor $(P/A\ i,n)$ and the single-period-present-worth factor $(P/F\ i,n)$ we can write

$$P = A(P/A\ i,4)(P/F\ i,3)$$

With a little practice one can become adept at such *time shifting*. Remember that the present worth of an equal-payment series is defined as of one interval before the first payment in the series. Therefore, multiplying an equal-payment amount A by the "pain" factor, with n being the number of payments, gives the worth as of one time-interval before the first payment. This worth can be discounted to time zero by multiplying by β^τ where τ is the time of the worth.

E42. Write a present worth formula for the cash-flow set as in the diagram.

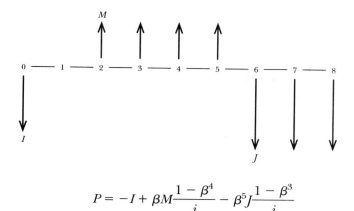

$$P = -I + \beta M \frac{1 - \beta^4}{i} - \beta^5 J \frac{1 - \beta^3}{i}$$

The vast majority of engineering economy problems uses only lump sums and equal-payment series. For such problems the only formulas needed are the "pain" factor to discount a series back to one interval before its inception and the β^t factor to discount a lump sum or a worth back to time zero.

For computing *future worth* (or worth at an arbitrary time) of a cash-flow set, it is only necessary to compute the present worth and "undiscount" it to the required time, say m, by multiplying by $\beta^{-m} = (1 + i)^m$.

E43. Write a formula for the future worth (at time 8) of the cash-flow set in the previous example.

$$F = F_8 = P(1 + i)^8 = P\beta^{-8}$$

$$= \beta^{-8}(-I) + \beta^{-8}\beta\frac{1 - \beta^4}{i} - \beta^{-8}\beta^5 J\frac{1 - \beta^3}{i}$$

$$= (1 + i)^8(-I) + (1 + i)^7\frac{1 - \beta^4}{i} - (1 + i)^3 J\frac{1 - \beta^3}{i}$$

E44. One way to write a formula for the present worth of a series of L beginning-of-year payments of C dollars each is to consider the time-zero payment separately from the $L - 1$ remaining payments:

$$P = C + C\frac{1 - \beta^{L-1}}{i}$$

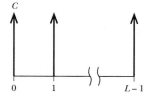

Another way is to find the worth at time -1 and "undiscount" the result to time 0. Do this.

$$P = \beta^{-1} C \frac{1 - \beta^L}{i}$$

For computing the *periodic equivalent* or annual worth of a cash-flow set, it is only necessary to compute the present worth and apply Eq. 2-15 (multiply by the reciprocal of the "pain" factor).

E45. **Maintenance charges (considered as positive) of {$500, $0, $250, $100, $100, $0} are expected for six typical months of operating a machine. At monthly interest of $i = 1\%$, what is the equivalent monthly maintenance cost?**

$$P = 500\beta + 250\beta^3 + 100\beta^4 + 100\beta^5 \qquad \text{where} \qquad \beta = \frac{1}{1.01}$$

$$= 928.941645$$

(This is not greatly different from the $950 sum.)

For $n = 6$ months,

$$A = P\left(\frac{i}{1 - \beta^n}\right) = P\left(\frac{1}{5.79547648}\right) = \underline{\$160.29}$$

(This is not greatly different from the $158.33 average.)

2.8.2.3 Time Scaling Consider the following example of a cash-flow set such as arises in replacement or scheduled maintenance problems:

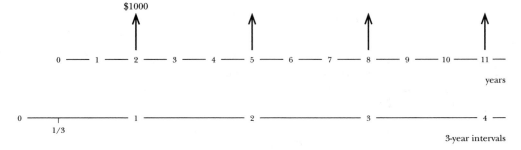

The problem of determining the present worth at $i_{\text{eff}} = 15\%$ is indistinguishable from that of determining the worth at time $1/3$ on the three-year altered time-scale shown, where $i = (1 + i_{\text{eff}})^3 - 1 = 0.520875$, so that the sought present worth is the worth of a four-payment equal-payment series, shifted to the right $1/3$ of an interval:

$$P = \beta^{-1/3} 1000 \frac{1 - \beta^4}{i} \qquad \text{where} \qquad \beta = \frac{1}{(1 + i)}$$

$$= (1.15)1000(1.56101339) = \$1795.17$$

The time-shift could be considered as one year to the right using i_{eff}, rather than 1/3 of an interval to the right using i. Such use of two interest rates and time scales in one problem might become confusing if there were further complications such as superimposing a geometric gradient. A general formula in terms of the original interest rate can be derived for a series of N equal payments at intervals of k years (k can be less than 1 as well as greater), with the first payment at time t:

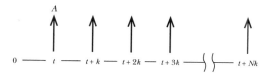

Using the same equivalence concepts as solved the concrete problem, we can write $i = (1 + i_{\text{eff}})^k - 1$ and

$$P = \beta^{-1+t/k} A \frac{1 - \beta^N}{i} \qquad \text{where} \qquad \beta = \frac{i}{(1 + i)}$$

Recalling $i = (1 - \beta)/\beta$, we can eliminate i:

$$P = \beta^{t/k} A \frac{1 - \beta^N}{\beta - 1}$$

Substituting β_{eff}^k for β, we can eliminate β, and obtain a formula for the *present worth of N payments of A dollars each at intervals of k years, with the first payment at time t:*

$$P = \beta_{\text{eff}}^t A \frac{1 - \beta_{\text{eff}}^{kN}}{1 - \beta_{\text{eff}}^k} \qquad (2\text{-}47)$$

E46. **At $i_{\text{eff}} = 10\%$ and assuming no future cost changes, if two brands of light bulb give the same light and use the same energy, which is cheaper: brand A, which costs \$6 and lasts nine years, or brand B, which costs \$0.70 and lasts 0.9 years?**

For nine years of service we can spend \$6 now on a single brand-A bulb. Alternatively, we can spend \$0.70 now for a brand-B bulb and also spend $A = \$0.70$ for each of a series of $N = 9$ future brand-B bulbs at intervals of $k = 0.9$ years, starting at $t = 0.9$ years. From Eq. 2-47 with $\beta_{\text{eff}} = 1/1.10$, the present worth of the costs of future brand-B bulbs is

$$\beta_{\text{eff}}^{0.9} \times 0.70 \times (1 - \beta_{\text{eff}}^{0.9 \times 9}) \div (1 - \beta_{\text{eff}}^{0.9}) = 4.20409 \cong \$4.20$$

Adding the \$0.70 cost of the initial bulb, the present worth of costs for nine years of service with brand-B bulbs is about $0.70 + 4.20 = \$4.90$. Since the cost for brand A is \$6.00, brand B is cheaper. Note that if interest had been ignored as in Example E4 of Chapter 1, the opposite result would have been obtained: Brand A has an annual cost of $6/9 \cong \$0.67$ per year, which would appear cheaper than $0.70/0.9 \cong \$0.78$ for brand B. But to ignore interest is to ignore the great disadvantage of having to pay for all of brand A's service in advance.

The foregoing example solved a simple *replacement* problem. But how would we solve such a problem if future costs were subject to monetary inflation or to escalation? Chapter 3 will provide the required methods. How would we account for differences in benefits (e.g., different amounts of light given by alternative bulbs) and differences in operating costs (e.g., different energy requirements for alternative bulbs)? Chapters 4 and 5 will provide the required methods. How would we account for unequal service lives (e.g., lack of the convenience of having 10 bulbs of one kind serve exactly as long as one bulb of another kind)? The second half of Chapter 5 will cover replacement problems in detail, including cases where the alternatives have replacement costs that will change in the future, have different benefits, have different operating costs, and do not cover the required service time with an integer number of replacements.

2.9 EXERCISES

1. Determine the repayment for a six-year loan of $1000:
   (a) For an annual interest rate of 10%.
   (b) For an annual interest rate of 15%.
   (c) For an annual interest rate of 20%.
   (d) For a semiannual interest rate of 10% (6 years is 12 intervals).
   (e) For a monthly interest rate of 1.25% (6 years is 72 intervals).

2. If there is to be a lump-sum repayment of $1000, at an annual interest rate of $i = 0.14$, to be paid at the end of n years, determine the appropriate loan amount:
   (a) When $n = 4$ years.
   (b) When $n = 8$ years.
   (c) When $n = 1.5$ years.
   (d) When repayment is at the end of 260 days, with a year considered to have 365.25 days.

3. If a loan of $1000 is repaid by a single payment of $1331.00 three years later:
   (a) What is the annual interest rate?
   (b) What is the monthly interest rate?

4. Determine the monthly interest rate charged by a lender who requires an interest payment of 5% of the principal of a loan along with repayment of the principal, when the length of the loan is six months.

5. Your cousin says, "I will lend you $100 if you will pay me back the $100 plus $5 interest six months from now." What is the annual compound interest rate?

6. Your father-in-law offers to lend you $100. If you keep it six months, he asks that you repay $105; if you keep it a year, $110. Is one of these options better than the other? (An option is better for a borrower if it has a lower interest rate and is better for a lender if it has a higher interest rate; here you are a borrower.)

7. A savings account pays 2.5% quarterly interest. If you make a deposit at time zero, how long does it take for the balance to grow to double the deposited amount? Answer the question under two different assumptions: First, that the savings institution pays "daily interest" so that a fraction of a quarter is meaningful, and second, that the interest is posted quarterly with no interest paid for a fraction of a quarter.

8. If a lender receives approximately a $360 lump-sum repayment for a $300 loan, what is the approximate term of the loan at 1% monthly interest?

9. What is the annual "rate of return" (interest rate) earned if an investment of $1000 yields a lump-sum receipt of $1041 after 0.38 years?

10. At 12% annual interest, what is the future worth at $n = 10$ years of a $100 present amount?

11. Determine the annual interest rate at which $100 now has a future worth of $110.25 after two years.

12. Determine the time it takes for $1000 to grow at 10% annual interest to a compound amount of $1500.

13. Determine the present worth at 11% annual interest of a $2000 payment to be made 3.20 years from now.

14. If money is worth 12% annual interest, what is the present worth of a promissory note that obligates a company to pay $1000 two years hence?

15. Determine the combined compound amount at time $n = 6$ years of $1000 invested at time 0 and $1600 invested at time 4 in a savings account that pays 8% interest annually. Do this both by applying Eq. 2-1 twice, with two different time scales, and by applying Eq. 2-2.

16. Omar habitually deposits most of his "Christmas" bonus in a special account that pays 7.52% annual interest. He made annual deposits of $2300, $1400, $500, and $900. Determine the balance (it was initially zero) just before and just after the $900 deposit. How much of the balance, at the time of the $900 deposit, was due to the $1400 deposit?

17. Determine the present worth at $i = 0.01$ of the following set of cash flows (these cash flows could represent the situation enjoyed by a credit-card holder who can spend $1000 of "plastic money" and wait a month before paying the bill).

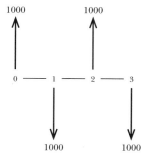

18. At 12% annual interest, what is the loan at time zero that would be repaid by the following payments?

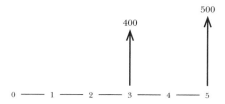

19. A $1500 loan is to be repaid at 9% annual interest by a $1000 payment after one year and another payment, A_2, after two years. Determine A_2 using Eq. 2-3.

20. A $3000 loan is repaid by a set of two payments: $2000 at time 1 and $1384.30 at time 2. Sketch the cash-flow diagram, with the lender as protagonist, for the three cash flows. Also sketch the cash-flow diagram with the borrower as protagonist. Using Eq. 2-3, determine which interest rate—8%, 9%, or 10%—is the correct interest rate for the loan.

21. Simplify the following cash-flow diagrams by combining coeval cash flows, and determine the present worth at 12% interest (amounts are in thousands of dollars):

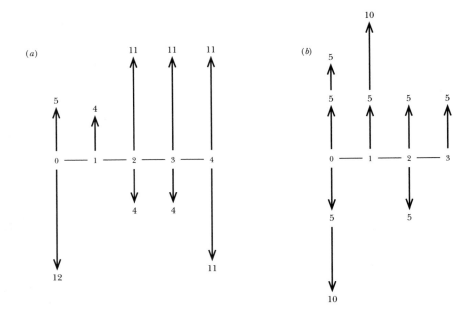

22. The following cash-flow diagram shows the net cash flows at each time. By splitting some of the cash flows into two or more coeval ones, redraw the diagram so that it shows (among other cash flows) a cost of 5 at each time except time zero.

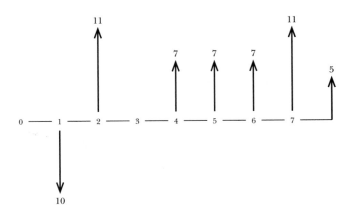

23. From Eq. 2-4, determine the present worth (worth at $m = 0$) and future worth (worth at $m = n = 5$) of the following set of cash flows, with 1.5% interest per period (amounts in dollars):

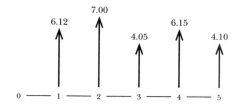

24. By reducing Eq. 2-4 to Eq. 2-3, show that present worth and worth at time zero are the same.

25. By reducing Eq. 2-4 to Eq. 2-3, show that future worth and worth at time n are the same.

26. From Eq. 2-3, prove that the present worth of a cash-flow set at zero interest equals the algebraic sum of the cash flows.

27. From Eq. 2-2, prove that the future worth of a cash-flow set at zero interest equals the algebraic sum of the cash flows.

28. From Eq. 2-4, prove that the worth of a cash-flow set at zero interest equals the algebraic sum of the cash flows, regardless of the evaluation time m.

29. From Eq. 2-4, prove that, given an interest rate, if two cash-flow sets $\{A_t^{(a)}\}$ and $\{A_t^{(b)}\}$ have equal worths at any evaluation time m, they also have equal worths at any other evaluation time m'.

30. At a given positive finite interest rate, is it possible for a finite non-null cash-flow set $\{A_t\}$ to have the same worths $F_m = F_{m'}$ at two distinct times m and m'? From Eq. 2-4, identify the necessary conditions for this.

31. Consider the contribution of a positive cash flow A_t to worth as computed in Eq. 2-4, with a positive interest rate. Determine and interpret the conditions on the evaluation time m and the cash-flow time t such that the worth contribution of the positive cash flow decreases with increasing interest rate.

32. Recall the cash-flow set of Example E10 in Section 2.2.2.1. Determine its worth at time 1 for five interest rates, {5%, 10%, 15%, 20%, 25%}, and sketch a plot of worth as a function of interest rate.

33. Recall the cash-flow set of Example E10 in Section 2.2.2.1. Determine its worth at time 3 for five interest rates, {5%, 10%, 15%, 20%, 25%}, and sketch a plot of worth as a function of interest rate.

34. Recall the cash-flow set of Example E10 in Section 2.2.2.1. At the interest rate $i = 0.1483314775$, determine its worth at evaluation times $m = 0$ and $m = 2$. Note that if a cash-flow set has a zero worth at every evaluation time m in Eq. 2-4, it has a zero worth at any evaluation time. The interest rate that makes a cash flow have zero worth is called its rate of return. Verify whether the given value of i is the cash-flow set's rate of return.

35. Determine the present worth at 25%, 30%, and 35% interest of the following cash-flow set and draw a sketch of present worth versus interest rate. From the results, roughly estimate (to the nearest 1%) the interest rate that makes the present worth zero (called the rate of return of the cash-flow set).

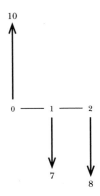

36. Determine the present worth at 5%, 10%, and 15% interest of the following cash-flow set and draw a sketch of present worth versus interest rate. From the results, roughly estimate (to the nearest 1%) the interest rate that makes the present worth zero (called the rate of return of the cash-flow set).

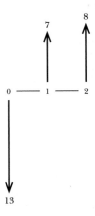

37. Sketch the cash-flow diagram of a cash-flow set that is indistinguishable from the following cash-flow set but has a subset consisting of the equal-payment series of cash flows of amount 3 at every time 1, 2, . . . , 8.

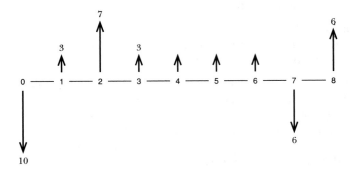

38. Sketch the cash-flow diagram of a cash-flow set that is indistinguishable from the following cash-flow set but has a subset consisting of the equal-payment series of cash flows of amount 3 at every time 1, 2, . . . , 10.

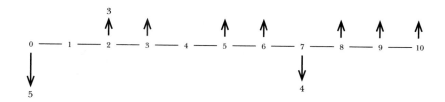

39. At 10% interest, what loan at time zero would a lender make to a borrower in return for the following repayment set? (The negative payment is indistinguishable from a second loan—the borrower receives money from the lender.) Repayment set:

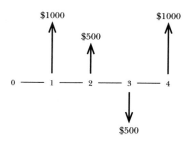

40. "At the interest rate of a loan, the net present worth of the loan and its repayments is zero" (Section 2.2.2.2). At 10% interest, a borrower proposes to *prepay* $1000 at time zero, take a loan of L dollars at time 1, and pay $1000 at time 2:

Making the (commercially unrealistic) assumption that the lender would pay the same interest rate as it charges, determine the loan amount that makes the arrangement fair.

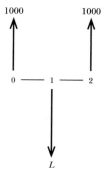

41. At 10% interest, a borrower agrees to pay X dollars at time 1, $2X$ dollars at time 2, and X dollars at time 3. If the loan (at time zero) is $1000, what are the payment amounts?

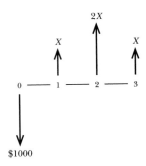

42. Determine the cash flow X such that the cash-flow sets a and b are equivalent at 9% interest.

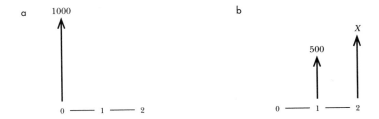

43. Determine the time of the $1200 payment if a $1000 loan is to be repaid by a $472.58 payment at time 2 and a $1200 payment later, to make the interest rate equal 9%.

44. A cash-flow set has a present worth of $801.56 at 12% interest. What is its future worth at time 17?

45. A cash-flow set consisting of 17 payments at times 1, . . . , 17 has a future worth of $1000, computed at 10% interest. What is its present worth, computed at the same interest rate?

46. Verify by long division that the infinite geometric series $\{1, x, x^2, x^3, \ldots\}$ has the sum $1/(1 - x)$.

47. Determine the interest rate at which an infinite series of $1 payments at times $\{1, 2, 3, \ldots\}$ has a present worth of $61.40. (*Note:* There is no payment at time zero.)

48. Use the infinite geometric series (Section 2.4.1) to derive a formula for the present worth of the following infinite-horizon cash-flow set:

(Such cash-flow sets arise in replacement problems, where a receipt or disbursement occurs every n years.) Express the result in terms of i or β, whichever gives a simpler expression.

49. In Chapter 10 the declining-balance depreciation schedule allows a depreciation charge of a fraction α of the current book value of an asset each year. The average dwell time of a depreciation schedule is a measure of the average delay between the time an asset is purchased and the time the resulting depreciation charges are allowed. It is defined for this schedule as

$$L = \sum_{t=1}^{\infty} t\alpha(1 - \alpha)^{t-1}$$

Using the precursor to Eq. 2-28 (Section 2.6.1), verify that $L = 1/\alpha$.

50. In Chapter 10 there is a declining-balance depreciation schedule with a half-year convention. At the end of each tax year, the depreciation charge is a fraction α of the previous book value, except that the first-year depreciation charge is only $\alpha/2$ of the original cost of the asset being depreciated; this halved first-year charge is meant to account for the assumption the asset was acquired at midyear instead of at the beginning. The average dwell time of this schedule measures its delay compared to an ideal delay of zero if all the depreciation charges were at time zero rather than according to the schedule. The average dwell time is defined for this schedule as

$$L = 1\left(\frac{1}{2}\alpha\right) + 2\alpha\left(1 - \frac{1}{2}\alpha\right) + 3\alpha\left(1 - \frac{1}{2}\alpha\right)(1 - \alpha) + 4\alpha\left(1 - \frac{1}{2}\alpha\right)(1 - \alpha)^2 + \ldots$$

Note that the expression is regular from the second term onward; that is, except for the first term, the tth term is $t\alpha(1 - \alpha/2)(1 - \alpha)^{t-1}$. Verify that $L = (1 - \alpha/2)/\alpha$, using the precursor to Eq. 2-28 (Section 2.6.1).

51. Recall Eq. 2-3:

$$P = \sum_{t=0}^{n} A_t\beta^t \qquad t = 0, 1, \ldots, n$$

This equation requires payments only at integer times. To allow payments at arbitrary times, let us index payments by a counter h.

Let a cash-flow set consist of H payments, numbered $h = 1, 2, \ldots, H$, having amounts $\{X_h\}$ and times $\{t_h\}$. Under continuous compounding, a loan at time zero of P_h dollars would be repaid at arbitrary time h by an amount X_n equal to P_h times $(1 + i)$ raised to the t_h power. Hence the present-worth contribution (loan repaid) by each amount X_h is X_h times β raised to the t_h power, and the sum of the loans repaid by the cash flows, is the present worth of the cash-flow set:

$$P = \sum_{h=1}^{H} X_h\beta^{t_h} \qquad \text{where} \qquad \beta \frac{1}{1 + i} \tag{2-48}$$

Of course, Eq. 2-48 reduces to Eq. 2-3 when the times $\{t_h\}$ are 1, 2, . . . , n. When times are arbitrary, there is seldom a reason not to express time in years, but Eq. 2-48 is valid for any i and β, not just for $i = i_{\text{eff}}$ and $\beta = \beta_{\text{eff}}$.

Recall Example E15, where the closing payment for an open-account loan was determined as the payment X such that the final balance would be zero. Another basis for determining the final payment would be to make it such that the cash-flow set consisting of all five transactions has a net present worth of zero (or alternatively, that the transactions after the $2000 loan have a present worth of $2000). Using Eq. 2-48, determine X this way and compare the result to the result given in Example E15.

52. An airline has a contract with a bank for daily cash management by which the bank earns daily interest at rate i when the balance is positive, and pays interest at the same rate when the balance is negative. The bank charges a fixed fee for the service; the interest simply serves to neutralize the effect of fluctuations on the bank's daily cash position. The daily interest rate is $i = 0.03\%$. Compute and interpret the interest and balance for the following three days of operation (payments reduce the balance):

Day	Payments	Advances	Interest	Balance
0	—	—	—	24,101.44
1	174,231.15	100,441.27		
2	101,475.16	129,388.40		
3	118,031.22	101,276.99		

53. A borrower borrows $1000 at time zero. One month later the borrower makes a $700 repayment; the next month the borrower makes a repayment of A_2 dollars; the third month the borrower makes a repayment of $71.44, which retires the loan. The interest rate is 1% per month. Determine A_2 two ways: first, by tracing the transaction sequence and solving for A_2 that makes the final balance zero, and then by applying Eq. 2-3.

54. Using a transaction sequence, show that if a borrower who borrows P dollars makes an interest-only payment iP at the end of each of n compounding intervals, the balance does not depend on n.

55. Using a transaction sequence, determine the payment that will retire a loan P after n intervals at an interest rate i, if at the end of each interval $t = 1, 2, \ldots, n - 1$ the borrower pays an interest-only payment iP.

56. At 1.25% monthly interest, John borrows $1000. He is to repay $400 each month until the loan is retired. How many months does it take, and what is the amount of the final payment?

57. Here are the first few and the last few rows of the amortization schedule for a $61,600 mortgage loan made November 1, 1986, to be repaid by a series of 300 equal monthly payments at 0.75% monthly interest. *Note:* An amortization schedule is a transaction sequence where the balance and interest payments are shown as positive. The payments are $516.95 each, as determined from Eq. 2-16 to the next higher cent, and the final payment corrects for the cumulative effect of roundoff error. The interest for each month is rounded to the nearest cent, so

that the new balance each month is an integer number of cents. From Eq. 2-16 and 2-11, determine what the balance (to the nearest cent) would have been after the August 1, 2011, payment if monthly payments and interest charges had been exact rather than rounded.

Payment Number	Payment Date	Interest Amount	New Balance	Cumul. Cal-Yr Interest
			61600.00	
1	Dec 1, 1986	462.00	61545.05	462.00
2	Jan 1, 1987	461.59	61489.69	461.59
3	Feb 1, 1987	461.17	61433.91	922.76
4	Mar 1, 1987	460.75	61377.71	1383.51
5	Apr 1, 1987	460.33	61321.09	1843.84
.	.	.	.	.
.	.	.	.	.
.	.	.	.	.
296	Jul 1, 2011	18.92	2024.24	209.31
297	Aug 1, 2011	15.18	1522.47	224.49
298	Sep 1, 2011	11.42	1016.94	235.91
299	Oct 1, 2011	7.63	507.62	243.54
300	Nov 1, 2011	3.81	0	247.35

Last payment: 511.43
Total payments: 155,079.48
Total interest: 93,479.48

58. A $61,600 loan can be made at a 0.75% monthly interest rate. The term of the loan is 25 years (300 monthly payments). By comparing the compound amount of the monthly payment series with the compound amount of the original principal, estimate the adjustment needed in the final payment if the monthly payments are rounded to $516.94, and if rounded to $516.95. (This exercise assumes that interest charges are *not* rounded.)

59. In borrowing $16,451.22 to buy a new car, Margarita gets the dealer to reduce the interest rate from 1.0125% monthly to 1.01% monthly. If she repays the loan in 48 equal monthly installments, how much does the interest reduction reduce her monthly payment amount?

60. "I borrowed money and payed it off in 60 equal monthly installments. I was shocked to learn that my payments ended up totaling 12 times the loan." If this statement were true, what would be the monthly compound interest rate? (Choose from 2%, 10%, 20%, 50%.)

61. Juaquin agreed to pay his father $10 per month for 12 months to repay a $100 loan. Another lender would have charged 1% monthly interest. Did his father charge more, or less, than that interest rate?

62. At 1.5% monthly compound interest, how many monthly $100 payments will bring a credit-card balance from $3000 down to zero?

63. An automobile dealership offers loans at 0.84% monthly interest for terms of 24, 30, 36, 42, 48, 54, or 60 months. If a customer can pay up to $400 per month for a $13,000 automobile loan, what should be the term of the loan?

64. A prepaid maintenance contract costs $4721 at time zero and covers two years of service. The customer has been paying monthly maintenance costs. To compare the prepaid contract with these costs, determine the contract's 24-month-horizon monthly equivalent at 1% monthly compound interest.

65. A fuel savings of $200 annually (end-of-year) is expected to last for many years. At 15% interest, what amount does its present worth approach?

66. At 1% monthly interest, what is the lower limit on the amount of each equal monthly repayment on a $1000 loan as the number of payments increases?

67. Equation 2-15 is not defined for $i = 0$, since its denominator vanishes. Prove $A = P/n$ for $i = 0$.

68. Determine the infinite-horizon annual equivalent of $2500 at 13% interest.

69. As a rule of thumb, an energy conservation group advised homeowners to install insulation if the prospective annual savings were at least 10% of the investment. Determine the implied interest rate if this rule is interpreted as specifying an infinite-horizon annual equivalent.

70. A newly installed piece of equipment will have to be replaced in eight years with a replacement that will cost $41,000. What annual amount must be deposited at the end of each of eight years into a sinking fund at 9% interest to yield a compound amount just sufficient to provide the replacement cost?

71. Aziz drives his own car on company business. Since the company estimates the car will last 10 years and will cost $14,000 to replace then, Aziz expects the company to reimburse him $1400 per year for depreciation. However, the company's accountants assume an interest rate of 8% and reimburse him the appropriate sinking-fund amount at the end of each year. What is the amount, and in what sense is it fair to Aziz?

72. A charity wants to purchase a van six years from now at a cost of $60,000. What monthly pledge from contributors would be enough to finance this expenditure if contributions are invested at 0.9% monthly interest?

73. If money could be invested at 0.8% monthly interest, how long would it take a family to save $40,000 at a rate of $100 per month?

74. Recall the equal-payment-series compound amount factor and its use in computing a compound amount given the amount, interest rate, and number of payments for an equal-payment series:

$$F = A\left[\frac{(1 + i)^n - 1}{i}\right] \qquad \text{(Equation 2-13, Section 2.4.1)}$$

Consider the issue of user performance for problems where i is a two-digit, three-keystroke entry, such as [decimal, zero, nine] for 9% or [decimal, one, six] for 16%; where n is a two-digit, two-keystroke entry, such as [one, two] for 12; and where A is a three-digit, three-keystroke entry, such as [one, zero, zero] for 100. Two examples of such a problem are

    (i) Determine F when $A = 240$, $i = 0.11$, $n = 10$.

    (ii) Determine F when $A = 101$, $i = 0.09$, $n = 15$.

(a) For your hand calculator, determine the number of keystrokes to solve such a problem.

(b) A normal time for skilled hand-calculator operations is about 0.6 seconds per keystroke. Practice on arbitrary problems or on (i) and (ii) above; when ready, have someone time your performance on one or both of the following two sample sets of 10 problems each. When the answer appears in the window, immediately solve the next problem; the monitor should compare your answers to the correct ones, and have you stop and start over if a mistake is made. After the total elapsed time for 10 error-free calculations is recorded, divide by 10 and divide by the number of keystrokes per problem; compare the result to the normal time per keystroke mentioned above.

Sample Set 1:

. . . .

A	i	n	(answer F)
100	5%	41	(12783 . . .)
994	13%	10	(18309 . . .)
700	12%	11	(14458 . . .)
532	11%	14	(16010 . . .)
463	25%	12	(25098 . . .)
112	14%	20	(10194 . . .)
700	13%	31	(232620 . . .)
205	4%	13	(3408.5 . . .)
338	1%	95	(53185 . . .)
896	19%	10	(22139 . . .)

Sample Set 2:

. . . .

A	i	n	(answer F)
161	9%	22	(10122 . . .)
704	8%	11	(11718 . . .)
242	10%	19	(12380 . . .)
656	5%	10	(8251.0 . . .)
829	7%	17	(25566 . . .)
315	11%	16	(12344 . . .)
970	12%	12	(23409 . . .)
133	6%	23	(6250.4 . . .)
588	19%	14	(32246 . . .)
497	20%	13	(24102 . . .)

75. Refer to the problem samples in the previous exercise. Such problems were formerly solved with the aid of interest tables. For most students and most calculators, about 12 seconds of calculator operation is required per problem of this type; to compare calculator use with interest-table use, assume that it takes 10 seconds to compute just the $(F/A\ i,n)$ factor by calculator, without multiplying by A. The comparable effort by interest table is the effort to find the page for the interest rate, look up the factor in the n row of the $(F/A\ i,n)$ column, and enter

the result into the calculator (the last step is necessary because the result must be multiplied by A, and under the alternative the result is already in the calculator ready to be multiplied).

(a) Pretending there were interest tables at the end of this book, make a personal estimate of the normal time to find the page for the interest rate, the time to look up the factor, and the time to enter the result into the calculator. Draw a conclusion about which is faster, hand calculator or interest tables.

(b) Interest tables rarely include interest rates such as 13%, or values of n such as 95, and they seldom are accurate enough for determining payments to the nearest cent. Would these facts constitute disadvantages of interest tables for the problem samples of Exercise 74(b)?

76. To the nearest 1%, find the rate of return of the following cash-flow set:

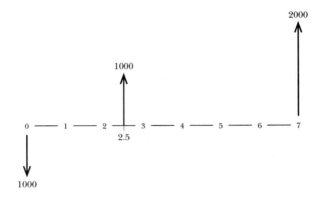

77. Erthgard borrowed $1000 at time 0, made a repayment of $1000 at time 2.5, and had to make a further repayment of $2000 at time 7. Starting with trial interest rates of 24.7% and 24.8%, determine the interest rate to at least six-figure accuracy by using the bracketing interpolation procedure.

78. Determine the effective interest rate for:
   (a) 1.02% monthly interest.
   (b) 12% annual interest, compounded monthly.
   (c) Interest at a rate such that $1 deposited for three months compounds to $1.045.

79. Determine the nominal interest rate for:
   (a) 1.02% monthly interest.
   (b) 12% effective interest when compounding is monthly.
   (c) 12% effective interest when compounding is 365.25 times per year.
   (d) A loan contract with monthly compounding whose annual percentage rate (APR) is advertised as 12.217%.

80. Determine the nominal continuous interest rate for an effective rate of 12%, and determine whether it is appreciably different from the nominal interest rate for daily (365.25 times per year) compounding.

81. Suleyman's bank pays 12.1% effective interest on a savings account, and he can write a check on it at any time without penalty. He deposits $5000. Determine

how much he can withdraw 122 days later (which is exactly one-third year under the bank's rules). Obtain the answer in three ways: (1) using daily interest with $m = 366$ days per year, (2) using the continuous compound interest rate, and (3) using Eq. 2-1 with noninteger n.

82. To help expedite a construction project in which he had a financial interest, Faid agreed to act as the construction lender. He granted a line of credit at 1% monthly interest to the contractor, with no penalties for payments or withdrawals at any time. The contractor withdrew money as she needed it during construction, and also used the account as a temporary repository for an advance payment from another customer on a different job. Transactions in her account with Faid proceeded as in the table.

Complete the missing quantities in the transaction sequence table and determine the closing payment. Verify the result using Eq. 2-48 (given in Exercise 51).

Time in Months	Interest	Payment	Balance
0	—	−61,000	−61,000
0.32		−40,000	
0.38		−15,000	
0.42		196,000	
0.91		−196,000	
1.30		−10,000	
2.21		74,211.15	
3.01			

83. Amalia Contreras, a gastroenterologist, purchases an endoscope. After partial payment, she owes a balance of $9210.48. She agrees to repay the balance in daily installments at a daily interest rate of $i = 0.00038$, paying $100 per use each day until the balance is paid off. She and the other doctors in her group practice use the endoscope 4 times the first day, 21 times the second day, 14 times the third day, none the next two days (weekend), and 15 times the sixth day.
    (a) Determine the balance she owes at the end of the sixth day if she made daily payments as agreed.
    (b) If each daily funds transfer costs $0.50, would Dr. Contreras have been better off simply paying the total $5400 the sixth day, assuming that, to her, very-short-term money has no time value?

84. A new boiler plant is expected to be needed in 3.5 years. It will cost $3,400,000. An investment available right now (and not available later) would allow the need for the boiler plant to be delayed 2.5 years to time 6. The investment would cost $86,000. If money has a time value of $i_{eff} = 21\%$ and the only effect of the expenditure now would be to delay the later expenditure, is the investment worthwhile?

85. A contractor borrows money at 19% interest on a large-scale plant. The owner is reimbursing expenses as they occur, but the $100,000 fee that will furnish the contractor's profit will be paid upon completion. What is the worth to the contractor of avoiding a 19-week delay (assuming 52 weeks per year)?

86. A tooling investment of $12,000 will reduce all fabrication costs in a project by 12%. These costs are estimated (without the tooling investment) as

Time, yr	Cost, $
1	86,420
2	97,100
4	105,630

    (a) Determine whether the tooling investment is worthwhile if done immediately, given an interest rate of 14%.
    (b) If there is a delay in the tooling investment, it will still cost $12,000 (at time 1 rather than at time 0) but will not earn the first year's savings. What is the present-worth cost of the delay?

87. Which is better, to receive $1000 in one year, or to receive $500 now and $500 in two years? Does this illustrate the maxim that "early" helps more than "late" hurts?

88. The maxim that "early" helps more than "late" hurts is based on $\beta^{-\tau} + \beta^{\tau} > 2$, for $0 \le \beta < 1$, $\tau > 0$. Prove the inequality.

89. A local electrical contractor frequently works at our plant. A typical job will involve our paying 50% of the cost 10 days in advance of the completion date and the remainder 10 days after the completion date. At an interest rate of 0.02% daily, for a $6,000 job to be completed 30 days from now, compare the present worth (a) ignoring the payment split and (b) taking it into account.

90. At 15% interest (annual compound or "effective" interest rates are assumed when not otherwise specified), a payment that will occur in six months is treated by the end-of-year convention as if it will occur in 12 months. Let the payment amount be $1000. Determine the resulting absolute and percentage error in the payment's present worth.

91. Su earns 15% interest on her investments. Her manager proposes two alternative versions of a new investment. Both require the same expenditure now. Alternative A will return $31,000 at the end of one year. Alternative B will return $2500 at the end of each of 12 months. If B is evaluated using the end-of-year convention, will Su choose the wrong version? If so, what will be the cost of the wrong choice, in present-worth terms?

92. For services of equal benefit to our plant, two contractors have submitted bids. Erthgard Blandish proposes to charge $30,000 per year, payable at the beginning of each year. E. P. Blatt proposes to charge $32,000 per year, payable at the end of each month. Our bid analysis software uses the end-of-year convention; it will place the Blandish proposal's payments accurately at year beginnings, and will treat the Blatt proposal's payments as if they occurred at year ends. The interest rate is 18%. Does the software make a wrong decision, and if so, how much does the wrong decision cost in present-worth terms, considering that renegotiation is possible after one year?

93.

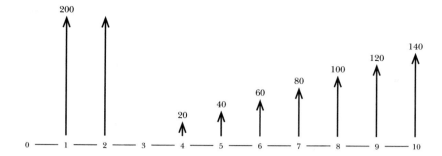

At 10% interest, determine the present worth of the above set of cash flows. (*Note:* Eq. 2-29 gives the worth of the gradient series at time 3 with $A_1 = 20$, $n = 7$; or at time 2 with $A_1 = 0$, $n = 8$.)

94. Maintenance costs for a radio for five years are expected to increase linearly from $100 the first year to $500 the fifth year. If our enterprise uses $i = 8\%$, would a $1200 prepaid five-year maintenance contract be effectively cheaper?

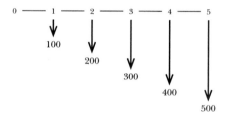

95. Corrosion is diminishing the profit from a reactor approximately linearly. The profit for the year starting today is estimated as $102,400. If the profit decreases by $8900 each year, how long should the reactor be operated, and what is the estimated present worth, at 18% interest, of its lifetime profits?

96. When a linear gradient series declines from a positive first payment A_1, having a negative G, its "positive life" L is defined (Eq. 2-30) as $L = A_1/(-G)$. A peculiarity of Eq. 2-30 (present worth of a linear gradient series) is that it gives the same value of P for $n = L$ and for $n = L + 1$. Certainly this makes sense when $-G$ divides A_1, so that L is an integer; in that case, the cash flow at time L is $-G$ (e.g., if $G = -20$ it is 20), and the cash flow at time $L + 1$ is zero. P is the same when a final cash flow of amount zero is excluded or included. Prove that $n = L$ and $n = L + 1$ give the same P even when L is not an integer.

97. A machine had maintenance costs of $9420 for the year just ended. If maintenance costs are escalating at 10% per year, what is the present worth, at $i = 12\%$, of the next five years of maintenance costs?

98. Sales revenues for a new product are estimated to be $13,400 the first year and to escalate at 7% annually. At 15% interest, determine the present worth of revenues if they continue for 10 years.

99. Recall that with $i = 0$, the present worth of a cash flow set is its sum. Use Eq. 2-35 to determine the five-year total of the revenues of a county that collected

$16.2 million in the year just ended and has passed a law to increase taxes by 0.5% each year.

100. If a new product has first-year sales of $220,000 and is anticipated to have a 12% annual decline in sales, determine its anticipated total sales (a) forever, and (b) for 10 years.

101. A set of prospective warehousing expenses for a chemical distributor has been estimated acording to the following cash-flow diagram (time in years, costs considered as positive in units of $1000):

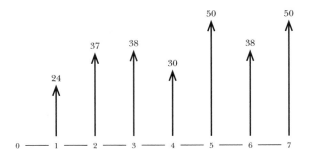

The distributor uses $i = 20\%$, and the present worth has been computed (for $\beta = 1/1.20$):

$$P = 24\beta + 37\beta^2 + 38\beta^3 + 30\beta^4 + 50\beta^5 + 38\beta^6 + 50\beta^7$$
$$= 128.92686 \quad \text{or} \quad \$128,926.86$$

However, it is discovered that the estimate was on the basis of a static market. Expenses are anticipated to be proportional to market volume, and the market is expected to increase at 4% annually; thus, for example, the first year's expenses would be 24(1.04) instead of 24. Correct the present worth accordingly.

102. There is an *asymptotic growth* present worth formula that gives the present worth for a cash-flow series that grows asymptotically to a level of R dollars per year:

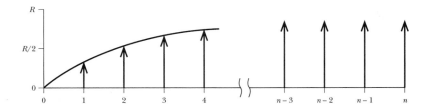

In the cash-flow series $\{A_t\}$ the cash flow in year t is $A_t = R[1 - (1 - a)^t]$, where the parameter a is obtained from another parameter τ called the half-growth time by the formula

$$a = 1 - (0.5)^{1/\tau}$$

The present worth at interest rate i is

$$P = R\left[\frac{1 - \beta^n}{i} - \frac{1 - \gamma^n}{q}\right]$$

where $\gamma = (1 - a)/(1 + i)$ and $q = 1/\gamma - 1$.

Using this as an example of a present-worth formula, we can use the general geometric gradient to get the present worth of a related cash-flow set.

To illustrate, consider that the Flatt Gas Company sees its revenues in a small subdivision as rising asymptotically from zero to $300,000 per year and estimates that they will reach half the level in 3.0 years. For a horizon of $n = 20$ years and with money worth $i = 15\%$, the present worth of prospective revenues can be computed as follows:

First, $a = 1 - (0.5)^{1/3} = 0.206299474$
$\quad\quad R = 300{,}000$
$\quad\quad\quad \gamma = (1 - a)/(1 + i) = 0.69017437$
$\quad\quad q = 1/\gamma - 1 = 0.448909207$

The resulting present worth of revenues is $P = \$1{,}209{,}914.78$.

Now, suppose the Flatt Gas Company has estimated the present worth of revenues from a small subdivision as above. However, it is believed that the potential level is not fixed at $300,000 per year but is increasing 7% per year (starting with $300,000 at time zero). Since in the formula R is a multiplicative factor, each cash flow A_t will become $A_t(1.07)^t$; that is, the required correction can be accomplished using the general geometric gradient. Perform the correction.

103. In Eq. 2-41, Section 2.7.1, it is seen that the present worth of n years of continuous cash flow at a constant rate of $\bar{A}$ dollars per year has the present worth

$$\bar{A}\frac{1 - \beta^n}{r}$$

where $r = \ln(1 + i)$ is the nominal continuous interest rate. By comparing this expression with the corresponding discrete expression involving the "pain" factor, determine the factor by which the end-of-year timing convention underestimates the worth of uniform continuous cash flows.

104. As a sales incentive, an energy management company offers to operate your heat plant for "free": you continue to pay bills for coal shipments, and so on, at old levels to the management company, which in turn pays the actual reduced bills, and at the end of the year the management company reimburses you for the full audited total of savings that it realized throughout the year. If the management company uses $i = 20\%$ and realizes $21,000 of savings essentially continuously throughout the year and pays you $21,000 at the end of the year, what present worth does the management company see for the year of operation?

105. Does the "normally distributed" cash-flow profile in Figure 2-6 bear out the maxim that "early" helps more than "late" hurts? Explain.

106. A vapor collection system for a group of naphtha storage tanks is expected to save $10,450 annually for 4.5 years, but the system will take 1.4 years to install. The installation will be done at a steady rate and have a total cost of $16,400; while the installation proceeds, the rate of savings will ramp up linearly. At 18% interest, determine the present worth of the project if it is abandoned without cost or salvage at the end of its life.

107. For each of the following substitutions, identify whether it expresses the metaphor of *equivalence*, the metaphor of *indistinguishability*, or neither.

   (a) A loan of $1000 for six years is repaid in a simple lump sum, the amount of which is the same as if there had been a series of one-year loans in which, for all but the last one, the borrower repaid in full and immediately borrowed the same sum.

   (b) A loan of $1000 is repaid in several payments, the amounts of which are determined by considering the series of transactions as a series of loans, each following the last.

   (c) A loan of $1000 is repaid in several payments, the amounts of which are determined by considering the payments as each being a lump-sum repayment of part of the loan.

   (d) In evaluating the worth of a cash-flow set, the present worth of a subset is substituted for the cash flows in the subset, thus simplifying the cash-flow set.

   (e) In evaluating the worth of a cash-flow set, some cash flows are replaced by coeval pairs, as in the following example, to allow use of convenient formulas:

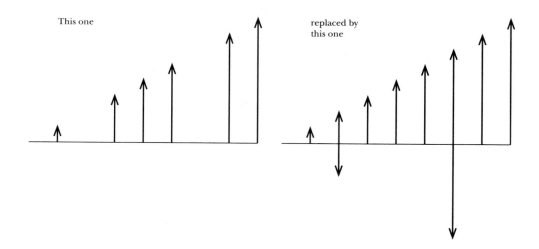

   (f) An engineering investment is likened to moneylending.

   (g) One cash-flow set is substituted for another in a way that would give them the same worth at a given interest rate.

   (h) One cash-flow set is substituted for another in a way that would give them equal worths at every interest rate.

108. At what interest rate is $1000 now equivalent to $1200 a year from now?

109. At what interest rate is $1000 now equivalent to:
    (a) $100 at the end of every year forever?
    (b) $100 continuously uniformly forever?
    (c) A pair of cash flows: $600 at time 1 and $700 at time 2?

110. Billy-Bob considers a project opportunity as ——————— picking up a windfall of $14,420.15 because by considering his ordinary course of business to be a ———————, he could define a set of transactions that would convert the project's cash-flow set to one ——————— the windfall. (Insert the phrases "surrogate banker," "equivalent to" and "indistinguishable from" in the appropriate blanks.)

111. Maria has a substantial savings account that pays interest at 10% annually. She has an opportunity to buy a frabjous widget for $100 and sell it for $150 in two years. At $i = 10\%$ the present worth of the opportunity is $-100 + 150(1/1.10)^2 = \$23.97$. Show how, using her savings account as a surrogate banker, Maria could convert the opportunity to a $23.97 windfall, or vice versa.

112. Ahmad has a substantial balance that he owes on his credit-card account, which charges interest at 1% monthly. He has an opportunity to buy a piano for $1500 and sell it for $1650 twelve months later. At $i = 1\%$ monthly, the present worth of the opportunity is $-1599 + 1650(1/1.01)^{12} = -\$35.71$. Thus it is a bad investment according to present-worth analysis. Show how, using his credit-card account as a surrogate banker, Ahmad could convert the opportunity to a $35.71 present loss, or vice versa.

113. Three vendors have responded to a request for a quotation for a grinder your company wishes to purchase. Bids will be analyzed on the basis of price, delivery date, and features. Your company uses $i = 20\%$ interest.
    (a) To simplify the price portion of the analysis, convert the following price quotations to discounted prices:

Vendor	Price	Terms
1	40,500	Payable on delivery
2	42,300	Payable within 90 days (0.25 years)
3	43,100	1% discount if paid within 30 days, or must be paid within 90 days

    (b) Analysis of the quotations reveals that Vendor 2 offers a grinder that will need $90 annual servicings not required by the other grinders. The grinders are all expected to last five years. Express the servicing requirement as a correction to the discounted price. (Assume the fifth servicing is needed, even though its cost is treated as being paid at the time of abandonment.)

114. Worth formulas are unique: A cash-flow set has a unique worth formula, and a worth formula represents a unique cash-flow set. For example, the present-worth formula

$$P = -1000 + 200\left(\frac{1 - \beta^3}{i}\right) + 900\beta^3$$

or any formula algebraically identical to it, such as $-100 + 200\beta + 200\beta^2 + 1100\beta^3$, gives the present worth of only this cash-flow set

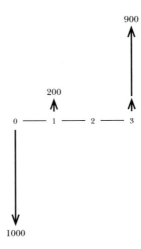

or one indistinguishable from it. For each of the following present-worth formulas, sketch the corresponding cash-flow diagram:

(a) $P = 200\beta^3 - 100\beta^4$

(b) $P = -1000 + 600\left(\dfrac{1 - \beta^4}{r}\right)$ where $r = \ln(1 + i)$

(c) $P = -1000 + \beta^4 600\left(\dfrac{1 - \beta^3}{i}\right)$

115. In Example E44, Section 2.8.2.2, two formulas were given for the present worth of a series of L beginning-of-year payments of C dollars each. Show algebraically that they are the same.

116. A janitorial service has been billing a customer $350 at the end of each month. Partly for tax reasons, the customer wants to pay for a year in advance. For $i = 15\%$ annually, determine the annual bill. Is it substantially less than $350(12) = \$4200$?

117. Verify Eq. 2-47, Section 2.8.2.3, by applying it to the numerical example in its development.

After World War I, German prices soared to the point where it took 100,000 marks to equal a U.S. dollar.

ESCALATION AND INFLATION

This chapter offers a unified treatment of the combined effects of monetary inflation and geometric escalation or deescalation, made simple by use of the *general geometric gradient* developed in Section 2.6.3.

3.1 MONETARY INFLATION

Monetary inflation is a *general increase in the level of prices* in an economy, and *monetary deflation* is a *general decline in prices*. For many fascinating and incompletely understood reasons, inflation is endemic while deflation is rare. A limited understanding follows simply by noting that everyone wants to charge more money for the goods and services he or she provides. There is a sort of hysteresis by which the market reacts incompletely to small price increases, because the reactions are not cost-free; if I insist on slightly higher wages or fees, you may pay them rather than go to the trouble of finding a new source. Economically immune segments of a society can cause inflation, the classic example being that a government can simply print (or borrow) more money.

An alternative definition of inflation is that inflation is a general decline in the value or purchasing power of money.

E1. A country has 2 billion units of wealth, measured in a foreign anthropologist/economist's arbitrary units for valuation of goods and services. The wealth remains constant, but the country's government suddenly prints extra money, raising the amount of money in circulation by 10%, from 10 billion xu to 11 billion

xu. By what resulting percentage do prices, in xu, generally increase? By what resulting percentage does the purchasing power of the xu decrease?

The price per unit of wealth goes from $10/2 = 5$ xu per unit to $11/2$ xu per unit, an increase in prices of 10%.

The purchasing power of the xu goes from $2/10$ units per xu to $2/11$ units per xu, a decrease in purchasing power of 9.0909%.

The alternative definition is not as easy to apply directly as is the price-rise definition, because money itself is our habitual measure of value. It is more convenient to avoid defining a metameasure of value and simply measure inflation by measuring prices.

3.1.1 Inflation Rate

Let L_t be the price, at time t, of something that is considered to be representative of a class of goods or services. If in the time interval 0 to n the price changes from L_0 to L_n, then the inflation rate j is defined such that

$$L_n = L_0(1 + j)^n \tag{3-1a}$$

$$j = (L_n/L_0)^{1/n} - 1 \tag{3-1b}$$

For example, if the price of gasoline is indicative of a segment of the economy, and the average price of gasoline went from $0.36 per gallon in 1955 to $1.20 in 1990, then the annual inflation rate is estimated from Eq. 3-1b as

$$j = (1.20/0.36)^{1/(1990-1955)} - 1 = 3.5\%$$

(Here we temporarily take gasoline as representative of all goods and services; in Section 3.3 we will consider escalation of each price category separately.)

There was, of course, no steady inflation rate, but a fluctuating one. Consider, for example, the *consumer price index* (CPI) published by the U. S. government as the most widely used "market basket of goods and services" indicative of the U. S. economy as a whole. One unit of this mix of goods and services was priced at $100 in 1967 and at $374 in 1990, indicating 5.9% annual inflation over the 23-year period. Yet the CPI rose in a fluctuating manner such that the steady inflation modeled by Eq. 3-1a rarely gave prices equal to those given by actual inflation. See Figure 3-1.

Engineering economy applications always involve the *future*, not the past. Lacking any practical basis for assuming that future inflation rates will be different in one year than another, we use a single estimated inflated rate as in Eq. 3-1a and 3-1b. In estimating such a rate, or in judging competing estimates advocated by others, we keep several points in mind: One is that general inflation depends on factors much broader than the characteristics of one project or even one industry. Another is that costs and revenues specific to a project can have their own escalation rates (Section 3.3). The engineering economy analyst, therefore, should probably spend little time questioning consensus projections of general inflation, but pay close attention to estimating specific escalation rates (say for fuel or for labor) directly applicable to the decision problem being analyzed.

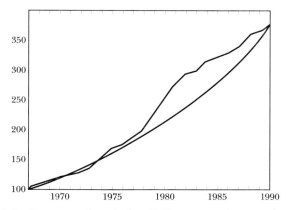

FIGURE 3-1. Consumer Price Index (CPI) compared to steady inflation.

Another point that needs to be kept in mind when dealing with past data, either in general inflation or on escalation of a specific price category, is that escalation or inflation rates have geometric rather than arithmetic averages. If we define j_t as the inflation rate for the one-interval time span $t-1$ to t, Eq. 3-1a gives

$$L_t = L_{t-1}(1 + j_t) \tag{3-1c}$$

If n intervals pass, and j is the rate defined by Eq. 3-1a, then

$$L_n = L_0(1 + j_1)(1 + j_2) \cdots (1 + j_n) = L_0(1 + j)^n \tag{3-1d}$$

E2. The consumer price index (CPI) was published as 125.3 for 1972, 133.1 for 1973, and 147.7 for 1974. By definition of CPI as the price level at the end of a year compared to the end of the previous year, Eq. 3-1c gives

$$\text{CPI}_{1973} = \text{CPI}_{1972}(1 + j_{1973})$$

and

$$\text{CPI}_{1974} = \text{CPI}_{1973}(1 + j_{1974})$$

Determine the inflation rate of each of years 1973 and 1974, determine the composite inflation rate j for the two-year time span, and determine whether an arithmetic average of the two one-year rates would have accurately estimated j.

Solving Eq. 3-1c for j_i:

$$j_{1973} = (\text{CPI}_{1973}/\text{CPI}_{1972}) - 1 = (133.1/125.3) - 1$$

$$= \underline{6.225\%}$$

$$j_{1974} = (\text{CPI}_{1974}/\text{CPI}_{1973}) - 1 = (147.7/133.1) - 1$$

$$= \underline{10.9692\%}$$

The arithmetic average of these two rates is 8.597%.

From Eq. 3-1b for the two-year span:

$$j = (CPI_{1974}/CPI_{1972})^{1/2} - 1 = (147.7/125.3)^{1/2} - 1$$
$$= \underline{8.571\%}$$

The difference is small, but it demonstrates the inaccuracy of using arithmetic averaging where geometric averaging (that is, use of Eqs. 3-1a–3-1d) is correct.

Inflation is one of several reasons that money has a time value. The anticipated inflation rate contributes to the overall *market interest rate i*, because one of the reasons a loan or investment P should be smaller than its repayment or return F is that P dollars at time n will purchase less in goods and services than it would have purchased at time zero.

E3. Your uncle, for religious or moral reasons, does not believe in interest. He wants to give you money to purchase a car, which you will pay back one year later, without interest. However, it is agreed that your repayment will be adjusted upward if an equivalent car costs more at the time of repayment. You borrow $12,000 from this uncle, and at the end of the year an equivalent car costs 2% more than what you paid; therefore you repay 12,000(1.02) = $12,240. What interest rate could have been charged that would have had the same effect as this correction for inflation?

Given $P = 12,000$, $F = 12,240$, $n = 1$, Eq. 2-1b of Chapter 2 gives

$$i = (F/P)^{1/n} - 1 = \underline{2\%}$$

The example illustrates the principle that the market interest rate i is at least as great as the inflation rate j in order for a lender or investor to prosper. Note that the rationale depends on the assumption of a *general* rise in prices; in the example, the rise in price of a car was taken to indicate inflation that presumably would apply to things the uncle would buy with the repayment F or had forgone buying with the loan amount P.

3.1.2 Real and Market Interest Rates

The interest rate i that is used in engineering economy calculations is called the market interest rate or the *combined interest rate*, so called because it combines the effects of inflation, risk, and other influences on the time value of money. It is also called the *opportunity value* or opportunity cost of money; given a particular investment opportunity, i is considered to be the proper rate at which to discount its cash flows in evaluating it, based on the rationale that if this opportunity is not taken, the money can otherwise be lent or invested at rate i.

We define the *real interest rate d*, also called the "inflation-free" interest rate, according to this basic relationship:

$$1 + i = (1 + d)(1 + j) \tag{3-2}$$

Below is a list of the explicit formulas for determining any one of these rates given the other two:

$$i = (1 + d)(1 + j) - 1 = d + j + dj \tag{3-2a}$$

$$d = \frac{1 + i}{1 + j} - 1 = \frac{i - j}{1 + j} \tag{3-2b}$$

$$j = \frac{1 + i}{1 + d} - 1 = \frac{i - d}{1 + d} \tag{3-2c}$$

E4. Determine the real interest rate if $i = 15\%$ and there is 5% annual inflation.

From Eq. 3-2b:

$$d = \frac{1 + i}{1 + j} - 1 = \frac{1.15}{1.05} - 1 = .095238$$

$$= \underline{9.52\%}$$

3.2 INDEXED AND CURRENT CASH FLOWS

When a future cash flow is estimated, the resulting number (such as "$3790.15") represents one of two things: on one hand, it can represent a *current* cash flow, one that explicitly takes into account the impact of inflation (e.g., $3790.15 in the cheaper future dollars). Current amounts are often called *then-current* amounts to emphasize that the word "current" is applied to a future time.

On the other hand, an *indexed* or *constant-worth* cash flow is one that does not explicitly take inflation into account (e.g., whatever amount in current dollars will buy the same goods and services as $3790.15 at the index time.) Unless otherwise stated, the index time will always be time zero.

Current-dollar amounts are sometimes called *inflated* or *after-inflation* amounts, and indexed amounts are sometimes called *inflation-free* or *before-inflation* amounts.

An example of a *current* cash flow estimate is the repayment of a loan or a payment that is fixed by contract. For example, if I have signed a five-year maintenance contract for $3790.15 per year, I will pay $3790.15 the fifth year even if that is a typical price of a hamburger at that time.

"Wake up, sir. When you died in an accident sixty years ago we cryogenically preserved your body and have applied the newest technology to resuscitate you. Your relatives put your IBM stock in trust. Shall I get your broker on the telephone?"

"Hello, how have my stocks done?"

"Very well, sir. Your holdings are currently about twenty million dollars."

"That's great . . ."

(Click) "Please deposit two thousand dollars for the next three minutes."

An example of an *indexed* cash flow is an ordinary maintenance cost. If I estimate maintenance costs at $3790.15 per year because that is what they now cost, and the need for maintenance will stay the same every year, then "$3790.15" represents the value in today's dollars of a future year's costs. This is what is meant by an indexed cash flow.

The cash flows in many engineering economy studies are mostly indexed numbers. In a study to upgrade facilities in a manufacturing plant, for example, the estimated future cash flows involve such things as revenues from sale of product and various kinds of costs—labor, materials, supplies, services. If there is 4% inflation, we expect that in two years we will sell our product at a price 8.16% higher and pay 8.16% more for labor and materials. On the other hand, a company may pay *current* dollars as interest on long-term debt or as payments under long-term supply contracts. One company built a major natural gas pipeline in 1963. It was financed with 30-year bonds at a low fixed interest rate and the company also took advantage of a 50-year agreement with Mexico to sell natural gas at a price fixed in current American dollars; as a result, the company enjoys paying 2.5 times less for debt service and gas than it would if making a similar deal today.

Cash flows are ordinarily expressed in current dollars. Let a cash flow occurring at time t be denoted A_t, expressed in current (then-current) dollars. Let W_t denote the same cash flow expressed in indexed dollars—that is, expressed as L_0 if L_t is A_t. From Eq. 3-1a, we get a relationship between current and indexed cash flows:

$$A_t = W_t(1 + j)^t \qquad \text{(3-3a)}$$

$$W_t = A_t(1 + j)^{-t} \qquad \text{(3-3b)}$$

E5. A maintenance fee to be paid two years from now is estimated as $1444 on the basis that it would cost $1444 to do the same amount of work today. Assuming 4% annual inflation, express the fee in current and in indexed dollars.

By its definition, it is already expressed in indexed dollars as $W_2 = \underline{\$1444}$. From Eq. 3-3a with $j = 0.04$:

$$A_2 = W_2(1.04)^2 = \underline{\$1561.83} \quad \text{(then-current)}$$

An estimate made as if no inflation were to occur is an estimate made in indexed dollars (today's dollars).

E6. A contracted maintenance fee obligated to be paid two years from now is $8079. Assuming 5% annual inflation, express the fee in current and in indexed dollars.

By its definition, it is already expressed in current dollars (the check will be written for $8079 two years hence). Thus $A_2 = \underline{\$8079}$. From Eq. 3-3b with $j = 0.05$:

$$W_2 = A_2(1.05)^{-2} = \underline{\$7327.89}$$

Note that W_2 is not the present worth of the fee; rather, it is what is sometimes called the purchasing power of the fee: In today's dollars, $8079 two years hence will have the power to purchase goods and services that would cost $7327.89 today, if there is to be 5% annual inflation.

To justify the definition of the real interest rate d (Eq. 3-2), recall the defining equation for the present worth of a cash-flow set (Eq. 2-3):

$$P = \sum_{t=0}^{n} A_t \beta^t = \sum_{t=0}^{n} A_t \left(\frac{1}{1+i} \right)^t$$

Using Eq. 3-3a to express the present worth in terms of the set of *indexed* cash flows $\{W_t\}$:

$$P = \sum_{t=0}^{n} W_t (1+j)^t \left(\frac{1}{1+i} \right)^t = \sum_{t=0}^{n} W_t \left(\frac{1+j}{1+i} \right)^t \tag{3-4}$$

Now we can motivate the definition of the real interest rate d as the *interest rate that discounts indexed cash flows*. Let d be such that $(1+j)/(1+i) = 1/(1+d)$, which is in fact the d defined by Eq. 3-2. Then Eq. 3-4 becomes

Present worth of indexed cash flows:

$$P = \sum_{t=0}^{n} W_t \left(\frac{1}{1+d} \right)^t \tag{3-5}$$

E7. A maintenance fee to be paid two years from now is estimated as W_2 = \$1444 in indexed dollars (today's dollars). Assuming 4% annual inflation, determine its present worth at 10% interest by determining the fee amount expressed in current dollars and discounting at i, and by determining d and discounting the indexed amount at d.

Discounting A_2 at i: $A_2 = W_2(1.04)^2 = \$1561.83$; $i = 10\%$.

$$P = A_2 (1/1.10)^2 = \underline{\$1290.77}$$

Discounting W_2 at d: $1 + d = (1+i)/(1+j) = 1.10/1.04$, so that the real interest rate is $d = 5.76923\%$.

$$P = W_2 [1/(1+d)]^2 = \underline{\$1290.77}$$

To take inflation into account in engineering economy analysis, it is convenient to use *present worth* as the worth measure rather than future worth or annual equivalent, because *present worth is the same whether expressed in indexed or current dollars*: $W_0 = A_0$ in Eqs. 3-3a and 3-3b. If future worths or annual equivalents are computed, it is necessary to distinguish between future worth in indexed dollars and future worth in current dollars, and between annual equivalent in indexed dollars using d or in current dollars using i.

Some cash flows are most naturally estimated in indexed dollars, others in current dollars. Both kinds of estimates may be used in the same problem, following this simple rule:

> Discount current-dollar cash flows at i;
> Discount indexed-dollar cash flows at d.

The inflation-free or real interest rate d is a special case of the substitute interest rate s introduced in Section 2.6.3. Later in this chapter (Section 3.3) we will show how to combine the effects of inflation and geometric growth or decay.

It should be noted that since Eq. 3-5 is general, that is, since it is valid for any set of indexed cash flows $\{W_t\}$, and since it is identical to Eq. 2-3 of Chapter 2 with $i \rightarrow d$ and $A_t \rightarrow W_t$, then *every formula derived from Eq. 2-3 of Chapter 2 is also valid with $i \rightarrow d$ and $A_t \rightarrow W_t$*. In particular, recall the "pain" factor, which allows us to compute the present worth at i of n equal payments of current amount A:

$$P = A(P/A\ i,n) = A\frac{1 - 1/(1 + i)^n}{i}$$

By letting $A \rightarrow W$ and $i \rightarrow d$, we can derive a corresponding factor that allows us to compute the present worth at d of n payments whose indexed values are all equal to an amount W:

Equal indexed-amount-series present worth:

$$P = W(P/W\ d,n) = W\frac{1 - 1/(1 + d)^n}{d} \tag{3-6}$$

E8. We just finished reloading a reactor with fresh catalyst at a cost of $9075. We must do the same thing at the end of each of the next three years. The future costs will probably be higher, because they include labor, materials, and energy, all of which will inflate at the general inflation rate that is estimated as 6% annually. Using Eq. 3-6, determine the present worth of the next three years' catalyst reloading costs, at $i = 15\%$.

From Eq. 3-2b with $i = 15\%$, $j = 6\%$:

$$d = \frac{i - j}{1 + j} = 8.490566\%$$

From Eq. 3-5, with $W = 9075$ indexed dollars per year:

$$P = 9075\left(\frac{1 - 1/(1 + d)^3}{d}\right) = 9075(2.5544545)$$

$$= \underline{\$23,181.67}$$

The same answer (and same numerical procedure) would result from applying the geometric gradient series formulas from Section 2.6.2.

Converting all cash flows in a problem to either indexed or current cash flows would be tedious and unnecessary. Estimates such as leases, contract revenues or payments, fixed fees, and so forth naturally arise in current-dollar form. Other estimates such as future sales revenues or expenses for labor, materials, energy, and so forth naturally arise in indexed-dollar form. The following example problem illustrates a present-worth calculation using a mixture of current and indexed estimates.

E9. A proposed spa can be opened for $20,000, and 600 fixed-fee memberships can be sold if an additional $10,000 sales effort is undertaken immediately. The memberships would bring in a total of $45,000 of membership revenue per year. (Use an end-of-year conventional treatment of annual revenues and costs.) Operating costs are estimated (ignoring inflation) as $15,000 per year. There is a lease available for five years at a fixed cost of $10,000 per year (end-of-year). The memberships would expire in five years, when the lease expires. At $i = 15\%$, determine the net present worth of this investment opportunity, assuming 5% annual inflation.

The membership revenues are in current dollars (we cannot raise the fees along with inflation). The operating costs are in indexed dollars. The lease is in current dollars. If we drew a cash flow diagram showing current-dollar amounts, as has been done so far, the operating costs would show an increase with time. However, let us simply adopt the convention of labeling any indexed cash flows as "indexed" instead of depicting the geometric growth of their corresponding current amounts (after all, our method allows us to avoid actually calculating the current amounts, so we will also avoid graphing them). Let amounts be expressed in thousands of dollars.

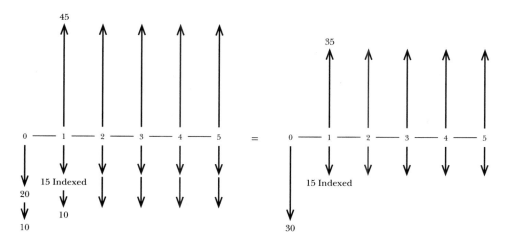

The present worth (in thousands of dollars), with the current net revenues discounted at $i = 15\%$ and the indexed costs discounted at $d = (1 + i)/(1 + j) - 1$ with $j = 0.05$, is

$$P = -30 + 35\left(\frac{1 - [1/(1 + i)]^5}{i}\right) - 15\left(\frac{1 - [1/(1 + d)]^5}{d}\right)$$

$$= \$29,765.08$$

3.3 REAL AND COMPOSITE GEOMETRIC ESCALATION

In this chapter, we have defined the inflation rate j, the real interest rate d, and the *indexed* cash-flow amount W_t. These new quantities, along with the familiar ones (the market or interest rate i and the current cash-flow amount A_t), allow convenient treatment of monetary inflation.

In Section 2.6.3 of Chapter 2, we introduced the gradient cash-flow amount G_t, the geometric growth rate g, the zero projection amount a_0, and the substitute interest rate s, with its corresponding substitute discount factor $\alpha = 1/(1 + s)$.

We require only one additional quantity in order to be able to handle cash flow sets under any combination of geometric growth (or decay) with monetary inflation (or deflation), where the available numerical estimates of cash-flow amounts either express or ignore any combination of those considerations. The new quantity is the real escalation rate.

The *real escalation rate* v is the geometric rate of change in the *indexed* amounts of a cash-flow set. The real escalation rate v contrasts with g, which we shall call the *composite escalation rate*; g is the geometric rate of change in the current amounts of a cash-flow set.

As examples of v, if the need for maintenance of a machine increases 3% per year and the cost follows general inflation, then $v = 0.03$; or if the yield of goods or services from an aging facility decreases 6% per year and the revenues per unit follow inflation, then $v = -0.06$. The real escalation rate excludes inflation and is the rate of escalation in W_t, while the composite escalation rate includes inflation and is the rate of escalation in A_t. We define v through the relationship

$$1 + g = (1 + v)(1 + j) \tag{3-7}$$

E10. **During a period of 4% annual inflation, the cost of computers fell 3% per year. Determine the real escalation rate in the cost of computers.**

From inverting Eq. 3-7, with $g = -0.03$ (since the costs were current-dollar costs) and $j = 0.04$,

$$1 + v = \frac{1 + g}{1 + j} = \frac{1 - 0.03}{1.04} = 0.9326923$$

$$v = 0.9326923 - 1 = \underline{-0.0673}$$

The real cost of computers was dropping 6.73% annually.

Let us review the present worth of a *geometric gradient series* and incorporate the real escalation rate, the real inflation rate, and indexed cash-flow amounts. In a geometric gradient series (Section 2.6.2) the current cash flows $\{A_1, A_2, \ldots, A_n\}$ are $A_1 = a_0(1 + g)$, $A_2 = a_0(1 + g)^2$, and so on, where a_0 is the zero projection amount. At combined interest rate i, we found (Eq. 2-35 of Chapter 2) that the present worth was

Present worth of geometric gradient series given a_0, i, and g:

$$P = a_0 \left[\frac{1 - \alpha^n}{s} \right] \qquad \text{where} \qquad \alpha = \frac{(1 + g)}{(1 + i)} \tag{3-8}$$

$$s = \frac{1}{\alpha} - 1$$

If one of the current cash flows A_t is estimated, the zero projection follows from

$$a_0 = A_t(1 + g)^{-t} \tag{3-9}$$

In particular, A_1 may be estimated, so that $a_0 = A_1/(1 + g)$.

Obviously, Eqs. 3-8 and 3-9 can also be used if, instead of estimating g, the analyst estimated the real escalation rate v and the inflation rate j, from which Eq. 3-7 would give g. But the analyst could avoid dealing with g at all. Substituting $(1 + v)(1 + j)$ for $1 + g$ (Eq. 3-8) into the definition of the substitute discount factor and the substitute interest rate, we see $\alpha = (1 + v)(1 + j)/(1 + i)$. In fact, we can solve Eq. 3-8 using g and i, or v, j, and i, or even v and d, depending on which estimates can be obtained more accurately or easily. The relationships among quantities contributing to the substitute discount factor and interest rate can be summarized as follows:

TABLE 3-1. Substitute Interest Rates for Geometric Gradient Series

Substitute interest rate:

$$1 + s = \frac{1 + i}{1 + g} = \frac{1 + i}{(1 + v)(1 + j)} = \frac{1 + d}{1 + v}$$

$$s = \frac{i - g}{1 + g} = \frac{d - v}{1 + v} = \frac{1}{\alpha} - 1$$

Substitute discount factor:

$$\alpha = \frac{1}{1 + s} = \frac{1 + g}{1 + i} = \frac{(1 + v)(1 + j)}{1 + i} = \frac{1 + v}{1 + d}$$

E11. A reactor that is expected to last 10 years will have escalating maintenance costs with 7% real escalation and 4% inflation. Costs in the year just ended were $1000. Determine, at $i = 30\%$, the present worth of the 10 years of (end-of-year) escalating costs.

Given $v = 0.07$, $j = 0.04$, $i = 0.30$, from Table 3-1

$$\alpha = \frac{1.07(1.04)}{1.30} \qquad s = \frac{1}{\alpha} - 1$$

From Eq. 3-8, with $n = 10$, $a_0 = 1000$

$$P = 1000\left(\frac{1 - \alpha^{10}}{s}\right) = \$4688.85$$

The estimation of a_0 can be from an estimate of a current cash flow A_t and the composite escalation rate g, or from an estimate of an indexed cash flow W_t and the real escalation rate v. We can give an alternative form of Eq. 3-9:

$$a_0 = A_t(1 + g)^{-t} = W_t(1 + v)^{-t} \tag{3-10}$$

E12. **A finishing machine that is expected to run for five years will have a production rate that declines at 4% annually as the machine deteriorates. The vendor guarantees a production of 300,000 finished widgets for the first year. The widget-finishing operation brings revenue of $1.21 per widget in today's market. Estimate a_0 for use in determining the present worth of widget-finishing revenues.**

$W_1 = 300,000(1.21) = \$363,000$ per year (indexed).
$v = -0.04$. From Eq. 3-10,

$$a_0 = W_1(1 + v)^{-1} = 363,000\left(\frac{1}{1 - 0.04}\right)$$

$$= \underline{\$378,125}$$

Intuitively, one could reason alternatively as follows: If the production declines 4% per year, it would have to start at $300,000/0.96 = 312,500$ widgets for year zero, which at $1.21 each would be worth $378,125.

E13. **For the finishing machine of Example E12, determine the present worth of five years of revenues at a real (not market) interest rate of 12% annually.**

From Table 3-1 with $v = -0.04$ and $d = 0.12$

$$\alpha = \frac{1 - 0.04}{1.12} \qquad s = \frac{0.12 - (-0.04)}{1 - 0.04}$$

$$\alpha = 0.85714286 \qquad s = 16.6667\%$$

From Eq. 3-8 with a_0 as computed previously and $n = 5$:

$$P = 378125\left(\frac{1 - \alpha^5}{s}\right) = \underline{\$1,219,080.22}$$

Recall the rules that were quoted in Section 3.2 for discounting current-dollar cash flows (A_t) at the market rate i and discounting indexed-dollar cash flows (W_t) at the real interest rate d. But here, we always discount geometric gradient series cash flows at the substitute interest rate s. To reconcile the previous rules with this procedure, note that if an indexed cash flow W_t is given and the real escalation rate is $v = 0$, then from Eq. 3-7 we get $g = j$, so that from Table 3-1 we get

$$1 + s = \frac{1 + i}{1 + g} = \frac{1 + i}{1 + j}$$

But from Eq. 3-2b, $(1 + i)/(1 + j)$ is $1 + d$. Hence $s = d$ when there is no real escalation. The rule to discount indexed cash flows at d is thus verified.

Similarly, if a current cash flow A_t is given and the composite escalation rate is $g = 0$, then from Eq. 3-7 we get

$$(1 + v)(1 + j) = 1$$

But from Table 3-1, this implies $1 + s = 1 + i$, or $s = i$. The rule to discount current cash flows at i is thus verified.

From this result, we can further note that *if there is inflation, an estimate of an equal-payment series* $\{A_t\}$ *implies a real decline.* $g = 0$ implies $(1 + v)(1 + j) = 1$, so $j > 0$ implies $v = -j/(1 + j)$. For example, if revenues are estimated to be $1000 per year in current dollars, and inflation is 4% annually, the revenues in *indexed* dollars must escalate at $v = -0.04/(1.04) = -3.846\%$ annually, that is, decline 3.846% per year. (If, under inflation, widgets should fetch a 4% higher price each year, to assume constant revenues is to assume a 3.846% annual decline in sales.) This consideration becomes important in Chapter 6, where we tune the "minimal attractive rate of return" (interest rate at which discounting should be done), and in Chapter 7, where we examine the meaning and consequences of the 10% interest rate mandated for public-sector decision making for most situations in the United States.

The end-of-year (eoy) convention underestimates worths when cash flows treated at the end of the year actually occur at more frequent intervals or continuously. For example, the lease payments and membership revenues in Example E9 would probably occur monthly. Note that all the definitions given so far in this chapter are compatible with any discrete time scale: just as i can be for intervals having lengths other than a year, the same is true of j, d, v, g, and s. If we define j_{eff}, d_{eff}, and so on, as the respective rates for an interval of one year, then the corresponding rates for an interval of $1/m$ years are given by equations analogous to Eq. 2-26 for i and i_{eff}:

$$j = (1 + j_{\text{eff}})^{1/m} - 1 \tag{3-11a}$$

$$d = (1 + d_{\text{eff}})^{1/m} - 1 \tag{3-11b}$$

$$v = (1 + v_{\text{eff}})^{1/m} - 1 \tag{3-11c}$$

$$g = (1 + g_{\text{eff}})^{1/m} - 1 \tag{3-11d}$$

$$s = (1 + s_{\text{eff}})^{1/m} - 1 \tag{3-11e}$$

If $a_0^{(\text{eff})}$ is the zero projection in dollars per year, then the zero projection in dollars per $1/m$ years is

$$a_0 = \frac{a_0^{(\text{eff})}}{m} \tag{3-11f}$$

E14. Membership revenues for a health spa are $45,000 annually, in current dollars. Operating costs are $15,000 annually, in indexed dollars. Assuming 5% inflation, compare the present worth at $i = 15\%$ for the net of membership revenues minus operating costs under two timing conventions: end-of-year (eoy) and end-of-month (eom).

For eoy, with $j = 0.05$, $i = 0.15$, $d = (1 + i)/(1 + j) - 1$ (amounts in thousands of dollars):

$$P^{(\text{eoy})} = 45\left(\frac{1 - 1/(1 + i)^5}{i}\right) - 15\left(\frac{1 - 1/(1 + d)^5}{d}\right) = \underline{\$93,286.64}$$

For eom:

$$j = (1.05)^{1/12} - 1 \quad\quad = 0.004074124$$

$$i = (1.15)^{1/12} - 1 \quad\quad = 0.011714917$$

$$d = (1 + i)/(1 + j) - 1 = 0.007609790$$

Monthly amounts (in thousands) are $45/12$ current and $15/12$ indexed. $n = 5(12) = 60$ months.

$$P^{(eom)} = \frac{45}{12}\left(\frac{1 - 1/(1 + i)^{60}}{i}\right) - \frac{15}{12}\left(\frac{1 - 1/(1 + d)^{60}}{d}\right) = \underline{\underline{\$100{,}924.46}}$$

The end-of-month convention gives a net present worth about <u>8.2% greater</u> than that given by the end-of-year convention.

It is often both accurate and convenient to use continuous cash-flow modeling for applications involving such things as sales revenues or energy consumption, where costs occur daily or weekly. Section 3.4 covers the continuous versions of the models discussed in this chapter.

3.4 CONTINUOUS GRADIENT SERIES

We will now develop the continuous gradient series that can be used when the end-of-year (eoy) convention introduces unacceptable inaccuracy, or when a worth is to be *time-convention bracketed*. (To bracket a worth by time convention is to compute a worth according to two time conventions, one known to treat cash flows later than they actually occur, and the other known to treat cash flows earlier than they actually occur.)

Figure 3-2a depicts a geometrically increasing cash-flow series (from Section 2.6.2), which has a present worth at $i = 15\%$ of $4635.28. Now assume this cash-flow set arose from an estimate of maintenance savings, where the savings would have totaled $900 in the year just ended and are expected to increase 10% each year for six years. If the maintenance savings, and their growth, actually occur throughout the years (rather than suddenly occurring at the end of each year), the worth is underestimated. We can improve on the eoy-convention estimate by computing the worth of an *equiponderous* continuous cash-flow profile—one that has cash flows equal to those of the series in every full year. The continuous profile will have a greater worth, because it assumes earlier cash flows.

Figure 3-2b depicts the continuous profile that is equiponderous with the cash-flow series of Figure 3-2a. The profile is the *exponential increase profile* continuous gradient series (Section 2.7). It starts at an instantaneous cash-flow rate of R dollars per year at time zero and has an instantaneous rate of $Re^{\bar{g}t}$ dollars per year from time $t = 0$ to time $t = 6$, where $\bar{g}$ and R can be determined from the requirement that it must have the same annual totals as the eoy cash-flow set.

Let T_n represent the total cash flow in n years. Since the eoy set has cash flows $\{a_0(1 + g)^t: t = 1,...,n\}$, its total cash flow is

Total geometric gradient series cash flow:

$$T_n = \sum_{t=1}^{n} a_0(1 + g)^t = a_0 \frac{1 + g}{g}[(1 + g)^n - 1] \qquad (3\text{-}12)$$

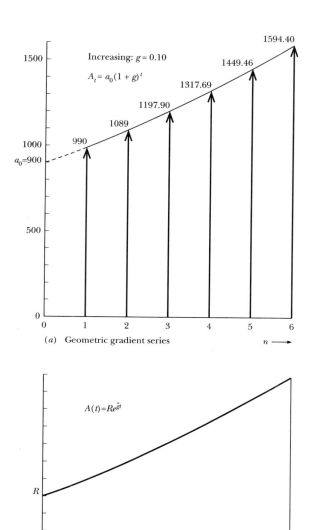

FIGURE 3-2. Equiponderous geometric gradient series and profile.

(The closed form of the sum is derived just as the "pain" factor was and follows directly from Eq. 2-7 of Chapter 2.)

The total cash flow in n years for an exponential increase or continuous gradient profile is

Total continuous gradient profile cash flow:

$$T_n = \int_0^n Re^{\bar{g}t}dt = \frac{R}{\bar{g}}[e^{\bar{g}n} - 1] \tag{3-13}$$

Note that in both Eq. 3-12 and Eq. 3-13 there is a factor in brackets that depends on n. If the two equations are to give the same T_n for every integer value of n, as is required for the profile and series to be equiponderous, then the factors that vary with n must be identical. Thus

$$(1 + g)^n - 1 = e^{\bar{g}n} - 1$$

$$\bar{g} = \ln(1 + g) \tag{3-14a}$$

$$g = e^{\bar{g}} - 1 \tag{3-14b}$$

Note the similarity to the relationship between i and the nominal continuous interest rate $r = \ln(1 + i)$; $\bar{g}$ is the continuous analog of g, just as r is the continuous analog of i.

Finally, the non-n factors in Eqs. 3-12 and 3-13 must also be equal:

$$\frac{R}{\bar{g}} = a_0\frac{1 + g}{g}$$

$$R = a_0(\bar{g}/g)(1 + g) \tag{3-15a}$$

$$a_0 = R(g/\bar{g})(1 + g) \tag{3-15b}$$

Equations 3-14a and 3-15a allow going from a geometric gradient cash-flow series to the equiponderous continuous gradient profile; Equations 3-14b and 3-15b allow the opposite conversion.

E15. Determine R and $\bar{g}$ for Figure 3-2b, so that the profile represents the same cash-flow totals as the series in Figure 3-2a.

From Figure 3-2a, the series has $a_0 = 900$ and $g = 0.10$. Equation 3-14a gives

$$\bar{g} = \ln(1 + g) = \underline{0.09531018}$$

Equation 3-15a gives

$$R = a_0(\bar{g}/g)(1 + g) = \underline{943.57}$$

The present worth of a geometric gradient series was given in Eq. 3-8. To contrast this with the present worth of the equiponderous profile, we label it "eoy" to denote that it arises from using the end-of-year timing convention:

$$P^{(eoy)} = a_0 \left[\frac{1 - \alpha^n}{s} \right] \qquad \text{where} \qquad \alpha = \frac{(1 + g)}{(1 + i)}$$

$$s = \frac{1}{\alpha} - 1$$

The present worth of the equiponderous profile, which arises from using the continuous ("con") timing convention, is (as in Eq. 2-14, Chapter 2)

$$P^{(con)} = \frac{R}{r - \bar{g}} (1 - e^{-(r - \bar{g})n}) \qquad (3\text{-}16)$$

E16. **The two parts of Figure 3-2 both represent six annual cash flows of $990, $1089, . . . ,$1594.40, but in Figure 3-2b the money is received throughout the year rather than at year end. Compare the present worths at $i = 15\%$ under the eoy and continuous timing conventions.**

eoy: $a_0 = 900, n = 6, i = 0.15, g = 0.10, \alpha = (1 + g)/(1 + i) = 0.956521739, s = 1/\alpha - 1 = 0.4545$. Equation 3-8 gives

$$P^{(eoy)} = a_0 \left[\frac{1 - \alpha^6}{s} \right] = \$4635.28$$

con: with $r = \ln(1 + i) = 0.139761942$, and with $\bar{g}$ and R as given in Example E15, Eq. 3-16 gives

$$P^{(con)} = \frac{R}{r - \bar{g}} (1 - e^{-(r - \bar{g})6}) = \$4969.32$$

The continuous timing convention gives a present worth about 7.2% greater.

An insight available from continuous gradient profiles is the *additivity of interest, inflation, and escalation* when expressed in continuous form. Let us define continuous versions of all geometric rates (the first two have already been defined):

$r = \ln(1 + i)$	the nominal continuous interest rate	(3-17a)
$\bar{g} = \ln(1 + g)$	the continuous escalation rate	(3-17b)
$\bar{j} = \ln(1 + j)$	the continuous inflation rate	(3-17c)
$\bar{d} = \ln(1 + d)$	the continuous real interest rate	(3-17d)
$\bar{v} = \ln(1 + v)$	the continuous real escalation rate	(3-17e)
$\bar{s} = \ln(1 + s)$	the continuous substitute interest rate	(3-17f)

The inverses of these definitions are

$i = e^r - 1$	$g = e^{\bar{g}} - 1$	$j = e^{\bar{j}} - 1$
$d = e^{\bar{d}} - 1$	$v = e^{\bar{v}} - 1$	$s = e^{\bar{s}} - 1$

The additivity properties of interest, inflation, and escalation can be derived as follows. Recall Eq. 3-2:

$$1 + i = (1 + d)(1 + j)$$

From the inverses of the definitions 3-17a, 3-17c, and 3-17d, we can write

$$e^{\bar{r}} = e^{\bar{d}} e^{\bar{j}} = e^{\bar{d}+\bar{j}}$$

which implies that *the nominal continuous interest rate is the sum of the continuous real interest rate and the continuous inflation rate*:

$$r = \bar{d} + \bar{j} \tag{3-18}$$

Similarly (from Eq. 3-7), *the continuous escalation rate is the sum of the continuous real escalation rate and the continuous inflation rate.*

Finally, recall the substitute interest rate from Table 3-1, which can be used in Eq. 3-8 to combine the effects of inflation and escalation:

$$\bar{g} = \bar{v} + \bar{j} \tag{3-19}$$

$$1 + s = \frac{1 + i}{1 + g} = \frac{1 + d}{1 + v}$$

The substitute interest rate can be expressed in continuous form:

$$e^{\bar{s}} = \frac{e^{\bar{r}}}{e^{\bar{g}}} = \frac{e^{\bar{d}}}{e^{\bar{v}}}$$

from which we see two additive relationships. *The continuous substitute interest rate is the nominal continuous interest rate minus the continuous escalation rate*:

$$\bar{s} = r - \bar{g} \tag{3-20a}$$

and also *the continuous substitute interest rate is the continuous real interest rate minus the continuous real escalation rate*:

$$\bar{s} = \bar{d} - \bar{v} \tag{3-20b}$$

E17. During a period of high inflation, a credit officer remarked, "With inflation at 10%, I have to charge 15% to earn 5%." Clarify the remark.

If the remark referred to continuous rates, it was true. Equation 3-18 is satisfied by $r = 15\%$, $\bar{j} = 10\%$, *and* $\bar{d} = 5\%$:

$$r = \bar{d} + \bar{j}$$

$$0.15 = 0.10 + 0.05$$

In more standard terminology, if inflation were at $j = 10\%$ (so that $\bar{j} = \ln 1.10 = 9.531018\%$) and it was desired to earn a real interest rate of $d = 5\%$ (so that

$\overline{d} = \ln 1.05 = 4.879016\%$), the market interest rate i that would be needed would be (Eq. 3-2a) $i = d + j + dj = \underline{15.5\%}$, not 15%. But if the credit officer was speaking in terms of continuous rates, the remark could be translated into a true statement in more standard terminology: "With inflation at $j = e^{0.10} - 1 = 10.5170918\%$, I have to charge $i = e^{0.15} - 1 = 16.183424\%$ to earn $d = e^{0.05} - 1 = 5.12711\%$."

The exercises give some applications of inflation and escalation, but more extensive applications will be found throughout the remainder of the book. This chapter and Chapter 2 have presented nearly all the basic definitions and formulas needed for engineering economic analysis, except those needed for risk analysis (Chapters 8 and 9) and after-tax analysis (Chapter 10). Most of the rest of the book concerns applications and the concepts and procedures of economy-based engineering decision making.

3.5 EXERCISES

1. Consider a simplified economy in which wages are raised an average of 7% every year, and prices of other things besides labor are also raised an average of 7% every year. There is no other substantial segment of the economy. If a pair of shoes costs $80 this year, and one day's wage is $100 this year, how much money will a pair of shoes cost 10 years from now, and how many day's wages will the cost represent?

2. Assuming a political and economic climate such as that prevailing in the United States since the 1940s, discuss briefly who would be hurt worse by inflation that exceeded prior expectations: "widows and orphans" on "fixed" incomes, or mortgage lenders at fixed rates?

3. A price index was 403 for year 1990. The index was based on 100 for year 1967. What inflation rate does this index's growth imply?

4. The CPI (Consumer Price Index, published by the U. S. Department of Commerce) was 181.5 for year 1977 and 311.1 for year 1984. An economist was quoted as saying these years constituted a time span she expected to be rather typical for the next few decades. The CPI was 343.1 for 1987. Compare this to the quoted economist's expectations.

5. In the time span from the end of 1977 to the end of 1984, during which inflation in the CPI occurred at an overall rate of almost exactly 8%, the annual published CPI-determined inflation rates were as follows:

1978	7.66%
1979	11.26%
1980	13.52%
1981	10.37%
1982	6.13%
1983	3.22%
1984	4.26%

How well would an arithmetic average represent inflation rates during this span?

6. If inflation in one year was 3% and in the next year was 11%, was it at 7% for the two years?

7. In 1941 the prices of many things (cars, houses, cola drinks) were about 0.1 of what they were in 1992. Estimate the general inflation rate on this basis.

8. The CPI is graphed for the years 1967 through 1990 in Figure 3-1. If this 23-year span is typical, a long-term estimate for the annual inflation rate j was asserted to be 5.9%, based on $CPI_{1967} = 100$ and $CPI_{1990} = 374$.
   (a) Verify the assertion (that is, compute j implied by the two CPI values).
   (b) If a long-term estimate for j was based on an eight-year span, examine Figure 3-1 and identify which eight-year span would presumably give the greatest estimate of j and which eight-year span would presumably give the least estimate of j.

9. In 1992 an economist speculated that the years 1973 to 1982 provided an example of the inflationary behavior to be expected for the United States in the coming decade. One published inflation index had a value of 133.1 for 1973 and 289.1 for 1982. Estimate the coming decade's average inflation rate based on this economist's concept.

10. If $CPU_{1982} = 289.1$ and $CPI_{1987} = 343.1$, what was the overall annual inflation rate during those "Reagan" years in the United States?

11. In Idealia, the accepted index of inflation is the price of shoes. In 1990, 100 ideals would buy 5 pairs of shoes; in 1993, 100 ideals would buy only 4 pairs. Thus the purchasing power of the ideal fell by 20% in three years. What annual inflation rate is implied?

12. In two successive years in Idealia, prices generally escalated 40% the first year and 20% the next. Was the average inflation rate 30%? If not, what was it?

13. If money is lent at 14% annual compound interest and inflation is at 4% annually, what is the real or "inflation-free" interest rate?

14. A lender has been lending at 11.5% annual compound interest, expecting 5% annual inflation. How should the interest rate for loans be revised if the lender begins to expect 7% annual inflation?

15. A consumer lender likes to charge the same interest rate, currently a nominal 12% compounded monthly (that is, 1% per month), for all consumer lending regardless of economic conditions (the stability and relatively low level of the rate is part of the desired marketing image for this lender). If the lender's policy is to leave the rate unchanged unless the real annual compound interest rate falls below 10%, what maximum annual inflation rate does the policy tolerate?

16. Refer to the scenario described in the box near the beginning of Section 3.2.
   (a) If a phone call 60 years prior to the scenario cost $0.80, what inflation rate is implied?
   (b) Determine the indexed value, indexed to 60 years before the scenario, of the protagonist's stock holdings. Interpret the result.

17. A natural gas distribution company secures a contract allowing it to purchase gas for 50 years at $1.7124 per unit. There is no provision for inflation or renegotiation in the contract. Assuming 3% annual inflation, determine A_{50} and W_{50} as

measures of the amount of a cash flow that would purchase one unit of gas at the end of the contract. Interpret the result.

18. Having just completed a $6088.14 furnace cleaning for you, the contractor offers to perform the next cleaning, due one year from now, for the same price, if you will pay $100 in advance. You expect inflation at a 5% annual rate, and you consider money to be worth 15% interest (i). The alternatives are (1) to pay $100 now and $6088.14 − 100.00 next year, or (2) to pay next year's price next year. Choose.

19. A cash flow that will occur three years from now can be expressed as $4121.15 in indexed dollars or as $4702.92 in then-current dollars.
    (a) Determine the assumed annual inflation rate.
    (b) Prove that, regardless of i, the cash flow's present worth can be calculated either by discounting its indexed amount at d or by discounting its current amount at i, giving identical results.

20.

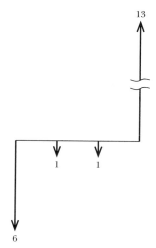

Calvin enjoys customizing and restoring automobiles. He can purchase a well-preserved car for $6000, put a total of $2000 into it, and sell it for $13,000 after three years, according to the cash-flow diagram shown. Money is worth 15% interest. He does not charge himself for labor.
    (a) Is the project worthwhile to Calvin?
    (b) If Calvin assumes 4% annual inflation, what real interest rate would he use to discount indexed cash flows?
    (c) Calvin comes to realize that when he estimated his costs and the sales price, he was estimating them in today's dollars! That is, the cash flows −1, −1, and 13 (in thousands) are indexed estimates, not current-dollar estimates. Determine the revised present worth of the prospective car restoration project.
    (d) Not quite trusting his engineering economic instincts, Calvin decided to analyze the project again, this time using current cash flows and discounting with i. Draw the revised cash-flow diagram and verify that the present worth will be the same when the 4% inflation is treated this way as when accounted for by using d.

(e) An article in the Kustom Kar Korner Kolumn asserts that prices for custom-ized cars are escalating at 6.5% rather than merely at the general inflation rate. If this is true, what is the corrected present worth of the project? (Customizing costs escalate at only 4%.)

21. The Gilbertson House distributes a line of liqueurs whose sales are declining linearly, so that the estimated present worth of sales revenues for the next 10 years is (in K$)

$$\frac{50}{i} - \frac{3}{i^2} - \left(\frac{1}{1+i}\right)^{10}\left[\frac{50}{i} - \frac{30}{i} - \frac{3}{i^2}\right]$$

(a) Using $i = 15\%$, determine the present worth.
(b) The above estimate was based on assuming the current dollar amounts would be 50, 47, and so on, because it was based on sales records. (If the estimate had been based on assuming a decline in indexed amounts, the interest rate would have been d, not i.) Now it appears that price competition will cause the revenues to decline 3% per year due to falling prices, a decline that is superimposed on the linear decline in sales volume. Correct the present worth accordingly.

22. In Example E8 a present worth involving indexed-dollar amounts was determined by first determining d and using it to discount an equal-payment series of indexed-dollar amounts. Demonstrate numerically that the same result is obtained by the brute-force approach of first determining the current-dollar amount of each cash flow, then discounting at i.

23. In Example E9 a present worth involving both indexed-dollar and current-dollar amounts was determined. Membership revenues, operating costs, and lease payments were treated according to the end-of-year timing convention. Revise the analysis to treat them as end-of-month cash flows.

24. In Example E9 a present worth included a lease that had fixed payments. As in the example, continue to assume that revenues and costs all occur at year-end. Revise the analysis if the landlord insists on a renegotiation clause in the lease, under which the rent is expected to inflate so that the first end-of-year payment will be $10,000(1.05)$ dollars, the second $10,000(1.05)^2$ dollars, and so on.

25. Determine the real escalation rate in labor costs for a company that paid average wages of 67 ideals per labor hour in 1990 and 92.5 ideals per labor hour in 1992, if the company's operations were in Idealia, where prices generally rose during the same interval by 45%.

26. When inflation is expected at 9% per year:
(a) If widget sales volume is expected to increase at 3% per year and the revenue per widget is expected to follow general inflation, what is the resultant escalation rate in widget sales revenues?
(b) If widget sales volume is expected to increase at 3% per year but the revenue per widget is fixed at $3 (current) per widget, what is the resultant escalation

rate in widget sales revenues? Also, what real escalation rate is needed to give this result?

(c) If widget sales volume is to remain steady and the indexed revenue per widget is to increase at 3% per year, what is the resultant escalation rate in widget sales revenues?

27. Widgets now can be purchased for $2 each. One of the cash flows in a project analysis is the expense of an annual consumption of 25,000 widgets. The company uses a real interest rate of $d = 0.25$ and expects 4% annual inflation, but the price of widgets is expected to rise 5% per year. Determine the present worth of six years of widget consumption.

28. An annual end-of-year expense is estimated as $10,000 per year in indexed dollars. Under 5% inflation, with zero real growth, determine at $i = 15\%$ the present worth of five years of this expense. Show that the same computation is done whether the present worth is computed by discounting indexed-dollar cash flows at d or by using Eq. 3-8.

29. Recall the rule given in Section 3.2: *Discount current-dollar cash flows at i. Discount indexed-dollar cash flows at d.*

The rule allows the equal-payment series present worth formula to be applied when either the current-dollar cash flows A_t are constant $\{A_t = A: t = 1,...,n\}$ or the indexed-dollar cash flows are constant $\{W_t = W: t = 1,...,n\}$.

(a) Under what conditions on escalation rates g and v does the first line of the rule apply?

(b) Under what conditions on escalation rates g and v does the second line of the rule apply?

(c) Write a third line of the rule, applying not to "current-dollar" nor to "indexed-dollar" cash flows, but to "escalating" cash flows.

30. A geologist's study concludes the Omega-4 oilfield, which produced 24.1 million barrels of crude oil in 1991, will decline in production to 10.3 million barrels in 2001. Assume the decline is exponential (geometric). Assume 4% annual inflation. Assume an annual 1% real growth in unit revenue at the well head, starting at $21 per barrel in 1991. The revenue is the product of production and price, so that the revenue in year t, with $t = 0$ for 1991, is (in millions of dollars)

$$A_t = 21(24.1)(1 + v_{\text{prod}}^t)(1 + v_{\text{price}}^t)$$

where v_{prod} is the escalation rate for production and v_{price} is the escalation rate for price.

(a) Estimate the real growth rate v so that $A_t = 506.1(1 + v)^t$.

(b) At $i = 20\%$, estimate the present worth of the production in the five-year period 1992 to 1996, inclusive.

31. A cost totaled 100 in the year just ended. It will total 110 this year.

(a) Determine R and $\bar{g}$ for the continuous gradient profile that would give these totals.

(b) At $i = 12\%$, determine the present worth of four years of this continuous gradient profile.

(c) Revise the present worth to follow the eoy convention.

32. Recall the decreasing geometric series of cash flows from Figure 2-5:

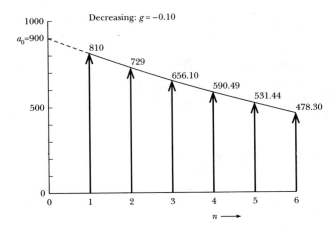

At 15% interest its present worth was determined to be $2495.59. Determine the revised present worth if the cash flow was continuous rather than end-of-year.

33. The zero projection of an end-of-year gradient cash flow series is $1000. If its present worth for n years turns out to be $1000n$ dollars, what is the relationship between i and g?

Efficiency can be a misleading concept.

4

EFFICIENCY MEASURES

. . . .

Chapter 1 introduced engineering decision making, and Chapters 2 and 3 introduced methods of determining worths. This chapter introduces worth-related *efficiency measures* such as rate of return and benefit/cost ratio. Efficiency measures indicate not worth itself but its relationships to other quantities such as time, scope, or capital requirements. Section 4.6 compares worth measures with efficiency measures. Use of both kinds of measure in choosing among alternatives will be covered in Chapter 5.

In general, a protagonist faced with a decision among alternatives should *choose the alternative having greatest worth* at the interest rate (minimal attractive rate of return, or MARR, defined and interpreted in Section 5.1.4) for which the protagonist effectively has a *surrogate banker* (Section 2.8.1). However, there are situations, particularly where one is screening or doing rough evaluation, where certain quantities needed for worth evaluation—MARR, or the scope (size or extent) of an alternative, or the amount of capital available for investment, or the length of the relevant time horizon, or the money value of benefits—may be unclear or irrelevant. In such cases, *efficiency measures* such as *rate of return* (ROR), *benefit/cost ratio* (B/C), *net present value (worth) index* (NPVI), or *payback time* are useful.

To simplify the discussion of efficiency measures, let us define a *simple investment project* as one that begins with an investment of I dollars at time zero, followed by a positive equal-payment series of returns, and possibly terminated by a positive salvage return, as in Figure 4-1.

Many important properties of efficiency measures are particularly clear for simple investment projects and are true for more complex projects that follow the general pattern of negative cash flows ("investment") followed by positive cash flows ("returns"). One such property is that *the worth of an investment project decreases with interest rate*. We can prove $dP/di < 0$ for all the present-worth formulas in Figure 4-1. Intuitively it is clear that $dP/di < 0$ for any simple investment project, because all the dis-

(a) Discrete simple investment project

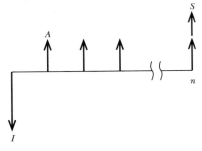

$$P = -I + A\left(\frac{1-\beta^n}{i}\right) + S\beta^n$$

(b) Continuous simple investment project

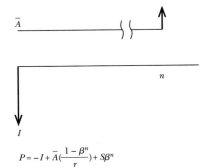

$$P = -I + \bar{A}\left(\frac{1-\beta^n}{r}\right) + S\beta^n$$

(c) Discrete, with zero salvage

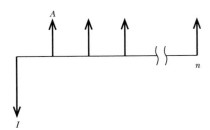

$$P = -I + A\left(\frac{1-\beta^n}{i}\right)$$

(d) Continuous, with zero salvage

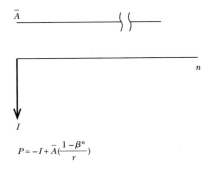

$$P = -I + \bar{A}\left(\frac{1-\beta^n}{r}\right)$$

(e) Discrete, infinite-horizon

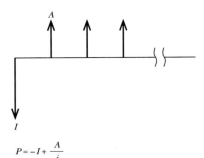

$$P = -I + \frac{A}{i}$$

(f) Continuous, infinite-horizon

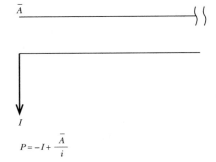

$$P = -I + \frac{\bar{A}}{i}$$

FIGURE 4-1. Simple investment projects.

counted contributions to P are positive, each of them making less contribution to P as the interest rate increases.

Let us define a *pure investment project* as having a negative cash flow at time zero, with all subsequent cash flows nonnegative and at least one positive.

Present worth of a pure investment project:

$$P = -I + \sum_{t=1}^{n} A_t \beta^t \quad \text{where} \quad I > 0, \quad \text{all} \quad A_t \geq 0 \quad (4\text{-}1)$$

For a pure investment project, it is easy to show (see Exercises) that the worth decreases with interest rate.

4.1 RATE OF RETURN

The *rate of return* (ROR) of a cash-flow set is *the interest rate at which the set has zero worth.* Let the present worth of a cash-flow set $\{A_t: t = 0,...,n\}$ be defined as in Eq. 2-3:

$$P = \sum_{t=0}^{n} A_t \beta^t \quad \text{where} \quad \beta = \frac{1}{1 + i}$$

P is a polynomial in β. We define the rate of return i^* as *the value of i such that P = 0, provided that i is real and nonnegative.* (The relationship between β and i is well behaved for $i > -1$, but we will expand the definition to negative i only in specific cases where it is useful and meaningful.) The equation $P = 0$ can have complex, imaginary, or negative roots in β, but we are interested only in positive real roots, in the range $0 < \beta \leq 1$, which correspond to $0 \leq i < \infty$. Given a β root β^*, the corresponding rate of return is $i^* = 1/\beta^* - 1$; i^* is undefined if β^* is outside the given range. Computation of rates of return has already been introduced in Section 2.3.4. ROR is sometimes called *internal* rate of return to distinguish it from the *external* rate of return defined at the end of this section.

Unless otherwise noted, we will cite rates of return in terms of i_{eff}, using the symbol i_{eff}^*, or i^* when it is clear that time is measured in years.

Rate of return is a measure of how fast returns recover an investment. To see this, consider the discrete infinite-horizon simple investment project of Figure 4-1e:

$$P = -I + \frac{A}{i}$$

Let i^* be i such that $P = 0$:

$$P = 0 \Rightarrow i = \frac{A}{I} \equiv i^*$$

Thus, for example, if you invest $1000 and receive annual returns of $200 forever, the rate of return is $i^* = 200/1000 = 20\%$; the returns recover 20% of the investment each year.

For the discrete zero-salvage simple investment project of Figure 4-1c, the rate of return i^* is less than A/I, because the returns do not continue forever. For example, if you invest $1000 and receive annual returns of $146.76 for only 12 years, the ROR is $i^* = 10\%$, not $A/I = 14.7\%$. However, ROR is still a measure of how fast the returns recover the investment, in the sense that of two zero-salvage simple investment projects, both having returns for $n = 12$ years, the one with greater $i*$ would have greater A/I.

The opposite of an *investment project* is an *obligation project*, in which the protagonist is not a lender to the project but a borrower from it. For an obligation project, ROR measures how fast the later negative cash flows must pay back the earlier positive cash flows. For an obligation project (Section 4.1.5) the protagonist prefers a smaller ROR rather than a larger one.

Just as a lender would ordinarily want to accept an opportunity to lend at higher than the usual rate, *an investment project having $i* > MARR$ is ordinarily a desirable project.* There are exceptions, however:

E1. If you give me $1 and I almost immediately give you $2 in return, what is the approximate ROR on your $1 investment, and what is the approximate net present worth at a reasonable interest rate?

The cash flows are as shown in the diagram, with τ a very small time measured in years.

$$P = -1 + 2\beta^\tau = -1 + 2\left(\frac{1}{1 + i}\right)^\tau$$
$$P = 0 \Rightarrow 2 = (1 + i)^\tau \Rightarrow i = 2^{1/\tau} - 1 \equiv i*$$

For concreteness, assume $\tau = 1/8760$ years (one hour). This gives $i* = 2^{8760} - 1$, or about 10^{2637}, <u>approximately infinite rate of return.</u>

For concreteness, assume a reasonable interest rate is $i = 10\%$:

$$P = -1 + 2(1/1.10)^{1/8760} = \$0.999978, \text{ \underline{approximately \$1 present worth.}}$$

Example E1 demonstrates that *ROR ignores project size, scope,* or *scale.* Nothing worth only $1 can be called more than mildly desirable.

Where a project is not a unique opportunity but can be scaled up or repeated, ROR is a good indication of its desirability.

E2. Vidalia onions could be sold as late as December if kept fresh under a cool nitrogen atmosphere in a special cargo container. On a sufficiently large scale, containers should cost about $61,000 each and would last about five years. After

subtracting operating costs, an operating profit of about $19,000 per container per year could be realized. How desirable is the prospect of extending the season by investing in the special cargo container?

Using the discrete simple investment model from Figure 4-1c, with no salvage value, with $n = 5$ years, we can compute a rate of return with $P = 61$ and $A = 19$ (the investment and returns for each thousandth of a container, scaled down from the unknown project size).

$$P = -61 + 19\left(\frac{1 - \beta^5}{i}\right)$$

$$P = 0 \Rightarrow i* = \underline{16.85\%}$$

(See Section 2.3.4 for computation methods.)

The prospect appears desirable for an investor whose MARR is less than $i*$; but for an investor with, say, MARR $= 20\%$, this prospect would not pass screening.

Not all projects are simple. The following example shows complications that can make ROR misleading.

E3. **A dishwasher manufacturer considers the prospect of launching a maintenance contract sales drive. A typical dishwasher requires no maintenance in the first 4 years but requires $5 annual maintenance for the rest of its 25-year life. The sales drive would require an initial investment of about $10 per contract sold; the customer would pay a one-time charge of $30 and would typically buy the contract when the dishwasher was 2 years old. The typical cash flows and present worth formula, per dishwasher are as shown in the diagram.**

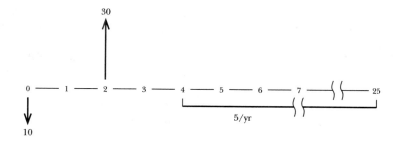

$$P = -10 + 30\beta^2 - \beta^4 5\left(\frac{1 - \beta^{21}}{r}\right) \qquad \text{where} \qquad r = \ln(1 + i), \qquad \beta = \frac{1}{1 + i}$$

Determine and interpret the rate of return.

P can be computed for various i (see Section 2.3.4 for computational methods). There are two values of i for which $P = 0$: $i = 24.65\%$ and $i = 61.13\%$. Figure 4-2 gives a sketch of P versus i. Note that P increases with i (contrary to the situation for simple investment projects), then decreases with i, and there are two rates of return. Interpretation for a rate of return of 24.65%: If the surrogate banker

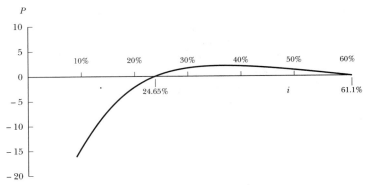

FIGURE 4-2. Anomaly in rate of return.

(ordinary course of business) is at 24.65%, then the initial $10 investment takes $10(1.2465)^2 = \$15.54$ out of the business by time 2; then the $30 receipt puts the manufacturer $30 - 15.54 = \$14.46$ ahead, which when invested in the ordinary course of business builds up by time 4 to $22.47, which is just enough to fund the $5/yr continuous maintenance costs. At less than 24.65%, the surplus at time 4 is insufficient, not only because it didn't build up enough from time 2, but because the portion not spent in the first few years after time 4 doesn't grow fast enough. At more than 24.65%, the surplus at time 4 is more than sufficient. At a very high interest rate, however, the $30 return at time 2 provides only a small surplus; at greater than 73.2% interest, the amount taken out of the business by the initial $10 investment would be $10(1.732)^2 = \$30$ by time 2, so that the $30 receipt would fail to provide any surplus at all.

4.1.1 Rate-of-Return Scale Complications

We already saw in Example E1 that rate of return is an unimportant measure for fixed-scale projects that are very small (a 2-for-1 trade has an infinite rate of return but a present worth of only 1).

When the cash flows are estimated *per unit of economic activity*, the usefulness of ROR depends on the validity of scaling. Often scaling is not a sensitive issue. For example, a roadway engineer found that a new type of pavement expansion joint that would save $2000 per year in maintenance cost per lane-mile of roadway would cost $5000 extra per lane-mile to install. Roughly guessing the savings would continue for at least 10 years, the engineer computed that the rate of return would be at least 38.45%. The new joint was included in the next revision of roadway construction specifications, after an appropriate design review. Scaling was not an issue in the review, because the decision would be a sound one whether the number of lane-miles of new roadway was to be 10 or 1000.

> I lose money on every sale, but I make it up in volume.
> —*Erthgard Blandish, bankrupt businessman*

When there are economies of scale, such as when engineering or development costs need to be amortized over the whole project, scale assumptions are simply incorporated into the estimates, as illustrated in the next example.

E4. **If \$145,000 automatic insertion machines are installed, each having the capacity to handle insertion of axial-lead components on 300 circuit boards per hour, it will save \$0.15 of labor cost per circuit board, after subtraction of other continuing costs. The machines should last five years. There are 8000 operating hours per year. It is not known whether demand will be enough for four machines, or as many as 12. An additional investment of \$90,000 is required to prepare the plant for the new technology; this is independent of how many machines are to be installed. Estimate the rate of return.**

Assuming four machines, the annual net savings would be $4(300)(0.15)(8000) = \$1,440,000$. The investment would be $4(145,000) + 90,000 = \$670,000$. Considering this as a discrete simple investment with zero salvage (Figure 4-1d), the present worth is (in millions):

$$P = -0.67 + 1.44\left(\frac{1 - \beta^5}{i}\right)$$

The rate of return is about $i^* = \underline{214.2\%}$ at a four-machine scale.

Assuming 12 machines, the annual net savings would be $12(300)(0.15)(8000) = \$4,320,000$. The investment would be $12(145,000) + 90,000 = \$1,830,000$.

$$P = -1.83 + 4.32\left(\frac{1 - \beta^5}{i}\right)$$

The rate of return is about $i^* = \underline{235.5\%}$ at a 12-machine scale.

The large estimates of ROR in Example E4 would probably not tend to mislead an engineer, because the project is a savings project, dependent on and limited by the circuit-board manufacturing activity that it would improve. Scaling issues are more misleading when the project is typical of the enterprise's main activity. Let us return to the maintenance-contract situation of Example E3, this time viewing it as a main activity rather than a subsidiary one:

E5. **An entrepeneur proposes to go into the dishwasher maintenance contract business, selling contracts for \$30, with a typical cash-flow set per contract as in Example E3. The cash-flows and present worth formula are as repeated in the diagram.**

$$P = -10 + 30\beta^2 - \beta^4 5\left(\frac{1 - \beta^{21}}{r}\right) \qquad \text{where } r = \ln(1 + i), \quad \beta = \frac{1}{1 + i}$$

The entrepeneur has no other ordinary course of business, and assumes this project will *be* the ordinary business, so that its rate of return—the smaller one, 24.65%—will be the rate of return in the ordinary course of business. With this project's typical per-contract cash flows as the only available surrogate banker, show how the entrepeneur's fortunes would proceed, starting with a $1000 investment. (For convenience, assume end-of-year maintenance expenses rather than continuous ones.)

Invest $1000, which is enough to sell $1000/10 = 100$ contracts, so that $30(100) = \$3000$ is received at time 2. Immediately invest this to sell 300 contracts, which will bring in $30(300) = \$9000$ at time 4. Now maintenance obligations begin. Invest only $8500, expending $500 on obligations, and sell 850 new contracts, which will bring in $25,500 at time 6. At time 6, spend $500 on the obligations from the first batch of contracts, set aside $2000 for the obligations at time 7 from the first two batches, and invest $23,000 to sell 2300 contracts.

Obviously, the transaction sequence is a "kiting" sequence that must grow or collapse. By investing {$1000, $3000, $8500, $23,000, $67,075, $158,250, $408,875, . . .} at times {0, 2, 4, 6, 8, 10, 12, . . .}, the entrepeneur can try to generate enough new business to keep up with the growing obligations. But the kiting cannot continue forever.

Examples E3 and E5 can be interpreted as evidence that *a high ROR by itself is meaningless.* There must be another business activity in which to reinvest funds, because trying to reinvest by scaling up a high-ROR project leads to kiting. Note from Example E3 and Figure 4-2 that an investor having MARR in a range of 30% or 40% would make money on each maintenance contract; to do so requires being able to make good use of the temporary surplus funds from the $30 contract sale.

4.1.2 Multiple Rates of Return

As Examples E3 and E5 show, a cash-flow set can have more than one interest rate at which the worth is zero. P is a polynomial in β,

$$P = \sum_{t=0}^{n} A_t \beta^t \tag{4-2}$$

and by the theory of polynomials (Descartes' Rule) we know that there can be as many positive values of β giving $P = 0$ as there are sign changes in the successive sums

$$\left\{ \sum_{t=0}^{m} A_t : m = 0, 1, 2, \ldots, n \right\}$$

Note that simple investment projects (Figure 4-1) and pure investment projects (Eq. 4-1) have *one sign change* if the sum of returns exceeds the investment; this means they have a single rate of return. If the returns equal the investment, so that all the cash-flow amounts sum to zero, the ROR is zero:

$$\sum_{t=0}^{n} A_t = 0 \Rightarrow \beta^* = 1 \Rightarrow i^* = 0 \qquad (4\text{-}3)$$

By combining theory with practical considerations we can explore the relevant cases of multiple rates of return quite deeply. To have multiple rates of return, a cash flow set must exhibit certain easily recognized properties. Descartes' Rule shows that to have two positive β values that give $P = 0$, there must be two sign changes in the successive sums. In Examples E3 and E5, the investor first was a net lender to the project (investing \$10 at time zero), became a net borrower from the project (receiving \$30 at time 2), and then became a net lender again (by the end of year 8, the maintenance expenses overtook the \$20 surplus). This kind of reversal, where you are behind, then ahead, then behind again (or ahead, then behind, then ahead again), is necessary in order for there to be two positive β roots to $P = 0$. Further, if there are two positive β roots, one or both of them may have $\beta > 1$, which corresponds to a negative interest rate [recall $\beta = 1/(1 + i)$; as i goes from zero to infinity, β goes from 1 to zero].

As a simple specimen of a two-ROR cash-flow set, consider Figure 4-3. The set consists of an investment of \$1 at time zero, a receipt of C dollars at time 1, and a disbursement of T dollars at time 2. From its present worth formula, setting $P = 0$ gives a quadratic expression for β^* (see Eq. 4-4, top of following page).

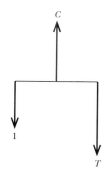

$C > 0, \ T > 0$

The first return is C times the investment; the final disbursement is T times the investment.

This cash-flow set (or its opposite, with reversed directions) has two positive rates of return when

$$C > 2$$

and

$$C - 1 < T < C^2/4$$

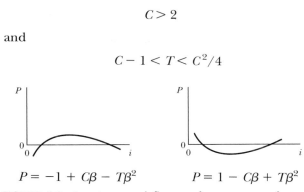

$$P = -1 + C\beta - T\beta^2 \qquad\qquad P = 1 - C\beta + T\beta^2$$

FIGURE 4-3. Specimen cash-flow set for two rates of return.

$$\beta* = \frac{C \pm \sqrt{C^2 - 4T}}{2T} \tag{4-4}$$

$$i* = \frac{1}{\beta*} - 1 \tag{4-4a}$$

To get two positive rates of return, both roots of Eq. 4-4 must be real, which requires $C^2 - 4T > 0$; also, both $\beta*$ values must obey $\beta* < 1$ (for $i* > 0$), which requires $T > C/2$ and $T > C - 1$. Combining the requirements (details are left to the Exercises) gives the requirements listed in Figure 4-3: the cash flow C at time 1 must be at least twice the investment, and the negative cash flow T at time 2 must have a magnitude between $C - 1$ and $C^2/4$.

Figure 4-3 determines the general nature of the requirements that must be obeyed for any cash-flow set to have two positive rates of return. In Example E3, for instance, the \$30 needed to be more than \$20 (twice the investment) for the problem to have two rates of return, and the maintenance costs needed to be neither too small nor too large; if too small, there would be only one rate of return, and if too large, P would have been negative at every interest rate.

E6. **In the 1980s a division of Harris Corporation offered satellite downlink equipment to newspapers who subscribed to United Press International (UPI) services. At the time, private satellite communication was cheaper than using common carriers. From the newspaper's standpoint, a simplified version of a typical deal had these cash flows (amounts in thousands of dollars).**

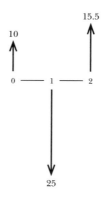

Show that the deal meets the conditions for having two positive rates of return, and discuss whether the deal would be a good one for a newspaper whose MARR is $i = 12\%$.

Comparing the cash flows to Figure 4-3, $C = 25/10 = 2.5$, and $T = 15.5/10 = 1.55$. $C = 2.5$ meets the criterion $C > 2$, and with this C the criterion for T is

$$2.5 - 1 < T < (2.5)^2/4$$
$$1.5 < T < 1.5625$$

Since T is within the range, the deal <u>meets the conditions</u>.

From Eq. 4-4 and 4-4a with $C = 2.5$, $T = 1.55$:

$$\beta^* = \frac{C \pm \sqrt{C^2 - 4T}}{2} = 0.878582838 \qquad \text{and} \qquad 0.734320388$$

$$i^* = \frac{1}{\beta^*} - 1 = \underline{13.82\% \text{ and } 36.18\%}$$

The directions of the cash flows indicate the bowl shape in Figure 4-3 (not the inverted bowl shape) for the P-versus-i curve. Thus $P > 0$ for $i < 13.82\%$, which means the deal is a good one at $i = 12\%$.

To check the result, with $\beta = 1/1.12$:

$$P = 10 - 25\beta + 15.5\beta^2 = 0.03507653$$

or $35.08, which is slightly better than an investment in the ordinary course of business.

Let us suppose we could factor Eq. 4-2 into two factors $f_1(\beta)$ and $f_2(\beta)$:

$$P = \sum_{t=0}^{n} A_t \beta^t = f_1(\beta) f_2(\beta) \tag{4-5}$$

By the elementary theory of the real roots of a polynomial, we know that any root of one of the factors is a root of P; that is, any β that satisfies $f_1(\beta) = 0$ also satisfies $P = 0$. This gives us an easy method to generate multiple-ROR cash flow sets at will.

Let a_k be any value of β that corresponds to an interest rate i_k:

$$a_k = \frac{1}{1 + i_k} \tag{4-6}$$

Then if the P equation has $\beta - a_k$ as a factor, it is guaranteed to have i_k as a rate of return. Thus, if we want a cash-flow set to have K different nonnegative rates of return $(i_1, i_2, \ldots, i_k, \ldots, i_K)$, we can simply write a *generating formula for P*:

$$P = C\left(\beta - \frac{1}{1 + i_1}\right)\left(\beta - \frac{1}{1 + i_2}\right) \cdots \left(\beta - \frac{1}{1 + i_k}\right) \tag{4-7}$$

where C is an arbitrary constant or an arbitrary function of β.

E7. Using $C = 1716$, use Eq. 4-7 to generate a cash-flow set that has rates of return of 10%, 20%, and 30%. Draw a sketch of the cash-flow set and draw a sketch of its P-versus-i curve.

$$P = 1716\left(\beta - \frac{1}{1.10}\right)\left(\beta - \frac{1}{1.20}\right)\left(\beta - \frac{1}{1.30}\right)$$

Expanding and simplifying:

$$P = 1716\beta^3 - 4310\beta^2 + 3600\beta - 1000$$

In this form, the P formula obviously is that of the following cash-flow set:

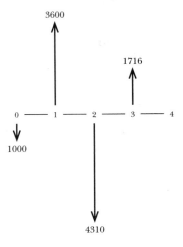

It is rare for cash-flow sets to arise in practice having as many as three rates of return. The following example demonstrates one situation in which this can arise: cheap acquisition of temporary profitable use of an asset, followed by very expensive permanent acquisition, and finally extremely profitable use or disposal.

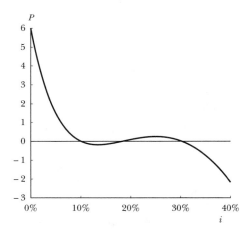

E8. **For a very small deposit, the Soapstone Art Center can borrow a collection of French Impressionist paintings for exhibition. The collection can be exhibited at a profit for two years, after which the art center can begin purchasing the collection at a preset price, on preset time and interest terms, while continuing to exhibit. It is believed the collection can then be sold for a very high price. Estimated cash flows, in thousands of dollars, are as shown in the diagram.**

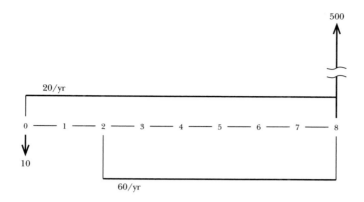

$$P = -10 + 20\left(\frac{1 - \beta^8}{r}\right) - 60\beta^2\left(\frac{1 - \beta^6}{r}\right) + 500\beta^8$$

Determine the rates of return and sketch the *P*-versus-*i* curve.

It is convenient to solve with a small computer program such as this one written in the Basic language, which asks the user to input an interest-rate range and prints ten (i,P) pairs in that range:

```
10   PRINT "min, max interest %";
20   INPUT I1, I2
30   I1 = I1*0.01: I2 = I2*0.01
40   D = (I1 − I2)*0.05
50   FOR I = I1 TO I2 STEP D
60   B = 1/(1 + I)
70   R = LOG(1 + I)
80   P1 = (1 − B^38)/R
90   P2 = (1 − B^36)/R
100  P = −10 + 20*P1 − 60*B^2*P2 + 500*B^8
110  PRINT 100*I;"% ";P
120  NEXT I
```

Repeated use, involving perhaps 50 evaluations of *P*, yields the three rates of return

$$i^* = 40.7\%, \ 108.7\%, \ \text{and} \ 537.5\%$$

and the *P*-versus-*i* curve of Figure 4-4.

As Figure 4-4 shows, rates of return themselves are virtually meaningless. They are simply places where the *P*-versus-*i* curve crosses $P = 0$. The *P*-versus-*i* curve is more informative, although in most cases a wise decision would best be made on the basis of *P* at the decision-maker's MARR.

Example E8 showed a remarkable constancy of *P* at interest rates. It would appear that an enterprise that normally earns almost any high rate of return in the ordinary

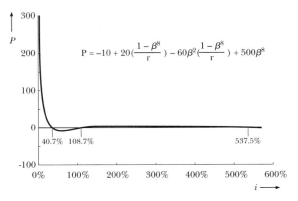

$$P = -10 + 20(\frac{1 - \beta^8}{r}) - 60\beta^2(\frac{1 - \beta^8}{r}) + 500\beta^8$$

FIGURE 4-4. Meaningless multiple rates of return.

course of business would find the opportunity a ho-hum one. How is it that the worth is just slightly positive (a maximum of $2222.82 at 206.5% interest) for all interest rates from about 109% to 537%? To see the balancing of influences here, let us examine the contributions of various terms in the worth formula.

E9. **For the Soapstone Art Center of Example E8, determine the contributions to worth of the individual terms of the worth formula, for the following interest rates:**

$i = 12\%$ **a typical MARR reflecting ordinary opportunities**
$i = 40.7\%$ **the smallest ROR**
$i = 58.8\%$ **a rate giving a local minimum worth**
$i = 108.7\%$ **the middle ROR**
$i = 206.5\%$ **a rate giving a local maximum worth**
$i = 537.5\%$ **the greatest ROR**
$i = 2000\%$ **a very high interest rate**

The contribution of the initial $10,000 deposit is always -10. The other contributions are as follows (in thousands to the nearest thousand):

Interest Rate, i	Contribution of Exhibition Revenues	Contribution of Purchase Cost	Contribution of Disposal Revenue	Total Worth, P
12%	105	−208	202	89
40.7%	55	−77	33	0
58.8%	42	−48	12	−4
108.7%	27	−18	1	0
206.5%	18	−6	0	2
537.5%	11	−1	0	0
2000%	7	0	0	−3

Note that at 12% interest the disposal revenue is the key benefit. During the years of purchasing the collection, the art center would have to borrow money (at 12% interest) or curtail other profitable operations, because exhibition revenues provide only one-third of the required purchase payments. The high disposal value, however, is an asset against which the money could be borrowed, and all-in-all the art center is ahead by about $89,000.

At 40.7% interest we must envision that $20,000 annual exhibition revenues for eight years are worth only about $55,000, and the $500,000 disposal price is worth only about $33,000; the purchase expenses, starting up after a two-year delay and totaling $360,000 are worth only $77,000. All this makes sense only if the surplus in the first two years is reinvested (in something else) at 40.7% and the money borrowed in the middle years is borrowed at 40.7%. At higher interest rates the situation is even stranger.

The remarkable near constancy of P with i is an artifact of the arrangement and relative sizes of the four contributions to P. Each contribution is bigger than, later than, and opposite to the preceding contribution.

4.1.3 External Rate of Return

We have taken pains to make it clear that to determine P at some i is to assume there effectively exists a surrogate banker willing to lend and borrow at i. Thus, to determine a rate of return for an opportunity is to identify an interest rate i^* at which the opportunity would be an ordinary one ($P = 0$) *if all shortfalls were financed at i^* and all surpluses were invested at i^*.* All the rates of return for the Soapstone Art Center example were unrealistic, because their computation assumed that the Center would borrow the initial $10,000 at i^* until exhibition revenues repaid it and would then put the excess exhibition revenues to work at i^*, use the returns to pay for the first part of the shortfall of purchase expenses' being $40,000/yr more than exhibition revenues, and then borrow at i^* to cover the remaining time, until the $500,000 disposal revenue would be just adequate to repay the loan. But in fact an art center would never borrow or divert money at such a high rate as 40.7% interest, nor could it invest its surplus at such a rate.

Because of these unrealistic assumptions inherent in using rate of return, the *external rate of return (ERR) method* has been advocated for the purpose of computing an interest rate i' similar to i^* but free of the assumption that surpluses are reinvested at the same interest rate. Given a net cash-flow set $\{A_t\}$, define two signed cash flow sets $\{A_t^+\}$ and $\{A_t^-\}$, where if $A_t > 0$ then $A_t^+ = A_t$ and $A_t^- = 0$, and if $A_t < 0$ then $A_t^+ = 0$ and $A_t^- = |A_t|$. For example, the following cash-flow set

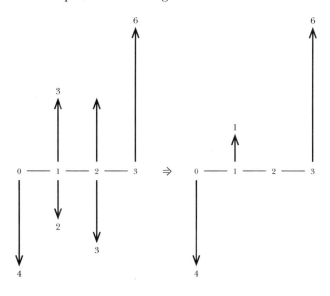

implies

$$\{A_t\} = \{-4, 1, 0, 6\}$$
$$\{A_t^+\} = \{0, 1, 0, 6\}$$
$$\{A_t^-\} = \{4, 0, 0, 0\}$$

The positive cash flows are assumed to be reinvested at a fixed interest rate i (usually MARR) and have a future worth or compound amount as of time n:

Compound amount of reinvested funds at rate i:

$$F_i^+ = \sum_{t=0}^{n} A_t^+ (1 + i)^{n-t} \tag{4-8a}$$

The negative cash flows have a compound amount $F_{i'}^-$ at the external rate of return i':

$$F_i^- = \sum_{t=0}^{n} A_t^- (1 + i')^{n-t} \tag{4-8b}$$

The external rate of return (ERR) is defined as the interest rate i' such that $F_i^+ = F_{i'}^-$:

Definition of external rate of return (ERR):

$$\text{ERR is } i' \text{ that satisfies } \sum_{t=0}^{n} A_t^+ (1 + i)^{n-t} = \sum_{t=0}^{n} A_t^- (1 + i')^{n-t} \tag{4-9}$$

For example, the ERR for a cash-flow set $\{A_t\} = \{-4, 1, 0, 6\}$ with a reinvestment rate of $i = 12\%$ can be determined from Eq. 4-9 as follows, with $n = 3$:

$$1(1.12)^2 + 6 = 4(1 + i')^3 \Rightarrow i' = 21.95\%$$

E10. The following sets of cash flows are known to have the two rates of return

$$i^* = 10\% \quad \text{and} \quad 60\%$$

(we call i^* the internal rate of return when it is necessary to contrast it with the ERR i').

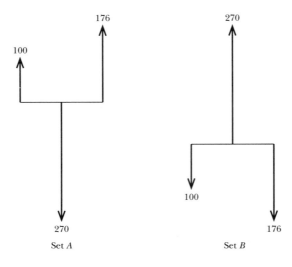

Set A   Set B

For a decision maker whose surplus funds earn 12% interest in the ordinary course of business, determine and interpret i' for both sets of cash flows.

Set A: $\{A_t^+: t = 0, 1, 2\} = \{100, 0, 176\}$. $\{A_t^-\} = \{0, 270, 0\}$

From Eq. 4-9 with $i = 12\%$:

$$100(1.12)^2 + 176 = 270(1 + i')^1 \Rightarrow i' = 11.64\overline{4}\%$$

Interpretation: This A project allows us to collect $100 at time 0 and $176 at time 2 by incurring the obligation to disburse $270 at time 1. If we invest the $100 in the ordinary course of business at 12% interest for two years, it grows to $125.44; combined with the $176 return at time 2, a total of $301.44 at time 2 results from a $270 investment at time 1, which implies a rate of return of 11.64$\overline{4}$%.

Set B: $\{A_t^+: t = 0, 1, 2\} = \{0, 270, 0\}$. $\{A_t^-\} = \{100, 0, 176\}$

From Eq. 4-9 with $i = 12\%$:

$$270(1.12) = 100(1 + i')^2 + 176 \Rightarrow i' = 12.428\%$$

Interpretation: This B project allows us to collect $270 at time 1 by investing $100 at time 0 and incurring the obligation to pay $176 at time 2. If we invest the $270 in the ordinary course of business at 12% interest for one year, it grows to $302.40; combined with the $176 disbursement, there is a net return of $126.40 at time 2 from a $100 investment at time zero, which implies a rate of return of 12.428%.

Note that Set A is less profitable than the ordinary course of business, whereas Set B is more profitable.

4.1.4 True Cash Flows

The ERR method, like other methods that use two interest rates to clarify ROR anomalies, is a version of the more general method of *true cash flows*. The conflict that gives rise to multiple (internal) rates of return is lack of specific assumptions about the interest rates at which surpluses are reinvested and deficits are financed. The ROR method identifies one or more interest rates i^* such that, if you can both borrow and lend (finance and reinvest) at a given i^*, the cash flows are at the boundary between profitability and unprofitability relative to that i^*. The ERR method replaces the lack of specific assumptions with the specific assumption that all positive cash flows are invested at the reinvestment rate i until the end of the project. If that specific assumption is reasonable, the ERR method thus resolves the confusion engendered by multiple ROR.

However, the ERR reinvestment assumption is not necessarily the best or most realistic one. Another assumption that would resolve the confusion of multiple ROR would be to assume that all negative cash flows are financed at a fixed cost of capital until the end of the project, allowing determination of a rate of return that would identify a reinvestment rate needed for the project to be barely profitable.

In general, in a multiple-ROR situation the confusion caused by lack of specification of how funds are reinvested and how deficits are financed is best resolved simply by *specifying explicit financing or reinvestment plans.* This direct approach is called *true cash flows.*

The key step in true-cash-flow analysis is to *replace unusual cash flows with their consequences.* That is, if it will actually be necessary to borrow money to cover all or part of a large deficit, replace the financed part of the deficit with its repayments. Similarly, if it will actually be necessary to invest part or all of a large return in other than the ordinary course of business, replace the unordinary part of the return with its special yields.

Remarkably, the true-cash-flow method can always be applied to reduce a multiple-ROR situation to an unambiguous one. In fact, it can be claimed that every multiple-ROR situation in practice is a poorly defined one that can be remedied by more explicit cash-flow estimation. The true-cash-flow method reduces to the ERR method when the true situation is that which underlies the ERR method (reinvestment of all returns at i).

E11. Recall the dishwasher-maintenance-contract Example E3, in which there were two rates of return. In this project, a $10 initial investment caused a $30 return at time 2 and a $5/yr continuous disbursement starting at time 4 and continuing for 21 years. Suppose the true situation is that the manufacturer can borrow against the prospective contract sales proceeds at an interest rate of 9%; that is, instead of paying $10 per contract at time zero, the manufacturer can instead pay $10(1.09)^2 = \$11.881$ at time 2, reducing the net returns at time 2 to $30 - 11.881 = \$18.119$. Draw the true-cash-flow diagram and determine the resulting unique ROR. Interpret the result, assuming MARR for the manufacturer is 15%.

The true-cash-flow diagram is

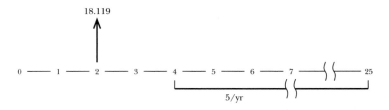

Note that this is the opposite of a pure investment project (Eq. 4-1); it is a pure "obligation project" (Section 4.1.5 will discuss obligation projects). Recall from Section 4.1 that the protagonist for an obligation project prefers a smaller ROR to a larger one.

$$P = 18.119\beta^2 - 5\beta^4\left(\frac{1 - \beta^{21}}{r}\right) \qquad \text{where} \qquad \beta = \frac{1}{1 + i}, \quad r = \ln(1 + i)$$

$$P = 0 \Rightarrow \beta^2\left(\frac{1 - \beta^{21}}{r}\right) - 3.6238 = 0 \Rightarrow \underline{\underline{i^* = 20.4796966\%}}$$

Note: At $i = 15\%$, $P = -\$5.67$ per contract, which is very poor. Interpretation of ROR: Selling these contracts is like borrowing money at i^*. Since money can be "borrowed" out of the ordinary course of business at 15% interest, borrowing at over 20% is very unprofitable.

E12. Recall the Soapstone Art Center's project, Example E8, in which there were three rates of return. Suppose the true situation is that the Center will mitigate the cash drain in the middle years by establishing a line of credit against which it will borrow $40,000 per year continuously, with repayment in a lump sum at 12% interest upon disposal of the art collection. As shown in an exercise at the end of the chapter, the loan repayment would be $343,716.22 at time 8, so the net proceeds are reduced from $500,000 to $156,283.78. The true cash flows become (in thousands):

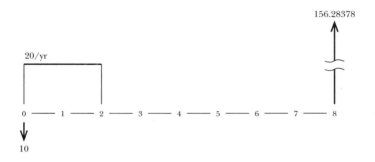

Determine the rate of return.

Note that this is a pure investment project (Eq. 4-1).

$$P = -10 + 20\left(\frac{1 - \beta^2}{r}\right) + 156.28378\beta^8 \Rightarrow \underline{\underline{i^* = 610.181467\%}}$$

The preceding examples show how the true-cash-flow method—use of explicit assumptions about reinvestment of surpluses or financing of deficits—simplifies complicated ROR situations. Let us now return to the cash flows of Example E10 to show that the ERR method is merely one version of the true-cash-flow method.

E13. Recall Set A in Example E10, which had rates of return of 10% and 60%, and was shown to have an external rate of return (ERR) of $i' = 11.64\overline{4}\%$ when the reinvestment rate was $i = 12\%$.

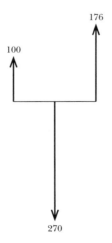

Assume that the true situation is that the $100 initial return is invested at 12% until the end of the project (this is the same assumption that underlies the ERR method). Determine the ROR for this situation.

The $100 cash flow at time 0 is replaced by $100(1.12)^2 = \$125.44$ at time 2, so that the true cash flows are to spend $260 at time 1 and receive $125.44 + 176 = \$301.44$ at time 2.

301.44

0 —— 1 —— 2

70

(Pure investment project: $i^* > i$ desirable)

$$P = -270\beta + 301.44\beta^2$$

$$P = 0 \Rightarrow \beta^* = \frac{270}{301.44} \Rightarrow i^* = \frac{1}{\beta^*} - 1 = \underline{11.64\overline{4}\%} \text{ as before.}$$

This demonstrates that the true-cash-flow method yields the ERR when the ERR's underlying assumptions are used.

Suppose, on the other hand, that the true situation is that the initial $100 return is invested at 12% for only one year, and its proceeds are used to reduce the required disbursement at time 1. Determine the ROR for this situation.

The $100 cash flow at time zero is replaced by $100(1.12) = \$112$ at time 1, so the net expenditure at time 1 is $270 - 112 = \$158$.

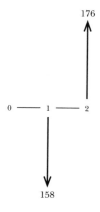

176

0 —— 1 —— 2

158

(Pure investment project: $i^* > i$ desirable)

$$P = -158\beta + 176\beta^2$$
$$P = 0 \Rightarrow \beta^* = 158/176 \Rightarrow i^* = 1/\beta^* - 1 = \underline{11.3924\%}$$

This rate of return is slightly different.

Note that both of these alternative "true situations" show that the cash flows of Set **A** do not return capital at as fast a rate as 12%, so the project is not a good one for someone who can invest at 12%. The complication of multiple rates of return simply does not arise.

4.1.5 Obligation Projects and Investment Projects

Most opportunities analyzed in engineering economy are investment projects, in which money is invested in order to gain returns that occur afterward. *Pure* investment projects were defined in Eq. 4-1; a pure investment project has a cash-flow set consisting of a single negative cash flow followed by at least one positive cash flow and any number of nonnegative cash flows. In terms of guaranteeing that P decreases with i, Eq. 4-1 is overly restrictive, since *any cash-flow set having all nonpositive cash flows before some time m and all nonnegative cash flows after time m is guaranteed to have P decrease with i*, provided there is at least one negative and at least one positive cash flow. We define an *investment project* as follows:

An investment project is a project having cash flows such that P decreases with i for i within the range of concern. For an investment project, $dP/di < 0 \Rightarrow dP/d\beta > 0$.

This definition is quite unrestricted. For example, the Soapstone Art Center example, whose P-versus-i curve was given in Figure 4-4, is an investment project at low interest rates, because P does in fact decrease with i for all i below about 58.8%.

An interest rate should not be "within the range of concern" unless it is a rate at which it would be conceivable to lend or to borrow. Thus, for the Soapstone Art Center, let us assume that it is unreasonable for any of the project's early surplus to be reinvested at more than 50% interest, or for any of the project's deficits to be financed by borrowing at more than 50% interest or by diverting funds that could otherwise be invested at more than 50% interest. If the decision maker has adopted this view in advance, the ROR problem becomes a simple one. The project is an *investment project*; its only ROR "within the range of concern" is 40.7%. Investing in this project is like lending money at 40.7% interest. (The higher rates of return are irrelevant, since any rates of return greater than 50% would involve borrowing or reinvesting at rates greater than 50%.)

As the following example shows, many projects that do *not* meet the "pure" criterion of having all negative cash flows before all positive cash flows can nevertheless be investment projects; a project can even have a strictly decreasing P-versus-i without meeting the "pure" criterion, and for relatively simple cash-flow diagrams, such strict monotonicity of P versus i can be recognized without sketching the whole curve.

Recall that for P to decrease with i means $dP/di < 0$. Also recall that from the definition $\beta = 1/(1 + i)$, it follows that $di/d\beta < 0$, so that $dP/d\beta > 0$.

E14. Show that the following cash flows constitute an investment project.

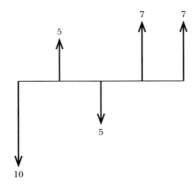

The project is not a pure investment project because of the negative cash flow at time 2. Its P equation is

$$P = -10 + 5\beta - 5\beta^2 + 7\beta^3 + 7\beta^4$$

No "range of concern" is given, so assume the widest range: $0 \le i < \infty \Leftrightarrow 0 < \beta \le 1$. Taking the derivative with respect to β, we seek to show $dP/d\beta > 0$:

$$\frac{dP}{d\beta} = 5 - 10\beta + 21\beta^2 + 28\beta^3$$

The only negative term is the second term. Obviously for $\beta \le 0.5$ the second term cannot exceed even the constant 5:

$$\beta \le 0.5 \Rightarrow \frac{dP}{d\beta} > 5 - 10\beta > 0$$

Now for $\beta > 0.5$,

$$\frac{dP}{d\beta} > 5 - 10\beta + 21(0.5)^2 + 28(0.5)^3 = 5 - 10\beta + 8.75 = 12 - 10\beta$$

But since $\beta \le 1$,

$$\beta > 0.5 \Rightarrow \frac{dP}{d\beta} \ge 12 - 10(1) > 0$$

Thus $dP/d\beta > 0$ everywhere, which implies $dP/di < 0$ everywhere; <u>P decreases with i</u>, so the cash flows constitute an investment project.

The opposite of an investment project is an *obligation project*, defined as a project for which $dP/di > 0$ for i within the range of interest. For an obligation project, P increases with i (and decreases with β). Just as an investment project can be likened to lending money, an obligation project can be likened to borrowing money. Just as $i^* > i$ indicates desirability for an investment project, $i^* < i$ indicates desirability for an obligation project.

We can show by example how, for a protagonist having a surrogate banker at interest rate *i, any opportunity to borrow money at an interest rate less than i is a profitable project.*

E15. **For each of the following situations, show that the obligation-project opportunity has $P > 0$ at i (and hence is desirable by the absolute measure P), show that it has $i^* > i$ (and hence is desirable by the efficiency measure i^*), and trace surrogate-banker transactions to show that the protagonist ends with increased wealth.**

1. **Kristen's surrogate banker is her credit-card account, on which she pays monthly interest at a rate of 18.9% APR on a balance that fluctuates between $1000 and $3000. She is offered the chance to take out a $1000 signature loan at 11.5% APR with 12 equal monthly payments.**

    Kristen's obligation-project opportunity is to receive $1000 at time zero and to pay 12 monthly payments at $11.5/12 = 0.95833\%$ monthly interest. The monthly payment amount is

    $$1000\left(\frac{0.009583\overline{3}}{1 - (1/1.009583\overline{3})^{12}}\right) = \$88.62$$

    The cash flows are shown in the diagram (with time in months).

    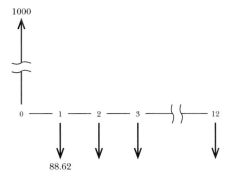

    The present worth is

    $$P = 1000 - 88.62\left(\frac{1 - \beta^{12}}{i}\right)$$

    At $i = 18.9/12 = 1.575\%$ monthly,

    $$P = 1000 - 962.12 = \underline{\$37.88}$$

    The rate of return is $i^* = i$ such that $P = 0$; since the only cash flows are those of the loan, the ROR is the interest rate of the loan: $i^* = i_{\text{eff}}$ corresponding to 11.5% APR. $i^* = (1 + 0.115/12)^{12} - 1 = \underline{12.1259\%}$; or, monthly, $i^* = 0.9583\overline{3}$.

    Transactions: Assume Kristen uses the $1000 to reduce her credit-card balance by $1000. This reduces her monthly credit card payments by

$$1000\left(\frac{0.01575}{1 - (1/1.01575)^{12}}\right) = \$92.11$$

Thus the obligation-project opportunity has the concrete effect of reducing her net required monthly payments by $92.11 - 88.62 = \underline{\$3.49}$ each month for 12 months.

2. **O'Lester's surrogate banker is his savings account, which pays 8.15% interest. He can write checks at any time to withdraw up to \$1000, and can make deposits at any time. He is offered the chance to borrow \$800 at 5% effective interest, to be repaid in a lump sum after one year.**

O'Lester's obligation-project opportunity is to receive \$800 now and repay $800(1.05) = \$840$ after a year. The cash flows are as shown in the diagram (with time in years). The present worth is

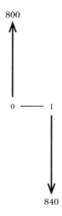

$$P = 800 - 840\left(\frac{1}{1 + i}\right)^{1}$$

At $i = 8.15\%$,

$$P = 800 - 840\left(\frac{1}{1.0815}\right)^{1}$$

The rate of return is $i^* = i$ such that $P = 0$; since the only cash flows are those of the loan, the ROR is the interest rate of the loan: $\underline{i^* = 5\%}$.

Transactions: Assume O'Lester deposits the \$800 in his savings account. In one year it grows to $800(1.0815) = \$865.20$. He writes a check for \$840 to repay the loan, and he ends up $\underline{\$25.20}$ wealthier than he otherwise would have been.

Obligation projects sometimes occur in ordinary engineering contexts where moneylending plays no role:

E16. **For a carpet mill that uses 25% (annual) MARR, is it worthwhile to run a rug loom harder than customary if the consequences are that monthly profits (end-of-month) are increased by $1500 but the necessary maintenance costs at the next overhaul, scheduled 12 months from now, will be increased by $20,000?**

The cash flows are as shown in the diagram. The present worth is

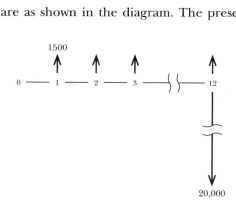

$$P = 1500\left(\frac{1 - \beta^{12}}{i}\right) - 20{,}000\beta^{12}$$

This is an obligation project, having positive cash flows before negative. MARR on a monthly basis is

$$i = (1.15)^{1/12} - 1 = 0.011714917$$

On an absolute basis, the present worth at MARR, with i as given above, is

$$P = 1500\left(\frac{1 - \beta^{12}}{i}\right) - 20{,}000\beta^{12} = \underline{\$-690.19}$$

so this is not a good project on an absolute basis.

On an efficiency basis, the rate of return (monthly) is

$$P = 0 \Rightarrow i^* = \underline{1.89521\%}$$

or 25.269% on an annual basis. This rate of return is greater than MARR. Since this is an obligation project, $i^* > i$ is unfavorable, and it indicates the project is not a good one.

4.2 PAYBACK TIME OR RECOVERY PERIOD

Cash has the quality called *liquidity*; it can be used for many purposes. Capital tied up in a project, whether already spent or obligated, is *illiquid*; little can be done with it but to leave it in the project to generate the project's returns. Consider an investment project having the following cash flows (in dollars, with time in years):

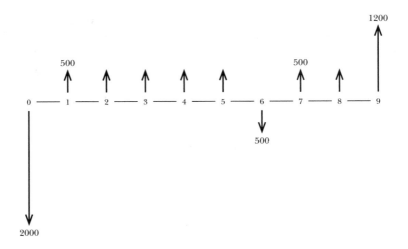

By time 5 the returns sum to $2500, which equals the $2500 sum of investments. Thus the project's illiquidity, suffered from spending $2000 and being obligated to spend $500 more, will have been offset by the project's returns by time 5, and the project's *payback time* is said to be 5 years. (It does not matter that the last negative cash flow occurs after time 5, since obligations that have already been covered are not a net drain on liquidity.)

4.2.1 Determination of Payback Time

Splitting a project's cash flows into its positive and negative sets $\{A_t^+\}$ and $\{A_t^-\}$ as in Section 4.1.1.3, we define the *payback time Y* as the earliest time when the (undiscounted) sum of positive cash flows up to that time equals or exceeds the (undiscounted) sum of all negative cash flows:

Definition of payback time Y:

$$Y \text{ such that } \quad \sum_{t=0}^{Y} A_t^+ \le \sum_{t=0}^{n} A_t^- \tag{4-10}$$

Y is defined only for investment projects; obligation projects improve liquidity rather than cause illiquidity.

E17. In Example E8 (Section 4.1.2), the project of acquiring an art collection for exhibit and later disposal at a profit was considered to be an investment project (P decreases with i except for i unreasonably large). The project's net cash flows are as shown in the diagram (in thousands). Determine and interpret the payback time.

The sum of all negative cash flows is

$$\sum_{t=0}^{8} A_t^- = 10 + 40(6) = 250$$

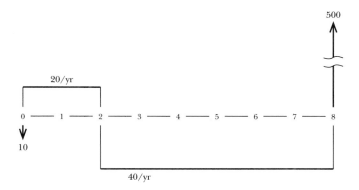

The sum of positive cash flows is $20(2) = 40$ by time 2, and does not increase until time 8, where it becomes 540. Hence, by Eq. 10 the payback time is $Y = \underline{\underline{8}}$ years.

Interpretation: This project detracts from the art center's liquidity for 8 years.

Payback time is a crude measure in that it only identifies when a project recovers its investment, without regard to such issues as whether it almost pays for itself earlier, or whether any profits remain after it pays for itself. Payback time ignores both interest and compounding of interest, and it takes into account neither the absolute nor relative excess of returns over investment. Nevertheless, payback time measures an aspect of a project (liquidity) that is not covered by other measures. As we shall see below, 8 years is an unusually long payback time for a project with high ROR and highly positive present worth. The Soapstone Art Center project, for example, has a rate of return of 40.7%, and a present worth of $98,300 if the art center uses MARR of 11%; despite a rate of return that shows the project makes money rapidly, and a present worth that shows the project makes a substantial amount of money, the 8-year payback time shows the project ties up capital for an inconveniently long time.

4.2.2 Payback Time for Simple Investment Projects

Recall the *simple investment project* of Figure 4-1a, in which an initial investment of I dollars produces an equal-payment series of end-of-year returns each of A dollars, continuing for n years with a nonnegative salvage value at time n. If the total returns $nA + S$ equal or exceed the investment I, then a payback time Y exists and is given by

Payback time for simple investment projects:

$$Y = \begin{cases} \lceil (I/A) & nA \geq I & \text{(4-11a)} \\ n & nA < I \leq nA + S & \text{(4-11b)} \end{cases}$$

(The $\lceil$ operator rounds its argument up to the next integer.) For continuous returns (Eq. 4-1b), the payback time exists if the total returns $n\bar{A} + S$ equal or exceed I:

$$Y = \begin{cases} I/\bar{A} & n\bar{A} \geq I & \text{(4-11c)} \\ n & n\bar{A} < I \leq n\bar{A} + S & \text{(4-11d)} \end{cases}$$

For other cases of simple investment projects $(n \rightarrow \infty$ or $S = 0)$, the payback time is given by Eq. 4-11a or 4-11c.

E18. Determine the payback time for each of the following simple investment projects:

Project Identifier	Required Investment	Returns	Salvage Value
A	$1000	$300/yr eoy for 6 years	$400
B	$1000	$150/yr eoy for 6 years	$400
C	$1000	$150/yr eoy for 6 years	$50
D	$1000	$300/yr continuous for 6 years	$400
E	$1000	$150/yr eoy forever	—
F	$1000	$150/yr continuous forever	—

Project A: $nA = 6(300) = \$1800 > \$1000.$
$Y = \lceil(1000/300) = \lceil(3.3\overline{3}) = 4$ years

Project B: $nA = 6(150) = \$900. \ nA + S = 900 + 400 = \$1300.$
$Y = n = 6$ years

Project C: $nA + S = 900 + 50 = \$950 < I. \ Y$ does not exist

Project D: $n\bar{A} = 6(300) = \$1800 > \$1000.$
$Y = 1000/300 = 3.\overline{33}$ years

Project E: $Y = \lceil(1000/150) = \lceil(6.\overline{66}) = 7$ years

Project F: $Y = (1000/150) = 6.\overline{66}$ years

4.2.3 Relation of Payback Time to Liquidity, Rate of Return, and Horizon

Recall that the quantity A/I is the rate of return for a discrete infinite-horizon simple investment project (Eq. 4-1e). That is, for $P = -I + A/i$, $i^* = A/I$ is the interest rate for which $P = 0$. For such a project $Y = \lceil(I/A)$, so *the payback time, before rounding up, is the reciprocal of the rate of return for discrete infinite-horizon simple investment projects.* Similarly, a continuous infinite-horizon simple investment project (Eq. 4-1f) has $r^* = \bar{A}/I$, so the payback time $Y = I/\bar{A}$ is the reciprocal of the ROR when ROR is expressed as a nominal continuous rate. For most investment projects there is an inverse relationship between Y and ROR. The quantity A/I (or $\bar{A}/I$), which is the reciprocal of Y except when the salvage value is high compared to the returns, is sometimes informally called a "rate of return" since it is the rate at which the returns recover the investment. Enterprises often use a maximum desirable value of Y as a rule of thumb; if this is set at 4 years, for example, projects whose payback time is 4 years or less are considered desirable under this rule, and projects whose payback time exceeds 4 years are considered undesirable. In practice, such a rule may not have the primary intent of setting an upper limit on the length of time that a project is allowed to diminish liquidity, but rather of setting an approximate lower limit on rate of return.

   Payback time also has a bearing on risk in situations in which the economic life of a project is uncertain. By its definition, Y directly answers the question, "How long must the returns continue in order for the project to be profitable (ignoring interest)?"

E19. At Blandish Corporation, most projects are simple investment projects that have a life of about 8 years and have negligible salvage value. Most projects are considered attractive if their payback time is at most 4 years. Interpret this perception as an approximate lower limit on rate of return.

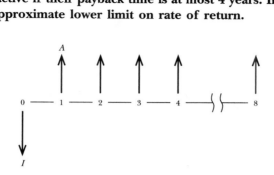

$$P = -I + A\left(\frac{1 - \beta^8}{i}\right), \qquad \beta = \frac{1}{1 + i}$$

Given $Y = I/A \le 4$, the ROR-defining requirement $P = 0$ implies

$$\frac{1 - \beta^8}{i} \le 4$$

This is satisfied by $i^* \le 18.6237\%$. A project with a rate of return not less than this value will have a payback time of not more than four years. The 4-year payback-time requirement corresponds to MARR.

On the other hand, suppose that a MARR of $i = 15\%$ is used, but the maximum payback time is nevertheless set at four years. Interpret this set of policies as a hedge against short economic life.

$$P = -I + A\left(\frac{1 - \beta^n}{i}\right)$$

Given $i = 0.15$ and $I/A \le 4$, we can determine a lower limit on n such that $P \ge 0$.

$$0 \le -4 + \frac{1 - \left(\frac{1}{1.15}\right)^n}{0.15} \Rightarrow n \ge 6.556 \quad \text{or} \quad \underline{\underline{7 \text{ years}}}$$

If a project estimated to have a life of eight years has a payback time of not more than four years, its present worth at 15% interest will be nonnegative if its life is as little as seven years.

4.3 BENEFIT/COST RATIO (B/C)

The ratio of benefits to costs is an efficiency measure that is conceptually simple and is versatile. It measures *cost efficiency* (in contrast to ROR and payback time, which measure time efficiency). This ratio, denoted B/C, will be utilized extensively in Chapter 7 ("Public Sectior Decision Making").

Let two opportunities denoted A and B have respective values $B^{(A)}$ and $B^{(B)}$ of a *benefit indicator*, and let them have respective values $C^{(A)}$ and $C^{(B)}$ of a *cost indicator*. The benefit indicator is a positive real number intended as a scalar measure of benefit relative to zero benefit, so that, for example, a benefit of 10 is considered twice as beneficial as a benefit of 5. It is required that $B^{(A)}$ and $B^{(B)}$ have *identical time profiles*; if $B^{(A)}$ is a present worth at interest rate i, then $B^{(B)}$ must also be a present worth at interest rate i, and if $B^{(A)}$ is an annual benefit amount assuming benefits persist for 8 years and decline 3% per year, then $B^{(B)}$ must also be in identical units with an identical horizon and identical rate of decline.

Let the cost indicator be a positive real number intended as a scalar measure of cost in monetary units. $C^{(A)}$ and $C^{(B)}$ must have identical time profiles with each other, but their units and their time profile can be different from those for benefits. For example, $C^{(A)}$ and $C^{(B)}$ could both be annual costs in dollars while $B^{(A)}$ and $B^{(B)}$ were measured in non-monetary units of benefit.

With benefit indicators and cost indicators that meet the abovementioned requirements, the benefit/cost ratios for opportunities A and B are defined as

$$(B/C)_A = \frac{B^{(A)}}{C^{(A)}} \tag{4-12a}$$

and

$$(B/C)_B = \frac{B^{(B)}}{C^{(B)}} \tag{4-12b}$$

Neither $(B/C)_A$ nor $(B/C)_B$ is meaningful in an absolute sense, but

$$(B/C)_A > (B/C)_B \text{ implies A is more cost efficient than B.}$$

E20. Which life insurance policy is more cost efficient for a person who uses $i = 8\%$ annual interest: a \$100,000 policy whose premium (cost) is \$7000 paid in advance, or a \$120,000 policy whose premium is paid in 10 beginning-of-year installments of \$825 each? Interpret the results.

Benefits: Let $B^{(A)} = 100,000$ and $B^{(B)} = 120,000$. Policy A will pay \$100,000 at some unknown time in the future, and policy B will pay \$120,000 at the same unknown time, so the benefit indicators have identical time profiles as required.

Costs: The cost indicators do not have the same time profiles as each other. Let $C^{(A)} = 7000$, a present worth. The present worth of the cost for B is

$$C^{(B)} = 825 + 825\left(\frac{1 - \beta^9}{i}\right) \text{ where } i = 0.008, \ \beta = \frac{1}{1 + i}$$
$$= 5978.682528$$

which has the same time profile as $C^{(A)}$.

From Eqs. 4-12a and 4-12b:

$$(B/C)_A = \frac{100,000}{7000} = \underline{\underline{14.2857}}$$

$$(B/C)_B = \frac{120,000}{5978.682528} = \underline{\underline{20.0713}}$$

Since $(B/C)_B > (B/C)_A$, the $120,000 policy is more cost efficient.

From a cost efficiency standpoint, the $120,000 policy is better; but it is important to realize that the result says nothing about whether the better insurance policy is worthwhile compared to alternatives such as no insurance. Note that the B/C method allows sidestepping of the question of life expectancy, but to bring in other alternatives such as the no-insurance alternative would require explicit resolution of that question.

Ratios of benefit/cost ratios are meaningful. If $(B/C)_B = 1.4(B/C)_A$ (as is approximately the case for Example E20), it is possible to assert that B is "40% better" or "1.4 times as good" as A, per dollar of cost.

B/C ignores project size, scope, or scale. In Example E20, if the person needed a $120,000 life insurance policy, choosing alternative B included an implicit assumption that the $100,000 policy of alternative A could be scaled up 20% in size and that it would cost 20% more when so scaled. If a $120,000 policy from the insurer who offered the $100,000 were to cost less than $8400, the B/C advantage of the other policy was overestimated. If a very small project has a very high B/C, the B/C is meaningless if the project cannot be scaled up to the same size as alternatives with which it is being compared.

E21. **A maintenance shop purchases dozens of new generators per year at a cost of $720 each. A generator of equal value can be built from scrap materials at a cost of $150. Right now the shop has enough scrap materials to build several generators. Determine B/C for the alternatives of purchasing (A) and building from scrap (B), and interpret the result.**

Benefits: Let $B^{(A)} = 1$ and $B^{(B)} = 1$; the benefit of each alternative is to build one generator, and the number of generators built is a convenient measure of benefit.

Costs: Let $C^{(A)} = 720$ and $C^{(B)} = 150$, reflecting the costs of building one generator under the respective alternatives.

$$(B/C)_A = \frac{1}{720}$$

$$(B/C)_B = \frac{1}{150}$$

Since $(B/C)_B$ is much greater than $(B/C)_A$, **B is much more cost efficient.**

However, method **B** cannot be scaled up to provide dozens of generators, so the result is misleading; the result is valid only while scrap materials are freely available.

B/C methods are used extensively in public-sector decision making. See Chapter 7, especially Section 7.4.2, for more B/C theory and applications.

For a simple investment project with zero salvage (Figures 4-1c and 4-1d) or with an infinite horizon (Figures 4-1e and 4-1f), the ratio of returns to investment A/I (or $\bar{A}/I$) is a properly-defined B/C ratio for alternatives having equal lives n. Let I be the measure of cost, and let the present worth of benefits be the measure of benefit. From Figure 4-1a, the benefit/cost ratio is defined as

$$B/C = \frac{A[(1 - \beta^n)/i] + S\beta^n}{I} \tag{4-13}$$

If $S > 0$ no simplification arises. Assume that $S = 0$ and that n is the same for all alternatives; of course i and β are the same for all alternatives. For alternatives **A** and **B**, we have, from Eqs. 4-12a and 4-12b:

$$(B/C)_\mathsf{A} = \frac{A^{(\mathsf{A})}[(1 - \beta^n)/i]}{I^{(\mathsf{A})}}$$

$$(B/C)_\mathsf{B} = \frac{A^{(\mathsf{B})}[(1 - \beta^n)/i]}{I^{(\mathsf{B})}}$$

But since $(1 - \beta^n)/i$ is a positive constant,

$$(B/C)_\mathsf{A} > (B/C)_\mathsf{B} \Leftrightarrow \frac{A^{(\mathsf{A})}}{I^{(\mathsf{A})}} > \frac{A^{(\mathsf{B})}}{I^{(\mathsf{B})}}$$

This illustrates that any measure of benefit can be used if it has a fixed time profile and is a scalar measure of benefit relative to zero benefit.

4.4 NET PRESENT VALUE (WORTH) INDEX

Capital is distinct from cost, both because of the need to consider its availability (capital scarcity may rule out capital-inefficient projects or those that require too much capital) and because of its special treatment in income-tax accounting. Leaving legalistic definitions of capital for tax purposes to Chapter 10, we offer here a definition of capital adequate for discussing capital efficiency: Capital is the portion of cost that is expended immediately and that is viewed as facilitating returns that occur after a substantial delay. If you purchase a more efficient furnace in order to save fuel, you may also need to maintain the furnace to keep up its fuel efficiency. The *capital* invested is only the purchase cost, while the *costs* of the project include not only the capital cost but other costs such as maintenance.

To measure *capital efficiency* in capital budgeting (Chapter 6), an index called the net present value index (NPVI) is defined as the ratio of net present value (''value'' is a widely used synonym for "worth") of a project to its immediate capital requirements. NPVI is defined for *investment projects* only:

Definition of NPVI:

$$\text{NPVI} = \frac{\displaystyle\sum_{t=0}^{n} A_t \beta^t}{-\displaystyle\sum_{t=0}^{m} A_t} = \frac{P}{\text{investment}} \qquad (4\text{-}14)$$

The numerator of NPVI includes the investment (unlike the numerator in B/C). The denominator is the undiscounted sum of the negative cash flows in the investment phase of the project, times 0 through m (usually time zero only).

E22. The following investment project was shown to have a payback time of five years:

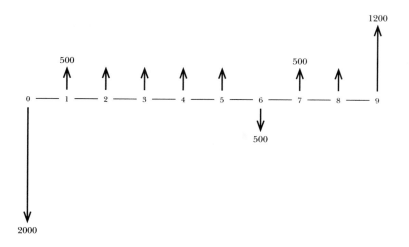

Assume the investment phase is considered to be time zero only. At $i = 12\%$, determine NPVI and compare NPVI to B/C for this project.

NPVI: The numerator is (treating time 6 as having -1000 and $+500$ flows):

$$P = -2000 + 500\left(\frac{1 - \beta^8}{i}\right) - 1000\beta^6 + 1200\beta^9, \quad \text{where } i = 12\%, \quad \beta = \frac{1}{1 + i}$$

$$= 409.92$$

The denominator for NPVI is $-A_0 = -(-2000) = 2000$.

$$\text{NPVI} = \frac{P}{2000} = \underline{\underline{0.20496}}$$

B/C: Let the numerator be the present worth of positive cash flows:

$$B = 500\left(\frac{1 - \beta^8}{i}\right) - 500\beta^6 + 1200\beta^9 = 2663.24$$

Let the denominator be the present worth of negative cash flows.

$$C = 2000 + 500\beta^6 = 2253.32$$

Thus $B/C = \underline{\underline{1.18}}$.

The NPVI shows that the wealth increase is slightly over 20% of the immediate required investment. The B/C shows that the wealth increase from the receipts is about 18% more than the wealth decrease from the disbursements.

NPVI is more closely related to payback time than to B/C, because NPVI deals with liquidity. Capital is a scarce commodity. Because of the surrogate-banker assumption behind the definition of worth, worth alone is not the only consideration in decision making. It may be impossible, or too risky, to borrow enough money to take advantage of a high-worth project. *NPVI is the ratio of the long-term positive effects of a project to its short-term negative effects.* It is not a perfect measure, especially if the long-term or the short-term or both are too long, but it indicates to some extent the worthiness of a project per unit of its capital consumption.

E23. Recall the Soapstone Art Center example, whose net cash-flow diagram is repeated here from Example E17 (in thousands, with time in years).

The present worth is

$$P = -10 + 20\left(\frac{1 - \beta^2}{r}\right) - 40\beta^2\left(\frac{1 - \beta^6}{r}\right) + 500\beta^8$$

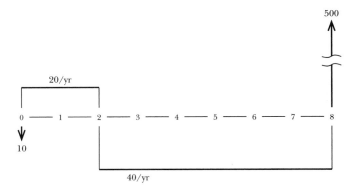

Assume the art center's surrogate banker is its existing long-term debt, at $i = 11.5\%$ annual interest; $r = \ln 1.115$, $\beta = 1/(1.115)$. At this interest rate, the present worth is

$$P = \$93,494.35 \cong \$93,500$$

We have already seen that the relevant rate of return is 40.7% and that the payback time is eight years. Determine the NPVI and describe the overall decision picture given by the absolute measure P and the efficiency measures i^*, Y, and NPVI.

If the investment phase were considered to be time zero only, NPVI would be $P/10 = 9249$, which is huge. However, although the capital budget may allow $10,000 to be spent now, an acceptance of the project obligates the art center to find capital in large amounts later. The investment phase is actually eight years, and the denominator of NPVI should be the undiscounted negative sum $10 + 40(6) = 250$, or $250,000. Thus

$$\text{NPVI} = \frac{93.49435}{250} \cong \underline{\underline{0.374}}$$

NPVI for all simple investment projects (Figure 4-1) is P/I.

4.5 TYPICAL EFFICIENCY VALUES FOR SIMPLE INVESTMENT PROJECTS

To use efficiency measures effectively, a decision maker must have benchmarks that indicate approximately what degree of desirability or undesirability is indicated by particular values of each measure. Let us postulate a set of typical simple investment projects and determine the efficiency values—ROR, Y, B/C and NPVI—that would be associated with such projects when they are (1) borderline-attractive and (2) moderately attractive. Recall Figure 4-1a, which gives the following present worth for a discrete simple investment project:

$$P = -I + A\left(\frac{1 - \beta^n}{i}\right) + S\beta^n$$

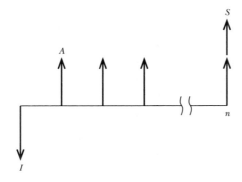

Obviously, $P = 0$ for the project to be borderline-attractive at MARR. We take "borderline-attractive" as meaning "equivalent at MARR to the ordinary course of business." Also, for a project to be borderline-attractive implies $i^* = \text{MARR}$ and $B/C = 1$ at MARR.

Arbitrarily we fix $i^* = \text{MARR} + 2\%$ as the meaning of "moderately attractive." Also arbitrarily, we fix $S = 0$; this simplifies computations and accords with the notion that environmentally sound cessation of an economic activity can be costly. With $S = 0$, we have (as for Figure 4-1c):

$$P = -I + A\left(\frac{1 - \beta^n}{i}\right) \qquad (4\text{-}15)$$

The horizon (n) and MARR (i) vary, and we will study a range of "typical" values. Recall from Chapter 3 that an equal-payment series in current dollars is a decreasing series in indexed dollars. Each "typical" result will be valid for two situations: MARR expressed as the market interest rate i with returns whose indexed value declines with inflation to remain steady in inflated dollars, and (for $i \rightarrow d$ and $A \rightarrow w$) MARR expressed as the real interest rate with returns whose indexed value remains steady.

As a *base case*, let us assume $i = 15\%$ and $n = 8$ years. *Borderline-attractive base-case projects* have NPVI = 0, ROR of $i^* = 15\%$, and at 15% interest have B/C = 1. To determine payback: $Y = \lceil [(1 - \beta^n)/i] = \lceil (4.4873) = 5$ yr.

Moderately attractive base-case projects, arbitrarily designated as those with a rate of return 2% above MARR, have ROR of $i^* = 0.15 + 0.02 = 17\%$. Letting $P = 0$ in Eq. 4-15 with $i = 17\%$ yields a payback time of $Y = \lceil (4.2072) = 5$ yr. It can be shown (see Exercises) that B/C becomes the ratio of "pain" factors for the old to new rate of return:

$$B/C = \frac{(P/A\ 15\%,8)}{(P/A\ 17\%,8)} = 1.06659$$

It can also be shown (see Exercises) that the NPVI is B/C $- 1$:

$$\text{NPVI} = B/C - 1 = 0.06659$$

For a decision maker who discounts at 15% interest, then, and for whom a typical project lasts eight years, a "moderately attractive" project would be one having a benefit cost ratio near 1.06659 and a net present "value" index near 6.659%. Also, a payback time near 4.2072 before rounding is "moderately attractive."

Figure 4-5 gives the values of various efficiency measures corresponding to a "moderately attractive" project having various economic lives n, for various values of MARR.

E24. **An energy conservation project that involves double glazing of windows and upgrading of HVAC (heating, ventilation, and air conditioning) controls for a given office building is estimated to require a \$400,000 investment and to save \$80,000 annually in fuel expenditures. From Figure 4-5, estimate whether the project would be attractive if the office building is owned by:**

   An electric power utility that uses MARR = 8% and expects a 20-year economic life.

   A manufacturing company that uses MARR = 12% and expects a 10-year economic life

   A real estate developer that uses MARR = 15% and expects to sell the building in five years, for a price that will not be significantly influenced by whether the project is undertaken.

The estimation can be done using any one of the four indicators. The project has $A/I = 80/400 = 0.20$ and $I/A = 5 = Y$. From the definition of B/C as the present worth of positive cash flows divided by the present worth of negative cash flows, the project has a benefit/cost ratio that depends on i and n:

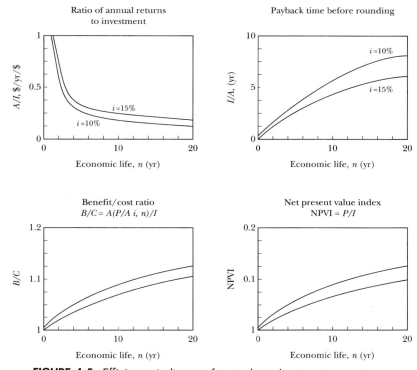

FIGURE 4-5. Efficiency indicators for moderately attractive projects.

$$B/C = \frac{80(P/A\ i,n)}{400}$$

Also, it has

$$NPVI = P/I = \frac{-400 + 80(P/A\ i,n)}{400} = B/C - 1$$

Comparisons are summarized as follows:

Owner	Efficiency Indicator	Value of Indicator for This Project	Moderately Attractive Value from Figure 4-5	Comparison
Electric power utility	A/I	0.20	~0.12	Attractive
i = 8%, n = 20	I/A	5	~8.5	Attractive
	B/C	1.9636	~1.15	Attractive
	NPVI	0.9636	~0.15	Attractive
Manufacturing company	A/I	0.20	~0.19	Moderately attractive
i = 12%, n = 10	I/A	5	~5.2	Moderately attractive
	B/C	1.1300	~1.1	Moderately attractive
	NPVI	0.1300	~0.1	Moderately attractive
Real estate developer	A/I	0.20	~0.31	Unattractive
i = 15%, n = 5	I/A	5	~3.2	Unattractive
	B/C	0.6704	~1.05	Unattractive
	NPVI	-0.3296	~0.05	Unattractive

All efficiency indicators are scale-independent; that is, if all cash flows in a project are multiplied by a positive constant X, the efficiency indicators keep their same values.

The definition of NPVI allows us to interpret the notion of a moderately attractive project in absolute (dollar) terms. From Eq. 4-14, for a simple investment project, we have

$$P = I \times (\text{NPVI}) \qquad\qquad (4\text{-}16)$$

Recall that for "base-case" projects (for $i = 15\%$, $n = 8$) a moderately attractive project was seen to have NPVI = 0.06659. Thus a "moderately attractive" project requiring an investment of \$10,000 would have a present worth of 10000(0.06659) $\cong$ \$666, while a "moderately attractive" project that increases the protagonist's wealth by the equivalent of \$1000 (that is, a project having $P = \$1000$ at the protagonist's MARR) is one that requires an investment of about 1000/0.06659 $\cong$ \$15,000.

4.6 WORTH VERSUS EFFICIENCY

The various indicators P, ROR, Y, B/C, and NPVI reveal different aspects of desirability. To clarify the distinctions let us examine contrasting cash-flow sets, illustrating how projects can have very different values of some indicators while having identical values of others.

At 8% interest, all three of the projects in Figure 4-6 have identical present worths (\$204.30). Yet they tie up money for payback times of 10 years, 6 years, and 1 year, respectively. Although each adds the same amount to wealth, the "quick" project is much more flexible. For most kinds of risk or uncertainty (see Chapter 8) the "quick" project would be preferred; if the main risk were that a similar opportunity might never again arise, the "long range" project would be preferred. Payback time Y distinguishes well among these equal-worth projects.

It is shown in the chapter-end exercises that ROR also distinguishes among these equal-worth projects, and that Y distinguishes among equal-ROR projects (as ROR remains constant when greater returns occur after longer time spans, Y responds more to the time spans than to the returns).

B/C and NPVI are identical for the projects in Figure 4-6 because the projects have identical investments. The contrasting projects in Figure 4-7 show how B/C and NPVI indicate aspects distinct from worth.

At 8% interest, all three of the projects in Figure 4-7 have identical present worths (\$204.30). Yet they have varying investments, and thus they have NPVI values of 20.43% for the "long range" project, 13.26% for the "steady" project, and 9.27% for the "quick" project. If capital is scarce, the "long-range" project, being much more capital-efficient than the others, may be the only feasible choice. The B/C values are simply 1 + NPVI for these projects.

Now we have reviewed the *capabilities* of efficiency indicators, except for the special capabilities of the benefit/cost ratio (Chapter 7). To complete the discussion of worth versus efficiency before turning to specific decision-making procedures, we must compare the *limitations* of worth and efficiency indicators.

The chief limitation of efficiency indicators is a *scale independence;* if all cash flows are multiplied by a positive constant, we have seen that the efficiency indicators are unchanged. As a consequence, efficiency indicators can be highly favorable for a

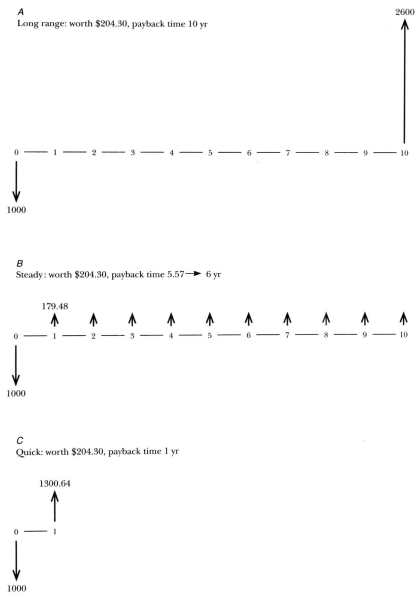

FIGURE 4-6. Varying liquidities for equal worths.

project that is too small to affect wealth, so that efficiency indicators by themselves can be misleading.

Worth by itself can also be misleading. The chief limitation of worth as an indicator is an *additive independence from project size.* Additive independence is an immediate consequence of the definition of worth. Let there be a project with cash flows $\{A_t: t=0,...,n\}$; let us suppose it has a positive present worth, is an investment project with a relatively small investment, and has relatively quick returns, so that we call it an "efficient" project. Now let there be an "inefficient" project whose cash flows are identical, except that the "inefficient" project has an extra investment J_0 at time zero and an

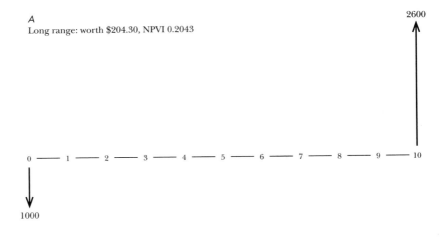

A
Long range: worth $204.30, NPVI 0.2043

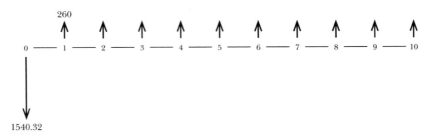

B
Steady: worth $204.30, NPVI 0.1326

C
Quick: worth $204.30, NVPI 0.0927

FIGURE 4-7. Varying capital efficiencies for equal worths.

extra return R_n at time n. The present worth of the "inefficient" project is shown in Figure 4-7.

$$P = \sum_{t=0}^{n} A_t \beta^t - J_0 + R_n \beta^n$$

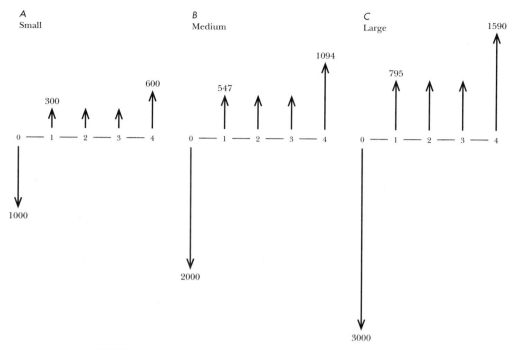

FIGURE 4-8. Additive independence of worth from project size.

But if $-J_0 + R_n\beta^n = 0$, that is, if the present worths of the extras offset each other, the "inefficient" project has the same worth as the "efficient" project. This is a severe limitation: if a small, quick project has a \$500 worth, it is efficient, but if a huge, slow project has the same \$500 worth, it is inefficient. The efficiency indicators can detect such conditions, as we can see from the final set of contrasting projects given in Figure 4-8.

The three projects in Figure 4-8 have approximately identical present worths (\$214.15, \$213.79, \$217.49) at 8% interest. Yet the "small" project is more efficient; if it could be doubled or tripled in size, or if two or three such projects could be implemented, more money would be made. All the efficiency measures show the efficiency advantages of the "small" project. For example, the rates of return of the three projects are 16.2297%, 12.1918%, and 10.8625%, respectively.

4.7 EXERCISES

1. By showing $dP/d\beta > 0$, which implies $dP/di < 0$, prove that the worth of a discrete simple investment project (Figure 4-1a) decreases with increasing interest rate. (*Note:* It may be convenient to express the "pain" factor as $\beta + \beta^2 + \cdots + \beta^n$.)

2. By showing $dP/dr < 0$, prove that the worth of a continuous simple investment project (Figure 4-1b) decreases with increasing interest rate. *Note:* Substituting e^{-rn} for β^n, the "parn" factor $(1 - e^{-rn})/r$ can be shown to have a negative derivative with respect to r by reducing the derivative to an expression M/r^2 where M is an expression in n and r. It will be found that M is negative if $(1 + rn)e^{-rn} < 1$ is true; but this is certainly true since by Taylor expansion $e^{rn} = 1 + rn + \cdots > 1 + rn$.

3. Determine a value for S (as a function of other parameters) such that a discrete simple investment project (Figure 4-1a) has the same present-worth formula as if it had an infinite horizon. Interpret the result.

4. A discrete simple investment project (Figure 4-1a) has a salvage value S that is independent of n; that is, the asset acquired by the expenditure of I dollars suddenly acquires a new value S (hopefully greater than I), and then never appreciates or depreciates in the value for which it can be sold. By determining dP/dn, find a critical value for S (as a function of other parameters) such that the investor should sell immediately if the salvage value is greater, or sell as late as possible if the salvage value is smaller.

5. A continuous simple investment project with zero salvage (Figure 4-1d) is to have a rate of return of $i^* = 10.5170918\%$, or $r^* = 0.10$ expressed as a nominal continuous rate. Determine n if $\bar{A}/I = 0.20$.

6. Prove that the present worth of a pure investment project (Eq. 4-1) decreases with interest rate. That is, prove $dP/d\beta > 0$, which implies $dP/di < 0$.

7. In the solution to Example E3, an interpretation was given for the 24.65% rate of return, in terms of how much the initial \$10 investment took out of the business by time 2, and how much surplus was built up by time 4. Provide a similar interpretation for the 61.13% rate of return for the same set of cash flows.

8. Prove that for any cash-flow set having a rate of return i^*, its opposite cash-flow set—the set in which all cash flows have the same amounts but opposite signs to those in the original set—has the same rates of return. Also prove that a cash-flow set has the same rate of return when measured in any monetary units (dollars, yen, marks, pesos, etc.).

9. In the pavement expansion joint illustration in Section 4.1.1, a rate of return was reported as 38.45%. The engineer was using one of the simple investment project models of Figure 4-1. Determine whether the model was the discrete model of Figure 4-1c, or the continuous model of Figure 4-1d.

10. A \$5000 investment is followed by 10 end-of-year returns of \$2000 each. Determine the rate of return. Also determine what the rate of return would be if the returns continued forever instead of ceasing after 10 years. Based on these results, are the returns after 10 years greatly important in determining the approximate desirability of the investment?

11. Prove or disprove that if all the cash flows for a project are multiplied by a finite constant other than zero, the rate(s) of return remain unchanged. In light of the result, is it possible to change a project's rate of return by simple scaling? Can the statement, "I lose money on every sale, but I make it up in volume" be valid?

12. A magazine article showed how a solar-energy-retention wall could be built cheaply by filling discarded glass bottles with water and using them as "bricks" in the wall. Another article advocated using butane as an automobile fuel, noting that butane is sold more cheaply than gasoline. A third article advocated substituting ethanol for most of the gasoline in motor fuel, with the ethanol to be manufactured from high-sugar agricultural waste not usable as livestock feed. For at least one of the three situations, point out a weakness in scaling up from a small profitable project to a large one.

13. A $5000 investment is followed by 10 end-of-year returns of $2000 each. There is also a disposal and cleanup cost of K dollars, so that the final net cash flow is $2000 - K$ dollars. For large enough K, the "salvage value" is, then, negative. Determine K such that the rate of return would be 10%. For protagonists interested in rates from zero to 25%, would this be an "investment project" as defined in Section 4.1.5 if K were as calculated?

14. A $5000 investment is followed by 10 end-of-year returns at $2000 each, but there is also a $20,000 disposal and cleanup cost at time 10.

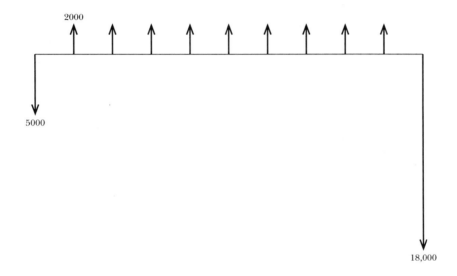

$$P = -5000 + 2000(P/A\ i,9) - 18000\beta^{10}$$

   (a) Verify that there are two rates of return, 13.4774% and 24.8556%.
   (b) Verify that the project is an "investment project" for interest rates greater than 18.4%.
   (c) Briefly explain, using the surrogate banker, how a protagonist makes or loses money on this project, compared to the ordinary course of business, when the protagonist's MARR is each of these values: 10%, 20%, 30%.
   (d) If there were no ordinary business opportunities, but this one could be "kited," briefly explain how this would be done and what the eventual outcome would be.

15. Generate a cash-flow set whose cash flow at time zero is $-$1000$ and that has rates of return of 50% and 100%. Determine its present worth at $i = 12\%$.

16. Sketch the P-versus-i curve for the cash-flow set that results from using Eq. 4-7 to generate a set having three rates of return all equal to 10% (let $c = 1331$).

17. For the cash-flow set of Example E6, estimate the smallest possible present worth this cash-flow set can have and the interest rate that minimizes worth.

18. The Soapstone Art Center in Example E8 would have financed the original $10,000 investment by taking it out of the ordinary course of business or by bor-

rowing it. If this financing had been done at 40.7% interest (as assumed implicitly in computing a 40.7% rate of return):

(a) How long would it take the exhibition revenues of \$20,000/yr (continuous) to repay the investment at interest?

(b) Given the foregoing result, determine the compound amount of the excess exhibition revenues from that time to time 2 (determine the worth at time n of 20/yr for $2 - n$ years and multiply by $\beta^{-(2-n)}$). This is the excess, available at time 2, to finance the first part of the shortfall between purchase expenses and exhibition revenues.

(c) Given the two foregoing results, determine the length of the shortfall of $60 - 20 = 40/yr$ that can be financed by the compound amount of excess revenues, and determine the time at which the shortfall will start causing a deficit.

(d) Given the three foregoing results, determine the compound amount of the deficit at time 8.

19. To illustrate Eq. 4-9, a cash-flow set $\{A_t: t = 0,...,3\} = \{-4, 1, 0, 6\}$ was shown to have an external rate of return (ERR) of 21.95% when the reinvestment interest rate was given as $i = 12\%$.

(a) Determine ERR for $i = 21.95\%$.

(b) Determine ERR for $i = 25\%$.

(c) Determine the (internal) rate of return ROR for this cash-flow set.

(d) Determine ERR for i equal to the ROR determined above.

20. Prove that if the reinvestment rate is equal to the ROR for a cash-flow set, the ERR is also the same.

21. In Example E10 the external rate of return (ERR) was determined for each of the following two cash-flow sets.

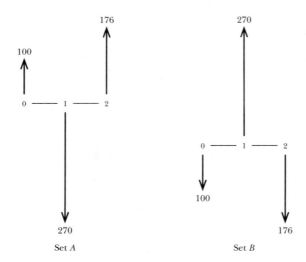

One value of the internal rate of return (ROR) is $i^* = 60\%$. For each of the sets, determine the external rate of return i' when the reinvestment rate i is 60%.

22. In Example E6 a newspaper could receive \$10,000 at time zero by contracting to pay \$25,000 at time 1 to buy equipment that would yield a \$15,500 savings at time 2. In thousands of dollars, the cash-flow diagram is:

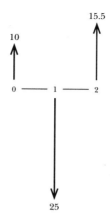

This cash-flow set has two rates of return. Assume that the newspaper earns a 12% rate on capital invested in the ordinary course of business.

(a) If the actual situation were that the initial $10,000 would be invested in the ordinary course of business for one year, draw the true-cash-flow diagram and determine the unique ROR.

(b) If the actual situation were that the initial $10,000 would be invested in the ordinary course of business for one year and a special loan at 9% interest were made available to finance $8000 of the $25,000 obligation at time 1 (to be repaid in full at time 2), draw the true-cash-flow diagram and determine the unique ROR.

23. The discrete equivalent of Example E11, with end-of-year cash flows, would have the following cash-flow diagram and present worth formula:

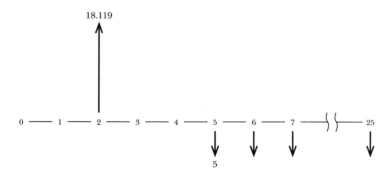

$$P = 18.199\beta^2 - 5\beta^4\left(\frac{1 - \beta^{21}}{i}\right) \text{ where } \beta = \frac{1}{1 + i}$$

Verify that the rate of return is between 18.9% and 19%, and conclude whether the result indicates the project is desirable or undesirable given a 12% MARR.

24. In Example E12 the Soapstone Art Center borrows $40,000 per year continuously for six years at 12% interest. Determine the lump-sum repayment. The cash flow is

shown below, in thousands of dollars. (Note that the time scale is offset from that in the example.)

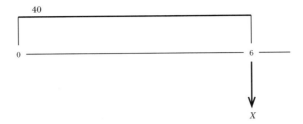

25. In Example E13 two alternative "true situations" were applied to Set **A** of cash flows from Example E10. These "true situations" incorporated specific assumptions about reinvestment of surpluses at 12% interest. Now consider Set **B** from Example E10. In the spirit of Example E13, concoct two alternative "true situations" to simplify the determination of ROR and interpret the results. The assumptions can concern financing of deficits at 12%, reinvestment of surpluses at 12%, or both.

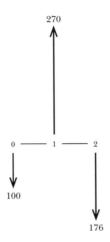

26. In Example E14 it was shown that the following cash flows constitute an investment project as defined in Section 4.1.5.

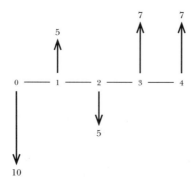

Determine the rate of return to the nearest 0.1%, and conclude whether the ROR indicates that the project is desirable for a decision maker whose MARR is $i = 12\%$.

27. The following project has rates of return near 10% and near 50%.

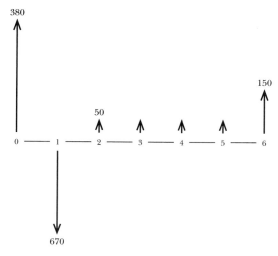

(a) Determine whether this is an investment project, an obligation project, or neither, for a protagonist for whom interest rates in the range 12% to 20% are of concern.

(b) For a protagonist whose surrogate banker gives and takes interest in the given range, is the project profitable?

28. A company earns at about a 13% annual interest rate in the ordinary course of business. Money can be borrowed at 10% interest and invested in the ordinary course of business. To maximize worth, would it be better to accept a 10% loan that would be repaid in 5 equal end-of-year installments, or accept an 11% alternative loan to be repaid in 10 equal end-of-year installments?

29. A water treatment plant that costs $6700 per year to operate has kept corrosion rates low in a water pipeline. The pipeline will be completely replaced in two years, and it could not corrode to failure in that time even without the plant. Is it worthwhile to shut down this plant for two years, realizing it will cost $13,400 to recommission it? (No interest rate is given specifically.)

30. At Moder Knitting nearly all cost-saving projects consist of an investment at time zero, followed by a series of six equal end-of-year returns, and no salvage value:

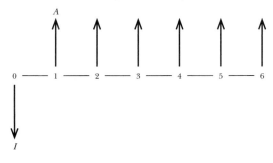

For simplicity, the knitting plant engineers are told that capital investments having a four-year payback time or less are acceptable. If an engineer desires to analyze a project that has a different horizon or profile of returns, what is the implied ROR?

31. Consider the two alternative projects, A and B:

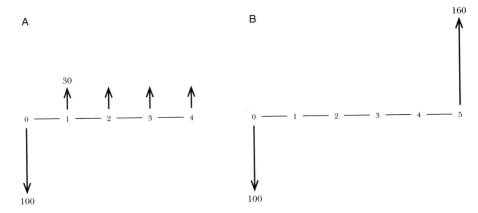

(a) Determine the payback times. Which project has greater liquidity?
(b) Which project has greater monetary efficiency (rate of return)?

32. It is easy to prove that *if two investment projects have equal investments, the one with a greater ROR has greater worth.*

Proof: Let i_A^* and i_B^* be the respective RORs of A and B, and let $\beta_A = 1/(1 + i_A^*)$ and $\beta_B = 1/(1 + i_B^*)$. Let the equal investment be I and let the respective cash flows after the investment be $\{A_t^{(A)}\}$ and $\{A_t^{(B)}\}$. From the definition of ROR:

$$0 = -I + \sum_t A_t^{(A)} \beta_A^t \quad \text{and} \quad 0 = -I + \sum_t A_t^{(B)} \beta_B^t$$

whence

$$\sum_t A_t^{(A)} \beta_A^t = \sum_t A_t^{(B)} \beta_B^t$$

Now let B have the greater ROR: $i_B^* > i_A^*$. Because B is an investment project, its worth at the smaller rate i_A^* must be greater:

$$\sum_t A_t^{(B)} \beta_A^t > \sum_t A_t^{(B)} \beta_B^t = \sum_t A_t^{(A)} \beta_A^t$$

which proves that the worth of B is greater than that of A when both are computed at i_A^*. Similarly it can be shown that the worths have the same relationship at i_B^* as well, and at any interest rate for which the projects both retain the "investment" character. Now, prove or disprove the proposition that if two investment projects have equal investments, the one with lesser payback time has greater worth.

33. Of two pension plans, plan A collects 6% of an employee's income and uses a 0.02 multiplier in the formula to compute retirement income as a function of years of

service and late-career income. Plan **B** collects 7% and uses a 0.023 multiplier. Which plan is more cost efficient?

34. Of two pension plans, plan **X** is more cost efficient than plan **Y**.
    (a) If plan **X** requires greater employee contributions during the working years, which plan has the greater worth?
    (b) If plan **X** requires smaller employee contributions during the working years, which plan has the greater worth?

35. Show that, for a simple investment project with zero salvage (Figure 4-1*c*),

$$\text{NPVI} = B/C - 1$$

36. For a discrete simple investment project with zero salvage (Figure 4-1*c*),
    (a) Show that if $B/C = 1$ at an interest rate i_1 (where B and C are the present worths at i_1 of the positive and negative cash flows, respectively), then if the returns increase so that the rate of return is a greater interest rate i_2, the benefit/cost ratio (still at i_1) increases to

$$B/C = \frac{(P/A \ i_1, n)}{(P/A \ i_2, n)}$$

    (b) Show that if NPVI $= 0$ at an interest rate i_1, then if the returns increase so that the rate of return is a greater rate i_2, the NPVI (still at i_1) increases to

$$\text{NPVI} = \frac{(P/A \ i_1, n)}{(P/A \ i_2, n)} - 1$$

37. In Section 4.1.5 a "moderately attractive" project was arbitrarily defined as a project having ROR = MARR + 2%. Using the "base-case" version (MARR of $i = 15\%$, $n = 8$ years) of a discrete simple investment project with zero salvage, determine the project scale—dollar values of I and A—that would give (at $i = 15\%$) a present worth of $1000. Do the results accord with the notion of "moderately attractive"?

38. In Example E24 an energy conservation project had these cash flows (in thousands, with time in years):

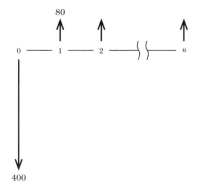

(a) Verify the results of Example E24 by determining the worth of the project for each of the three alternative protagonists: ($i = 0.08$, $n = 20$; $i = 0.12$, $n = 10$; and $i = 0.15$, $n = 5$)

(b) Verify the results of Example E24 by determining the rate of return for the project and comparing it to MARR for each protagonist.

39. The three projects in Figure 4-6 have identical present worths at 8% interest. Do their rates of return illustrate that ROR is "a measure of how fast returns recover an investment" (Section 4.1)?

40. Consider three cash-flow sets having the same general characteristics as those in Figure 4-6, but with identical rates of return (rather than identical present worths at 8%):

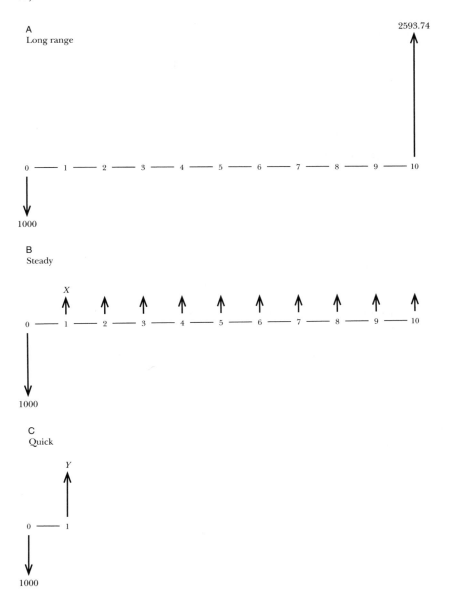

Sometimes it is not easy to choose what to do.

EVALUATION OF ALTERNATIVES

This chapter explains how to use both worth measures and efficiency measures to make engineering economic decisions. It has two major sections: Section 5.1 on Evaluation Procedures covers how to define mutually exclusive alternatives and independent opportunities, how to identify relevant consequences of a decision, how to establish planning horizons, and how to compare alternatives. It includes material on how to use available cost-accounting data, how to avoid double-counting, how to treat sunk costs, and how the choice of interest rate (MARR) affects decisions. This section constitutes a mini-course in engineering economy for someone who knows the basic definitions, concepts, and quantities discussed in the preceding chapters.

The second half of the chapter, Section 5.2 on Replacement and Timing Decisions, gives a unified treatment of the special techniques that can be used to clarify decision making where sequencing or timing of consequences is the major consideration. This includes a modern and comprehensive treatment of equipment replacement decision techniques, with a modern treatment of after-tax analysis that does not require the detailed depreciation-accounting methods covered in Chapter 10.

5.1 EVALUATION PROCEDURES

Engineering economy concerns the future, not the past. For every engineering economic decision, there is an exhaustive set of feasible, mutually exclusive alternatives. There is a set of consequences of each alternative. There is a minimal attractive rate of return (MARR) that allows a worth to be assigned to each set of consequences. The assignment of worth to consequences is usually performed under several simplifying assumptions concerning risk, financial environment, constituencies, taxation, and nonmonetary values. Subject to modifications to mitigate the effects of these simplifying assumptions, there is a single basic decision procedure in engineering economy: *to select the alternative having greatest worth.*

The remainder of this chapter concerns how to generate and evaluate alternatives according to the basic maximum-worth criterion. Then the following five chapters will concern modifications (Chapter 6 for financial environment, Chapter 7 for constituencies and nonmonetary values, Chapters 8 and 9 for risk, and Chapter 10 for taxation).

5.1.1 Mutually Exclusive Alternatives

Every decision problem has a *scope*, which is a definition of the limits of the problem: limits as to which kinds of alternatives can be considered, which kinds of consequences can be considered, and what is the time horizon beyond which benefits and costs will be ignored. Often the scope is severely limited. In a *make-or-buy* decision, for example, the design of the thing to be made or bought is considered fixed. Similarly, in a *buy-or-lease* decision, the characteristics of the thing to be bought or leased are considered fixed. In a *bid analysis* or a *replacement* problem, it is usual to consider most or all benefits to be identical for all alternatives that are within the scope.

Appropriate scope limitations and simplifying assumptions are what make a decision problem manageable and determine its intellectual content. For example, if all consequences occur within a small time span and benefits are considered to be identical for various alternatives, worth maximization boils down to cost minimization: to pick a 67¢ can of noodle soup over a 79¢ can, when both are of equal quantity and judged to be of equal quality, you need no MARR, and you need no estimate of benefits. On the other hand, if risk considerations are important, it may be appropriate to replace worth maximization with the more elaborate procedures of maximizing *expected* worth (Chapters 8 and 9).

Given a problem's scope and simplifying assumptions, the first step in problem solving is to define an exhaustive set of feasible, mutually exclusive alternatives. An *exhaustive* set of alternatives does not omit any alternatives that are in the scope, such as the do-nothing alternative, if feasible. A *feasible* alternative is one that is assumed possible to implement; it is *infeasible*, for example, to invest more money than you have or can borrow. Infeasible alternatives are usually described as those that violate *constraints*. There are constraints that render infeasible an alternative that includes murdering your grandmother; more quantifiably, a constraint on an investment may be expressed mathematically in a form such as $I \leq B$, where I is the required investment amount for an alternative, and B is the maximum amount you are assumed able to beg, borrow, or retain from previous earnings. Alternatives are *mutually exclusive* when they are defined such that to accept one is to reject all others. Some brief examples can illustrate the concepts of exhaustiveness, feasibility, and mutual exclusivity.

E1. Machine A costs $400 and will save $75 per year for five years, whereas machine B costs $500 and will save $80 per year for six years. Choose.

Regardless of MARR, both alternatives have negative worth, because their returns do not equal or exceed their investments. If the do-nothing alternative is feasible, yet A and B are the only alternatives considered, then the set of alternatives will *fail to be exhaustive.* Following the maximum-worth rule with an incomplete set would have the consequence here of unnecessary acceptance of a money-losing alternative.

E2. Texas engineer Bill Lesso tells the story of bringing a fresh sheaf of computer output to a meeting, only to find it told the client to open 1.5 mineshafts at Carlsbad and put 26 ton/day of ore back into the ground at Deming. What was wrong?

Two common types of constraint had been omitted: an *integer* constraint that should have kept the program from considering fractional numbers of mine-shafts, and a *nonnegativity* constraint that should have kept the program from considering negative production rates from mines.

E3. An uninsulated pipe carries hot oil and loses heat. Pipe insulation is available in integer-inch thicknesses from 1 to 5 in. Define the exhaustive set of feasible, mutually exclusive alternatives.

There are six alternatives: insulate the pipe with 0-in. (do-nothing), 1-in., 2-in., 3-in., 4-in., or 5-in. insulation.

5.1.2 Independent Opportunities

Each of an exhaustive set of feasible, mutually exclusive alternatives is a *version* of a project or opportunity. The decision problem is to choose this version. An enterprise may be faced with many different decision problems, each having its own scope and assumptions. Two opportunities are said to be *independent* if their consequences are independent, so that the consequences of neither one are dependent on which alter-native version of the other one is chosen. Independence is a convenient concept, because if opportunities could not be treated as independent, the enterprise would have only one opportunity, and every combination of versions of every choice would be a separate alternative. For example, Henry must decide about his health insurance, and he must decide about his furnace. Since health-insurance benefits do not depend on the furnace choice and fuel savings do not depend on the choice of health plan, Henry can make the two decisions separately. Otherwise, if there were 4 alternative health plans and 3 alternative furnace choices, Henry would have to consider 12 alternatives—health plan A with furnace X, health plan A with furnace Y, and so on. A dozen problems, each with 3 alternatives, requires only 36 worth evaluations if the problems are independent; but if they are not treated as at least partially independent, there are $3^{12} = 531,441$ worth evaluations, one for each different set of alternatives.

Usually, by careful definition of scope and assumptions, most decisions can be treated as independent, with some *partial dependence* as illustrated in the following example.

E4. Blandish Company engineers have identified that vapor-recovery equipment and elutriators can abate their plant's air pollution. A minimal (A) and a more elabo-rate (B) vapor-recovery system are under consideration. One large elutriator (1) or several smaller elutriators (2) are possible options. The large elutriator is not compatible with the minimal vapor-recovery system. To get by with only a vapor-recovery system or only an elutriator system, the plant would have to be operated at only 72% of its present capacity. Short of shutting the plant down completely,

these are the only alternatives. Define the exhaustive set of feasible, mutually exclusive alternatives.

The alternatives are:

1. **A2**—minimal vapor-recovery system with smaller elutriators
2. **B1**—elaborate vapor-recovery system with large elutriator
3. **B2**—elaborate vapor-recovery system with smaller elutriators
4. **A**—minimal vapor-recovery system with 72% capacity operation
5. **B**—elaborate vapor-recovery system with 72% capacity operation
6. **1**—large elutriator with 72% capacity operation
7. **2**—smaller elutriators with 72% capacity operation
8. **X**—complete shutdown

Note that this project cannot be truly independent of others. Its costs and benefits assume the environment of a plant operating at a given capacity, yet other decisions could change that capacity. Conversely, this pollution abatement project apparently contemplates within its scope something as drastic as reducing plant throughput to 72% of capacity. Other decisions, such as whether to enlarge an overloaded vapor pump, would surely depend on capacity.

In practice, such conflicts are avoided by managerial coordination and careful project definition. There is a hierarchy of decisions, according to which a decision such as selection of the most profitable plant capacity is at a higher level and decisions about vapor-recovery equipment are at a lower level. "The right hand must know what the left is doing"; in practice, a simplified version of the problem of Example E4 would be solved with various fixed-capacity assumptions, and the results would be used as data in a higher-level plant-capacity decision, where it is necessary to know the pollution-abatement costs at various capacities.

Sometimes a group of projects that are effectively independent is tied together by a single interdependence, such as contention for capital. Chapter 6 treats such problems.

5.1.3 Decision-Relevant Consequences

After isolating a decision problem by defining its scope and assumptions under an assumed environment, and defining its exhaustive set of feasible, mutually exclusive alternatives, the next step is to *define the decision-relevant consequences.*

A cash-flow set will be assigned to each alternative. If a decision procedure such as the basic one of selecting the alternative having greatest worth is to be both valid and convenient, the cash-flow sets must estimate the values of all the decision-relevant consequences without requiring unnecessary or redundant cash-flow estimation and calculation.

5.1.3.1 Planning Horizon The planning horizon, which often provides a value for the parameter n in worth formulas, is *the time beyond which all further consequences are either ignored or replaced with a salvage value.*

One basis for setting a planning horizon is inconstancy of the environment. Investments in computers were traditionally made on a five-year basis in the 1980s. At an office automation conference in 1985, the most-quoted bit of wisdom was a keynote-speech remark that "computers are a great expense but a lousy investment." The obsolescence resulting from rapid advances in hardware, software, and communication effectively means that no further savings or benefits from any computer alternative are reliably predictable beyond a few years. Other horizon-limiting inconstancies of the environment include such things as prospective loss of a lease on business property or planned expansions, relocations, or shutdowns.

E5. A plant is expected to operate for five more years and then shut down. Various projects are available that will save operating and/or maintenance costs for the plant. Define the planning horizon.

Obviously, $n = 5$ years.

Benefits from an alternative will cease either when the environment changes or when the assets created by the investment wear out or are used up, whichever occurs earlier. A planning horizon reflecting these considerations is called an *economic life*. Economic life can sometimes be estimated, independently of estimating its deterioration and obsolescence aspects, by examining the history of previous investments considered comparable. A variation on obsolescence is pure uncertainty; the protagonist may simply doubt ability to estimate long-term advantages or disadvantages because the future is considered unpredictable.

E6. A plant will probably operate for 20 or 30 years, but beyond 8 years the analyst does not estimate any particular differences between alternatives. There is one exception: the building that is part of alternative G will still be worth $40,000. Define the horizon and suggest how to handle alternative G.

The horizon should be n = 8 years, with a salvage value of $40,000 at time 8 for alternative G.

Example E6 illustrates the use of salvage values to represent the effects of all consequences beyond time n. Consider an alternative for which cash flows are estimated for times $\{0, 1, \ldots, n, \ldots, m\}$. We can show that the worth is easily expressed in cash flows that do not extend beyond time n by adding a salvage value at time n equal to the worth at n of all later cash flows:

$$P = \sum_{t=0}^{m} A_t \beta^t = \sum_{t=0}^{n} A_t \beta^t + \sum_{t=n+1}^{m} A_t \beta^t \tag{5-1}$$

The second term on the right is

$$\sum_{t=n+1}^{m} A_t \beta^t = \beta^n \sum_{t=n+1}^{m} A_t \beta^{t-n}$$

Note that the last sum is the worth at time n of the cash flows at times $\{n+1, n+2, \ldots,$

m} (see Eq. 2-4 of Chapter 2, where the meanings of symbols m and n are interchanged). We define that sum as the *salvage value* S_n:

$$S_n = \sum_{t=n+1}^{m} A_t \beta^{t-n} = \sum_{\tau=1}^{m-n} A_{\tau + n} \beta^{\tau} \tag{5-2}$$

where the second form of the sum, with the change of index variable to τ, shows that the salvage value is what on the τ scale will be the *present* worth of the cash flows that occur after $t = n$, $\tau = 0$.

Thus we have a salvage-value rule for the treatment of consequences beyond the planning horizon: *determine the worth at time n of beyond-horizon consequences, and treat this worth as a salvage value at time n.* From Eqs. 5-1 and 5-2:

$$P = \sum_{t=0}^{n} A_t \beta^t + \beta^n S_n \tag{5-3}$$

The philosophy of Eq. 5-3 is very widely used to simplify decision problems of many kinds. For example, an artificial-intelligence program that plays the game of chess analyzes the possibilities n moves ahead; then a value is estimated for each alternative board situation remaining after the nth move ahead. This value substitutes for the huge tree of possibilities remaining for further moves. As example E6 showed, the salvage-value approach is easy to apply. It is quite useful (see Section 5.2) for replacement problems and problems where different alternatives have different economic lives.

Infinite-horizon analysis, with $n \to \infty$, can be useful not only where economic lives are extremely long, but where consequences decay with time or are cyclic. First, let us note the oddity of the "full" salvage value; if net returns of a simple investment project are the equal payment series $\{A_t = A: t = 1,...,n\}$ and the salvage value is the "full" salvage value $S_n = A/i$, then from Eq. 5-3

$$P = \sum_{t=0}^{n} A \beta^t + \frac{\beta^n A}{i}$$

$$= A_0 + A\left(\frac{1 - \beta^n}{i}\right) + \frac{\beta^n A}{i}$$

$$= A_0 + \frac{A}{i} = -I + \frac{A}{i}$$

where $I = -A_0$ is the investment. This is the same present worth as if returns continued forever. Note that if the salvage value of an asset is always A/i, P is independent of the time the asset is planned to be sold; this is often the case for such assets as land or an entire enterprise.

E7. A timber tract yields $30,000 of annual operating profit. Determine its value to a prospective buyer whose MARR is $i = 12\%$. Suppose it can be acquired for 90% of this value, and the buyer assumes that sooner or later it can be sold for 100% of

this value. Show that if the buyer sells the tract when it can first be sold for 100% value, the present worth of the investment is independent of that time.

For $A = 30,000$ and $i = 0.12$, the value of the infinite-horizon stream of operating profits is $A/i = \underline{\$250,000}$.

If the acquisition price is 90% of this, or $225,000, and the tract is held for n years, then the present worth of buying the tract, operating it for n years, and selling it at time n for full value is [with $i = 0.12$, $\beta = 1/(1 + i)$]:

$$P = -225,000 + 30,000\left(\frac{1 - \beta^n}{i}\right) + 250,000\beta^n$$

But recall that $250,000 = 30,000/i$ where $i = 0.12$. Hence

$$P = -225,000 + 30,000/i - 30,000\beta^n/i + 30,000\beta^n/i$$
$$= -225,000 + 250,000 = \underline{\$25,000}$$

The present worth is identical no matter when the tract is sold.

For a deteriorating asset that operates until no longer profitable and then is abandoned, or for an investment whose benefits decline with time, the demands of simplicity and understandability have often caused engineers to use an approximate equal-payment-series model, accounting for decay with either a reduction of net returns A or a reduction of the time horizon n. As the following concrete example shows, an infinite-horizon geometric decay model is probably simpler, more understandable, and more accurate.

E8. An electric power utility is designing a substation to serve a new industrial park. Customers' induction motors will depress the power factor. This will be mitigated by a bank of capacitors that will be included in the substation and by a billing charge that will encourage customers to balance their electrical loads. Five years ago a similar bank of capacitors was installed in a similar substation, and the annual contributions of the capacitors to the operating profit of the substation were estimated to be as follows (in thousands, with time in years):

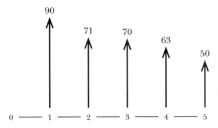

The decline is due to customers' gradual balancing of their own loads. The new substation is expected to show similar performance for a horizon of 10 years. The interest rate is 10%. Compare three approximations of present worth: (1) $90,000

for a shortened number of years, (2) a reduced equal-payment series for 10 years, and (3) an infinite-horizon geometric decline.

A panel of three registered engineers was asked for a consensus for (1), (2), (3), and an "ideal" method.

Approximation (1): They agreed that if the equal-payment series had to have a level of \$90,000, it should go for 5 years. (A smaller n would account for the greater importance of the earlier cash flows, but a larger n would account for the level remaining above zero at time 10.) The resulting worth is

$$P^{(1)} = 90\left(\frac{1 - \beta^5}{i}\right) = \underline{\underline{\$341,171}}$$

Approximation (2): They agreed that if the equal-payment series had to have a length of 10 years, its level should be \$50,000. The resulting present worth is

$$P^{(2)} = 50\left(\frac{1 - \beta^{10}}{i}\right) = \underline{\underline{\$307,228}}$$

Approximation (3): They agreed that an infinite-horizon geometric decline should have a_0 and g such that it would have a cash flow of \$90,000 the first year and \$45,000 the fifth year. The resulting calculations are

$$(1 + g)^4 = \frac{45}{90} \Rightarrow g = -0.159103585$$

$$a_0 = 90(1 + g)^{-1} = 107.02864$$

$$P^{(3)} = \frac{a_0}{s} \qquad \text{where} \qquad s = \frac{(1 + i)}{(1 + g) - 1}$$

$$= \underline{\underline{\$347,351}}$$

"Ideal" method: They agreed that the "ideal" method was a geometric decline with a horizon of 10 years. They agreed that the best way to use the data was to fit a_0 and g by linear regression:

$$A_t = a_0(1 + g)^t$$
$$\ln A_t = \ln a_0 + t\ln(1 + g)$$

This straight line has intercept $\ln a_0$ and slope $\ln(1 + g)$. Given the five data points of $t = \{1, \ldots, 5\}$ and $\ln A_t = \{\ln 90, \ln 71, \ln 70, \ln 63, \ln 50\}$, the least-squares intercept and slope are 4.601764 and -0.12951185. These values give $g = -0.1214758$ and $a_0 = 99.6599667$. The present worth is

$$P = a_0\left(\frac{1 - \alpha^{10}}{s}\right) \qquad \text{where} \qquad s = \frac{(1 + i)}{(1 + g) - 1} \qquad \text{and} \qquad \alpha = \frac{1}{(1 + s)}$$

$$= \underline{\underline{\$353,579}}$$

Various engineers would make various approximations, but for this problem it appeared to be easier and more accurate to guess an appropriate point through which the cash-flow series would pass (45 at time 5) rather than an appropriate horizon or an appropriate average amount for an equivalent nondeclining cash-flow series.

It is believed that in practice many engineers either shorten the horizon or use a reduced cash-flow amount to offset the effect of using an equal-payment series when a declining geometric series would be more realistic. An ideal correction would simply be to estimate the rate of decline and increase the interest rate accordingly.

If there is no basis for a finite horizon other than the decline, an infinite-horizon model can be used. This amounts to substituting $1/s$ for the "pain" factor. *For every finite-horizon equal-payment series, there is an equivalent infinite-horizon geometric gradient series.* The equal-payment series $\{A: t = 1,..., n\}$ has present worth $A(P/A\ i,n)$; there exists a substitute interest rate such that the geometric gradient series $\{A(1 + g)^t: t = 1,...,\infty\}$, whose present worth is A/s where $s = (1 + i)/[(1 + g) - 1]$, has the same present worth.

Equating present worths of an equal-payment series with its equivalent infinite-horizon geometric gradient series, we have

$$A\left(\frac{1 - \beta^n}{i}\right) = \frac{A}{s}$$

$$s = \frac{i}{1 - \beta^n} = \frac{1}{(P/A\ i,n)} \tag{5-4}$$

Conversely, if a cash-flow set has present worth A/s, there is a family of equivalent finite-horizon equal-payment series cash flow sets having amount A and $(P/A\ i,n)$ factor $1/s$. At a given interest rate i, assuming $i < s$, the horizon of the equivalent set is

$$n = \frac{\ln[1 - (i/s)]}{\ln \beta} \tag{5-5}$$

E9. Determine the infinite-horizon substitute interest rate for an equal payment series that has horizon $n = 10$ years, under interest rate $i = 10\%$.

From Eq. 5-4:

$$s = \frac{1}{(P/A\ 10\%,10)} = \underline{\underline{16.2745\%}}$$

E10. A company whose MARR is $i = 12\%$ uses a horizon of $n = 8$ years, not because projects suddenly die at age 8, but rather so that their geometric decay with time can thus be accounted for. Under this policy, what actual cash flows in the first three years are assumed for a project whose returns are estimated as $6000 per year?

The present worth at $i = 12\%$ of 8 years of $6000 annual savings is

$$P = 6000\left(\frac{1 - \beta^8}{i}\right) = \$29,805.8386$$

The present worth of a geometric gradient series of cash flows with an infinite horizon is (Eq. 3-8 with $n \rightarrow \infty$)

$$P = \frac{a_0}{s}$$

If the formula $6000/s$ is to give this value of P, then (of course, s can be computed from Eq. 5-4 without evaluating P)

$$s = \frac{6000}{P} = 0.20130284$$

Given s and i, from Chapter 3 we recall the gradient g is

$$g = \frac{1 + i}{1 + s} - 1 = -0.06767889$$

The geometric gradient series cash flows are $\{a_0(1 + g)^t\} = \{6000(1 + g), 6000(1 + g)^2, 6000(1 + g)^3, \text{etc.}\} = \underline{\$5593.93}, \underline{\$5215.34}, \underline{\$4862.37}, \text{etc.}$

For $i = 12\%$, an infinite-horizon geometric series having these first three cash-flow amounts has the same present worth at s as the equal-payment series of $6000 per year for 8 years has at i.

Figure 5-1 allows approximate selection of an infinite-horizon substitute interest rate for representing a finite-horizon equal-payment series. It also can be used to determine approximate rate of return for simple investment projects.

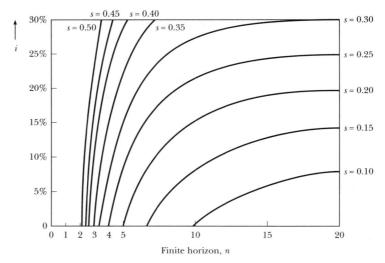

FIGURE 5-1. Substitute interest rate to convert finite equal-payment series to infinite horizon.

E11. Determine the rate of return of this discrete simple investment project:

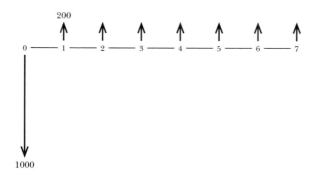

$P = -1000 + 200(P/A\ i,7)$. $P = 0 \Rightarrow (P/A\ i,7) = 5 \Rightarrow s = 1/5 = 0.20$. From Figure 5-1, for $n = 7$ and $s = 0.20$, we read $i \cong 9.2\%$. The rate of return is more accurately 9.196%.

5.1.3.2 Comparison of Alternatives: Relative and Incremental Worth   Costs and benefits of alternatives are expressed as cash flows. Costs and benefits for all alternatives in a given decision problem must be on the same basis. A cash-flow set is *project centered* if it is defined so that there is a do-nothing alternative whose worth is zero. The do-nothing alternative is often implicit, and it amounts to ignoring the opportunity and continuing with the ordinary course of business. When cash-flow sets are absolute, the worth of an alternative represents the wealth added to the enterprise and measures how much better it is to accept the opportunity than to do nothing.

E12. A dry-cleaning plant can purchase new machines at a cost of $60,000 to reduce cleaning-fluid losses by $8000 per year for 10 years (alternative A). Alternatively (alternative B) the plant can modify existing machines at a cost of $10,000 to reduce cleaning-fluid losses by $1200 per year for the same number of years. The plant normally earns a 12% ROR on capital investments. Make a decision.

$$P^{(A)} = -60,000 + 8000(P/A\ 12\%,10) = \underline{-\$14,798.22}$$

$$P^{(B)} = -10,000 + 1200(P/A\ 12\%,10) = \underline{-\$3,219.73}$$

From the context, there is an implicit do-nothing alternative whose present worth is zero. Choose do-nothing, because it has the greatest (least negative) worth.

As the example illustrates, the rule for project-centered cash flows is to choose the alternative with greatest positive worth, or choose do-nothing if no alternative has positive worth.

A cash-flow set is *environment centered* if there is no do-nothing alternative or its worth is not zero.

E13. For the alternative opportunities in Example E12, assume the plant has been spending $13,000 per year for cleaning fluid, and that the savings for alterna-

tives A and B are described as reducing the annual cleaning-fluid cost to $5000 or to $11,800, respectively. Choose.

$$P^{(A)} = -60,000 - 5000(P/A \ 12\%,10) = -\$88,251.11$$

$$P^{(B)} = -10,000 - 11,800(P/A \ 12\%,10) = -\$76,672.63$$

Given the environment-centered costs, it is necessary to define an explicit do-nothing alternative (alternative zero), whereby no capital expenditure is made and the cleaning-fluid expenditures remain as is:

$$P^{(0)} = -13,000(P/A \ 12\%,10) = -\$73,452.90.$$

So again, choose do-nothing, because it has the greatest (least negative) worth.

As this example illustrates, *environment-centered* cash flows require do-nothing alternatives to be made explicit. Also, the worths have only relative meanings.

A common type of environment-centered analysis is *cost minimization*, which is often used for evaluating bids. Example E13, with algebraic signs reversed, would be an example of cost minimization: it minimizes the present worth of the sum of costs for cleaning fluid (including investment in fluid-saving).

All cash-flow sets are relative, because there is always some sort of status quo against which all alternatives are measured. To demonstrate this we can expand the situation of Examples E12 and E13 to include other benefits and costs of the basic system.

E14. **The plant of Examples E12 and E13 has been spending not only the mentioned $13,000 per year for cleaning fluid, but also $31,000 per year in other costs; the revenue brought in by these operations is $58,000 per year. Choose.**

The crucial thing to notice here is that the scope of the decision has been expanded. The problem now is a project-centered one in which the alternatives are to invest $60,000 and operate at low fluid consumption (A), invest $10,000 and operate at moderate fluid consumption (B), invest $0 and operate at high fluid consumption (0), or—the expanded problem's additional alternative—abandon the dry-cleaning operations (X). The newly-mentioned costs and revenues are assumed to be independent of the investments; otherwise the previous examples would have wrongly omitted some decision-relevant consequences. Note that the new status quo is not to operate the dry cleaning plant at all, so that the new option X is the true do-nothing alternative:

$$P^{(A)} = -60,000 - 5000(P/A12\%,10) - 31,000(P/A12\%,10) + 58,000(P/A12\%,10)$$
$$\qquad\qquad \text{(investment)} \qquad \text{(fluid costs)} \qquad \text{(other costs)} \qquad \text{(revenues)}$$

$$\qquad = \$64,304.91$$

$$P^{(B)} = -10,000 - 11,800(P/A \ 12\%,10) -$$
$$\qquad\qquad\qquad\qquad 31,000(P/A \ 12\%,10) + 58,000(P/A \ 12\%,10)$$

$$\qquad = \$75,883.39$$

$$P^{(0)} = -31,000(P/A \ 12\%,10) - 13,000(P/A \ 12\%,10) + 58,000(P/A \ 12\%,10)$$

$$= \$79,103.12$$
$$P^{(X)} = \underline{\underline{\$0}}$$

Since the present worth of the true do-nothing alternative is zero, the expanded problem formulation meets the requirements of being *project centered*, and the alternative X could have been left as implicit (not specifically mentioned). *Choose* 0, because it has greatest worth.

Note that all valid formulations yield the same decision; in the above examples, neither of the fluid-saving alternatives was worthwhile, and the one called A was always $11,578.49 worse than the one called B (verify by computing $P^{(A)} - P^{(B)}$ from each of the three examples).

A convenient formulation is that of *incremental* cash flows. If alternative A has cash flows $\{A_t^{(A)}\}$ and alternative B has cash flows $\{A_t^{(B)}\}$, then the incremental alternative A − B has cash flows $\{A_t^{(A)} - A_t^{(B)}\}$, which are differences that are often easier to define directly than to define by subtraction; for example, an add-on may cost $50,000 "extra" and give $6800 "extra" annual savings, as in this now-familiar example.

E15. Compared to the alternative B, the dry-cleaning plant of example E12 can spend an additional $50,000 to increase the annual savings by $6800 to implement alternative A. Determine the present worth of the incremental alternative A − B.

$$P^{(A-B)} = -50000 + 6800(P/A\ 12\%,10) = \underline{-\$11,578.48}$$

The present worth of an incremental investment A − B is denoted $P^{(A-B)}$ and is interpreted as the present worth of implementing A instead of B, forgoing the returns and avoiding the costs of B:

Present worth of incremental investment A − B:

$$P^{(A-B)} = P^{(A)} - P^{(B)} \tag{5-6}$$

Equation 5-6 follows directly from the definition of present worth and is valid regardless of the basis—project-centered or environment centered—used in defining alternatives. Excluding the convenient practice of changing signs to represent costs as positive in cost minimization problems, *all valid formulations of a given decision problem have the same incremental worths, and have worths of alternatives that differ from one formulation to another only in an additive constant.* The additive constant that distinguishes various project-centered and environment-centered formulations from one another is the worth of a cost or a benefit that is the same for all alternatives and that hence can validly be either included or omitted.

E16. Identify and interpret the additive constant that distinguishes the formulation of Examples E12 and E13.

The present worth of the $13,000 current annual expenses for cleaning fluid is included in E13 and excluded in E12. This worth is

$$-13,000(P/A\ 12\%,10) = \underline{-\$73,452.90}$$

Note that the corresponding worths in the two examples vary by this amount.

If there are K alternatives in a decision problem, there are

$$\binom{K}{2} = \frac{K!}{(K-2)!2!}$$

different incremental worths. But an incremental-worth decision problem can be solved by evaluating only K worths. The alternatives must be ordered. The order of *increasing required investment* is conceptually clear, because it allows interpretation of the successive increments in terms of "spending x more to gain y more." (Any ordering that starts with an acceptable candidate works equally well mathematically.) There must be either an explicit feasible do-nothing alternative or an alternative known to be acceptable, and this alternative must be initially designated as the acceptable candidate. The incremental-worth decision procedure is as follows:

Incremental-worth decision procedure:
. . . .

1. Given the current acceptable alternative "+", identify the next unevaluated increment N; if none, stop, designating "+" as the final choice.
2. Determine the increment worth of N over "+". If the worth is positive, designate N as the new "+". Go to 1.

E17. **The decision problem of Examples E12 to E16 can be formulated in incremental terms as follows:**

Alternatives in increasing-investment order after initial acceptable candidate:

Alternative	Investment	
0 (continue as is)	0	initial acceptable alternative
X (abandon)	0	
B	$10,000	
A	$60,000	

Choose the best alternative by incremental-worth analysis.

Recall $i = 12\%$, $n = 10$ years, and cost data from previous examples.

Step 1: The next unevaluated increment is X − 0.

Step 2: Compared to 0, the X alternative avoids the $13,000 annual fluid costs and the $31,000 other annual costs, and abandons the $58,000 annual revenue:

$$P^{(X-0)} = (13,000 + 31,000 - 58,000)(P/A\ 12\%,10)$$
$$= \underline{-\$79,103.12}$$

This worth is not positive; 0 continues as the current acceptable alternative.

Step 1: The next unevaluated increment is B − 0 (*not* B − X).

Step 2: Compared to 0, the B alternative reduces annual fluid costs by $1200 and requires a time-zero investment of $10,000:

$$P^{(B-0)} = -10,000 + 1200(P/A\ 12\%,10) = \underline{-\$3219.73}$$

This worth is not positive; 0 continues as the current acceptable alternative.

Step 1: The next unevaluated increment is A − 0 (*not* A − B).

Step 2: Compared to 0, the A alternative reduces annual fluid costs by $8000 and requires a time-zero investment of $60,000:

$$P^{(A-0)} = -60,000 + 8000(P/A\ 12\%,10) = \underline{-\$14,798.22}$$

This worth is not positive; 0 continues as the current acceptable alternative.

Step 1: There is no unevaluated increment. <u>The final choice is 0.</u>

Note that in incremental-worth analysis, if the alternatives are numbered $1, 2, \ldots,$ K in increasing-investment order, it is not generally possible to know in advance that the needed incremental worths will be $P^{(2-1)}$, $P^{(3-2)}$, $P^{(4-3)}$, and so on. For example, if $P^{(2-1)} < 0$, then $P^{(3-1)}$ is the next incremental worth to be evaluated, not $P^{(3-2)}$.

5.1.3.3 Comparison of Alternatives: Incremental Rate of Return

An obsolete procedure that has intuitive appeal is the *incremental rate-of-return* method. It is valid for a set of alternatives that are all *investment* alternatives (P decreases with i for every rate of return $i = i^*$ that may arise during the procedure).

Incremental-ROR decision procedure:

1. Given the current acceptable alternative "+", identify the next unevaluated increment N; if none, stop, designating "+" as the final choice.
2. Determine the rate of return of N over "+". If the rate of return exceeds MARR, designate N as the new "+". Go to 1.

E18. Apply the incremental-ROR procedure to the decision problem of Examples E12 to E16.

MARR is $i = 12\%$. Recall data from previous examples. The initial acceptable alternative is 0.

Step 1: The next unevaluated increment is X − 0.

Step 2: Compared to 0, the X alternative has worth:

$$P^{(X-0)} = (13,000 + 31,000 - 58,000)(P/A\ i,10)$$
$$= -14,000(P/A\ i,10)$$

$$P^{(X-0)} = 0 \Rightarrow \underline{\underline{i^* = -\infty}}$$

This rate of return does not exceed MARR; 0 continues to be the current acceptable alternative.

Step 1: The next unevaluated increment is B − 0.

Step 2: Compared to 0, the B alternative has worth:

$$P^{(B-0)} = -10,000 + 1200(P/A\ 12\%,10)$$
$$P^{(B-0)} = 0 \Rightarrow \underline{\underline{i^* = 3.460154\%}}$$

This rate of return does not exceed MARR; 0 continues as the current acceptable alternative.

Step 1: The next unevaluated increment is A − 0.

Step 2: Compared to 0, the A alternative has worth:

$$P^{(A-0)} = -60,000 + 8000(P/A\ 12\%,10)$$
$$P^{(A-0)} = 0 \Rightarrow \underline{\underline{i^* = 5.604464\%}}$$

This rate of return does not exceed MARR; 0 continues as the current acceptable alternative.

Step 1: There is no unevaluated increment. <u>The final choice is 0.</u>

5.1.3.4 Cash-Flow Treatments for Evaluation

We have seen that all cash flows are relative and that all formulations and procedures for comparing worths of alternatives give the same resulting worth-maximizing decision.

Deficiencies in formulation can invalidate comparisons, and the common pitfalls are identified here. Little more can be said about the most basic pitfalls: omitting feasible alternatives by defining the scope and assumptions too narrowly (ignoring feasible do-nothing alternatives is the most common version of this), omitting necessary costs, omitting incidental benefits, and including benefits or costs that are not really consequences of the decision. However, certain pitfalls deserve separate mention: these are the treatment of sunk costs, the treatment of marginal versus total costs, double-counting, and inappropriate linking.

5.1.3.4.1 Treatment of Sunk Costs

No alternative can include undoing an irreversible action. A *sunk cost* is a cost that will occur regardless of the decision, or has already occurred. A *sunk benefit* is a benefit that will occur regardless of the decision, or has already occurred. The rule for treating sunk costs and benefits is to *ignore sunk costs and benefits, or include them in every alternative.*

E19. **A $50,000 conveyor that was expected to save $12,000 per year in warehouse-operation expenditures turns out to operate in such a way that it will only save $2000 per year. Company policy forbids investments having a payback time of more than five years. Should it be abandoned if someone is willing to cart it away for free?**

Ignoring the sunk $50,000 cost, and assuming the only alternatives are to abandon or to continue, the decision problem faced *now* is to save $0 per year (abandon) or save $2000 per year (continue). *Choose to continue.*

E20. A benefit of using contractor A is that this contractor performs thorough site cleanup upon completion of the job. With contractor B it has been necessary to perform a $15,000 cleanup after each past job. For the job whose contract is now being let, contractor A has bid $37,000 and contractor B has bid $34,000. Immediately after this job a major demolition job will be performed on the same site. Which contractor should be chosen?

Assuming the demolition need not start with a cleaned-up site, the cleanup benefit of contractor A is sunk. Unless contractor A can reduce the bid by at least $3000 for being allowed to skip normal cleanup, the bid for contractor B is cheaper.

5.1.3.4.2 Marginal Costs and Economies of Scale

Engineering projects often involve *idle capacity*. For example, just after a major plant expansion there are opportunities for *bottleneck-removal* projects; of all the systems that must work together to produce a product or service, one system may turn out to be the limiting one, so that the production rate of the entire plant can be increased by extra investment in the one limiting system. Spare capacity can usually be found somewhere in any ongoing enterprise: The warehouse is not full, not all employees are utilized to the desired extent, the plant is not operating 24 hours per day, and so on. There are free goods or free services available, and the costs to be used in an engineering economy study should be limited to out-of-pocket costs.

E21. At the Peachtree Door plant, the crew at a workstation that finishes storm doors includes three workers. A door comes to the station, all three workers do their jobs simultaneously, and the door leaves. The tasks are split among the workers so that worker 1 takes 59 seconds per door, worker 2 takes 55 seconds per door, and worker 3 takes 40 seconds per door. As the tasks are currently defined, any naive reassignments of tasks would only make the balance worse. However, Erin Waters has identified a 15-second task that could be added to the procedure for worker 3; doing this task would save money downstream in the process. In her analysis of the task assignment, how many seconds of labor per door should she consider to be a cost in the new procedure?

Worker 3 had $59 - 40 = 19$ seconds of unavoidable idle time per door under the old procedure, and that idle time is a free good. There is no out-of-pocket cost, so she should consider the task as having zero cost.

Since some goods and services are free, cost-accounting records can be misleading as data sources. Consider the story told by Delal Aoki about her first assignment as an engineer in an oil refinery. She was asked to specify insulation for some steam-heated hot-oil storage tanks. After assembling weather records, heat-loss insulation performance formulas, and insulation prices and installation costs, she asked cost accountants for the cost of steam. The steam utilized to heat the tanks was 15-psig steam, which was produced as exhaust from processes that used higher-pressure steam. These procedures went on at an inexorable rate, and there was always enough 15-psig steam to do all the required heating, with extra steam simply vented to the atmosphere. The cost accountants gave her a reasonable figure that had been derived according to a formula whereby 15-psig steam was much less costly than 900-psig steam because it contained much less heat energy per pound of mass. Did she use this cost?

The cost she used was zero, because 15-psig steam was a free good. It would save nothing to insulate a tank; more steam would just be vented to the atmosphere.

Now suppose there was excess steam, available 8000 hours per year, while extra steam would have to be generated for hot-oil heating the remaining 766 hours per year. Then, for 766 hours per year, the cost accounting figure would apply. If overcapacity is intermittent, it is free only part of the time.

In an environment of expanding capacity, utilization of overcapacity may be costly through its hastening of the time when further expenditures are needed.

E22. **Seeing that steam was a nearly free good, Delal Aoki proposed using a steam-turbine driver instead of the usual electric-motor driver for a new pump that was to be installed. This alternative, she believed, would cause a planned boiler expansion program to be undertaken at time $m - 1$ rather than at time m. The expansion would cost H dollars either way. Sketch the cash flows that should be included in the cash-flow set to reflect this aspect of the cost situation for this alternative.**

The cash-flow set is:

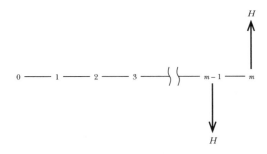

The alternative avoids an expenditure of H dollars at time m and causes an expenditure of H dollars at time $m - 1$.

If idle labor can be used, it has value. For worker 3 in Example E21, it would have been very difficult to do something else useful in the 38-second interval available every two minutes. But when the situation is not a rigid one, idle labor can have up to its full value.

E23. **In an automated carpet mill, where operators watch for a loom to jam and quickly fix it, there are four operators for 19 machines. In a proposal to add a twentieth machine, Angie claims there is no labor cost, because a fifth operator will not be hired until there are 21 machines. Benjy claims the labor cost is that of 20% of an operator. Which is correct?**

Unless the situation is very rigid, Benjy is more nearly correct. To see this, consider the contradiction of adding a twentieth machine and refusing to add a twenty-first machine that would incrementally contribute equally to profits. The operators are there to fix jams, which occur randomly. In attention units per machine, their capacity to fix jams is reduced from 4/19 to 4/20, which is exactly a 5% reduction. If the wage-plus benefits cost per operator exactly offsets the benefit per operator from jam-fixing, then the twentieth machine reduces jam-fixing benefits by an amount equal to 5% of the cost of four operators, or 20% of an operator.

In nearly all situations where labor utilization is somewhat fluid, a person-hour of labor saved or used is worth the wage-plus-benefits cost of a person-hour of labor, without regard for whether a given alternative identifiably causes a worker to be hired or fired. To assume otherwise is to assume that the given alternative is the *only* thing that can change labor requirements. As a further example, consider four new projects that are added to a consulting company's load at the same time, causing the need for one additional clerical worker. If the net profit on each project, before considering clerical labor, is equal to one-half the cost of a clerical worker, which project should be rejected? (None, of course, but if the clerical worker is considered a consequence of only one of the projects, that project will be rejected.)

Cost accounting concepts include the useful one of *fixed* and *variable* costs. The cost $C(x)$ of producing x units of a good or service is considered to consist of two components, f_M dollars and $v_M x$ dollars, where f_M is the *fixed cost* when x is in the range denoted M, and v_M is the *unit variable cost* when x is in the range denoted M:

$$C(x) = f_M + v_M x \qquad x \in M \tag{5-7}$$

Equation 5-7 is applicable at any level of aggregation of cost. Figure 5-2 shows a typical way in which costs are classified in a cost-accounting system. There can be a *fixed price* and a *variable price*; there can be a *fixed total cost* and a *variable total cost*, and so on, down to *fixed direct wages* and *variable direct wages*.

Fixed and variable costs are often cited on a unit basis:

$$u(x) = \frac{C(x)}{x} = \frac{f_M}{x} + v_M \qquad x \in M \tag{5-8}$$

E24. When Prism Packaging Services packages 16,000 copies per day of Word Wonder 5.2, it receives (at no cost) diskettes and books from another enterprise and packages them. Classify each of the following cost items into a node in the cost-accounting structure of Figure 5-2, and also state whether the item is fixed, variable, or has both fixed and variable components.

1. **The bill from the temporary labor service for daily packaging labor.**
2. **The wages and employee benefits for the receiving clerk (there are two receiving clerks during the busiest season).**
3. **The air conditioning and lighting bill.**
4. **The bill for cardboard boxes (one per copy) that hold the diskettes and book.**
5. **The bill for rolls of plastic film (one roll provides shrink-wrap for 240,000 copies).**

Typical Manufacturing Cost-Accounting Structure:

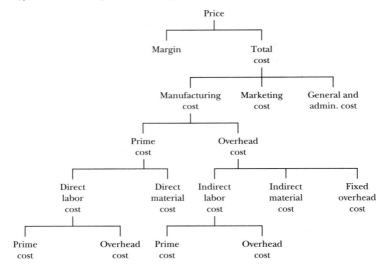

Relation of Cost Accounting Structure to Some General Accounting Quantities:

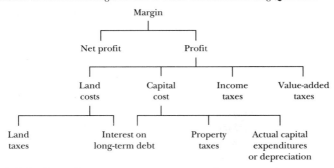

FIGURE 5-2. Typical cost-accounting structure for a manufacturing enterprise.

6. **The bill for separately metered electrical power for the shrink wrap machines.**
7. **Rent for the building.**
8. **Wages and benefits for the president's secretary.**
9. **Wages and benefits for the plant engineer.**
10. **Income taxes.**

1. (daily labor)	"direct labor cost"	variable
2. (receiving clerk)	"indirect labor cost"	fixed
3. (electricity)	"fixed overhead cost"	fixed
4. (boxes)	"direct material"	variable
5. (plastic film)	"direct material"	variable
6. (machine power)	"direct material"	fixed and variable
7. (rent)	"fixed overhead cost"	fixed

8. (pres.'s secretary)   "general and admin. cost"   fixed
9. (plant engineer)   "indirect labor cost"   fixed
10. (income taxes)   not in cost accounting   —

The receiving clerk is indirect rather than direct labor because it is not useful or convenient to match receiving tasks to packaging jobs; the receiving clerk is a fixed cost because the amount paid would not change with modest changes in production rate.

Engineering economy's requirements for estimates of consequences of alternatives are distinct from the historical monitoring and control requirements served by cost accounting procedures. This distinction is so profound that cost-accounting quantities can be more misleading than helpful. Very generally, *if an alternative causes an increase in a level of activity, the decision-relevant cost of the increase is more than the variable cost and less than the fixed-plus-variable cost.* Recall Example E22, in which the value of steam was at issue. We saw first that there could be activity (saving steam by insulating heated tanks) that *did not cause* an increase or decrease in the amount of steam generated, so that steam savings could cause no decision-related benefits. Then we saw that an increase in the usage of steam could cause an increase in fixed costs for boiler capacity; in the example the boiler-capacity expenditures were estimated directly, but an accounting-oriented estimation might have used the difference in the boiler expenditures per pound of steam under the two ranges of steam usage rates. Finally, the increase in steam usage contemplated in the example would eventually (by year $m - 1$) actually require an increase in the amount of steam generated; obviously the out-of-pocket fuel costs for generating the steam, reflected in the cost-accounting variable-cost figure, would apply. This illustrates that an alternative should "pay" for *all* its consequential variable costs, and for the consequential increase in its fixed costs.

E25. A maintenance shop for a widget manufacturer has expenditures per widget shown in cost-accounting records to be "$45,000 per year plus $3.50 per widget." Current production is 150,000 widgets per year. A decision alternative proposes to raise production to 200,000 widgets per year. Determine (1) a lower limit for the annual maintenance cost of the alternative, (2) an upper limit for the annual maintenance cost of the alternative, and (3) an estimated annual maintenance cost of the alternative based on "$55,000 per year plus $3.50 per widget" as the maintenence shop's fixed and variable costs in the production range above 170,000 widgets per year.

In the current range, with Eq. 5-7 expressed in $/yr units, we have $f_M = 45,000$ $/yr, $v_M = 3.50$ $/widget, and $x = 150,000$ widget/yr:

$$45,000 + 3.50(150,000) = \underline{\underline{\$570,000}} \text{ /yr}$$

In the new range, fixed costs can at best (1) stay the same, as they would if the higher production rate put no new load on the shop, or at worst (2) increase in proportion to the production rate, as they would if everything in the shop had zero usable overcapacity and zero economy of scale, or, more realistically (3), increase less than in proportion to the production rate.

1. Considering no increase in fixed cost, the increase in annual maintenance cost would be

$$3.50(200{,}000 - 150{,}000) = \$175{,}000/\text{yr}$$

2. Considering full increase in fixed cost, the increase in annual maintenance cost would be

$$570{,}000(200{,}000/150{,}000) = \$760{,}000/\text{yr}$$

3. Considering the new fixed cost of $55,000 per year, the increase in annual maintenance cost would be the new annual cost minus the old annual cost:

$$[55{,}000 + 3.50(200{,}000)] - [45{,}000 + 3.50(150{,}000)] = 755{,}000 - 570{,}000 = \$185{,}000/\text{yr}$$

Economies of scale occur in a wide range of activities. A human operator can operate a 12-row harvester, or an 18-row harvester that reaps almost 50% more crop per minute. A 45-passenger bus consumes the same fuel as 4 or 5 automobiles, and an automobile can carry 6 passengers while consuming only 10% more fuel than when carrying a single passenger. A pipeline's carrying capacity increases with nearly the square of its diameter, but its cost increases not much more than linearly. An oceangoing ship requires a crew only 15% larger if you double its payload. Almost any coordinated system has some usable overcapacity, so an increase in throughput can be achieved by enlarging less than all its components. There is a "six-tenths rule" that applies approximately to the capacity-versus-cost relationship for a large variety of process-industry equipment such as reactors, distillation columns, pressure vessels, and pumps:

E26. **The "six-tenths rule" says that cost increases as the 0.6 power of capacity. If a 300-horsepower turbine can be purchased for $20,000, what is the approximate cost by this rule of a 500-horsepower turbine?**

The approximate cost is

$$20000\left(\frac{500}{300}\right)^{0.6} = \$27{,}173.10 \cong \$27{,}200$$

The counter to economy of scale is *diminishing returns*—diseconomy of scale or intensity when the scale or intensity gets too large. At a given hydroelectric dam site, for example, nature provided a limit to the power that can be generated; two turbine generators (or one that is $2^{0.6} \cong 1.5$ times larger) may generate more power per dollar of investment than one, but eventually the limit of potential energy is reached and there is no more water to fall through another generator. A rancher can raise beef more cheaply at 1.0 animal per acre than at 0.5, but above 1.5 the grass crop fails and free grass must be supplemented with expensive grain to feed the cattle.

Because of the ubiquity of the interplay of economy of scale and diminishing returns, nearly every project has an optimal or most appropriate scale close to the size or intensity at which a key resource reaches its limit. Accordingly, decision problems do

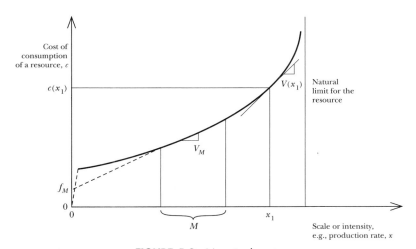

FIGURE 5-3. Marginal cost.

not usually involve alternative scales. The best scale is as big as is natural. Rather, alternatives usually differ in approach or procedure.

Closely related to fixed and variable costs are *marginal, average* and *total costs.* From the discussion of economy of scale and diminishing returns, it is clear that the linear model of fixed and variable costs, which is valid only for a given range, is typically part of a nonlinear relationship such as is illustrated in Figure 5-3. *The marginal cost V(x) for a given resource is the instantaneous slope of the unit cost curve for that resource.* It is not taken from cost accounting records but is estimated directly for output quantities x in a fairly narrow range. For output quantities near a given quantity x_1, which has a corresponding cost c_1, the estimated cost for a different quantity x_2 is

$$c(x_2) \cong c(x_1) + V(x_1)(x_2 - x_1) \tag{5-9}$$

A common mistake is to substitute *average cost* where marginal cost is valid. Average cost $\bar{c}(x)$ is $c(x)/x$.

E27. It has been necessary to add a heat exchanger to cool a mill that is now operating at 135% of its original design capacity. Two alternative versions of a proposed improvement project would (incidentally to their main purpose) slightly increase and slightly decrease the mill throughput, respectively, to 137 and 130 (measured in percent of original capacity). The current cooling cost is $4500 per year, and the cooling cost for a third alternative that runs the mill at 145 has been directly estimated as $5000 per year. Which of the following estimates are more valid?

1. $c(137) = \$4566.67/\text{yr}$ and $c(130) = \$4333.33/\text{yr}$
2. $c(137) = \$4600.00/\text{yr}$ and $c(130) = \$4250.00/\text{yr}$

Using the average cost of $4500/135 = 33.\overline{3}$ \$/yr/unit, the estimated costs of the two alternatives are $137(33.33) = \$4566.67/\text{yr}$ and $130(33.33\beta) = \$4333.33/\text{yr}$.

Using $(5000\text{-}4500)/(145\text{-}135) = 50$ \$/yr/unit as the estimate of $V(x)$, the estimated costs of the two alternatives are, from Eq. 5-9:

$$c(137) = c(135) + V(x)(137 - 135) = 4500 + 50(2) = \$4600/\text{yr}$$
$$c(130) = c(135 + V(x)(130 - 135) = \$4250/\text{yr}$$

The estimates denoted (2) are more valid.

The principle of using marginal rather than average costs in estimating cost differences is a simple one, and it is probably misused intentionally more than unintentionally. A diet charlatan convinced clients that eating 15% less would cause 15% weight loss. A "financial advisor" told clients in the 30% income-tax bracket, who were paying a total of 23% of their income in taxes, that their after-tax earnings would be 77% of total earnings; when challenged by a client who realized he would keep only 70% of each *additional* dollar in earnings, the "advisor" indignantly replied, "How can you consider your January earnings to be tax-free, and your December and stock earnings to be taxed at 30%?"

5.1.3.4.3 Double-Counting

Just as alternatives must form an exhaustive, feasible, mutually exclusive set, there are similar logical requirements for costs and for benefits for each alternative.

Costs must be exhaustive, unavoidable, and exclusive. It is easy to fail to include costs that have to do with *offsite work* or *infrastructure.* Engineering economy is a branch of micro-economics; we assume or estimate a given environment for a project and focus on one project or one group of projects at a time. Since we do not perform macroeconomics analysis to study the dynamics of the economic environment and how a project may influence its own economic climate, it is important that we at least consider offsite work and infrastructure—elements that might seem to be outside the project.

E28. A project on a factory floor involves some new raw materials that must be received and stored, greater use of some raw materials already used in the plant, and a new finished product to be stored and shipped. Name some offsite and infrastructure costs to be considered.

Besides the need for utility hookups (power, air, water, data connections) at or adjacent to the project's facilities, and the possibility that it may reduce local floor access, interfere with sightlines, and the like, the statement implies offsite costs in receiving, shipping, and warehousing: some improvements may need to be made in shipping and receiving docks, and in the warehouse, and in material handling between the warehouse and the factory floor.

Given an exhaustive consideration of offsite and infrastructure matters, there is the decision between *direct costing* and *overhead costing.* When installation of a new compressor is being considered, for example, the direct-costing approach might involve estimating all the costs of adding to the electrical distribution system, in which case the appropriate cost of electrical power should *exclude any fixed-cost portion that reflects overhead costs for the items treated specifically.* The overhead-costing approach might involve ignoring all distribution-system costs; the project would "pay" for the compressor's motor controller and hookup, and the full fixed-plus-variable cost of electrical power would be used.

E29. **The project of Example E28 has been estimated to require specific throughputs and inventory levels of several materials and products. Inventory holding and handling costs have been established, with fixed and variable components. It is known that this project's additional load will trigger remodeling of the shipping staging area and installation of more space-efficient racks in part of the warehouse. How much of these remodeling and installation costs should be ascribed to the project if the analysis uses full fixed-plus-variable inventory holding and handling charges?**

None; to "pay" for capacity both directly and through overhead would be double-counting. Costs must be mutually exclusive.

Some side effects that often are neither reflected in overhead charges nor considered directly are loss of flexibility, pilferage, noise, safety, and pollution. The extent to which these should be considered depends on *conservation* policies of the enterprise. Conservation policies also determine the extent of completeness of offsite and infrastructure costing. An enterprise can have a conservative policy with respect to some resources or qualities and a liberal one with respect to others.

Consider the issue of electrical distribution for the compressor mentioned earlier. If the electrical distribution system is considered highly *demand-dynamic* and *substitute-inflexible*, a highly conservative policy might be chosen by which the compressor project should "pay" all costs necessary to restore the electrical distribution system to its former overcapacity and flexibility. *Under a highly conservative policy, full fixed-plus-variable costing is used if costing is done by the overhead approach, and total-restoration costs are estimated if costing is done by the direct approach.* This would be reasonable if the enterprise sees a dynamic demand, so that at any time there may be an attractive or necessary opportunity to use *all* of the system's current level of flexibility and overcapacity, and if (as is reasonable for electric power) there is no alternative resource that could be substituted if a sudden or large demand occurs.

The opposite stance is a *liberal* conservation policy, appropriate when a resource or quality is considered *demand-static* or *substitute-flexible*. For example, the new compressor may be the only major new power user contemplated, or it may be easily possible to drive the next compressor with a steam turbine instead of electricity. In such a case the enterprise may have a liberal conservation policy that regards the distribution system's current overcapacity and flexibility as a free good. *Under a highly liberal conservation policy, variable-only costing is used if costing is done by the overhead approach, and infrastructure costs are ignored if costing is done by the direct approach.*

E30. **In a fairly quiet corner of a noisy truck-assembly plant, a noisy spot welding robot was installed. The plant manager insisted it be moved, for two reasons: it was too noisy, and it cut off the view of a workstation from its supervisor. The engineer who had chosen the robot and its location noted that the new location was an already-noisy one (but the robot would not bring its noise level above the established limit), and that several supervisors had views of their workstations that were already obstructed. What side effects and policies had come in to conflict here?**

The plant manager apparently had a *more conservative* policy than the engineer realized, with respect to two qualities: *noise and sightlines*. (A highly liberal policy would consider quiet and unrestricted views as overcapacities that were free goods until exhausted.)

Just as costs must be exhaustive, unavoidable, and exclusive, *benefits* must be *exhaustive, otherwise unobtainable,* and *exclusive*. It is easy to fail to include benefits that have to do with esthetics, infrastructure, flexibility, noise, safety, and pollution. The estimation and treatment of hard-to-quantify benefits will be covered in Chapter 7. To the extent that benefits are simply negative costs, or savings, the issues of exhaustiveness, exclusiveness, direct or overhead costing, and conservation have already been discussed.

There must be a cause–effect relationship between costs and benefits. Any costs (negative cash flows) that could be avoided while reaping the same benefits should be excluded; similarly, any benefits (positive cash flows) that would be obtained without incurring the costs should be excluded.

E31. **Bink Batterly recorded six original songs at Doppler Studio in 1992. They are not enough to fill an album. His manager and producer both urge him to record two "cover songs" (songs already recorded by someone else) to fill out a releasable album, and to make a video of one of the original songs. This would not require any new writing (songwriter's block is the difficulty), and would cost (in addition to the $400,000 already expended) a total of $55,000, of which $20,000 would pay for royalties and recording expenses for the two cover songs, and the remaining $35,000 would produce the video. Describe the decision alternatives, and state what benefits would need to be estimated.**

Of course, by the sunk-cost principle, no alternative would include undoing the $400,000 expenditure. By the requirement that benefits be otherwise unobtainable, we are warned against linking video benefits to album costs, and vice versa.

Making no assumptions about whether video and album benefits are linked, the decision alternatives are

0. Do nothing.
1. Record the cover songs.
2. Produce the video.
3. Record the cover songs and produce the video.

The required benefits to be estimated are

1. The value of the album if there is no video.
2. The value of the video if there is no album.
3. The combined value if there are both the video and the album.

If (as would not actually be the case) the benefits of album and video were unrelated, there would be two *independent* decision problems.

Inclusion of avoidable costs or otherwise-available benefits is sometimes called *unnecessary linkage*. It is manifested not only when projects are inappropriately linked together but when unprofitable add-ons called *riders* are added to profitable alternatives. It is very common, when a large, profitable project is undertaken, for people to be tempted to add smaller pet projects onto it as riders. For example, when a new rubber mill was added to a tire factory, requiring relocation of other mills, the opportunity was seized to thoroughly modernize the mill area to include amenities that could not have otherwise been justified; since approval of such details as the esthetics of an alarm-display panel was handled at a much lower level than approval of the overall project, and the benefits but not the costs of such details would touch the low-level employees, money was inevitably wasted. (That said, it should be remarked that every experienced engineer can recount situations in which the only way to get needed things done was to bypass approval channels.)

E32. There are 10 printing presses at Czech Cheque, and 8 of them are operated on a typical production day. A project to automate the delivery of paper to the presses will cost $40,000 and will save $12,000 of operator time per year for 6 years. The savings are due to operators' no longer needing to get up and fetch paper between runs. Since operators will be sitting longer, 10 new ergonomic chairs are provided. They cost $240 each (already included in the cited project cost), and will last 6 years, and operator comfort will be improved to an extent considered to be worth $75 per year per operator. Given a 15% interest rate, are the 10 chairs worthwhile?

Since only 8 presses are operated on a typical production day, a *rider* has been snuck in, in that the need for the two additional chairs is questionable. Let p_9 and p_{10} be the proportion of days that 9 and 10 presses are in use, respectively. The annual benefit for 10 chairs is $8(75)(1 - p_9 - p_{10}) + 9(75)p_9 + 10(75)p_{10} = 600 + 75p_9 + 150p_{10}$. We write the overall present worth for 10 chairs:

$$P^{(10)} = -40,000 + (12,000 + 600 + 75p_9 + 150p_{10})(P/A\ 15\%,6)$$

Define alternatives 9 and 8, in which 9 and 8 chairs are purchased, and write their present worths:

$$P^{(9)} = -39,760 + (12,000 + 600 + 75p_9 + 75p_{10})(P/A\ 15\%,6)$$
$$P^{(8)} = -39,520 + (12,000 + 600)(P/A\ 15\%,6) = \underline{\$8164.48}$$

We see that the project with 8 chairs is worthwhile. We can determine the present worth with no chairs:

$$P^{(0)} = -37,600 + 12,000(P/A\ 15\%,6) = \underline{\$7813.79}$$

Since $P^{(8)} > P^{(0)}$ we know 8 chairs is better than no chairs.

Now for 9 chairs to be better than 8 chairs, $P^{(9)} > P^{(8)}$:

$$-39,760 + (12,000 + 600 + 75p_9 + 75p_{10})(P/A\ 15\%,6) > 8164.48$$

which implies $p_9 + p_{10} > \underline{0.84556}$.

But if there are "typically" only 8 presses in operation, we know $p_9 + p_{10} < 0.5$. Hence <u>9 chairs cannot be better than 8 chairs</u>, and it is obvious as well that <u>10 chairs cannot be optimal</u>.

When an alternative saves money by reducing the consumption of a resource, it may offer the opportunity to increase the production rate. This occurs only when the production rate is limited by availability of this resource. To avoid double-counting, remember that a resource-consumption savings can cause benefits due to *reduced consumption at existing production, or increased production at existing resource consumption, but not both.* Only rarely is the latter benefit—increased production—the operative one; in such cases the project should be clearly recognized as a "bottleneck removal" project in its intent.

E33. **At the Peachtree Door plant, Erin Waters redesigned tasks at a storm door assembly workstation and reduced the cycle time from 59 seconds per door to 56 seconds per door. The station operates 7.5 hours per day, 260 days per year. The station adds a value of $1.32 per door. Wages-plus-benefits labor cost at the station averages $66 per hour. Determine the annual benefit from this reduction in cycle time.**

An invalid but reasonable-seeming approach is to estimate the benefits of increased production. When the cycle time is c seconds per door, the annual production rate is

$$\frac{7.5(260)}{c/3600} = \frac{7,020,000}{c} \text{ doors per year}$$

Thus the benefit per year, at $1.32 value added per door, might seem to be

$$1.32\left(\frac{7,020,000}{56} - \frac{7,020,000}{59}\right) = \$8413.80/yr$$

Note that the wages-plus-benefits does not enter into the above calculations, because the same labor is assumed.

The more valid approach is to estimate the labor savings for the same production rate, which is $7,020,000/59 = 118.983$ doors per year. The labor cost goes from $66 per hour to $66(56/59) = \$62.6440678$ per hour. Thus the annual benefit is

$$\left[66 - 66\left(\frac{56}{59}\right)\right](7.5)(260) = \underline{\underline{\$6544.07/yr}}$$

Note that the value-added figure does not enter into the calculation, because the same production rate is assumed. Unless the reduction in cycle time will actually cause more doors to be produced and sold, this benefit estimation is the valid one.

5.1.4 Interest Rate and MARR

Worth evaluations to select among alternatives are meaningful only when they use a meaningful interest rate. We have seen that the project centered worth of a cash-flow set is the amount of a windfall or increase in wealth that is *equivalent,* at the interest rate, to the cash-flow set. The concept of equivalence assumes existence of a surrogate banker that stands ready to convert a cash-flow set to its worth. This requires the *surrogate banker* to lend and borrow arbitrary amounts at arbitrary times, both charging and paying interest, when required, at the given interest rate. We have seen (Section 2.8.1) that having a fairly flexible ordinary course of business or being either a chronic debtor or a chronic creditor does provide a financial environment close to the ideal of having a surrogate banker. We have informally introduced the minimal attractive rate of return (MARR) and have identified it as the interest rate charged and paid by the surrogate banker, so that worth could be interpreted as increase in wealth.

However, worth evaluation is more robust and general than the above assumptions imply. *Whether or not a decision protagonist enjoys financial flexibility anywhere near that of having a surrogate banker, worth evaluation usefully clarifies alternatives.* We will now operationally define MARR and use it as a basis for a weaker but more general interpretation of worth.

Operational Definition of MARR:

The minimal attractive rate of return (MARR) is the interest rate chosen such that, under local circumstances and assumptions, a project having positive worth is attractive.

"Attractive" means that the project should be undertaken unless it is infeasible or there exists a feasible, mutually exclusive alternative that has greater worth.

"Having positive worth" means that a project-centered cash-flow set that represents the project has positive worth at MARR.

The restriction to "local circumstances and assumptions" means that MARR can be "tuned" to a specific set of decisions or estimation practices or assumptions about inflation, future business conditions, or anything else. Section 6.2 in the next chapter is devoted to methods for choosing appropriate values of MARR for specific situations.

As will be seen in Section 6.2, MARR can be quite different (usually greater) than the rate of return actually earned in the ordinary course of business, or than the interest rate charged and paid by whatever serves approximately as a surrogate banker. Reasons for this discrepancy abound: As Chapter 6 will discuss, scarcity of capital may restrict attention to the most efficient projects, so that the rate of return of project X becomes MARR if there is enough capital to invest in X and in all investment projects more efficient than X, but not in any projects less efficient than X. Even when scarcity of capital is not an issue, MARR may be tuned to allow cash-flow sets to be estimated ignoring inflation, or ignoring risk (especially geometric risk, Section 8.4), or ignoring taxes (Chapter 10), or even being subject to chronic optimism.

E34. N. J. Neary has to approve all capital appropriations requests for the controls division of a manufacturing company. He is told that investment proposals for

projects having rates of return of at least 14% should be accepted. A typical investment project is of the discrete simple-investment form with a 15-year horizon and a salvage value one-tenth the investment:

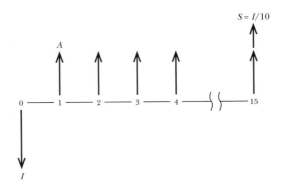

$$P = -I + A(P/A\ i,15) + 0.1I\beta^{15}$$

From experience, however, he knows that the people under his supervision, despite guidance, habitually underestimate the required investment by 9% and overestimate the annual returns by 8%. What MARR should he publish to his people so that they will send up only truly attractive proposals?

MARR should be i such that $P = 0$ when I and A are the figures estimated by Mr. Neary's people, while the actual worth is zero at $i = 14\%$ for an investment of $I/0.91$ and annual returns of $A/1.08$:

$$P^{(\text{actual})} = -I/0.91 + (A/1.08)(P/A\ 14\%,15) + 0.1(I/0.91)(1/1.14)^{15}$$
$$P^{(\text{actual})} = 0 \Rightarrow A/I = 0.190516826$$

Substituting this actual A/I into the equation solved by Mr. Neary's people:

$$P = 0 = -1 + (A/I)(P/A\ i,15) + 0.1\beta^{15} \Rightarrow i = \underline{17.51470\%}$$

Thus Mr. Neary could publish MARR of 17% or 18%, so that people who overestimate returns and underestimate investments will see $P > 0$ at MARR for projects whose actual worth is positive at 14%.

Tuning MARR as in this example has a futile and circular aura, like setting your watch 10 minutes ahead to fool yourself into being on time. Nevertheless, it has always been true that the audited rates of return on investment for almost any enterprise are chronically several percentage points less than the rates of return considered minimally attractive. Apparently, as in the example, to earn 14% you have to think you will earn 17% or 18%.

Along with our operational definition of MARR as being exactly what its name implies—the rate of return minimally considered attractive—we can offer an operational definition of worth.

> **Operational Definition of Worth:**
> . . . .
> The (project-centered) worth of a project is a scalar measure in monetary units (e.g., dollars) of the project's desirability compared to that of a minimally attractive project.

Note that this operational definition of worth is much weaker than the ideal interpretation of worth as wealth increase. To the question, "How good is this project?" the worth at MARR is not an ideal answer but merely the best single answer routinely available.

5.2 REPLACEMENT AND TIMING DECISIONS

When *timing* of cash flows is the major way in which alternatives differ, or when the amounts and timing of cash flows are interrelated, interesting considerations arise in estimating the relevant consequences of decisions. In this final section of the chapter, we will discuss the evaluation of alternatives in *delay* problems (the worth of preventing delay), problems in which the alternatives have *unequal economic lives*, problems in which the *timing of an action* is the decision variable, and problems in *equipment replacement*.

To avoid distracting attention from the issues at hand we will use the familiar market interest rate i and current cash flows in some situations where it would make more sense, because costs in current dollars would inflate with time, to use the *real* interest rate and *indexed* cash flows.

5.2.1 Delay Decisions

In such contexts as the management of a construction project, a decision maker may be faced with many opportunities to speed up or delay individual activities. Normally the time value of money touches a contractor in a very direct way: a *construction loan* provides money in advance to pay for labor and materials for a portion or phase of the project, and it must be repaid with interest, while a *partial payment* is received from the owner upon successful completion of a portion or phase of the project. Partial payments are each intended to be enough to repay the corresponding construction loan with interest, plus profit; sometimes they are modified by bonuses for early completion or penalties for delay.

E35. **A bridge builder is nearing one of the phases of a bridge construction project in which a large rental crane is required for erecting vertical sections of the bridge. The crane arrives by rail, and $4000 daily rent is paid until it leaves. At a time when some of the sections are ready to be erected and the others are nearly ready, the builder must tell the crane provider when to deliver the crane. Describe the decision problem, the nature of the trade-offs among costs and benefits, and the general character of the optimal solution.**

The decision problem is when to receive the crane. If too early, unnecessary crane rental and operator labor is expended; if too late, unnecessary delay is caused in receiving the partial payment for the phase of the project, perhaps also with loss of a bonus or imposition of a penalty. Generally the optimal crane arrival time is as late as possible while allowing timely completion.

Given a cash flow amount X, what is the cost of delay if the timing of X is delayed for one interval (such as a day or week) and the interest rate per interval is i?

The present worth goes from X to $X\beta = X/(1 + i)$. However, note that the worth at time 1 goes from $X(1 + i)$ to X; the difference is iX, which is the interest on a loan of X dollars for one interval. If the length of an interval is short, such as a day or a week, there is little difference between the worths at times 0 and 1; therefore we assert

---

For short intervals, the cost of a delay (or benefit of a speedup) of a payment is the interest on the payment for the time span of the delay (or speedup).

For a small number m of short intervals, since $(1 + i)^m \cong 1 + mi$, we can add rather than compound the interest, incurring little error.

E36. Tansel Buyukakten has a MARR of $i_{\text{eff}} = 12\%$. By difficult replanning she could delay a \$9100 maintenance expenditure four days (at 365.25 days per year) without having any adverse effect on operations. To see whether the difficult replanning effort would be worthwhile, she needs to know the benefit of the prospective delay. Compare ways of determining this.

The interest rate for one day is $i = (1 + i_{\text{eff}})^{1/365.25} - 1 = 0.000310325$. The most intuitive approach would be to say that four days of daily interest on \$9100 at i is $4(0.000310325)(9100) = \$11.30$.

A slightly more elaborate approach is to compute the worth of the delay as of the fourth day, which can be done using either the daily time scale at i or the yearly time scale at i_{eff}

$$9100(1 + i)^4 - 9100 = 9100(1 + i_{\text{eff}})^{4/365.25} - 9100 = \underline{\$11.30}$$

The present worth approach, again using either time scale:

$$9100 - 9100[1/(1 + i)^4] = 9100 - 9100[1/(1 + i_{\text{eff}})^{4/365.25}] = \underline{\$11.29}$$

Since \$11.29 or \$11.30 would pay for very little difficult replanning, Tansel should abandon the idea of a delay.

Delay of an entire cash-flow set is important in project management, action timing, replacement, and capital budgeting (where an investment opportunity may be delayed until capital is available). There are two easily handled types of delay: *shift delay* and *truncated delay*. Consider an arbitrary set of cash flows $\{A_t: t = 1,...,n\}$ as in Figure 5-4. (*Note:* If the time intervals are long enough for inflation to affect the cash flows, the current cash flows $\{A_t\}$ should be replaced by indexed cash flows $\{W_t\}$ and i should be replaced by d.)

A shift delay of a cash-flow set for m intervals occurs when all the cash flows retain their amounts and occur m intervals late. A truncated delay occurs when all the cash flows beyond time m retain their amounts and timings, positive cash flows at times $0, \ldots, m$ are lost, and negative cash flows at times $0, \ldots, m$ are replaced by their (not compounded) sum at time m. See Figure 5-4.

E37. **A manufacturing plant is under construction in Nebraska and its benefits are expected to be worth $15,000,000 when complete. It is expected to have a 20-year economic life. If the owner uses MARR of 15%, what is it worth to speed up the construction so that it can open at the beginning of the next canning season rather than a year later?**

A set of cash flows equivalent to $15,000,000 at time zero (beginning of next canning season) would undergo a one-year shift delay unless the speedup occurs. From Figure 5-4, given $P = \$15$ million, the present worth of avoiding the delay is

$$P(1 - \beta^1) = 15[1 - (1/1.15)] \cong \underline{\$1.96 \text{ million}}$$

It is worth nearly $2 million to speed up the construction.

E38. **A 36-month manufacturing contract has the following estimated tooling costs (in thousands, with time in months) for the first few months:**

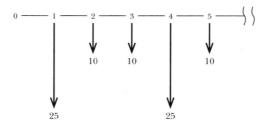

A $50,000 diemaking improvement can save 40% of these costs, and its present worth at a MARR of 11% has been determined to be $140,530. At $i = (1.11)^{1/12} - 1$, $= 1/(1 + i)$:

Undelayed cash-flow set: the present worth is

$$P = \sum_{t=0}^{n} A_t \beta^t$$

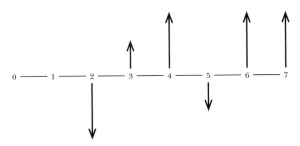

Shift delay ($m = 2$): The delayed present worth is $P\beta^m$.

The present worth of avoiding a shift delay is $P(1 - \beta^m)$

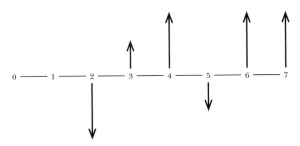

Note: If shifted cash flows are subject to inflation, replace $\{A_t\}$ with $\{W_t\}$ and let $\beta = 1/(1 + d)$.

Truncated delay ($m = 2$): The delayed present worth is

$$P - \sum_{t=0}^{m} A_t^{+} \beta^t + \sum_{t=0}^{m} A_t^{-} (\beta^t - \beta^m)$$

where $\{A_t^{+}\}$ are positive cash flows and $\{A_t^{-}\}$ are positive numbers representing negative cash flows, as in Section 4.1.1.3. The present worth of avoiding a truncated delay is

$$\sum_{t=0}^{m} A_t^{+} \beta^t - \sum_{t=0}^{m} A_t^{-} (\beta^t - \beta^m)$$

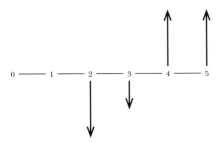

FIGURE 5-4. Shift-delay and truncated cash-flow sets.

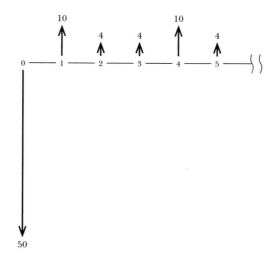

$P = -50 + 10\beta + 4\beta^2 + 4\beta^3 + 10\beta^4 + 4\beta^5 + o = 140.530$, where o is the present worth of the cash flows beyond month 5. Determine the present worth if the diemaking improvement is delayed 3 months.

This is a truncated delay, since the benefits have a time schedule (that of the construction contract) independent of that of the diemaking improvement. A delay will shift the $50,000 investment to time 3 (months) and forgo the first 3 returns. From Figure 5-4, the present worth after a truncated delay is

$$P^{(\text{delay})} = P - \sum_{t=0}^{3} A_t^{+}\beta^t + \sum_{t=0}^{3} A_t^{-}(\beta^t - \beta^3)$$

$$= 140.530 - [10\beta + 4\beta^2 + 4\beta^4] + 50(\beta^0 - \beta^3) = \underline{\$124{,}076.24}$$

Let X_t be either a cash flow scheduled to occur at time t or the worth at time t of a set of cash flows. Let P be the present worth of X_t:

$$P = X_t\beta^t$$

The instantaneous rate of change of P as X_t is shift-delayed is

$$\frac{dP}{dt} = X_t\beta^t\ln\beta = X_t e^{-rt}(-r) \tag{5-10}$$

where $r = \ln(1 + i) = -\ln\beta$ is the nominal continuous interest rate.

E39. An alternative in a decision problem has two returns whose timing can be influenced:

$$P = -\cdots + 263\beta^{3.1} + \cdots + 463\beta^{4.4} + \cdots$$

For $\beta = 0.87$, which return is it more beneficial to speed up by a small amount?

Let the timings of the two returns (currently 3.1 and 4.4) be denoted t_1 and t_2.

$$\frac{dP}{dt_1} = 263\beta^{3.1}(\ln\beta) = \underline{\underline{-23.7873}}$$

$$\frac{dP}{dt_2} = 463\beta^{4.4}(\ln\beta) = \underline{\underline{-34.93804, \text{ more beneficial}}}$$

(If t_2 is speeded up by a small amount, say $\Delta t_2 = -0.01$, P increases by approximately $\Delta t_2(dP/dt_2) = 0.349$.)

5.2.2 Unequal Economic Lives

When the *duration* of a decision consequence varies, not only does its contribution to worth vary, but there is a delay or speedup in the consequences that follow afterward.

Consider, for example, the choice of catalyst for a catalytic reactor that is expected to last for 8 years. At a cost of $7500, activation with catalyst A will last 1.5 years before the reactor needs to be activated again. Alternatively, at a cost of $10,000, activation with catalyst B will last 2.5 years before requiring reactivation. Assuming MARR is $i_{eff} = 18\%$, which catalyst should be used? (Without changing notation, we will assume the costs are *indexed*, and MARR is given as the *real* interest rate; otherwise the repeatability assumption to be made about costs would be invalid.)

Amazingly, there is substantial confusion in the literature that can be easily cleared up here. There are three techniques—*annual equivalent, infinite horizon,* and *common life*—that are mathematically indistinguishable, yet authors debate their merits and misunderstand their underlying assumptions. There are two others—*explicit salvage* and *sequencing*—useful when the underlying assumptions are different.

5.2.2.1 Annual Equivalent and Related Techniques
First, let us assume *repeatability*: the activations will all be done with the same catalyst at the same cost. Second, assume the eight-year horizon is a *vague horizon*. This assumption is that the horizon is substantially longer than the economic life of any alternative, and that the unused life of the catalyst on the abandonment of the reactor could be anything from zero to the alternative's life. The *annual equivalent* technique is to determine the annual worth (of the cost) of each alternative over its economic life and choose the alternative with greatest annual worth (least annual cost):

A: $7500(A/P\ 18\%,1.5) = 7500/(P/A\ 18\%,1.5) = \$6140.49399/\text{yr}$

B: $10,000(A/P\ 18\%,2.5) = 10000/(P/A\ 18\%,2.5) = \$5311.96518/\text{yr}$

B has the lower equivalent annual cost and is chosen. Note that the ratio of the (cost) worths for A and B is 1.155974067; A costs 15.6% more than B. Assuming repeatability as defined above, for each alternative the same annual cost can be extended for as many activations as is necessary to cover the horizon. This is realistic, of course, only if cash flows are in indexed dollars and $\beta = 1/(1 + d)$ where d is the real interest rate.

The infinite-horizon technique is to compare the present worths of infinite sequences of each alternative. Let C represent the present worth of the cost of an infinite series of disbursements of X dollars each at times $\{0, k, 2k, \ldots\}$.

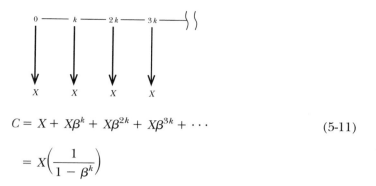

$$C = X + X\beta^k + X\beta^{2k} + X\beta^{3k} + \cdots \qquad (5\text{-}11)$$

$$= X\left(\frac{1}{1 - \beta^k}\right)$$

(Eq. 5-11 is a specialization of Eq. 2-51 of Chapter 2 with the first payment at time zero and an infinite horizon.)

Applying Eq. 5-11 to the catalyst problem, we have infinite-horizon present costs as follows ($\beta = 1/1.18$):

A: $7500\left(\dfrac{1}{1 - \beta^{1.5}}\right) = \$34{,}113.85550$

B: $10{,}000\left(\dfrac{1}{1 - \beta^{2.5}}\right) = \$29{,}510.91766$

Recall that the infinite-horizon annual equivalent of a present worth is i multiplied by the present worth (Eq. 2-16). The annual equivalents are:

A: $34{,}113.85550(0.18) = \$6140.49399/\text{yr}$

B: $29{,}510.91766(0.18) = \$5311.96518/\text{yr}$

These are identical to the previous annual equivalents, showing that the annual equivalent and infinite-horizon techniques are mathematically indistinguishable.

The much maligned and unnecessary *common life* technique consists of determining a horizon (ignoring the given one) such that both alternatives can end with an integer number of catalyst activations:

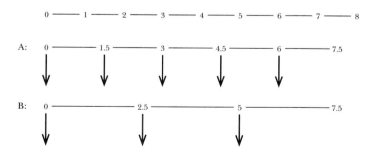

A horizon of 7.5 years allows 5 activations of A and 3 activations of B. Then we compare any measure of worth, say annual worth, at this horizon. Instead of using Eq. 2-51 of Chapter 2, note that the annual worth of the cost of the first activation certainly equals that of the second activation (same amount, same time span), so the annual worth remains the same for the whole horizon and may be computed as that of the first activation:

A: $7500(A/P\ 18\%,1.5) = \$6140.49399/\text{yr}$

B: $10{,}000(A/P\ 18\%,2.5) = \$5311.96518/\text{yr}$

These are the same results obtained twice before. This demonstrates that the *annual equivalent, infinite horizon,* and *common life* techniques are mathematically indistinguishable. The specific assumptions that lead directly to each of the techniques can be questioned: the annual equivalent technique blithely compares alternatives that are not explicitly put on a common basis; the infinite-horizon technique assumes that the repeated expenditures continue forever; the common life technique uses an intuitively meaningless horizon. Yet a valid solution is not made invalid by the fact that faulty arguments lead to it. If we have *repeatability* (costs and lives are the same for each cycle of a given alternative) and a *vague horizon* (in the specific sense that there is a uniform probability distribution of where the abandonment time falls within the cycle), these techniques can be shown to be correct, in the sense that the annual equivalent cost is mathematically equal to the expected annual cost. *For unequal economic life comparisons, use the annual equivalent technique when there is repeatability and the horizon is vague.*

5.2.2.2 Explicit Salvage Technique

When the horizon is *sharp*—the abandonment is assumed to occur at a time when various alternatives will have various unused economic lives remaining in the last cycle—explicit data are needed on salvage values. Suppose, for example, abandonment of the reactor were to occur at exactly $n = 6$ years (not a vague 8 as before), and the 1.5- and 2.5-year lives of the two alternatives were considered exact. At time 6 the catalyst in alternative A will be "fully spent" and, we assume, valueless; let S represent the salvage value of catalyst in B when it is one year old and has 1.5 years of remaining life. Let C represent the present worth of costs at 18% interest:

$$C^{A} = 7500 + 7500\beta^{1.5} + 7500\beta^{3} + 7500\beta^{4.5} = \$21{,}477.00751$$

$$C^{B} = 10{,}000 + 10{,}000\beta^{2.5} + 10{,}000\beta^{5} - S\beta^{6} = \$20{,}982.51573 - S\beta^{6}$$

We see that the advantage of B over A depends on the salvage value. For *zero* salvage value, the ratio of (cost) worths for A and B would be $C^{(A)}/C^{(B)} = 1.023566849$. This 2.4% excess cost of A is considerably smaller than the 15.6% excess cost of A determined earlier for the vague-horizon techniques. Because $n = 6$ is a time at which the catalyst in alternative B has considerable unused life already paid for, which if not recoverable, the advantage of B is reduced.

We can compute the *salvage value implied by the annual-equivalent technique.* It is S such that $C^{(A)}/C^{(B)}$ is the same 1.155974067 as was given by the annual equivalent technique:

$$\frac{21477.00751}{20982.51573 - S\beta^{6}} = 1.155974067 \Rightarrow S = \$6487.89$$

Now if this salvage value is *reasonable,* we can use it and get exactly the same answer as by the annual equivalent and related techniques; if it is not reasonable, we can estimate a more reasonable value and get a specific answer.

This *explicit salvage technique* is recommended by the famous industrial engineer John A. White and by other authors. In practice, it amounts to using the annual-equivalent technique unless the salvage value that it implies is unreasonable. However, if n is *vague* it is incorrect to consider salvage values at all, since using smaller-than-implied salvage values would discriminate against the alternative having the greatest unused value at the exact n assumed. To make this clear, let us compute the annual worth of the advantage of B over A for various horizons n.

If the horizon is n, the number of additional activations after the activation at time zero is the greatest integer less than $n/1.5$ for A or $n/2.5$ for B; for example, at $n = 6$ there are $N_A = 3$ additional activations for A and at $n = 6.001$ there are $N_A = 4$, and at both these times $N_B = 2$. The present-worth cost advantage of B over A is

$$C^{(A)} - C^{(B)} = 7500(1 + \beta^{1.5} + \beta^3 + \cdots + \beta^{1.5 N_A}) - 10{,}000(1 + \beta^{2.5} + \beta^5 + \cdots + \beta^{2.5 N_B})$$

where N_A and N_B depend on n as described above.

At a given n, the annual-worth advantage is the annual equivalent (for that n) of the present-worth cost advantage defined before. It is computed as $(C^{(A)} - C^{(B)})/(P/A$ $i, n)$. As n increases, it converges to the difference between the annual worths computed by the vague-horizon techniques; recall that the annual equivalent costs of A and B were computed as \$6140.49399/yr and \$5311.96518/yr, so the annual-worth advantage must converge to their difference: \$828.53. Figure 5-5 shows this convergence. If the horizon is anything greater than about 6 years, the equivalent annual cost of A will be greater than that of B by about \$828.53, and to say the advantage of B over A is much greater or less than that is to assume the horizon will be some exact value of n.

5.2.2.3 Sequencing
The *repeatability* assumption—that the horizon will be covered by a series of replications of the same alternative—is justifiable for vague horizons, but not strictly justifiable for sharp horizons. Given some particular sharp horizon n, a mixed sequence of alternatives may be optimal. Suppose, for example, you had solved the catalytic reactor activation problem several years ago at some sharp horizon greater than $n = 3$, so that you would have chosen B (see Figure 5-5, in which B has an advantage over A for all $n > 3$). Now suppose that at time $t = 4.5$ you learn that the actual abandonment, with no salvage, will be at $n = 6$. The second (sunk) B activation will serve until time 5. Obviously, at that time it will be better to spend \$7500 than \$10,000 for the final year's operation. Therefore, if there is no salvage, the explicit salvage technique would have given a suboptimal answer for $n = 6$. (As will be shown in the exercises, the same would be true for any reasonable salvage values.)

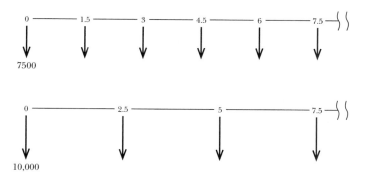

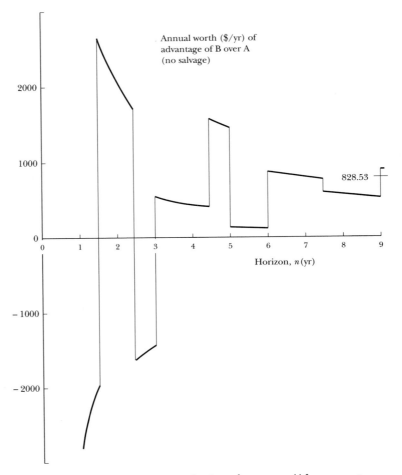

FIGURE 5-5. Exact versus vague horizon for unequal-life comparison.

This problem for fixed n and no salvage is a simple version of a *sequencing problem:* to fill a time span with a sequence of activities at minimal discounted cost, given a duration and cost for each candidate activity. Given a measure of efficiency (equivalent annual cost) for each candidate activity, the general solution is to schedule the candidates in decreasing order of efficiency until the horizon is approached; near the horizon, less efficient candidates may be optimal if more efficient candidates would go beyond the required time span. In the catalytic reactor activation problem, the optimal solution would be expected to be the sequence {B,B, . . .} with perhaps one or two As at the end if the 2.5-year life of the final B would extend beyond n. Table 5-1 shows the optimal sequences and equivalent annual costs for various horizons. Note that except for very short horizons the sequences have the expected form, and for any horizon exactly filled by a sequence of Bs the optimal equivalent annual cost is the $5311.97 originally computed as the equivalent annual cost for B. Since the object of the decision problem is to make only the initial decision (the repetitions or sequences constitute only assumptions about what will be decided later), we can conclude that *the simple annual-equivalent technique is valid except where the horizon is very short and accurately known.* The explicit-salvage technique can be used for short horizons; if it is necessary to consider the possibility of juggling alternatives to fit into a horizon, the problem may be treated as a sequence problem.

TABLE 5-1. Optimal Sequence Solutions for Catalytic Reactor Activation

Horizon, n (yr)	Optimal Sequence	Equivalent Annual Cost at $i = 18\%$	Horizon, n (yr)	Optimal Sequence	Equivalent Annual Cost at $i = 18\%$
1.5	A	6140.49	5	B, B	5311.97
2	B	6387.16	5.5	B, A, A	5670.70
2.5	B	5311.97	6	B, B, A	5686.68
3	A, A	6140.49	6.5	B, B, A	5432.79
3.5	B, A	6123.45	7	B, B, B	5505.01
4	B, A	5506.68	7.5	B, B, B	5311.97
4.5	B, B	5693.42	8	B, B, A, A	5508.08

For a fixed horizon n, we showed in Chapter 2 that the *annual equivalent* (periodic equivalent or annual worth, Section 2.3.2) was a *worth measure*: at a given interest rate, the ratio of the worths of two alternatives is identical whether those worths are measured by present worth, worth at some fixed time, or annual equivalent at some fixed n, where n is not necessarily the time of the last cash flow in any of the alternatives.

In the last two subsections, however, we have seen that for *variable n*, representing the duration of an activity, the annual equivalent is a kind of *efficiency* measure. For example, we identified B as the more efficient way to cover catalyst needs for a reactor, based on its annual equivalent cost compared to that of A. We can make the efficiency interpretation more specific by stating and proving the *sequencing theorem*.

Let there be two activities **1** and **2** having durations d_1 and d_2 and costs c_1 and c_2. These activities are to be sequenced so that one starts at time zero and the next one starts when the first one's duration is complete. The problem is whether to choose the sequence **1, 2** or the sequence **2,1**. We can interpret the costs c_1 and c_2 as the costs associated with each activity, discounted to the activity's start time. The alternative sequences can be diagrammed using the conventions of an activity-on-arc graph (as in critical-path scheduling):

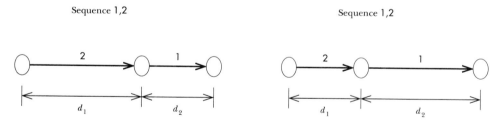

Associated with each sequence is the corresponding cash-flow diagram:

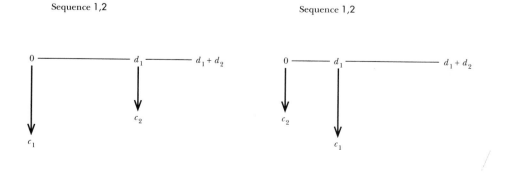

The present costs of these two cash-flow diagrams are

***Sequence* 1,2**   ***Sequence* 2,1**

$$C^{(1,2)} = -P^{(1,2)} = c_1 + c_2\beta^{d_1} \qquad C^{(2,1)} = -P^{(2,1)} = c_2 + c_1\beta^{d_2}$$

Given the two costly activities that can follow each other in either sequence, we want to choose the cheaper sequence, which of course is the sequence with smaller present cost. If 1, 2 is the optimal sequence, then

$$C^{(1,2)} < C^{(2,1)} \Leftrightarrow c_1 + c_2\beta^{d_1} < c_2 + c_1\beta^{d_2}$$

We can rearrange the inequality, divide by positive quantities, and multiply by i (if the costs are indexed, the real interest rate would be used):

$$c_1(1 - \beta^{d_2}) < c_2(1 - \beta^{d_1})$$

$$\frac{c_1}{1 - \beta^{d_1}} < \frac{c_2}{1 - \beta^{d_2}}$$

$$c_1\frac{i}{1 - \beta^{d_1}} < c_2\frac{i}{1 - \beta^{d_2}}$$

$$c_1(A/P\ i,d_1) < c_2(A/P\ i,d_2) \tag{5-12}$$

This proves the *sequencing theorem* and states it mathematically. (For c_1 and c_2 in indexed dollars, replace i in Eq. 5-12 with the real rate d.)

Sequencing Theorem:

If two activities can be sequenced in either order, worth is maximized by scheduling first the one with greater annual worth over its duration.

Applying the sequencing theorem to the catalyst activation problem, where B has a greater annual worth (lesser equivalent annual cost) than A, we see that it requires that no sequence can be optimal if B follows A anywhere in it; therefore the only As allowed in an optimal solution would be in a group at the end of the sequence (this group could have no As or one A, or could be the entire sequence, depending on n and the data).

E40. **The owner of the historic building that houses the San Mateo Gallery must paint the building with one of the following paints:**

Paint Type	Coverage (sq ft/gal)	Paint Cost (per gal)	Labor Cost (per sq ft)	Estimated Life (yr)
L: latex	625	$15.00	$0.11	4
O: oil	550	$33.00	$0.12	7

There is no difference in appearance and protection qualities. The lease runs for 10 more years, immediately after which remodeling will occur. MARR is 10% real interest (d), and future costs will have the same amounts in indexed dollars as now. By the annual-equivalent technique, the explicit-salvage technique, and the sequencing technique, determine the optimal paint type. Compare results.

A convenient basis is an area of 100 square feet, since the area to be painted is not given, and all costs are proportional to area. The salvage value is assumed to be zero at $n = 10$ yr because of the remodeling. Let $\beta = 1/1.10$.

Annual equivalent

L: $(15.00/6.25 + 11) = \$13.40$ cost every 4 years (per 100 ft^2)

O: $(33.00/5.50 + 12) = \$18.00$ cost every 7 years (per 100 ft^2)

The annual equivalents over the lives are

L: $13.40(A/P\ 10\%,4) = \$4.227308770/\text{yr}$

O: $18.00(A/P\ 10\%,7) = \$3.697298995/\text{yr}$ (O cheaper)

Explicit salvage

$C^{(L)} = 13.40(1 + \beta^4 + \beta^8) = \$28.80357920$ present cost (per 100 ft^2) for (L,L,L)

$C^{(O)} = 18.00(1 + \beta^7) = \$27.23684612$ present cost (per 100 ft^2) for (O,O)

O is cheaper.

Sequencing

Since O is more efficient, and the sequences (L,L,L) and (O,O) have already been evaluated, the only sequences that could be optimal are (O,O), which has present cost $C^{(O)}$ determined above, and (O,L), which provides $7 + 4 = 11 > 10$ years of coverage; (L,O) would violate the sequencing theorem. Obviously (O,L) is optimal, since it differs from (O,O) only in spending \$13.40/sq ft rather than \$18.00/sq ft at time 7.

$C^{(O,L)} = 18.00 + 13.40\beta^7 = \$24.87631879$ *present cost (per 100 ft^2) for* (O,L)

Comparison: The annual-equivalent technique ignores the possibility of abandonment at a time that leaves unused economic life. The explicit-salvage technique ignores the possibility of a mixed sequence of alternatives, which turns out to be cheapest. Note that all three techniques, for this problem, give the same answer to the immediate problem: use oil paint.

5.2.3 Action Timing

Consider an activity whose duration may be selected as a decision variable τ, so that its net present worth excluding salvage value at τ is $V(\tau)$, a function of τ. Its salvage value, which also depends on τ, is denoted $S(\tau)$ and in general may be the net present worth of some future activity that begins at time τ.

Action timing activity diagram:

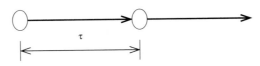

Action timing cash-flow diagram:

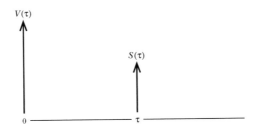

The present worth, as a function of the selected duration τ, is

$$P^{(\tau)} = V(\tau) + S(\tau)\beta^\tau \tag{5-13}$$

The action-timing problem is to select τ to maximize $P^{(\tau)}$. If $S(\tau)$ is given in current dollars, let $\beta = 1/(1 + i)$; if in indexed dollars, let $\beta = 1/(1 + d)$ where d is the real interest rate.

5.2.3.1 Optimal Abandonment
Where, due to deterioration or obsolescence, returns from an economic activity are decreasing, the activity obviously should be abandoned when the net returns switch from positive to negative—*if* no further economic activities are affected by the abandonment's timing. Delay of a positive salvage value is a cost that speeds up optimal abandonment, as the following example shows.

E41. A crew works an old mine whose ore brings in

$$W_t = 180(0.80)^t$$

of revenue, in thousands of indexed dollars, at the end of each year. The cost of the crew and land-taxes is 100 each year (indexed). When abandoned, the land can be restored and the land sold for 200 more than the cost of restoration (indexed). Determine the (integer year) best time to abandon the mine and sell the land if the real interest rate is 10%.

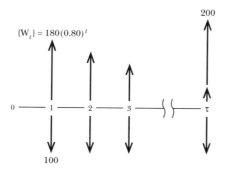

The declining series has $v = -.020$ (recall from Chapter 3 that the real escalation rate v is the geometric rate of change of indexed cash flows). $d = 0.10$.

$$\alpha = \frac{1 + v}{1 + d} = \frac{0.8}{1.10} \qquad s = \frac{1}{\alpha - 1} = 0.375$$

$$P^{(\tau)} = 180\left(\frac{1 - \alpha^\tau}{s}\right) - 100\left(\frac{1 - (1/1.10)^\tau}{0.10}\right) + 200\left(\frac{1}{1.10}\right)^\tau$$

To find τ to maximize $P^{(\tau)}$ is a one-dimensional search problem:

τ	0	1	2
$P^{(\tau)}$	200	<u>221.28</u>	217.85

The mine should be operated one year and then abandoned. In the exercises it will be shown that optimal abandonment would seem to occur after two years if the delay in selling the land were not considered.

An alternative approach to optimal abandonment (and other action timing) problems is the *differential* approach. If $P^{(\tau)}$ has a maximum, it occurs where $\Delta P^{(\tau)}/\Delta\tau$ or $dP^{(\tau)}/d\tau$ crosses zero.

If τ is integer, let the integer h denote the optimal abandonment time so that $\Delta P^{(h)}/\Delta\tau$ is positive or zero and $\Delta P^{(h+1)}/\Delta\tau$ is negative or zero. Let the cash flows except for the salvage value be $\{R_t\}$. Then

$$P^{(\tau)} = \sum_{t=0}^{\tau} R_t \beta^t + S(\tau)\beta^\tau \tag{5-14a}$$

$$P^{(\tau + 1)} = \sum_{t=0}^{\tau+1} R_t \beta^t + S(\tau + 1)\beta^{\tau + 1} \tag{5-14b}$$

Now as τ increases from 0, h is the first value of τ such that $P^{(\tau + 1)} - P^{(\tau)} \leq 0$. Subtracting Eq. 5-14a from 5-14b we have

$$0 \geq P^{(\tau + 1)} - P^{(\tau)} = P_{\tau + 1}\beta^{\tau + 1} + S(\tau + 1)\beta^{\tau + 1} - S(\tau)\beta^\tau \tag{5-15}$$

Dividing by β we have the *differential criterion for optimal abandonment time:*

$$0 \geq R_{\tau + 1}\beta + S(\tau + 1)\beta - S(\tau) \tag{5-16}$$

The optimal abandonment time h is the smallest (earliest) value of τ for which Eq. 5-16 holds. But Eq. 5-16 has intuitive meaning: *at time h, $R_{h+1}\beta$ is the discounted value of next period's returns,* $S(h + 1)\beta$ is the discounted value of the salvage value if abandonment is at next period, and $S(h)$ is the salvage value for immediate abandonment. Thus the differential criterion for abandonment is to *operate until the next period's returns do not offset the delay and decrease in salvage value.*

E42. Show that the differential criterion gives the same answer as present-worth maximization for the mine abandonment problem of Example E41.

> At $\tau = 0$, let us determine if Eq. 5-16 is satisfied: Next year's discounted returns are $R_1\beta = [180(0.80)^1 - 100]\beta$, next year's discounted salvage value is $S(1) = 200\beta$, and the immediate salvage value is $S(0) = 200$. Thus operation for the next year is worth (at $\beta = 1/1.10$, with amounts in thousands)
>
> $$[180(0.80)^1 - 100]\beta + 200\beta - 200 = \$21{,}818.18$$
>
> This is positive, so do not abandon. Then at $\tau = 1$:
>
> $$[180(0.80)^2 - 100]\beta + 200\beta - 200 = -\$4363.64$$
>
> <u>Abandon at time 1</u>.
>
> The exact correspondence between the numerical answer here and the earlier answers in Example E41 will be verified in the exercises at the end of the chapter.

The salvage value can be a net profit from sale of what is abandoned, as in the example, and it can be assumed to increase or decrease with time. It can also represent the net present worth, as of inception, of an activity or investment that starts upon this abandonment. The salvage value may be negative.

For abandonment to occur optimally at the time when returns go to zero, it is not necessary for the salvage value to be zero. Suppose the salvage value increases at a geometric rate i (or d, if measured in indexed dollars), so that its growth rate just offsets the time value of money. Let the salvage value be $S(\tau) = S_0(1 + i)^\tau$, so that its present worth is constant. Equation 5-14a becomes

$$P^{(\tau)} = \sum_{t=0}^{\tau} R_t\beta^t + S_0(1 + i)^\tau\beta^\tau$$

$$\tag{5-17}$$

$$= \sum_{t=0}^{\tau} R_t\beta^t + S_0$$

Then the salvage value's contribution to present worth is unvarying with the abandonment time τ, and the τ that maximizes $P^{(\tau)}$ depends only on the returns. The criterion expressed in Eq. 5.16 becomes $0 \geq R_{\tau + 1}$, and abandonment occurs when next period's returns are negative.

At times some assets such as gold, antiques, art works, and land may grow in value even faster than money grows at compound interest. In such cases Eqs. 5-14 and 5-16 can give infinite optimal abandonment times.

E43. **The Soapstone Art Center's collection of Kurdish tapestries is believed to contribute to patronage just enough to offset its upkeep and insurance costs each year. MARR is $i = 12\%$. The appraised value is increasing 14% per year. What is the best time to sell?**

The annual net returns are zero: $\{R_t\} = 0 = \beta 1/1.12$. The salvage value is $S(\tau) = S_0(1.14)^\tau$, where S_0 is not given. Equation 5-14a gives

$$P^{(\tau)} = S_0(1.14)^\tau \beta^\tau = S_0(1.017857143)^\tau$$

$P^{(\tau)}$ increases with τ, so its maximum is at $\underline{\underline{\tau = \infty}}$ ("never sell").

To interpret infinite optimal abandonment times, keep in mind first that the result says only that you should not abandon *now*, given the assumption that the salvage appreciation rate and the interest rate will remain as estimated. The imputed decisions about what would be decided in future periods are merely assumptions that are included in the method. To see this, note how the differential criterion (Eq. 5-16) would treat the Kurdish tapestry problem of Example E43: Abandonment would occur when $0 \geq 1.14\beta - 1$. If the interest rate were temporarily greater than 14% but expected to return to being below 14%, we obviously should not sell even though the differential criterion would recommend it; this makes clear that β in Eq. 5-16 is an estimate of the long-run time value of money, not a temporary time value.

One general change in the economic climate for engineering economy since the 1960s has been a widespread reduction of salvage values. Not only does the pace of technological obsolescence accelerate, but in our shrinking world there are many costs of abandonment that were often ignored or inoperative in the past: site restoration, disposal of hazardous materials, tax reclassification, and loss of "grandfathered" immunities. Salvage values can be negative and can get more negative with time.

E44. **The power plant that takes cooling water from Idaho's ironically named New Clear Creek operates at a $30,000 net annual profit in indexed dollars. The real interest rate is 8%. The abandonment cost would be $3,000,000 today; assume it will be $3000\gamma^\tau$ (in thousands of dollars) for abandonment at time τ, where γ is unknown. Explore the effect of γ on optimal abandonment time.**

From Eq. 5-14a, with $\beta = 1/1.08$ and amounts in thousands

$$P^{(\tau)} = 30(P/A \; 8\%, \tau) - 3000 \; \gamma^\tau \beta^\tau \qquad \text{where} \qquad \beta = 1/1.08$$

More informative than searching for the optimal τ at various values of γ is to examine the differential criterion of Eq. 5-16. The returns are $R = 30$ for all τ, and the (negative) salvage values are $-3000\gamma^{\tau + 1}$ and $-3000\gamma^\tau$, so Eq. 5-16 becomes

$$0 \geq 30\beta - 3000(\gamma^{\tau+1}\beta - \gamma^{\tau})$$
$$0 \geq 30\beta - 3000\gamma^{\tau}(\gamma\beta - 1)$$

We see immediately that unless $\gamma\beta > 1$ the expression is never negative. Hence the optimal abandonment time is "never" when $\gamma \leq 1.08$. Only if the abandonment cost grows faster than money at compound interest will the annual profits eventually be overcome by the annual increases in the abandonment-cost obligation.

For immediate abandonment at $\tau = 0$, the expression becomes

$$0 \geq 30\beta - 3000(\gamma\beta - 1) \Rightarrow \alpha \geq 1.09$$

Hence the optimal abandonment time is immediate when $\alpha \geq 1.09$. If the abandonment cost grows faster than 9% annually, the annual profits are already being overcome by the annual increase in the abandonment-cost obligation.

In the range $1.08 < \alpha < 1.09$ there is a finite positive optimal abandonment time. From Eq. 5-16 we can solve for it:

$$0 \geq 30\beta - 3000\gamma^{\tau}(\gamma\beta - 1)$$

$$\gamma^{\tau} \geq \frac{1}{100\gamma - 108}$$

$$\tau \geq \frac{-\ln(1000\gamma - 108)}{\ln \gamma}$$

Immediate abandonment costs $3,000,000. The optimal abandonment time can be interpreted as follows: Let there be an abandonment fund that grows at compound interest but not as fast as the abandonment cost grows; the operating profits can be added to the fund so that the fund grows faster, but there comes a time when the abandonment cost's (geometric) growth outstrips the profits' (arithmetic) contribution; of all possible abandonment times τ, this is the optimal one h. Some numerical examples can be computed from the results:

Abandonment-cost growth rate, $\gamma - 1$:	8%	8.25%	8.5%	8.75%	9%
Optimal abandonment time, h:	never	18 yr	9 yr	4 yr	now

5.2.3.2 Horizon-Coverage Switchover Timing

Figure 5-6 shows the cash flows for an important family of *switchover* problems. In a switchover problem there are two mutually exclusive activities x and y; the decision problem is when to abandon x and switch over to y. In the *horizon-coverage* family of switchover problems, there is a finite horizon n. The *general alternative* is to abandon x at some time τ and abandon y at time n; a special *no-switch alternative* is to abandon x at time n; and a special *immediate-switch alternative* is to begin with y at time 0 and abandon it at time n. Activity x has an investment I, returns $\{X_t: t = 1,...,n\}$ (the last $n - \tau$ of which will be discarded), and a salvage value $S(\tau)$ that can depend on the switchover time τ. Activity y has an investment J, returns $\{Y_\theta: \theta = 1,...,n\}$ (the last τ of which will be discarded), and a salvage

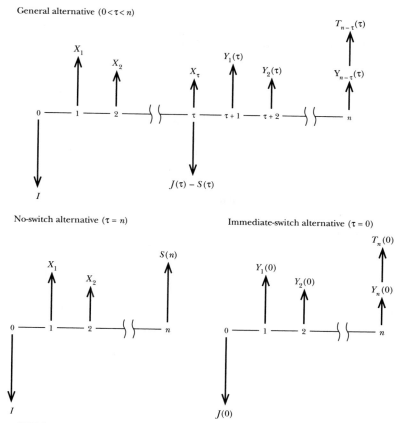

FIGURE 5-6. Cash flows for horizon-coverage switchover timing.

value T_θ. The relative time index θ for activity y is $\theta = t - \tau$ where t is the actual calendar time. It is possible for the cash flows of activity y to depend on the switchover time; when they do, we use the functional notation $J(\tau)$, $\{Y_\theta(\tau)\}$, and $T_\theta(\tau)$.

The horizon-coverage switchover timing model unifies problems in investment timing, maintenance planning, plant expansion, and equipment replacement. For example, x may repesent the continued operation of an existing machine whereas y represents replacement by an alternative machine; the model allows representation of technological improvement by letting the alternative's investment cost $J(\tau)$ decline with τ and letting its returns $\{Y_\theta(\tau)\}$ increase with τ.

The present worth of the general alternative is

Present worth of horizon-coverage-switchover general alternative:

$$P^{(\tau)} = -I + \sum_{t=1}^{\tau} X_t \beta^t + S(\tau)\beta^\tau - J(\tau)\beta^\tau + \sum_{t=\tau+1}^{n} Y_{t-\tau}^{(\tau)} \beta^t + T_{n-\tau}^{(\tau)} \beta^n$$

$$= -I + \sum_{t=1}^{\tau} X_t \beta^t + S(\tau)\beta^\tau - J(\tau)\beta^\tau + \beta^\tau \sum_{\theta=1}^{n-\tau} Y_\theta^{(\tau)} \beta^\theta + T_{n-\tau}^{(\tau)} \beta^n \qquad (5\text{-}18)$$

If the cash flows are in indexed dollars, $\beta = 1/(1 + d)$, where d is the real interest rate; if in current dollars, $\beta = 1/(1 + i)$, where i is the market interest rate.

Note that the first three terms of Eq. 5-18 define the present worth, as given in Eq. 5-14a of activity x when abandoned at time τ, and the last three terms, when β^τ is factored out, similarly define the worth at time τ of activity y when abandoned after $\theta = n - \tau$ periods:

$$P^{(\tau)} = P_x^{(\tau)} + \beta^\tau P_y^{(n-\tau)} \tag{5-19}$$

where $P_x^{(\tau)}$ is Eq. 5-14a for x and $P_y^{(n-\tau)}$ is Eq. 5-14a for y with the appropriate change of time index (in Eq. 5-14a for y, t becomes θ and τ becomes $n - \tau$).

E45. **Maintenance and operation costs for a fleet of air-parcel transport planes are 22% above the industry standard and are increasing 3% per year. An immediate revamp project would cost 1.88c, where c is the industry-standard annual cost; the required revamp investment will increase 3% per year. The benefit of revamp is to bring costs back down to c, so that they will be 1.03c, $(1.03)^2 c$, and so on, in the years after revamp as they resume 3% growth. The horizon is eight years, after which consequences are ignored; there is no salvage value at $n = 8$. If the revamp were undertaken at $\tau = 3$, the cash flows would be as follows (in multiples of c):**

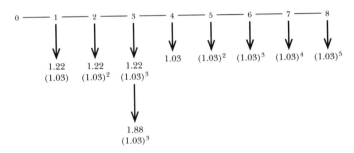

Assuming a real interest rate of 10% (costs are indexed), determine the optimal time to undertake the revamp project.

The geometric gradients have $v = 0.03$. Given $d = 0.10$, the substitute interest rate is $s = (1 + d)/(1 + v) - 1 = 0.067961165$, and the substitute discount factor is $\alpha = 1/(1 + s) = 0.936363636$.

For the no-switch alternative the costs simply continue for eight years:

$$P^{(8)} = -1.22\left(\frac{1 - \alpha^8}{s}\right) = -7.342895572$$

For the immediate-switch alternative, 1.88 is invested and the costs escalate for eight years from the 1 level:

$$P^{(0)} = -1.88 - 1\left(\frac{1 - \alpha^8}{s}\right) = -7.898766862$$

For the general alternative $(0 < \tau < 8)$, Eq. 5-18 could be used, but let us illustrate Eq. 5-19 instead. The present worth of the current costs if the switchover is at τ is

$$P_x^{(\tau)} = -1.22\left(\frac{1 - \alpha^\tau}{s}\right)$$

The worth at time τ of the new costs, including the revamp cost, is

$$P_y^{(n-\tau)} = -1.88(1.03)^\tau - 1\left(\frac{1 - \alpha^{8-\tau}}{s}\right)$$

Equation 5-19 combines these:

$$P^{(\tau)} = P_x^{(\tau)} + \beta^\tau P_y^{(n-\tau)} = -1.22\left(\frac{1 - \alpha^\tau}{s}\right) - \beta^\tau 1.88(1.03)^\tau - \beta^\tau\left(\frac{1 - \alpha^{8-\tau}}{s}\right)$$

The results are, for $\tau = 0, 1, \ldots, 8$:

τ	$P^{(\tau)}$
0 (immediate switch)	−7.8998
1	−7.8371
2	−7.8246 local minimum
3	−7.8545
4	−7.9209
5	−8.0185
6	−8.1426
7	−8.2889
8 (no switch)	−7.3429 optimal

Note that although it is better to switch at time 2 than at time 1 or at time 3, it is best not to switch at all. In general, optimal horizon coverage switchover timing can occur at either extreme as at an intermediate time. Short horizons (as in this problem) often favor the no-switch extreme; great savings often favor the immediate-switch extreme.

5.2.4 Equipment Replacement

The techniques in Section 5.2.1 on delay, Section 5.2.2 on unequal economic lives, and Section 5.2.3 on action timing provide a sound basis for replacement decisions of most kinds, but *equipment replacement* decisions have special characteristics of *technological progress* and *depreciation tax consequences* that deserve special attention. In 1949 George Terborgh of the Machinery and Allied Products Institute (MAPI) published a model (the MAPI replacement analysis system) that explicitly considered these characteristics. Although the MAPI model is obsolete (it is tedious, it lacks clarity of assumptions, it uses linear cost and revenue trends instead of geometric trends, and it uses built-in inappropriate values of income tax rates, interest on borrowed money, MARR, and depreciation schedules), its basic concepts are still useful. The following subsections will begin with simple *age-deterioration* replacement (5.2.4.1), continue with replacement under technological change (5.2.4.2), and finally consider the effects of depreciation tax consequences on replacement decisions (5.2.4.3).

Replacement problems contemplate replacing a *defender* asset that is already in service and has a viable remaining economic life with a *challenger* asset (the terms "challenger" and "defender" were coined by George Terborgh). The decision problem in practice is whether to continue with the defender for one more period, although we find it convenient to view the problem as one of *when to replace*. If the challenger has a viable economic life much shorter than the horizon, or the horizon is vague, repeatability simplifications arise (as in Section 5.2.2.1); otherwise, sharp-horizon methods apply (as in Sections 5.2.2.2 and 5.2.2.3), or the problem is one of optimal abandonment (Section 5.2.3.1) or switchover timing (Section 5.2.3.2).

5.2.4.1 Age-Deterioration Replacement (ADR)

When the challenger is identical to the defender, the (inflation-corrected) environment is constant, and the horizon is vague, we have the simple *age-deterioration replacement* (ADR) problem, which is closely related to the unequal-life problems that were solved in Section 5.2.2 by the annual-equivalent technique. (Those problems chose a challenger from a set of challengers each of whose economic lives could have been optimized by this ADR problems's method.)

The ADR problem is this: *Given a defender whose cash flows eventually decrease with age, determine the optimal time to replace it with a challenger having identical age-dependent cash flows.* There is no dependence on calendar time, only on age; obviously we must use indexed cash flows and discount at the real interest rate d. We use the term "deterioration" to indicate that the reason for replacement is a decrease in benefits or increase in costs with age—consequences that imply economic, if not necessarily physical, deterioration.

Let $\{W_\theta: \theta = 0,...,n\}$ be the age-dependent cash-flow set. We can consider integer replacement ages τ from $\tau = 1$ to $\tau = n$, where n is the maximal age for which cash flows are defined. There is no salvage value. The decision is to choose τ to maximize the worth of an indefinite sequence of successors, each replaced at age τ:

$$P^{(\tau)} = \sum_{t=0}^{\tau} W_t \beta^t + \beta^\tau \sum_{\theta=0}^{\tau} W_\theta \beta^\theta + \beta^{2\tau} \sum_{\theta=0}^{\tau} W_\theta \beta^\theta + \cdots \tag{5.20}$$

Define $P_1^{(\tau)}$ as the present worth of the cash flows of *one* challenger in the series, as of that challenger's age zero:

$$P_1^{(\tau)} = \sum_{\theta=0}^{\tau} W_\theta \beta^\theta \tag{5.21}$$

$P_1^{(\tau)}$ is also the defender's present worth. (The index t is used instead of θ in the first term of Eq. 5.20 because the defender's age is also calendar time.) With the definition 5-21, Eq. 5-20 becomes

$$P^{(\tau)} = P_1^{(\tau)} + \beta^\tau P_1^{(\tau)} + \beta^{2\tau} P_1^{(\tau)} + \cdots$$

$$= \frac{P_1^{(\tau)}}{1 - \beta^\tau} = \frac{\sum\limits_{\theta=0}^{\tau} W_\theta \beta^\theta}{1 - \beta^\tau} \tag{5-22}$$

E46. Ursa Tsarte plans advertising campaigns. She uses indexed cash-flow estimates and a real interest rate of 1% monthly. A typical campaign for her most successful client has an initial cost of 9; it brings in revenues-less-costs of {4, 5, 4, 2, 1, 0.9, 0.7} in the following seven months. After seven months there is a sharp dropoff from staleness of the campaign, so campaigns have been run every seven months. Is there a shorter campaign replacement age that would be even better?

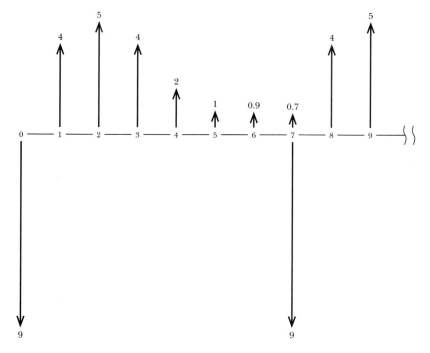

The best replacement age τ maximizes $P^{(\tau)}$ in Eq. 5-22. $\beta = 1/1.01$. Surely the campaign should run at least three months (why?).

$$P^{(3)} = \frac{-9 + 4\beta + 5\beta^2 + 4\beta^3}{1 - \beta^3} = 127.3123328$$

$$P^{(4)} = \frac{-9 + 4\beta + 5\beta^2 + 4\beta^3 + 2\beta^4}{1 - \beta^4} = \underline{145.2139312}$$

$$P^{(5)} = \frac{-9 + 4\beta + 5\beta^2 + 4\beta^3 + 2\beta^4 + 1\beta^5}{1 - \beta^5} = 136.3502011$$

$P^{(6)}$ and $P^{(7)}$ are smaller. _Four months_ is the optimal replacement age.

Now recall that $\beta = 1/(1 + d)$, and that $d/(1 - \beta^\tau)$ is the _periodic equivalent_ factor. Multiplying Eq. 5-22 by d and defining $A^{(\tau)}$ as the annual equivalent of $P_1^{(\tau)}$, we have a formula for the annual (or periodic) equivalent:

$$A^{(\tau)} = P_1^{(\tau)}\left(\frac{d}{1 - \beta^\tau}\right) = \left(\sum_{\theta=0}^{\tau} W_\theta \beta^\theta\right)(A/P \; d, \tau) \qquad (5\text{-}23)$$

Since d is a constant, whatever τ maximizes $A^{(\tau)}$ also maximizes $P^{(\tau)}$, and we have the ADR decision rule:

For simple age-deterioration replacement over a vague horizon, choose the replacement age τ that maximizes the annual equivalent cash flows (or minimizes annual equivalent cost) for one successor.

The infinite-horizon present worths of Eq. 5-22 are not as easy to interpret as the annual equivalents of Eq. 5-23.

E47. Solve example E46 by Eq. 5-23 and clarify why replacement ages less than three months or more than five months would not be optimal.

The monthly equivalents in Eq. 5-23 can be obtained from the present worths of Eq. 5-22 simply by multiplying by the interest rate. Multiplying the former results by $d = 0.01$, we have

$$A^{(3)} \cong \underline{1.273} \qquad A^{(4)} \cong \underline{1.452}, \text{ optimal} \qquad A^{(5)} \cong \underline{1.364}$$

Recall from Chapter 2 that at zero interest, the periodic (here monthly) equivalent is simply the total cash flow divided by the time span. For $\tau = 3$, the total is $-9 + 4 + 5 + 4 = 4$, so the zero-interest monthly equivalent would be $4/3 \cong 1.333$; for $\tau = 4$, $6/4 = 1.5$; and for $\tau = 5$, $7/5 = 1.4$. We see that the zero-interest analysis would have given the same optimal replacement age, on an obvious profit-per-month basis.

$\tau = 1$ or $\tau = 2$ could not be better than $\tau = 3$, because they give zero-interest monthly equivalents of $-5/1 = -5$ and $0/2 = 0$, respectively.

To see why $\tau = 6$ and $\tau = 7$ could not be optimal, imagine the limit that $A^{(\tau)}$ would approach if the returns continued $\{1, 1, 1, \ldots\}$ forever. Obviously $A^{(\tau)}$ would approach 1, since almost all the months would have a return of 1. Thus it is clear that adding a month with a return of 1 will bring $A^{(\tau)}$ closer to 1, so there is no need to check $A^{(6)}$ and $A^{(7)}$; they are obviously less than $A^{(5)}$ since $A^{(5)}$ is greater than 1.

It is possible to see from Examples E46 and E47 how Eqs. 5-22 and 5-23 are valid for making *dynamic* ADR decisions as well as time-zero ones. At the end of month 3, for example, when the cost of the current campaign is sunk and the returns for the first three months have already been collected, the *dynamic* ADR decision is whether to wait to the end of month 4 or immediately replace the campaign at age 3; if it is decided to wait, the dynamic decision at time 4 is again whether to wait or replace. If we expand $P^{(3)}$ term-by-term, it is the present worth of the infinite series $\{-9, 4, 5, (4 - 9), 4, 5, (4 - 9), 4, 5, (4 - 9),\ldots\}$:

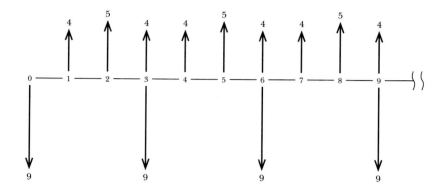

Now consider the dynamic ADR decision at time 3, where the past cash flows $\{-9, 4, 5, 4\}$ are sunk. If we subtract these sunk cost flows from both $P^{(3)}$ and $P^{(4)}$, we cannot change $P^{(3)} - P^{(4)}$. The method does not fail to treat sunk cash flows properly; recall from Chapter 1 that sunk cash flows "must either be ignored or be included in every alternative." Here they are included in every alternative.

Recall that in the age-deterioration (ADR) problem returns eventually decrease with age. For τ sufficiently large, $A^{(\tau)}$ increases with τ, reaches a maximum, then decreases with τ. We can derive a *differential criterion* by subtracting $A^{(\tau)}$ from $A^{(\tau + 1)}$, because the first τ for which $A^{(\tau + 1)} - A^{(\tau)}$ is negative must be that τ that maximizes $A^{(\tau)}$. Figure 5-7 illustrates the incremental project of replacing at age 4 months rather than 3 months for examples E45 and E46. Note that $A^{(4-3)} = A^{(4)} - A.^{(3)}$ Since $A^{(4-3)}$ is not negative, $\tau = 3$ is not optimal. We will now derive a formula for $A^{(\tau + 1)} - A^{(\tau)}$, which is the partial worth of the incremental project of continuing one further period.

Considering Eq. 5-20 and 5-21 term-by-term for τ and for $\tau + 1$, we can reach this result:

$$P^{(\tau + 1)} - P^{(\tau)} = W_{\tau + 1}(\beta^{\tau + 1} + \beta^{2(\tau + 1)} + \cdots) - P_1^{(\tau)}(\beta^{\tau} + \beta^{2\tau} + \cdots) \quad (5\text{-}24)$$
$$+ P_1^{(\tau)}(\beta^{\tau + 1} + \beta^{2(\tau + 1)} + \cdots)$$

The closed form is

$$P^{(\tau + 1)} - P^{(\tau)} = \frac{W_{\tau + 1}\beta^{\tau + 1}}{1 - \beta^{\tau+1}} - \frac{P_1^{(\tau)}\beta^{\tau}}{1 - \beta^{\tau}} + \frac{P_1^{(\tau)}\beta^{\tau + 1}}{1 - \beta^{\tau+1}} \quad (5\text{-}25)$$

Multiplying both sides by d and expressing in terms of $A^{(\tau)}$ from Eq. 5-23, the difference in periodic equivalent is

$$A^{(\tau + 1)} - A^{(\tau)} = W_{\tau + 1}\beta^{\tau + 1}(A/P\ d,\tau + 1) - A^{(\tau)}\beta^{\tau + 1}(A/P\ d,\tau + 1) \quad (5\text{-}26)$$

The first term accounts for the effects of the returns $W_{\tau + 1}$ added by extending the replacement age; the other term accounts for the progressive delay whereby the successive age-θ cash flows are repeated every $\tau + 1$ periods rather than every τ periods. Eq. 5-26 leads directly to a very straightforward *differential criterion* for replacement age. If the optimal replacement age τ is the smallest value of τ (after deterioration begins) for which $A^{(\tau + 1)} - A^{(\tau)}$ is negative, then after age deterioration begins, it is the smallest τ for which $W_{\tau + 1} \leq A^{(\tau)}$.

Age-deteriorating cash flows (ages in months):

$$\{W_\theta: \theta = 1,...,7\} = \{-9, 4, 5, 4, 2, 1, 1, 1\}$$

Replacement age $\tau = 3$:

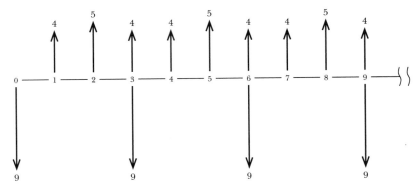

Monthly equivalent for $\tau = 3$: $A^{(3)} = 1.273123$ at $\beta = 1/1.01$, for time spans of the first 3, first 6, first 9, first 12, etc., months.

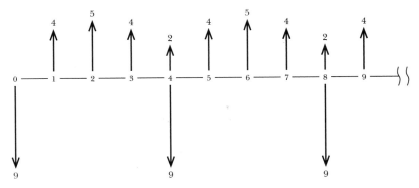

Monthly equivalent for $\tau = 4$: $A^{(4)} = 1.452139$ at $\beta = 1/1.01$, for time spans of the first 4, first 8, first 12, etc., months.

Cash flows for incremental project "$\tau = 4$" − "$\tau = 3$":

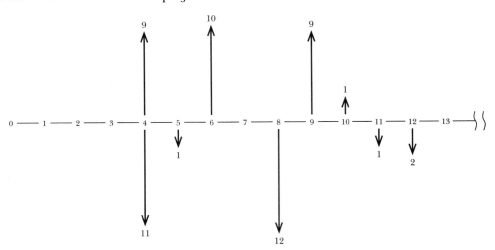

Monthly equivalent for increment: $A^{(4-3)} = 0.179016$ at $\beta = 1/1.01$, for time spans of the first 12, first 24, etc. months.

FIGURE 5-7. Periodic equivalents for replacement-age cycles.

> **Differential criterion for age-deterioration replacement (ADR):**
>
> $$W_{\tau+1} \leq A^{(\tau)}$$ (5-27)

Recall the ADR assumption that after deterioration begins, $A^{(\tau)}$ increases with τ, then decreases. Given that assumption, it is optimal to *replace at the first deteriorating age for which the returns for an additional period of operation are less than the periodic equivalent for operating to that age.*

E48. A plant that uses $d = 12\%$ annual real interest has been replacing cooling coils every four years at a cost of \$4000, which holds down total costs (replacement coils) to an annual equivalent of $-A^{(4)} = \$4131.67$. The extra pumping costs would be \$4497.92 for the fifth year. Should the replacement intervals be changed to five years?

$-W_{\tau+1} = \$4497.92$, so $W_{4+1} < A^{(4)}$. By Eq. 5-27, the optimal replacement time is four years (if it is not earlier). Do not change to five years.

The following example will demonstrate how $A^{(\tau)}$ reaches a maximum when the next-age return is no longer great enough to maintain the annual equivalent.

E49. A machine yields $7420(0.91)^\theta$ dollars (indexed) of net operating returns (value added to product, less operating costs and maintainence) considered to be collected at the end of each year when it attains the age θ. It costs \$14,450 (indexed) to replace it with a similar one. How often should this be done if $d = 18\%$? If $d = 6\%$?

Where $\beta = 1/(1 + d)$ and d is either 18% or 6%, the annual equivalent if replaced at age τ is given by Eq. 5-23 as

$$A^{(\tau)} = P_1^{(\tau)}(A/P\ d,\tau) \qquad \text{where} \qquad P_1^{(\tau)} = \sum_{\theta=0}^{\tau} W_\theta \beta^\theta$$

$$P_1^{(\tau)} = -14450 + \sum_{\theta=1}^{\tau} 7420(0.91)^\theta \beta^\theta$$

$$= -14450 + 7420 \sum_{\theta=1}^{\tau} (0.91)^\theta \beta^\theta$$

Note that the last term is the present worth of a geometric gradient series with $a_0 = 7420$ and $1 + v = 0.91$. The substitute discount factor (see Table 3-1 of Chapter 3) is $\alpha = (1 + v)/(1 + d) = 0.91/(1 + d)$, and the substitute interest rate is $s = 1/\alpha - 1$.

$$A^{(\tau)} = \left[-33000 + 7420\left(\frac{1 - \alpha^\tau}{s}\right) \right](A/P\ d,\tau)$$

From Eq. 5-27, the optimal replacement age is the smallest such that $W_{\tau + 1} \leq A^{(\tau)}$, where $A^{(\tau)}$ is as given above and $W_{\tau+1} = 7420(0.91)^{\tau + 1}$.

$d = 18\%$				$d = 6\%$	
τ, yr	$A^{(\tau)}$	$W_{\tau + 1}$	τ, yr	$A^{(\tau)}$	$W_{\tau + 1}$
12	1971.85	2177.42	9	2817.37	2889.47
13	1976.72	1981.45	10	2822.84	2629.42
14	1976.82	1803.12	11	2809.92	2392.77
15	1973.97	1640.84	12	2785.19	2177.42

Note from the example that the *optimal replacement age increases with interest rate*. $A^{(\tau)}$ decreases with interest rate (recall that it is a worth, and worth was shown in Chapter 2 to decrease with interest rate). Suppose τ is optimal, which is recognized by $W_{\tau + 1} \leq A^{(\tau)}$; if the interest rate is increased, the same $W_{\tau + 1}$ may no longer be smaller than $A^{(\tau)}$. In the example $W_{13} = 2177.42$. At $d = 6\%$, $A^{(12)}$ exceeds W_{13}, whereas at $d = 18\%$, $A^{(12)}$ is less than W_{13}; thus age 12 is too old an age to replace if $d = 6\%$, but too young if $d = 18\%$.

We can see from Eq. 5-27 that the ADR problem does *not* require the challenger to be identical to the defender, except that its cash flows at and beyond the age τ must be identical to those of the defender. All future challengers must have cash flows identical to those of the first challenger. In the next section we consider the effects of obsolescence or technological improvement, where successive challengers can be better than previous ones.

5.2.4.2 Replacement Under Technological Change

Under technological change, replacement decisions depend on assumptions about future challengers. One common assumption is that indexed equipment prices will decline for the same net revenues or costs; this will increase the worth of the stream of future challengers, and will tend to decrease the optimal replacement age of the defender. A second common assumption is that indexed net revenues will increase (or costs decrease) for the same indexed equipment prices; this will have similar effects. *Technological improvements* have one or both of these progressive positive effects, and they encourage the defender to be replaced somewhat sooner than in a static situation. It is difficult to provide simple procedures for analyzing these situations, because *repeatability* cannot be exploited as simply as in ADR problems.

The only change pattern that perfectly preserves repeatability is *geometric scale change*. Suppose a machine produces a product for which the demand is steadily growing, or steadily shrinking, so that the successive challengers should have capacities that follow the same trend. If the trend is measured by a scale increase factor u, it is reasonable to assume that a challenger installed t years from now would require $(1 + u)^t$ times as much investment as now and that a cost or return occurring in year t would be $(1 + u)^t$ times as great as now.

If we superimpose a geometric trend on all cash flows, so that each cash flow is multiplied by $(1 + u)^t$, where t is the calendar time of the cash flow, Eq. 5-20 becomes

$$P^{(\tau)} = \sum_{t=0}^{\tau} W_t \beta^t (1 + u)^t + \beta^{\tau} \sum_{\theta=0}^{\tau} W_{\theta} \beta^{\theta} (1 + u)^{\tau + \theta} + \beta^{2\tau} \sum_{\theta=0}^{\tau} W_{\theta} \beta^{\theta} (1 + u)^{2\tau + \theta} + \cdots$$

$$= \sum_{t=0}^{\tau} W_t[\beta(1 + u)]^t + [\beta(1 + u)]^{\tau}\sum_{\theta=0}^{\tau} W_\theta[\beta(1 + u)]^{\theta} + \cdots \qquad (5\text{-}28)$$

Thus, as in Section 2.6.3 of Chapter 2, this defines a *general geometric gradient*, where β is replaced by $\beta(1 + u)$. We can compute $P^{(\tau)}$ at a changed interest rate $d \to (1 + d)/(1 + u) - 1$, and all mathematical results remain as developed previously. However, the optimal replacement age and the resulting annual equivalent will be changed. For example, consider Exercise E49 with various general gradients, referred to the baseline real interest rate of $d = 6\%$:

All Cash Flows Multiplied By $(1 + u)^t$, Where u Is	Changed Interest Rate, $d \to$	Optimal Replacement Age	Optimal Annual Worth
−0.04	10.42%	11 yr	$2539.42
−0.02	8.16%	10 yr	$2687.50
0	6%	10 yr	$2822.84
0.02	3.92%	9 yr	$2946.58
0.04	1.92%	9 yr	$3061.49

This general geometric scale change is the only model of future trends that will preserve the validity of the assumption that all future challengers will have identical optimal replacement ages.

E50. A railroad company has a real MARR of $d = 10\%$ and uses an established procedure for all equipment replacement decisions, from rolling stock to office equipment. The company expects to experience a general decline in business at a rate of about 4% per year. What specific change can be made in the replacement-decision procedure, and what general effect will there be on optimal replacement ages?

Given $n = -0.04$ and $d = 0.10$, the real interest rate used in replacement decisions should become

$$d \to (1 + d)/(1 + u) - 1 = \underline{14.58\%}$$

This is the appropriate real interest rate for equipment whose appropriate size, scale, initial cost, operating benefits, and operating costs will decline 4% annually. The effect, as already seen in example E49, where 6% interest gave $\tau = 10$ years and 18% interest gave $\tau = 14$ years, will be to keep equipment somewhat longer.

Declining equipment prices is a welcome effect of technological progress. The response of optimal replacement age to declining replacement costs is subtle: one popular textbook gets it backwards, claiming you should keep the defender longer if future challengers are expected to be better than the current challenger.

First, we should say that if you expect an imminent *sudden* improvement, it can be optimal to wait for it. No special methods are required beyond those already covered in Section 5.2.1 ("Delay Decisions"). For example, if a project using $d = 10\%$ has a $1000 investment and has returns worth $1100, so that its present worth is $100, a 5% decrease in the investment along with a shift delay of one year makes the present worth $\beta(-950 + 1100) = \$136.36$, which is attractive.

For an expected *downward trend in investment cost*, let us assume that the investment costs for a sequence of challengers decline with calendar time, while the returns from the investments decline with age but not with calendar time. Let $I(t)$ denote the required investment at replacement time, to be followed by returns $\{W_\theta\}$ where θ is the age after investment. With the variation of investment cost, we can no longer assume that all the investments have the same optimal replacement age, even if the horizon is vague; for instance, if investment costs fall rapidly at first and later fall more slowly, early challengers may be replaced more often than later ones.

We will let the defender be null (to be restored to the analysis later). Let the successive challengers be installed at times τ_0, $\tau_0 + \tau_1$, $\tau_0 + \tau_1 + \tau_2$, and so forth, so that τ_k is the replacement age of the kth challenger and τ_0 is the replacement age of the (null) defender. (Visualize a type of machine that at time zero is too expensive to be profitable; as prices decline, one is purchased at time τ_0, that one is replaced at age $\theta = \tau_1$, which is at time $t = \tau_0 + \tau_1$, etc.)

The decision problem is to choose τ_0, τ_1, τ_2, and so on, to maximize the worth of the sequence of successors. The worth to be maximized is a generalization of that in Eq. 5-20, with investment cash flows treated separately:

$$P = \beta^{\tau_0}[-I(\tau_0) + R_1(\tau_1)] + \beta^{\tau_0+\tau_1}[-I(\tau_0 + \tau_1) + R_2(\tau_2)] + \cdots \qquad (5\text{-}29)$$

where $R_k(\tau_k)$ is the worth of the returns for the kth challenger at its inception:

$$R_k(\tau_k) = \sum_{\theta=1}^{\tau_k} W_\theta \beta^\theta \qquad (5\text{-}30)$$

For example, the following cash-flow diagram shows a solution $\tau_0 = 2$, $\tau_1 = 4$, $\tau_2 = 4$:

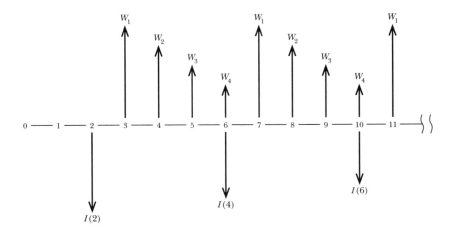

To solve the problem of determining $\{\tau_0, \tau_1, \tau_2, ...\}$ to maximize P in Eq. 5-29, it is not fruitful to do a blind search. We can borrow ideas from the exact optimization procedure called *dynamic programming* to get a near-optimal solution quickly, which can then be refined. Arbitrarily select a fixed horizon, say $n = 20$, and define a *final-coverage problem* to choose a final-machine start time so that the coverage of the final segment of the horizon is done as efficiently as possible—that is, let the last machine be replaced at an age that maximizes its annual equivalent over its age. Then, given that we make as much money as possible on the final ("ultimate") machine, we have a new final-coverage problem to choose a replacement age for the next-to-last ("penultimate") machine, to cover the penultimate segment of the horizon as efficiently as possible. This can be continued back toward time zero; if an awkwardly long or short replacement age is obtained for the first challenger, the horizon can be shortened or lengthened appropriately and the process repeated.

The result from this series of final-coverage computations is very close to the optimal, and the true optimal can be verified or found by trying minor changes. The next two examples will illustrate.

E51. **For a protagonist with MARR of $d = 10\%$, a machine is available to earn annual returns whose indexed-dollar amounts decline linearly with machine age:**

$$W_\theta = 2000 - 100\theta$$

The machine is too expensive now, but its indexed-dollar cost is expected to decline geometrically with calendar time:

$$I_t = 2000 + 7000(0.85)^t$$

For a horizon in the general neighborhood of $n = 20$ years, the decision problem is when to expect to purchase the first machine so as to optimize the worth of the sequence of machines.

(a) **As a first step in making the decision, determine the replacement time t of the penultimate machine to maximize the annual equivalent of net earnings from the ultimate machine.**

Let F_t be the worth at time t of the ultimate machine's cash flows to $n = 20$:

$$F_t = -[2000 + 7000(0.85)^t] + \sum_{\theta=1}^{20-t} (2000 - 100\theta)\beta^\theta$$

$A_t = F_t(A/P\ d, 20 - t)$ is the annual worth over the machine's life from its inception at time t to its abandonment at time 20 at age $\tau = 20 - t$. For various t the results are

t	F_t	A_t	
12 yr	$5537.80	$1038.03/yr	
13 yr	$5127.35	$1053.19/yr	almost as efficient; $\tau = 7$ yr
14 yr	$4587.19	$1053.25/yr	most efficient; $\tau = 20 - 14 = 6$ yr
15 yr	$3904.84	$1030.09/yr	
16 yr	$3065.18	$966.97/yr	

The most efficient coverage of the last segment of the 20-year horizon is by a machine installed at time 14 (or time 13) and replaced at age 6 (or age 7).

(b) Given the result for the ultimate machine, determine the most efficient coverage by the penultimate machine.

Let F_t be the worth at time t of the penultimate machine's cash flows to $n = 14$ (taking 14 as the previous result). F_t and A_t are as before except with the 20-year horizon changed to 14 years. Results:

t	F_t	A_t
7 yr	$3729.64	$766.09/yr
8 yr	$3399.14	$780.47/yr most efficient; $\tau = 14 - 8 = 6$ yr
9 yr	$2895.00	$763.70/yr

(c) Continuing with final-coverage computations, the most efficient coverage for a third-from-last machine to be replaced at time 8 turns out to be from $t = 3$ ($\tau = 8 - 3 = 5$ yr). Interpret the results in terms of the overall decision problem.

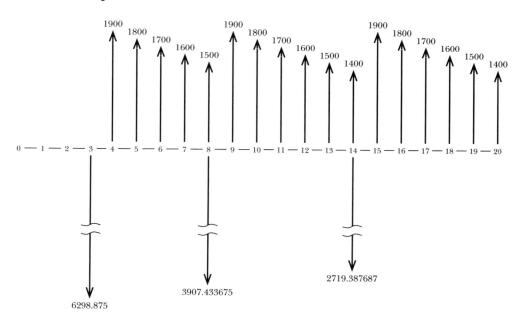

The overall decision problem is to choose τ_0, τ_1, τ_2, and so on, to maximize the worth of the sequence of successors (Eq. 5-29). The final-coverage problems give a solution, sketched above, that replaces the null defender and successive challengers at ages $\tau_0 = 3$, $\tau_1 = 5$, $\tau_2 = 6$, $\tau_3 = 6$.

This solution is not guaranteed to be the optimal solution for the exact horizon $n = 20$, but it provides the most efficient possible coverage of each section of that horizon for all machines except the first one.

Given the suggested solution from a sequence of final-coverage problems, the next step to solving the actual replacement problem depends on whether the horizon is vague or exact. If the horizon is vague, and the early coverage is awkward, the final-coverage problems can be solved again with a changed horizon. For example, the final coverage problems for $n = 20$ in example E51 had the first challenger being installed at time 3 and replaced at time 8. If $n = 20$ is awkwardly short for coverage by three successive challengers, the procedure could have shortened the first challenger's replacement age, or made it start earlier, or both, compared to the optimal solution. Let us examine the final-coverage solutions for various horizons:

Horizon, years	20	21	22	23	24	25	26	(27)
Ultimate challenger start	14	14	15	16	17	18	19	(20)
Penultimate challenger start	8	8	9	10	11	12	13	(14)
Earlier challenger start	3	3	3	4	5	6	7	(8)
								(3)

Note how the final-coverage solutions form a cycle: for a horizon of 19 or 26, the first challenger would be installed at time 7, and for a horizon of 20 or 27, the first challenger would be installed at time 3; the former horizons "squeeze" the first challenger and the latter horizons "stretch" it. If the horizon is vague, the best answer we can obtain from final-coverage solutions is to install the first challenger at time 4, which is the time given by the horizon that is in the middle of the cycle.

Given the final-coverage solution for one or more horizons, it is not out of the question to search for the exact optimal solution.

E52. For the machines of Example E51, starting with the final-coverage solution for $n = 20$, seek the true optimum for $n = 20$.

If the challengers are installed at times τ_0, $\tau_0 + \tau_1$ and $\tau_0 + \tau_1 + \tau_2$, the present worth of the whole sequence is given by Eq. 5-29. Recall Eq. 5-30 and the I_t and W_θ formulas from Example E51:

$$P = \beta^{\tau_0}[-I(\tau_0) + R_1(\tau_1)] + \beta^{\tau_0+\tau_1}[-I(\tau_0 + \tau_1) + R_2(\tau_2)]$$
$$+ \beta^{\tau_0+\tau_1+\tau_2}[-I(\tau_0 + \tau_1 + \tau_2) + R_3(\tau_3)]$$

where

$$R_k(\tau_k) = \sum_{\theta=1}^{\tau_k} W_\theta \beta^\theta$$

and

$$I(t) = 2000 + 7000(0.85)^t$$
$$\tau_3 = n$$
$$W_\theta = 2000 - 100\theta$$
$$\tau_3 = 20 - (\tau_0 + \tau_1 + \tau_2)$$

With $\beta = 1/1.10$, we try various solutions $(\tau_0, \tau_0 + \tau_1, \tau_0 + \tau_1 + \tau_2)$ and compute P for each solution, starting with $(3, 8, 14)$ as given by the final-coverage solutions. Instead of reporting P, let us report the annual equivalent over the 20-year horizon:

$$A = P(A/P\ 10\%,20)$$

Results (from a small computer program written to avoid tedious hand computation):

Replacement times, yr	A		Replacement times, yr	A
3, 8, 14	347.33		4, 10, 16	388.83
3, 9, 15	382.31		4, 11, 17	403.98
⋮	⋮		⋮	⋮
3, 12, 17	417.76 optimal		4, 13, 18	411.03

Note that the truly optimal solution for $n = 20$ is the same as the final-coverage solution for the most neutral horizon $n = 23$. However, in general the most-neutral-horizon's final-coverage solution is *not* guaranteed to give the truly optimal solution for any horizon. In particular, the final-coverage solutions ignore the advantage of replacing a machine later or earlier so that its *successor* will be cheaper or more profitable (final-coverage solutions just cover each machine's own segment most efficiently). It turns out, for example, that for $n = 23$, for which the final-coverage solutions are (3, 8, 14), the truly optimal replacement times are (3, 12, 19).

The same plan is recommended for solving both declining-equipment-price problems and *increasing-benefit problems*, or problems in which successors have both lower costs and higher returns: solve a sequence of final-coverage problems at one or more horizons, and use the solution as a starting solution for a search for the true optimum (for one or more horizons) by trying various solutions in Eq. 5-29.

Computations for Eq. 5-29 should be done with an interactive computer program, which can be quite simple and should require no more than about 30 lines of code, with the following structure (assuming three challengers to cover the horizon):

Initialization: Set values of d, β and n.

Trial: Input values of τ_0, τ_1, and τ_2 (or of τ_0, $\tau_0 + \tau_1$, $\tau_0 + \tau_1 + \tau_2$).

Compute $\{R_k\}$: Compute returns $R_1(\tau_1)$, $R_2(\tau_2)$, $R_3(\tau_3)$, where $\tau_0 + \tau_1 + \tau_2 + \tau_3 = n$, either individually or in a loop.

Compute $\{I(t)\}$: Compute investments at times $t = \{\tau_0, \tau_0 + \tau_1, \tau_0 + \tau_1 + \tau_2\}$ either individually or in a loop.

Compute P and/or A: Compute the worth at time zero from Eq. 5-29 given $\{R_k\}$ and $\{I(k)\}$, either individually or in a loop. Compute A; note that this annual equivalent is for the span from 0 to n, not τ_0 to n, because initial coverage is by the null-machine defender.

Report and loop: Display or print results and return to trial input. Vary the inputs by changing τ_0, τ_1, and τ_2 by

one period individually or together. It would
rarely take more than 10 trials to be sure of the
optimal answer.

For the problem in Examples E51 and E52, it turns out that τ_0, the optimal time to
install the first challenger, is three years for every horizon.

5.2.4.3 Effects of Taxes, Incentives, and Depreciation on Replacement

Income taxes
and value-added taxes are largely *decision-neutral* with respect to equipment replacement decisions, but property taxes and the depreciation provisions of property and
income taxes introduce a bias against replacement of capital equipment, while tax
incentives often mitigate or even reverse the bias. Chapter 10 treats taxes, depreciation, and incentives in detail, but their effects on replacement decisions can be reviewed here.

In countries that levy income taxes on enterprises, the strongest anti-replacement
bias comes from the contrast between depreciation of capital investments and "expensing" of noncapital outlays such as repairs or maintenance. A replacement outlay
of C dollars is a capital investment, which through a *depreciation schedule* is replaced in
tax accounting computations by a series of later expenses called *depreciation charges*
$\{D_t\}$, which sum to C (they are shown here as occurring at successive times 0.5 yr,
1.5 yr, etc.):

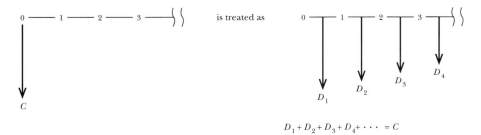

$$D_1 + D_2 + D_3 + D_4 + \cdots = C$$

The tax-levying entity is a "silent partner" that takes a proportion T of net income
as determined by tax accounting. If there were no depreciation schedule, and $\{A_t\}$ were
the returns and expenses following an investment C, then the present worth before
taxes would be

$$P_{\text{bt}} = -C + \sum_t A_t \beta^t \tag{5-31}$$

With income taxation at rate T, after a taxation lag λ (commonly 0.5 yr), this investment's returns would each contribute to net profit λ years after collection, and its
expenses would each reduce net profit λ years after being incurred. If the investment
C is "expensed," it reduces net profit by C dollars, and thus reduces taxes by TC
dollars after lag λ. With taxes included in the cash flows, the *after-tax* present worth
with *expensing* becomes

$$P_{\text{at}}^{(\exp)} = -(1 - T\beta^\lambda)C + (1 - T\beta^\lambda)\sum_t A_t \beta^t \tag{5-32}$$

$$= (1 - T\beta^\lambda)P_{\text{bt}}$$

Since $1 - T\beta^\lambda$ is a constant, we see how *income taxation with expensing of investments is decision-neutral*: if $P_{at}^{(\exp)} \geq 0$ then $P_{bt} \geq 0$, and vice versa, so all decisions would be the same before and after taxes, and the rate of return would be identical before and after taxes.

With depreciation, however, C does not reduce the net taxable profit after λ years; instead, the depreciation charges $\{D_t\}$ reduce the net profits at times λ, $1+\lambda$, $2+\lambda$, and so on. The after-tax present worth with *depreciation* becomes

$$P_{at}^{(dep)} = -C + T\beta^{\lambda-1} \sum_{t=1}^{\infty} D_t \beta^t + (1 - T\beta^\lambda) \sum_t A_t \beta^t \tag{5-33}$$

The first term is the actual investment at time zero; the second term is the worth of tax relief from the investment's reduction of net taxable income through depreciation charges; the third term is the worth of returns less the worth of taxes on them.

To compare depreciation with expensing we define the *efficiency of a depreciation schedule*, Ω, as the present worth of the actually timed depreciation charges per dollar of investment:

$$\Omega = \frac{\beta^{\lambda-1} \sum_{t=1}^{\infty} D_t \beta^t}{C} = \frac{\beta^{\lambda-1} P\{D_t\}}{C} \tag{5-34}$$

where $P\{D_t\}$ is the present worth of the nominally timed depreciation charges, known as the *present worth of the depreciation schedule*:

$$P\{D_t\} = \sum_{t=1}^{\infty} D_t \beta^t \tag{5-35}$$

(By convention, $P\{D_t\}$ is defined so as effectively to assume a taxation lag of one year. Eq. 5-34 is the same as Eq. 10-33 of Chapter 10, and Eq. 5-35 is the generic form of all the specific depreciation worth formulas in Chapter 10, such as Eq. 10-22, 10-23, 10-24, and 10-28.)

With the depreciation schedule efficiency Ω, Eq. 5-33 may be expressed as

$$P_{at}^{(dep)} = -C + TC\Omega + (1 - T\beta^\lambda) \sum_t A_t \beta^t$$

$$= (1 - T\Omega) C + (1 - T\beta^\lambda) \sum_t A_t \beta^t \tag{5-36}$$

The depreciation schedule efficiency is the equivalent fraction of the expenditure that the depreciation schedule recognizes. Note that for *expensing* of an expenditure $\Omega = \beta^\lambda$. For depreciation by any method, for any interest rate, Ω can be determined from Chapter 10; for example, a piece of equipment in the "MACRS life class" 10 (considered to have a depreciable life of 10 years) has a depreciation efficiency of 0.7567 for a taxpayer who uses $i = 10\%$ interest.

Let us subtract Eq. 5-36 from Eq. 5-32 to get the *depreciation disadvantage compared to expensing* for an investment of C dollars:

$$P_{at}^{(exp)} - P_{at}^{(dep)} = TC(\beta^\lambda - \Omega) \tag{5-37}$$

E53. **A machine that should be replaced for $40,000 could perhaps be repaired instead. What is the greatest repair charge that could be as cheap after taxes as the replacement? Assume a tax rate of 40%, a taxation lag of 0.5 yr, a MARR of $i = 10\%$, and a depreciation efficiency at i of 0.7567.**

With $T = 40\%$, $C = 40,000$, $\beta = 1/1.10$, $\lambda = 0.5$, and $\Omega = 0.7567$, Eq. 5-37 gives

$$P_{at}^{(exp)} - P_{at}^{(dep)} = TC(\beta^\lambda - \Omega) = \$3148$$

If the repaired machine would be equal to a new one in every relevant way, a repair would be better than replacement if it cost less than $3148 extra; the greatest attractive repair charge is 40,000 + 3148 = $43,148.

Incredibly, the general feeling about depreciation rules are that they *encourage* capital investment and modernization. The only depreciation rules that would not discourage capital investment would be to allow expensing—that is, *immediate full depreciation.*

E54. **Recall example E52. Assume a $T = 40\%$ income tax rate, a depreciation schedule whose efficiency is $\Omega = 0.62$, and a $\lambda = 0.5$ taxation lag. To avoid additional complication, assume that Ω and λ are already corrected for the fact that tax relief amounts are in current dollars (keep $\beta = 1/(1 + d)$). Before-tax analysis yielded optimal replacement times of {3, 12, 17} for a 20-year horizon. Does after-tax analysis give the same answer?**

In the after-tax analysis, each investment is multiplied by $1-T\Omega = 0.752$ and each return is multiplied by $1-T\beta^\lambda = 0.618614964$. When these simple changes are made to the computer program for example E52, the results are:

Replacement times, yr	After-tax A	Replacement times, yr	After-tax A
(1) 3 12, 17	161.78	4, 12, 17	170.86
3, 12, 18	162.44	4, 12, 18	172.57
3, 13, 18	162.97	4, 13, 18	174.16 after-tax optimum

(1) was the before-tax optimum; the after-tax optimum delays all the replacements by one year and is about 7.6% more profitable than if the before-tax analysis result had been used. After-tax analysis gives a different answer—one that demonstrates how depreciation slightly discourages replacement.

If $1 - T\Omega$ and $1 - T^\lambda$ had been equal to each other, after-tax analysis would have given the same replacement schedule as before-tax analysis.

5.3 EXERCISES

1. Some or all of the following decisions misapply the basic principle of selecting the alternative having greatest worth. Identify and explain the misapplications.
   (a) Benny has $10,000 to invest. He rejects project **A** (to purchase a $5000 treasury bond) in favor of project **B** (to invest $4000 in a real estate deal).
   (b) Ibn-Oerkan buys a 1/4-in. drill at a mall; it is too light-duty for his application, and it soon fails irreparably. He buys a different 1/4-in. drill at a hardware store; it also fails. Although it is very expensive to do so, he decides to farm out his drilling work, because buying new drills every few days would be even more expensive.
   (c) Otto cannot justify spending $750 for a used oxcart, because a stolen one would cost only $300. However, he would not buy a stolen item.
   (d) An ink-jet printer has been analyzed as having a net present worth of $3400 at 15% interest. An alternative laser printer has been analyzed as having a net present worth of $2300 at 12% interest. The ink-jet printer is chosen.

2. Constance Alter does maintenance planning for a chemical plant (**A**) and a nearby power plant (**B**). She notices that pipes carrying hot fluids tend to be more heavily insulated at **B** than at **A**, and that the pipes themselves are bigger at **B** than they are at **A** for the same rate of fluid flow.
   (a) If investments in plant **A** generally have the same economic life as in plant **B**, which plant apparently uses the greater MARR?
   (b) If plant **A** and plant **B** are known to use the same MARR, which plant generally has a greater economic life for its projects?

3. At the Lone Star Brewery, several projects are under consideration. Water quality affects taste; heating rate affects taste and yield. The projects are

   A: Water treatment efficiency improvement to produce treated water of same quality at lower cost.
   B: Water treatment effectiveness improvement to produce better quality of water by additional treatment. **B** has same costs and benefits regardless of acceptance or rejection of **A**.
   C: Taste improvement by vat instrumentation upgrade.
   D: Increase in heating rate to improve yield.
   E: Maintenance labor-saving improvements for vat cleaning.

   Determine the sets of independent and of mutually exclusive opportunities.

4. The division of Science Atlantis that manufactured cable TV selection equipment was "expecting the bottom to drop out of the market" for its products, owing to competition from cable-ready TV sets and cable-ready VCRs. The economic life of any cost-saving project was thought to be limited to n years. Such projects were ordinary investment projects with no salvage value, with a series of n equal net annual returns of W indexed dollars each. MARR was $d = 12\%$. If Science Atlantis engineers were told to propose only those capital investments having a three-year payback time or less, determine n to the nearest integer.

5. Will Rogers offered the investment advice, "Buy land; they aren't making it anymore." Ignoring taxes, the indexed cash flows for a land investment might follow

this pattern, where the land is sold at the same (indexed) price at which it was bought:

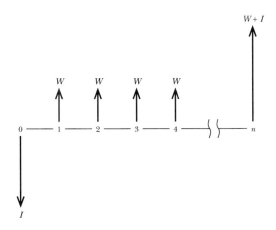

where W is the annual return earned from the land. Suppose $W/I = d$ (where d is the minimally attractive real interest rate), so that the land investment would be barely attractive if the horizon were infinite (with an infinite horizon, $P = -I + W/d$, so $P = 0$ implies $W/I = d$). With the finite horizon, what is the rate of return of the land investment?

6. A lift truck can be purchased for use in a warehouse. Because of a planned warehouse revamp, the project of which the lift truck is a part will have an economic life of only two years. (Except for the project, a lift truck would not be needed until the revamp is complete.) There is a question as to the proper salvage value to use in evaluating the two-year project. It is estimated that the truck could be sold in two years for $14,000; if the truck were not purchased now, a two-year old one could be purchased in two years for $16,000; its usefulness in the revamped warehouse would be so great that even $18,000 would not be too much to pay if a cheaper truck were not available. Determine the proper salvage value.

7. A series of end-of-year returns will have current amounts (in thousands of dollars) of {99, 89.1, 80.19, . . .}, decreasing geometrically forever. At $i = 15\%$, what horizon n will make an equal-payment series of payments of 110 current amount have the same worth?

8. At Burgher Buhn Bakery the management wishes to instruct its engineers to compute present worths of equal-payment series simply by dividing the annual amount A by a substitute interest rate s.
   (a) If typical projects were to have an economic life of 10 years and MARR is $i = 13\%$, what value of s should be published?
   (b) Verify the answer by using Eq. 5-5.
   (c) What geometric gradient g is implied by the substitute interest rate calculated above?
   (d) In using the substitute interest rate, does the annual amount A equate to a_0, or does it equate to A_1?

9. An agricultural equipment company, for whom MARR is $i = 15\%$, uses a horizon of 10 years for projects whose economic lives may be much longer. It is felt that

the company's engineers do not realize that actual returns decay geometrically with time, so the given horizon is an attempt to correct for that. A project's estimated annual returns are $9340. What first-year return A_1 does the attempted correction imply?

10. At Sopworth Industries a study of past investments concluded that a typical investment has returns, measured in current dollars, that decline geometrically at a 21% annual rate and continue for a very long time. Where $g = -0.21$, the returns at times $\{1, 2, \ldots\}$ are $\{a_0(1 + g), a_0(1 + g^2), \ldots\}$. The first return is $A_1 = a_0(1 + g)$.

Engineers analyzing factory-floor cost-savings investments at Sopworth are asked to estimate the first return A_1 and to compute present worths at the company's MARR as if the returns were A_1 dollars per year for n years (not declining, but constant over a short horizon instead).

(a) Derive a formula for n such that, if the engineers are told to use n, they will compute the correct present worth for a typical project. Express n in terms of g and i.

(b) If MARR for the company is $i = 10\%$, determine the integer horizon closest to n given by the formula.

(c) A typical project at Sopworth will have first-year returns of $2150. At $i = 10\%$, determine the present worth assuming an infinite-horizon geometric decline at 21% per year. Compare this to the present worth computed in the manner proposed to be used.

11. Use Figure 5-1 to estimate the rate of return for the following project:

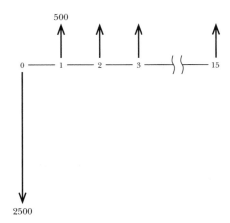

12. Show that in the three different formulations of examples E12, E13, and E14, all the incremental present worths are unaffected by the changes in formulation.

13. Because modifying existing radios would cost a total of $700,000, a feasability study for a proposed new radio, the **XB-B**, was performed at a cost of $160,000. The **XB-B** was found feasible, and the study concluded that it could be developed and fielded for an additional $650,000 (so that the total cost would be $810,000). Should the **XB-B** be developed? Explain.

14. You have committed $45,000 of the construction cost of a craneway, and the contractor suddenly informs you the total cost will be $133,000, not the $100,000 that was originally estimated. The benefits of the completed craneway have a

present worth of $90,000, so the craneway would not have been an attractive investment anyway. Should you abandon or continue?

15. Frambient feculators are normally quite expensive—about $80 apiece—but this week they are on sale for $60. We need 600 of them. We hear that in Shanghai they can be obtained for $28 apiece; to take advantage of this opportunity we must send a buyer to Shanghai, incurring expenses of $8000.

    (a) Should the buyer be sent (without considering risk that the $28 price is wrong)?

    (b) The price at home has reverted to $80. The buyer calls from Shanghai with bad news: the price is $68. Your office mate advises not making the Shanghai buy: "It is easier to justify spending $48,000 to buy 600 feculators at $80 apiece than to justify paying for an $8000 trip to save $7200." What is wrong with that argument?

16. A heat exchanger for waste-heat recovery can be purchased and installed in any one of several alternative sizes:

Size	Required Investment	Annual Net Heat Savings (indexed)
#4	1097	375
#5	1254	414
#6	1434	449
#7	1639	483

    MARR in real-interest terms is $d = 12\%$. The savings will continue for $n = 9$ years. Apply the incremental-ROR decision procedure to determine the best size.

17. Apply the incremental-worth decision procedure to Exercise 16.

18. Recall that an investment project is defined as one whose worth decreases with interest rate. Consider two investment projects. Project A has a $1000 investment at time 0, followed by $400 annual returns forever. Project B has a $1500 investment at time 0, followed by a single $5400 return at time 4.

    (a) In the range $10\% < i < 30\%$, is the incremental project B − A an investment project?

    (b) For MARR of $i = 18\%$, determine the present worths of A and B and conclude whether the incremental project B − A is attractive.

    (c) Show that for a decision maker using MARR of $i = 18\%$, the incremental-ROR procedure would give the wrong answer. (*Note:* In the $10\% < i < 30\%$ range, there is a rate of return of 15.3373% for the incremental project B − A.)

19. In Section 5.1.3.4 the most basic pitfalls in cash-flow treatments were mentioned:

    1. Omitting feasible alternatives.
    2. Omitting necessary costs.
    3. Omitting incidental benefits.
    4. Including benefits or costs that are nonconsequences.

For each of the following invalid cash-flow treatments, list the basic pitfall that it illustrates:

A. Diego forgot that a database management system would require annual maintenance fees in addition to its first cost.

B. Suzan designed a material handling system with a "sky hook" (she forgot to consider how an overhead crane would be supported).

C. Donny signed the drawings for a $40,000 pump, unaware that a pump meeting the specifications was already in place and idle.

D. Hanif used the freeway at rush hour because it saved 5 minutes compared to the back roads (at other times of day it would save 20 minutes), unaware (or uncaring) that his choice caused other motorists an additional delay of about 15 vehicle minutes.

E. Rose Ann decided against a vapor recovery system that would reduce air pollution and reduce stock losses, because the value of the recovered vapor stock was insufficient to pay for the system.

F. Matilda used overtime and extra personnel to make ahead 410,000 circuit boards to be put into inventory so that sales would not be lost during a two-week shutdown to install new equipment. The new-equipment project analysis assumed two weeks of lost sales.

G. Spartacus recommended a new computer when the old computer's disk drive failed.

H. Part of the justification for a mezzanine for material storage above a factory floor was the value of floor space saved, although there was plenty of idle space already.

I. Helene asked for funds to beautify the lobby of the building, since the art council had recently awarded the building a $7000 appearance prize.

J. Pierre included insurance and depreciation in the estimated costs for company travel, but not fuel, because when employees would use their cars for company travel they were allowed to fill their fuel tanks at the company pump and were reimbursed only for insurance and depreciation.

20. A $45 million expansion project in a chemical plant consisted of a $30 million reactor and $15 million of piping, controls, pumps, and miscellaneous equipment. Product yield from the reactor was difficult to estimate, so the process engineers were conservative; the reactor was the one thing that could not be easily enlarged if necessary. Which of the following situations was most likely? Explain.

A. There was no significant opportunity for bottleneck-removal projects.

B. Several bottleneck-removal opportunities arose, and their rates of return were greater than that of the original project.

C. Several bottleneck-removal opportunities arose, although their rates of return were less than that of the original project.

21. At an assembly line, partial assemblies move past fixed stations at a rate of one unit per minute. John's task requires 59 seconds per unit; Henry's task requires 45 seconds per unit. The industrial engineer proposes a new 12-second task that can

be added to Henry's station and adds $0.05 value to each unit produced. Workers like Henry, at this assembly-line pace, cost $0.07 per unit. No capital investment is required.

(a) If the line will continue to run basically as is, should the new task be added?
(b) If a new assembly line is being designed, its specific stations are not known, and a task that adds $0.05 value per unit and requires $0.07 labor cost per unit is proposed, should it be included in the design?

22. G. R. Badge Industries produces 3.7 ton/day of sawdust as an unavoidable by-product. There is a buyer for 2.1 ton/day at a net revenue of $21/ton. The excess is carted away by a hauler who charges $0.60/ton. For purposes of analyzing projects that produce more sawdust by-product, what is the value, or cost, of sawdust per ton? Explain.

23. Cold-Sure Meats employs six chemists at a "loaded" (wage-plus-benefits-plus-overhead) cost of $26 per hour per chemist. The chemists analyze incoming meat, meat in process, and product for fat content, sodium content, bacteria, and so forth. They also analyze scrapings from many environmental surfaces. A new test becomes available to analyze for a bacterium that is not dangerous but is associated with a rancid smell in chicken meat. Regular analyses would help suppress this bacterium and contribute to shelf life and quality. The proposed testing program would cost 2.0 chemist hours per day and $16 of materials per day; its benefits would be worth $45 per day. The chemists are considered to be fully utilized, but it is likely the new work would be absorbed through adjustments, not actually causing additional chemist hours to be paid for. Is the project attractive?

24. A new machine and some associated improvements are proposed. The benefits of the proposal would be that the widget-making process would produce 3.7 widgets per minute rather than the current 2.9. The widget-making process has been operating from 5 hours to 9 hours per day, depending on demand; the average annual production has been 360,000 widgets. Which of the following is the best basis for evaluating the benefits? Explain.

A. Multiply the $3.7 - 2.9 = 0.8$ widget-per-minute production increase by the net profit per widget, and convert the result to an annual increase in profit.
B. Determine the old and new net profit per widget, multiply each by its production rate, take the difference, and convert the result to an annual increase in profit.
C. Determine the old and new net production cost per widget (many of the cost elements are multiplied by 2.9/3.7), take the difference, and multiply by 36,000 to convert to an annual decrease in cost.

25. Oester Oenology, the California quality-control service for vineyards, can produce up to 135,000 analyses per year with existing equipment and facilities. The operating costs of the testing division are considered to consist of a $62,000 annual fixed cost and a variable cost of $3.50 per analysis. Gary Oester, the president and chief chemist, has always followed the policy of pricing analyses at 15% above fixed-plus-variable cost.

(a) Determine the price per analysis for a period during which Gary expects to perform analyses at a 120,000/yr rate.

(b) Determine the price per analysis for a period during which Gary expects to perform analyses at the maximum rate.

26. Hans K. ("Hank") Gustanov, the automatic identification (bar coding) innovator, was puzzled when friends and business acquaintances suddenly started calling him "Mark"; a local gossip columnist had noted his physical resemblance to the famous basketball player Mark Price and the fact that his products mark prices on packages. His company manufactures and ships 3000 readers, 2500 hand-held printers, and 1700 cartons of custom labels in a typical month. Production is mostly to order, but an inventory of about 2000 readers and 5000 printers is kept. Temporary workers are sometimes employed on day shift. Classify each of the following cost items into a node in the cost-accounting structure of Figure 5-2, and also state whether the item is fixed, variable, or has both fixed and variable components.

   1. Mr. Gustanov's salary and benefits.
   2. Wages and benefits for reader-line production workers.
   3. Wages and benefits for secretarial and clerical workers.
   4. The bill from the advertising agency.
   5. The bill for office air conditioning upgrades.
   6. Shrink-wrap film for packaging of labels.
   7. Shipping cartons for printers.
   8. Lift-truck expenses in the warehouse.
   9. Wages and benefits for delivery truck drivers.
   10. The bill for water and sewage.

27. A boiler that provides utility steam for heating and cleanup in a food-service operation has fixed costs of $63,000 annually and variable costs of $0.16 per meal, where the current annual number of meals served is 38,000. Under a new proposal, the annual number of meals served will increase by 20%. Above 40,000 meals per year, the boiler is inadequate, and the fixed costs are estimated to be $65,000 annually. If this estimate is accepted, what is the annual increase in boiler-related costs caused by the new proposal if implemented?

28. Crystal Ball Cologne produces 1000 to 1500 bottles per minute of its popular "Oh!" eau, depending on demand. The only suitable possibilities for automation of packaging are boxing machines that cost $10,000 and can box 350 bottles per minute, and wrapping machines that cost $4000 and can wrap 265 bottles per minute. A student design group has suggested installing 5 boxing machines and 6 wrapping machines; this automation alternative would allow automated boxing and wrapping of up to 1590 bottles per minute (with some idle overcapacity in boxing). The chief engineer realizes that unit fixed costs will be proportional to the investment divided by the actual production rate and is unconvinced that it is wise to install so many machines. To generate alternatives that may possibly be more attractive, please identify the two most efficient machine balances within the capacity range of 1000 to 1500 bottles per minute—those balances for which the machine cost per production rate is least. Are they both more efficient than the suggested alternative, which costs $74,000 and has a capacity of 1590 bottles per minute, yielding a machine-cost-per-production-rate efficiency of 46.54?

29. A total industrial furnace capacity of 10 megatherms must be added in a process plant. Furnaces are available in sizes of 2, 4, 6, and 8 megatherms, and their costs

follow the "six-tenths rule." A 2-megatherm furnace has a cost of $104,000. Determine the cheapest combination of furnaces to provide at least 10 megatherms.

30. A taxpayer inspected the income-tax records for her small business. She noted she had paid $4560 on her last $12,000 of income (38%) and had paid $11,960 on her entire $52,000 of income (23%). To take income taxes into account, she wants to begin computing after-tax present worths. In after-tax analysis, each noncapital cash flow is multiplied by $(1 - T\beta^\lambda)$ where $\lambda = 0.5$ yr, and where T is a tax rate. The factor works for both positive and negative cash flows. For positive cash flows, it expresses the fact that, λ years after the taxpayer receives an extra dollar, the tax on the extra reported income is paid at rate T. For negative cash flows, it expresses the fact that, λ years after the taxpayer incurs an extra dollar of expense, the income tax is reduced by the tax rate T on the dollar, since the reported income is a dollar less than otherwise. Thus, if the taxpayer has a project in which she spends $475 as a noncapital expense and it earns $1000 a year later, the after-tax present worth is

$$P_{at} = -475(1 - T\beta^\lambda) + 1000(1 + T\beta^\lambda)\beta^1$$

Supposing her after-tax MARR to be $i = 15\%$, decide whether she should use the marginal (38%) or the average (23%) tax rate as T in the equation. Verify your answer by estimating the actual after-tax cash flows and showing their present worth to be identical numerically to the one computed using the equation.

31. In each of the situations described, quote one or more principles from Section 5.1.3.4.3 that is violated, and explain how the violation could be costly.

   A. McKinley, not knowing whether sufficient power was available to feed a new motor control center, ignored the issue.

   B. Szu chose the greatest insulation thickness that made a whole insulation project have ROR > MARR.

   C. Renée accepted some suggestions for small improvements desired by plant operators for their general convenience, and she added them to a big, profitable project proposal. They increased the project cost slightly; their benefits seemed substantial but hard to quantify, and the project was profitable enough that their inclusion would not have any significant impact, so she ignored them.

   D. Leah proposed and received approval for a "study" that actually constituted most of the engineering design for a new distribution terminal for petroleum products. With this cost study, she was now able to propose the terminal itself as a profitable project.

   E. Shashi found a new warehouse office to be unjustified because of labor costs. Two new warehouse workers were to be hired, and they were costed at wages plus benefits plus overhead; overhead included such items as one copier for every 32 workers and one secretarial or clerical worker for every 18 functional workers. In addition to the two new warehouse workers, Shashi included the cost of 4 hours per day of secretarial and clerical work.

32. Insulation of a jacketed vessel can be done at various thicknesses. The required investment increases roughly linearly with thickness. The savings, in indexed dollars, are considered to be an equal-payment series of savings at the ends of years 1 to 8, with no further economic consequences. The enterprise uses MARR of $d = 12\%$. The specific investments and savings for various thicknesses are as follows:

Thickness (in.)	Investment	Savings/yr	Thickness (in.)	Investment	Savings/yr
1	2,340	899	7	7,360	2,107
2	3,120	1,362	8	8,332	2,128
3	3,906	1,687	9	9,301	2,137
4	4,707	1,894	10	10,301	2,143
5	5,510	2,014	11	11,298	2,146
6	6,410	2,074			

Determine the insulation thickness that makes the project most profitable, and determine the greatest insulation thickness for which the project is profitable. Which insulation thickness should be chosen?

33. If "piecemealing" leads to a wrong decision, it must be either dishonest or inaccurate. The most common abuse of this type is the "foot-in-the-door" ploy whereby a feasibility study or other first step is taken, after which the elimination of sunk costs makes the further steps attractive even if in retrospect the whole project would have been unattractive. In a classic case, a large southern utility company began building a nuclear power plant in the 1980s. A generous estimate of the benefits would be an annual net savings of $100 million in fuel costs, based on high prices for coal, the alternative fuel. At $d = 8\%$ and a horizon of 20 years, the savings would justify an investment of $100(P/A\ 8\%,20) = \$981.81474$ million. Although it was patently obvious to outside observers that the plant would cost at least $2000 million ($2 billion) more than an equivalent coal-fired plant, the go-ahead was given. Call the incremental investment compared to a coal-fired plant C.

   After enough construction money had been spent so that this southern utility company could not stop construction and abandon the plant without *already* having spent $2000 million more than on a coal-fired plant, it became known to outsiders that C was going to total at least $4000 million—at least $2000 million remained to be spent to complete the plant and reap the benefits. It later turned out that the costs were much greater even than that, but the actual decision was to continue, not to abandon. Some combination of dishonesty and inaccuracy by the company and its regulatory overseers caused C to be underestimated again. Determine the greatest estimate of C that could have justified a go-ahead at that point.

34. At Marshall Choka's company, all kinds of excess capacity are considered to be valuable resources, whose existence makes the company better able to gear up quickly for sudden changes in demand. At Perry Stoker's company, the attitude is that excess capacity is wasted capacity. At each company, there is an opportunity to install a $60,000 machine that will earn $18,000 annually (indexed dollars) for five years. Let $d = 10\%$ for each company. The machine requires 200 square feet of floor space, valued at $45 per square foot by MC (Marshall Choka's company) and available free at PS.

   (a) What adjective describes the conservation policy at MC, and what contrasting adjective describes it at PS?
   (b) Does the difference in treatment of the value of offsite and infrastructure resources affect the decision described above?
   (c) Which of the two companies behaves like a rapidly expanding company?

35. Recall Example E8 of Chapter 4, in which the Soapstone Art Center could borrow a collection of French Impressionist paintings, exhibit them, and later purchase them for eventual profitable resale. Suppose the indivisibility assumption for this project did not hold; that is, suppose the center could pay the $10,000 fee, exhibit the collection for two years, and then decide separately whether or not to purchase the collection. If this were the case, the previous analysis of the project violates the principle of avoiding unnecessary linkage. Assuming a 12% interest rate, analyze each of the separate projects and make separate decisions.

36. A crew of three clerks produces 4000 units of database work per month, at a wage-plus-benefits-plus-overhead cost of $3840 per month per clerk. A new DBMS (database management system) would effect a 20% reduction in the clerical time required per unit of database work. Idle clerks will not be laid off but will be utilized elsewhere (in other words, any labor savings will be fully realized).

   (a) Determine the monthly benefit in clerical-labor savings from the DBMS.
   (b) Postulate a value v per unit of database work such that the current monthly net profit on database work with a crew of three is $4000v - 3(3840)$. With the same crew, the new DBMS could produce $4000/(1 - 0.20) = 5000$ units per month, giving a monthly net profit of $5000v - 3(3840)$. Determine v so that the new net profit would exceed the old net profit by at least the benefit computed above. Interpret the result.
   (c) Postulate a value w per unit of database work such that the old monthly net profit on database work was barely profitable. Now if the value w is valid for additional database work and the same crew of three keeps working, determine whether the monthly benefit of the new DBMS is smaller, the same, or greater than if the crew was reduced to just enough to do 4000 units per month.

37. Assume that a fledgling company can invest $1000 and collect a return of $1100 after one year. Further assume that the $1100 return can be invested to earn a $1210 return a year later, and that such bootstrapping can be continued for 10 years at a 10% rate of return, so that the net cash flow diagram would be as follows:

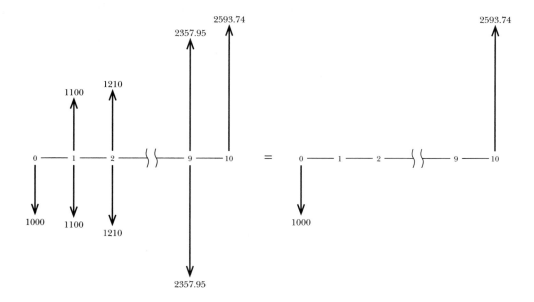

What is it that is misleading or invalid about presenting the opportunity in the form shown? Does the cash-flow diagram properly represent the alternatives available at time zero?

38. Since MARR can be "tuned" according to capital availability (Chapter 6), estimation practices (Example E34), risk (Chapter 8), or taxes (Chapter 10), the question arises as to sensitivity of worth evaluation to interest rate. That is, if the interest rate is uncertain or mistaken, are costly wrong decisions likely? To shed light on this issue, consider two alternatives that differ greatly in their time profiles and thus should be sensitive to interest rate:

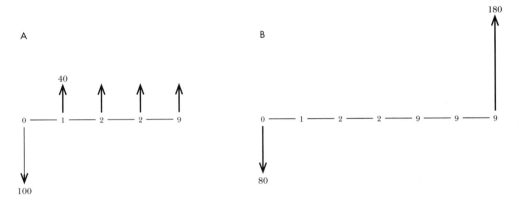

$$P^{(A)} = -100 + 40(P/A \ i, \ 4) \qquad P^{(B)} = -80 + 180\beta^6$$

(a) Without performing any compound-interest computations, claim or refute that **B** is more attractive at lower interest rates, and **A** at higher.

(b) Both **A** and **B** are investment projects, so their worth decreases with interest rate. It turns out that **B** is more attractive than **A** for low interest rates; they are equally attractive (present worth is 31.647) at 8.28563% interest; **A** is more attractive than **B** up to 21.8623% interest, where **A** has zero worth, beyond which neither **A** nor **B** is attractive, although **B** becomes the lesser evil after they both have the same present worth (-79.725) at 194.671% interest. Assume the alternatives are do nothing, **A**, or **B**. Would a decision maker for whom MARR could be anything from $i = 10\%$ to $i = 20\%$ make the correct decision regardless of using any MARR within the range?

39. Consider two same-horizon, no-salvage investment projects **A** and **B**:

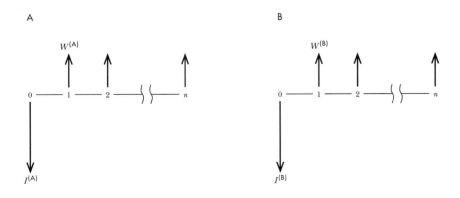

Let A have a rate of return (in real-interest terms) d:

$$0 = -I^{(A)} + W^{(A)}(P/A\ d,n) \tag{1}$$

Let B have rate of return o:

$$0 = -I^{(B)} + W^{(B)}(P/A\ o,n) \tag{2}$$

Let the rate of return of B be greater than that of A:

$$o > d \Rightarrow (P/A\ o,n) < (P/A\ d,n)$$

(a) Show that the project with greater ROR has shorter payback time (not rounded to integer).

(b) Determine whether the project having the greater rate of return is guaranteed to have the greater present worth at the smaller interest rate (the rate of return of the other project).

40. Consider the following two same-horizon, no-salvage investment projects A and B:

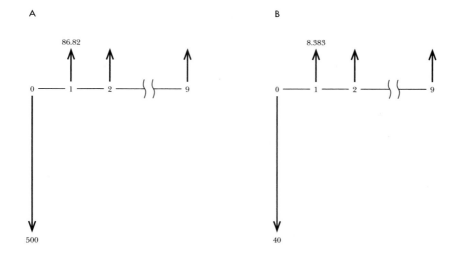

(a) Verify that B is the more efficient project (greater ROR); specifically verify that the rate of return of B is about 15% and of A about 10%.

(b) In general, a larger project (A is larger here) that has a smaller ROR (as A has here) can have a greater worth than a smaller project that is more efficient (B is more efficient here). However, among projects with similar time profiles, the more efficient one has greater worth than the larger one except at interest rates smaller than either project's ROR. Demonstrate that here, by comparing worths at interest rates 0%, 10%, 15%, and ∞.

(c) Determine the interest rate at which A and B have identical worths.

41. A construction project has tasks A, B, and C, where A is a predecessor to both B and C (A must be completed when B and C begin). With time in weeks, two schedules are shown below; the schedule on the left is an *early-start schedule*, in which each activity starts as early as possible, and the schedule on the right is a

late-start schedule, in which each activity starts as late as does not delay project completion.

Early-start schedule

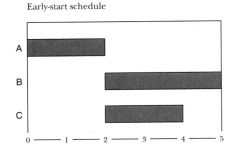

Late-start schedule

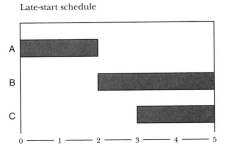

The early-start schedule is used when it is desired to minimize the chance of delaying project completion. The late-start schedule is used when it is desired to spend money as late as possible. If the cost of task C is $21,450, the interest rate is 16%, and a week is taken to equal 7/365.25 years, how much money is saved by the late-start schedule?

42. At a United Parcel Service (UPS) terminal that has 800 loading berths, there are three "sorts" per day. Each sort takes five hours, during which packages are loaded into outbound trucks according to a carefully optimized plan that is different for each sort because the mix of packages going to various destinations is different at different times of day. Between sorts, partly full trucks are moved to the berth specified in the next sort's plan; for example, if six trucks bound for Memphis are loaded and dispatched from berth 78, and the seventh truck is left partially full, this truck is moved to whatever berth is for Memphis on the next sort. A *universal outbound sort* plan has been proposed. It would provide, to the greatest practical extent, for the same berths to correspond to the same destinations for every sort. The proposed plan has advantages and disadvantages, but one advantage is that it would reduce jockeying between sorts, thus allowing sorts to be extended in time, or merged or overlapped. The resulting increase in capacity would have the benefit of delaying a planned expansion. If the terminal expansion were planned for 1996 and could be delayed until 1998 as a consequence of the proposed plan, and if it were estimated to have a cost of $2.21 million in 1993-indexed dollars, determine the present worth (in 1993) of this benefit at a 10% real interest rate.

43. An accounting change in the treatment of a recent expenditure can delay a $48,371.42 tax obligation by six months. If it costs $1500 to implement the change, what is the smallest interest rate such that a taxpayer having MARR equal to the interest rate would find the change worthwhile?

44. A discounted second lien has monthly payments of $442.19 through June 13, 1998. The final payment is payment 360. Immediately after receipt of payment 302, the lienholder offers to sell the lien for $18,396.65. This is the firm price, but the buyer must raise the cash, which may take a month or two. If the buyer uses $i_{\text{eff}} = 10\%$, how much is it worth to avoid a one-month delay in raising the cash,

given that the lienholder will collect the next payment and not reduce the price nor turn the payment over to the buyer?

45. In Example E38 the present worth of a diemaking improvement after a truncated delay was determined using the formula from Figure 5-4 for truncated delay.
    (a) Determine o, the present worth of the cash flows beyond month 5. Using this, verify the delayed present worth by directly comparing the present worth of the truncated delay cash-flow set.
    (b) It would be worth $16,453.76 to avoid the prospective delay. If the delay had been mistakenly treated as a shift-delay (that is, if it had mistakenly been assumed that all costs and savings would occur, delayed by three months), by how much would the worth of avoiding delay have been underestimated?

46. You use about a pound of black peppercorns annually in your pepper grinder. The DeKalb Farmer's Market charges $3.99 per pound for a vial containing 0.18 pounds, or $2.99 per pound for a bag containing 4.80 pounds. Ignoring the prospects of deterioration, cost of storage space and all other inventory holding costs except capital, determine which package—the vial or the bag—has the smaller equivalent annual cost for a decision maker for whom MARR is:
    (a) $d = 5\%$.
    (b) $d = 25\%$.
    (c) $d = 0\%$.
    (d) The present worth of the cost of an indefinite sequence of vials is $0.7182 + 0.7182/o$, where 0.7182 is the cost of a vial and o is the interest rate for a time interval of 0.18 years.

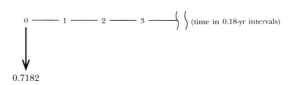

    If d is the real annual interest rate, then

$$1 + o = (1 + d)^{0.18} \quad \text{or} \quad d = (1 + o)^{1/0.18} - 1$$

    Similarly, the present worth of the cost of an indefinite sequence of bags is $14.352 + 14.352/u$, where u is the interest rate for a time interval of 4.8 years.

$$1 + u = (1 + d)^{4.8} \quad \text{or} \quad d = (1 + u)^{1/4.8} - 1$$

    The present worth of the incremental investment of purchasing an indefinite sequence of bags rather than vials would be the difference:

$$P_{\text{bags}-\text{vials}} = 0.7182 + 0.7182/o - [14.352 + 14.352/u]$$

    The incremental investment **bags** − **vials** has cash flows as shown in the diagram.

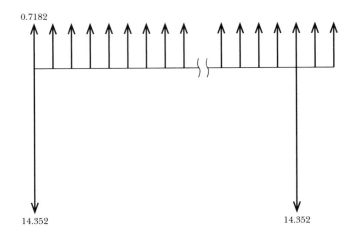

Determine the rate of return of the incremental investment.

(e) Verify that at the rate of return determined above, the two alternatives have identical equivalent annual costs (solve as in the first two parts of the exercise, with this value of d).

(f) Do the results exemplify the maxim that decision makers with smaller MARR accept less attractive investments? Explain.

47. In the simplest economic order quantity (EOQ) model, an inventory is replenished at regular intervals to satisfy a constant "demand" rate of D units per year. If the cost of each replenishment is $K + Cy$ dollars, where K is the "ordering cost," C is the cost per unit, and y is the number of units replenished, and if the annual cost of keeping an average inventory of $y/2$ units is $hy/2$ dollars, then the (undiscounted) total annual cost is

$$DC + \frac{K}{y/D} + \frac{hy}{2}$$

which is minimized by setting y to the value y^*:

$$y^* = \sqrt{\frac{2KD}{h}}$$

The unit annual holding cost h covers such things as space rent, deterioration, utilities, and the cost of capital. Assuming all costs are in indexed dollars, h is taken to include a term Cd, where d is the real interest rate, because $Cd \times y/2$ represents the interest on the average amount of capital, $Cy/2$, tied up in inventory. Note y/D is the number of years between replenishments, so y^*/D is the optimal replenishment interval according to the EOQ model.

(a) A restaurant uses 100 pounds of black peppercorns per year. Peppercorns can be purchased for \$2.00 per pound, and each replenishment order for peppercorns adds \$0.35 to the restaurant's overall replenishment costs. Peppercorn shelf space is considered negligible, but the restaurant uses a real interest rate of $d = 15\%$ in economic decision making. Using the EOQ model, determine the optimal replenishment interval.

(b) Determine the total annual cost, according to the EOQ model, for replenishing every month (1/12 year), replenishing EOQ-optimally, and replenishing every 2 months (1/6 year).

(c) The EOQ model ignores the timing of orders in its treatment of the time value of money. The annual-equivalent technique can be applied to the peppercorns problem as follows: If y is the order size and $y/100$ is the replenishment interval, and the cost of an order is $0.35 + 2y$ dollars, then the equivalent annual cost of a replenishment cycle is

$$A^{(y/100)} = (0.35 + 2y)(A/P\ 15\%, y/100)$$

Verify that this equivalent annual cost is minimized to $219.43 by an order size of about 15.8 lb. Based on the results and the shallowness of the optima (an optimum is said to be shallow if moderate variation from it does not cost much), does the EOQ model seem to do an adequate job of recommending an appropriate replenishment interval?

48. A truck terminal operator can buy either Acme or Buta tires for his 12-wheel trailers. An Acme tire costs $384 and lasts 16 months. A Buta tire costs $445 and lasts 20 months. The real interest rate is 11%.

(a) As a matter of general policy, which tire is more economical?
(b) Used tires can be sold for $70 plus $10 per month of remaining tread life. A particular trailer that will be scrapped 35 months from now needs a tire. Which is more economical, ignoring the possibility of switching brands in the sequence of replacements?
(c) For the particular trailer described above, considering the possibility of switching brands, what sequence of replacements is optimal?

49. The optimal-sequencing solution to the "catalytic reactor activation" problem was given in Table 5-1, Section 5.2.2.3, for various horizons. This problem has zero salvage values. For the horizon 5.5 years, determine the explicit-salvage solution and compare it to the optimal-sequencing solution.

50. In Example E41, a rapidly declining mine was to be abandoned after one year. Show that if the delay of the salvage value was ignored, optimal abandonment would seem to occur after two years.

51. Reconcile the numerical result of Example E42 to that of Example E41.

52. Derive a differential criterion for optimal abandonment time for the horizon-coverage switchover model of Eqs. 5-18 and 5-19, assuming that the cash flows of alternative y do *not* depend on the switchover time and the salvage value of alternative y is zero.

53. In Example E44 the New Clear power plant has a geometrically increasing abandonment cost (negative salvage value). If the annual growth rate in abandonment cost is 8.05%, determine the optimal abandonment time (integer year) and compute the net present worth of operating profits and abandonment cost for abandonment one year earlier, then, and one year later.

54. Let an investment project, whatever its earlier cash flows, have a time t after which its salvage value grows geometrically with abandonment time

$$S(\tau) = s_0\gamma^\tau, \qquad s_0 > 0, \qquad \gamma > 1$$

and its returns each period are a positive constant R.

(a) Derive a formula for the optimal abandonment time h.

(b) From the derived formula or its derivation, show that

    (i) If the salvage value grows as fast as money at compound interest, it would "never" be optimal to abandon.

    (ii) If s_0 is great enough (how great?) it would be optimal to abandon immediately.

(c) For monthly indexed returns of $1000, a salvage value at abandonment time τ of $200,000(1.01)^\tau$, and a real monthly interest rate d such that $\beta = 1/(1 + d) = 1/1.0125$, determine the optimal abandonment time.

55. Solve the revamp timing problem of Example E45 using a horizon of 13 years (rather than 8), with all other data remaining as is.

56. Verify Eq. 5-26 for $\tau = 3$ and $\tau + 1 = 4$ for Example E46.

57. The annual-equivalent technique for dealing with unequal economic lives and replacement problems makes routine use of the $(A/P\ i,n)$ factor for values of n that are not necessarily integer. Let us develop an interpretation of what it means for an equal-payment series of A dollars per year to be continued for, say, 2.5 years. Let us deal with the "pain" factor $(P/A\ i,n)$, which is the reciprocal of the $(A/P\ i,n)$ factor.

(a) At $i = 10\%$, $\beta = 1/1.10$, show that $(P/A\ i,2.5)$ lies between $(P/A\ i,2) = \beta + \beta^2$ and $(P/A\ i,3) = \beta + \beta^2 + \beta^3$, thus providing a small illustration of how $(P/A\ i,n)$ values for non-integer n provide a smooth curve that goes through the points for integer n.

(b) The above values are the worths of $1 per year for 2, "2.5," and 3 years. Recall that with continuous time a continuous cash flow at rate $1 per year would have present worth $(1 - \beta^n)/r$ where $r = \ln(1 + i) = -\ln \beta$. Comparing this with $(1 - \beta^n)/i$, we see that the end-of-year convention, applied to a cash flow that actually was continuous, underestimates its worth by the factor r/i. Now the present worth would also be underestimated if we viewed *every* infinitesimal payment as delayed λ years. Equate this to r/i, and solve for λ.

(c) Using the above result, determine the effective delay by the end-of-year convention when $i = 10\%$.

(d) According to the above arguments, the factor $(P/A\ 10\%,2.5)$ can be interpreted as the present worth at 10% interest not of "2.5" payments of $1 each, but of either of the following two cash-flow sets:

Demonstrate numerically that each of the two cash-flow sets has worth $(P/A\ 10\%,2.5)$.

58. From the results of Example E46 for $\tau = 3$ and $\tau = 4$, verify Eq. 5-25 numerically.

59. Refer to Example E46. Let the revenues-less-costs be {3, 4, 3, 1, 1, 1, 1} rather than those previously given. Determine how long a campaign should run, using Eq. 5-23.

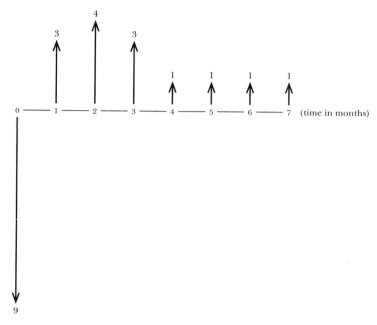

Note: Without age deterioration, if the returns are equal for a set of periods (as in months 4, 5, 6, and 7 here), the differential criterion (Eq. 5-27) would be the same for each period after the first period in the set. Hence we can conclude that if the campaign should run four months, it should run seven.

60. A process plant undergoes a maintenance shutdown once per year. Cooling coils are replaced by cleaned ones when observed to be appreciably clogged by scale buildup on their inside walls. Clogging increases power consumption in pumping cooling water through the coils; the indexed annual pumping costs are estimated to obey the growth curve

$$X_\theta = 81.5 \ (8 - 0.6\theta)^{-1.8}$$

where X_θ is the annual pumping cost in thousands of dollars when the set of coils is θ years "old" at the end of the year.

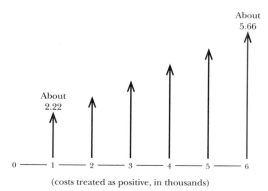

(costs treated as positive, in thousands)

The plant uses a real annual interest rate of 12%. If a replacement has an indexed cost of 4 (that is, $4000), including the worth of the cost of descaling the replaced coils for future reuse, determine the best age at which to replace clogged coils.

61. Solve the age-deterioration replacement problem of Example E49 for 18% real interest and a replacement cost of $10,000 (as opposed to $14,450). The results should illustrate that a decrease in investment causes a decrease in optimal replacement age.

62. Solve the age-deterioration replacement problem of example E49 for 6% real interest and a replacement cost of $10,000 (as opposed to $14,450). The results should illustrate that a decrease in investment causes a decrease in optimal replacement age.

63. A project has the following current-dollar cash flows:

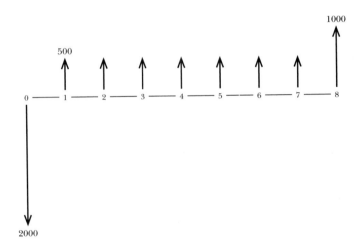

(In estimating equal annual returns, the analyst is aware of assuming that real productivity declines at an inflation-offsetting rate.) The owner uses $i = 15\%$ in worth calculations. A shift delay of one year is contemplated because the investment cost is expected to be 30% less, while the returns' current-dollar amounts would be unaffected (the analyst is aware of the slight reduction in real productivity implied by shifting the constant-dollar returns and salvage value). Determine whether the delay is worthwhile.

64. Considering an expected reduction in equipment cost and increase in productivity for a proposed project for Blatzworth Industries, it is estimated that the indexed-dollar worth of the project at its inception will be 9% greater if there is a one-year delay in undertaking it. What must be known about Blatzworth in order to decide whether it is better to delay than to act immediately? State a definite condition under which the delay is chosen.

65. Let the instantaneous gross operating revenue R_t be increasing according to the asymptotic growth profile in Chapter 2 from R_0 \$/yr to R \$/yr with continuous gradient parameter $a > 0$:

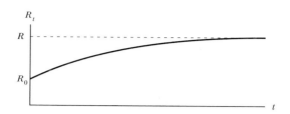

Let the instantaneous gross operating cost C_t be decreasing from C_0 to C according to the same parameter:

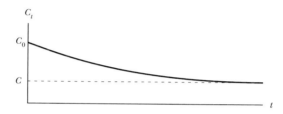

The net operating profit is $W_t = R_t - C_t$. Show that the net operating profit increases according to the asymptotic growth profile from $R_0 - C_0$ to $R - C$ with continuous gradient parameter a.

66. Write a computer program to solve Eq. 5-29 for the problem of Examples E51 and E52. Use it to search for a set of three machine start times to cover a horizon of $n = 22$.

67. Determine the best time to purchase a machine like the one in Example E51 if the horizon is 10 years and there will be only one machine (no replacement).

68. Determine the best time to purchase a machine like the one in Example E51 if the horizon is 13 years and there will be only one machine (no replacement).

69. Solve the problem of Example E52 for a horizon of $n = 22$.

70. To illustrate the depreciation bias against investment, consider a \$1000 machine that earns \$400 each year for five years. Assume zero inflation, so i and d are the same.

Before taxes:

$$P_{bt} = -1000 + 400\left(\frac{1 - \beta^5}{i}\right)$$

Let the income tax rate be $T = 40\%$, let the tax lag be $\lambda = 0.5$ years, and let the depreciation efficiency be as given in this extract from Table 10-11 of Chapter 10:

i	1%	5%	10%	15%	20%	25%	30%
Ω	97.75%	89.62%	81.10%	74.01%	68.04%	62.96%	58.59%

The before-tax rate of return of the project is 28.64929%. Without necessarily determining the after-tax rate of return accurately, demonstrate that it is substantially smaller (it would not be smaller without depreciation, so the depreciation bias against investment will be thus demonstrated).

The after-tax present worth of the project is

After taxes:

$$P_{at} = -1000(1 - T\Omega) + 400(1 - T\beta^{\lambda})\left(\frac{1 - \beta^5}{i}\right)$$

71. Philips Lighting offered its Earth Light™ light bulb at a cost of $18. It is said to last for 7670 hours, to draw 18 watts of electricity, and to provide illumination equivalent to that of a regular 75-watt bulb. Assume that a regular 75-watt bulb lasts for 1000 hours and draws 75 watts. Assume that electrical energy is purchased at a cost of $0.077 per kilowatt-hour and that there is a requirement for 1000 hours per year of this amount of illumination. Assume that there is no inflation, so i and d are the same.
    (a) With $i = 10\%$, if a regular bulb costs $1, which bulb—the Philips or the regular—has the smaller equivalent annual cost before taxes?
    (b) Repeat the calculation on an after-tax basis with an income-tax rate of $T = 40\%$ and a tax lag of $\lambda = 0.5$ years, assuming light bulbs are an expense (not depreciated, so that $\Omega = \beta^{\lambda}$). Show that the after-tax ratio of the equivalent annual costs of the two bulbs is identical to the before-tax ratio, which demonstrates decision neutrality.
    (c) Repeat the calculation on an after-tax basis with the same rate and lag as before, but assuming that the tax authority has ruled that light bulbs that last for at least seven years must be depreciated according to a schedule for which the depreciation efficiency is $\Omega = 0.8110$ for a decision maker who uses $i = 10\%$. Show that the requirement for depreciation introduces a bias against the investment in the longer-lived bulb, by comparing after-tax ratios.

Mechanical leverage magnifies force; financial leverage magnifies investment capital.

LEVERAGE AND CAPITAL BUDGETING

Whereas Chapter 5 concerned mutually exclusive alternatives, this chapter concerns the array of *independent opportunities* facing a decision maker.

Obviously an investor would like to accept all desirable opportunities. We have already established worth at MARR as a measure of desirability. The question for this chapter is how or whether an investor can manage to accept all desirable opportunities if the supply of investment capital is not unlimited.

Broadly, there are two answers to this question. For one thing, the investor can enhance the available capital supply by long-term borrowing. *Leverage*, or the use of borrowed capital, is the subject of Section 6.3.

The other answer to how one can accept all desirable opportunities is that one "tunes" MARR, the parameter that measures desirability, until the population of desirable opportunities is small enough not to demand too much capital. This sour-grapes approach to the matter (recall Aesop's fable in which the Fox concluded that the grapes he couldn't reach were probably sour) is the subject of Section 6.2. Section 6.1 introduces the issues and reviews formal and informal allocation procedures.

6.1 CONTENTION FOR CAPITAL

Civilization arose after agriculture produced enough capital to enable routine, large-scale investments. Once there was money, backed by stored grain, there must have been many projects (water supply, warehousing, roads, housing) contending for capital, and only the most attractive could be funded. The following example clarifies some of the issues in contention for capital.

E1. You visit two plants that manufacture electronics products. Plant A has semiauto-mated assembly, automated testing, more floor space, and, in general, many extras that increase its investment but decrease its ongoing operating costs. Plant B seems to minimize investment. List and discuss possible explanations for the difference.

The observation is that Plant A has accepted several investment projects, while Plant B has not accepted the corresponding opportunities. Apparently the extras give more benefits or require smaller investments at Plant A, or Plant B could not accept the corresponding opportunities or did not see them as desirable. Some specific possibilities are:

1. If Plant A has high labor costs, perhaps by being unionized or in an affluent neighborhood, while Plant B has low labor costs, perhaps by being in an economically depressed area, laborsaving projects may be more beneficial to Plant A.

2. If Plant A is on cheaper land, its greater investment may be due to less costly floor space.

3. If the company that owns Plant B is short of available investment capital, the difference would be explained.

4. If Plant B is to be torn down sooner than Plant A, the shorter-lived benefits may not justify the investments.

5. If the company that owns Plant B is very profitable and normally earns a high ROR, while Plant A normally earns a lower ROR, and if ROR for these investments was between the two, the difference would be explained.

Shortage of capital (point 3) and differences in MARR (point 5) are the business of this chapter. As we shall see, the two points may be related; shortage of capital can cause a company to increase its perceived MARR.

The undistributed after-tax earnings of an enterprise (those not paid out as stock dividends) are available for investment or for reducing long-term debt; these funds, if used for either purpose, are called *equity capital* or "plowback" capital. Obviously the equity capital available for investment is limited by the returns recently earned on previous investments.

The additional *borrowed capital* lenders may be willing to lend for investment is limited by lenders' perceptions of the risks of not being repaid.

There are other sources of capital—diluting ownership by issuing stock, and selling off assets—but we will confine discussion in this chapter to equity capital and borrowed capital.

6.1.1 Combinations of Independent Projects

Two project opportunities are *independent* if their required investments and their consequences are, for each, independent of whether the other opportunity is accepted. For example, in an office the costs and benefits of a copier may be independent of the costs and benefits of a computer but not independent of those of a laser printer.

Given a set of independent project opportunities, there is a *corresponding set of mutually exclusive alternatives* representing all the combinations of accepting from none to all of the independent opportunities.

E2. **A company's board has not decided what its investment budget will be for the coming fiscal year. Besides many opportunities to invest various amounts in the ordinary course of business at a rate of return of about 15%, there are these extraordinary opportunities (independent of each other, in thousands of dollars):**

Project	Required Investment	Net Present Worth at $i = 15\%$
1	30	26
2	40	30
3	90	100

Determine the corresponding set of mutually exclusive alternatives, and for each give its required investment and its present worth.

Each alternative is a combination of independent opportunities, and has a required investment equal to the sum of their required investments and a present worth equal to the sum of their present worths (in thousands of dollars):

Alternative	Required Investment	Present Worth
0	0	0
1	30	26
2	40	30
3	90	100
1, 2	70	56
1, 3	120	126
2, 3	130	130
1, 2, 3	160	156

The set of mutually exclusive alternatives corresponding to a set of independent opportunities typically exhibits *diminishing returns* in that an increase to a small investment budget earns more worth increase than the same increase to a larger budget.

E3. **Suppose the investment budget can be anything from $50,000 to $180,000, in steps of $10,000. Prepare a graph showing how the present worth increases with the budget.**

Since all the alternatives have been completely enumerated in the answer to Example E1, the graph is simple to prepare. It is shown in Figure 6-1.

With practical numbers of independent opportunities it is not feasible to enumerate all alternatives. For example, with 10 independent opportunities there are 1024 different alternatives: 1 alternative that includes none of them, 10 that include one of them, 45 that include two of them, and so on. If one must consider the alternative versions of each independent opportunity, the problem size grows further. If each of the projects had 3 alternative versions, the number of mutually exclusive alternatives would be multiplied by 3, becoming 2442 for 10 independent opportunities each having 3 versions. The problem size grows even further when the possibilities of delay—

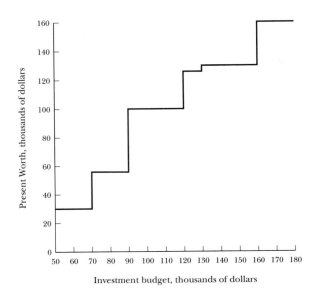

FIGURE 6-1. Diminishing returns of an investment budget.

implementing a project next year instead of now—are considered. The following two sections show how capital budgeting can be done in ways that avoid exhaustive enumeration.

6.1.2 Basic Capital Budgeting

Given a set of J independent opportunities numbered $j = 1, 2,...,J$, each having a required investment I_j and a net present worth P_j at a given interest rate, and given an investment budget limit B, the basic capital budgeting problem is to determine the set of opportunities that maximizes the sum of the worths of the included opportunities, among those sets for which the sum of the required investments of the included opportunities does not exceed the budget. Let the decision variable x_j have value zero if opportunity j is excluded, or value 1 if opportunity j is included. Then the basic capital budgeting problem can be formulated as a constrained optimization problem:

Basic capital budgeting problem:

$$\text{Maximize} \sum_{j=1}^{J} P_j x_j \tag{6-1}$$

$$\text{subject to} \sum_{j=1}^{J} I_j x_j \le B \tag{6-2}$$

$$\text{and } x_j \in \{0,1\} \qquad \text{for} \qquad j = 1, 2,...,J \tag{6-3}$$

E4. Formulate the problem of Examples E2 and E3 as a basic capital budgeting problem, for a budget of 100.

From Example E2, the projects are numbered $j = 1, 2, 3$; the required investments are $I_1 = 30$, $I_2 = 40$, and $I_3 = 90$; the present worths are $P_1 = 26$, $P_2 = 30$, and $P_3 = 100$. For $B = 100$, the formulation is

$$\text{Maximize } 26x_1 + 30x_2 + 100x_3$$

$$\text{subject to } 30x_1 + 40x_2 + 90x_3 \leq 100$$

$$\text{and } x_j \in \{0,1\} \quad \text{for} \quad j = 1, 2, 3$$

6.1.2.1 Exact Capital Budgeting Solutions The basic capital budgeting problem of Eq. 6-1, 6-2, and 6-3 is mathematically a *knapsack* problem, which can be solved efficiently by an optimization technique called *dynamic programming*. Dynamic programming is efficient for this problem in the sense that the solution effort grows only linearly with J (recall that J is the number of decision variables). Thus if we have twice as many independent opportunities, dynamic programming uses only about twice as much computer time; other methods are less efficient, having effort that grows exponentially with J.

Any introductory operations research textbook that covers dynamic programming specifically covers basic capital budgeting; for example, Chapter 9 of Handy A. Taha's *Operations Research* (Macmillan), Third Edition, opens with this problem.

In this chapter we will restrict attention to problems so small that the exact solution can easily be found by exhaustive enumeration, if necessary. As we shall see, exact solutions are often beside the point in practical situations.

6.1.2.2 NPVI Ordering If it were not for the impossibility of partially accepting an opportunity (ruled out by Eq. 6-3), the problem expressed by Eq. 6-1 and 6-2 would have an exact solution that is very easy to obtain. Given $0 \leq x_j \leq 1$ instead of $x_j \in \{0, 1\}$, the solution to Eqs. 6-1 and 6-2 would be to sort the opportunities in decreasing order of the ratio P_j/I_j and accept as many as possible. P_j/I_j is the NPVI for opportunity j as defined in Chapter 4; the *NPVI-ordering* procedure is to go down the NPVI list until the budget is exhausted. This is sometimes called the "bang-for-buck" heuristic (a heuristic is a procedure that is not guaranteed to find an optimal solution).

E5. Four independent projects are contending for an investment budget of 30 (all amounts in thousands of dollars):

Project, j	P_j	I_j
1	52	22
2	42	14
3	15	8
4	12	6

The optimal alternative is to accept projects 2, 3, and 4, earning a present worth of 69 for an investment of 28. Apply NPVI ordering. Does it give the optimal solution?

$$P_1/I_1 = 2.3636$$
$$P_2/I_2 = 3$$
$$P_3/I_3 = 1.8750$$
$$P_4/I_4 = 2$$

Sorting the P_j/I_j values in decreasing order, the opportunities should be considered in the order 2, 1, 4, 3.

Accept Project 2, leaving an unused budget of $30 - 14 = 16$; consider Project 1, which is infeasible because $I_1 > 16$; accept Project 4, leaving an unused budget of $16 - 6 = 10$; accept Project 3, leaving an unused budget of $10 - 8 = 2$. This procedure accepts Projects 2, 3, and 4, which is the same as the optimal solution.

The NPVI-ordering procedure can fail to identify the optimal solution, as the next example demonstrates.

E6. The following independent projects are available:

Project	Required Investment	Net Present Worth
A	$110,000	$ 6,700
B	120,000	8,400
C	70,000	4,000
D	130,000	10,000

Because of a shortage of capital, no more than $300,000 can be invested. The optimal solution is to accept projects A, B, and C, earning a net present worth of $19,100 and using the entire $300,000 budget. Apply NPVI ordering. Does it give the optimal solution?

$$P_A/I_A = 0.0609$$
$$P_B/I_B = 0.0700$$
$$P_C/I_C = 0.0571$$
$$P_D/I_D = 0.0769$$

Sorting the P_j/I_j values in decreasing order, the opportunities should be considered in the order D, B, A, C.

Accept D, leaving $170,000 in the budget; accept B, leaving $50,000 in the budget; reject A; reject C. This procedure accepts projects D and B, which is not the same as the optimal solution.

The NPVI-ordering procedure earns a present worth of $18,400, which is smaller than the optimal $19,100.

It should be noted that the unused investment budget amount, if any, is assumed to be invested in the ordinary course of business, earning zero worth.

Despite its mathematical suboptimality, the NPVI-ordering procedure has some practical advantages over exact solution. Suppose we recognize the inexactness of the data; in real life, we would expect errors of 5% to 10% in P_j, I_j, and B. When variation is great enough, the NPVI-ordered solution turns out to be *better* than the solution that is exactly optimal when all quantities are at their average values. Look at Example E6, and consider the optimal solution's rejection of the most efficient project, D. If the budget were 10% greater, the NPVI-ordered solution (B, C, D) would be better than the identified optimal solution; in fact, the identified optimal solution is best only for a few isolated sets of values out of the many that would result from tweaking the numbers randomly. The most efficient project, D, is more likely than any other to be in the best set.

More important than random variation is the dynamic nature of budgeting. New opportunities can arise at any time. If this occurs to a great extent, the decision maker who accepted the more efficient projects is almost sure to enjoy a better final outcome than the one who filled a "chink" in the budget with a less efficient project that happened to fit well (that is what the optimal solution does). The budget itself is not really a random variable; instead it can be influenced by the opportunities. As we will see in Section 6.3, a profitable investment opportunity often creates its own borrowing opportunity. For all these reasons, the exact approach to capital budgeting is not widely used.

6.1.2.3 ROR Ordering A widely used heuristic for capital budgeting is to sort the opportunities in decreasing order of *rate of return* and accept as many as are both possible (within budget) and profitable (ROR > MARR).

To compare this ROR-ordering procedure with NPVI ordering, let us examine the three independent projects whose data are given in Figure 6-2.

E7. The projects shown in Figure 6-2 are the independent opportunities available to a decision maker who has a capital budget of $10,000. Consider two separate cases: the ordinary course of business yields a 12% rate of return, or the ordinary course of business yields an 18% rate of return. For each of the cases, determine the set of projects to be recommended by the ROR-ordering procedure, the set recommended by the NPVI-ordering procedure, and the optimal set.

Case 1: MARR = 12%

From Figure 6-2, the projects sorted in decreasing ROR order are B, C, and A. Since they each require a $10,000 investment and the budget is $10,000, the ROR-ordering procedure recommends B.

Since from the graph in Figure 6-2 it is clear that $P^{(C)} > P^{(B)}$ at 12% interest, and $\text{NPVI}^{(C)} = P^{(C)}/10,000$ is greater than $\text{NPVI}^{(B)} = P^{(B)}/10,000$, the NPVI-ordering procedure recommends C.

The optimal set is obviously C. At 12% interest, with $\beta = 1/1.12$, the present worth is

$$P^{(C)} = -10,000 + 2800(P/A\ 12\%,\ 10) + 4700\beta^{11} = \$7171.76$$

The present worth of B at 12% is

$$P^{(B)} = -10,000 + 6000\beta + 4000\beta^2 + 9700\beta^3 + 1000\beta^4 = \$6085.70$$

Using the ROR-ordering procedure would cause a wrong decision that reduces the present worth by $1086.06.

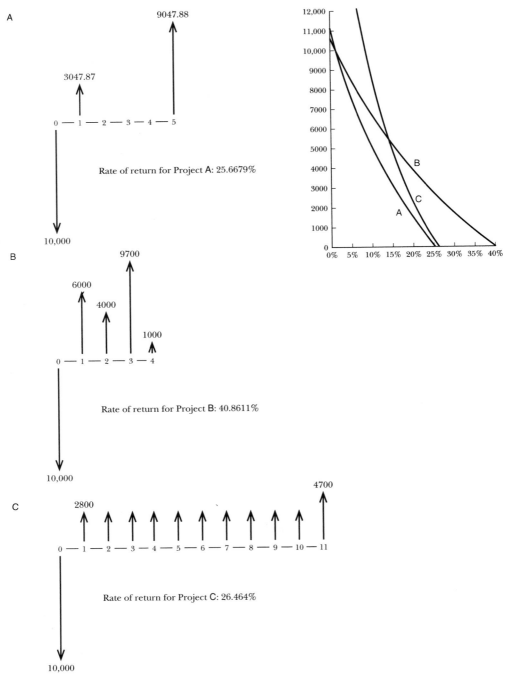

FIGURE 6-2. Three independent projects having contrasting *P*-vs-*i* curves.

Case 2: MARR = 18%

The ROR-ordering procedure, which ignores MARR, recommends **B** as before. From Figure 6-2 it is clear that $P^{(B)} > P^{(C)}$ at 18% interest, and $\text{NPVI}^{(B)} = P^{(B)}/10{,}000$ is greater than $\text{NPVI}^{(C)} = P^{(C)}/10{,}000$; hence the <u>NPVI-ordering</u>

procedure recommends B. The optimal set is obviously B. At 18% interest, with $\beta = 1/1.18$, the present worth is

$$P^{(B)} = -10{,}000 + 6000\beta + 4000\beta^2 + 9700\beta^3 + 1000\beta^4 = \underline{\$4376.99}$$

Example E7 has shown that ROR-ordering does not necessarily fill a budget in the most profitable way. Comparing B and C, we note that B *returns less money faster, while* C *returns more money slower.* This causes B to have a greater ROR and to be better for a high-MARR impatient investor, while C is better for a low-MARR patient investor.

Now let us explore a weakness of the capital budgeting problem itself, which is that it *ignores future opportunities.* We shall see that although ROR-ordering fails to do well in solving a basic capital budgeting problem, it does better than NPVI-ordering in allocating capital over the long run.

E8. For a decision maker with MARR = 12%, Example E7 showed that the ROR-ordering procedure would choose B, whereas C would maximize worth and would be chosen by NPVI-ordering. Now assume that project opportunities like B and C may arise occasionally in the future. Specifically, assume that an opportunity will again be available whenever at least three years have passed since its last acceptance, and its payback time has elapsed. (This assumption recognizes that returns from current investments create future equity capital.) Under this assumption, does the ROR-ordering recommendation maximize worth?

Project B has a payback time of two years, so it can be repeated every three years. Project C has a payback time of $10{,}000/2800 = 3.57 \rightarrow 4$ years, so it can be repeated every four years.

The cash flows of the indefinite stream of repetitions of B are equivalent at 12% interest to $P^{(B)} = \$6085.70$ every three years, having the annual equivalent

$$A^{(B)} = P^{(B)}(A/P\ 12\%,3) = \underline{\$2533.78/yr}$$

The cash flows of the indefinite stream of repetitions of C are equivalent at 12% interest to $P^{(C)} = \$7171.76$ every four years, having the annual equivalent

$$A^{(C)} = P^{(C)}(A/P\ 12\%,4) = \underline{\$2361.19/yr}$$

The result is remarkable: Although C has greater worth, the greater-ROR project B is a better choice under capital scarcity if similar future opportunities will arise and the returns from current projects will finance them.

Example E8 gives quantitative support to the widespread practice of accepting all investment projects with high ROR. Table 6-1 summarizes the conclusions from this section as to which capital budgeting approaches are applicable to ration scarce investment capital under various conditions and assumptions.

To review the applicability of the various capital budgeting approaches, let us consider several sample situations for a protagonist with MARR = 12%:

1. No scarcity of capital: Available are A, B, and C from Figure 6-2 and many ordinary ROR = 12% projects. The investment budget is $40,000.

TABLE 6-1 Recommended Capital Budgeting Approaches

Recommended Capital budgeting approach	Precision of budget, worths, required investments	Expectation of future opportunities
Exact solution (dynamic programming)	exact data	ROR = MARR only
NPVI-ordering	inexact data	ROR = MARR only
ROR-ordering	exact or inexact data	occasional ROR > MARR opportunities

2. Exact data, ROR = MARR future: Available are A, B, and C from Figure 6-2 and many ordinary ROR = 12% projects, with all data considered exact and no expectation of any future ROR > MARR opportunities. The investment budget is $28,000. An additional opportunity D has a required investment of $5000, a present worth of $1000 at 12% interest, and ROR = 15%.

3. Inexact data, ROR = MARR future: The situation is the same as 2 above, except that the data are considered inexact.

4. ROR > MARR future: Available are A, B, and C from Figure 6-2 and many ordinary ROR = 12% projects. The investment budget is $10,000. Occasional ROR > MARR opportunities are expected to arise in the future.

In situation 1, capital is not scarce. There is enough capital to accept all ROR > MARR opportunities. The protagonist should do as recommended in Chapter 5: Invest in all opportunities having ROR > MARR (which is the same, for investment opportunities, as $P > 0$ at MARR), and put all remaining capital into the ordinary course of business.

In situation 2, with a budget of $28,000 and an additional available opportunity D, the exact solution method would accept B, C, and D. Although A is much more efficient than D, there is not enough capital for A. The present worth earned by B, C, and D is $6085.70 + $7171.76 + $1000 = $14,257.46. If $2000 of additional capital were available, the set of accepted projects would be B, C, and A, which would earn a worth of $6085.70 + $7171.76 + $6120.90 = $19,378.36. Too bad! (As we will see in Section 6.3, it would be worthwhile to borrow the additional $2000 even if the interest rate were huge.)

In situation 3, since D has a very small NPVI compared to the others, the NPVI-ordering procedure would identify C first, then B, then A. A would bring the total required budget $2000 over the available $28,000, which would be allowable if the budget limit were considered to be inexact.

In situation 4, the ROR-ordering procedure would recommend project B, whereas the exact solution and the NPVI-ordering procedure would have recommended C. As shown in Example E8, B would be better in this situation.

If we reexamine Figure 6-2, we note that B has quick returns. Although it adds less total wealth to a MARR = 12% enterprise than does C, it quickly yields returns that can be reinvested. Thus **B** is the sort of project that is desirable if other ROR > MARR project opportunities are expected to occur in the future. If, on the other hand, ROR > MARR opportunities will not recur, the protagonist cannot do better than investing in **C**.

6.1.3 Global Versus Hierarchical Selection

Most organizations have specialization such that not all opportunities can be considered together. For example, a warehouse engineer may be aware of opportunities to automate picking, to save floor space, to optimize lift truck routes, and to use demand forecasting to set more accurate stock levels. A shipping engineer working at a neighboring workstation in the same office may be aware of opportunities to save fuel by better routing, to improve the cost effectiveness of delivery truck maintenance, and to redesign the loading dock to save loading labor. Even for these closely related functions—warehousing and shipping—it is obvious that no one person or entity would weigh all the versions of all the opportunities together in a single decision process.

There is a hierarchical scheme for letting all the decisions at different places in the organization be made separately. The best versions of each warehouse project may be aggregated into a single warehouse-improvements budget. This may be aggregated with its shipping counterpart into a single finished-goods budget. In turn, this may be aggregated with others at the same level in the hierarchy into a manufacturing improvements budget, which with the marketing and other budgets is aggregated into the corporate capital-expenditures budget. See Figure 6-3.

To coordinate all the decisions made at various places, upper management promulgates an investment selection policy. Part of the policy is an efficiency-measure value. A theoretically deficient but widely used efficiency measure value is payback time. Suppose upper management orders that "all proposed capital improvements should have a payback time of four years or less."

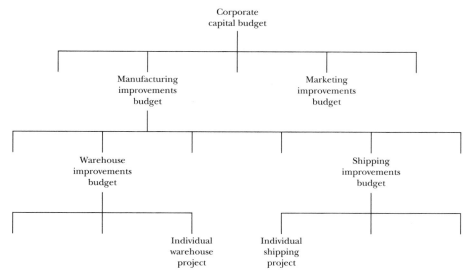

FIGURE 6-3. Capital budget hierarchy.

The payback-time criterion acts throughout the organization as a shadow price, causing consistent decisions to be made. Each project in the warehouse is adjusted to include all increments that pay off faster than four years and to exclude those that do not. When all the proposals reach the corporate level, their total required investment either is roughly the amount of capital available for investment, or, if it is too large or too small, upper management can "tune" the criterion. MARR can be used in exactly the same manner as payback time, with more consistent results.

MARR is the efficiency measure that functions best in coordinating engineering economic decision making. Section 6.2 discusses the important question of how to "tune" MARR for best results.

6.2 MINIMAL ATTRACTIVE RATE OF RETURN (MARR)

The most useful definition of MARR is a very simple one:

> MARR is defined as the interest rate for use in project evaluation.

Included in a specification of MARR, of course, are characteristics of the decision procedures in which it is used. Especially important is whether cash flows are indexed (calling for MARR expressed as a real interest rate d) or current, and (if current) what inflation rate is assumed. It must be clear whether a specified MARR is for before-tax or after-tax analysis. There must be a standard riskiness, and it must be clear whether cash-flow estimation procedures are nonbiased expected cash flows or hoped-for cash flows (see Chapter 8).

Determining the appropriate MARR is not trivial, because the choice should depend partially on how it is used—that is, different policies and procedures for estimating costs and benefits and different rules for accepting or rejecting projects imply different MARRs. We will review practices and criteria, examine their effects on decisions by solving some illustrative problems, and review the issues and advice given in the engineering economy literature for choosing MARR. Since *risk, taxes,* and *leverage*—three topics not yet covered—affect MARR, some of this discussion will foreshadow material to be learned in more detail later.

6.2.1 How MARR Is Used

The first question to answer in setting MARR is the "Why?" question: Why do we need a value for MARR? That is, What is MARR used for?

We already know that *MARR is the basis for selecting the best among mutually exclusive investment opportunities.* If there is a right or wrong way to set MARR, the wrong way should set MARR too high or too low in some situations, leading to wrong decisions that interfere with the pursuit of maximal profitability. Here we will assume that MARR is used to screen out unattractive opportunities, to choose the "live candidate" version of each project, and to select the set of candidates chosen for investment. This last use is that of capital budgeting.

> **The assumed hierarchical use of MARR:**
> . . . .
>
> 1. To screen candidate opportunities.
> 2. To select the best version of each opportunity.
> 3. To select the set of accepted opportunities.

Hierarchical decision procedures are known mathematically to be suboptimal. At each step in the hierarchical scheme some candidates are eliminated from further consideration, and it is possible that the best final outcome could be achieved by using eliminated candidates. Our assumed hierarchical use of MARR is hierarchical in several ways: *screened-out opportunities are eliminated, second-best and worse versions of opportunities are eliminated,* and *the procedure separates time periods* in that selection of accepted opportunities is for a given budget period without regard to next year. Despite their weaknesses, hierarchical decision procedures are actually used in real enterprises, for the simple reasons that (1) full centralized coordination is impractical (as the Soviet system has demonstrated) and (2) new opportunities arise and old ones change or disappear, so that there is never a complete set of valid data.

E9. Candidate Screening. Four investment opportunities are independent. Their costs and benefits have been estimated, giving results shown in the table (present worth is in *K$.*):

Independent Project	ROR	*Present worth in K$ at i =*				
		10%	*15%*	*20%*	*25%*	*30%*
A	24.95%	600.5	346.2	151.1	−1.3	−122.6
B	10%, 40%	0	0.1	0.2	0.2	0.2
C	19.90%	756.9	331.9	−6.3	−278.8	−501.2
D	10.32%	11.2	−142.3	−257.9	−346.1	−414.1

For an enterprise having MARR of $i = 20\%$, apply two screening rules:

1. **Accept all independent opportunities having positive present worth at MARR, and**

2. **Accept all independent opportunities having ROR > MARR.**

(Recall that these rules are guaranteed to give identical choices if all projects are investment projects.)

By the first rule, <u>select A and B</u> and screen out C and D.

By the second rule, <u>select A</u> and screen out C and D. <u>B is not an investment project</u>; its worth does not decrease with i throughout the investigated range.

We see from Example E9 that *attention must be confined to investment projects.* Obligation projects, or projects that are neither investment nor obligation projects, must be converted to their "true cash-flow" versions (Section 4.1.4) before being considered.

Example E9 illustrated the use of MARR to screen candidate opportunities. The next hierarchial use of MARR, to select the best version of each opportunity, was thoroughly illustrated in Chapter 5.

It remains to examine the use of MARR to select the set of accepted opportunities.

Since formal optimal capital budgeting is inappropriate in most enterprises, the usual situation leading to appropriation of funds for a project is this: first, the project survived screening because the present worth at MARR of some version of it was positive (or because ROR > MARR for some version of it); then the best version of the project was identified as that having greatest present worth at MARR (or the largest version for which the incremental investment had ROR > MARR). Now the candidate project joins other, independent candidates in competing for investment capital. The third step in this hierarchical decision process is to accept the project, or to reject it, or to defer it to compete in a future batch of candidates.

Obviously, if it were feasible, a desirable policy would be to accept *all* candidates at this final stage in the hierarchical process, since each project is estimated to tend to increase the wealth of the enterprise. This is the key concept in setting MARR:

The Tuning of MARR:

· If there is not enough capital (or personnel or other resources) to accept all candidates, MARR may have been set too low.
· If there is more than enough capital and other resources to accept all candidates, MARR may have been set too high.

Of course, MARR would seldom be set so accurately that there is always just enough capital. It is usual that there are more candidates than can be accepted, and the usual rule at this third stage in the hierarchical decision process is one of the following:

---

1. Accept the candidates with greatest NPVI, or
2. Accept the candidates with greatest ROR.

Recall from Example E8 and Table 6-1 that the NPVI rule is better if future ROR > MARR candidates are not anticipated, and the ROR rule is better if they are.

It is important to realize that many of the candidates have smaller versions with greater NPVI and greater ROR. The mistake is often made that an investment opportunity is rejected or deferred while others are fully implemented, whereas it would be better to implement smaller versions of all.

E10. Hierarchical use of MARR. An enterprise uses a MARR of $i = 20\%$. Three independent investment opportunities have been identified, and their best versions have been selected (amounts in thousands):

	Selected Version		Alternative Version	
Opportunity	Present Worth	Required Investment	Present Worth	Required Investment
Project 1	30	100	22	80
Project 2	100	200	90	190
Project 3	28	150	20	100

Unfortunately, it turns out that only $390,000 of investment capital can be made available in the current budget cycle. Which opportunities would be accepted by the NPVI rule applied to selected versions only? Which opportunities would be accepted if alternative versions were also considered?

The NPVIs are 0.30 for Project 1, 0.50 for Project 2 and 0.1866 for Project 3. Hence, the NPVI rule would choose Projects 2 and 1, for a total present worth of 130; the total required investment would be 300, leaving 90 to be invested in the ordinary course of business at MARR, earning zero worth.

With alternatives also considered, the NPVIs sorted in decreasing order are those for Projects 2, 2A, 1, 1A, 3A, 3. Since mutually exclusive alternatives are included, we do not have a set of independent projects. An obvious extension of the NPVI-ordering procedure would choose projects 2, 1, and 3A, for a total present worth of 142; the total required investment would be 380, leaving 10 to be invested in the ordinary course of business at MARR, earning zero worth.

Example E10 illustrates that smaller or more efficient alternatives can enhance profitability when capital is scarce. For this reason, it is better to repeat allocation with an adjusted MARR than to reject or delay whole projects. Some large enterprises ask for more than one version to be sent up; there are exact optimization techniques ("integer programming") that can select from a set that includes alternative versions of independent projects.

6.2.2 How MARR Is Established

The following example will show that MARR should be "tuned" rather than have alternatives be evaluated at a MARR that sizes projects less accurately.

E11. Consider the same projects and alternatives given in Example E10. The table in Example E10 gave the present worths at 20% interest. Now we give the present worths at 23% interest:

	"Selected" Version		"Alternative" Version	
Opportunity	P at 23%	Required Investment	P at 23%	Required Investment
Project 1	20	100	21	80
Project 2	87	200	89	190
Project 3	15	150	18	100

The "alternative" versions are those that have greatest worth at 23% interest. For each project, the "preferred" version that has greatest worth at 20% interest includes an increment whose ROR is about 21% or 22%.

(a) **Determine the range of budgets for which the "alternative" versions of all three projects would be chosen.**

Since each "alternative" has greater worth than the corresponding "selected" version, and the minimum budget to accept all the "alternative" versions is 80 + 190 + 100 = 370, any budget of 370,000 or more would cause choice of the "alternative" versions.

(b) **Now consider a fixed investment budget of $410,000. If a MARR of 20% had been published and *only* the "selected" versions had been sent forward, identify what set of projects would have been chosen and how much would have been invested in the ordinary course of business.**

The budget is enough for two but not three of the "selected" projects, and (as previously found in Example E10) the best set would be Projects 2 and 1, giving a total present worth of $130,000 at 20% interest ($107,000 at 23% interest), leaving 410 − (200 + 100) = $110,000 to be invested in the ordinary course of business.

(c) **For the same fixed budget of $410,000, consider on the other hand that a MARR of 23% had been published and *only* the "alternative" versions had accordingly been sent forward. Identify what set of projects would have been chosen and how much would have been invested in the ordinary course of business.**

The budget is enough for all three "alternative" Projects 1A, 2A, and 3A, giving a total present worth of $128,000 at 23% interest ($132,000 at 20% interest), and leaving 410 − (80 + 190 + 100) = $40,000 to be invested in the ordinary course of business.

(d) **Now suppose that the actual ordinary course of business yields a 20% ROR, so that a MARR of 20% would be the MARR that best fits the surrogate-banker assumption and best fits the wealth-increase interpretation of worth. Given the results above for a budget of $410,000, determine which MARR— 20% or 23%—would best have allocated capital.**

Certainly the 20% interest rate is correct for making evaluations. At this interest rate we can compare the results of the capital allocations. (The worths at 20% are given in the table in Example E10.)

If 20% had been the published MARR, the larger "selected" versions would have been sent forward, and Projects 1 and 2 would have been chosen, yielding a wealth increase (at 20%, the correct evaluation rate) of $130,000.

If 23% had been the published MARR, the smaller "alternative" versions would have been sent forward, and Projects 1A, 2A, and 3A would have been chosen, yielding a wealth increase (at 20%, the correct evaluation rate) of $132,000.

Thus, because use of the ordinary-course-of-business MARR caused proposals to exceed the budget, a better overall result was obtained by increasing MARR to cause proposals to be pared back. Note that the portions of the proposals forgone were increments that actually yielded 21% or 22% ROR, so better-than-ordinary increments were rejected, but otherwise it would have been necessary to forgo an entire project.

We have just seen that an artifically high MARR can give better results than the ordinary-course-of-business MARR when capital is scarce, because MARR coordinates project sizing. Now consider this: if increments having ROR of 21% or 22% are trimmed from proposals to meet a budget while allowing all proposals to be accepted, then *a surrogate banker at 21% or 22% is thereby created.* There may have been an ordinary course of business yielding a 20% rate of return. But if there is a large backlog of available project increments yielding 21% or 22%, the restoration of one of them would be the "ordinary" use of any new available capital. If MARR had been published as 23%, the most profitable rejected increment in a large group of trimmed projects would pay almost 23%. Therefore, *if MARR is tuned correctly for capital allocation, it also is only a slight overestimate of the rate of return that can be earned routinely,* because routine use of available capital would be to restore a trimmed increment.

Since the capital allocation process creates its own surrogate banker, the basic rule for establishing MARR is a managerial one, not a mathematical one.

Basic rule for establishing MARR:
. . . .

Set MARR so that the screened, refined investment proposals (that are expected to perform better than the ordinary course of business) collectively demand capital or other investment resources at approximately the level available.

As MARR is increased, some proposals are screened out, and other proposals are scaled down.

E12. Reconsider the four independent projects proposed in Example E9. If MARR had been reset to 20% after previously being established as 15%, what proposals would be removed from candidacy?

Project C in Example E9 has a positive worth at 15% interest and a negative worth at 20% interest; it would be removed from candidacy. (If a "leaner" version of project C having positive worth at 20% interest were available, it would have been better to consider it rather than the full-size Project C.)

E13. A group of old machines can be replaced with a single new machine that is available in three models. The least expensive model is fairly efficient, has a low scrap rate, and can handle most of the work, leaving some requirements for overtime and for sending out a few jobs to be done by a subcontractor. The middle model is more efficient, requiring less overtime. The most expensive

model is almost as efficient as the middle model, has a near-zero scrap rate, and is more versatile, almost eliminating the need for subcontracting.

The results of estimates and economic calculations for these alternatives are given in the following table at the enterprise's MARR of 20% and also at two neighboring interest rates. Data for the alternatives in incremental form is also included.

Alternative Version	ROR	*Present worth ($000) at i =*		
		18%	*20%*	*22%*
0	25.99%	2.173	1.574	1.014
1	20.34%	0.891	0.125	−0.590
2	27.54%	4.368	3.333	2.366
1 − 0	6.34%	−1.282	−1.449	−1.604
2 − 0	29.83%	2.196	1.759	1.352
2 − 1	65.10%	3.478	3.208	2.956

(a) **At MARR = 20%, which alternative version will be selected for consideration and sent forward to compete for investment funds?**

Version 2 would be selected, not because it has high ROR, but because it has greatest present worth at 20%.

(b) **If too many project proposals have been sent forward and the proposers are asked to reappraise their proposals at a high MARR, how high would the higher MARR have to be to change the proposed version of this project? Is this a typical "diminishing returns" project in which each add-on is less profitable than the previous add-on?**

If MARR gets to 27.54%, *no* version is sent forward. No value of MARR would cause 1 or 0 to be sent forward—because this is *not a "diminishing returns"* project in which successive increments are less profitable.

(c) **If too many project proposals have been sent forward and the upper management has no time to reconsider versions but simply goes down the list of ROR until the budget is exhausted, and if it happens that the cutoff occurs at 26%, is this project implemented or not?**

Yes, since version 2 was sent forward with ROR = 27.54%. Note that if version 0 had been sent forward (perhaps in an effort to ask for a smaller amount of capital), the project would not be implemented.

(d) **Data on the required investments of the alternatives is as follows:**

Alternative Version	Required Investment at Time 0 ($000)	Present Worth at 20% ($000)
0	10	1.574
1	13	0.125
2	15	3.333

If upper management simply goes down the list of NPVI until the budget is exhausted, and it happens that the cutoff occurs at 0.20, is this project implemented?

NPVI

0	$1.574/10 = 0.1574$
1	$0.125/13 = 0.009615$
2	$3.333/15 = 0.2222$ greater than 0.20

Yes, the project is implemented if version 2 was the one sent forward.

(e) **If upper management uses a capital budgeting algorithm to maximize total present worth at MARR = 20% for a specific total investment limit, suppose the solution procedure reaches a point where $13,000 of investment capital is left and no other versions of other projects are available having positive present worth. What version of this project will be accepted?**

There is enough money for version 0 or version 1, but not for version 2. Since version 0 contributes more present worth, it is chosen (leaving $3000 in the budget). (If version 1 had been chosen, using all the remaining budget, $1.574 - 0.125 \cong \$1,450,000$, of present worth would be lost compared to accepting version 0.)

6.2.3 Considerations Affecting MARR

Here is a list of considerations that actually affect managers' choice of MARR, or should affect it, or are claimed in the literature to be relevant:

· Inflation
· Risk
· Cost of capital
· Optimism, advocacy bias
· Taxes
· Nonmonetary considerations—broad goals, public relations, social concern, etc.
· Liquidity, cash management

We have discussed MARR thus far as a managerial tool—a shadow price set by management to cause the collection of local decisions to approach global optimality. It can be tuned by trial and error. However, it is good to be able to prescribe MARR before the fact by considering ways of estimating its ideal level and its ideal upper and lower limits.

The *ordinary project* approach to setting MARR is usable when an enterprise can identify a typical kind of ordinary-course-of-business project. If there is a plenitude of "ordinary" projects available, all having about the same rate of return, then the enterprise would invest all available capital in these if there were no better proposals available. Suppose this ordinary rate of return were set as MARR. Then if only a limited set of opportunities having ROR > MARR is available, those are accepted and the remaining capital is put into "ordinary" projects.

If, on the other hand, there are too many profitable opportunities available, the "ordinary" projects would be irrelevant. All available capital would be put into the more profitable opportunities, and (as discussed previously) MARR should be raised to weed out the appropriate proportion. Thus *the rate of return earned in the ordinary course of business is a lower limit on MARR.*

For similar reasons, which can be discussed in detail later in connection with leverage and borrowed capital, *the cost of borrowed capital is a lower limit on MARR.*

Now since an enterprise would generally not borrow money at a higher interest rate than it can earn with the borrowed money, the cost of borrowed capital is generally less than the rate of return earned in the ordinary course of business. This fact causes many authors to claim that a MARR based on the cost of capital is too low a standard. However, highly leveraged enterprises that are aggressively managed (Coca-Cola is an example) often find that each major proposal creates a new opportunity to borrow more money, secured by that proposal. In such a situation capital is not really rationed; each proposal largely creates its own capital, and the discounted cash flow analysis is unique to the proposal, almost as if it created an autonomous enterprise separate from the other parts of the company. If a project makes money compared to its own costs of capital, why not undertake it? Why not indeed, if the project is not taking capital or other resources away from the rest of the enterprise! Thus *the interest rate on borrowed money is an appropriate value for MARR when projects create their own new sources of capital.*

Economists point out, however, that there *are* hidden connections by which new projects do take resources away from the rest of an enterprise; overextension can rob parts of an enterprise of executive talent and can reduce its ability to borrow further. Most economists in the United States agree, for example, that the federal government should not undertake projects having rates of return below 10% even when it is paying under 9% for borrowed capital. Most analysts feel the cost of capital is almost always too low a value for MARR.

Let us now look at the setting of MARR as influenced by considerations of inflation, risk, cost of capital, optimism or advocacy bias, taxes, nonmonetary considerations, and cash management.

E14. An "ordinary" project for XYZ Company is to invest $1000 and receive $1210 two years later. The $1210 is an estimate in indexed dollars. Inflation is expected at 5% annually.

    (a) Determine MARR based on this "ordinary" project and express it in both i and d terms.

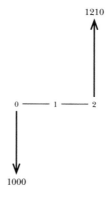

Since indexed dollars are discounted at the d rate, we have

$$P = -1000 + 1210\left(\frac{1}{1+d}\right)^2$$

$$P = 0 \Rightarrow 1 + d = \sqrt{1.21} = 1.1 \Rightarrow \underline{d = 10\%}$$

$$1 + i = (1+d)(1+j) \Rightarrow 1 + i = (1.1)(1.05) = 1.155 \Rightarrow \underline{i = 15.5\%}$$

MARR = 15.5% in market-rate terms or 10% in inflation-free terms.

(b) Suppose cash-flow estimates for the "ordinary" project were provided by one analyst but converted to MARR by another analyst who mistakenly assumed the $1210 was in current dollars. What MARR, in i terms, would the second analyst mistakenly compute?

The mistaken analyst, assuming current dollars, would compute

$$P = -1000 + 1210\beta^2$$

$$P = 0 \Rightarrow \beta = \sqrt{1.21} = 1.1$$

$$\underline{i = 10\%} \quad \text{(mistaken MARR in } i \text{ terms)}$$

Note that for many enterprises that produce goods or services, it is natural to estimate most cash flows in inflation-free indexed terms. Surely when Merry Djinin, P. E., signs an estimate that says energy cost savings will be $2000 per year, she means the amount of energy saved will be the amount that at today's prices is worth $2000. She does not intend to deny that prices may increase, or to imply that the then-current amount will be steady.

E15. A savings is estimated in current dollars as $2000 per year. If 5% inflation is expected, what real rate of (de)escalation is assumed?

$$g = 0 \quad \text{(the current amount } A_t \text{ is constant).}$$

But

$$1 + g = (1+v)(1+j) \qquad for \qquad j = .05$$
$$1 + v = 1/1.05 \Rightarrow v = \underline{-4.7619048\%}$$

If the *cause* of savings is declining at 4.76% annually, this just makes up for 5% inflation and keeps the current-dollar value constant.

For most enterprises the only cash flows that are known or estimated in *current* dollars are debt payments, payments under long-term supply contracts or leases, and those proportions of tax payments that are tied to past events, such as depreciation or tax credits. Everything else is subject to inflation and is naturally estimated in *indexed* dollars: if inflation is expected at 4%, then revenue next year for selling a $100 widget is expected to be $104 in current dollars, and the current-dollar cost for a $15 hour of skilled labor is expected to be $15.60.

Despite the $1 + i = (1+d)(1+j)$ relationship made clear in all major engineering economy textbooks, the fact is that *most practicing engineers make computations in terms of d while calling the interest rate i.* There is no harm in this unless the analyst fails to take into account that fixed-dollar obligations are much better than obligations subject to inflation and that fixed-dollar revenues are much worse than inflatable revenues. The explicit distinction between discounting fixed-dollar (current) amounts at i and discounting inflatable (indexed) amounts at d, as recommended in Chapter 3, automatically takes care of these issues.

By the way, as a consequence of the informal use of d for i, it turns out that the 10% interest rate mandated by Congress for analyzing federal governmental expenditures (see Chapter 7) is in practice sometimes treated as a d rate rather than an i rate. With 4% inflation, the i rate is $(1.10)(1.04) - 1 = 14.4\%$, or about 5.4% more than the cost of borrowed money. This is appropriate, as we shall see in discussing the effects of risk and optimism.

Risk is widely acknowledged to affect MARR, and the common wisdom is that in riskier situations MARR should be higher. We will study two kinds of risk effect in Chapter 8: ordinary risk and geometric risk.

"Ordinary risk" is a name for the phenomenon that estimates are deterministic numbers that represent what are really random variables. We can deal with the simplest cases of ordinary risk easily.

E16. Consider a project in which a $2000 investment yields returns of $800 at the ends of the five years beginning at the end of year 2:

> **The returns are in indexed dollars, so we discount them with a d rate. Let $d = 0.10$, and let the inflation rate be $j = 0.04$. We compute**

$$P = -2000 + \left(\frac{1}{1 + d}\right)(800)\left(\frac{1 - (1/(1 + d)^5)}{d}\right) = \underline{\$756.94}$$

> **Now suppose there is a 5% risk that the $800 returns will not materialize at all. This will make the *expected returns* be not $800 but $760 (computation of expected values will be covered in Chapter 8). Thus the expected *present worth* will be smaller. Determine the expected present worth by using 760 instead of 800 in the above formula.**

> Using $E(P)$ as the symbol for the expected value of P, the formula becomes

$$E(P) = -2000 + \left(\frac{1}{1 + 0.1}\right)(760)\left(\frac{1 - (1/1.1)^5}{0.1}\right) = \underline{\$619.09}$$

E17. Now suppose the above project were an "ordinary" project being used to set MARR. Without the risk the rate of return turns out to be 19.8967572%. With the risk (that is with 760 substituted for 800), the rate of return turns out to be 18.226198%. Determine MARR expressed as a d rate for analysts who will correct for risk by reducing hoped-for amounts to expected amounts, and also for analysts who will use hoped-for amounts such as $800/yr rather than the expected value of $760/yr.

> This project gives an expected $760 return, so its ROR is $\underline{d = 18.23\%}$. If this project is the model of an "ordinary" project, and if analysts will use expected

returns (not hoped-for returns), then this is the correct MARR. On the other hand, if analysts will use hoped-for returns, so that they will call such a return "$800" although its expected value is less, MARR should be set at $\underline{d = 19.9\%}$.

From the last two examples we see that if hoped-for values are used instead of expected values, the computed present worth of a project will be too high, and also the computed rate of return of a project will be too high. This clarifies the claim that MARR should be increased with risk: *If the estimating procedures used in determining project data do not fully account for risk, then MARR should be increased* (because risky projects will look better than they really are).

Geometric risk is a risk at each time period (constant over time) that the project's further cash flows will not occur. It represents situations such as a 2% risk each year that the plant in which a project is installed will be abandoned. It will be shown in Chapter 8 that geometric risk can be handled much like inflation, with an easily computed change in the interest rate. The result will be an increase in the interest rate (and in the appropriate MARR) for situations in which estimates do not already take geometric risk into account.

Since many enterprises have situations in which the same people who perform cost estimates are those who advocate the project, there is a tendency toward optimism or "advocacy bias." As a result, projects generally look a little better than they actually are. The combination of unaccounted-for risk and this optimism or bias explains why enterprises whose actual financial performance indicates a growth in wealth of, say, 8% annually will regularly use a 15% or greater MARR. You have to invest in projects that look as if they will yield 15% or better in order actually to achieve an 8% yield. As was remarked in Chapter 4, acknowledging this is a little like setting a watch 10 minutes ahead in order to be on time; an analyst aware of optimism might "discount" it and report a project as much better than it really is because a project that seems "only wonderful" will be rejected.

6.3 LEVERAGE: THE USE OF BORROWED CAPITAL

The use of borrowed capital is an important feature of enterprise. There are major segments of capitalistic societies that accumulate cash beyond what can be profitably plowed back into the business without going outside the boundaries of the familiar. They are willing to lend. Other segments need capital, having identified good opportunities but having insufficient capital to invest in them. They are willing to borrow.

Those willing to lend are, on the one hand, financial institutions that concentrate excess capital from sources as small as individuals, and on the other hand, direct sources of capital such as real estate and insurance companies or the largest companies in any "mature" industry. Those willing to borrow are small businesses and businesses of any size in growth situations.

Leverage is the use of borrowed capital in investment. The basic facts about leverage are that *it magnifies profitability and magnifies risk.* Since risk is a future topic, it will be treated lightly and informally here.

We will distinguish between a "project" and a "leveraged project." Without regard to its sources of capital a project has a set of cash flows and has the associated characteristics such as present worth at an interest rate, rate of return, and so on. These characteristics of the project itself are what have been discussed all through the book up to this point.

6.3.1 Leverage Magnifies Profitability

Suppose you could borrow money at 8% interest and invest it in an enterprise that has MARR ≅ 10%. Let a typical ordinary-course-of-business project be this one (in thousands of dollars):

Project cash flows:

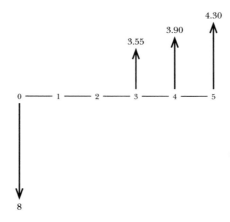

Let a lender be willing to lend you 8 at an interest rate (approximately 8%) such that the repayments would be 2.00 per year for five years. The net cash flows with respect to your own equity capital would be these:

Leveraged project cash flows:

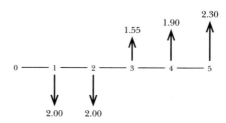

The rate of return of this leveraged project, or the *rate of return on equity capital*, is 14.9666%. The present worth at MARR = 10% is 0.419308. This demonstrates that leverage magnifies profitability: you had a project whose rate of return was 10%, and by borrowing you increased its rate of return to about 15% and increased its worth at 10% interest from zero to about $419.

A *leveraged project* is defined, when a specific loan and repayment schedule is associated with a project, as *the combined project whose cash-flow set is the sum of those of the loan and those of the project*. In the foregoing example the cash flows of the loan are

Loan cash flows:

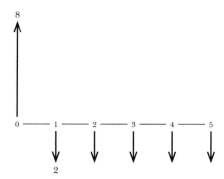

These loan cash flows plus the project cash flows sum to the leveraged cash flows.

Usually a leveraged project is meaningful only if the project creates its own borrowing opportunity. The loan itself has a present worth at 10% interest of

$$8 - 2(P/A\ 10\%,5) = 0.418426$$

The project has a present worth at 10% interest of

$$-8 + 3.55\beta^3 + 3.90\beta^4 + 4.30\beta^5 = 0.000882$$

Their sum, of course, is the same 0.419308 as was given for the leveraged project. If you could do the borrowing and invest the proceeds in the ordinary course of business, whether or not there was a specific project at hand, it would pay to do so.

There is an intimate connection between leveraged cash flows and the *true cash flows* of Section 4.1.4. If a large negative cash flow is wholly or partly financed by borrowing, the leveraged project's cash flows include the loan proceeds and repayments. Thus they are the true cash flows. (Recall, however, that the true-cash-flow method can also make corrections other than for leverage: specific reinvestment of project proceeds other than at MARR or to retire leverage debt, and specific acquisitions of investment funds other than borrowing, such as by selling off existing assets.)

The next few examples will illustrate leverage and will make clear that borrowing at an interest rate less than MARR is profitable, and that borrowing at an interest rate greater than MARR is unprofitable unless it makes it possible to accept a profitable investment opportunity for which the required capital is otherwise unavailable. In the discussion we will use the terms "leveraged present worth" and "leveraged rate of return" referring to the leveraged project's cash-flow set; "return on equity capital" is a synonym of leveraged rate of return, where "equity capital" is the amount invested less the amount borrowed.

E18. Jonah can buy and remodel a building for $200,000, and sell it for $300,000 one year later. A lender is willing to lend $150,000 to Jonah, with the building as collateral, at 11.5% interest with a single lump-sum repayment after one year.

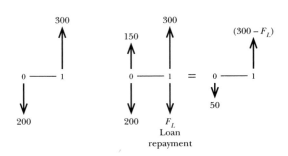

(a) Determine the present worth, at Jonah's MARR of $i = 15\%$, of the project and of the leveraged project.

$$P = -200 + 300\left(\frac{1}{1 + 0.15}\right) = \$60{,}869.57$$

$$P_L = -50 + (300 - F_L)\left(\frac{1}{1.15}\right)$$

But

$$F_L = 150(1.115) = 167.25$$

Hence

$$P_L = -50 + (300 - 167.25)\left(\frac{1}{1.15}\right) = \$65{,}434.78$$

Note that the leveraged project is more profitable than the unleveraged one. This is a consequence of borrowing at 11.5% some money that would otherwise have been taken out of the ordinary course of business and hence would effectively have been "borrowed" at MARR = 15% interest.

(b) Determine the rate of return of the project and the rate of return on equity.

For the project:

$$P = 0 \Rightarrow -200 + 300\left(\frac{1}{1 + i^*}\right) = 0$$

$$1 + i^* = \frac{300}{200}$$

$$i^* = 50\%$$

For the leveraged project:

$$P_L = 0 \Rightarrow -50 + (300 - 167.25)\left(\frac{1}{1 + i^*}\right) = 0$$

$$1 + i^* = \frac{132.75}{50} = 2.655$$

$$i^* = 165.5\%$$

Note that the leveraged project has a faster rate of return. There are two kinds of capital put into the project: the borrowed capital, which has a rate of return to the lender of 11.5%, and the equity capital. The mixture of borrowed and equity capital earns a 50% rate of return, so if the borrowed capital in the mixture earns at a slower rate than 50%, the equity capital must earn at a faster rate than 50%. (Think of the lender and investor as partners. The lender earns 11.5% on the lent portion of capital, while the investor earns 165.5% on the equity portion; the project itself has an intermediate ROR of 50%.)

6.3.2 Leverage Magnifies Risk

We have just seen how leverage magnifies profitability. To see how it magnifies risk, we must start by considering the possibility of a "poor outcome" in which the leveraged project will still make more money than the nonleveraged one even if the project earns at a rate below both MARR and the cost of borrowed money. This will show that leverage does *not* magnify risk on a per-project basis; then we will show that it *does* magnify risk on a per-dollar-of-equity-capital basis.

E19. Suppose there is a "poor outcome" possible, under which the remodeled house might sell for only 220K$.

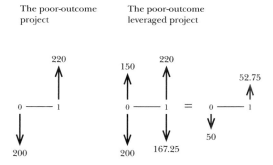

(a) **Determine the present worth, at Jonah's MARR of $i = 15\%$, of the "poor outcome" project and of the "leveraged poor outcome" project.**

$$P_{POP} = -200 + 200\left(\frac{1}{1 + 0.15}\right) = \underline{-\$8695.65}$$

$$P_{LPOP} = -50 + 52.75\left(\frac{1}{1.15}\right) = \underline{-\$4130.43}$$

Thus we see that leverage does *not* necessarily increase risk in the sense of the owner's being worse off when the outcome of the investment is poor. In fact it *protects* the investor somewhat in this case, due to the good effect of borrowing money at a rate less than MARR and risking less equity capital. (The equity capital not invested continues to earn at MARR.)

(b) Determine the rate of return of the "poor-outcome" project and its rate of return on equity.

$$P_{POP} = 0 \Rightarrow -200 + 200\beta = 0$$

$$\beta = \frac{200}{220} = \frac{1}{1.1} \Rightarrow i^* = 10\%$$

$$P_{LPOP} = 0 \Rightarrow -50 + 52.75\left(\frac{1}{1 + i^*}\right) = 0$$

$$1 + i^* = \frac{52.75}{50} \Rightarrow i^* = 5.5$$

We see here that the rate of return earned on the leveraged project is worse than if no money had been borrowed. However, since the *size* of the leveraged project is small in terms of owner's equity capital invested, the investor is protected from loss by the leverage.

We can now ask what outcome, if any, could be disastrous enough to make borrowing money unwise for the building-remodeling project.

E20. Let i be MARR and let X be the price for which the remodeled building is sold.

Determine the relationship between MARR and the selling price such that the leveraged project has a smaller present worth than the unleveraged project.

Given $P_L < P$,

$$-50 + (X - 167.25)\left(\frac{1}{1 + i}\right) < -200 + X\left(\frac{1}{1 + i}\right)$$

$$\frac{X}{1 + i} - \frac{167.25}{1 + i} - \frac{X}{1 + i} < -150$$

$$\frac{167.25}{1 + i} > 150$$

(Note that the selling price drops out of the equation.)

Thus, if MARR $< 11.5\%$ and money is borrowed at a higher rate, then $P_L < P$.

$$1.115 = \frac{167.25}{150} > 1 + i \Rightarrow i < 11.5\%$$

A leveraged project always has a smaller present worth than an unleveraged one if money is borrowed at a rate exceeding MARR. The leveraged project always earns less than if it were not leveraged.

The results seem so far to belie the claim that leverage magnifies risk. No matter how disastrous the outcome of a project, the investor is better off using as much borrowed money for it as possible, if the money is available at a rate below MARR. However, the comparison basis—a given project—is misleading, because the leveraged project requires less equity capital. The following example shows what happens if an investor puts *all available equity capital* into a poor-outcome situation.

E21. **Jonah has $200,000 available to invest. As before, he can buy and remodel a building for $200,000 and sell it for a profit. If he borrows money at 11.5% interest, which is less than his MARR of 15%, and the lenders are willing to lend $150,000 for each such building, it takes only $50,000 of his equity capital for each remodeling project. Thus he can (assuming availability of the opportunities) remodel four such buildings; let this be the leveraged alternative.**

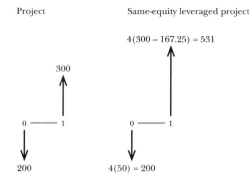

(a) **If the outcomes are "good"—each building sells for $300,000—determine the unleveraged and leveraged present worths at MARR.**

$$P = -200 + 300\left(\frac{1}{1.15}\right) = \underline{\$60,869.57}$$

$$P_L = -200 + 531\left(\frac{1}{1.15}\right) = \underline{\$261,739.13}$$

which is, of course, four times the previously computed answer for a good outcome. *Note:* the RORs are still $\underline{50\%}$ for the good project and $\underline{165.5\%}$ for the good leveraged project:

$$P_{\text{4-building good project}} = 4\,P_{\text{1-building good project}}$$

so $P = 0$ gives the same interest rate for both.

The foregoing example shows leverage in a truer light than before, because it compares equity investments of the same size. With borrowing, the investor was able to tackle four times as much activity and increase his wealth by 4.3 times as much as without using leverage.

Now we will consider the effect of leverage if the outcomes are poor.

E22. Suppose Jonah invests in one building without borrowing, or alternatively in four buildings with borrowing, and the buildings end up selling for only $220,000 each.

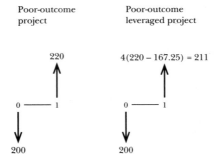

Poor-outcome project

Poor-outcome leveraged project

Determine the unleveraged and leveraged present worths.

$$P_{POP} = -200 + 220\left(\frac{1}{1.15}\right) = \underline{-\$8695.65} \quad \text{as before}$$

$$P_{LPOP} = -200 + 211\left(\frac{1}{1.15}\right) = \underline{-\$16{,}521.74}$$

which is four times the worth of single-building poor outcome.

Note that a poor outcome is more harmful to the investor's wealth (1.9 times as bad in the example) than if no borrowed capital had been used—*if* the same amount of equity capital was involved in both cases. *Leverage magnifies risk per dollar of equity capital.*

Recall the previous results for a single project, in which the investor was better off using leverage if money could be borrowed at an interest rate less than MARR, regardless of whether the single project's outcome was good or bad. Let us determine the corresponding results for multiple projects, in which the same amount of equity capital is invested with or without leverage.

E23. Let Jonah invest in remodeling one building at a cost of $200,000 or, alternatively, invest in remodeling four such buildings, borrowing $150,000 at 11.5% interest on each building, so that the equity capital invested is still $200,000. Let i = MARR and let X be the price for which each remodeled building is sold.

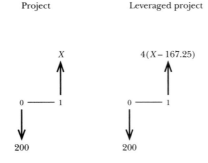

Project

Leveraged project

Determine the relationship between MARR and the selling price such that the leveraged project has a smaller present worth than the unleveraged project.

$$P = -200 + X\beta \quad \text{where} \quad \beta = \frac{1}{1+i}, \quad i = \text{MARR}$$

$$P_L = -200 + 4(X - 167.25)\beta$$

Let $P_L < P$.

$$-200 + 4(X - 167.25)\beta < -200 + X\beta$$
$$(4X - 669)\beta < X\beta$$
$$3X < 669$$
$$\underline{X < 223}$$

For this example, the leveraged alternative is worse if the remodeled buildings sell for less than $223,000 each.

E24. For the current example, verify or refute the maxim that it is unwise to borrow at an interest rate exceeding the project's rate of return.

When $X = 223$,

$$P = -200 + X\beta$$
$$P = -200 + 223\beta$$
$$P = 0 \Rightarrow \beta = \frac{200}{223} \Rightarrow i^* = 11.5\%$$

Thus we see that the leveraged project is worse than the unleveraged one when the outcome gives a rate of return less than the cost of borrowed money. The maxim is true, dollar for dollar of equity capital; it is unwise to borrow at a rate greater than MARR. (The only time it is wise to borrow at a rate greater than MARR is when borrowing is the only way to finance a profitable activity.)

If it is unwise to borrow at an interest rate greater than the rate of return, how do we explain *usury*—the practice of lending and borrowing at very high interest rates—which is accepted by borrowers in special circumstances?

Previous examples showed that if you can borrow at less than MARR, it can pay to do so even if the money is put to work at a rate not only less than MARR but even less than the interest rate on borrowed capital! But this was true only if borrowing reduced the amount of owner's capital involved. (Recall Example E19, in which a "poor-outcome" project had ROR = 10%. It reduced a MARR = 15% investor's wealth by $8695.65 if $200,000 was invested, but reduced the investor's wealth by only $4130.43 if only $50,000 of equity capital was invested while the remaining $150,000 was borrowed at 11.5% interest.)

When the amount of equity capital is not reduced, and leverage is used to increase the size of a project that can be implemented with a given amount of equity capital, previous examples showed that the increased-size project must have a rate of return at least equal to the cost of borrowed money in order for borrowing to be advantageous.

(Recall Example E24.) This teaches us that high interest rates for borrowed capital can be justified only if the borrowing reduces capital requirements.

To explain usury, let us return to the "good" version of the building remodeling project:

E25. **Jonah can buy and remodel a building for $200,000, and sell it for $300,000 one year later. Jonah's MARR is 15%. This is a unique business opportunity, and Jonah has only $180,000 to invest. He must borrow $20,000 or be unable to undertake the project. What would be the highest interest rate he could pay for the loan (call this interest rate h) and still prefer the project to doing nothing?**

The leveraged project

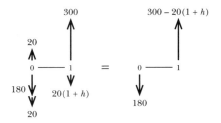

$$P_L = -180 + [300 - 20(1 + h)]\left(\frac{1}{1 + .15}\right)$$

Find h for $P_L > 0$. This makes the project better than investing the $18,000 in the ordinary course of business at 15%.

$$(1.15)P_L = -180(1.15) + 300 - 20(1 + h)$$
$$P_L > 0 \Rightarrow -180(1.15) + 300 - 20(1 + h) > 0$$
$$93 > 20(1 + h)$$
$$1 + h < \frac{93}{20} = 4.65$$
$$h < 365\%$$

At 365% interest, the net return at time 1 is 207, which is 180(1.15).

Thus we see that high interest rates are attractive to borrowers when a small amount of additional capital is needed to allow acceptance of a good business opportunity.

A general rule that can be derived from all these examples is that leverage is useful when, and only when, it frees up capital.

If you can borrow money at less than MARR, you should do so to the extent possible, within the limits of (1) running out of ordinary projects (so that MARR would decline to the level of what previously would have been worse-than-ordinary projects) or (2) overextending so that there is significant risk of financial ruin if outcomes are worse than estimated.

For a project that creates its own borrowing opportunity (such as involving equipment that can serve as loan collateral), you can afford to borrow at greater than MARR but less than the project's rate of return. That is, it is better to borrow in this situation than to use your own capital, even if you have the capital. Here again, risk limits the wise amount of borrowing.

Finally, if a unique and uniquely profitable opportunity arises and you do not have enough capital to accept it, you can afford to borrow small amounts of additional capital at rates exceeding its rate of return. Risk, as always, limits the wise size of the repayment obligation that should be undertaken.

6.3.3 Leveraged Buyouts and Takeovers

Consider a company that has been refusing to incur any long-term debt. This year it has C dollars of capital available for investment. After investing in the best identifiable opportunities, the company is left to invest the remainder of its capital in a group of investment opportunities having a 14% after-tax rate of return. Thus the after-tax MARR is considered to be 14% for this conservative company.

After the available C dollars of capital have been invested, let D be the additional investment that could yield a 14% after-tax rate of return. We have already seen that if money can be borrowed at less than MARR, it would pay to borrow D dollars to invest a total of $C + D$ dollars. Yet suppose the company refuses to do this, and suppose the company's entire assets have a value V, which we assume to equal the present worth at a smaller interest rate—let it be 12%—of the company's future income, assuming it continues to operate in the established conservative manner. The interest rate that determines V is smaller because the potential purchasers of the company require only a smaller rate of return.

Now certainly to purchase and operate a company constitutes an "investment project" in the sense of Chapter 4. Since worth of an investment project decreases with interest rate, the current owners value the company, according to their MARR of 14%, at some smaller value $V - Q$.

Obviously there is some range of prices $V - pQ$, where $0 < p < 1$, at which a sale of the company would be perceived as benefiting both the current owners and the purchasers:

$$\text{Gain to current owners:} \quad (V - pQ) - (V - Q) = (1 - p)Q > 0$$
$$\text{Gain to purchaser:} \qquad V - (V - pQ) = \quad pQ \quad > 0$$

For a concrete example, in millions of dollars, let the company's market value be $V = 10$, let its owners value its future prospects at $V - Q = 8$ (so that $Q = 2$), and let the agreed purchase price be $V - pQ = 9$ (so that $p = 0.5$; the owners and purchaser share equal perceived benefits).

Now suppose the purchaser leverages the purchase, putting up 4 and borrowing the remaining 5. The purchaser has equity of $10 - 5 = 5$ in return for having had to pay only 4 of cash—a million-dollar windfall.

How high an interest rate would the purchaser be willing to pay? The loan would be in the form of "junk bonds" issued by the company. Suppose they were seven-year bonds with half-yearly payments:

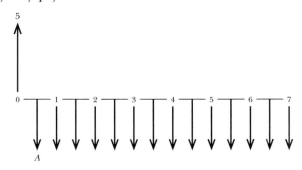

Let the effective interest rate on the junk bonds be 15%. This is 7.2380529% per half-year, so that the loan repayments are $5(A/P\,7.238\%,14) = 0.5799$ per half year or about 1.16 per year. How heavy are these payments? Recall that in the original owners' hands the company was a 14% cash cow valued by the owners at 8, which implies an annual profit of about $8(0.14) = 1.12$; on the other hand, recall that it was valued at 10 for MARR = 12% prospective buyers, which implies it has a potential annual profit of about $10(0.12) = 1.20$. The loan repayments of 1.16 are more than the former profits but less than the potential profits.

The formerly conservative company is now "living on the edge," needing to pour most of its profits into interest on long-term debt. However, assuming it weathers the seven-year debt period, the purchaser ends up owning all of the company, free of debt. If it is sold for 10 at that time, the purchaser's net equity transactions will have been

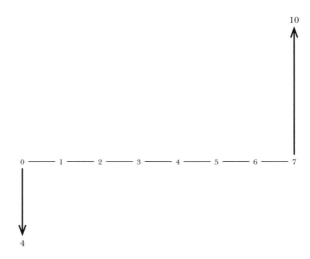

This yields approximately an overall 14% rate of return for the purchaser. Note that the purchaser was willing to pay high interest on the junk bonds—even higher than the company's rate of return. This is because the junk bonds made it possible for the purchaser to enjoy a million-dollar windfall.

6.4 EXERCISES

1. Verify point 1 of Example E1 by examining this labor-saving project at Plant A:

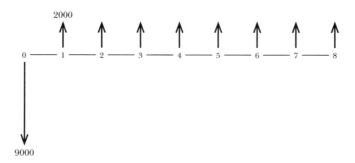

Assuming that both plants use $d = 12\%$, the returns are in indexed dollars at Plant A's cost of labor, and wages at Plant B are \$9.60 per hour compared to \$14.00 per hour at Plant A, is the point verified?

2. Verify point 4 of Example E1 by examining this labor-saving project at Plant A:

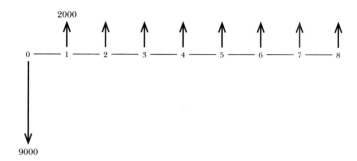

Assuming that both plants use $d = 12\%$, the returns are in indexed dollars at both plants' cost of labor, and Plant B will be torn down at the end of year 6, is the point verified?

3. Verify the claim made at the end of Section 6.1.1 that if there are 10 independent opportunities to consider, the number of different combinations of zero or more of them is 1024.

4. To the set of independent opportunities in Example E2, add the following independent opportunity and formulate as a basic capital budgeting problem for a budget of 100. (Do not solve; just formulate.)

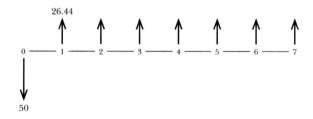

5. Consider the problem formulated in Exercise 4: the set of four independent opportunities from Exercise 4 and Example E2.
   (a) Determine how many different alternatives there are to accept zero or more projects from the set (not using the budget amount to eliminate infeasible alternatives).
   (b) By enumerating all alternatives, determine the maximum-worth set of opportunities for a budget of 100.

6. Consider the problem formulated in Example E2, with the addition of an opportunity that requires an investment of 50 and has a present worth of 60.
   (a) For a budget of 140, apply NPVI ordering to select a feasible set of projects that tries to maximize worth.
   (b) For a budget of 200, apply NPVI ordering to select a feasible set of projects that tries to maximize worth. Show that there is a better set than the one selected.

7. Apply NPVI ordering to the projects in Example E5, but with a budget of 22. Show that it finds the best solution.

8. Consider the following independent projects:

Project	Investment	Worth	NPVI
A	20	5	0.250
B	30	6	0.200
C	40	7	0.175
D	50	8	0.160

(a) Determine the worth-maximizing set of projects that stays within a budget of 90. Does the NPVI-ordering procedure recommend this set?

(b) Determine the worth-maximizing set of projects that stays within a budget of 130. Does the NPVI-ordering procedure recommend this set?

9. For the independent projects of Exercise 8, determine the optimal set for every budget, in increments of 10, from 0 to 140. Count the number of budgets that contain each project. Do the results tend to verify the claim that projects with greater NPVI are more likely to be in the optimal solution for an arbitrary budget?

10. In an enterprise whose MARR is $i = 14\%$, two independent projects were available for a budget of $55,000:

Project	Required Investment	Present Worth	NPVI
1	$53,000	$7840	0.1479245
2	41,000	7420	0.1809756

One year later, it turned out that $25,000 was newly available for investment, and two further projects were available:

Project	Required Investment	Present Worth	NPVI
3	$48,200	$9440	0.1958506
4	36,000	5780	0.1605556

The enterprise chose a project set and invested the investment-budget remainder in the ordinary course of business, where it grew at $i = 14\%$ and became available plowback capital a year later, to be added to the newly available capital. Consider the following two scenarios:

Scenario A: The worth-maximizing set was chosen the first year
Scenario B: The NPVI-maximizing set was chosen the first year

Under which scenario would the enterprise have fared better? Does the result support the claim that capital budgeting should choose efficient projects if new opportunities can arise?

11. Consider the following table:

Project	Net Present Worth	Required Investment
A	7	12
B	9	13
C	30	15
D	25	17
E	33	18

(a) Determine the worth-maximizing portfolio of independent projects for an investment budget of 30.

(b) The listed worths are at MARR of $i = 18\%$. It is hoped that a scaled-down version of C will become available, which would allow a present worth of 14 to be earned for an investment of 7. How long would it be profitable to wait for the scaled-down version, where waiting N years means to omit a project from the worth-maximizing portfolio so that there will be enough money to invest in the scaled-down version when it becomes available after a wait of N years?

12. An enterprise can raise not more than B dollars for capital investment now. In addition to essentially unlimited opportunity to invest all or any part of B dollars at an interest rate $i = $ MARR, three major projects have been identified as independent investment opportunities:

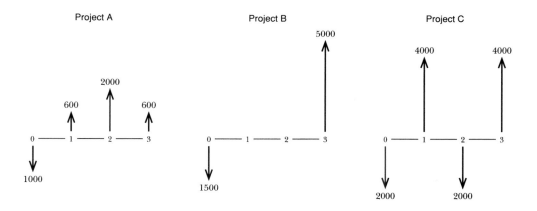

Here are the results of some calculations made for these projects:

Project, j	Investment, I_j	ROR	Present Worth P_j and $(P/I$ ratio$)$ at $i =$				
			10%	20%	30%	40%	50%
A	1000	85.36%	1649 (1.65)	1236 (1.24)	918 (0.92)	668 (0.67)	467 (0.47)
B	1500	49.38%	2257 (1.5)	1394 (0.93)	776 (0.52)	322 (0.21)	−19 (−0.01)
C	2000	100%	2989 (1.49)	2259 (1.13)	1714 (0.86)	1294 (0.65)	963 (0.48)

(a) For MARR = 10% and an investment budget of $B = 3500$, determine the worth-maximizing portfolio.

(b) Determine the portfolio recommended by the NPVI-ordering procedure for the given budget and MARR. Does this agree with the worth-maximizing result?

(c) Determine the portfolio recommended by the ROR-ordering procedure for the given budget. Does this agree with the worth-maximizing result?

(d) In comparing A and C for a MARR = 10% investor, note that A has the greater NPVI while C has the greater ROR. Answer these questions with a response of either "ROR" or "MARR" for each:

   (i) Under ROR methods, reinvestment is at what rate?

   (ii) Under worth methods, reinvestment is at what rate?

   (iii) For an investor who will have no future high-ROR opportunities, reinvestment at what rate is realistic?

   (iv) For an investor who will always have a few high-ROR opportunities, reinvestment at what rate is realistic?

13. To the set of projects in Exercise 12 add a project D identical to A but independent. A, C, and D are opportunities that must be either accepted now or lost. B can be delayed. Enough capital has been raised to accept either AD or C now.

(a) Which choice is better, assuming that the enterprise has MARR of 20% and B can be accepted as soon as the worth of the returns from the initial portfolio exceeds the worth of its investment(s) by at least $1500?

(b) Repeat the analysis for a MARR of 10%.

14. For a company with MARR = 18%, three independent project proposals are available:

Project	Description	Required Investment	Present Worth of Net Benefits	Net Present Worth	Rate of Return
A	Energy conservation	$47,500	$53,500	$6,000	20%
B	Yield improvement	$51,600	$58,700	$7,100	27%
C	Maintenance facility	$60,200	$72,600	$12,400	40%

(a) Given an inflexible $100,000 total budget for investment, which portfolio of projects maximizes immediate worth?

(b) Because it is efficient, the maintenance facility project could be implemented now, and both of the other two projects could be implemented next year. On the other hand, if the other two projects were implemented now, it would take two years before the maintenance facility project could be implemented. Assuming no inflation or loss of profitability of delayed projects, is it better in this case to go with efficiency, or should immediate worth maximization prevail?

15. Recall the data from Exercise 12.

(a) If there were no way to scale any of the three projects up or down, and the investment budget were $3500, what "tuned" value of MARR could have been published to filter the proposals so that they would not contend for capital?

(b) Assume that after one year there will be enough capital to fund any rejected candidate. Worth maximization would have rejected a different candidate than was rejected by tuning MARR. If returns actually are reinvested at 10% interest and rejected candidates can be shift-delayed without change in their cash flows, which basis for rejecting a candidate—MARR tuning or worth maximization—happens to work best in this case?

16. A job of cleaning scale from some furnace tubes can be done at three different levels, to save fuel until the next cleaning opportunity a year from now:

Level of cleaning: 1   2   3
Savings: 3841 3986 4079
Cost: 3148 3322 3471
Cash-flow diagram:

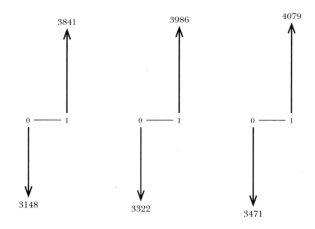

(a) Determine the level of cleaning that should be proposed by an engineer who is given MARR of 18%, 20%, 22%, and 24%. (Compute present worths.)
(b) If upper management published MARR of 14%, which level would be proposed?
(c) Determine the greatest MARR for which level 2 would be proposed.

17. As part of a plant upgrade, a spray-paint booth must be designed. The basic design (A) has an initial cost of $34,712 and consumes $201,371 in materials, labor, and energy per year, according to estimates prepared by the plant engineer. An alternative design (B) has an initial cost of $45,189 and consumes $198,171 per year. Costs are in indexed dollars and are expected to remain constant. The booth will operate for five years. What MARR (in real-interest terms to the nearest 1%) will be small enough to cause the engineer to incorporate B instead of A into the plant upgrade?

18. At lower levels of the Girl-Ella Salon management there exist the following alternative versions of investment opportunities (amounts in thousands):

Opportunity	Investment and ROR of "leanest" version	Incremental investments and incremental RORs of larger versions
1	10, 19%	2, 22%; 2, 15%; 2, 12%
2	18, 36%	1, 20%; 2, 14%; 4, 12%
3	9, 40%	4, 18%; 4, 13%; 8, 18%
4	10, 21%	none
5	9, 14%	4, 13%; 12, 12%
6	20, 16%	3, 13%; 3, 12%
7	21, 25%	2, 20%; 2, 18%; 1, 14%
8	21, 24%	2, 20%; 2, 16%; 3, 12%

Note that most of the incremental investments have diminishing returns. The exception is Opportunity 3: its largest version has incremental investments and RORs of (16, 16%) compared to the leanest version, (12, 15%) compared to the first increment, and, as listed, (8, 18%) compared to the second investment.

(a) If upper management publishes MARR of 13%, what total amount of capital investment requests should be received from lower levels? (Assume that projects earning exactly MARR are accepted.)

(b) If the capital available for investment turns out to be $136,000, what published MARR would give the most appropriate set of requests?

(c) What MARR (to the nearest 1%) would be great enough to cause the originator of Opportunity 3 to submit other than the largest version? At that MARR, which version of Opportunity 3 would be submitted?

19. Morgan knows that the estimators who work for her are set in their ways. An estimated cash flow set that they perceive as $1000 per year for five years, in current dollars to be discounted at i, is the same one she perceives as a declining geometric gradient series of indexed-dollar amounts, the first one being $1000 (indexed). She perceives the real escalation rate to be -0.05, the inflation rate to be 0.07, and MARR to be such that the real interest rate should be $d = 0.15$.

(a) As Morgan perceives it, determine the substitute interest rate, the zero projection, and the present worth of the series.

(b) Determine to the nearest 1% the value of i that Morgan could publish so that her estimators would compute the same present worth she does.

(c) What value of i would Morgan presumably have given to her estimators if she assumed that they would perceive cash flows as she did?

20. For the Flower Construction Firm, a typical job for which J is the estimated cost is bid at $1.18J$ dollars. Nominally, the firm spends J dollars and gets paid $1.18J$ a year later. Actually, the firm spends $J(1 + o)$ dollars and gets paid $(1 + i + c)J$ dollars $1 + y$ years later, where o is the cost overrun rate, c is the contingency rate, and y is the lateness. All amounts are in current dollars. Bob Flower considers his MARR to be 15% (he buys and sells 15%-yielding oil leases that constitute a surrogate banker). He tunes bids and proposals by telling his people to add a contingency rate to bids. The contingency rate is currently $c = 0.03$. Recent cost statistics indicate estimators generally underestimate jobs so that there is a 5% average cost

overrun, and the time lag between spending and getting paid is 0.85 years. To the nearest 1%, what should the new contingency rate be?

21. Leverage is the use of borrowed capital in investment. Consider a simple project for an investor with MARR = 15%: Invest $1000 at time zero, and receive $1200 at time 1.

    Since $P = -1000 + 1200[1/(1 + i)^1]$, the present worth is 43.48 at 15%, and the rate of return is 20%.

    Now consider that the investor can borrow part of the $1000 investment at 18% interest (which is greater than MARR but less than the rate of return of the project). Let L be the amount borrowed and let Y be the amount of the investor's own "plowback" capital; $L + Y = 1000$. The loan will be repaid by a payment of $L(1.18)$ dollars at time 1, and by taking out the loan the investor is, in effect, substituting this expenditure for L of the initial investment.

    (a) Draw a cash-flow diagram for the leveraged project, where the net investment is $1000 - L$ and the net return is $1200 - 1.18L$. Also write the present worth formula for the leveraged project, in terms not of L but of the investor's capital Y.

    (b) Sketch a graph of the net present worth as a function of Y, for $Y = 0, 500$, and 1000. (Show numerical values either on the sketch or in an accompanying table.)

    (c) Derive an expression for the rate of return on investor's capital as a function of Y.

    (d) Sketch a graph of the rate of return on investor's capital as a function of Y for $Y = 0.01, 0.1, 1, 10, 100, 200, 500, 1000$. (Show numerical values in an accompanying table.)

22. These independent projects are available:

Project	Required Investment	Returns at Time 1
A	$30,000	$40,000
B	$40,000	$60,000
C	$50,000	$80,000

You have $70,000 of capital available to invest at time 0. In addition, you can borrow $10,000 at 40% interest (repayment $14,000 at time 1). Any capital not invested in one or more of the above projects will be invested in the ordinary course of business at a 20% rate of return.

    (a) Compute the (unleveraged) rates of return for each of the projects and for any combinations that are feasible without borrowing.

    (b) Compute the leveraged rate of return for C (borrow $10,000).

    (c) Compute both the leveraged and the unleveraged present worths for C (at the MARR implied in the problem statement).

    (d) Do the results already illustrate that an alternative having a lower rate of return can have a higher present worth? If so, point out how.

    (e) Compute the (unleveraged) present worth for the feasible portfolio AB.

    (f) Are there any portfolios that are not feasible with your capital but become feasible if you borrow? If so, compute their leveraged present worths.

    (g) Make and justify a recommendation for a specific alternative.

23. These independent projects are available:

Project	Required Investment	Returns at Time 1
A	$20,000	$30,000
B	$30,000	$40,000
C	$40,000	$50,000

You have $40,000 of capital available to invest at time zero. In addition, you can borrow $10,000 at 30% interest (repayment $13,000 at time 1). Any capital not invested in one or more of the above projects will be invested in the ordinary course of business at a 20% rate of return.

(a) Compute the (unleveraged) rates of return for each of the projects.
(b) Using the MARR implied in the problem statement, compute:
    (i) The present worth of **A** (unleveraged).
    (ii) The present worth of **A** leveraged (borrow $10,000).
    (iii) The present worth of the portfolio **AB** leveraged, if feasible.
(c) Compute the rate of return of **A** leveraged (borrow $10,000).
(d) How (or how not) do the above results illustrate (or fail to illustrate) that an alternative having a higher rate of return can have a lower present worth?
(e) The mutually exclusive alternatives are to invest in any feasible combination of projects (including the "do-nothing" portfolio), where feasibility is determined by availability of capital including borrowed capital. Which alternative do you recommend, and why?

24. For a company with MARR = 18%, three independent project proposals are available:

Alter-native	Description	Required Investment	Present Worth of Net Benefits	Net Present Worth	Rate of Return
A	Energy conservation	$10,000	$22,200	$12,200	97%
B	Yield improvement	$46,600	$61,000	$14,400	21%
C	Maintenance facility	$52,800	$68,600	$15,800	20%

(a) Verify that for an inflexible $100,000 budget a maximum net present worth of $30,200 can be obtained.
(b) The company's credit rating is such that borrowed funds are not normally available even at junk bond rates. However, for a bonafide energy conservation project, the creditors will agree to lend at 20%, requiring repayment in 10 equal end-of-year payments. The loan will be of the amount ($9400) just needed to fund the energy conservation project. Is it worthwhile to take this greater-than-MARR loan?

25. There are four independent projects available, each one the best version of its kind at a MARR of 15%.

Project	Required Investment	Present Worth
1—energy	10	4
2—process	6	2.1
3—whse.	5	1.5
4—mtls.	3	0.6

(a) If there is an inflexible budget of 15, what combination would be selected?

(b) If the budget is considered approximate, what projects would be selected, and how much additional budget would be used over the estimated 15?

(c) Suppose that the alternatives are these: (A) Borrow the additional budget computed above and invest in the resulting portfolio, or (B) invest now only in the portfolio computed for a budget of 15. In either case, any projects not accepted now will be accepted next year and will earn the same worth then as they would have earned now. If the only loan available were at 25% interest, to be repaid in 10 equal end-of-year payments, would the loan be worthwhile?

26. A capital shortage threatens to prevent you from investing in a very good project that yields $12,200 in net present worth at MARR = 18%. You are only $6500 short of the required investment capital. The project's returns will allow repayment of a loan in two equal end-of-year payments.

    If you wait one year you will have the necessary capital, but the project will not only be delayed but will have a net worth of only $9000 at that time. If Fiendly Loan Company is the only lender willing to help, what is the highest interest rate (to the nearest 1%) that could be charged without making you decide to wait?

    Hint: At 18% you would borrow if $P_{wait} < P_{nowait}$, where P_{wait} is the present worth of $9000 delayed one year, and P_{nowait} is $12,200, plus $6500 (remember that the $12,200 includes investment, and you now do not pay this part of the investment), minus the present worth (at 18%) of the two repayments.

27. Upon auditing your economic analyses of project proposals, an investment banker familiar with your company and industry offers to lend you the additional capital necessary to invest in attractive projects for which you lack adequate capital. The investment banker's stipulation is that the loan be at an opportunity-dependent interest rate. For simplicity, since these negotiated rates are such that the banker gets about half of the total advantage, assume that you will have to pay the investment banker an amount that is half the present worth (at your MARR) gained; for example, if you could borrow an extra $1000 to get an extra net present worth of $200, you really gain a present worth of only $100.

    Your MARR is 18%, you have only $100,000 of available capital, and the following independent project proposals are available:

Alternative	Description	Required Investment	Present Worth of Net Benefits	Net Present Worth	Rate of Return
A	Energy conservation	$47,500	$53,500	$6,000	20%
B	Yield improvement	$51,600	$58,700	$7,100	27%
C	Maintenance facility	$60,200	$72,600	$12,400	40%

(a) Make a recommendation based on the assumption that any opportunity not taken now will disappear.

(b) Make a recommendation based on the assumption that any opportunity not taken now will be available one year from now, and that you will then have adequate capital for all projects whose rates of return exceed MARR.

Henry J. Kaiser celebrates completion of the Hoover Dam in 1935, under budget and ahead of schedule.

PUBLIC-SECTOR DECISION MAKING

This chapter treats considerations that arise when an engineer performs design or consulting work where the values to be placed on consequences of a decision are unclear or controversial. Such considerations arise in the public sector because decisions are being made on behalf of a larger constituency than just the owners of an enterprise, and because it is in the public sector that many difficult decisions are made regarding health, safety, and public welfare. Public-sector considerations also arise in the private sector when there are questions regarding pollution, public endangerment, workplace safety, environmental risk, archeological or historical preservation, and the like.

It should be emphasized that only in totalitarian societies would there arise situations in which an important decision hinging on human values would be made solely or even mainly on the basis of an engineering economic analysis, no matter how comprehensive or well-founded the analysis might be. Nevertheless, it is worthwhile to base recommendations on the best available methodology.

Whereas private-sector decisions are in principle made to maximize net benefits to the *owners* of an enterprise, public-sector decisions are in principle made to maximize net benefits to whomever they may accrue. Recall from the first chapter the list of those affected:

> **Constituencies Affected by a Decision:**
>
> Owners (shareholders, partners)
>
> Management
>
> Employees
>
> Customers
>
> Suppliers
>
> The public, future generations, mankind
>
> Governments (surrogate for all nonowners)

7.1 LIMIT REGULATIONS AND INCENTIVES

In most societies there are two links between public and private decision making: *limit regulations* and *incentives*. Both these links tend to cause private decision makers to behave in such a way that the interests of nonowners are represented. Ideally, an enterprise should be influenced by limit regulations and incentives so that the decisions made in self-interest are substantially the same ones as would be made in the public interest.

Incentives work better than limit regulations, in general. For example, a study was made in 1972 of 10 industrial enterprises on the Houston Ship Channel, which were emitting a total of about 58,000 tons per year of particulates into the atmosphere while spending about $1.3 million in annual particulate emission control costs. The enterprises were obeying limits imposed by the Texas Air Control Board and federal and local authorities. It was estimated that the emission limits could be fine-tuned to cause a shift to a total emission of about 49,000 tons per year and an annual control cost of about $1.0 million—better air for less money. At the same time, it was estimated that a $6/ton-year emission fee would cause a shift to 40,000 tons per year and an annual control cost of about $0.8 million—even better air for even less money. The "secret" of incentives over regulations is that enterprises' marginal costs of compliance vary; those who can more easily take an incentive-encouraged action will do so to a greater extent, while others will find it more economical to respond to a lesser extent. Specific numerical examples to demonstrate this are given in the first two exercises at the end of the chapter.

Limits and incentives are established by governments in the form of laws and regulations. Examples of limit regulations are a legally established minimum wage, a speed limit for vehicles on a highway, or a maximum allowable fat content in a processed food product. Incentives include excise taxes on luxury items (a negative incentive), tax credits for favored classes of capital investment, or subsidies for certain industries or economic activities.

The role of limit regulations is to represent the interests of nonowners through *constraints*. The owners choose alternatives to maximize their wealth, but the choice is from a set of *feasible* alternatives; an alternative is infeasible if it violates limits against paying substandard wages, making fraudulent claims, erecting unsafe structures, and the like. The role of incentives is to represent the interests of nonowners by creating additional costs and benefits that the decision maker must take into account; an alternative becomes worse if it includes incurring fines or penalties, better if it includes taking advantage of tax incentives or free governmental services.

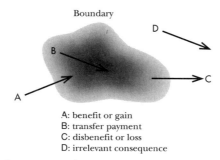

A: benefit or gain
B: transfer payment
C: disbenefit or loss
D: irrelevant consequence

FIGURE 7-1. Payments with respect to a welfare-economy boundary.

7.2 THE WELFARE ECONOMY PRINCIPLE

The basic principle for deciding what is best in the public sector, whether the purpose is to recommend limits and incentives or to recommend actions to be taken by public agencies, is the *principle of welfare economy: to maximize net benefits to whomever they may accrue.* In the United States, the Flood Control Act of 1936 seems to mark the first official adoption of the principle. The main idea, which is also embodied in the phrase "greatest good for the greatest number," is based on the notion of a *welfare economy boundary* that encompasses all the constituents whose interests are to be considered relevant in the decision. Figure 7-1 depicts a welfare economy boundary and payments with respect to it. Arrow **A** represents a monetary receipt or a benefit (expressed as money) coming into the system from outside: This is a *gain.* Arrow **B** represents a *transfer payment,* representing a gain by one part of the system and an offsetting loss by another part of the system. Arrow **C** represents a monetary disbursement or a dis-benefit—a *loss.* Arrow **D** is something outside the system, such as payments from Floridians to Georgians as viewed by the Alabama Board of Trade if it considers only the welfare of Alabamians.

7.2.1 Welfare Economy Decision Making

Once a welfare economy boundary is adopted for a given decision, the welfare economy rule is to decide on the basis of gains (arrow **A**) and losses (arrow **B**), ignoring transfer payments (arrow **C**) and payments outside the system (arrow **D**). If the welfare economy boundary is adopted to include only the owners of the enterprise, welfare-economy decision making reduces to the owner-wealth maximization that has been assumed throughout this book. A particular boundary choice is called a *viewpoint;* there is the owners' viewpoint, the public's viewpoint, and others.

E1. A proposed factory would earn its owners $1 million and would generate harm from pollution. Assuming the harm is estimated as equivalent to a $1 cost incurred by each of 2 million surrounding residents, and that the harm is ignored by or unknown to the owners, determine the worth of the proposed factory from the owners' viewpoint and from the public's viewpoint.

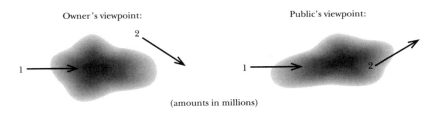

Owner's viewpoint: Public's viewpoint:

(amounts in millions)

$$P = \$1 \text{ million to owners} \qquad\qquad P = 1 - 2 = -\$1 \text{ to public}$$

The word "society" is often used to denote either everything within a welfare-economy boundary or everything within the boundary that is not otherwise designated. Note that by definition the owners of an enterprise are part of society. By the same token, a governmental agency is defined as within society, and a prison population is defined as within society. A project is considered worthwhile if the worth of its estimated gains exceeds the worth of its estimated losses.

Work done or effort exerted is a *loss* (the entropy sump of the universe is outside the boundary); harvests, fruits of creativity, or anything of value earned as a result of work or effort are *gains*. Property theft provides an interesting example of welfare-economy bookkeeping: Although the value of the stolen item is traditionally considered to be the measure of a theft's harm to society, the change of possession itself is a transfer payment; the loss is the diminishment of society's valued state of order.

E2. **A student intern working for her village council estimates that a one-person police force would cost $90,000 per year and would save $120,000 per year, classified as follows: reduce thefts 15% from $330,000 level; reduce traffic congestion, saving 1000 person-hours of travel time valued at $7/hr; reduce violence, saving 400 treatment-days valued at $150/day; and provide miscellaneous benefits valued at $3500/yr.**

(a) Why is the $90,000 annual salary a cost rather than a transfer payment?

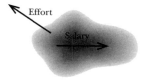

The money paid by the village to the public person *is* a transfer payment. However, the presumably equal effort exerted by the police person is a loss.

(b) Accepting the estimates, is a police person worthwhile?

Yes. The worth is

$$-90,000 + 120,000 = \$40,000/\text{yr} > 0 \Rightarrow \text{worthwhile}$$

(c) The intern estimated that $50,000 of the costs but only $20,000 of the benefits accrue to the residential area, so establishing the police force would effec-

tively constitute establishing a $30,000 subsidy of the business area by the residential area. Why is this not relevant to the basic decision on whether a police force would be worthwhile?

The subsidy, being a transfer payment, is irrelevant to the welfare-economy decision.

7.2.2 Equity Restoration by Transfer Payments

Welfare-economy analysis would not be reasonable without the further notion of *equity-restoring transfer payments*. (Here, the word "equity" is used in its meaning of "fairness" rather than in its meaning of "owners' capital.")

Segments of a society value their sense of equity or fair treatment. The extensive structure of governmental services and taxes constitutes a set of transfer payments that tend to preserve an existing level of satisfaction or dissatisfaction with the overall fairness of society. Implementation of a new project will change the net level of equity satisfaction as some segments feel better treated and some worse. The *equity disbenefit* of a project is the amount by which the project decreases net equity satisfaction.

Now it is obvious that if a project's net benefits, excluding its equity disbenefit, exceed its net costs, *it is always possible to devise an equity-restoring set of transfer payments so that all segments are better off than before*, unless the equity-restoring adjustments themselves cost too much.

Therefore, we can assert a justifying equity assumption that allows evaluation of projects on a welfare-economy basis:

Equity Assumption for Welfare Economy Decision Making:

The rule of accepting a project whose net benefits exceed net costs assumes that one of the following situations holds:

1. The project does not decrease net equity satisfaction.
2. The project decreases net equity satisfaction by an amount less than the margin by which its benefits exceed its costs.
3. The project, after implementation of a full or partial equity-restoring set of transfer payments, decreases net equity satisfaction by an amount such that this amount, plus the cost of administering the set of transfer payments, is less than the project's benefits-less-cost margin.

In practice, the transfer payments that attempt to restore equity do *not* closely approach the ideal of making everyone better off. A typical set of equity-restoring transfer payments is represented by a toll booth on a bridge. If a bridge were financed out of general tax revenues, people who seldom used it would complain; the collection of tolls makes at least part of the cost correlate with usage. It is very difficult to agree on an equity definition; should the prior state be preserved, or should new works generally favor the disadvantaged? It is also very difficult to agree on valuations of consequences; how much does a citizen who does not personally use a new road nevertheless gather benefits such as reduced prices for goods whose shipping costs are thereby reduced? The theory of welfare economy assumes that the economic and social system has many ways to spread benefits, so that a two-phase decision process is justified: first identify the alternative having greatest benefits-less-cost, and then devise any necessary equity-restoring transfer payments.

E3. A new access ramp costing $400,000 will serve the Blandish Plant, benefiting its employees to an extent whose present worth is estimated as $800,000, but also disbenefiting freeway drivers to an extent whose present worth is estimated as $200,000.

$800K $400K
               $200K

(a) Suggest a set of transfer payments that would make everybody better off.

Since hundreds or thousands of individual motorists are involved, complete equity resoration would be impossible, even with a voucher or toll system measuring every use of the ramp.

(b) Suggest a practical set of equity-restoring transfer payments for this project.

The Blandish Plant could pay both the $400,000 cost and an additional fee between $200,000 and $400,000. Say this additional fee were $300,000, so that the net benefit to the Blandish Plant and the net benefit to the public are equal at $100,000 each. It is impractical to identify which freeway drivers are inconvenienced and by how much. The additional fee could go into general tax coffers, or partly or wholly be used for freeway improvements or beautification.

The issues of efficiency and accuracy of equity-restoring transfer payments can be understood in terms of the bookkeeping system defined in Figure 7-2 for a simple society that consists of protagonist, regulator, and public.

In terms of the quantities defined in Figure 7-2, we can define a *good* project and an *equitable* project:

A project is good if society profits from it.

$$B - C = R_B - C_B - C_A - (1 - \eta)X \geq 0 \qquad (7\text{-}1)$$

A project is equitable if everyone profits from it. Both

$$(B - C)_B = R_B - C_B + T_{AB} - X \geq 0 \qquad (7\text{-}1\text{a})$$

and

$$(B - C)_A = \eta X - C_A - T_{AB} \geq 0 \qquad (7\text{-}1\text{b})$$

Recall, for instance, the Blandish Plant's access ramp of Example E3. Let **A** be the freeway drivers, **B** the Blandish Plant, and **R** an agency whose transfer efficiency is $\eta = 0.85$ and which collects a $300,000 fee from **B** in addition to requiring **B** to pay

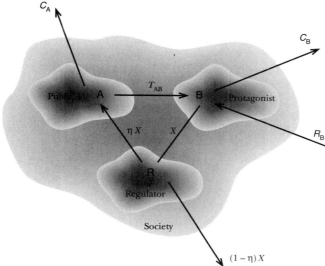

Protagonist "B" undertakes a project that has cost C_B and brings returns R_B, but also causes an involuntary transfer payment T_{AB} from "A" to "B" and an involuntary loss C_A by "A". Regulator "R" exacts a fee X from "B" and transfers ηX to "A", where η is the regulator's transfer efficiency.

FIGURE 7-2. Gains, losses, and transfers in a simple regulated society.

the cost of the ramp. From the viewpoint of the protagonist B, Eq. 7-1 is (amounts in thousands)

$$(B - C)_B = 800 - 400 + 0 - 300 = \$100,000$$

From the viewpoint of the public A, Eq. 7-2 is

$$(B - C)_A = 0.85(300) - 200 - 0 = \$55,000$$

Since benefits exceed costs from both viewpoints A and B, the project is equitable. Further numerical examples are given in the chapter-end exercises, where it is also proved that every equitable project is good.

7.2.3 MARR for Public Expenditures

Public agencies borrow money, and thus, like any enterprise, should use a minimal attractive rate of return (MARR) that is at least the cost of capital. Public agencies also are short of capital, so MARR should be tuned as recommended in Chapter 5 to make the proposed versions of projects contain the appropriate incremental subprojects. A local or provincial government or agency, then, can select MARR just as any enterprise does.

The situation is somewhat different for agencies of a national government, where the agency does not stand alone but is tied into an interlocking web of finances and services. Although one agency in a national government may be capital-rich while another is capital-poor, it would seem that all should use the same MARR. One can argue, for example, that every dollar spent by the United States government is a dollar taken out of the economy, where it would otherwise contribute to the nation's wealth at some grand, overall rate of return. That MARR, for the United States, has been set at 10%.

Circular A-94, "Discount Rates to Be Used in Evaluating Time-Distributed Costs and Benefits," was last published by OMB (Office of Management and Budget) in 1972 and was still in effect as of 1992. It specifically requires an interest rate of 10% for evaluating federal investment decisions, with certain exceptions (water resource projects can sometimes use a lower rate). The rate is based on the notion that all governmental expenditures take capital away from the private sector, which over the long term tends to earn a rate of return of about 10% before taxes and after inflation. The major stock market price indexes in the United States have increased just at this rate over the recent decades, so if the stock market is a surrogate banker for society, the 10% rate is accurate.

"After inflation" means the rate is applicable to cash flows that already include inflation, which are those measured in A_t or "current" (inflated) dollars. Thus, by regulation this is an i rate. However, an accepted practice appears to be to ignore inflation, so that cash flows that may be "billed" as A_t are really W_t, meaning that the rate is treated as a d rate. We will examine the relevant issues by solving problems that show that ignoring inflation tends to introduce a bias against investment.

E4. **An analyst's analysis of a public-sector proposal shows benefits of $11 million per year for 15 years, which fail to justify the proposed $85 million investment at $i = 10\%$.**

$$P = -85 + 11(P/A\ 10\%,15) = -\$1.333 \text{ million}$$

However, you notice in reviewing the analysis that the benefits are savings in citizens' time spent waiting in queues, valued at $7.50 per hour, and monetary savings for fuel and other goods and services that should be expected to inflate. Thus you conclude the $11 million per year is really a W_t (indexed) estimate. Using the customary 4% annual anticipated inflation rate, recompute P.

$$1 + i = (1 + d)(+j) \Rightarrow 1 + d = \frac{1.10}{1.04} \Rightarrow d = 0.057692308$$

$$P = -85 + 11\left(\frac{1 - (1/1 + d)^{15}}{d}\right) = -85 + 11(P/A\ 5.7692808\%,15)$$

$$= -85 + 11(9.860386)$$

$$= \$23.464 \text{ million}$$

Based on your results, would the proponent of a project favor ignoring inflation or taking inflation into account?

Assuming that the proponent is biased in favor, he/she would want to take inflation into account.

E5. In Example E4, benefits of $11 million per year were estimated. It was assumed that the benefits were in W_t terms although reported as if they were in A_t terms, and this assumption caused a correction that greatly increased the desirability of the investment. Now let us assume, to the contrary, that the analyst really meant the benefits expressed as A_t would be $11 million each year, so that the original unfavorable analysis at $i = 10\%$ was correct.

(a) What real rate of decline in benefits is implicit in the analyst's figures if 4% inflation was expected?

$$v = \frac{1}{1.04} - 1 = \underline{-3.846\%} \quad \text{escalation} \quad (3.846\% \quad \text{decline})$$

(b) Under the assumption that the analyst expected a decline in W_t, what are the indexed amounts for years 1 and 2 corresponding to $A_1 = A_2 = \$11$ million? (Use v computed above.)

$$A_0 = A_1 = A_2 = \$11 \text{ million}$$
$$W_t = a_0(1 + v)^t$$

Hence

$$W_1 = a_0(1 + v)^1 = 11(0.961538462)$$
$$= \underline{\$10.577 \text{ million}}$$
$$W_2 = 11(0.961538462)^2 = \underline{\$10.170 \text{ million}}$$

(c) Determine the substitute interest rate for $i = 10\%$, $j = 4\%$ and $v = (1/1.04) - 1$. Does this verify that the analyst was originally using the correct rate if anticipating a decline that would just offset inflation? Explain.

$$1 + s = \frac{1 + i}{(1 + v)(1 + j)} = \frac{1.10}{(1/1.04)(1.04)} = 1.10 \Rightarrow \underline{s = 10\%}$$

Yes. The analyst originally used 10%; this result shows 10% as the correct rate for real escalation that just offsets inflation, so that $(1 + v)(1 + j) = 1$.

7.3 MEASURABILITY AND COMMENSURABILITY OF BENEFITS AND COSTS

If all desirable and undesirable consequences of a decision could be converted to money, public-sector decisions would not constitute a separate topic. However, there are levels of difficulty that depend on how well the consequences of a decision can be quantified.

SPECTRUM OF DIFFICULTY OF PUBLIC DECISIONS

Level of Difficulty	Analysis Method
0: Benefits and disbenefits firmly convertible to money	Standard (same as for private sector)
1: Benefits and disbenefits uncertainly convertible to money	*B/C* ratio
2: Benefits and disbenefits convertible not to money but to a measure of effectiveness	Effectiveness/cost ratio (*B/C* ratio with benefits in nonmonetary units)
3: Benefits and disbenefits too vague	Legal and political processes

For decisions at the 0 level of difficulty, where benefits and disbenefits are firmly convertible to money, the main special characteristic of public decisions is the wide view—the necessity of considering side-effects on all constituencies included within the welfare-economy boundary. At this level of difficulty, the wider viewpoint is the only real distinction between public-sector and private-sector decision making.

For decisions at the 1 level of difficulty, where benefits are uncertainly convertible to money, there are some special conventions and assumptions used in estimating the monetary equivalents of benefits and disbenefits. For example:

· If there is a market in a benefit, the market price is the measure. Thus the benefit of eliminating travel time or waiting time is valued at minimum wage for high school students or charity patients, or median wage (about $7.50 an hour in 1991) for a cross section of citizens.

· If there is no market, a benefit's monetary equivalent can sometimes be established by investigating willingness to pay. For example, recreational benefits of a park project could be estimated on the basis of a reasonable admission price.

· Economic multipliers are ignored, and double-counting of all kinds is avoided. For example, the necessity for a new employee is a quantifiable disbenefit measured by the outlay. The money may change hands many times as transfer payments; the only net effect is the extra effort expended by an extra employee, and the measure of effort is the wage. Similarly, loss of property value after a flood is a measure of damage, but it would be double-counting also to count the cash damages.

· In every area of benefits there are special assumptions or rules of thumb. For example, theft is an involuntary transfer payment (the thief, fence, and receivers gain what the victim loses), but conventionally the harm to society from a theft is considered to be equal to the value of the item stolen. As another example, the insertion of a car into rush-hour traffic causes delay not only of that car but of other cars; the total delay is conventionally estimated as twice the inserted car's delay.

E6. (a) An irrigation project would improve Aiville's apples to the quality of Beeville's, whose apples command $0.14 more per bushel. If Aiville produces 95,000 bushels per year, estimate the annual benefit.

$$95,000(0.14) = \underline{\$13,300}$$

(b) A market survey established that Aiville's citizens favored a park improvement about as much as a recent library improvement, if they knew the cost of neither. The library improvement's cost was actually $2 million, and its benefits were generally perceived as appropriate to the cost. Estimate the park improvement's benefits, in present-worth dollars.

Equating benefits to costs, the estimate is $2 million.

(c) A proposed Academy Bowl Game would bring an estimated 10,000 extra visitors to the Highland Falls area. Each visitor would spend an average of $220 locally on food, lodging, and entertainment in addition to that spent for tickets and at the game itself. The local authorities and boosters consider their welfare-economy boundary to include local residents and exclude others (so extra visitors' expenditures count as input). Since money received locally by retailers tends to be spent locally (a dollar may go from hotelier to butcher to music teacher to grocer . . .), the Middletown newspaper runs a story quoting an estimate that $15.4 million will be added to the local economy as the total of all increased receipts in the last week of December. Estimate the benefit from extra visitors' cash infusion to the local area's economy.

$$10,000(220) = \$2.2 \text{ million}$$

Ignore the multipliers.

Special conventions and assumptions, however, cannot clear up all the difficulties of benefit estimation. The benefit/cost ratio allows hard-to-estimate benefits to be used in decision making in an appropriate way.

7.4 BENEFIT/COST RATIOS IN PUBLIC SECTOR DECISION MAKING

7.4.1 Stability of B/C Ratios

When there is *substantial difficulty in estimating the monetary value of benefits*, there is some objection to using the usual worth measures. Consider the situation illustrated in Figure 7-3, where $B^{(A)}$ and $B^{(B)}$ represent the present worths, in thousands of dollars, of visitors' time saved by alternative improvements A and B to a hospital's system for handling visitors, and $C^{(A)}$ and $C^{(B)}$ represent the respective present worths of the costs of implementing the alternatives.

Note that project A has the greater B/C *ratio* (benefit/cost ratio), a ratio defined as the present worth of benefits divided by the present worth of costs. Note also, on the other hand, that project B has the greater $B - C$ *difference*, a difference defined (with costs conventionally considered as positive) so as to be identical to the *present worth of the project*. A gives 1.05 times as much "bang for buck" as B although it gives less "bang minus buck."

Now by standard analysis project B is the better alternative (its present worth is $4000 more than that of A). However, let the "substantial difficulty in estimating the

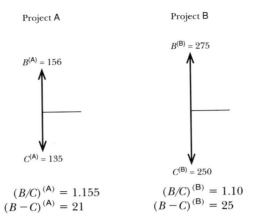

$$(B/C)^{(A)} = 1.155 \qquad (B/C)^{(B)} = 1.10$$
$$(B-C)^{(A)} = 21 \qquad (B-C)^{(B)} = 25$$

FIGURE 7-3. Alternative hospital visitor-handling improvements.

value of benefits'' be expressed in terms of a parameter M, so that the *true* benefits are $156M$ and $275M$. We will show that small changes in M from its assumed value of 1 can change the decision if the decision is based on the B/C ratio. This will clarify why public-sector decision makers frequently use the benefit/cost ratio (B/C) while using $(B-C)$ to a lesser extent: It is because they distrust the exact valuation of benefits.

E7. **In the situation of Figure 7.2, suppose the value of visitors' time was $M = 95\%$ of what was estimated; that is, under A the time saved was worth $156M = 148.2$ and under B the time saved was worth $275M = 261.25$. Show that this small change in benefit estimation reverses the decision if based on $B - C$ but leaves it the same as before if based on B/C.**

Under $M = 0.95$, the two alternatives have cash flows as follows:

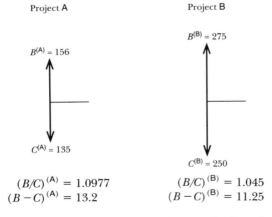

$$(B/C)^{(A)} = 1.0977 \qquad (B/C)^{(B)} = 1.045$$
$$(B-C)^{(A)} = 13.2 \qquad (B-C)^{(B)} = 11.25$$

Note that **A** is favored by the B/C ratio, as before. In fact the *ratio* of B/C ratios, $(B/C)^{(A)}/(B/C)^{(B)}$, remains as before; **A** gives 1.05 times as much benefit per unit cost as **B**.

But whereas with $M = 1$ the $B - C$ difference favored **B** by \$4000, with $M = 0.95$ it now favors **A** by $13.2 - 11.25 = \$1950$.

What has been demonstrated is that a size-independent measure such as the B/C ratio tends to be more stable than a quantity measure such as present worth when there exist scaling difficulties such as uncertainty in the dollar value of a nonmonetary benefit. If we are uncertain as to the "unit price" of an important benefit, we know the benefit per dollar more accurately than we know the present worth. Using B/C, we can compare two projects with similar benefits (such as health benefits, recreational benefits, esthetic benefits) much more surely than we can compare them, using $B - C$, with dissimilar opportunities. This concept, carried to the extreme of not assigning money values to benefits, leads to the simplest case of *cost-effectiveness* analysis.

The foregoing arguments do not, of course, change the fact that B/C is an efficiency measure, as shown in Chapter 4. It is inappropriate to choose the alternative having greatest B/C if benefit valuations are not questionable. For example, if alternative A has benefits of 30 and costs of 20, then $P^{(A)} = (B - C)^{(A)} = 30 - 20 = 10$, and $(B/C)^{(A)} = 1.5$; and if alternative B has benefits of 40 and costs of 28, then $P^{(B)} = (B - C)^{(B)} = 40 - 28 = 12$, and $(B/C)^{(B)} = 40/28 = 1.42857$. B has more worth and should be chosen, although A is more efficient. To make this clear, some public-sector agencies use the *incremental B/C ratio*. The incremental project $B - A$ has incremental benefits of $40 - 30 = 10$ and incremental costs of $28 - 20 = 8$, so its incremental B/C ratio is $(B/C)^{(B-A)} = 10/8 = 1.25$. Since this is greater than 1, the increment $B - A$ would be accepted. The incremental B/C ratio uses the rule of accepting all increments having an incremental B/C ratio exceeding 1; this is shown in the exercises to be equivalent to maximizing the worth $B - C$.

7.4.2 The *B/C* Ratio in Cost-Effectiveness Analysis

Health and safety benefits are much easier to quantify in appropriate units such as "lives saved" than to evaluate monetarily. Besides reluctance to place a monetary value on such a thing as an individual human life and to suffer the perception that to make a decision is tantamount to deciding how many people to kill or let die, there is the more general difficulty that benefit-related measurable quantities are often only *indicators* of benefits. If a new court-scheduling procedure can reduce average delay from indictment to trial for a class of criminal cases, we may despair of monetarily estimating the benefits to society from speedier justice, yet we may be quite confident that a procedure that saves an average of 4.7 days is better than one that saves an average of 3.2 days if they both have the same cost. Similarly, if a traffic-safety project saves 15 lives, then even if we could confidently say each lifesaving success is worth X dollars, we still would not know the benefits, because for every fatal traffic accident there are many nonfatal accidents involving injury, disability, property damage, shortening of life expectancy, and so forth. Still, if these other consequences are highly correlated with traffic deaths, we may be confident that saving 15 lives is better than saving 10 if the projects able to do each both have the same cost.

Consider a B/C ratio in which the numerator is measured in some arbitrary benefit unit such as "air-quality index" or "recreation hours provided." Then if $(B/C)^{(A)} > (B/C)^{(B)}$ we say A is more *cost effective* (or cost efficient) than B. This is taken to imply that A should be preferred to B, but not that either one should necessarily be preferred to doing nothing.

The assumption necessary to support the cost-effectiveness notion is that the arbitrary benefit quantity is directly proportional to a scalar measure of "true" benefit, so that twice the measure means twice the benefit.

E8. **Air bags promise to save 800 lives per year and would cost $2 billion per year to install in all new cars. Seat-belt safety laws promise to save 1000 lives per year and would cost $0.8 billion per year to promote and administer. Compute the B/C ratio for each alternative. Ignoring the do-nothing and do-both options, and ignoring the difference in providers (air-bag costs would be $200 per car, incurred by the manufacturer and added to the price paid by the consumer, whereas seat-belt safety laws would be administered and promoted by a mixture of local and federal agencies), which is better?**

Project	Benefits	Costs	B/C Ratio
Air bags	800 lives/yr	$2 billion/yr	400 lives/$ billion
Seat-belt laws	1000 lives/yr	$0.8 billion/yr	1250 lives/$ billion

Since $1250 > 400$, seat-belt laws are more cost-effective than air bags.

Cost effectiveness as indicated by a B/C ratio remains a useful notion if extended so that the *denominator* is in arbitrary units, as the following example illustrates.

E9. **A memo within a regulatory agency states, "We can bring 15 companies into compliance with 2 more people in Department A. If Department B were given 3 more people, instead of giving 2 people to Department A, we could bring 22 companies into compliance." The memo goes on to recommend the addition of 2 people to Department A as being more cost-effective. Show why.**

Project	Benefits	Costs	B/C Ratio
A	15 companies	2 people	7.5 compliances/employee
B	22 companies	3 people	7.33 compliances/employee

Since $7.5 > 7.33$, adding 2 people to Department A is more cost-effective.

Note that the denominator's arbitrary cost quantity is directly proportional to the ''true'' cost, because twice as many people would cost twice as much.

The limitation that a B/C ratio says nothing about absolute desirability of an alternative can be overcome in some instances by comparison with the B/C ratio of a project already concluded to be marginally desirable. Thus, for example, an aviation safety agency indicates the benefits of many of its actions and programs in terms of reduction in a defined ''incident rate,'' whereas ''incident'' is any (1) accident, (2) near miss, (3) monitored occurrence of an unsafe condition, (4) validated complaint, or (5) inspection result that meets published definitions. The agency's funding limitations provide a benchmark B/C value. If in recent years the agency has been able to fund actions and programs having B/C of at least 0.017 but not less, then the effectiveness-to-cost ratio of a new proposal does indeed indicate its desirability.

The limited cost-effectiveness technique we have covered here is a small part of an extensive family of cost-effectiveness techniques that are built on the theory of multiattribute decision analysis. The more elaborate cost-effectiveness techniques are complex and subtle, and they rest on shaky theoretical foundations, but the basic B/C ratio with nonmonetary benefits is simple and sound. Consider, for example, the problem of deciding between two field artillery weapons systems that are identical in most attributes (mobility, etc.) except firepower and cost. If firepower is measured in appropriate units (say, rounds per minute where the rounds are of equal effectiveness per round), so that the measure is agreed upon as representing well the intuitive notion of "amount of firepower," then clearly the system having the greater firepower per dollar of cost ("bang per buck") is the better system.

When more than one nonmonetary measure of benefit is available, first check to see if they are highly correlated. If so, either measure can be used alone as the indicator of benefit. If, on the other hand, two measures seem to be independent or negatively correlated (the more of one, the less of the other), seek a basis for deriving a weighted average of them, and use the weighted average as the benefit indicator. (If neither of these approaches is appropriate, the problem is a multicriterion problem that requires techniques beyond the scope of this chapter.) Note that the most usual basis for a weighted average is to estimate that money value of each benefit.

When benefits are nonmonetary, it is important to use *all* costs in the B/C denominators for every alternative. It is *not* valid to eliminate any nonsunk cost that is the same for all alternatives.

7.4.3 Classification of Benefits and Costs

Public-sector decision making is not a game of government versus citizen. Taxes, user fees, tolls, and the like are transfer payments and are neither costs nor benefits. For example, if a bridge is built with public funds and half its revenues are financed by taxes and the other half by user tolls, the user tolls are not a cost or disbenefit to the public nor a negative cost or benefit to the government. Note that the public pays for *all* this project anyway; certainly the part paid as user fees rather than general taxes is not relevant in deciding whether one bridge is better than another.

For similar reasons, in such decisions as prison improvements, it is important to remember that the prisoners are part of society.

Classification of benefits and costs is fraught with definitional difficulties. There are three basic rules in common use for splitting benefits from costs:

1. The *user/provider* B/C split puts all benefits, disbenefits $(-)$, and nontransfer monetary costs $(-)$ to the using and affected public in the numerator ("benefits"), and puts all costs to the governmental providing agency in the denominator ("costs").
2. The *later/now* B/C split puts all continuing ($/yr) benefits, disbenefits $(-)$, and nontransfer monetary costs $(-)$ or profits $(+)$ in the numerator, and puts all immediate costs $(+)$ and benefits $(-)$ in the denominator.
3. The *nonmonetary/monetary* B/C split puts all nonmonetary benefits and disbenefits $(-)$ in the numerator (not necessarily expressed as dollars), and puts all monetary consequences (including benefits and disbenefits that *are* expressed as money) in the denominator.

E10. A project at a college puts a heavy-duty laser printer in an academic building, where previously the only one was at the computer center. It saves many walking trips to get output—benefit B_1. It costs money to purchase and install—cost C_1. It costs money to operate—cost C_2. It encourages more use of the computer, considered beneficial to intellectual development—benefit B_2. By reducing

walking, it detracts from student fitness—(dis)benefit B_3. **Under the three rules, classify the items.**

	Numerator	*Denominator*
User/provider:	*User*	*Provider*
B_1	✓	
B_2	✓	
B_3	✓	
C_1		✓
C_2		✓
Later/now:	*Later*	*Now*
B_1	✓	
B_2	✓	
B_3	✓	
C_1		✓
C_2	✓ $(-)$	
Non-monetary/monetary:	*Non-monetary*	*Monetary*
B_1	✓	
B_2	✓	
B_3	✓	
C_1		✓
C_2		✓

7.4.4 Size Scaling of Projects in B/C Analysis

Many public-sector projects are capable of being size-scaled. That is, some projects can be scaled up or scaled down in size while keeping the investment, other costs, benefits, and disbenefits all (linearly) proportional to their values at one size. Examples of linear size scaling would be an immunization program where fewer or more patients could be included, yielding proportional benefits (the same benefit per patient) and proportional costs (a constant cost per patient); a weapons procurement program where the unit cost and unit effectiveness per copy would remain constant over a range of number of copies procured; or a safety-device retrofit program for automobiles, where bringing in or excluding various model years (e.g., retrofitting cars from model year 1985 to 1987 versus from 1984 to 1988) would incur equal unit costs and unit benefits.

We can easily prove that the worth-maximizing version of a linearly scalable project is simply its largest or smallest version: Let a project have cash flows (including benefits and disbenefits measured as money) constituting the set $\{A_t: t = 0,...,n\}$, where A_0 would often be negative and would be the investment, whereas the other A_t amounts would often be positive. The project's present worth is

$$P = \sum_{t=0}^{n} A_t \beta^t$$

Now if the project is linearly scalable, another version exists that is x times as big as this version; its investment and all costs and benefits can be multiplied by x. Let the scaled present worth be denoted P_x:

$$P_x = \sum_{t=0}^{n} (A_t x)\beta^t = xP$$

Thus the scaled present worth is maximized if P is positive by using the greatest x or if P is negative by using the least x.

In reality, projects cannot be size-scaled very far and maintain linearity, but *approximate scalability increases the applicability of size-independent efficiency measures.* If a project consists generally of early costs and disbenefits followed by later returns and benefits, so that P decreases with i, then we can easily prove that *if two projects can be scaled to similar size, the one with the greater rate of return will also have the greater worth.* A similar result is true for other size-independent measures: The project with the greater B/C ratio, or the greater NPVI, or the shorter payback time, will generally have the greater worth if the projects can be scaled to similar size.

E11. **Let Project 1 save 50 lives for $50,000, while Project 2 saves 10 lives for $100. (These data are unrealistically extreme for illustrative purposes.) Let the parameter V represent the present worth of the benefits of saving one life.**

(a) Show that the B/C ratio prefers Project 2.

$(B/C)_2 = 0.1V$, while $(B/C)_1 = 0.001V$, so that Project 2 is 100 times more cost effective. Note that the relative sizes of the B/C ratio are *independent* of the price V.

(b) Show that present-worth maximization prefers Project 1 unless a life is worth $1247.50 or less.

$P_2 > P_1$ implies $10V - 100 > 50V\text{-}50,000$ which implies $V < 1247.50$.

(c) Is it reasonable for Project 1 and 2 to be considered as mutually exclusive alternatives?

Suppose, for example, Project 1 consists of searching out and treating 50 victims of a rare disease, while Project 2 consists of treating only those 10 victims for whom it is not necessary to search. They are by definition mutually exclusive—to implement both would be to treat the same 10 easy-to-find victims twice.

Results of the foregoing problem reinforce the distinction between size-independent measures (e.g., B/C) and worth measures (e.g., present worth). Project 2 is hugely cost effective and also cheap. Evidently it cannot be scaled up; no one would consider saving 10 lives for $100 if there was an alternative to save 20 lives for $200. Its present worth is positive if a life is worth more than $10. If a life is worth more than $1247.50, Project 1 is even better, because it is far larger in size than Project 2. Assuming the projects are mutually exclusive

- The fact that the B/C ratio favors Project 2 means that if money were extremely limited it could be possible to reject projects saving "only" 1 life per $1000 expenditure while accepting projects saving 1 life per $10 expenditure.
- The fact that the $B - C$ present worth favors Project 1 for any reasonable monetary valuation of human life means that saving 50 lives for $50,000 provides more net benefit to society than saving 10 lives for $100.

7.5 EXERCISES

1. Enterprises **A** and **B** currently emit an air pollutant at the legal maximum of 10 ton/day each, thereby incurring equivalent annual control costs (at 10% interest) of $13,600 + $4600 = $18,200. As the curves below show, control costs vary with emission rates. There are 250 operating days per year. Under consideration is a plan to drop the regulation that limits maximum emission rates and to replace the regulation with an emission fee of $6/ton. Each enterprise will prefer to emit an amount that will minimize the annual total of its emission control cost and its emission fee.

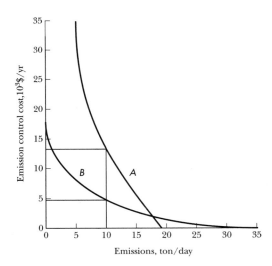

   (a) Under the plan, which of the following alternative amounts will **A** prefer to emit: 10 ton/day or 15 ton/day?
   (b) Under the plan, which alternative amount will **B** prefer to emit: 10 ton/day or 2 ton/day?
   (c) Do the results support the claim that "incentives work better than limit regulations" in the sense of achieving tighter pollution control for less control cost (no control cost)?
   (d) Although **A** and **B** as a group achieve lower total emission control costs, the emission fees paid to the government are expensive. Determine the annual

net loss seen by each enterprise and the annual net gain seen by the government in switching to the emission-fee system. If the emission fees are all returned to the enterprises in the form of governmental services shared equally by all enterprises, how close an approach is made to the ideal of net gain for all entities?

2. The Wood Authority has decided to encourage use of recycled paper in paper mills. Options are (1) to publish a limit regulation requiring each paper mill to use at least 40% recycled paper in its feed stream, or (2) to levy a fee of $5/ton on wood, with no fee for recycled paper. There are two mills, A and B. A uses 41 ton/day of wood feed; options for A are to switch to using a mix of 11 ton/day of recycled paper and 30 ton/day of wood, incurring extra costs of $50/day; or to switch to using a mix of 25 ton/day of recycled paper and 16 ton/day of wood, incurring extra costs of $160/day. These options, and options for B, are shown in the following table:

Mill, alternative	Ton/day of wood in feed mix	Ton/day of paper in feed mix	Extra cost $/day
A current	41	0	0
A option 1	30	11	50
A option 2	16	25	160
B current	60	0	0
B option 1	35	25	110
B option 2	14	46	160

(a) Under the 40% limit regulation, determine how A and B will choose to operate, and report the overall proportion of recycled paper and the total daily extra operating costs incurred.

(b) Under the $5/ton fee for wood, determine how A and B will choose to operate, and report the overall proportion of recycled paper, the total daily extra operating costs incurred, and the total fees paid.

(c) Do the results confirm the claim that "incentives work better than limit regulations" in the sense of achieving a greater proportion of recycled paper usage while reducing the extra operating costs? (The emission fees are not extra operating costs.)

(d) Assume the emission fees were supplemented with a rebate transfer payment paid back to each mill by the Wood Authority in approximate proportion to the mill's production rate. Let this transfer payment be $85/day to mill A and $125/day to mill B. Would everyone—mill A, mill B, the Wood Authority, and the public—thereby be better off under the rebate-supplemented $5/ton fee system than under the 40% limit regulation?

3. It is generally agreed that since the middle of the nineteenth century the world's most powerful economic nations have tended toward increased egalitarianism. Name several constituencies that may be more likely to be included within welfare-economy boundaries now than formerly for public-sector decision-making from a national viewpoint.

4. From Chapter 1 or the beginning of this chapter, review the list of constituencies on whose behalf decisions are made. In a capitalistic society, decisions are usually considered to be made on behalf of one of these constituencies. The net benefit to this constituency is to be maximized, subject to constraints expressing the minimum benefits to other constituencies. Which constituency has this special status in a capitalistic society? Also, which constituency has the special status in a socialistic or communistic society?

5. (a) What is the name given to the principle of balancing all benefits to whomever they may accrue against all costs, to whomever they may accrue?
   (b) Explain the term "transfer payment."
   (c) Some people are excluded from "whomever" in the abovementioned principle. Name several kinds of people who are ignored in decisions made:
      (i) With respect to a toll road within a State.
      (ii) By a city's tourist bureau.
      (iii) By economic planners.
      (iv) By health care officials.
      (v) With respect to automobile safety regulations.

6. A housing development will bring its developers a profit of $6 million (in present-worth terms). There are assumed to be negligible benefits to residents of the development (because they pay for their housing) and to contractors, suppliers, and so forth (because they earn the money paid to them). Assume that the development lowers the quality of life for 400 neighbors who each value this loss at $500.
   (a) If the neighbors organize and successfully block the development from being built, is the result the same as a public-sector decision maker would have calculated?
   (b) If the project is implemented and the developers are forced by the local government to distribute $300,000 to a neighborhood beautification association, about how much money can the association presumably waste or steal without tending to decrease the neighbors' net equity satisfaction?

7. By undertaking activities that cost B $20 and deprive A involuntarily of $30, B can create $70 of wealth.

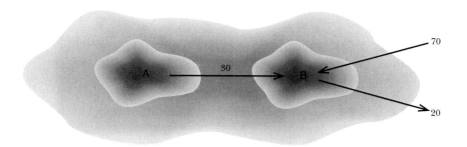

   (a) Determine $B - C$ from the viewpoint of A, B, and of society.
   (b) A regulatory agency R can levy a tax of X dollars on B, out of which it will expend $0.15X$ dollars of effort and will pay the remaining $0.85X$ dollars to A. Determine the smallest tax that will barely redress A.

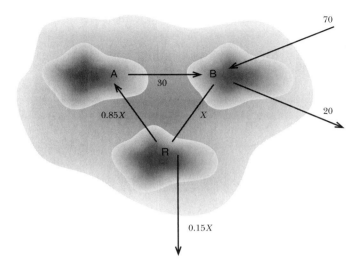

(c) Determine the greatest tax that allows **B** to profit.
(d) Determine the greatest tax that allows society to profit, if **B** can freely choose whether to undertake the wealth-producing activities.
(e) Determine the tax that makes **A** and **B** profit equally from these wealth-producing activities of **B**.
(f) Assume that the tax is $X = \$40$. The efficiency of the regulatory agency is 85%. To what value of η can the efficiency drop before society or some segment of it fails to profit?

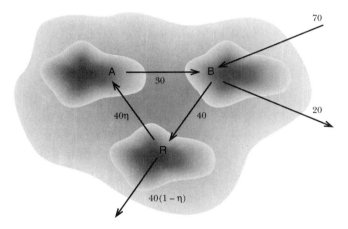

8. The health minister and tax minister of Idealia agree to estimates that Idealians purchase about 6 million stogies per year, and the adverse health effects are valued at 3 million ideals per year. The retail price is currently 2.5 ideals per stogie. If the health ministry receives the proceeds of a new excise tax of x ideals per stogie, and achieves a transfer efficiency of 80% in generating health benefits, what is the minimum tax needed to make the public (everyone except the stogie industry) better off? Assume the stogie industry absorbs all the tax without a price increase, and the consumption of stogies does not decrease. Determine the loss to the stogie industry and the loss to society if the minimum tax is enacted.

9. From Eqs. 7-1 and 7-2, prove that every equitable project is good.

10. A $70 million dam gives *indexed* annual net benefits of $4 million for 50 years. Compare its desirability at 10% interest after inflation with its desirability at 10% interest before inflation, if inflation is at 4%.

11. A $90 million highway is estimated to give net benefits of $10 million annually for 20 years. The estimation of benefits is in *current* dollars; the estimator expects the underlying benefits to decay at a rate that just offsets inflation. Inflation will be at 4% annually. Compare the highway's desirability at 10% interest after inflation with its desirability at 10% interest before inflation.

12. A public-works analyst estimates the worth of a sewage treatment plant as follows, in millions:

$$P = -60 + 9\left(\frac{1 - (1/1.10)^{17}}{0.10}\right) = \$12{,}193{,}979.80$$

   (a) If the analysis obeys United States federal-expenditure practices, the benefits are in what kind of dollars—*indexed* or *current*? Explain.
   (b) Illustrate with this problem the maxim that "ignoring inflation tends to introduce a bias against public investment."

13. In Example E7, there were two projects, **A** and **B**, having a somewhat uncertain valuation of their benefits. The benefits were estimated as 156 and 275 (in thousands of dollars), respectively, while the respective costs were estimated as 135 and 250. The uncertainty in benefit estimation was represented by a parameter M, so that the true benefits were $156M$ and $275M$, respectively, with M unknown but thought to be near 1.

   (a) Determine the range of M for which the B/C ratio favors **A** and the range for which it favors **B**.
   (b) Determine the range of M for which the $B - C$ difference favors **A** and the range for which it favors **B**.
   (c) Based on the above results, which measure (B/C, or $B - C$) is more stable in the face of uncertainties in benefit estimation?

14. A federal hydroelectric dam project in the United States has three alternatives, each with an estimated life of 50 years. Estimated benefits and costs, in thousands of indexed dollars, are as follows (the user/provider B/C split is used):

	Alternative A	Alternative B	Alternative C
Benefits:			
From flood control	500/yr	700/yr	1,000/yr
From irrigation	700/yr	900/yr	1,200/yr
From recreation	200/yr	400/yr	700/yr
Costs:			
First cost	50,000	70,000	100,000
Operation and maintenance costs	400/yr	500/yr	700/yr
Revenue from sale of power	−2,000/yr	−2,400/yr	−3,600/yr

(a) At an interest rate appropriate for the expectation of 4% annual inflation, determine $P = B - C$ and B/C for each alternative.

(b) Based on the results, which alternative is best, and/or which alternative is closest to being attractive?

(c) Repeat the determination of $P = B - C$ and B/C for an interest rate appropriate for the expectation of 5% annual inflation.

(d) Based on the results for 5% inflation, which alternative has greatest worth, and which alternative is most efficient?

(e) Knowing that the estimates are not really accurate, and not knowing whether inflation will be at 4% or 5%, which alternative should be chosen, if the do-nothing choice is out of the question?

15. The environmental impact study for a proposed recreation center in a city park has been published. Using its results along with the architectural and engineering estimates, the city engineer has compiled the estimated benefits and costs for the three live alternatives, using a user/provider B/C split. Amounts are in thousands of present-worth dollars at the city's 8.75% cost of capital.

	Alternative A	Alternative B	Alternative C
Benefits:			
Recreation	200	300	400
Congestion	−40	−70	−100
Pollution	−2	−5	−18
Costs:			
Construction	150	250	325
Fee revenue	−15	−40	−55

(a) Determine $P = B - C$ and B/C for each alternative, and make a selection.

(b) A dissenting consultant reviews the alternatives and concludes that fee revenues should be doubled while everything else remains as estimated. Upon reflection, the city engineer agrees. Revise the $P = B - C$ and B/C results, and make a selection based on worth.

(c) In preparing revised plans for the recreation center, based on the increase in fee revenues, the city engineer comes to a further realization: The benefit estimates for recreation, congestion, and pollution could easily be inaccurate so that the total benefits could really be 15% greater or 15% less than estimated.

16. Consider the recreation-center data given in the table for Exercise 15 above. Suppose the recreation benefits were to increase by a multiplicative factor M while all other data remained as given.

(a) Determine the range of M for which C would have greater worth than that of the other two alternatives.

(b) Determine the range of M for which C would be more efficient than the other two alternatives.

17. Let there be two alternative projects with benefits and costs as follows:

Alternative	Worth of Benefits	Worth of Costs
1	$B^{(1)}$	$C^{(1)}$
2	$B^{(2)}$	$C^{(2)}$
2 − 1	$B^{(2)} - B^{(1)}$	$C^{(2)} - C^{(1)}$

(a) The *incremental B/C ratio rule*, given a current acceptable alternative, say 1, is to accept an increment, say 2 − 1, if its *incremental B/C* ratio exceeds 1:

$$\frac{B^{(2)} - B^{(1)}}{C^{(2)} - C^{(1)}} > 1 \Rightarrow \text{accept } 2 - 1$$

Prove that this rule is the same as worth maximization.

(b) An alternative incremental *B/C* ratio is defined and used by some agencies. The first cost *I* is separated from the remaining costs *K*; let $C = I + K$. Define the ratio $(B - K)/I$. The rule is to accept an increment whose *incremental* $(B - K)/I$ exceeds 1. Prove that this rule is the same as worth maximization.

18. Grant applications have been received for two literacy programs. Program 1 asks for $5,743,221 and promises to teach 35,740 clients to read. Program 2 asks for $17,741,209 and promises to teach 124,000 clients to read.

(a) Which program is more cost effective?

(b) The agency receiving the grant applications has $6 million that could be spent on literacy programs. Which of the following actions is least appropriate? Why?

   (i) Fund Program 1.

   (ii) Fund a scaled-down version of Program 2.

   (iii) Ask for revised applications that stay within budget.

19. A disease dangerous only to newborn infants is carried by children and pregnant women. It kills 2500 infants per year. Two annual public health programs are under consideration. Program 1 is to screen all pregnant women and treat those having the disease; this would reduce infant deaths by 44%. Program 2 is to screen all schoolchildren and treat those having the disease; this would reduce infant deaths by 57%. Screening costs $12 per person, whether it is pregnant women or schoolchildren who are screened. Treatment has a cost of $32 for a pregnant woman and $40 for a schoolchild. There are 3.2 million pregnant women and 5.8 million schoolchildren. It is estimated that 0.12% of the screened pregnant women and 0.08% of the screened schoolchildren will have the disease. Which program would be more cost effective?

20. A member of Congress asks for your help. She wants to vote responsibly in the public health and safety area, rather than follow the wishes of the party leadership (which wants her to vote for every health and safety bill) or the wishes of her primarily conservative constituents (who want her to vote against every one). She gives you a list of several bills, with cost and number of lives to be saved. For the

bills in this batch, total benefits can be assumed to be roughly proportional to number of lives saved. You are to rank the bills so that she can go down the list, voting "yes" to a certain point and "no" below that point. Produce the list and document the basis for it.

Bill	Annual lives saved	Cost ($000)
1 (Auto safety omnibus)	1700	6900
2 (Auto air bags)	650	5890
3 (Hospital care for certain indigents)	150	600
4 (Medicare supplement)	8420	16475
5 (VA hospitals)	740	22800
6 (Center for Disease Control)	3000	10500
7 (Natal research)	2500	4070

21. Two immunization programs are under consideration for fighting a flu epidemic. Program 1 would save 30,000 hospital patient-hours and 16 lives per 100,000 immunizations. It is applied to whole populations and has a direct cost of $14; to administer an immunization under Program 1 also requires a minimal no-diagnosis visit by the patient to a clinic, health-fair station, or doctor's office. Let the cost of such a visit be $20.

    Program 2, which is applied only to a self-selected high-risk group, is expected to save 95,000 hospital patient-hours and 55 lives per 100,000 immunizations; each would cost $20 and some diagnostic effort adding $35 in doctor and patient effort beyond that of a typical Program 1 immunization.

    (a) Without assuming specific money values for human lives or for hospital hours, is there a clear basis for choosing one program over the other?

    (b) By eliminating the $20 cost of a minimal no-diagnosis visit, which is a part of the costs that is the same for both alternatives, use this problem to illustrate the invalidity of eliminating such costs.

22. Veterinarians are debating the relative merits of two ways to control Gallblatz' disease, which attacks pregnant cows, newborn calves, and older calves. One can screen and treat the population of pregnant cows at an average cost of $12 each, or screen and treat all the population of older calves at an average cost of $8 each. There are 350,000 pregnant cows and 658,000 older calves. The main outcome of the disease is 3000 annual deaths of mostly newborn calves. The screen-and-treat program for pregnant cows would reduce this measure to approximately 280, and the program for older calves would reduce it to approximately 122.

    (a) Show which program is more cost effective, without inferring a money value for a calf.

    (b) Given that the money value of a calf is roughly $400, make a decision.

23. An academic department of a university finds that its 1000 students are spending about 4 hours per year apiece walking to and from the nearest laser printing station available to them. This could be reduced to 1.5 hours per student per year if a $70,000 printer were purchased; the printer could be leased, maintained, and

operated for $14,000 per year over current costs (so the $70,000 purchase cost can be considered irrelevant).

(a) What implicit valuation of the worth of student's time corresponds to barely accepting this printer?

(b) For comparison with other projects whose benefits are in terms of student hours saved per year and whose costs are in terms of dollars per year, what is the B/C ratio for this project?

24. There are two air-pollution-abatement programs under consideration. One would reduce the particulate count from its current 50.1 to 37.2 and would cost the emitters $37 million in extra abatement costs (in present-worth terms), while also justifying a budget increase for the Air Pollution Control Board equivalent to $17 million in present-worth terms.

The other abatement program would reduce particulates to 29.1 and would cost emitters $50 million and the Board $21 million.

Harm from pollution is considered approximately proportional to particulate count.

(a) Compare the two abatement programs. Identify your assumptions and method.

(b) What specific data or estimates are missing so as to prevent using a user-provider split in B/C analysis for this problem?

25. A municipal government is considering two alternative library projects; call them C for "centralized improvements" and D for "distributed improvements." C is mainly to upgrade the downtown main library, with some improvements at branches; D is mainly to upgrade the branch libraries and add more branches.

The main benefit of a library is the cultural and literacy services it provides, a measure of which is a *usage* statistic expressed in user hours. The usage statistic is essentially a weighted average of circulation (volume of book lending) and visitorship, averaged under the concept that a borrower reads two hours per week per checked-out book, which counts the same as visiting for two hours.

Present worths of relevant costs have been estimated at $i = 10\%$. The following data are available for the incremental benefits and costs compared to the present system.

Project	Usage, user hours per week	Present worth of construction costs, K$	Present worth of operating costs, K$	Present worth of access costs, K$
C	7000	300	800	790
D	4000	420	960	310

The centralized improvements would add greatly to usage and would be cheaper, but would be more difficult for citizens to reach (the access costs assume $7.50 per user hour spent getting to and from the central or branch library). The operating costs include a proportion (30% for C, 20% for D) paid directly by users in card fees, borrower's fees, and fines.

(a) With the user/provider B/C split rule for classifying benefits and costs, the usage and access amounts are in the (B) numerator because they concern the users or public and the construction and operating costs are in the (C) denominator because they concern the providers or government. The portion of operating costs paid directly by users is irrelevant, since the user/provider rule excludes transfer payments. Assume a usage hour's benefits to be worth $2.50, and assume 50 weeks per year and a $(P/A\ i,n)$ factor of 6.2 to convert $/yr to present worth. Determine the B/C ratios under the user-provider B/C split rule, and choose the better alternative.

(b) With the later/now B/C split rule for classifying benefits and costs, the construction costs are in the (now) denominator, and everything else is in the (later) numerator. Assume the same conversion of usage to present-worth dollars as previously. Determine the B/C ratios under the later/now B/C split rule, and choose the better alternative.

(c) With the nonmonetary B/C split rule for classifying benefits and costs, the usage benefits do not need conversion to money. Determine the B/C ratios under the nonmonetary/monetary B/C split rule, and choose the better alternative.

26. (a) A bridge will collect tolls from vehicles that cross it. In benefit/cost analysis, is this toll revenue a benefit, or is it a cost? Why?

(b) Before the 10% interest rate was mandated for federal projects in the United States, many public works agencies were using interest rates as low as 3% or 4%. Did the mandate make it easier or harder for proponents to justify projects?

(c) A public project will cost taxpayers an equivalent of $40 million and bring benefits worth an equivalent of $100 million. However, because of land-use patterns and ownerships, $75 million of the benefit will go directly to A. P. Jones Jr., and his family and associates. Is the project justified? Why?

(d) A public project in a city will bring $6 million benefits and will cost $4 million, of which the Federal Government will pay $3.6 million. Calculate two B/C ratios for it, one from the viewpoint of a "regional statesman" and one from a national viewpoint.

27. (a) In 1970 the Metropolitan Atlanta Rapid Transit Authority (MARTA) had an opportunity to ask for federal funding of two major portions of its proposed rail transit system. It was felt that federal funding for additional major portions could be asked for later, but that perhaps the probability of obtaining funding might be lower later, or the criteria tougher. From strictly a local point of view, if the **East** portion had a B/C ratio of 2.47, the **Airport** portion had a B/C ratio of 2.94, the current federal system would accept anything with a B/C ratio of 2.3 or more, and the federal system was assumed to be likely to go to a 2.6 cutoff later, which portion should have been asked for first, and why?

(b) With all figures in present-worth equivalents, a road will cost $30 million to install, will save motorists $40 million in fuel and time, and will save the Highway Department $6 million in reduced maintenance. Calculate the B/C ratio using the user/provider split.

(c) A road will cost a city only $3 million, because the federal government will pay 70% of the cost, and will bring benefits of $7 million to city residents and $5 million to travelers passing through. Is it justified? Why?

W. C. Fields plays it close to the vest. Will three deuces beat him?

RISK AND UNCERTAINTY

Since engineering economy concerns the future, the numbers used in engineering economy calculations are estimates. Throughout this book we have been using estimates of parameters such as interest rates and amounts and timings of cash flows to obtain *point estimates* of worths and efficiency measures. When a decision is made on the basis of point estimates, we cannot be sure that it is the decision the future will vindicate, but point estimates do yield decisions that are good in the sense of being more likely right than those that could have resulted by any different methods using no additional information.

This and the next chapter concern where and how to obtain and use more information about the future in order to make better decisions.

There are several approaches to confronting risk and uncertainty. A bull-by-the-horns approach is that of *probabilistic decision making*, to be introduced in Chapter 9, where instead of using estimates of parameters to obtain a point estimate of a result, one uses probability distributions of parameters to obtain a probability distribution of the result. Probabilistic decision making is powerful, but it is difficult and very demanding of additional hard-to-estimate data.

In the present chapter we introduce approaches that are less elaborate—breakeven analysis, sensitivity analysis, expected worth, dispersion of worth, geometric risk, and geometric delay. These approaches to risk and uncertainty are essentially in the nature of modest enhancements to the deterministic methods of the first seven chapters—how to correct for risk and uncertainty.

8.1 BREAKEVEN AND SENSITIVITY ANALYSIS

Around 1960 the GIGO concept—"garbage in, garbage out"—became popular as people began to realize that computers would be unable to fulfill their vast decision-aiding potential unless fed better data. The obvious but unwarranted philosophical implication was that the way to improve decisions was to expend more effort to obtain more accurate point estimates.

Once any wild guesses have been replaced with reasonable estimates, however, there is little to be gained by further pencil-sharpening. Stimulated by the ease with which what-if questions could be posed and answered by Gerald R. Wagner's IFPS financial planning language and the spreadsheet progams that later mushroomed, decision makers came to realize that it's *always* "garbage in": the point is to search for a robust decision that will be the right one under a wide variety of reasonably possible futures. Such a search is called *sensitivity analysis*. It uses information handy to the decision maker but difficult to incorporate into a point estimate: judgment as to what variations from estimated values are likely to occur.

8.1.1 Breakeven Analysis

The simplest sensitivity-analysis technique is that of *breakeven analysis*, which has already been illustrated several times, starting with part e of Example E3 of Chapter 1. A breakeven problem has a *breakeven parameter* that is singled out for study, and it has an *assertion*. For example, suppose we have the worth formula

$$P = -100 + 25.01\beta + 21\beta^2 \left(\frac{1 - \beta^5}{i} \right) + 51\beta^5$$

in which $i = 0.11$ and the parameter "51" in the final term is the estimated salvage value, and let the breakeven problem be to ascertain the smallest salvage value for which the worth is positive. The *breakeven parameter* is the salvage value, and the *breakeven assertion* is $P > 0$.

The general procedure for solving a breakeven problem is as follows:

Breakeven Analysis Procedure:

1. Assign a symbol to represent the breakeven parameter's value.
2. Express the assertion (replace the breakeven parameter's estimated value with the symbol and write equalities or inequalities as required) and solve for the symbol.

For example, we assign S as the symbol for the salvage value, express the $P > 0$ assertion substituting S for 51, and solve for S:

$$P = -100 + 25.01\beta + 21\beta^2 \left(\frac{1 - \beta^5}{i} \right) + S\beta^5 > 0$$

$$S > 24.39178454$$

Thus the answer to the breakeven problem is that 24.39 is approximately the smallest salvage value for which the worth is positive. This answer would be useful if the salvage value estimate of 51 had been considered unreliable and the correctness of a decision depended on the worth's being positive.

E1. The *Stella Lykes,* an oceangoing American merchant marine vessel, fills up her fuel tanks with $37,000 worth of bunker fuel at each major stop. She uses an extra amount of fuel keeping the fuel tanks and lines warm enough so the fuel will flow. This is estimated as $33,000 in a typical operating year. She is going into drydock, and much of the fuel system hardware is due for replacement, so this would be a good time to add insulation. Lykes Brothers uses MARR = 10% on a *d* basis (fuel costs are expected to move with general inflation). A "fancy" insulation job would save perhaps 80% of the present fuel-warming costs. The vessel will last about eight years more and be scrapped. How much could a fancy insulation job profitably cost?

Let X be the cost of a fancy job. The prospective savings, in indexed dollars, are $0.80 \times 33,000 = \$26,400$ per year for eight years. Thus the present worth of a fancy insulation job that would yield these savings is, at $d = 0.10$ and $\beta = 1/(1 + d)$,

$$P = -X + 26,400(P/A \ d,8)$$

The breakeven assertion is $P \geq 0$, which implies

$$-X + 26400(P/A \ d,8) \geq 0$$

$$X \leq 26,400 \times 5.3349262$$

$$X \leq \underline{\$140,842.05}$$

This example illustrates why breakeven analysis is sometimes worthwhile. Perhaps the analyst had no idea of what an insulation job would cost. Given the breakeven result, there is a triage: If $141,000 is recognizable as far too little to pay for a major insulation job in drydock, the proposal can be abandoned without further effort. If, on the other hand, $141,000 is recognizable as more than the cost of a major job, an immediate go-ahead decision can be made. Only if $141,000 is "in the right ballpark" is further analysis needed. This illustrates how breakeven analysis can prevent needless estimation effort by identifying a prospect as hopeless, obviously good, or just a prospect.

Economic life is a particularly difficult parameter to estimate, since the returns from an investment can be terminated by outside factors such as obsolescence or relocation.

E2. An investment of $1000 promises to earn returns of $400 per year. The prospective life is uncertain. How many years would the returns need to continue for the investment to be attractive, if MARR is $d = 10\%$?

$$P = -1000 + 400\left(\frac{1 - \alpha^n}{d}\right) \qquad \text{where} \qquad d = 0.10 \text{ and } \alpha = \frac{1}{1 + d}$$

The breakeven parameter is n, and the assertion is $P > 0$.

$$P > 0 \Rightarrow -1000 + 400\left(\frac{1 - \alpha^n}{d}\right) > 0$$

$$1 - \left(\frac{1}{1 + d}\right)^n > 2.5d$$

$$0.75 > \left(\frac{1}{1.1}\right)^n$$

$$\ln(0.75) > -n \ln(1.1)$$

$$\underline{n > 3.018377 \text{ years}}$$

E3. Maintenance costs in our plant were $3000 last month. We expect inflation at a rate of 4% annually, and we expect the need for maintenance to increase at a rate of 3% annually. A five-year maintenance contract is under negotiation. The prospective maintenance vendor mentioned $3500 (current) per month, paid in advance each month, as an approximate fee. If we use MARR of 20% in i terms, is this a good deal, and how low would the figure need to be for it to be a good deal?

With time in months, the monthly inflation rate is $j = (1.04)^{1/12} - 1 = 0.00327374$. The monthly real escalation rate is $v = (1.03)^{1/12} - 1 = 0.00246627$. The combined monthly interest rate is $i = (1.20)^{1/12} - 1 = 0.015309470$.

If we continue to pay our own maintenance costs for 60 months, with $a_0 = 3000$, $\alpha = (1 + v)(1 + j)/(1 + i) = 0.99058279$, $s = 1/\alpha - 1$, the present worth of the maintenance costs is

$$P_{\text{own}} = \frac{a_0(1 - \alpha^{60})}{s}$$

$$P_{\text{own}} = \underline{136,696.10}$$

Let the monthly fee be x dollars, in current dollars. If we pay the fee for 60 months at the beginning of each month, the present worth of the contracted maintenance costs is

$$P_{\text{cont}} = X\beta^{-1}\left(\frac{1 - \beta^{60}}{i}\right) \qquad \text{where} \qquad \beta = \frac{1}{1 + i}$$

$$P_{\text{cont}} = 39.66736812X$$

The contract is less costly if

$$P_{\text{cont}} < P_{\text{own}} \Rightarrow 39.66736812X < 136,696.1 \Rightarrow \underline{X < \$3446.06}$$

The mentioned fee of $3500 is slightly above the breakeven point, and thus is <u>not a good deal</u>.

8.1.2 Sensitivity Analysis

Sensitivity analysis is the study of the sensitivity of an economic conclusion to changes or errors in parameters. It includes breakeven analysis but is more broad; often several parameters or combinations of parameters are manipulated, and the focus is not only on profitability boundaries but on other aspects of profitability such as how much the worth changes, and in which direction, for a unit change in a parameter. The "sensitivity" of a proposal to a parameter is often measured by the derivative of the present worth with respect to the parameter.

Tentative decisions in an enterprise are often ratified (or rejected) by authority groups in a "what-if" atmosphere. The proponent proposes a model of the situation, perhaps in the form of a present-worth formula, gives estimates of the parameters, and uses the model and parameters to support an assertion of profitability. The others ask what-if questions that challenge the estimated values of parameters. The model is repeatedly exercised, each time with different combinations of parameter values. At some point the decision or conclusion advocated by the proponent may be replaced by a different one that the group sees as wiser considering the array of possible conditions.

The act of repeatedly exercising the model to get different answers for different parameter estimates is a common form of sensitivity analysis, whether it is performed by a group as described above or by an analyst in advance. Sensitivity analysis greatly contributes to the believability and acceptance of a proposal, and no formal request for investment funds would be complete if based only on a point estimate of profitability without investigation of the conditions under which the advocated decision remains valid. This is really a definition of sensitivity analysis:

> Sensitivity analysis is the investigation of conditions under which a decision remains valid.

Figure 8-1 illustrates a method of displaying the results of many sensitivity analyses on a single graph. Consider the following simple investment project: At $i = 15\%$, we have

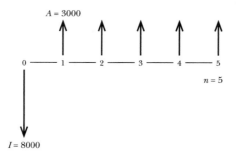

$$P = -8000 + 3000(P/A\ 15\%,5) = \$2056.46529$$

In general, letting all quantities be parameters, we have

$$P = -I + A(P/A\ i,n)$$

Now if we vary each of the four parameters (I, A, i and n) separately over a range of its estimated value plus or minus 40% of its estimated value, holding the other parameters constant at their estimated values while varying each one, the results can all be presented on a single graph giving present worth as a function of the relative varia-

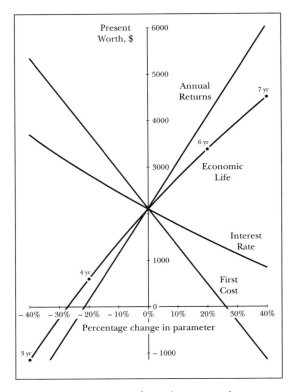

FIGURE 8-1. Sensitivity of worth to several parameters.

tion. Figure 8-1 shows this graph, which can readily be prepared using a spreadsheet program. The following example illustrates the what-if considerations that the combined graph conveniently supports.

E4. For the project described above, use the combined sensitivity analysis graph of Figure 8-1 to obtain approximate answers to the following what-if questions.

(a) The project has an estimated five-year life. How many additional years of life would double the project's worth?

Reading from an ordinate of about 4100 to the economic-life curve, the corresponding abscissa is about 34%, which gives 5 × 1.34 = 6.7 years. The additional years of life to double the worth would be about 6.7 − 5 = 1.7 years → 2 years.

(b) By how much could the annual returns decrease before the project became unattractive?

At zero worth, the annual-returns curve is at about −20%, or a decrease of about 3000 × 0.20 = $600 from the estimated $3000.

(c) If the first cost were 10% more than estimated, would the project still be attractive?

Yes. The first-cost curve does not cross the zero-worth line until the investment is about 26% above the $8000 estimate.

(d) For what range of interest rates would the present worth be at least $1000?

The interest-rate curve crosses the $1000 ordinate at an abcissa of about 32%, corresponding to $i = 0.15 \times 1.32 \cong 20\%$ interest. The range of $P > 1000$ is all interest rates less than about 20%.

(e) Suppose that in a discussion an alternative version of the project is brought up under which the economic life would be six years and the first cost would be $9600, other parameters remaining the same. From the formula for P, this alternative would have a worth of $1753.45. Could the graph be used to obtain a similar result?

From the graph, a six-year life gives $P \cong 3350$, while a $(9600 - 8000)/8000 = 20\%$ increase in first cost gives $P \cong 460$. Given $P \cong 2060$ originally, the additional life adds $3350 - 2060 = 1290$, and the additional first cost subtracts $2060 - 460 = 1600$, for a net subtraction of $1600 - 1290 = 310$, giving $P \cong 2060 - 310 = \$1750$. These computations are the same as using derivatives of P with respect to various parameters.

As Figure 8-1 illustrates, the response of worth to changes in parameters is approximately linear for relatively small changes in any parameter, even n or i. Let there be M parameters $\{p_m: m = 1,...,M\}$ of a cash-flow set. When each of these parameters undergoes a change Δp_m, we assume the present worth changes from P to $P + \Delta P$, where

Linear composite sensitivity of present worth to parameters:

$$\Delta P \cong \sum_{m=1}^{M} (dP/dp_m)\Delta p_m \qquad (8\text{-}1)$$

For example, consider a simple investment project of spending 10 at time zero to receive annual returns of 3 at the ends of each of 5 years, at 12% interest. Here the parameters can be identified as I, A, i, and n, having estimates of $I = 10$, $A = 3$, $i = 0.12$, and $n = 5$. The present worth is

$$P = -10 + 3(P/A\ 12\%,5) = 0.8143286$$

and, in general,

$$P = -I + A\left(\frac{1 - \beta^n}{i}\right) \qquad (8\text{-}2)$$

The linear composite sensitivity equation (Eq. 8-1) for this project is

$$\Delta P \cong (dP/dI)\Delta I + (dP/dA)\Delta A + (dP/di)\Delta i + (dP/dn)\Delta n \qquad (8\text{-}3)$$

To estimate the derivatives, we first note that the worth is linear in the cash-flow amounts, and the derivatives are simple:

$$dP/dI = -1 \quad \text{and} \quad dP/dA = \left(\frac{1 - \beta^n}{i}\right) = 3.6047762$$

The worth is nonlinear in i and n. For such parameters, we can estimate the derivative by computing the effect of a small change δ in the parameter. Let $P(p_m + \delta)$ denote the present worth when δ is added to parameter p_m. Then the difference in worth divided by δ is an *estimate of the derivative of P with respect to a parameter* p_m:

$$dP/dp_m \cong \frac{P(p_m + \delta) - P}{\delta} \tag{8-4}$$

For the project of Eq. 8-2 with $I = 10$, $A = 3$, $i = 0.12$, and $n = 5$, Eq. 8-4 can be used to estimate dP/di and dP/dn. Let $\delta = 0.01$.

$$dP/di \cong \frac{P(i + 0.01) - P}{0.01} = \frac{0.5516938 - 0.8143286}{0.01} \cong -26.26$$

and

$$dP/dn \cong \frac{P(n + 0.01) - P}{0.01} = \frac{0.8303959 - 0.8143286}{0.01} \cong 1.607$$

Thus Eq. 8-1 for this project becomes

$$\Delta P \cong -\Delta I + 3.605\Delta A - 26.26i\ 1.607n$$

The linear composite sensitivity relationship expressed by this equation can be quite inaccurate, as the following example shows.

E5. Given the above sensitivity-analysis equation for the project of Eq. 8-2 with estimates of $I = 10$, $A = 3$, $i = 0.12$, and $n = 5$, what if the investment were to increase by 1 and the economic life were to decrease to 4 years, while the returns increased by 0.3 per year and the interest rate went to 12.5%? Is sensitivity to a combination of parameters well approximated by the composite-sensitivity approach of Eq. 8-1?

$\Delta I = 1$, $\Delta A = 0.3$, $\Delta i = 0.125 - 0.120 = 0.005$, $\Delta n = 4 - 5 = -1$. According to the linear composite-sensitivity equation (Eq. 8-1):

$$\Delta P \cong -1 + 3.605 \times 0.3 - 26.26 \times 0.005 + 1.607(-1) \cong \underline{-1.657}$$

The present worth would change to approximately

$$P + \Delta P = 0.8143286 + (-1.657) \cong \underline{\underline{-0.842}}$$

We can check this answer directly by putting the changed parameter values into Eq. 8-2:

$$P = -(10 - 1) + (3 + 0.3)\left(\frac{1 - \beta^4}{i}\right) \quad \text{where} \quad i = 0.125, \quad \beta = \frac{1}{(1 + i)}$$

$$= \underline{\underline{-1.08139}}$$

The large discrepancy between $P = -1.08139$ and the estimate of -0.842 is due to interplay among the parameters. In particular, based on the original conditions of $i = 0.12$ and $n = 5$, each additional dollar-per-year return is estimated to increase the worth 3.605 dollars; however, at $i = 0.125$ and $n = 4$, the "pain" factor is only 3.00564, so the effect of additional returns is greatly overestimated by Eq. 8-1. The linear composite-sensitivity approach does not approximate the sensitivity well in this case.

The linear composite approach to sensitivity analysis is not generally recommended, because it is easier and more accurate to compute worth and efficiency measures separately for each set of parameters.

How should sets of parameters be chosen for investigation? First, note that best-case or worst-case scenarios are not very useful. They simply show that if everything goes very well a project will be wonderful, and if everything goes very poorly the project will be disastrous. In the project of Figure 8-1, for example, if every parameter changes 40% in the unfavorable direction the parameters are $I = \$11,200$, $A = \$1800/\text{yr}$, and $n = 3$ yr (we will leave i at 15%, since i measures the environment, not the project), giving a present worth of $-\$7090.19$; conversely, if every parameter changes 40% in the favorable direction the present worth is $\$12,673.76$. These extremes reveal little about likely prospects, and the worth is much more likely to be near its point estimate of about $\$2060$ than to be near either extreme.

The parameters investigated in sensitivity analysis should be those whose changes can be estimated most directly. This usually means that aggregate cash flows should be disaggregated. For example, suppose the cash flows of the project of Eq. 8-2 had been aggregated, so that the estimated investment of 10 can be disaggregated into a machine cost M and a design and installation cost Q, and the estimated annual returns of 3 can be disaggregated into revenues R and costs C:

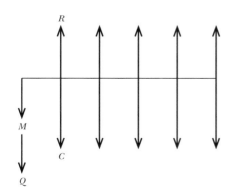

Parameter	Estimated Value
$(-)M$	$(-)6$
$(-)Q$	$(-)4$
R	5
$(-)C$	$(-)2$
n	5
i	0.12

$$P = -M - Q + R(P/A\ i,n) - C(P/A\ i,n)$$

E6. Show that if the parameters M and Q in the above disaggregated model vary 40% above or below their estimated values, the effect on worth is much less than if the aggregated parameter I varies in the same proportion.

If the machine cost M varies ±40%, then $M = 6 ± 0.40 × 6 = 6 ± 2.4$, or 3.6 to 8.4. If the design and installation cost varies ±40%, then $Q = 4 ± 0.40 × 4 = 4 ± 1.6$, or 2.4 to 5.6. Recall that $P \cong 0.8143$ with all parameters at their estimated values. In response to $M = 6 ± 2.4$, P varies $0.8143 ± 2.4$, and in response to $Q = 4 ± 1.6$, P varies $0.8143 ± 1.6$. If there is no reason to believe that *both* M and Q will simultaneously be at their upper limits in a reasonable scenario, then $P = 0.8143 - 2.4 = \underline{-1.5857}$ is the worst reasonable case. But a ±40% variation around the total investment of 10 would give $P = 0.8143 - 0.40 × 10 = -3.1857$ as the worst case considered.

The example illustrates a logical weakness in basing sensitivity analysis on aggregated parameters. However, as the next examples show, knowledge about likely variations is sometimes available only in aggregated form. To get maximal benefit from sensitivity analysis, the "what-iffing" should be done in terms of the most familiar quantities, so that people can apply their judgment and experience as effectively as possible. (In the following examples we will discuss money amounts in dollars rather than in thousands.)

E7. Ann Alice (known as "Sis") has participated in several projects of the same type and knows their total investment costs can easily be 5% more than estimated. Cy Burnett Hicks (known as "Hix") has participated in many machine purchases and knows machines can easily cost 10% more than estimated. If Sis and Hix attend a meeting considering the merits of the above project proposal, which is likely to bring up the more severe what-if question about investment cost?

Sis is likely to ask, "What if the investment is $500 more than estimated?" Hix is likely to ask, "What if the investment is $600 more than estimated?" Hix's question is the more severe. Note that it does not make sense to sum their suggested variations.

Although we saw in Example E5 that Eq. 8-1 is misleading when used with nonlinear parameters such as i or n, it is accurate and convenient to use derivatives with linear parameters such as cash-flow amounts.

E8. Sis and Hix bring further questions to the same meeting. Answer each of them in terms of effect on the estimated present worth of $814.33.

Sis: What if widgets sell for less than estimated, so that revenues decrease from the estimated $5000/yr to only $4000/yr?

Recall that $P = -M - Q + R(P/A\ i,n) - C(P/A\ i,n)$, so that $dP/dR = (P/A\ i,n)$. At $i = 0.12$, $n = 5$, we have $dP/dR = (P/A\ 12\%,5) = 3.6047762$. From Eq. 8-1, with $\Delta R = 4000 - 5000$, we have

$$\Delta P = (dP/dR)\Delta R = 3.6047762(-1000) = -\$3604.78$$

The present worth would go to $P + \Delta P = 814.33 - 3604.78 = \underline{-\$2790.45}$.

Hix: What if the design and installation cost increases by \$1000 over the estimate?

$dP/dQ = -1$. $\Delta P = (dP/dQ)\Delta Q = (-1)(1000) = -\$1000$ (obviously).
The present worth would go to $P + \Delta P = 814.33 - 1000 = \underline{-\$185.67}$.

Sis: What if we have to pay a \$2000 renewal fee at the end of the third year?

Recall that $\beta = 1/1.12$. Obviously the fee subtracts $2000\beta^3$ from P, so the present worth goes to $P + \Delta P = 814.33 - 2000\beta^3 = 814.33 - 1423.56 = \underline{-\$609.23}$. Note that the derivative of P with respect to a cash flow at time t is β^t.

Hix: What if half of the design and installation cost Q can be paid six months late?

Because P is not linear in n and dP/dn has no constant value, there is no reason to use derivatives here. We gain \$2000 (half of Q) at time zero and pay it at time 0.5:

$$\Delta P = 2000 - 2000\beta^{0.5} = 110.18$$

The present worth goes to $P + \Delta P = 814.33 + 110.18 = \underline{\$924.51}$.

Table 8-1 gives a summary of the most useful derivatives for parameters to which P responds linearly. $\{A\}$ or $\{A_t\}$ is in current dollars; $\{W\}$ or $\{W_t\}$ is in indexed dollars; $\beta = 1/(1 + i)$; $\alpha = 1/(1 + d)$; s is the substitute interest rate defined in Chapter 3.

E9. A project having an estimated present worth of \$9420.51 at $i = 10\%$ includes a geometrically increasing series of maintenance savings having current-dollar amounts of $\{\$321(1.02)^t: t = 1,...,9\}$. What if these savings are 15% less than estimated?

TABLE 8-1. Derivatives of Worth with Respect to Cash Flows

	Payment	$\Delta P/\Delta payment$	New P
Lump sum:	A_t at t	β^t	$P + (\Delta A_t)\beta^t$
Equal-payment series:	$\{A\}$ at $t = 1,...,n$	$(P/A\ i,n)$	$P + (\Delta A)(P/A\ i,n)$
	$\{W\}$ at $t = 1,...,n$	$(P/A\ d,n)$	$P + (\Delta W)(P/A\ d,n)$
Geometric gradient series:	$\{A_t\} = a_0(1 + g)^t,\ t = 1,...,n$	$(P/A\ s,n)$	$P + (\Delta a_0)(P/A\ s,n)$
	$\{W_t\} = a_0(1 + v)^t,\ t = 1,...,n$	$(P/A\ s,n)$	$P + (\Delta a_0)(P/A\ s,n)$
Delayed series:	$\{A\}$ at $t = t_1,...,t_1 + n$	$\beta^{t_1-1}(P/A\ i,n)$	$P + (\Delta A)\beta^{t_1-1}(P/A\ i,n)$
	$\{W\}$ at $t = t_1,...,t_1 + n$	$\alpha^{t_1-1}(P/A\ d,n)$	$P + (\Delta W)\beta^{t_1-1}(P/A\ d,n)$

Given $P = 9420.51$, $i = 0.10$, $a_0 = 321$, $g = 0.02$, $n = 9$, we compute (see Table 3-1, Chapter 3):

$$s = \frac{1 + i}{1 + g} - 1 = \frac{1.10}{1.02} - 1 = 0.078431373$$

The parameter change is $\Delta a_0 = (-015)321 = -48.15$.

The new present worth is

$$P + (\Delta a_0)(P/A\ s,n) = 9420.51 + (-48.15)(6.287842108)$$
$$= 9420.51 - 302.76 = \underline{9117.75}$$

The most important use of sensitivity analysis is to discover if an uncertainty really matters. If an uncertainty is found to be able to make a decision-reversing difference, sensitivity analysis by itself cannot do much more than identify the difficulty and give a rough idea of its magnitude. Sensitivity analysis can identify a need either to resolve uncertainties or to analyze them probablistically.

E10. An after-tax analysis of a project gives the following after-tax present worth, where $i = 0.12$ and T is the income-tax rate:

$$P_{at} = -10 + 7.9T + (1 - T)3(P/A\ 12\%,5) \quad \text{(amounts in thousands)}$$

Explanation of the formula: 10 is invested and is capitalized. The depreciation scheme reduces taxes in future years by amounts whose total present worth is $7.9T$ (the depreciation scheme's efficiency at $i = 12\%$ is 79%). The net returns of 3 per year for 5 years are taxed at rate T.

Determine the effect on P_{at} of a possible increase in the tax rate from $T = 34\%$ to $t = 36\%$.

The tax rate T appears in two terms that are linear in T, so dP_{at}/dT is constant and is easy to calculate:

$$\frac{dP_{at}}{dT} = 7.9 - 3(P/A\ 12\%,5) = -2.914329$$

Since $\Delta T = 0.36 - 0.34 = 0.02$, the present worth will decrease by

$$\Delta P_{at} = (dP_{at}/dT)\Delta T = \underline{-0.05828658} \text{ (a decrease of \$58.29)}.$$

8.2 EXPECTED WORTH

To go beyond breakeven and sensitivity analysis in judging how likely it is that a given decision is the right decision, we must introduce some notions from probability and statistics. In this chapter we will discuss only techniques that can be used and understood without a prior background in probability and statistics. First we will see that the point estimation methods we have been using all along are very close to what is called *expected-value* methods, and that by careful estimation (using expected values rather than most-likely values) we can ensure that the results of standard deterministic engineering economy procedures are well centered within their risk ranges.

An *event* is something described clearly enough that its occurrence or nonoccurrence can eventually be established. "The payment at time 2 does not exceed $50" is an event, and it is true, or it is false, or its truth or falsity (occurrence or nonoccurrence) can be unknown; if unknown, we can assign a *probability* to the event. The probability is a number between 0 and 1 that expresses belief that the event, when the outcome is known, is true. For example if we are fairly strongly of the opinion that the payment at time 2 will not exceed $50, we may assign a probability of, say, 0.85 to its not doing so; if we know it will not, or did not occur, its probability is zero; if we know it will or did occur, its probability is one.

An event of a particularly useful kind is one that describes the value of a *random variable*, which is any outcome that can vary and is measurable by a real-number value. We can assign probabilities to the various possible mutually exclusive outcomes of a random variable. Such probabilities sum to 1, because the random variable is certain to take on some particular value. Engineering economy parameters such as P, A, i, n, and so on, can be random variables.

A parameter X can have a value x that is a particular one of its possible values x_1, x_2, and so on, if X is discrete or is within its range if X is continuous. If we have a list of its possible values and a probability of each one, the list of probabilities is called the *probability distribution* of the parameter. Let the probabilities of the possible values x_1, x_2, and so on, be denoted by p_1, p_2, and so on. Then the *expected value* of X, denoted $E(X)$, is defined as

---

Definition of expected value:

· ·

$$E(X) = p_1 x_1 + p_2 x_2 + \cdots \tag{8-5}$$

The probabilities p_1, p_2, and so on, sum to 1. The expected value, then, is computed simply by taking each possible value, multiplying by its probability, and summing up the results. $E(X)$ has some interesting and important properties.

Probably the most significant property of $E(X)$ for decision making is that it constitutes a *central measure* or stand-in value for the variable X.

E11. There is a 0.2 probability that we will receive $1000 and a 0.8 probability that we will receive $5000 instead. Show that the expected value, if received with certainty in a large number of trials, would have approximately the same total as the expected total. First, compute the expected value of the receipt.

Let X be the value of the receipt; its possible values are $X_1 = 1000$ and $X_2 = 5000$.

$$E(X) = (0.2)(1000) + (0.8)(5000) = \underline{\$4200}$$

Now consider 100 cases of receiving either $1000 or $5000. From the probability distribution it would be typical for $1000 to be received in 20 of the cases and

$5000 to be received in 80 of the cases. Show that the typical total received in 100 cases is the same as if the expected value had been received every time.

$$20(1000) + 80(5000) = \underline{\$420,000} \quad \text{typical total}$$
$$100(4200) = \underline{\$420,000} \quad \text{total if expected value}$$
$$\text{is received every time}$$

It should be clear why expected value is sometimes called "certainty equivalent" or "average." If we say, for example, that the expected cost of a meal at a restaurant is $14.80, what we mean is that, even though the meal may sometimes cost much more or much less, the total cost of a large number of meals is expected to be the same as if every meal had a certain cost of $14.80 rather than having a variable cost. The concept of expected value as a certainty equivalent extends to all linear calculations, not just to straight summing.

E12.

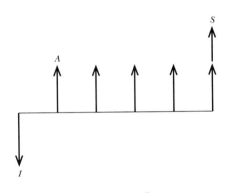

$$P = -I + A\left(\frac{1 - \beta^5}{i}\right) + S\beta^5$$

where $i = 0.20$, $\beta = 1/(1 + i)$.

PROBABILITY DISTRIBUTIONS:

Parameter	Possible Values	Probabilities
A	1000	0.3
	1100	0.3
	1600	0.4
I	2900	0.1
	3700	0.9
S	0	0.8
	800	0.2

A project has the data given above. Because the expected value of a linear combination of variables is the same as the linear combination of their expected values, the expected value of P is easy to compute. Do this.

$$E(A) = 0.3(1000) + 0.3(1100) + 0.4(1600) = 1270$$

$$E(I) = 0.1(2900) + 0.9(3700) = 3620$$

$$E(S) = 0.8(0) + 0.2(800 = 160$$

$$E(P) = -E(I) + E(A)(1 - \beta^5)/i + E(S)\beta^5$$

$$= -3620 + 1270(2.990612) + 160(0.4018775)$$

$$= \$242.38$$

A useful fact about probabilities is that if two events are *independent*, the probability that they both occur is the product of the probabilities that each occurs. This is used in the following example.

E13. **The accompanying table shows all the possible combinations of parameter values, their probabilities of occurring (assuming independence among parameters), and the resulting present worths.**

(a) **Identify the greatest and least present worths possible, and determine the present-worth *range* (their difference).**

Greatest P: 2206.48 (greatest A, least I, greatest S)
Least P: $-(-709.30)$ (least A, greatest I, least S)
Range: 2915.87

A	I	S	Probability	P
1000	2900	0	$(0.3)(0.1)(0.8) = 0.024$	90.61
1000	2900	800	$(0.3)(0.1)(0.2) = 0.006$	412.11
1000	3700	0	$(0.3)(0.9)(0.8) = 0.216$	−709.39
1000	3700	800	$(0.3)(0.9)(0.2) = 0.054$	−387.89
1100	2900	0	$(0.3)(0.1)(0.8) = 0.024$	389.67
1100	2900	800	$(0.3)(0.1)(0.2) = 0.006$	711.18
1100	3700	0	$(0.3)(0.9)(0.8) = 0.216$	−410.33
1100	3700	800	$(0.3)(0.9)(0.2) = 0.054$	−88.82
1600	2900	0	$(0.4)(0.1)(0.8) = 0.032$	1884.98
1600	2900	800	$(0.4)(0.1)(0.2) = 0.008$	2206.48
1600	3700	0	$(0.4)(0.9)(0.8) = 0.288$	1084.98
1600	3700	800	$(0.4)(0.9)(0.2) = 0.072$	1406.48
			1.000	

$$E(P) = 242.38$$
$$\text{Least } P = -709.39$$
$$\text{Greatest } P = 2206.48$$

(b) **The *midrange* is a statistic sometimes used as a central measure. It is the halfway point between minimum and maximum. Does this measure give a good approximation to the expected value for this problem?**

$$\frac{2206.48 + (-709.39)}{2} = \$748.54$$

No, this is not an approximation of $242.38.

(c) The *median* is another statistic sometimes used as a central measure. It is the value such that the probabilities are equal for the outcome to be above or below the value. If we sort the *P* outcomes from small to large, we see that *P* of −387.89 or less would occur in 48.6% of the trials and *P* of −88.82 or less would occur in 54.0% of the trials, so the median is a negative *P* somewhere between −88.82 and −387.89. For this problem, does the median statistic give a good approximation to the expected *P*?

No, this is not near $242.38.

(d) The *mode* or most likely value is a tempting but often invalid measure to use as a stand-in for a random variable. The mode is the typical value, and it seems reasonable to use it as the value in economic computations. This example project provides a good illustration of how the mode can be misused. First we note that there seems to be an identifiable mode. Determine the present worth that has the greatest probability of occurring, and also determine the present worth that results from using the mode of each parameter.

The *P* with the greatest probability of occurring, that is, the modal or most likely *P*, is $1084.98, which has a probability 0.288 of occurring.

The *P* that results from using the most likely $A = 1600$, the most likely $I = 3700$ and the most likely $S = 0$ is

$$-3700 + 1600\left(\frac{1 - \beta^5}{i}\right) + 0\beta^5 = \$1084.98$$

Clearly $1084.98 is a "typical" *P* for this problem.

Is the mode close to the expected value?

No, $1084.98 is not close to $242.38.

Actually for this problem the mode is not even a meaningful statistic. A histogram would show two main concentrations of probability: negative present worths when *I* is 3700 and *A* is either 1000 or 1100, with either *S*, occur 54% of the time and thus are more typical than the positive present worths that occur otherwise.

The various parts of Example E3 showed that other statistics do not approximate the expected present worth. We will now assert the basic principle of engineering economy risk analysis:

It is best in the long run to be an expected-value decision maker.

To illustrate how expected-value decision making outperforms other strategies, we introduce two simple cash-flow sets:

E14.

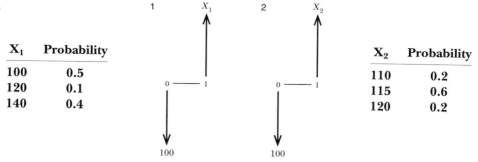

X_1	Probability
100	0.5
120	0.1
140	0.4

X_2	Probability
110	0.2
115	0.6
120	0.2

Given the data on cash-flow sets 1 and 2 shown, consider them to be mutually exclusive alternatives, and consider them to be typical of a series of alternatives, so that the decision maker will be faced many times with choosing between a project like 1 and an alternative project like 2. MARR is 15%.

(a) **Determine the typical (modal) return X_1 for 1 and that for 2; on this basis, compute a typical present worth for 1 and for 2 and determine which alternative would be chosen on a modal or most-likely basis.**

$X_1 = 100$ has the highest probability, giving a typical present worth for 1 or $-100 + 100(1/1.15) = \underline{\underline{-13.04}}$.

$X_2 = 115$ has the highest probability, giving a typical present worth for 2 of $-11 + 115(1/1.15) = \underline{\underline{0}}$.

On a modal decision-making basis either 2 or "do nothing" would be chosen.

(b) **Determine the expected X_1 and X_2 and determine $E(P_1)$ and $E(P_2)$, the expected values of the present worths of 1 and 2.**

$$E(X_1) = 0.5(100) + 0.1(120) + 0.4(140) = 118$$
$$E(X_2) = 0.2(110) + 0.6(115) + 0.2(120) = 115$$
$$E(P_1) = -100 + 118(1/1.15) = 2.61$$
$$E(P_2) = -11 + 115(1/1.15) = 0$$

(c) **Which alternative would be chosen on an expected-value basis?**

1 because $E(P_1) > E(P_2)$ and $E(P_1) > 0$.

(d) **Suppose three project opportunities arose, each with two mutually exclusive alternatives such as 1 and 2. Let Mo, a modal decision maker, choose the 2 version of each of the three, and let Ex, an expected-value decision maker, choose the 1 version of each of the three. Now three is hardly a large number of samples, but it is large enough for things to start to average out. For** alternative 1 there are 10 possible combinations of outcomes, from making 100 all three times to making 140 all three times. The most common sum is 340; there are three ways to make 340 from 100, 100, and 140, each way having a probability of $(0.5)^2(0.4)$, and there are three ways to make it from 100, 120, and 120, each way having a probability of $(0.5)(0.1)^2$; thus the probability of making 340 in three trials of 1 is $3(0.5)^2(0.4) + 3(0.5)(0.1)^2 = 0.315$. By contrast, what is the probability of making only 300 in three trials of 1?

$$(0.5)^3 \times 1 = 0.125$$

(only occurs once)

Thus Mo's modal basis for choosing the other alternative—the notion that, since 100 was the most typical profit for 1, 300 would be its most typical total profit—was wrong. Meanwhile, look at Mo's choice, alternative 2:

Sum of returns in three trials of 2	Probability
330	0.008
335	0.072
340	0.240
345	0.360
350	0.240
355	0.072
360	0.008
	1.000

While Ex (who chose 1) is basking in the expectation of making 354, Mo is probably going to make much less. How probable is it that three trials of 2 yield 350 or less?

$$1 - 0.072 - 0.008 = \underline{92\%} \text{ probable}$$

If there were 10 independent trials in the above example instead of 3, both Mo and Ex would be virtually certain to earn returns very close to 10 times their expectations: a sum of about 1150 for Mo and 1180 for Ex. The corresponding total present worths would be zero and 26.1.

Thus we see why expected-value decision making is wise: The advantage of expected-value choices grows as the number of trials increases.

A closely related concept is that it is inconsistent to single out any subset of decisions, hoping to "beat the odds just this once." Whenever there appears to be a wise exception to the expected-value rule, the exception is an illusion. Examples:

E15. An NFL quarterback, in the last few seconds of a game in which his team is behind by less than a touchdown but more than a field goal, rejects a play that could be expected to gain four or five yards, and instead calls a play whose expected gain is negative. How could this be wise?

Although yards gained is a good surrogate goal during most of the game, the real objective is to win the game. The expected present worth is pV where p is the probability of winning and *V* is the value of winning. To maximize this, one must maximize *p*. In the final seconds of the game, this would be done by selecting the play that has the greatest probability of yielding a touchdown, without regard to yardage.

E16. A company president rejects an alternative that has, with a very small probability, the potential to bankrupt the company. Yet the analyst's computations show its having a greater expected present worth than the alternative chosen. How could the president's decision be wise?

The analyst's computations must have neglected to include a large negative cash flow to represent the disruption and losses attendant to bankruptcy; including them would reduce the alternative's expected present worth. Another possibility is that the president may be maximizing his or her career rather than the company's fortunes; the benefit to a career of a $10 million profit may be nearly as large as that of a $20 million profit, leading an executive to be conservative. An executive would probably be a hero for bringing in a $10 million project. Why risk the company for being a little bit bigger hero at $20 million? From the executive's viewpoint, expected-value analysis says reject.

The following examples will illustrate the determination of expected values and their use in computing expected present worths.

E17. The PERT-Beta distribution, originally introduced to represent the variability of activity duration in project scheduling, is a three-parameter distribution especially convenient for encoding the results of an expert's experience or opinion. The three parameters are *a*, the smallest reasonably anticipated possible value, *m*, the most likely value, and *b*, the greatest reasonably anticipated possible value.

A real estate holding will be sold after 10 years as part of a project, and an expert has opined, "It would fetch at least $240,000; most probably it will sell for about $300,000, but it could go for as high as $600,000." The expert's figures are in today's dollars and do not include inflation. The enterprise uses *d* = 12% as its MARR.

The mean (expected value) of a PERT-Beta distribution is

$$\frac{a + 4m + b}{6}$$

Determine the expected contribution of the real estate sale to the present worth of the project.

$a = 240$, $m = 300$, $b = 600$ in K$.

$$\frac{a + 4m + b}{6} = 340\text{K\$}$$

Note the difference between expected value and mode; the expected value expresses the effects of the possibility of a very high price.

The present-worth contribution is $P = 340\delta^{10}$, $\delta = 1/1 + d$, $d = 12\%$. $P = \underline{109.47K\$}$. (Using the mode would have given an answer nearly 12% smaller.)

E18. The required investment for a project is described as "anywhere between $1 million and $1.6 million." Determine the expected investment.

Language that simply gives an upper and lower limit for a random variable is usually interpreted as implying the uniform probability distribution, whose mean (expected value) is halfway between the limits. Thus,

$$\frac{1 + 1.6}{2} = \underline{\underline{\$1.3 \text{ million}}}$$

is the expected investment. Any *symmetric* probability distribution would have its mean at the midpoint of the range, giving the same answer.

E19. At MARR = 20%, determine the expected present worth of an annual $3000 savings that will last "anywhere between 6 and 10 years." Use the end-of-year timing convention, and assume that it is equally likely for the savings to last 6, 7, 8, 9, or 10 years; compare the answer to the approximation of its lasting for the expected time of 8 years.

If the savings last n years, they have present worth

$$P_n = 3000\left(\frac{1 - \beta^n}{i}\right) \qquad \text{where} \qquad i = 0.20, \quad \beta = 1/1.20$$

The variable N takes on values $n = 6, 7,...,10$ with probability $\frac{1}{5}$ for each of the five possible values. Thus

$$E(P) = (\tfrac{1}{5})P_6 + (\tfrac{1}{5})P_7 + \cdots + (\tfrac{1}{5})P_{10}$$

This can be evaluated with or without prior algebraic simplification. Simplifying,

$$E(P) = \frac{3000}{5i}[(1 - \beta^6) + (1 - \beta^7) + \cdots + (1 - \beta^{10})]$$

$$= \frac{3000}{5i}[5 - \beta^5(\beta + \beta^2 + \cdots + \beta^5)]$$

$$= 3000\left[\frac{1}{i} - \frac{\beta^5}{5i}\left(\frac{1 - \beta^5}{i}\right)\right]$$

$$= \underline{\underline{\$11,394.42}}$$

The "simplified" formula, showing linear-gradient terms (note i^2 in the denominator), hints at a relationship whose simplest form is illustrated in the next example.

The approximation by considering the cash flow to last the average number of years is

$$E(P)_{\approx} = 3000\left(\frac{1 - \beta^8}{i}\right) = \underline{\$11,511.48}, \quad \text{fairly close}$$

E20. A $500 cash flow will be received at one of the times 1, 2, . . ., 5, each time having equal probability of occurring. Determine the expected value of its present worth at $i = 20\%$.

If the cash flow occurs at time n, it has the present worth

$$P_n = 500\beta^n$$

For n being 1, 2, . . ., or 5, each with probability $\frac{1}{5}$, the expected present worth is

$$E(P_n) = \tfrac{1}{5}P_1 + \tfrac{1}{5}P_2 + \cdots + \tfrac{1}{5}P_5$$

$$= \frac{500}{5}(\beta + \beta^2 + \beta^3 + \beta^4 + \beta^5)$$

$$= 100\left(\frac{1 - \beta^5}{i}\right) = \underline{\$299.06}$$

Note that the formula for $E(P_n)$ is the same as the formula for five payments of $100 at times 1, 2, . . . , 5. *Distribution of the probability of a payment over time has the same numerical effect as the same distribution of the payment itself.* Thus a five-year uniform spread of $500 has a present worth if physically spread into five equal payments, and it has a numerically equal *expected* present worth if the *probability* of its timing is the thing that is spread.

Note: An approximation to the expected present worth of the $500 payment would be its present worth at its expected time, which is three years (halfway between one and five years):

$$E(P)_{\text{approx}} = 500\beta^3 = \underline{\$289.35}$$

which is about 3% low.

This group of examples has illustrated that using expected values of parameters in computing present worths tends to give close approximations to the expected present worths. The results are exact when the variable is a cash flow amount or any parameter in which the present worth is linear; when the parameter is something like a time or an interest rate, in which the present worth is not linear, some error is introduced.

When expected values of parameters are used, ordinary deterministic discounted cash-flow computations tend to approximate expected-value results.

All the present-worth calculations done in earlier lessons can be viewed in this light: not only are the results valid when the data are not variable, but they are approximately valid when the data are variable. Results can be misleading or invalid when any other central measures are used for variables except their expected values and when the worth measure is a highly nonlinear function of the parameter.

8.3 DISPERSION OF WORTH

8.3.1 Variance and Standard Deviation

The amount by which the possible outcomes of a random variable can deviate from its expected value is expressed by the variable's *standard deviation*. Given a variable X and its expected value $E(X)$, there is an expected square error called the *variance* and denoted σ_X^2, which is the expected value of the square of the difference between an outcome x and the central measure $E(X)$; the square root of this is the standard deviation σ_X.

The standard deviation σ_X has the same units (years, dollars, etc.) as the variable has, and for most probability distributions it is very rare for an outcome to be more than three standard deviations (three "sigmas") above or below the mean. That is, it is almost sure that an outcome x falls in the range

$$E(X) - 3\sigma_X < x < E(X) + 3\sigma_X$$

An expected-value decision maker cannot ignore variance, because it is never practical to include the effects of very large but rare deviations, especially in the negative direction, into expected-value calculations.

E21. A large widget manufacturing project has a possibility of an investment cost so great or a widget price so low that massive failure of the project could have major consequences. Describe some possible major consequences and discuss why they would not just be included in the expected present worth formulas for various alternative versions of the project.

Massive failure could cause

· Loss of ability to meet contracted deliveries.
· Loss of the enterprise's capacity to borrow money.
· Bad will among employees or customers or suppliers, or any constituency whose future actions could harm the company.

All these consequences would not be included in the expected present worth formulas, because

(a) They are awkward to include, being conditional; the structure of one part of a formula should not depend on the numerical outcome of other parts. Thus, for example, if a $20,000 loss would trigger an extra $15,000 cost, the formula would not only include the terms to determine the loss, but also a term where $15,000 could be multiplied by the probability that the loss was greater than $20,000; this would require either repeating logic in the formula or converting it to an algorithm with defined steps and intermediate results.

(b) The necessity to bother with the estimation of disaster-relevant data and logic can be avoided if disaster is found to be negligibly probable.

E22. Without representing the consequences of disaster, an analyst has prepared estimates for alternative versions 1 and 2 of a project:

Version	E(P)	σ_P
0	0	0
1	$42,000	$10,000
2	$47,000	$13,000

(a) Determine the 3-sigma worst present worth for each version. By this measure, which alternative is more risky?

$$1: \quad 42,000 - 3(10,000) = \$12,000$$
$$2: \quad 47,000 - 3(13,000) = \$\ 8,000$$

Alternative 2 is more risky in that it has the smaller reasonably anticipated present worth. However, on this basis the do-nothing alternative is riskier still.

(b) If $P < \$35,000$, as computed by the formulas, it is believed the lenders will insist on a refinancing that will cost $16,000 in present-worth terms. The probability of this event is estimated as 0.24 for 1 and 0.18 for 2. Recompute the expected present worths accordingly.

1: With probability 0.24, the present worth is reduced by $16,000; thus it is reduced by an expected $(0.24)(16,000) = \$3840$ to

$$E(P_1) = 42,000 - 3840 = \underline{\$38,160}$$

2: Similarly, with probability 0.18, the present worth of 2 is reduced by $16,000:

$$E(P_2) = 47,000 = (0.18)(16,000) = \underline{\$44,120}$$

8.3.2 Statistical Independence

When there is statistical *independence* among projects or among parts of a single project, the variances of the combinations can be computed simply. Independence means that the conditions that make one variable great or small have no influences on the conditions that make another variable great or small.

The concept of *correlation* is closely related to independence. Two variables are correlated positively if large values of one tend to occur along with large values of another. An example of positive correlation is the relationship among durations of activities in a project; such things as rain, cold weather, or strikes will tend to lengthen the durations of all members of a class of activities, and so their durations will be positively correlated. An example of negative correlations is the relationship of sales volumes of competing products; if you sell two products that compete with each other, their sales may be negatively correlated, with the likelihood of large sales for one corresponding to the likelihood of small sales for the other. Independent variables have no expected correlation.

When variables X and Y are *independent*, we can easily compute the variance of $X + Y$ or of $X - Y$:

Variance of the sum or difference of two independent variables:

$$\sigma^2_{X+Y} = \sigma^2_{X-Y} = \sigma^2_{Y-X} = \sigma^2_X + \sigma^2_Y \qquad \text{(8-6)}$$

E23. **Consider two independent projects A and B having data as follows:**

Independent Project	$E(P)$	σ_P
A	106.3	10.0
B	100.0	2.5

(a) **Since the present worths are random variables, the present worth of a portfolio consisting of both the independent projects is also a random variable. Determine its expected value and its standard deviation.**

$$E(P_{A+B}) = E(P_A) + E(P_B) = 106.3 + 100 = \underline{206.3}$$
$$\sigma_{A+B} = \sqrt{\sigma^2_A + \sigma^2_B} = \sqrt{(10)^2 + (2.5)^2} = \underline{10.30776}$$

(b) **$P_A - P_B$ is a random variable that is the amount by which A would outperform B. Determine the mean and standard deviation of this difference.**

$$E(P_{A-B}) = E(P_A) - E(P_B) = 106.3 - 100 = \underline{6.3}$$
$$\sigma_{A-B} = \sqrt{\sigma^2_A + \sigma^2_B} = \sqrt{(10)^2 + (2.5)^2} = \underline{10.30776}$$

(c) **Using the 3-sigma rule, it is "rare" for an outcome to be more than 3σ above or below its mean, and "almost certain" for it to be within its mean plus or minus 3σ. Define the "anticipated minimum" present worth of a project or portfolio as present worth such that it would be "rare" to encounter a smaller one. Compute the anticipated minimum present worth for A, B, and AB.**

$$\text{A:} \qquad 106.3 - 3(10) = \underline{76.3}$$
$$\text{B:} \qquad 100 - 3(2.5) = \underline{92.5}$$
$$\text{AB:} \quad 206.3 - 3(10.307764) = \underline{175.3767}$$

(d) **Based on the results, which project, A or B, is "safer" from yielding a "disappointing" outcome of a 90 present worth?**

B is safer, since it is almost certain to have a present worth of at least 92.5. An outcome of 90 would be rare for B but not rare for A.

8.3.3 Portfolio Risk

A diversified portfolio can be much safer than its component projects. The following example will show that combining safer, lower-yielding projects into a portfolio actually is more risky than combining riskier, higher-yielding projects, if projects are independent and there are many of them.

E24. **Now suppose we had four independent project opportunities as follows:**

Independent Project	Required Investment	Expected Present Worth	Standard Deviation of Present Worth
A	150	106.3	10.0
A2	151	107.0	10.1
B	152	100.0	2.5
B2	151	101.0	2.6

Here we have added project A2 that is very similar to A and B2 very similar to B. Now suppose the available capital for investment is 305, so that *any two* of the independent projects can be accepted. To maximize expected present worth, we would obviously choose A and A2. However, suppose we would have a disaster, whose extra costs are not reflected in individual projects' data, if the *total present worth* of the portfolio of two projects was small.

(a) **Which portfolio is safer—the portfolio (A,A2) of higher-yielding risky projects, or the portfolio (B,B2) of lower-yielding safer projects?**

$$E(P_{(A,A2)}) = 106.3 + 107.0 = 213.3$$

$$\sigma_{(A,A2)} = \sqrt{(10)^2 + (10.1)^2} = 14.213$$

Anticipated minimum P for portfolio (A,A2):

$$213.3 - 3(14.213) = \underline{\underline{170.66}}$$

$$E(P_{(B,B2)}) = 100.0 + 101.0 = 201.0$$

$$\sigma_{(B,B2)} = \sqrt{(2.5)^2 + (2.6)^2} = 3.607$$

Anticipated minimum P for portfolio (B,B2):

$$201.0 = 3(3.607) = \underline{\underline{190.18}}$$

The portfolio of two projects is safer if it is made of two lower-yielding safer projects; with the riskier projects, at least 170.66 is anticipated, but with the safer projects, at least 190.18 is anticipated. Two-project portfolios are not diverse enough to exhibit the safety of diversity.

(b) **Now consider portfolios with greater numbers of projects. Let project A be typical of a group of similar projects; for simplicity, let them each have an expected present worth of 106.3 and a present-worth standard deviation of**

10.0. Let project B be typical of another group, one of slightly less profitable but much safer projects; for simplicity, let each member of this B group have an expected present worth of 100 and a present-worth standard deviation of 2.5.

The projects are all independent, and we can use them to demonstrate the safety of diversity ("safety in numbers"), which is a consequence of the rule for adding independent variances. Let there be a capital budget sufficient for accepting M projects, where all M of them can be the A type, or all M of the B type, or some of each. If the whole portfolio is of type A projects, let Y_A be the minimum anticipated total present worth:

$$Y_A = 106.3M - 3\sqrt{100M}$$

That is, the whole portfolio has an expected present worth that is M times 106.3, and the variance is M times that of one project (M times the square of 10), so that the 3-sigma downward deviation is 3 times the square root of the variance. Similarly, there is a minimum anticipated total present worth for a portfolio of B-type projects:

$$Y_B = 100M - 3\sqrt{6.25M}$$

Note that the expected advantage of the A-type portfolio increases linearly with the number of items in the portfolio, while the downward deviations (where B-type portfolios have the advantage) increase only as the square root of the number of items M. Thus, *for great enough M, a portfolio of M better-yielding risky independent projects must be safer than a portfolio of M lesser-yielding but individually safer projects.* Solve for the value of M that makes A-type portfolios safer than the B-type portfolio.

$Y_A > Y_B$. The A portfolio is to have the greater minimum anticipated total present worth.

$$106.3M - 3\sqrt{100M} > 100M - 3\sqrt{6.25M}$$

$$6.3M > 30\sqrt{M} - 7.5\sqrt{M}$$

$$7.3\sqrt{M} > 22.5$$

$$M > \left(\frac{22.5}{6.3}\right)^2 = \underline{\underline{12.755}}$$

Hence, $\underline{\underline{13}}$ projects is enough to make the bolder portfolio safer.

(c) **Show that a portfolio of 13 A-type projects is slightly safer (has a greater minimum anticipated total present worth) than a portfolio of 13 B-type projects.**

For $M = 13$,

$$Y_A = 106.3M - 3\sqrt{100M} = 1273.73$$

$$Y_B = 100M - 3\sqrt{6.25M} = 1272.96$$

A is slightly safer.

8.4 HOPED-FOR CASH FLOWS AND GEOMETRIC RISK

The principal cash-flow estimates that are made in engineering economy are those of a future lump sum A_t in current dollars or W_t in indexed dollars, or of an equal-payment series $\{A: t = 1,...,n\}$ in current dollars or $\{W: t = 1,...,n\}$ in indexed dollars, or of a geometric gradient series $\{a_0(1 + g)^t: t = 1,...,n\}$ in current dollars or $\{a_0(1 + v)^t: t = 1,...,n\}$ in indexed dollars. In each case, the *expected value* of the cash-flow parameter—A_t, W_t, A, W or a_0—is the correct estimate to use in worth calculations, so that the result is the expected worth. For example, consider estimating the zero projection of an escalating cash-flow series where there is a 0.90 probability that $a_0 = \$1000$ and a 0.10 probability that $a_0 = \$2000$; the expected worth of the series is the worth that is calculated if $0.90 \times 1000 + 0.10 \times 2000 = \$1100$ is the estimate of a_0 that is used in the worth formula. The possibility of a windfall or of a disaster is thus accounted for by using the expected-value definition of Eq. 8-5 to adjust the estimate up or down; the analyst is asked to use $\$1100$ as the estimate for an amount that will very probably be $\$1000$, the extra $\$100$ being added to account for a 10% chance that the amount will be doubled.

Now we turn to some simple instances of risk in which the analyst has *not* made such an adjustment; the worth can be corrected in a way other than adjusting the cash-flow amount to its expected value.

8.4.1 Hoped-For Cash Flows

Let H_t denote a *hoped-for cash flow* at time t. Let Π_0 denote the probability the cash-flow amount A_t will be zero and let Π_1 denote the probability the cash-flow amount A_t will be H_t. Let 0 and H_t be the only two possibilities, so that $\Pi_0 + \Pi_1 = 1$. Then the *expected value of a hoped-for cash flow* is

$$E(A_t) = \Pi_0 0 + \Pi_1 H_t = \Pi_1 H_t = (1 - \Pi_0) H_t \tag{8-7}$$

Π_0 is called the *risk* of H_t. If the hoped-for amounts of several different cash flows need to be distinguished, we use the functional notation $\Pi_0(H_t)$ to denote the risk of a particular one.

E25. A project has the following hoped-for cash flows:

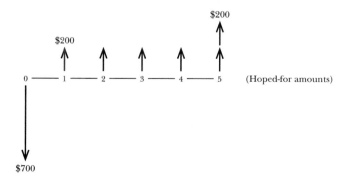

(Hoped-for amounts)

There is a 10% risk that the first-year return will not occur and a 20% risk that the salvage value will be zero instead of $200. The returns at times 2, . . ., 5 are not at risk. Determine the expected present worth at 12% interest.

Given $\Pi_0(A_1) = 0.10$, $\Pi_0(\text{salvage}) = 0.20$.   Replacing H_1 with $E(A_1) = \Pi_1(A_1)H_1 = 0.90 \times 299 = \$180$ and   the   hoped-for   salvage value with $0.80 \times 2000 = \$160$, we have

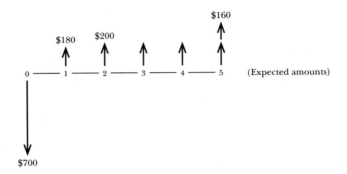

The expected present worth, with $i = 0.12$, $\beta = 1/(1 + i)$, is

$$E(P) = -700 + 180\beta + \beta200\left(\frac{1 - \beta^4}{i}\right) + 160\beta^5 = \underline{\$93.89}$$

This illustrates that to correct for the use of a hoped-for cash-flow estimate H_t, the hoped-for value is simply replaced by $\Pi_1 H_t = (1 - \Pi_0)H_t$; that is, the hoped-for value is multiplied by one minus its risk.

The same thing can be done to a hoped-for A_t, a hoped-for W_t, a hoped-for A, a hoped-for W, or a hoped-for a_0. When a hoped-for amount that represents a whole series (A, W, or a_0) is corrected by multiplying by one minus its risk, the risk being accounted for is that the whole series of cash flows will not occur.

E26. **A lender lends \$1000 to a borrower at $i = 0.945\%$ monthly interest (11.34 APR), thus hoping to receive 18 monthly payments in return. The lender's MARR is the same i, so the hoped-for monthly repayment of $1000(A/P\ i,18) = \$60.68$ gives a present worth of zero if the loan is repaid.**

(a) **Considering the two possibilities that the loan will be repaid in full on time, or that there will be no repayments at all, let there be a 0.1% risk of the latter. Determine the expected present worth of the loan from the lender's viewpoint.**

The present worth, where $i = 0.00945$ and A is the repayment amount, is

$$P = -1000 + A(P/A\ i,18)$$

The hoped-for value of A is \$60.68, and its expected value considering a 0.001 risk is $(1 - 0.001)60.68 = 60.61932$. Thus the expected worth is

$$E(P) = -1000 + 60.61932(P/A\ i,18) = \underline{-\$0.93258}$$

The lender loses an expected 93¢ compared to lending to a borrower certain to repay.

(b) Determine the interest rate at which the loan should be made so that the expected worth at 0.945% interest is zero.

At an unknown interest rate i, the hoped-for repayment is $H = 1000(A/P\ i,18)$. Putting $(1 - 0.001)H$ into the present-worth formula, we have the expected worth at 0.945% interest.

$$E(P) = -1000 + 0.999H(P/A\ 0.945\%,18)$$

$$= -1000 + 999(A/P\ i,18)(16.4810067)$$

$$E(P) = 0 \Rightarrow (A/P\ i,18) = 0.060736642 \Rightarrow i = \underline{0.95592435\%}$$

This rate is slightly higher than 0.945% and makes up for the risk.

8.4.2 Geometric Risk

There is one kind of risk that can be neatly accounted for by a simple change in the interest rate. This is *geometric risk*. The geometric risk model gives a straightforward, easily computed answer to potentially thorny questions about the risks associated with equipment reliability, changing economic conditions, natural disasters, obsolescence, and so forth.

Consider a series of hoped-for cash flows $\{H_t:\ t = 0,...,n\}$, where there is a risk q at each time period that no further cash flows will occur.

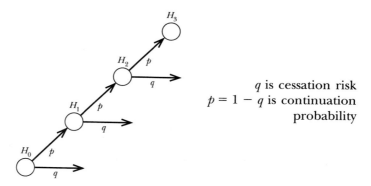

q is cessation risk
$p = 1 - q$ is continuation
probability

The cash flow H_0 is certain to occur. The hoped-for cash flow at time 1 has a probability $p = 1 - q$ of occurring, so the expected value of the cash flow at time 1 is pH_1. Now recall that in conjunction with Example E13 it was mentioned that if two events are independent, the probability that both of them occurs is the product of the probabilities that each occurs. For the cash flow H_2 to occur, two independent events must occur: The system must persist through the first time interval, and it must persist through the second time interval. The probability of each of these events is p, so the probability that cash flow H_2 occurs is p^2. Similarly, the probability that cash flow H_t occurs is p^t. Hence the *expected* cash flow at time t is $p^t H_t$ (see Figure 8-2) and the *expected present worth of a set of hoped-for cash flows under geometric risk* is

$$V = E(P) = \sum_{t=0}^{n} p^t H_t \beta^t = \sum_{t=0}^{n} H_t(p\beta)^t \tag{8-8}$$

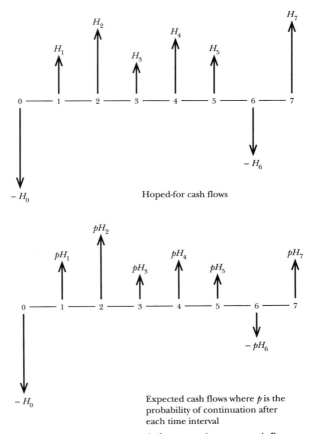

FIGURE 8-2. Geometric risk for an arbitrary cash-flow set.

Note that the formula for V has the same mathematical form as a formula for P, with $p\beta$ instead of β as the one-period discount factor. Thus this type of risk operates *geometrically* and can be handled similarly to the way that inflation and geometric escalation are handled through alteration of the interest rate. That is why this type of risk is called *geometric risk*.

Geometric risk occurs when there is a *continual cessation probability q*, and the hoped-for estimated cash flows $\{H_j\}$ ignore the cessation probability. The estimated cash flows can be in current $\{A_j\}$ dollars, or in indexed dollars $\{W_j\}$, or in amounts subject to escalation at real rate (inflation-free rate) v or combined rate g, or they can even be *expected values* of cash flows according to any probabilistic process that ignores the cessation risk and is independent of it.

Geometric risk can be handled informally by simply replacing β or α by $p\beta$ or $p\alpha$, or it can be handled formally. As an example of informal handling, consider the present worth of the proposed spa in Example E9 of Chapter 3, involving current-dollar fixed membership revenues and lease payments discounted at $d = 9.5238095\%$:

$$P = -30 + 35\left(\frac{1 - \beta^5}{i}\right) - 15\left(\frac{1 - \alpha^5}{d}\right) \text{ where } \beta = \frac{1}{1 + i} \text{ and } \alpha = \frac{1}{1 + d}$$

$$= \underline{\$29,765.08}$$

Suppose it were learned that there is a 0.5% risk each year of losing the necessary business permits, so there would be no further revenues or costs. To correct for this risk, we simply replace $\beta = 1/(1 + i)$ with 0.995β and replace $\alpha = 1/(1 + d)$ with 0.995α; of course, we also replace i and d with the corresponding quantities, or express them as $(1 - \beta)/\beta$ and $(1 - \alpha)/\alpha$ before replacing β and α:

$$E(P) = -30 + 35\left(\frac{\beta}{1 - \beta}\right)(1 - \beta^5) - 15\left(\frac{\alpha}{1 - \alpha}\right)(1 - \alpha^5)$$

Where $\beta = 0.995/1.15$ and $\alpha = 0.995/1.095238095$, the result is $E(P) = \$28{,}983.65$, about $781 smaller than before.

Formally, we define f as the substitute interest rate that takes geometric risk into account, and define ϕ as the corresponding one-period present-worth discount factor. ϕ is $p\beta = (1 - q)\beta = (1 - q)/(1 + i)$ in the special case where $s = i$. All the cases are summarized in Table 8-2.

E27. A bank expects to earn a nominal 11.5% interest, compounded monthly, on safe loans of a certain class. As a social service the bank agrees to provide loans in an itinerant community, where there is a risk of $q = 0.003$ each month that a customer will leave without paying any further payments.

(a) Determine the monthly interest rate that should be charged for the risky itinerant loans so that the expected present worth V is the same (zero) as the present worth of the usual loan at $i = 11.5\%/12 = 0.95833\%$ monthly.

$$1 + f = \frac{1 + i}{1 - q}\frac{1.0095833}{0.998} = 1.0116065 \Rightarrow f = 1.16065\% \quad \text{per month}$$

(*Note:* The APR would be $r = mf = 12(1.16065) = 13.927855\%$ compounded monthly.)

TABLE 8-2. Geometric Risk Combined with Inflation and Escalation

Geometric Risk: Cessation Probability $q = 1 - p$ Each Period

Determination of substitute interest rate f:

$$\phi = \frac{1}{1 + f} = \frac{1 - q}{1 + s} = \frac{(1 + g)(1 - q)}{1 + i} = \frac{(1 + v)(1 + j)(1 - q)}{1 + i} = \frac{(1 + v)(1 - q)}{1 + d}$$

$$1 + f = \frac{1 + i}{(1 + g)(1 - q)} = \frac{1 + i}{(1 + v)(1 + j)(1 - q)} = \frac{1 + d}{(1 + v)(1 - q)} = \frac{1 + s}{1 - q}$$

Special case of geometric risk only, with no escalation:

Current dollars, $g = 0$:	*Indexed dollars, $v = 0$:*
$\phi = \dfrac{1}{1 + f} = \dfrac{1 - q}{1 + i}$	$\phi = \dfrac{1}{1 + f} = \dfrac{1 - q}{1 + d}$
$f = \dfrac{1 + i}{1 - q} - 1$	$f = \dfrac{1 + d}{1 - q} - 1$

(b) **For a \$1000 loan to be paid in three equal monthly installments at** $i =$ **0.95833% monthly interest, the monthly payment would be** $A = \$339.74$. **Compute the (hoped-for) monthly payment at the risk-cognizant interest rate.**

At $f = 1.16065\%$ monthly,

$$\phi = \frac{1}{1+f} = 0.988526620$$

$$A = \frac{Vf}{1 - \phi^3} = \frac{1000}{2.931684767} = \underline{\$341.10} \quad \text{per month}$$

(c) **According to the principles behind the interest rate substitution, the expected present worth of the repayments, computed at the original interest rate** i, **should be \$1000. Verify this.**

For $A = 341.10$, where $\beta = 1/(1 + 0.115/0.12)$,

$$E(P_{A1}) = [0.998(341.10) + 0.002(0)]\beta^1$$

$$E(P_{A2}) = [0.998^2(341.10) + (1 - 0.998^2)(0)]\beta^2$$

$$E(P_{A3}) = [0.998^3(341.10) + (1 - 0.998^3)(0)]\beta^3$$

$$V = E(P_{A1}) + E(P_{A2}) + E(P_{A3})$$

$$= 337.186 + 333.3178 + 329.4935 = \underline{\$1000}$$

E28. Consider a project requiring an investment of \$1000 and yielding hoped-for returns of \$621.31 at the ends of each of the first two years.

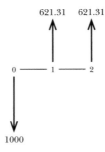

Let the investor have MARR = 10%. The hoped-for present worth of the project is

$$P = -1000 + 621.31(\beta + \beta^2) \quad \text{where} \quad \beta = 1/1.10$$
$$= \$78.31$$

(a) **Now suppose it turns out that there is a** $q = 0.05$ **geometric risk—each year there is a 5% chance of no further returns. Compute the expected present worth.**

$$E(P) = -1000 + 621.31(\phi + \phi^2)$$
$$= -1000 + 621.31(1.609504)$$
$$= \underline{\underline{0}}$$

where

$$\phi = \frac{1 + 0.05}{1 + 0.10} = 0.86\overline{3636} \qquad f = \frac{1}{\phi} - 1 = 15.7895\%$$

(b) Recall that MARR can be set on the basis of a typical "ordinary" project. Suppose this project is a typical "ordinary" project and that the enterprise wishes to publish MARR expressed two ways: as an i rate for the case in which the cash flows are already corrected for geometric risk, and as an f rate for the case in which the cash flows are hoped-for ones ignoring geometric risk. Determine the two rates, and demonstrate that this typical "ordinary" project has a zero present worth under each.

We have just seen that $P = 0$ for $f = 15.7894736\%$, in the case of the hoped-for cash flows of $621.31 each year. The i corresponding to this f, as we have already seen, is $i = 0.10$. To check,

$$1 + f = \frac{1 + i}{1 - q} = 1 + i = 1.1578947(0.95) = 1.10$$

The cash flows "already corrected for geometric risk" would be the expected cash flows given geometric risk:

$$\text{at } t = 1: \quad 621.31 \times 0.95 = 590.2445$$
$$\text{at } t = 2: \quad 621.31 \times 0.95^2 = 560.7322750$$

At $i = 10\%$,

$$P = -1000 + 590.2445\left(\frac{1}{1.10}\right) + 560.7322750\left(\frac{1}{1.10}\right)^2$$

$$= -1000 + 536.5859091 + 463.4151033$$

$$= \underline{\underline{0}}$$

E29. An oil refinery uses a MARR that in f terms is 20%. The plant is designed for a "200-year" earthquake, which implies, approximately, that each year there is a 0.005 probability that the plant will be damaged beyond repair. Plant improvement projects compete for capital against other projects not subject to earthquake risk. For projects not subject to earthquake risk, what would be the appropriate MARR in i terms?

$$1 + f = \frac{1 + i}{1 - q} \Rightarrow 1.2 = \frac{1 + i}{1 - 0.005} \Rightarrow \underline{\underline{i = 19.4\%}}$$

E30. The same oil refinery is considering replacing an existing jacketed pipeline that carries poisonous H_2S gas (pronounced "aitch-two-ess" or "hydrogen sulfide") to the neighboring chemical plant. It is realized that the pipeline operates essentially at the whim of environmental authorities, and that there is substantial risk, estimated at 9% per year, of losing the right to use it. The expected present worth of the revenues from the replacement project would otherwise be computed as

$$20\frac{1 - (1/1.23)^7}{0.23}\ \text{K\$}$$

without considering shutdown risk. What is the risk-corrected present worth?

The interest rate in the formula is 2.3%, which is either an i rate or an s rate. The corresponding f rate is

$$f = \frac{1 + 0.23}{1 - 0.09} - 1 = 35.1648352\%$$

The present worth becomes

$$V = 20\frac{1 - (1/1.351648352)^7}{0.351648352} = \underline{\underline{49.97458234}}\ \text{K\$}$$

For comparison, ignoring risk gives

$$20\frac{1 - (1/1.23)^7}{0.23} = 66.54\ \text{K\$}$$

The use of *conservative economic lives* is an (inferior) alternative way of accounting for one of the motivators of geometric risk—the possibility that a cash-flow set may terminate early.

E31. A cash-flow set is A dollars per year every year for $n = 15$ years. The interest rate is 15%. Determine (to the nearest whole year) a conservative economic life m that would have the same effect on (expected) present worth as a $q = 0.05$ geometric risk.

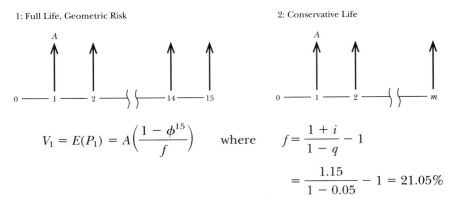

1: Full Life, Geometric Risk

2: Conservative Life

$$V_1 = E(P_1) = A\left(\frac{1 - \phi^{15}}{f}\right) \quad \text{where} \quad f = \frac{1 + i}{1 - q} - 1$$

$$= \frac{1.15}{1 - 0.05} - 1 = 21.05\%$$

$$V_1 = E(P_1) = A(4.479554294) \qquad \text{and } \phi = \frac{1}{1+f}$$

$$P_2 = A\left(\frac{1-\beta^m}{i}\right) \quad \text{where} \quad i = 15\% \text{ and } \beta = \frac{1}{1-i}$$

Find m so that $E(P_1) \cong P_2$, so that $P_2/A = 4.479554294$:

m	P_2/A	
10	5.0	too high; reduce m
8	4.49	about right, slightly high
7	4.16	

$\underline{m = 8}$. Thus if the economic life is reduced to 8 years from 15, the offset is about the same as a 5% geometric risk.

It would not be recommended to use conservative economic life in lieu of interest rate alteration, because the interest rate alteration gives a definite correction that is independent of the cash-flow amounts and the life.

One last example will combine the effects of inflation, escalation, and geometric risk.

E32. **An enterprise wants to earn a real interest rate of $d = 8\%$. It expects inflation of $j = 4\%$. A cash-flow set is $1000 per year for eight years, estimated in indexed dollars but subject to real escalation at rate $v = 2\%$.**

   (a) Determine the hoped-for present worth (ignoring risk).

$$\alpha = \frac{1+v}{1+d} = \frac{1.02}{1.08} \qquad s = \frac{1}{\alpha} - 1$$

$$P = 1000\left(\frac{1-\alpha^8}{s}\right) = \underline{\underline{\$6238.81}}$$

   (b) Determine the expected present worth if there is a $q = 6\%$ risk of cessation each year.

$$\phi = \frac{(1+v)(1-q)}{1+d} = \frac{(10.2)(1-0.06)}{1.08} \qquad f = \frac{1}{\phi} - 1$$

$$E(P) = 1000\left(\frac{1-\phi^8}{f}\right) = \underline{\underline{\$4858.36}}$$

8.4.3 Expected Life Under Geometric Risk

For a given continual cessation probability q, there is a corresponding *expected life L*, defined as the expected number of periods that a set of cash flows will endure.

If we define a special series of hoped-for payments, each of $1, at times 1, 2,... indefinitely,

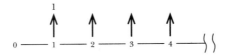

the expected present worth of this series at zero interest rate ($\beta = 0$) is its expected sum; and of course if \$1 is collected for every period endured, the expected sum equals the expected number of periods, or the expected life:

$$L = \sum_{t=1}^{\infty} p^t = p + p^2 + p^3 + \cdots = \frac{p}{1-p} = \frac{1-q}{q} \tag{8-9}$$

E33. **A machine has a 0.01 probability of failing in a period, and this probability is the same for every period. (Such a failure process is called a *geometric failure process*, or an *exponential failure process* if time is represented as continuous.) Determine the machine's expected life (number of periods to failure).**

$$L = \frac{1-q}{q} = \frac{1-0.01}{0.01} = \underline{\underline{99 \text{ periods}}}$$

Conversely, if the expected life L is known, the continual cessation probability can be determined as

$$q = \frac{1}{L+1} \tag{8-10}$$

E34. **Modifications to an unattended reactor system are expected to yield the following set of cash flows, in thousands of indexed dollars:**

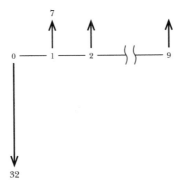

However, the reactor itself is considered to have an exponential (geometric) life expectancy whose expected value is 20 years. Determine the expected present worth at $d = 12\%$ of the modification project both before and after this consideration.

Before the consideration:

$$E(P) = -32 + 7\left(\frac{1-\delta^9}{d}\right) \qquad \text{where} \qquad \delta = \frac{1}{1.12}$$

$$= -32 + 7(5.32849)$$

$$= \underline{\$5,297.75}$$

(It is a good project if no risk is considered.)

Given $L = 20$, after the consideration:

$$q = \frac{1}{L+1} = \frac{1}{20+1} = 0.047619$$

$$\phi = \frac{1-q}{1+d} = \frac{0.95238}{1.12} = 0.85034$$

$$f = \frac{1}{\phi} - 1 = 0.176$$

$$V = -32 + 7\left(\frac{1-\phi^9}{f}\right) = \underline{-\$1,472.54}$$

(A bad project, considering risk.)

8.5 GEOMETRIC DELAY

Let A_τ represent a cash flow scheduled to occur at time τ. If there is a delay in the cash flow, the cash flow will occur at some actual time $\tau + t$, where t is the delay, which can be 0, 1, 2, . . . time units.

The delay is said to be *geometric*, or to have the geometric probability distribution, if it results from a try-and-try-again process similar to the process that gives rise to geometric risk.

Let there be a probability p at each time $\tau, \tau + 1, \tau + 2, \ldots$ that the cash flow fails to occur and is enabled possibly to occur at the next time period. Thus we have a process, like that for geometric risk, that continues with probability p and ceases with probability $q = 1 - p$, independently at each time period.

Now the cash flow occurs at some particular time $\tau + t$ only if the process continued at each of times $\tau, \tau + 1, \tau + 2, \ldots, \tau + t - 1$ and if it ceased at time $\tau + t$. The continuation events each occurred independently with probability p, and there were t of them. The cessation event occurred with probability q. By the rule of multiplying independent probabilities together, the combination of all these events has probability $p^t q$. Thus the delay is zero with probability q, one time period with probability pq, two time periods with probability $p^2 q$, and so forth.

The *expected geometric delay* is

$$E(t) = (q \times 0) + (p^2 q \times 1) + (p^3 q \times 2) + (p^4 q \times 3) + \cdots$$

$$= pq(1 + 2p + 3p^2 + \cdots) \quad \text{(\textit{recall the development of Eq.\ 2-11})}$$

$$= \frac{pq}{(1-p)^2} = \frac{p}{q} \tag{8-11}$$

Conversely, given the expected delay $E(t)$, the *continuation probability* p is

$$p = \frac{E(t)}{1 + E(t)} \tag{8-12}$$

E35. Mary Guido keeps her unpaid bills in a fishbowl. Every Wednesday she takes one out at random and pays it. There are 12 bills in the bowl each time, so a bill has a $\frac{1}{12}$ chance of being paid. Determine the expected number of weeks of delay before she pays a bill.

If she pays the bill the first Wednesday after it is received, there is considered to be no delay. The probability of cessation of the delay is $q = 1/12$, so $p = 1 - q = 11/12$. From Eq. 8-11,

$$E(t) = p/q = \tfrac{11}{12}/\tfrac{1}{12} = \underline{11 \ \ weeks}$$

The present worth of a payment A_τ scheduled at time τ is $A_\tau \beta^\tau$ if it is not delayed, $A_\tau \beta^{\tau+1}$ if it is delayed one period, $A_\tau \beta^{\tau+2}$ if it is delayed two periods, and so forth. These events occur with probabilities q, pq, p^2q, and so forth.

probability q, worth $A_\tau \beta^\tau$:

probability pq, worth $A_\tau \beta^{\tau+1}$:

probability p^2q, worth $A_\tau \beta^{\tau+2}$:

The expected present worth is computed by the usual method from equation 8-5; the probability of each worth is multiplied by the worth, and the results are summed:

Expected present worth of a payment A_τ subject to geometric delay:

$$E(P) = qA_\tau\beta^\tau + pqA_\tau\beta^{\tau+1} + p^2qA_\tau\beta^{\tau+2} + \cdots$$

$$= A_\tau\beta^\tau q(1 + p\beta + p^2\beta^2 + \cdots)$$

$$= A_\tau\beta^\tau \frac{q}{1 - p\beta} \tag{8-13}$$

Thus we have a *geometric delay correction factor*, given here expressed in three ways:

$$\frac{1}{1 - p\beta} = \frac{1}{1 + E(t) - \beta E(t)} = \frac{1 + i}{1 + i + iE(t)} \tag{8-14}$$

The factor reduces the undelayed or *scheduled* present worth $A_\tau\beta^\tau$ to account for geometric delay.

A delay of exactly $E(t)$ time periods would, of course, multiply the worth by $\beta^{E(t)}$. Thus $\beta^{E(t)}$ is an approximate correction factor for a delay that averages $E(t)$ periods. It is always smaller than the geometric delay correction factor of Eq. 8-14; that is, it reduces the worth too much, because the geometric delay includes the likelihood of very short delays.

E36. A shipping permit worth \$2 million is being applied for. Bureaucratic delays are possible; a consultant estimates an average of 6 one-month delays for such a permit. Determine the prospective effect on present worth of the permit for an enterprise whose MARR translates to 1.25% monthly.

With time in months, $E(t) = 6$, $\beta = 1/1.0125$, and the delay correction factor is (using the middle form in Eq. 8-14)

$$\frac{1}{1 + E(t) - \beta E(t)} = \frac{1}{1 + 6 - (6/1.0125)} = \underline{0.93103448}$$

Thus the expected worth of the shipping permit becomes

$$2 \times 0.93103448 \cong \underline{\$1.862 \text{ million}}$$

Note: To use the left-hand form of Eq. 8-14, we first compute q from Eq. 8-12:

$$q = 1 - p = \frac{1}{1 + E(t)} = \frac{1}{7}$$

Then

$$\frac{q}{1 - p\beta} = \frac{1/7}{1 - [(6/7)/1.0125]} = 0.93103448 \qquad \text{as before}$$

Compare the geometric-delayed worth with the worth if the delay were exactly six months.

$$2 \times \beta^6 = \underline{\$1.856 \text{ million}}, \qquad \text{roughly \$6000 less}$$

E37. **At every scheduled maintenance shutdown of the catalytic cracking plant of an oil refinery, a comprehensive effort is made to fix everything to allow an 18-month interval to the next scheduled shutdown. This has never been achieved; shutdowns have been scheduled every April. The maintenance manager believes it might happen this time: "We have a fifty-fifty chance of running to October next; if not, we'll have a similar chance next April, and so on. Once we acheive it, we will know how to keep it up, and at that time the worth (at 21% interest per year) of the future savings will be $3 million." Determine the expected present worth of the prospective savings.**

A savings worth $3 million is delayed geometrically according to $p = 0.50$. With $q = 1 - p = 0.50$ and $\beta = 1/1.21$, $A_\tau = \$3$ million, $\tau = 0$ (time is in years), Eq. 8-13 gives

$$E(P) = 3\beta^0 \frac{q}{1 - p\beta} = 3 \times 0.85211268 \cong \underline{\underline{\$2.556 \text{ million}}}$$

It should be noted that the context of delay problems (as in Chapter 5) is usually one in which *indexed* dollars are used, and so the interest rate should be a d rate and β should be $1/(1 + d)$.

8.6 EXERCISES

1. Recall the data from Example E3 in Chapter 1. Answer further breakeven questions.
   (a) The purchase price of the Duro-Lite X2500 bulb is high. At what purchase price would the Duro-Lite X2500 bulb become the best buy (assuming $1.00 additional costs associated with replacement for any brand of bulb)?
   (b) The GE Miser is a better buy than the GE Softwhite. If the Softwhite is on sale at a discount while the Miser is at regular price, what price makes the two bulbs an equally good buy? Also, state whether this result depends on the additional replacement cost (would it change if the additional replacement cost were more or less than $1.00?) and why or why not.

2. In Example E1 assume that the master of the *Stella Lykes* finds an insulation subcontractor willing to install insulation guaranteed to save 80% of the present fuel-warming costs, for a fee of $160,000. It now appears that the eight-year remaining life of the vessel is uncertain. What is the minimum remaining life for the insulation job to be worthwhile?

3. In Example E1 assume that the master of the *Stella Lykes* finds an insulation subcontractor willing to install insulation guaranteed to save 80% of the present fuel-warming costs, for a fee of $160,000. It now appears that fuel costs will immediately increase by some factor J and continue to follow inflation from the new level. How great a factor J would justify the insulation job?

4. A project has the following estimated worth

$$P = -10 + (R - C_M - C_L)\left(\frac{1 + \alpha^{12}}{d}\right) \quad \text{where } \alpha = \frac{1}{1 + d}$$

where cash-flow amounts are in thousands of indexed dollars, and the real annual interest rate d is 0.05. Estimates are that the annual returns are $R = 9.14$, the annual materials costs are $C_m = 2.94$, and the labor costs are $C_L = 5.04$. It is feared that labor costs will escalate at some real rate v. How great can this rate be for the project to remain attractive?

5. Paint that has an indexed cost of $300, including $89 of materials and $211 of labor, will protect a walkway for four years. The walkway will be in service for many years. An alternative paint that would take only $100 of labor to install has a materials cost of $105, but its economic life is in question. How long must the alternative paint last to be as economical as the four-year paint, if the real interest rate is $d = 0.06$?

6. Recall the data from Example E3 in Chapter 1. Assuming that the additional replacement cost introduced in parts d and e of that example is zero, and that the GE Miser has the lowest total cost when the electrical energy price is $0.077 per kilwatt-hour, answer these sensitivity-analysis questions:
   (a) Determine the sensitivity of the choice to the price of electrical energy.
   (b) Determine the sensitivity of the choice to the number of operating hours per year (with the price of electrical energy at $0.077/kW-hr).
   (c) A rational purchaser aware of all costs may choose the Softwhite over the Miser on the basis of light quality. At least how much per bulb per 1000 hours is such a person presumably willing to pay for this perceived quality difference?

7. Recall the data from Example E3 in Chapter 1. Assuming that the additional replacement cost introduced in parts d and e of that example is zero, sketch a graph of total energy-plus-replacement cost versus electrical energy price, for prices of 0.02 to 0.08 $/kW-hr. Write a brief statement summarizing the situation, with respect to energy price, that is shown by the graph.

8. Consider the project whose sensitivity of worth to several parameters is shown in Figure 8-1.
   (a) From the graph in Figure 8-1, estimate the decrease in annual returns that would just offset an increase in the economic life to six years.
   (b) Determine (from the P formula) the actual decrease in annual returns that would just offset an increase in the economic life to six years.
   (c) Explain the cause for the discrepancy between the graphical and actual answers.

9. In the project whose worth sensitivity to various parameters is shown in Figure 8-1, verify that the present worth is $12,673.76 when every parameter (except i) changes 40% in the favorable direction.

10. There are two major kinds of what-if questions that can be asked in sensitivity analysis: "What if the parameters change from their estimated values?" and "What if the model is incomplete?" The text and examples in Section 8.1.2 do not illustrate the latter kind of what-if question well. From your general knowledge and experience, write several brief illustrative examples, either general or specific, of sensitivity questions you might ask that could not be answered by merely adjusting parameter values or making trivial adjustments.

11. In Example E8, let Sis or Hix bring up the question, "What if a salvage value of $400 can be realized at time 5?" Determine the prospective effect on worth of the project.

12. For Example E10, verify the decrease in P_{at} by computing P_{at} at the two tax rates and subtracting. Why is there no discrepancy between this result and the result obtained by using the derivative dP_{at}/dT?

13. (a) If a venture has a 0.10 probability of having a net present worth of $60,000, and otherwise its net present worth is −$9000 (negative), what is the expected present worth?

    (b) If a cash flow of $100 has a 0.40 probability of occurring after 1.0 years, a 0.50 probability of occurring after 5 years, and a 0.10 probability of never occurring, what is its expected present worth at 15% interest?

    (c) Verify numerically whether or not the same result would be obtained by discounting $100 to the expected time of occurrence, and explain.

14. It seems to be boom or bust in the restaurant business. Sandy Spring, the former water boy, can envision his restaurant's turning out like Martino's (which would have about a $110,000 present worth if built today), or like Billy Klub's (built by the famous former bat boy for $60,000 and sold in three weeks for $40,000). Sandy feels the odds are 9 to 1 in favor of the latter alternative, and Sandy likes to play the odds, that is, Sandy is an expected-value maker. Should Sandy open his restaurant?

15. The long-run average number of jobs awaiting processing in a computer system has the following probability distribution:

Number of jobs	0	1	2	3	4
Probability	0.71	0.20	0.04	0.03	0.02

    (a) Determine the expected number of jobs in the system.

    (b) If the hourly cost of waiting for a job is $0.40, and there are 2000 operating hours per year, determine the expected annual cost.

    (c) A scheduling algorithm can change the unit distribution to the following:

Number of jobs	0	1	2	3	4
Probability	0.75	0.24	0.01	0.00	0.00

    Determine the maximum justifiable annual cost for maintaining and operating this algorithm.

16. A project has a 70/30 chance of outcome **A** versus outcome **B**.

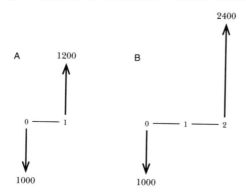

(a) Determine the project's expected present worth at 10% interest.

(b) Determine the interest rate at which the present worth is not a random variable.

17. A wood-products company plans a major expansion whose profitability depends heavily on success in trade negotiations that are beyond the company's ability to influence but are believed to have a 75% probability of success. Two alternative expansion plans are under consideration: conservative plan **A** will earn (a net present worth of) $1 million if the negotiations are successful, but will be ordinary (earn $0) otherwise, whereas bold plan **B** will earn $2.5 million if the negotiations are successful, but will lose $1 million otherwise. The decision is to be made by the company's Finance Committee.

(a) Assuming the Finance Committee truly represents the owner's interests, and a present-worth loss of $1 million is not really a disaster, which alternative is chosen?

(b) Suppose, on the other hand, the Finance Committee is dominated by a management team, and a typical member of the team stands to gain career enhancement worth $0.2 million if at least $1 million is earned, $0 if the outcome is ordinary, and −$0.2 million if at least $1 million is lost. Which alternative is chosen?

(c) In an effort to make executives more responsive to owners' interests, the company's board enacts a profit-sharing plan whereby, in addition to the career-enhancement incentives mentioned above, a share x of present-worth gain or loss is given to (or taken from) a typical member of the management team. How great need x be to cause a choice of **B** over **A**?

(d) If the profit-sharing is an additional cost not offset by base salary reductions, is the minimal profit-sharing plan worthwhile to the company?

18. At 5% annual real interest, the (indexed) future benefits from completion of a power plant were estimated to be worth $600 million upon completion, which was scheduled for June 3, 1994. Construction cost was estimated as $438 million, plus or minus $10 million per month, timed in months around the due date (the date of the 438 negative equivalent cash flow) as shown in the following examples:

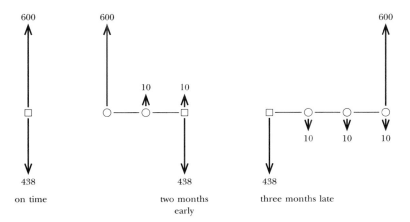

The best information available on completion times concluded that it was almost certain that plant completion would be not more than 16 months late or 2 months early, and that the most likely completion time would be 2 months late.

(a) Convert this information to an estimate of the expected net present worth of the power-plant project.
(b) Determine the expected completion time and determine the present worth if the project were certain to be completed at that time.
(c) Determine the present worth if the project were certain to be completed at the most likely completion time.

19. A $1000 payment will be received at an integer time "anywhere from time 6 to time 14." At $i = 20\%$, determine its expected present worth.

20. An estimated construction cost has an expected value of $2.114 million and a variance of 2.5×10^{11} $\$^2$. Is it almost sure that the construction cost will be (a) not greater than $3.7 million? (b) not less than $2 million? Explain.

21. An extremely major drought could cause permanent damage to an agribusiness's major asset—its land. The cost would be huge; the probability would depend on which of several water-resources investment alternatives was chosen. Which of the following two approaches would be used in analyzing the alternatives? (1) For each alternative, the expected-value estimate would include major drought as one of the possible outcomes, with a probability and cost. (2) Alternatives having too great a probability of permanent land damage from major drought would be rejected as too risky. Explain your choice by a quote or reference from Section 8.3.1.

22. Four statistically independent investments are undertaken, having the following expected values of present worth and standard deviations of present worth:

Independent Project	E(P)	σ_P
1	73.4	22.0
2	28.9	10.0
3	40.2	10.0
4	16.1	6.0

Determine the expected present worth of the portfolio of four independent projects, and determine the smallest anticipated contribution to the enterprise's wealth (that is, the anticipated minimum present worth).

23. Three independent risky projects are available for investment:

j	E(P_j)	Var(P_j)	
1	$40,000	100,000,000 $\$^2$	(σ_1 = $10,000)
2	$30,000	25,000,000 $\$^2$	(σ_2 = $5000)
3	$22,000	16,000,000 $\$^2$	(σ_3 = $4000)

This has been a conservative enterprise that usually confines itself to risk-free investments at MARR; investing in any risky projects would be unusual, and real harm might be done to the company's reputation (or so claim the managers, who may simply fear for their own careers) if a bold step were to lose money. Therefore, it is of interest to calculate which portfolio of risky projects (other than the do-nothing portfolio) is least likely to have a worth of zero or less. With a portfolio P, we need a statistic that indicates the probability of

$$\sum_{j \in P} P_j \leq 0$$

A useful such statistic is the z variate, which is the distance of a value from the expected value, measured in numbers of standard deviations:

$$z = \frac{0 - E\left(\sum P_j\right)}{\sqrt{\mathrm{Var}\left(\sum P_j\right)}}$$

(a) As z gets more negative, there is less probability of losing money. Therefore the problem reduces to finding the portfolio that maximizes the absolute value of z. What is this "safest" portfolio, and what is its $|z|$?
(b) Ignoring the managers' concerns about risk, which portfolio would you recommend, and why?
(c) Giving full consideration to the managers' concerns about risk, which portfolio would you recommend, and why?

24. Portfolio **A** has six independent risky projects, each with an expected present worth of 2.1 and a standard deviation 3.0. Portfolio **B** is a single "safe" project with an expected present worth of 8 and a standard deviation 1.0. Which portfolio has the greater risk of losing money?

25. Portfolio **A** has six independent risky projects, each with an expected present worth of 13.4 and standard deviation 4.1. Portfolio **B** is a single "safe" project with an expected present worth of 45.0 and a standard deviation σ_B perceived as small. How large can σ_B be if **B** remains safer from losing money than **A**?

26. A project has the following estimated cash flows in thousands of indexed dollars:

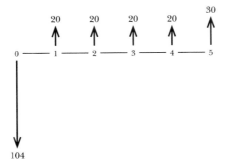

However, it is realized that the cash flows at times 4 and 5 are hoped-for cash flows; there is a 0.04 probability they will not occur. Determine the expected present worth at 10% real interest.

27. In Example E26, a lender lends $1000 and receives 18 monthly repayments. The rate of return would have been 0.945% monthly if the repayments had their

hoped-for value of $60.68, but due to risk the repayments have an expected value $60.61932. Determine the rate of return corresponding to their expected value.

28. A $1000 investment is hoped to yield perpetual returns of $180 (indexed) at the end of each year. At $d = 17\%$, determine the hoped-for present worth; the expected present worth if there is an annual geometric risk of $q = 0.01$; and the greatest annual geometric risk for which the project remains profitable.

29. Recall Example E40 of Chapter 5. The owner of the historic building that houses the San Mateo Gallery must paint the building with one of the following paints:

Paint Type	Coverage (sq ft/gal)	Paint cost (per gal)	Labor cost (per sq ft)	Estimated life (yr)
L: latex	625	$15.00	$0.11	4
O: oil	550	$33.00	$0.12	7

With a real interest rate $d = 10\%$, assuming that estimated lives are exact but that the horizon is vague, the oil paint is more economical. By the annual equivalent method, if f is a substitute interest rate, the oil paint is more economical when its annual equivalent cost is less than that of the latex paint:

Choose oil when

$$18.00(A/P\,f,\,7) < 13.40(A/P\,f,\,4)$$

If there is an annual geometric risk q that the Gallery will be sold or destroyed, f is greater than 10%. Given that $f = 24.5231525\%$ is the critical substitute interest rate that makes both annual equivalent costs equal, determine the annual risk q such that latex paint and oil paint are equally economical; also determine the corresponding expected life of the Gallery.

30. A fleet of delivery trucks distributes frozen food from a depot that is estimated to become inadequate for sales volume in five more years. A revamp project to improve loading facilities at the depot would cost $28,400 and would save $7750 per year (indexed). The real interest rate is 11%.
    (a) If the depot is to be abandoned in exactly five years, is the revamp project worthwhile?
    (b) If the depot is under annual geometric risk of abandonment such that its expected remaining life is five years, is the revamp project worthwhile?
    (c) For what geometrically distributed expected life L would the revamp project have the same expected worth as its worth for exactly a five-year life?

31. It can be shown that if a cash-flow set begins with an investment, continues with an equal-payment series, and ends with a salvage value equal to the investment, its rate of return is just the equal-payment amount divided by the investment. If we have hoped-for returns of H dollars per year for n years, for an investment of I dollars, with a hoped-for salvage value of the same amount at time n, the corresponding result is obtained:

$$E(P) = -I + \frac{H(1 - \phi^n)}{f + I\phi^n}$$

$$= (1 - \phi)^n \left(\frac{H}{f - I} \right)$$

Hence the rate of return in f terms is $f^* = H/I$.

An investment of \$100,000 in an art object allows a museum to earn a net of \$30,000 per year from lending it out. But there is a geometric risk of its falling out of fashion. If it does not fall out of fashion, it will continue earning at the same rate and can be sold for its original price plus inflation; otherwise the museum is stuck with a worthless object.

(a) Determine the rate of return in f terms.
(b) If $d = 10\%$, determine the greatest annual geometric risk q, and the corresponding life L, such that the art object is a good investment for the museum.
(c) A similar art object but with a more certain life can be purchased by the same museum for the same price, will bring in the same returns, and will suddenly becomes worthless at the end of five years. Determine the present worth of acquiring this object.
(d) Based on the above results, which is better: an investment that yields returns for exactly five years, or one that yields returns for a geometrically distributed life with an expected value of five years?

32. Example E27 showed that a bank that expects to earn nominal 11.5% interest should charge nominal 13.927855% interest to offset a $q = 0.002$ monthly geometric risk of default. This was illustrated using a three-month \$1000 loan. A risk-free loan at 11.5% interest would have the following amortization schedule:

Month	Balance	Interest	Payment
0	0	—	−1000
1	1000	9.58	339.74
2	669.84	6.42	339.74
3	336.52	3.22	339.74
Ending	0		

Prepare an expected amortization schedule for the risky loan whose hoped-for payments are \$341.10 per month. Show the expected balance, the expected interest, and the expected payment (recall that the expected payment at time t is p^t times the hoped-for payment). Verify that the expected balance ends at zero except for roundoff error.

33. If an asset earns A indexed dollars (at the end of) each period it survives, and its probability of survival each period is p, then the expected present worth of its earnings until failure can be shown to be

$$\frac{A\beta p}{1 - \beta p}$$

where $d = (1/\beta) - 1$ is the real interest rate per period.

(a) Show that when there is no survival risk the formula reduces to the appropriate formula. (State why it is appropriate.)

(b) When $A = 1$ (so that dollars count periods) and $\beta = 1$ (zero interest), the expected present worth of earnings until failure becomes the expected value of what?

(c) A conveyor system has a 0.025 risk of failure each week. How many weeks is it expected to last until failure?

(d) If the company's weekly real rate of return is $d = 0.004$, and the conveyor system earns \$200 per week, what is the present worth of the conveyor system's expected earnings until failure?

If the conveyor system is overhauled upon each failure and immediately returned to service, and the overhaul cost is K, it can be shown that the expected weekly net earnings are

$$\frac{\beta(1 - \beta)(pA - qK)}{1 - \beta p - \beta^2 q}$$

where $q \equiv 1 - p$.

(e) Determine the expected net weekly earnings for the conveyor system if each overhaul costs \$2000.

(f) A more expensive overhaul costing \$2400 would reduce the weekly risk of failure to 0.02. Would this be worthwhile?

34. An oil field's production is declining 4.5% per year. Revenues for the year just ended were 39.7 K\$. We use $i = 22\%$ and expect 4% annual inflation. Oil fields like this one run a 5% risk each year of going permanently dry. Determine the expected present worth of the next 10 years of revenue.

35. A geometric delay is 0 time periods with probability q, 1 time period with probability pq (where $p = 1 - q$), 2 time periods with probability $p^2 q$, and so forth. Verify that the sum of the probabilities of all these mutually exclusive delay times is one.

36. Verify that the first form of geometric delay correction factor from Eq. 8-14 can be expressed in terms of the expected delay $E(t)$ in these two forms:

$$\frac{1}{1 + E(t) - \beta E(t)} = \frac{1 + i}{1 + i + iE(t)}$$

37. The Flower Corps scheduled the completion of a major construction job for January 1994. Time zero, the start date, was scheduled for July 1993. It was felt that this kind of job would have a geometric delay, with the expected delay being 11 months. The completion date triggers the final receipt, which for this job was estimated as \$2.1 million. MARR is $i = 15\%$.

(a) Determine the expected worth (as of the start date) of the final receipt.

(b) Compare the expected worth to the approximation that would have been obtained by letting the delay be exactly its expected value of 11 months.

38. A company whose MARR is 21% has a chance to buy another company's accounts receivable. Their amount (after correction for risks) is \$744,000. The receivables consist mostly of due notes, with some 30-day and 60-day paper. Determine the expected present worth, assuming the further delay is geometrically distributed with an expected value of 40 days.

39. In Example E37, an annual 0.5 risk is run of not achieving a maintenance success valued at $3 million.
    (a) If we count the maintenance shutdown at time zero, how many shutdowns are expected to occur until the maintenance success is achieved?
    (b) If the delay were exactly the expected delay, what would be the present worth of the $3 million savings? Compare this to the result in Example E37.
    (c) The permanent extension of shutdown intervals from 1 year to 1.5 years was valued at $3 million. Assume future shutdown costs would grow with inflation, so that the interest rate is a d rate, $\beta = 1/(1 + d)$, and $3 million is an indexed-dollar value. Let the cost of a maintenance shutdown, in millions of indexed dollars, be X. The permanent extension, when it occurs, allows the **B** stream of costs to replace the **A** stream:

A

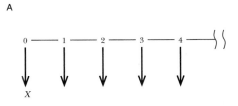

B

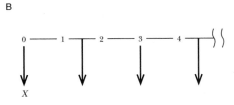

Assuming an infinite horizon, estimate X.

The laws of probability will not be denied.

PROBABILISTIC DECISION MAKING

This chapter applies some topics in probability and statistics that have direct relevance to engineering economy. The reader of this chapter is assumed to have a probability background equivalent to one course in the subject. To avoid conflict with the notation for present worth we will use $\Pi(\text{event})$ to denote the probability of an event; for example, in Eq. 9-1 the probability that an outcome x is between a and b will be denoted $\Pi(a < x \le b)$. We will use $E(X)$ or $E(x)$ to denote the expected value of the random variable whose name is X or whose value is x; for example, in Eq. 9-2 the expected value of the function g of the random variable X will be denoted $E(g(X))$.

A discrete random variable X has a discrete set of possible values $x_1, x_2, \ldots$. The set can be finite or infinite. A discrete random variable has a *probability mass function*, which is a list that assigns probabilities $p_1, p_2, \ldots$ to each of the values $x_1, x_2, \ldots$, or it is a formula that assigns a probability $p(x_m)$ to each value x_m. The probabilities sum to one.

A continuous random variable X has a continuum of possible values denoted simply by the symbol x. (See Figure 9-1.) The probability that the value of X falls in the infinitesimal range from x to dx is $f(x)\,dx$, where $f(x)$ is the *probability density function*, defined such that

$$\Pi(a < x \le b) = \int_a^b f(x)\ dx \qquad (9\text{-}1a)$$

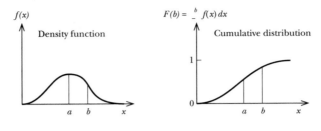

$$\Pi(a < xb) = \int_a^b f(x)dx = F(b) - F(a)$$

FIGURE 9-1. Density and cumulative distribution functions.

The probability that a random variable X does not exceed a given value b is called its *cumulative distribution function $F_x(b)$*:

$$F_x(b) = \Pi(X \le b) = \int_{-\infty}^{b} f(x)\ dx \qquad (9\text{-}1b)$$

The *expected-value theorem* states that the expected value of a *function* of a random variable is obtained by multiplying the probability of each possible value of the *random variable* by the corresponding value of the *function*, and summing the results. If X is a random variable taking on possible values x_1, x_2, and so on, with probabilities p_1, p_2, and so on, and $g(X)$ is any real-valued function of X, then we have

---

Expected value theorem:
. . . .
$$E(g(X)) = p_1 g(x_1) + p_2 g(x_2) + \cdots \qquad (9\text{-}2)$$

This is a straightforward extension of Eq. 8-5, since the probabilities of x_1, x_2, and so on, are the probabilities of the resulting $g(g_1)$, $g(x_2)$, and so on, except that more than one value of X may lead to a single value of $g(X)$; when this duplication occurs, summing the appropriate terms in Eq. 9-1 leads to Eq. 8-5 where the probability distribution is that of the function itself.

Given a continuous density function $f(x)$, the expected value of x is defined as

$$E(x) = \int_{-\infty}^{\infty} xf(x)\ dx \qquad (9\text{-}3a)$$

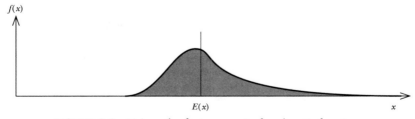

FIGURE 9-2. $E(x)$ as the first moment of a density function.

$E(x)$ is called the "first moment" of x; see Figure 9-2. From the expected-value theorem, if $g(x)$ is a function of x, the expected value of $g(x)$ is

$$E[g(x)] = \int_{-\infty}^{\infty} g(x) f(x) \, dx \tag{9-3b}$$

9.1   RANDOM TIMING OF CASH FLOWS

If a payment of X dollars occurs at a random time t, the expected present worth is

---

Expected present worth of a randomly-timed lump-sum payment:

$$E(P) = E(X\beta^t) = E(Xe^{-rt}) \tag{9-4}$$

---

where $\beta = 1/(1 + i)$ and r is the nominal continuous interest rate $r = \ln(1 + i)$. If X is deterministic, the right-hand side is $XE(e^{-rt})$. If X is random and independent of t, the right-hand side is $E(X) \times E(e^{-rt})$. If X is a function of t, the right-hand side $E(Xe^{-rt})$ can be determined, but if X is random and not independent of t, $E(P)$ cannot be determined without information on the correlation between X and t.

The expected value of the discount factor, $E(\beta^t) = E(e^{-rt})$, is the key quantity in two of the mentioned cases. For almost any possible probability distribution of t, continuous or discrete, the formula for $E(e^{-rt})$ can be easily obtained from the distribution's tabulated formula for its *moment generating function*, which is $E(e^{\phi t})$, or its *characteristic function*, which is $E(e^{\iota\phi t})$ where ι is $\sqrt{-1}$ (usually called i), or its *Laplace transform*, which is $E(e^{-st})$; simply substitute r for $-\phi$ or for $-\iota\phi$ or for s. Let us derive $E(e^{-rt})$ for some of the more important cases rather than just copy the formula.

9.1.1   Expected Discount Factor for Uniform Discrete Timing

Let X be paid at a time that is equally likely to be any integer time from 1 to n. That is, t is a random variable with probability mass function

$$p(t) = \begin{cases} \dfrac{1}{n} & \text{for} \quad t \in \{1,\ldots,n\} \\ 0 & \text{otherwise} \end{cases} \tag{9-5}$$

From the expected-value theorem (Eq. 9-1), we have

$$E(e^{-rt}) = E(\beta^t) = \frac{1}{n}\beta^1 + \frac{1}{n}\beta^2 + \cdots + \frac{1}{n}\beta^n$$

$$= \frac{1}{n}(\beta + \beta^2 + \cdots + \beta^n) = \frac{1}{n}(P/A \ i,n) \tag{9-6}$$

Thus if the payment amount X is deterministic, or independent of t,

$$E(P) = \frac{X}{n}(P/A \ i,n) \tag{9-7}$$

Note that if the payment X were replaced by n payments of X/n dollars each, the worth would be the same as this expected worth! Thus, for example, an expected-value decision maker would be indifferent to the difference between receiving a total of $1000 in n equal installments or receiving a lump-sum of $1000 at a time equally likely to be any of times 1, 2,..., or n. For any time interval and any interest rate, *the expected worth of a payment is the same whether the payment itself or its timing probability is uniformly spread over the interval.*

E1. After extensive information gathering, there are still some important facts Tex Arkin will simply not know in evaluating an operating oilfield for possible purchase. For example, although he knows that about $1.5 million in renovations (indexed dollars) will be due sometime within the next eight years, he has no idea when. With $d = 0.13$, determine the appropriate amount by which these renovations should decrement the value of the oilfield.

The uniform discrete timing distribution is appropriate for "no idea when." Eq. 9-7 is valid for indexed amounts when $i \to d$. For $X = \$1.5$ million, $n = 8$ years, and $d = 0.13$, the expected reduction in value is the expected present worth of the renovation cost:

$$E(P) = (1.5/8)(P/A \ 13\%,8) = \underline{\$0.89976943 \text{ million}}$$

For uniform discrete timing where the set of times is not 1 to n, let the possible times be $t = a$, $t = a+1$,..., $t = b$. The number of payments is $n = b - a + 1$, and Eq. 9-7 gives the worth at time $a - 1$, which can be multiplied by β^{a-1} to obtain the present worth.

E2. A pulpwood crop will be sold for $34,000 (indexed) whenever the land is required to be cleared for a planned highway. That time is estimated to be from three to seven years away. Assuming a uniform timing distribution and the end-of-year (eoy) convention, determine the expected present worth of the crop at 10% (real) interest.

There are $n = 7 - 3 + 1 = 5$ possible times. From Eq. 9-7, multiplied by $\beta^{3-1} = \beta^2$, where $\beta = 1/1.10$, the expected present worth is

$$\beta^2(34000/5)(P/A \ 10\%,5) = \underline{\$21,303.60}$$

9.1.2 Expected Discount Factor for Geometric Timing (Geometric Delay)

Let X be paid at a time t that has the *geometric distribution* (see Figure 9-3)

Probability mass function for geometric distribution:

$$p(t) = p^t q \qquad t = 0, 1, 2, \ldots \tag{9-8}$$

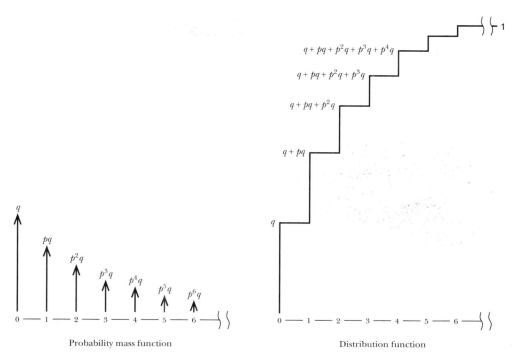

FIGURE 9-3. Geometric probability mass and distribution functions.

where p is the "continuation probability," $q = 1 - p$, and the expected time of payment is $E(t) = p/q$. The expected discount factor has already been developed as the *geometric delay correction factor* of Eq. 8-14 in Section 8.5.

9.1.3 Expected Discount Factor for Continuous Timing Distributions

Let X be paid at a time t that is distributed uniformly over the continuous interval 1 to n. The uniform continuous distribution over this interval has the probability density function

---

Probability density for $(0, n)$ uniform continuous timing:
....

$$f(t) = \begin{cases} \dfrac{1}{n} & \text{for} \quad 0 < t \le n \\[2mm] 0 & \text{otherwise} \end{cases} \tag{9-9}$$

Since the probability that the payment occurs in the infinitesimal interval from time t to $t + dt$ is $(1/n)\,dt$, and its present worth if paid at that time is Xe^{-rt}, the expected present worth is, by the expected-value theorem:

Expected present worth for $(0, n)$ uniform continuous timing:

$$E(P) = \int_0^n Xe^{-rt}\left(\frac{1}{n}\right) dt = X\left(\frac{1 - e^{-rn}}{rn}\right) \tag{9-10}$$

Thus the expected discount factor is $1/n$ of the "parn" factor, and the expected present worth is the same as the present worth would be if the payment itself were uniformly paid at continuous rate X/n throughout the interval.

More generally, let the timing be distributed uniformly in the continuous interval a to b. Then $f(t) = 1/(b - a)$ in the interval. The moment-generating function of this distribution is known to be

Moment-generating function for (a, b) uniform continuous distribution:

$$E(e^{\phi t}) = \frac{e^{\phi b} - e^{\phi a}}{\phi(b - a)} \tag{9-11}$$

Hence we can write the expected discount factor directly by letting $\phi \to -r$.

Expected discount factor for (a, b) uniform continuous timing:

$$E(e^{-rt}) = \frac{e^{-ra} - e^{-rb}}{r(b - a)} = \frac{\beta^a - \beta^b}{r(b - a)} \tag{9-12}$$

E3. In the previous example, the timing of the pulpwood crop sale was estimated according to the eoy convention. Making the corresponding estimate according to the continuous timing convention, determine the expected present worth.

The earliest eoy time was three years, which would apply to cash flows in the interval $(2, 3)$. Thus the continuous interval (a, b) is from $a - 2$ years to $b = 7$ years. The (real) nominal continuous interest rate is $r = \ln 1.10$. From Eq. 9-17, with $\beta = e^{-r} = 1/1.10$, the expected discount factor is

$$E(e^{-rt}) = \frac{\beta^2 - \beta^7}{r(7 - 2)} = 0.657407558$$

The expected worth of the $34,000 (indexed) payment is

$$34000E(e^{-rt}) = \underline{\$22,351.86}$$

This exceeds the previous result by the ratio of the discrete to continuous interest rates, as is usual when worths under the eoy and continuous timing conventions are compared.

The continuous analogue of the geometric timing or geometric delay distribution is the *exponential distribution*, often called the negative exponential distribution, which has the probability density function (see Figure 9-4).

Probability density for exponential timing:

$$f(t) = \begin{cases} \dfrac{1}{\theta} e^{-t/\theta} & t > 0 \\[2ex] 0 & \text{otherwise} \end{cases} \tag{9-13}$$

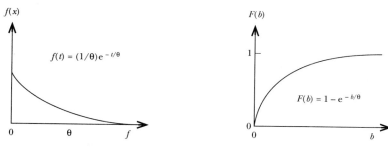

FIGURE 9-4. Exponential density and distribution function.

where the parameter θ is the expected value of t: $E(t) = \theta$. The moment generating function is known to be

Moment generating function for exponential distribution:

$$E(e^{\phi t}) = \frac{1}{1 - \phi\theta} \tag{9-14}$$

Hence we can write the expected discount factor directly by letting $\phi \to -r$.

Expected discount factor for exponential timing:

$$E(e^{-rt}) = \frac{1}{1 + r\theta} \tag{9-15}$$

E4. The delay until receipt of a $1000 payment has been treated deterministically as $n = 5$ years. Actually, the delay has an exponential distribution with a mean of five years. At $i = 15\%$, how much did the deterministic treatment underestimate the expected present worth of the payment?

At $\theta = 5$ and $r = \ln 1.15$, Eq. 9-14 gives

$$E(e^{-rt}) = \frac{1}{1 + r\theta} = 0.588647447$$

so $E(P) = 1000E(e^{-rt}) = \underline{\$588.65}$.

The deterministic treatment gave $1000(1/1.15)^5 = \underline{\$497.18}$, which is about a <u>15.5% underestimate</u>.

9.1.4 Expected Present Worth for Random Economic Life

If a constant continuous cash flow of $\overline{A}$ $/yr endures for t years, its present worth is $\overline{A}(1 - e^{-rt})/r$, as shown in Chapter 2. Now if t has a probability density function $f(t)$, the expected present worth is

$$E(P) = \int_0^\infty \overline{A}\left(\frac{1 - e^{-rt}}{r}\right)f(t) \ dt = \frac{\overline{A}}{r}\left[1 - \int_0^\infty e^{-rt}f(t) \ dt\right] \tag{9-16}$$

But the integral on the right is $E(e^{-rt})$.

Let the economic life t be exponentially distributed with expected life θ. Then, with $E(e^{-rt})$ from Eq. 9-14, the expected present worth becomes

---

Expected present worth of $\overline{A}$ \$/yr for exponential duration:

$$E(P) = \frac{\overline{A}}{r}\left[1 - \frac{1}{1 + r\theta}\right] = \overline{A}\left[\frac{1}{r + 1/\theta}\right] \tag{9-17}$$

E5. A reactor yields continuous annual profits of \$9471 (indexed). At 10% real interest, determine the expected present worth (a) if the reactor will last an expected seven years, exponentially distributed, and (b) if the reactor will last exactly seven years.

For $\overline{A} = 9471$, $r = \ln 1.10$, $\theta = 7$, Eq. 9-17 gives

$$E(P) = 9471\left[\frac{1}{r + 1/7}\right] = \underline{\underline{\$39,766.16}}$$

If the reactor lasts exactly 7 years,

$$P = 9471\left(\frac{1 - \beta^7}{r}\right) = \underline{\underline{\$48,377.62}}$$

The deterministic worth overestimates the expected worth by nearly 22%.

The example helps explain one of the main reasons why it is quite common to overestimate worths of investments. *If the economic life of an investment is exponentially distributed, its expected life gives a substantial overestimate of its profitability.*

9.1.5 Exponential Risk

We can generalize Eq. 9-16 quite readily to the continuous analogue of geometric risk. Recall Eq. 2-44 for the present worth of an arbitrary continuous cash-flow profile $F(t)$:

$$P = \int_0^\infty F(t)\,e^{-rt} \ dt \tag{9-18}$$

Now if there is an *exponential risk of cessation* of the cash-flow profile, such that the probability that $F(t)$ endures to at least time t is $e^{-t/\theta}$, then the expected infinitesimal payment in the interval t to $t + dt$ is not the hoped-for $F(t)\,dt$ but the expected $F(t)\,e^{-t/\theta}dt$. The sum of these expected infinitesimal payments (that is, the integral) is the expected present worth:

$$E(P) = \int_0^\infty F(t)\, e^{-rt} e^{-t/\theta}\, dt = \int_0^\infty F(t)\, e^{-(r+1/\theta)t}\, dt \qquad (9\text{-}19)$$

Comparing Eqs. 9-19 and 9-18 we see $r \to (r+1)/\theta$.

Now θ is the expected life of the cash-flow profile. Recall that $F(t)$ can represent any cash-flow set, with discrete elements expressed using the Dirac delta from Section 2.7.1. Exponential risk can be accounted for by replacing r by $r + 1/\theta$. This is valid whether the hoped-for cash flows are in *current dollars* with r representing the nominal continuous *real interest rate* $\ln(1 + d)$, or in indexed dollars with r representing the nominal continuous *market interest rate* $\ln(1 + i)$.

To account for an exponential risk of cessation, such that the expected cessation time is θ, discount the hoped-for cash flows using $r + 1/\theta$ instead of r, or $\beta e^{-1/\theta}$ instead of β.

Exponential risk applies to worth computations done using the continuous timing convention. For computations done using the eoy or end-of-period conventions, geometric risk from Chapter 8 is appropriate.

E6. In indexed dollars, the following are the hoped-for cash flows for a proposed project:

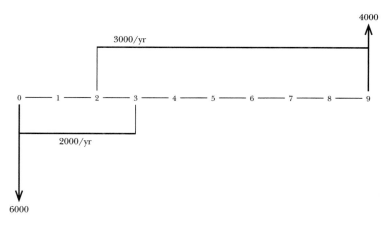

$$P = -6000 - 2000\left(\frac{1 - e^{-r3}}{r}\right) + e^{-r2}3000\left(\frac{1 - e^{-r7}}{r}\right) + 4000e^{-r9}$$

The enterprise uses a real interest rate of 10%, so $\beta = e^{-r} = 1/1.10$. At this interest rate the present worth of the hoped-for cash flows is $P = \$3142.35$. The project is part of a business activity that has an exponentially distributed life. If the expected life is $\theta = 20$ yr, what is the expected present worth of the project?

Replace r with $r + 1/\theta = \ln 1.10 + 1/20 = 0.14531018$. New $\beta = e^{-r+1/\theta} = 0.86475402$.

$E(P) = \underline{\$74.26}$, which is barely profitable.

9.1.6 Gamma-Distributed Life

Although the duration of a cash-flow set is seldom known exactly, it is not likely to be as extremely random as the exponential life distribution would imply. The gamma distribution provides the most practical treatment of uncertain economic life.

If the time to an event (such as cessation of a cash-flow set) is the time it takes for k successive "failures" or subevents to occur, and the time between successive subevents has the negative exponential distribution with mean θ, then the time to the event has the *gamma distribution* with mean $k\theta$ and variance $k\theta^2$. Most durations are those of a sequence of subprocesses. For example, for a bill to be paid, first the service or delivery of goods must occur, then the customer must be billed, then a bill-paying cycle must reach the proper point, then the payment must be mailed or delivered, and finally the payment must be received and posted. Although the various components of the total time are not all exponentially distributed and do not all have equal expected durations, the overall duration often has a sample distribution that can be fit fairly well by a gamma distribution. The parameter k need not be an integer in practice.

Consider a constant continuous cash-flow of A dollars per year for t years, where t is a random variable having the gamma distribution with mean $k\theta$ and variance $k\theta^2$. The moment-generating function for the gamma distribution is

Moment generating function for gamma distribution:

$$E(e^{\phi t}) = \left(\frac{1}{1 - \phi\theta}\right)^k \tag{9-20}$$

We write the expected discount factor directly by letting $\phi \rightarrow -r$.

Expected discount factor for gamma timing:

$$E(e^{-rt}) = \left(\frac{1}{1 + r\theta}\right)^k \tag{9-21}$$

From Eq. 9-16 we know the expected present worth of A dollars per year for t years is

Expected present worth of $\overline{A}$ \$/yr for gamma duration:

$$E(P) = \frac{\overline{A}}{r}[1 - E(e^{-rt})] = \frac{\overline{A}}{r}\left[1 - \left(\frac{1}{1 + r\theta}\right)^k\right] \tag{9-22}$$

E7. **A \$1000/yr continuous return is expected to have a gamma-distributed life with a mean of 7.2 years and a standard deviation of 1.4 years. Determine the expected present worth at 10% interest.**

The parameters of the gamma distribution are $k\theta = 7.2$ and $k\theta^2 = (1.4)^2 \Rightarrow 7.2\theta = 1.96 \Rightarrow \theta = 0.2722$ and $k = 26.44897959$. With these values, $r = \ln 1.1$, and $\overline{A} = 1000$, Eq. 9-22 gives

$$E(P) = \frac{1000}{r}\left[1 - \left(\frac{1}{1 + r\theta}\right)^k\right] = \underline{\underline{\$5328.86}}$$

9.2 MONTE CARLO SIMULATION OF PROJECT AND PORTFOLIO OUTCOMES

Given that cash-flow amounts and timings are random variables, the worth of a cash-flow set is a random variable. The most important thing to estimate about a worth is its expected value; additional information is gained from estimating its variance; and even more information is gained from estimating its entire probability distribution.

Given a worth formula, if we estimate the probability distributions of each parameter, and we assume independence or assume specific joint distributions, there follows a specific probability distribution of the worth. The expected worth can often be estimated readily; the variance is more difficult; and for practical cash-flow sets the only way to estimate the entire worth distribution is by *Monte Carlo simulation*, which samples the possible combinations of parameters in proportion to their probability of occurring.

The weaknesses of Monte Carlo simulation are that it requires a computer and that it does not provide an elegant, compact answer such as a formula, but rather gives tables and histograms. The strengths of Monte Carlo simulation are its great simplicity and the fact that its relatively heavy computation load, formerly burdensome for casual use, is easily handled by today's microcomputers.

9.2.1 Monte Carlo Sampling

Consider the following project:

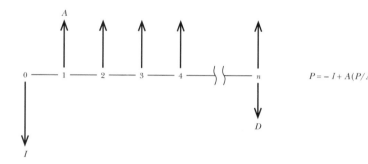

$$P = -I + A(P/A\ i,n) - D\beta^n$$

Let the interest rate be 10%, and let the investment I, the annual return A, the disposal cost D, and the economic life n have the following mutually independent probability mass functions:

I	$\Pi(I)$		A	$\Pi(A)$		D	$\Pi(D)$		n	$\Pi(n)$
3000	0.20		1000	0.75		300	0.90		4	0.60
4000	0.80		2000	0.20		3000	0.10		5	0.30
	1.00		3000	0.05			1.00		6	0.10
				1.00						1.00

In a single Monte Carlo experiment we observe a particular set of outcomes of all the parameters and compute the resulting worth. For example, one possibility is that the investment is $I = 4000$, the annual return is $A = 1000$, the disposal cost is $D = 300$, and the economic life is $n = 4$, giving a worth of -1035.04. This is a highly probable possibility, having a probability $0.80 \times 0.75 \times 0.90 \times 0.60 = 0.324$ of occurring. A second possibility, much less probable, is that the investment is $I = 3000$, the annual return is $A = 3000$, the disposal cost is $D = 3000$, and the economic life is $n = 6$, giving a worth of 8372.36. In Monte Carlo sampling we would run a moderate number of experiments, say 1000 of them. The sampling process should be such that in about 32.4% of the experiments the outcome would be the first possibility, because its probability of occurring is 32.4%, and the outcome would be the second possibility in about 0.01% of the experiments, because the probability of the second possibility is $0.20 \times 0.05 \times 0.10 \times 0.10 = 0.0001$ or 0.01%.

The Monte Carlo sampling process that satisfies these requirements is based on *random-generation* techniques described in the following sections. For each kind of probability distribution, there is a random-generation technique that guarantees that, in the long run, the possible values of the variable will be generated with frequencies reflecting their probabilities. In the current example, 20% of the experiments will have an investment of 3000, while the other 80% have an investment of 4000; 75% of the experiments will have an annual return of 1000, and so forth.

9.2.2 Random Generation

All modern random generation techniques are based on first generating one or more independent (0, 1) uniform variates u_1, u_2,..., which are outcomes of a random variable U whose density is $f(u) = 1$ on the interval 0 to 1, and whose cumulative distribution function is

$$\Pi(U \le u) = F_U(u) = \int_0^u 1 \, dx = u \tag{9-23}$$

Equation 9-23 says that the value of a (0, 1) uniform variate is equal to its probability of not being exceeded; 90% of these variates are at most 0.90, 30% of them are at most 0.30, and so forth. This is a very useful property.

9.2.2.1 Generation of (0, 1) Uniform Variates Another useful property of (0, 1) uniform variates is their ease of generation. The multiplicative congruential method built into most computer languages and scientific hand calculators multiplies a large *seed* number by a constant *multiplier*, discards the spillover bits to the left, and uses the result both to determine a u variate and to be the seed for the next variate. The process is deterministic and reproducible, but the sequence appears random to anyone lacking knowledge of the multiplier. The next seed appears equally likely to be any number from zero to the largest number the computer can store (the *modulus*). The variate is the current seed divided by the modulus.

E8. For a computer with 14-bit words, a seed of 3749, and a multiplier of 13947, generate three (0, 1) uniform pseudo-random variates by the multiplicative congruential method.

The modulus is $2^{14} = 16384$. We can multiply the seed by the multiplier and divide by the modulus:

$$3749 \times 13{,}947 = 52{,}287{,}303 \qquad 52{,}287{,}303/16{,}384 = 3191.363708$$

The integer part is what the computer would have spilled over, the fractional part is the new variate, and the new seed is the remainder. The remainder is an integer that the computer retains; we can recover its value by multiplying the new variate times the modulus. Thus the new variate is 0.363708 and the new seed is $0.363708 \times 16{,}384 = 5959$.

Next, $5959 \times 13{,}947 = 83{,}110{,}173$. $83{,}110{,}173/16{,}384 = 5072.642395$. The new variate is 0.642395 and the new seed is 10,525.

Again, $10{,}525 \times 13{,}947 = 146{,}792{,}175$. $146{,}792{,}175/16384 = 8959.483337$. The new variate is 0.483337 and the new seed is 7919.

Table 9-1 lists some (0, 1) uniform variates for use in examples to follow.

TABLE 9-1. Some (0, 1) Uniform Variates

0.4141	0.7459	0.3132	0.3093	0.7104	0.1777
0.3880	0.6232	0.1568	0.2303	0.2946	0.8759
0.6831	0.9711	0.7240	0.1995	0.5326	0.5646
0.4455	0.2379	0.4523	0.8297	0.0064	0.0078
0.0488	0.9880	0.9962	0.6504	0.5617	0.8615

9.2.2.2 Generation of Arbitrary Variates Given Eq. 9-23, if $F_X(x)$ is the cumulative distribution function for a random variable X, then x in $F_X(x) = u$ is the value of X whose cumulative probability is the same as that of u. For example, if an investment I is 3000 with probability 0.20 and is 4000 with probability 0.80, its cumulative distribution function is

$$F_I(x) = \begin{cases} 0 & x \le 3000 \\ 0.20 & 3000 < x \le 4000 \\ 1.00 & x < 4000 \end{cases}$$

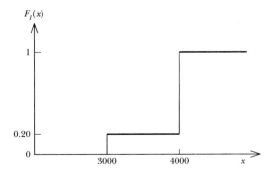

If we generate (0, 1) uniform variates u and let $u \le 0.20$ imply $x = 3000$ and $0.20 < u \le 1$ imply $x = 4000$, then we are guaranteed that 20% of the investment variates will be 3000 and 80% of them will be 4000, as required by their probability distribution.

E9. **Use the first row of Table 9-1 to generate six investment variates from the example project at the beginning of Section 9.2.1.**

$F_I(x)$ is as given above. $u \leq 0.20 \Rightarrow 3000$, otherwise 4000.

u:	0.4141	0.7459	0.3132	0.3093	0.7104	0.1777
x:	4000	4000	4000	4000	4000	3000

9.2.2.3 *Generation of Variates from Various Distributions* The *exponential distribution* has the cumulative distribution function as shown.

Cumulative distribution function for exponential distribution:

$$F_X(x) = 1 - e^{-x/\theta} \qquad x \geq 0 \tag{9-24}$$

Letting $F_X(x) = u$ and solving for x, we have

$$1 - e^{-x/\theta} = u \Rightarrow x = -\theta \ln(1 - u)$$

A nicety that can be applied here is that $1 - u$ is a $(0, 1)$ uniform variate just as u is; $1 - u$ has large values where u has small, and vice versa, so it is unnecessary to subtract u from 1. Thus we have the *formula for generation of exponential random variates:*

$$x = -\theta \ln u \tag{9-25}$$

E10. **An exponential variable has an expected value of 6.1. Using $(0, 1)$ uniform variates of 0.05, 0.50, and 0.95, generate three variates.**

$$x_1 = -6.1 \ln 0.05 = 18.274$$
$$x_2 = -6.1 \ln 0.50 = 4.228$$
$$x_3 = -6.1 \ln 0.95 = 0.313$$

(Note that small u causes large x, and vice versa, due to the reversal of $1 - u$ to u.)

The *gamma distribution*, when k is an integer (called the Erlang distribution), is the distribution of the sum of k exponential variables each having expected value θ. Thus we can generate a gamma variate by summing k exponential variates.

Generation of gamma variates having integer k, mean $k\theta$, variance $k\theta^2$:

$$x = \sum_{m=1}^{k} -\theta \ln u = -\theta \ln(u_1 \times u_2 \times \cdots \times u_k) \tag{9-26}$$

E11. **A cost is estimated to be a gamma-distributed random variable with a mean of 1.824 and a standard deviation of 0.912. Using the rightmost column of Table 9-1 as a source of $(0, 1)$ uniform variates, generate a variate from this distribution.**

$$k\theta = 1.824 \text{ and } k\theta^2 = (0.912)^2 \quad \text{implies } k = 4, \ \theta = 0.456$$
$$x = -\theta \ln(0.1777 \times 0.8759 \times 0.5646 \times 0.0078) = \underline{3.322}$$

The gamma distribution is able to give an accurate representation of the distributions of most kinds of delays or durations. For delays *past a scheduled time*, where occurrence is unlikely or impossible before the scheduled time, a useful random variable is the *offset exponential*, where the time is a constant c plus an exponential variable: $t = c + x$ where x is exponential. For cash-flow amounts, the *normal distribution* is widely used.

Statistics packages, some spreadsheet packages, simulation languages, and mathematics function libraries (e.g., IMSL) offer built-in random-variable generators for various distributions, usually including the normal distribution, the gamma distribution (including noninteger k), the Weibull distribution, the beta distribution, and others. The theory behind each kind of generator is explained in simulation textbooks such as *Simulation Modeling and Analysis* by Law and Kelton (McGraw-Hill).

9.2.3 Simulation Process

Let us simulate the worth of the project described at the beginning of Section 9.2.1. In simulating the worth of a cash-flow set, each *simulation experiment* consists of generating a random variate for each of the variable parameters and determining the resulting worth. This is one sample of the worth; further experiments give further independent samples, and a *run* of a sufficiently large number of experiments provides enough samples to estimate the distribution of the worth to whatever accuracy is required.

E12. Recall the project described at the beginning of Section 9.2.1. Using variates from Table 9-1 in row-wise order from the upper left, perform two Monte Carlo experiments.

The cumulative distributions for the project's parameters are:

I	$F_I(x)$	A	$F_A(x)$	D	$F_D(x)$	n	$F_n(x)$
3000	0.20	1000	0.75	300	0.90	4	0.60
4000	1.00	2000	0.95	3000	1.00	5	0.90
		3000	1.00			6	1.00

The interest rate is 10%. $\beta = 1/1.10$. Variates will be generated as in Section 9.2.2.2, and worth will be computed as

$$P = -I + A(P/A\ 10\%,n) - D\beta^n$$

First experiment:

$$
\begin{array}{cccccccc}
u & \Rightarrow & I & u & \Rightarrow & A & u & \Rightarrow & D & u & \Rightarrow & n \\
0.4141 & & \underline{4000} & 0.7459 & & \underline{1000} & 0.3132 & & \underline{300} & 0.3093 & & \underline{4}
\end{array}
$$

$$P = -4000 + 1000(P/A\ 10\%,4) - 300\beta^4 = \underline{-1035.04}$$

Second experiment:

$$u \Rightarrow I \qquad u \Rightarrow A \qquad u \Rightarrow D \qquad u \Rightarrow n$$
$$0.7104 \quad \underline{4000} \quad 0.1777 \quad \underline{1000} \quad 0.3880 \quad \underline{300} \quad 0.6232 \quad \underline{5}$$

$$P = -4000 + 1000(P/A \ 10\%,5) - 300\beta^5 = \underline{\underline{-395.49}}$$

Each experiment corresponds to one implementation of the project. To have much confidence in the results, it would be necessary to run a few hundred or a few thousand experiments. When this is done, the following results will be obtained:

· $E(P) \cong 345$. On the average, the project is slightly profitable.
· The standard deviation of P is about 2129.
· $\Pi(P < 0) \cong 0.642$. The outcome is negative more often than not.
· Maximum P is 9896.44, which occurs with probability 0.0009.
· Minimum P is -2879.17, which occurs with probability 0.0360.
· Most likely P is -1035.04, which occurs with probability 0.324.

How many experiments are enough? The variance of the difference between the true mean $E(P)$ and the simulated mean $\hat{E}(P)$ is approximately $\hat{\sigma}^2/M$ where $\hat{\sigma}^2$ is the simulated variance and M is the number of experiments. Thus the error due to too few experiments is almost sure to be in the 3-sigma interval

$$[\text{3-sigma error interval}] = \pm 3\sqrt{\hat{\sigma}^2/M} \qquad (9\text{-}27)$$

If important rare events are included in the possibilities, the simulation run should either be known to include them, or M should be great enough that the expected number of inclusions for the rarest one would be at least 3; if π_r is the probability of a rare event, $3/\pi_r$ is the corresponding minimum M.

Suppose, for example, $M = 1000$ experiments had been run, giving $\hat{E}(P) = 340$ and $\hat{\sigma}^2 = 4,600,115 \Rightarrow \hat{\sigma} = 2144.79$. From Eq. 9-27, the error should be no more than about

$$\pm 3\sqrt{4,600,115/1000} \cong 203$$

There are no important rare events in the example project (the rarest thing in the data is the 3000 value of A, which occurs about once in $1/0.05 = 20$ experiments). Hence $M = 1000$ passes both tests for being enough, unless an answer of 340 ± 203 is not close enough to support the required decision.

E13. A construction project has three parallel tasks and is complete when all four tasks are complete. Each task has an exponentially distributed duration with a mean of six months. The construction cost is \$4000 per month for each task, and the worth of the future returns from the completed project at its completion time is \$82,000. At 5% monthly interest, conduct two Monte Carlo experiments of the net present worth.

Let n_1, n_2, and n_3 represent the task completion times, and let $n = \max(n_1, n_2, n_3)$ represent the project completion time. For $\beta = 1/1.05$, $r = \ln 1.05$, with the continuous-timing convention the cash-flow diagram is, for one possible out-come:

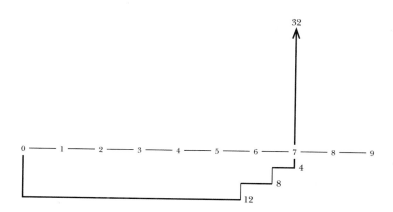

$$P = -4\left(\frac{1 - \beta^{n_1}}{r}\right) - 4\left(\frac{1 - \beta^{n_2}}{r}\right) - 4\left(\frac{1 - \beta^{n_3}}{r}\right) + 82\beta^n$$

As a source of $(0, 1)$ uniform variates, let us use the fourth row of Table 9-1, which gives the variates 0.4455, 0.2379, 0.4523, 0.8297, 0.0064, 0.0078.

First experiment:

$$u = 0.4455 \Rightarrow n_1 = -6 \ln u = 4.851348193$$

$$u = 0.2379 \Rightarrow n_2 = -6 \ln u = 8.615429172$$

$$u = 0.4523 \Rightarrow n_3 = -6 \ln u = 4.748530499$$

$$n = \max(n_1, n_2, n_3) = n_2.$$

$$P = -4\left(\frac{1 - \beta^{n_1}}{r}\right) - 4\left(\frac{1 - \beta^{n_2}}{r}\right) - 4\left(\frac{1 - \beta^{n_3}}{r}\right) + 82\beta^n = \underline{-\$8510.35}$$

Second experiment:

$$u = 0.8297 \Rightarrow n_1 = -6 \ln u = 1.120146536$$

$$u = 0.0064 \Rightarrow n_2 = -6 \ln u = 30.30874373$$

$$u = 0.0078 \Rightarrow n_3 = -6 \ln u = 29.12178927$$

$$n = \max(n_1, n_2, n_3) = n_2$$

$$P = -4\left(\frac{1 - \beta^{n_1}}{r}\right) - 4\left(\frac{1 - \beta^{n_2}}{r}\right) - 4\left(\frac{1 - \beta^{n_3}}{r}\right) + 82\beta^n = \underline{-\$111,153.30}$$

This example shows how simulation can handle a situation where deterministic calculations or even expected-value calculations would be almost meaningless because of the nonlinear dependence of the project completion time on the task durations. It also illustrates the use of a very high interest rate, such as could be used if there were a geometric risk of abandonment (but it would probably be better practice to simulate the abandonment rather than handle it thus). Finally, the example illustrates the use of an exponential distribution of a duration, such as could be used for tasks that essentially consist of a series of stabs at completion; tasks that behave this way include the startup of a new steel mill or oil refinery, or the first flight of a new spacecraft.

9.3 DECISION TREE ANALYSIS

In dealing with decision trees and Markov chains, we will assume that all cash flows are in indexed dollars, and $\beta = 1/(1 + d)$ will be the only measure of the time value of money. The symbols i and j will be used not to indicate interest rates, but as labels for states of a system.

9.3.1 States, Transitions, Rewards, Values

Let a system be in *state i* at time t. After dwelling in state i for a duration t_{ij}, it makes a transition to some state j at time $t + t_{ij}$. The probability that the system is in state i at time t is denoted $\pi_i(t)$, or simply π_i when the timing need not be noted. Of course the system is in *some* state at time t, so these *state probabilities* sum to 1:

$$\sum_i \pi_i(t) = 1 \tag{9-28}$$

Given that the system is in state i at time t, the conditional probability of its state's being j at the next epoch is denoted p_{ij}. Of course the system goes to *some* state, so these *transition probabilities* sum to 1:

$$\sum_j pij = 1 \tag{9-29}$$

Figure 9-5 shows how states and transitions can be depicted as a network whose nodes represent states and whose arcs represent transitions. Associated with each arc is not only the conditional probability of the transition it represents, and its dwell duration, but also a *transition reward* c_{ij}, which represents the expected value of a cash flow considered to occur (in accordance with the end-of-period convention) at the end of the swell duration t_{ij}. Associated with each node is a *state value* V_j, which is the expected worth of all transition rewards to be collected in the *future* (it excludes c_{ij}); V_j is the expected worth, at the beginning of the dwell duration t_{jk}, of whatever reward will be collected at the end of t_{jk}, and further rewards.

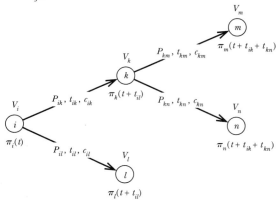

FIGURE 9-5. State transition tree.

All transition probabilities are assumed to be independent. When the state transitions form a tree, so that each state has only one possible preceding state, each state probability is related very simply to the preceding one:

$$\pi_j = \pi_i p_{ij} \tag{9-30}$$

As a consequence, the probability that a particular state occurs at its appropriate time is straightforward to compute.

E14. In studying policies for starting up a large process furnace, the following state transition tree was prepared and labeled with state probabilities and transition probabilities:

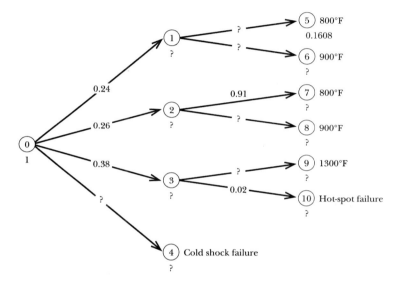

Supply the state and transition probabilities marked "?".

Applying Eqs. 9-28, 9-29, and 9-30:

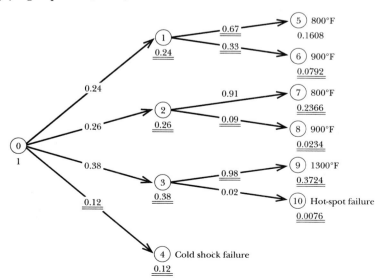

Given that the state is a particular state i at time t, and that there are several possible states j to which it may transit, then at time $t + t_{ij}$ two financial consequences occur: A transition reward having expected value c_{ij} is collected, and the future prospects are those indicated by V_j. The expected value of the transition reward is the sum, over all possible next states j, of the products $p_{ij}c_{ij}$ (by the definition of expected value). The expected value of the new future prospects, similarly, is the sum over j of $p_{ij}V_j$. Discounting both these consequences for the delay of t_i, we can compute V_i:

$$V_i = \sum_j p_{ij}c_{ij}\beta^{t_i} + \sum_j p_{ij}V_j\beta^{t_{ij}}$$

$$= \sum_j p_{ij}(c_{ij} + V_j)\beta^{t_{ij}} \tag{9-31}$$

In many cases (including Markov-chain analysis in Section 9.4 below) it is convenient to make two traditional simplifications. First, the dwell durations are traditionally all one period long, so that the discount factor across a transition is simply β. Second, the expected worth of the transition rewards is traditionally replaced by the *immediate expected reward* r_i:

$$r_i = \beta\sum_j p_{ij}c_{ij} \tag{9-32}$$

With these simplifications the traditional *state value equation* is

$$V_i = r_i + \beta\sum_j p_{ij}V_j \tag{9-33}$$

For decision trees we use Eq. 9-31 if time spans are long, and Eq. 9-33 with $\beta = 1$ if time spans are short.

9.3.2 Decision Trees with Discounting

A *decision tree* is any state transition tree for which it is possible to influence one or more of the transition probabilities.

As a first example of a decision tree, let us add some decision making to Example E14. Suppose the tree as given represents the usual policy for starting up the furnace, and that a failure (of either kind) incurs an expected cost of $17,000, while success of any kind is worth $5000. Since a furnace startup takes at most two days, we will ignore time (let $\beta = 1$). Labeling arcs with transition probabilities and costs, consolidating the irrelevant success portions of the tree, and labeling worths on final nodes, we have the state transition tree shown at the top of the next page.

The state values shown in italics are computed by a "foldback" procedure: at state 3, the immediate reward (from Eq. 9-32) is $r_3 = 0.98 \times 0 + 0.02 \times (-17,000) = -\$340$, and the state value (from Eq. 9-33) is $V_3 = r_3 + [0.98 \times 5000 + 0.02 \times 0] = \$4560$. Given this, we have the data to compute V_0. $r_0 = 0.50 \times 0 + 0.38 \times 0 + 0.12 \times (-17,000) = -\$2040$ and $V_1 = -2040 + [0.50 \times 5000 + 0.38 \times 4560 + 0.12 \times 0] =$

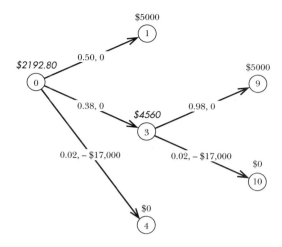

$2192.80. Now let us analyze other policies by turning this state transition tree into a decision tree.

E15. **Given the above costs and values for the usual startup policy for the furnace of Example E14, determine whether it would be worthwhile to spend $800 on a furnace-tube monitor that would improve the transition probabilities (p_{01}, p_{02}, p_{04}) from their usual (0.50, 0.38, 0.12) to (0.60, 0.30, 0.10).**

We represent the decision opportunity by a new *decision state* D that transits to either the usual state 0 or to the new set of possibilities:

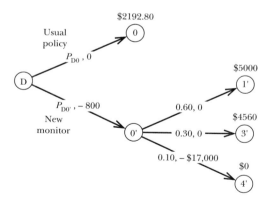

The decision maker is free to choose the transition probabilities from the decision node. Because of the linearity of Eq. 9-31, it maximizes expected state value to choose $p_{ij} = 1$ for one j and 0 for the others.

Folding back, we first evaluate node $0'$, whose state value is

$$V_{0'} = \underbrace{[0.60 \times 0 + 0.30 \times 0 + 0.10(-17{,}000)]}_{\text{immediate expected reward } r_{\text{D}}} + \underbrace{[0.60 \times 5000 - 0.30 \times 4560 + 0.10 \times 0]}_{\text{expected next-state value}}$$

$$= \$2668$$

Given this result, the choice is between $\underline{\$2192.80}$ for the usual policy and $-800 + 2668 = \underline{\$1868}$ for the new monitor. The monitor is <u>not worthwhile</u>.

E16. How much would it be worthwhile to pay for improved furnace startup probabilities in Example E15?

Given that state 0 has state value $\$2192.80$ and state $0'$ has state value $\$2668$, and letting the cost of improvement be X, the tree becomes (with renumbered nodes):

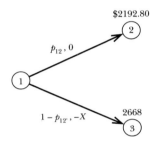

2192.80

We choose p_{12} to maximize $V_1 = p_{12} \times 2192.80 + (1 - p_{12}) \times (-X + 2668)$. V_1 is 2192.80 if the upper branch is chosen, or $-X + 2668$ if the improvement is chosen. For the improvement to be chosen, the assertion is $-X + 2668 > 2192.80 \Rightarrow X < \underline{\$475.20}$.

For decisions in multiyear capital budgeting or in facility planning, a decision tree can be used with discounting. Recall from Figure 9-5 how arcs are labeled: with the transition probability p_{ij} (which is left to choice if the arc comes from a decision node), the state dwell duration t_i, and the transition reward c_{ij}, which by convention is timed at the end of the duration. Thus (from Eq. 9-31) the state value V_i has the transition rewards and the next state values both discounted by the dwell duration t_{ij}.

Figure 9-6 illustrates a decision tree for facility sizing and expansion. Note that nodes 1, 5, 6, 7, and 8 are decision nodes, whose value is the maximum of the values obtained by setting any of its transition probabilities to 1. The values of the terminal states, such as 60 for state 9, represent the expected worth at the node time (which for state 9 is 2).

E17. Figure 9-6 has amounts in \$10,000 units and represents the decision problem of how large a plant to build and whether to react to market response by expansion or retrenchment under various outcomes. For example, a medium plant can be built for \$220,000 paid at the end of one year, and if it meets with "medium" market acceptance, a three-year expansion can be undertaken, or not. For a decision maker using a real interest rate of 10%, solve the decision tree and interpret the results.

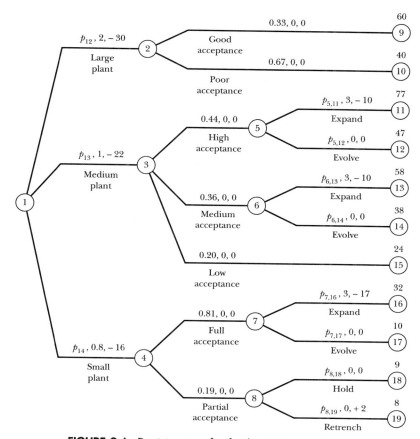

FIGURE 9-6. Decision tree for facility sizing and expansion.

Let $\beta = 1/1.10$ and apply Eq. 9-31 repeatedly, "folding back" from the rightmost nodes. The computations are simple, and it is usual to perform them on the diagram itself, marking each state value as it is computed, and marking the chosen branches from each decision node.

Node 2 has value $V_2 = 0.33 \times 60 + 0.67 \times 40 = \underline{46.6}$.

Node 5 is a decision node. If its upper branch is chosen it has value $\beta^3(-10 + 77) = 50.33809$; if its lower branch is chosen it has value 48; hence the upper branch is chosen, and $V_5 = \underline{50.33809}$.

Node 6 is a decision node. If its upper branch is chosen it has value $\beta^3(-10 + 58) = 36.06311$; if its lower branch is chosen it has value 38; hence the lower branch is chosen, and $V_6 = \underline{38}$.

Node 3 has value $V_3 = 0.44V_5 + 0.36V_6 + 0.20(24) = \underline{40.62876}$.

Node 7 is a decision mode. If its upper branch is chosen it has value $\beta^3(-17 + 32) = 11.269722$; if its lower branch is chosen it has value 10; hence the upper branch is chosen, and $V_7 = \underline{11.269722}$.

Node 8 is a decision node. If its upper branch is chosen it has value 9; if its lower branch is chosen it has value $2 + 8 = 10$; hence the lower branch is chosen, and $V_8 = \underline{10}$.

Node 4 has value $V_4 = 0.81 V_7 + 0.19 V_8 = \underline{11.028475}$.

Finally, node 1 is a decision node. If its top branch is chosen it has value $\beta^2(-30 + V_2) = 13.71901$. If its middle branch is chosen it has value $\beta(-22 + V_3) = 16.93524$. If its bottom branch is chosen it has value $\beta^{0.8}(-16 + V_4) = -4.606547$. Hence, the middle branch is chosen, and $V_1 = \underline{16.93524}$.

Interpretation: The expected value of the present worth of the facility is $\underline{\$169,352}$. To achieve this, a <u>medium</u> plant is built; if it gains high acceptance, the <u>expansion</u> should be undertaken, but if it gains medium acceptance the expansion should not be undertaken.

9.4 VALUED MARKOV CHAINS

In *infinite-horizon* situations or situations in which conditional probabilities and cash flows recur, we can combine the representation of states by defining *recurring states*. For example, in an equipment replacement problem, if every epoch that starts with installation of a new challenger has the same probabilities and costs, we define recurring states such as "new," whereas in a state transition tree the state "new in 1994" would be distinct from "new in 1998." A system of recurring states, with conditional probabilities that depend only on the state, is called a *Markov chain*. We will discuss discrete-time Markov chains, in which the state is observed at times 0, 1, 2,....

Consider a gas compressor that undergoes a 0.10 chance of breakdown each month. If it breaks down, it is repaired at a cost of $400, and its usual $25 monthly profit is still earned. The month that immediately follows a breakdown-and-repair month is similar to an ordinary month except that the probability of breakdown is only 0.05. Thus, if epochs are combined, there are really only two states—"not newly repaired" and "newly repaired."

Figure 9-7 represents this system three ways. First, Figure 9-7a shows a state transition tree in the manner of Figure 9-5; the redundancy is evident in the endless repetition of two sets of probabilities and costs. Figure 9-7b and 9-7c show the Markov-chain data for the same problem. Each transition has a transition probability p_{ij} (recall Eq. 9-29) and a transition reward c_{ij}, as already defined in Section 9.3.1.

Since a Markov chain is not a tree, so that there can be more than one preceding state for a given state, Eq. 9-30 is replaced with the *state probability transition equation.*

$$\pi_j(t+1) = \Sigma_i \pi_i(t) p_{ij} \qquad \text{for each state} \qquad (9\text{-}34)$$

This equation is just a form of the probability addition theorem: The probability of being in state j is the sum of the products of probabilities of being in a previous state multiplied by the conditional probability of transiting to j.

Figure 9-7c shows the *Markov transition matrix* $\mathbf{\Pi}$, which is a matrix of the conditional probabilities:

$$\mathbf{\Pi} = \{p_{ij}\} = \begin{pmatrix} p_{11} & p_{12} & \cdots \\ p_{21} & p_{22} & \cdots \\ \vdots & \vdots & \end{pmatrix} \qquad (9\text{-}35)$$

We define a row vector of state probabilities

$$\boldsymbol{\pi}(t) = (\pi_1(t) \ \pi_2(t) \ \pi_3(t) \ \ldots) \qquad (9\text{-}36)$$

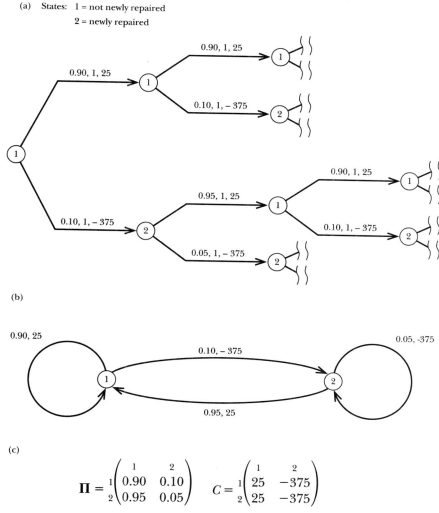

(a) States: 1 = not newly repaired
2 = newly repaired

(b)

(c)

$$\Pi = \begin{pmatrix} & 1 & 2 \\ 1 & 0.90 & 0.10 \\ 2 & 0.95 & 0.05 \end{pmatrix} \qquad C = \begin{pmatrix} & 1 & 2 \\ 1 & 25 & -375 \\ 2 & 25 & -375 \end{pmatrix}$$

FIGURE 9-7. Markov-chain representation of compressor maintenance states. (a) State transition tree. (b) State transition diagram with epochs combined. (c) Markov transition matrix and transition rewards matrix.

Matrix multiplication of $\pi(t)$ onto Π solves Eq. 9-34 for all states:

$$\pi(t + 1) = \pi(t)\Pi \qquad (9\text{-}37)$$

As an example of Eq. 9-37, let the gas compressor of Figure 9-7 start in a "not newly repaired" month (state 1) at time zero. We can determine its state probabilities in successive months:

$$\pi(1) = \pi(0)\Pi = (1 \quad 0)\begin{pmatrix} 0.90 & 0.10 \\ 0.95 & 0.05 \end{pmatrix} = (0.90 \quad 0.10)$$

$$\pi(2) = \pi(1)\Pi = (0.905 \quad 0.095)$$

$$\pi(3) = \pi(2)\Pi = (0.90475 \quad 0.09525)$$

$$\pi(4) = \pi(3)\Pi = (0.9047625 \quad 0.0952375)$$

$$\vdots \qquad \vdots$$

$$\pi(8) = \pi(7)\Pi = (0.9047619048 \quad 0.0952380952)$$

$$\pi(9) = \pi(8)\Pi = (0.9047619048 \quad 0.0952380952)$$

As often happens, long-run state probabilities independent of the initial state are approached within a few epochs.

We define a *transition rewards matrix* C.

$$C = \{c_{ij}\} = \begin{pmatrix} c_{11} & c_{12} & \cdots \\ c_{21} & c_{22} & \cdots \\ \vdots & \vdots & \end{pmatrix} \tag{9-38}$$

The immediate expected rewards $\{r_i\}$ can be computed from Eq. 9-32 by multiplying corresponding elements of Π and C and summing each row. For the example, the result is

$$\{r_i\} = \begin{pmatrix} r_1 \\ r_2 \end{pmatrix} = \begin{pmatrix} -15\beta \\ 5\beta \end{pmatrix}$$

The value equation, Eq. 9-33, can be solved for the example:

$$V_1 = r_1 + \beta(0.90\ V_1 + 0.10\ V_2)$$

$$V_2 = r_2 + \beta(0.95\ V_1 + 0.05\ V_2)$$

Let the interest rate be 10% annually, so that $\beta = (1/1.10)^{1/12}$ for time in months. Solution of the two linear equations yields

$$V_1 = -\$1644.01 \qquad \text{and} \qquad V_2 = -\$1625.11$$

These are the infinite-horizon expected present worths of the compressor's profits and repairs. Incidentally, the difference $V_2 - V_1 = \$18.90$ is the expected present worth of the advantage of starting with a newly repaired compressor.

The set of state value equations for a Markov chain is always linear and can always be solved by standard matrix-inversion techniques if $\beta < 1$.

E18. A whole jet engine is a very expensive spare part. It costs $3.6 million. Each month there is a 0.03 risk of needing one, but if one is not available, a $3.8 million substitution cost can be incurred instead. $\beta = (1/1.10)^{1/12}$ monthly. Because of the lead time to replace a spare, its replacement is not available until the beginning of the second month after it is used. The replacement spare is paid for in the month it is ordered. Does it pay to try to keep a spare on hand if one is already on hand?

Let Policy A = "No spare." There is already a spare on hand, so there are two states: 1 = "spare not yet used," and 2 = "spare already used." In state 1 with probability 0.03 we transit to state 2 and pay nothing (the spare already on hand is used). In state 2, we incur a 0.03 risk of paying $3.8 million, so the expected cost is $0.03 \times 3.8 = 0.114$ million; we stay in state 2.

$$\Pi^{(A)} = \begin{pmatrix} 0.97 & 0.03 \\ 0 & 1 \end{pmatrix} \qquad C^{(A)} = \begin{pmatrix} 0 & 0 \\ 0 & -0.114 \end{pmatrix}$$

The state value equations are

$$V_1^{(A)} = 0\beta + \beta(0.97V_1^{(A)} + 0.03V_2^{(A)})$$
$$V_2^{(A)} = -0.114\beta + \beta(0V_1^{(A)} + V_2^{(A)})$$

Note the $V_2^{(A)}$ equation simplifies to

$$V_2^{(A)} = \frac{-0.114\beta}{1 - \beta} = -14.2962$$

Solving for $V_1^{(A)}$ given $V_2^{(A)}$ yields $V_1^{(A)} = -11.2942$.

Since the system starts in state 1, $E(P^{(A)}) = V_1^{(A)} = \underline{-\$11.2942 \text{ million}}$.

Let Policy **B** = "One spare." Let the states of the system be 1 = "spare on hand" and 2 = "spare not on hand." In state 1, with probability 0.03 we transit to state 2 and pay for a replacement. In state 2, with probability 0.03 we transit again to state 2 and pay the substitution cost; otherwise we transit to state 1.

$$\Pi^{(B)} = \begin{pmatrix} 0.97 & 0.03 \\ 0.97 & 0.03 \end{pmatrix} \qquad C^{(B)} = \begin{pmatrix} 0 & -3.6 \\ 0 & -3.8 \end{pmatrix}$$

The state value equations are

$$V_1^{(B)} = 0.03(-3.6)\beta + \beta(0.97V_1^{(B)} + 0.03V_2^{(B)})$$
$$V_2^{(B)} = 0.03(-3.8)\beta + \beta(0.97V_1^{(B)} + 0.03V_2^{(B)})$$

The solution is $V_1^{(B)} = -13.5662$, $V_2^{(B)} = -13.5721$.

Since the system starts in state 1, $E(P^{(B)}) = V_1^{(B)} = \underline{-\$13.5662 \text{ million}}$.

Comparing $E(P^{(B)})$ with $E(P^{(A)})$, we see that $E(P^{(A)}) > E(P^{(B)})$, so it <u>does not pay</u> to try to keep a spare on hand.

E19. **An unattended solar power device has a control mechanism called a trigger. It is considered to be worth $400 per week to have an operable trigger. For system reliability, three triggers are installed. A trigger in service has a 0.04 weekly probability of failing; a trigger on standby has a 0.01 weekly probability of failing. For a weekly $\beta = 0.998$, determine the expected present worth of trigger operation until all are inoperable.**

Let the states of the system be denoted states 0, 1, 2, 3, meaning how many triggers are inoperable. Given state 0, we can determine the transition probabilities with the aid of a state transition diagram for the system of microstates for which specific triggers survive or fail:

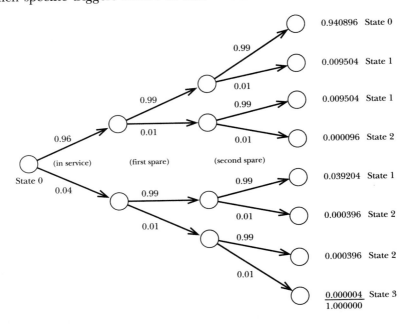

Adding up the various ways of getting to each state, we have

p_{00}	p_{01}	p_{02}	p_{03}	
0.940896	0.058212	0.000888	0.000004	(sum is 1)

From state 1, the microstates are simpler.

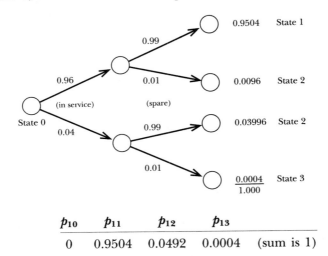

p_{10}	p_{11}	p_{12}	p_{13}	
0	0.9504	0.0492	0.0004	(sum is 1)

From state 2:

p_{20}	p_{21}	p_{22}	p_{23}
0	0	0.96	0.04

From state 3:

p_{30}	p_{31}	p_{32}	p_{33}
0	0	0	1

Given the probability data, we can write the Markov transition matrix. The reward matrix simply reflects a \$400 profit for any transition that ends in a state having a trigger in service.

$$\Pi = \begin{matrix} & 0 & 1 & 2 & 3 \\ 0 & \\ 1 & \\ 2 & \\ 3 & \end{matrix}\begin{pmatrix} 0.940896 & 0.058212 & 0.000888 & 0.000004 \\ 0 & 0.9504 & 0.0492 & 0.0004 \\ 0 & 0 & 0.96 & 0.04 \\ 0 & 0 & 0 & 1 \end{pmatrix}$$

$$C = \begin{matrix} & 0 & 1 & 2 & 3 \\ 0 & \\ 1 & \\ 2 & \\ 3 & \end{matrix}\begin{pmatrix} 400 & 400 & 400 & 0 \\ 400 & 400 & 400 & 0 \\ 400 & 400 & 400 & 0 \\ 400 & 400 & 400 & 0 \end{pmatrix}$$

The value equations are

$$V_0 = \beta \sum_{j=0}^{3} p_{0j}c_{0j} + \beta \sum_{j=0}^{3} p_{0j}V_j$$

$$= 399.1984032 + \beta(p_{00}V_0 + p_{01}V_1 + p_{02}V_2 + p_{03}V_3)$$

$$V_1 = \beta \sum_{j=0}^{3} p_{1j}c_{1j} + \beta \sum_{j=0}^{3} p_{1j}V_j$$

$$= 399.0403200 + \beta(p_{10}V_0 + p_{11}V_1 + p_{12}V_2 + p_{13}V_3)$$

$$V_2 = \beta \sum_{j=0}^{3} p_{2j}c_{2j} + \beta \sum_{j=0}^{3} p_{2j}V_j$$

$$= 383.2320000 + \beta(p_{20}V_0 + p_{21}V_1 + p_{22}V_2 + p_{23}V_3)$$

$$V_3 = 0 + \beta V_3 \Rightarrow V_3 = 0$$

The values are $(V_0 \quad V_1 \quad V_2 \quad V_3) = (22362.67 \quad 16464.33 \quad 9141.98 \quad 0)$

Starting with three operable triggers (state 0), the expected present worth is $V_0 = \underline{\$22,362.67}$.

E20. In the previous example a system of redundant triggers was found to have a \$22,362.67 expected present worth for earnings of \$400 per week for a weekly discount factor of 0.998. Determine the expected life of the operable trigger system.

One approach would be to solve with a discount factor approaching 1, so that the expected present worth approaches the expected sum. Then this divided by

$400/week would approach the expected life in weeks. For example, with $\beta = 0.9999999$, V_0 is 24230.33, so the life is estimated as $V_0/400 = 60.58$ weeks.

Another approach would be to solve exactly with a reward system that gives $1 for each week of survival, so the expected reward at $\beta = 1$ is the expected life. This is left to the exercises.

9.5 EXERCISES

1. An equipment life is anticipated to be any integer number of years from 6 to 10, each possible life having equal probability.
   (a) Determine the expected life.
   (b) From Eq. 9-2, if the equipment earns $100 at the end of each year starting from year 1, determine the expected present worth at 10% interest of the equipment's lifetime earnings.

2. A naphtha distillation unit is corroding. The inspector gives the survival probabilities as

Years	Probability
0	0
1	0.2
2	0.4
3	0.2
4	0.2
	1.0

   When the unit fails, it will cost $8740 to replace it. At 10% interest, determine the expected present worth of the replacement cost.

3. The normal (Gaussian) probability distribution—the one having the familiar symmetrical bell-shaped curve for its density function—has a Laplace transform of

$$E(e^{-st}) = e^{-s\mu + \sigma^2 s^2/2}$$

   where s is the Laplace transform variable, μ is the expected value, and σ^2 is the variance. A $1000 payment will be received at a time that is a normally distributed random variable with expected value 4 yr and variance 2.25 yr^2. At 10% interest ($r = \ln 1.10$), determine the expected present worth of the payment.

4. A tax agency is scheduled to receive $10,000 from each of 12 corporations. Each corporation must make the payment on the next anniversary of its original incorporation date. If incorporation dates are assumed uniformly distributed and the annual interest rate is 8% ($r = \ln 1.08$), determine the expected value of these receipts.

5. In Example E1, assume Tex Arkin receives additional information: The renovations cannot be due within the first two years. Reevaluate the decrement in the value of the oilfield.

6. In Example E2, the expected present worth of a pulpwood crop's revenue was determined using the eoy convention. At the same interest rate (10% real annual

interest), recompute the result using the continuous timing convention and letting the interval widen to the interval from two to eight years.

7. In a study of graduation rates for students who eventually graduate, it was estimated that 30% of students graduated four years after matriculation. Of those who did not, 80% graduated one year late; 80% of the remainder graduated one further year late, and the same 80% process held for additional delays.

   (a) Determine the expected delay, and from the result determine the expected number of years to graduate.
   (b) If a college education has an (indexed) worth of $100,000 upon graduation, at 5% real interest determine the worth at matriculation.

8. Using the continuous timing convention and 4% real interest, determine the expected present worth of seasonal heating-fuel savings of $100,000 at the time of a plant startup, given that the season at plant startup is unpredictable.

9. If an exponentially distributed delay has a mean of five years, what is the probability the delay will be:

   (a) At most 1 year?
   (b) At most 5 years?
   (c) At most 10 years?

10. At $r = 0.10$ nominal continuous interest, determine the expected present worth of a $1000 payment that is due at time 1 but will have an exponentially distributed delay averaging 0.6 years.

11. At $r = 0.10$ nominal continuous interest, determine the expected present worth of a $1000/yr continuous payment whose duration is 4 years plus an additional X years, where X is exponential with mean 1 year.

12. A warehouse is expected to continue to operate for seven years plus an additional life estimated as an exponential random variate with a mean of three years. At 16% real interest, if the indexed earnings of various projects are to be treated as having a deterministic life of n years, what is the most accurate integer n to use?

13. A project has been estimated as having the following cash flows:

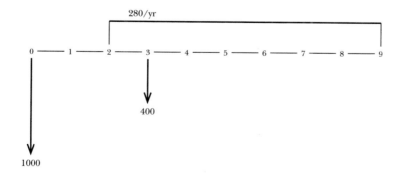

It now appears that the life of the plant in which the project is located has an exponentially distributed life of 15 years. At nominal continuous real interest of $r = 0.05$, compare the expected present worth of the project with and without this consideration.

14. A patent can earn royalties of $40,000 (indexed) per year until the year 2009, if a royalty agreement is approved. Approval was scheduled for 1994; it appears there will be a delay, which is estimated to be exponential with a mean of two years. Determine the expected worth as of 1994 at a real nominal continuous interest rate of $r = \ln 1.10$ (as the startup is delayed, the life is equally shortened).

15. If the reactor in Example E5 will last four years plus an exponentially distributed additional life so that the total expected life is seven years, what is the expected present worth?

16. The project in Example E6 is part of a business activity that has a limited life. How much would its expected worth increase or decrease if the life were certain to be at least three years, followed by an exponentially distributed duration averaging 17 more years?

17. The project in Example E6 is part of a business activity that has a limited life. How much would its expected worth increase or decrease if the life were gamma distributed with the same expected value as given but with half the standard deviation? (The standard deviation of an exponential random variable equals its mean.)

18. The life of a fuel cell in a spacecraft will last until five successive failures have occurred. Time between failures is exponentially distributed with mean 2.1 years. The spacecraft earns continuous communication fees of $475,000 (indexed) per year until the fuel cell dies. At a real nominal continuous interest rate of 0.05, determine the expected present worth of the fees.

19. Using (0, 1) uniform variates of 0.102, 0.943, and 0.786, generate three continuous uniform variates on the interval 101.7 to 396.8.

20. Using (0, 1) uniform variates of 0.507, 0.321, and 0.974, generate three discrete uniform variates in the set $\{6, 7,...,15\}$.

21. Generate three more pseudo-random (0, 1) uniform variates as in Example E8.

22. A computer that uses a 5-bit word can express positive integers from 0 to $2^5 - 1 = 31$. If two integers are multiplied to give a K-bit result, the most significant $K - 5$ bits are lost while the least significant 5 bits of the result remain (this automatically provides modulo arithmetic). *Note: x* mod *m* means the remainder when *x* is divided by *m*.

    Determine parameters *a*, *m*, and *c* of a pseudo-random-number generator of the form

$$Z_i = (aZ_{i-1} + c) \bmod m$$

    having the longest period that this computer's integer arithmetic is capable of producing.

23. (a) Use the second row of Table 9-1 to generate six annual-return variates from the example project at the beginning of Section 9.2.1.
    (b) Use the third row of Table 9-1 to generate six economic-life variates from the example project at the beginning of Section 9.2.1.

24. An investor is confronted with an opportunity to invest *I* dollars, which will enable him to receive *A* dollars throughout each of *k* years. (More properly, he will receive money at a rate of *A* dollars/yr from time zero to time *k*, where *k* is not

necessarily an integer number of years.) The investor can ordinarily earn at least $r = 10\%$ nominal compound interest. Under these assumptions he is interested in maximizing the present worth of the sum of all his projects, subject to whatever constraints are operating. The present worth of the above-described project only is

$$P = -I + \frac{A}{0.10}(1 - e^{-0.10k})$$

Let us assume that A is a constant, I is a random variable, and k is a random variable and that it is desired to estimate the expected value of P by simulation.

Data: The investment I has a normal Gaussian distribution with mean \$21,000 and standard deviation \$2000. Some typical random variates (divided by 1000 and rounded off) are 26, 18, 20, 23, 22, 23, 22, 19, 19, 16, 20, 21, 19, 18, 22, 24, 21, 20. The annual returns A will be \$2600 annually.

The cutoff time k has a negative exponential distribution with a mean of 20 years, so that the density function and cumulative distribution function are as follows:

$$f(k) = (1/20)e^{-k/20} \qquad F(k) = 1 - e^{-k/20}$$

A random variate from this distribution can be generated by using random variate u from a $(0, 1)$ uniform distribution:

$$k = -20 \ln u$$

However, since k appears only in the expression $\exp(-0.10k)$, we may as well avoid calculating natural logs and exponents.

(a) Give the random variate $\exp(-0.10k)$ as a function of the uniform variate.
(b) Some typical values of the uniform variate are

  0.266, 0.966, 0.584, 0.222, 0.455, 0.235, 0.055, 0.904, 0.300,
  0.401, 0.041, 0.802, 0.471, 0.255, 0.799, 0.608, 0.577, 0.346.

  Give a few typical values of P.

25. The truncated negative exponential distribution with parameters θ and α is the distribution of those values that do not exceed α from a negative exponential distribution with mean θ. Some properties of the truncated exponential are as follows:

Density:

$$f(x) = \begin{cases} \dfrac{1/\theta}{1 - e^{-\alpha/\theta}}e^{-x/\theta} & 0 \le x \le \alpha \\ \\ 0 & \text{otherwise} \end{cases}$$

Expected value:

$$\frac{\theta}{1 - e^{-\alpha/\theta}}[1 - (1 + \alpha/\theta)e^{-\alpha/\theta}]$$

(a) Starting with the standard uniform variate 0.31625, generate a truncated negative exponential variate having parameters $\theta = 20$ and $\alpha = 40$. Explain your method.

(b) If you were to generate many such variates, what value would their mean approach?

26. A cost is estimated to be gamma distributed with $k = 6$ and $\theta = 7140.22$. Using the last two rows of Table 9-1 as a source of uniform variates, generate two variates of this cost.

27. One simple way of generating approximately normally distributed random variates is based on the central-limit theorem, which says that a sum of independent random variables tends toward being normally distributed if there are enough of them. In particular, a sum of 12 (0, 1) uniform variates is approximately normally distributed with mean 6 and variance 1. From this, a method for generating a variate x from a normal distribution with mean μ and variance σ^2 is given by the formula

$$x = \mu + \sigma\left(\sum_{m=1}^{12} u_m - 6\right)$$

Use the last two rows of Table 9-1 to generate a random variate from a normal distribution having mean 32.1 and standard deviation 6.37.

28. In analyzing a computer improvement project, it is required to estimate the daily cost of diverted jobs. If this estimation is done by simulation, using knowledge of how the load of offered jobs varies through the working day, explain in general terms what one *experiment* would be and what a *run* would be.

29. Perform one additional Monte Carlo experiment for Example E12.

30. If $M = 200$ experiments are run for a project, given an estimate of expected present worth of $248.1475 with a standard deviation of $400, determine:

(a) The (3-sigma) minimum anticipated present worth of the project.

(b) The (3-sigma) minimum of the "true" expected value of the present worth.

31. Repeat Example E13 using the last row of Table 9-1 as the source of (0, 1) uniform variates.

32. In the following state transition tree, determine for each terminal node (a) its probability of occurring, (b) its time of occurrence if it does occur, and (c) the expected present worth of its rewards, at 10% interest. Finally, determine (d) the expected present worth of the whole tree.

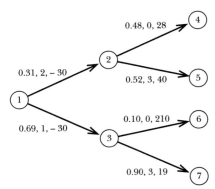

33. In the data of the previous exercise, make one change: The decision maker can choose the path from node 1, rather than risking it. Determine the expected present worth of this choice privilege.

34. Recall Example E14.
    (a) Verify that the probabilities of the terminal states sum to 1.
    (b) Determine the probability of failure (of either kind).
    (c) Determine the probability of succeeding with a temperature of 900°F or greater.

35. In Figure 9-6, with a 10% real interest rate, the expansion projects are estimated to take three years. If they could be speeded up to take one year, would any decisions change from those reported in Example E17?

36. A protagonist who uses a $d = 15\%$ real interest rate owns a plant that is now operating. It might be sold for $2.7 million this year or $2.4 million next year or $1.9 million the following year, if buyers are willing; each year, with probability 0.18, they are willing. It makes a profit of $0.2 million per year up to and including the year it is sold. Each year a quality-control project can be undertaken if the protagonist so chooses; it increases profits by $0.06 million for each of the following three years, but not in the year it is undertaken; in that year it decreases profits by $0.09. Effects of successive quality-control projects are cumulative and additive (e.g., the profit is $0.32 million if a quality control project was undertaken in each of the two previous years). If the plant is not sold in the first three years, it is certainly sold for $1 million in the fourth year. Assume that no quality control project will be undertaken in the third or fourth year, nor in the second year unless undertaken also in the first year; that is, consider quality control projects only for the first year or for the first and second years. Draw and solve a decision tree and report the expected worths.

37. Three risky projects are available:

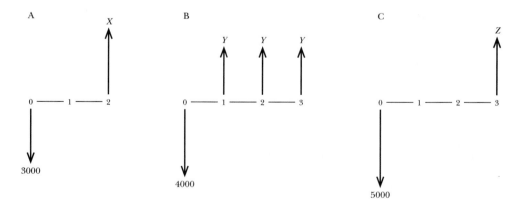

You have $6000 available to invest. Any returns or uninvested budget add to the budget for the next year. X, Y, and Z are independent random variables having the following probability distributions:

X	Probability		Y	Probability		Z	Probability
6000	0.2		2000	0.5		8000	0.6
7000	0.8		3000	0.5		9000	0.4

The interest rate is 10%. Any project not taken is still available the next year. Investments can be made at times 0, 1, and 2. Draw and solve a decision tree and report the expected worths (investments' future returns do count; leftover budget is worthless at the end).

38. For the following valued Markov chain determine the expected present worth of starting in the first state, at $\beta = 0.99$.

$$\Pi = \begin{pmatrix} 0.5 & 0.5 \\ 0.1 & 0.9 \end{pmatrix} \qquad C = \begin{pmatrix} 17 & -4 \\ 17 & -1 \end{pmatrix}$$

39. A shopping mall is laid out so that people move from area to area as follows:

$$\Pi = \begin{pmatrix} 0 & 0.5 & 0.5 \\ 0.2 & 0 & 0.8 \\ 0 & 0 & 1 \end{pmatrix}$$

Using β near 1, use valued Markov-chain analysis to determine the expected number of areas visited by a shopper, including revisiting the first area. Visiting the third (exit) area does not count (let rewards be $1 for each visit, so that the expected number of visits is the expected reward).

40. In the gas compressor repair example of Section 9.4, determine the greatest repair cost (instead of $400) such that the expected worth is nonnegative for both starting states.

41. In Example E18:
    (a) Would it be worthwhile to spend $1.6 million at time zero so that the monthly risk of needing a spare would be 0.02 instead of 0.03?
    (b) If the risk were 0.04 instead of 0.03, would it pay to try to keep a spare on hand?

42. Recompute the state values for Example E19 with the following Markov transition probabilities:

$$\Pi = \begin{pmatrix} 0.94 & 0.06 & 0 & 0 \\ 0 & 0.95 & 0.05 & 0 \\ 0 & 0 & 0.96 & 0.04 \\ 0 & 0 & 0 & 1 \end{pmatrix}$$

43. For Examples E19 and E20, with the data from the previous exercise, write the reward matrix C for $1 for each week of survival. Eliminate $V_3 = 0$ from the equations. Solve the remaining equations for V_0, V_1, and V_2 with $\beta = 1$, and interpret the result in terms of life of the trigger system.

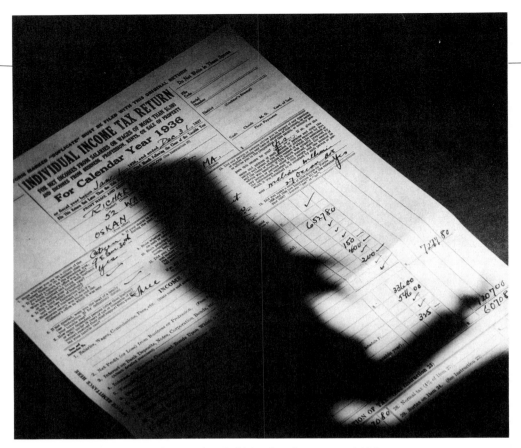

Uncle Sam has held his hand out since 1913.

TAXES, DEPRECIATION, AND INCENTIVES

Most taxes, such as excise taxes, property taxes, licenses, and sales taxes, are included as a matter of course even in what is called *before-tax* analysis. For example, a fleet operator would never ignore the cost of licensing the fleet's vehicles, and road taxes to a trucker are as ordinary as fuel costs. With 5% sales taxes, a $3150 retail sales register total is routinely considered to represent a receipt of $3000. The words "before tax" and "after tax" refer specifically to *income taxes,* which are sometimes ignored because they are complexly defined and are often irrelevant when all alternatives are taxed similarly.

This chapter concerns how to compute *after-tax* worth measures—those that take income taxes into account.

The aim of after-tax analysis is to maximize after-tax present worth. In the United States, it is official policy of the Internal Revenue Service (IRS) that a taxpayer should pay the smallest amount, and on the latest schedule, that the law allows. The IRS and the taxpayer are civil adversaries; under civil law, the IRS tries to collect as much as possible and the taxpayer tries to pay as little as possible. Tax practice distinguishes between *tax avoidance* (actions to minimize taxes, including actions viewed as unfair or unethical from the IRS standpoint, but not clearly illegal) and *tax evasion* (illegal actions). A brief examination of tax ethics is given in the first exercise at the end of the chapter. Figure 10-1 provides a preview of what is involved in after-tax analysis.

10.1 INCOME TAXATION

In the United States and most other industrial nations, income taxes are levied against *taxable income,* an accounting quantity that is carefully defined. Its definition changes from year to year and is intended partly to indicate net recent success of an enterprise

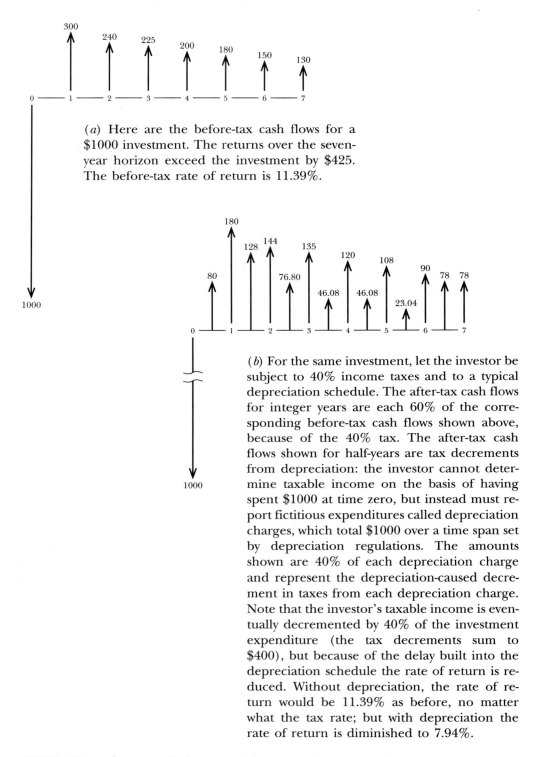

(*a*) Here are the before-tax cash flows for a $1000 investment. The returns over the seven-year horizon exceed the investment by $425. The before-tax rate of return is 11.39%.

(*b*) For the same investment, let the investor be subject to 40% income taxes and to a typical depreciation schedule. The after-tax cash flows for integer years are each 60% of the corresponding before-tax cash flows shown above, because of the 40% tax. The after-tax cash flows shown for half-years are tax decrements from depreciation: the investor cannot determine taxable income on the basis of having spent $1000 at time zero, but instead must report fictitious expenditures called depreciation charges, which total $1000 over a time span set by depreciation regulations. The amounts shown are 40% of each depreciation charge and represent the depreciation-caused decrement in taxes from each depreciation charge. Note that the investor's taxable income is eventually decremented by 40% of the investment expenditure (the tax decrements sum to $400), but because of the delay built into the depreciation schedule the rate of return is reduced. Without depreciation, the rate of return would be 11.39% as before, no matter what the tax rate; but with depreciation the rate of return is diminished to 7.94%.

FIGURE 10-1. Before-tax and after-tax cash flows. (*a*) Before-tax cash flows for a $1000 investment. (*b*) After-tax cash flows for the same investment.

for taxation purposes, and partly to provide economic incentives and transfer payments to achieve economic and social goals.

Income taxes are levied by governments at national, provincial, and local levels; for example, in the United States the federal government, many State governments, and some local governments (e.g., New York City) levy *personal income taxes* on individuals and *corporate income taxes* on corporations or businesses treated as corporations.

As examples of the effects of personal income taxes on individual decisions, consider the following scenarios:

· Henry concentrates his physical checkups, dental work, and elective surgery into even-numbered years, because personal medical expenses are tax-deductible only to the extent that they exceed 5% of gross personal income.
· Becky is awarded a piano, but lets it be given instead to her local art center, where she can enjoy it nearly as much but not have to pay income tax on its value.

As examples of effects of corporate income taxes on business decisions, consider these scenarios:

· A farmer repairs a fence rather than more cheaply replacing it, because repairs can be "expensed" while replacements must be "depreciated."
· A partnership invests in a losing "tax-sheltered" real estate deal whose losses are more than offset by its income-tax benefits.
· A warehouse chooses a less economical material-handling system because the more economical one involves equipment that has a longer depreciable life and thus gets less favorable tax treatment.

Personal taxable income consists of such items as wages, winnings, net profit from a personal business, pensions, interest on savings, withdrawals from tax-deferred accounts; less certain exclusions and exemptions; less personal deductions, which consist of such items as medical expenses, State and local taxes, charitable contributions, interest, and casualty losses. Corporate taxable income (and net profit from a personal business) consists of gross business receipts; less such deductions as advertising, salaries and wages, materials, supplies, shipping, interest, other taxes, insurance, repairs, travel, employee benefits, research, rent, and special items such as depreciation and depletion. Business deductions include practically anything that one would consider a cost of doing business, except bribes, criminal fines (civil judgments, and the costs of defending or insuring against them, are deductible), and capital expenses (which are handled through depreciation). Punitive damages in liability suits involving such subjects as pollution or safety can be defined as nondeductible in a civil judgment.

10.1.1 Marginal Tax Rate

The amounts of taxes paid are partly determined by the details of definition of taxable income, and partly determined by tax rates. For example, income taxes in the United States were changed to allow fewer deductions and exclusions in the late 1980s; tax rates were correspondingly lowered, and the amounts collected remained about the same.

Income tax rates usually follow a graduated scale. Let a taxpayer's income for the past year be R dollars. R falls in some range or *tax bracket* R_m to R_{m+1}, within which there is a tax rate t_m, so that the tax paid on the increment of income $R - R_m$ is $t_m(R - R_m)$. It is meaningful to use a combined income tax rate, since national, provincial, and local governments normally coordinate their income taxation. For example, if the federal income tax rate is 39% in a certain bracket, a State might levy 2% and a city might levy 1%, all based on the same taxable income definition and the same bracket limits, so that the taxpayer pays a combined rate of 42% on income in that bracket.

In the early 1990s, typical combined income tax rates for corporations in industrial countries were as given in Table 10-1. Actual rates vary with time and locality; we will use the rates in Table 10-1 for all numerical examples.

The table defines four tax brackets. The tax on the first $50,000 of taxable income is 18%, on the next $25,000 it is 25%, and so forth.

E1. A company has $85,000 of taxable income. Determine its combined income tax.

$R = \$85,000$, and the marginal tax rate is 35%. The combined income tax is $0.35R - 11,000 = \underline{\$18,750}$.

We define the anticipated marginal tax rate as T. Consider the after-tax analysis of an investment opportunity that will not by itself change the tax bracket. Then an additional receipt of $1 will increase taxable income by $1 and increase income tax by T dollars: The taxpayer keeps $1 - T$ of the additional receipts generated by a project. Similarly, an additional disbursement will reduce taxable income. If the disbursement is an ordinary expense, it reduces taxable income immediately. Capital expenditures are treated differently (taxable income is reduced later through depreciation charges), but the taxpayer pays $1 - T$ of the ordinary expenses generated by a project.

The government is a silent partner that pays part of the expenses and reaps part of the profits.

E2. Blandish Corporation is in the 40% bracket. By incurring an ordinary expense of $1000 it can reap a profit of $1300 one year later. Determine the before-tax and after-tax present worth at 15% interest, and the before-tax and after-tax rate of return.

The before-tax present worth is $P_{\text{bt}} = -1000 + 1300\beta^1$, where $\beta = 1/1.15$. This is $\underline{\$130.43}$.

TABLE 10-1. Typical Combined Income Taxes

Taxable Income R More Than	But Not More Than	Combined Income Tax, $
$0	$50,000	$0.18R$
$50,000	$75,000	$9000 + 0.25(R - 50,000) = 0.25R - 3500$
$75,000	$100,000	$15,250 + 0.35(R - 75,000) = 0.35R - 11,000$
$100,000		$24,000 + 0.40(R - 100,000) = 0.40R - 16,000$

The after-tax present worth is $P_{at} = -(1 - T)1000 + (1 - T)1300\beta^1$ where $T = 0.40$. This is $(1 - T)P_{bt} = \underline{\$78.26}$.

As a silent partner, the tax authority pays 40% of the expenses and reaps 40% of the rewards.

The before-tax rate of return is such that $P_{bt} = 0$. This is 30%. Since the after-tax present worth equals a constant $(1 - T)$ times the before-tax present worth, the after-tax rate of return is equal to the before-tax rate. Both the enterprise and the government enjoy a 30% rate of return on their respective shares of the project.

10.1.2 Effects of Depreciation and Incentives

The situation in the foregoing example is one in which the tax authority's silent partnership is a decision-neutral one. If all expenditures constituted deductible expenses and all receipts augmented taxable income, then present worths of all projects would be multiplied by the constant $(1 - T)$ and there would be no need for after-tax analysis; decisions about a project made on the basis of either a worth measure or an efficiency measure would be the same before and after taxes. However, capital expenditures cannot be treated as ordinary expenses. To see why, consider the following example:

E3. The King of Idealia newly decrees that all expenditures, including capital ones, shall be immediately deductible. The widget factory board notes that net profits will be 80 ideals this year, which will be taxed at $T = 40\%$. A year-end project is available:

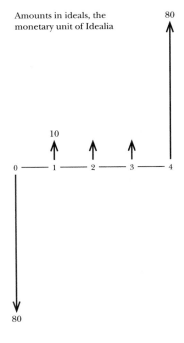

Under the decree the 80-ideal investment is an ordinary expense. The year-end project has a 12.5% rate of return whether computed before or after taxes. Assume the factory ordinarily enjoys a 15% rate of return, so the project is rejected.

However, the youngest board member brings up a new issue. "We are in business for ourselves, not the King," she points out. "There are two distinct ways we can benefit from this year's efforts: Take the profits, or plow them back to increase our owned wealth. Now the King confiscates 40% if we take the profits, but defers confiscation if we plow them back."

"Show me!" demands the board member who comes from Misery, one of the provinces of Idealia. In reply, the young one defines four alternatives:

A. Do nothing except pay the 40% tax on the 80 ideals.
B. Spend the 80 ideals on the year-end project.
C. Assuming that similar year-end projects will always be available (with rates of return at only 12.5%, not 15%), plan never to cash in the salvage value but keep earning 10 ideals per year forever.
D. As in C, keep earning 10 ideals per year forever, but do not pay taxes on this money; instead, spend it on amenities that are deductible but that will be enjoyed by the board members (owners' representatives) as much as if they were given the same (untaxed) amount each year.

Determine the four present worths at 15% interest, and interpret the results.

$$P_{at}^{(A)} = 80(1 - T) = \underline{48 \text{ ideals}}$$

$$P_{at}^{(B)} = 10(1 - T)(P/A\ 15\%,5) + 80(1 - T)\beta^5 = 0.60(73.29569) = \underline{43.9774}$$
$$\underline{\text{ideals}}$$

$$P_{at}^{(C)} = 10(1 - T)/i = \underline{40 \text{ ideals}}$$

$$P_{at}^{(D)} = 10/i = \underline{66.67 \text{ ideals}}$$

The results for the first three alternatives confirm that the immediate deductibility of capital expenditures gives a decision-neutral situation; the factory loses money on both its schemes to delay taxation by investing at less than MARR. Note that alternative B would have an after-tax present worth of 48 ideals if MARR were 12.5%; that is, if the project were exactly as good as an ordinary one, it would leave the after-tax situation unchanged. The fourth alternative is of a different character: It constitutes tax avoidance by granting perquisites to the owners in lieu of income, assuming the cost of the perquisites is deductible. This practice can easily become abusive. In the United States, the IRS has been reluctant to put severe limits on deductibility. The practical limits on this type of avoidance are imposed by auditing and prosecution of blatant excesses, and by a growing body of laws and regulations that restrict the preferential treatment of owners and managers as compared to ordinary employees.

Example E3 illustrates one of the reasons for not treating capital expenditures as ordinary expenses: Owners can to some extent live at company expense. Example E3 shows only about half of the advantage gained, because when deductible company benefits are substituted for taxable profits, not only does the company avoid corporate income taxes, but the owners avoid personal income taxes on the same amount of money.

A second reason for special treatment of capital expenditures is a need to limit fluctuations in tax collections.

E4. A small printing business runs a printing press very hard and must replace it every five years. Its profits before taxes are normally $30,000 per year, but in a year that the press is replaced (at a cost of $40,000) there is a loss of $10,000. Assume $T = 40\%$. Tax collections would fluctuate widely if capital expenditures were deducted as ordinary expenses. Devise a schedule of deductions totaling $40,000 in five years but yielding equal tax collections every year.

Obviously if $8000 were deducted each year, giving taxable income of $22,000 every year, the tax collections would be $8800 every year. Such a schedule, where the cost of a capital asset is treated as if it were spread out evenly over the asset's economic life, is *straight-line depreciation*.

Example E4 illustrated depreciation, which not only irons out fluctuations in tax collections, but also mitigates the concerns raised in Example E2. The next example illustrates the effects of depreciation.

E5. For a company with MARR = 15% and $T = 40\%$, the following project is available:

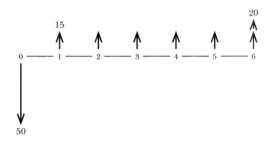

Amounts in K$

Compare its before-tax and after-tax present worths, both at 15% interest. Consider three depreciation schemes: (A) immediate depreciation (treatment of the investment as an expense); (B) straight-line depreciation of the entire 50 K$ investment, with the salvage value of 20 K$ treated as ordinary income; and (C) straight-line depreciation of the 30 K$ of investment-less-salvage.

Before taxes:

$$P_{bt} = -50 + 15(P/A\ 15\%,6) + 20\beta^6 = \underline{15.41379\ K\$}$$

A After taxes with immediate depreciation $(T = 0.40)$:

$$P_{at} = (1 - T)P_{bt} = \underline{9.24828\ K\$}$$

B After taxes with depreciation of the whole investment and salvage treated as income (depreciation charges 8.33333 K$ per year):

$$P_{at} = -50 + T8.33333(P/A\ 15\%,6) + (1 - T)15(P/A\ 15\%,6) +$$
$$(1 - T)20\beta^6 = \underline{1.86322\ K\$}$$

C After taxes with depreciation of the net investment (depreciation charges 5 K$ per year):

$$P_{at} = -50 + T5(P/A\ 15\%,6) + (1 - T)15(P/A\ 15\%,6) + 20\beta^6 = \underline{0.27586\ K\$}$$

The results show that the two nonimmediate depreciation schemes are much less favorable to the taxpayer than immediate depreciation. The after-tax present worth of an investment is diminished by an amount that depends on how much delay is in the depreciation schedule. The taxpayer spends the money up front, but the tax authority pays its share of the investment later than it collects its share of the fruits.

The project of Example E5 demonstrates the effects of depreciation. When capital expenditures are "expensed" rather than depreciated, there is no loss in financial efficiency. For example, the rate of return for scheme A in the example (immediate depreciation, or "expensing") is 24.62%, equal to that of the same project before taxes; the company earns less on the project because of being taxed, but it also invests correspondingly less by virtue of immediate tax deductions. In schemes B and C the tax authority grants the same total deductions but on a delayed schedule, thus in effect obtaining interest-free loans from the taxpayer.

E6. In Example E5, the rates of return are

    A. 24.62% for expensing (same as before taxes).
    B. 16.26% for depreciation of whole investment with salvage as income.
    C. 15.18% for depreciation of net investment.

    From these results, what can be said in general about the effects of depreciation on economic decisions?

    1. Delay built into every depreciation scheme except "expensing" depresses rate of return and present worth.
    2. The taxpayer should use the fastest depreciation scheme available, and should, if possible, treat salvage values as income rather than depreciate net investments.
    3. After taxes, a project whose capital expenditures can be depreciated faster may be better than a more profitable project that involves slower depreciation (Example E7 will illustrate this).
    4. Because of depreciation, MARR for after-tax analysis should be lower than MARR for before-tax analysis. (If the project of Example E5 were an ordinary-course-of-business project, it would imply a before-tax MARR of about 25% and an after-tax MARR of 15% or 16%.)

E7. Two robotics systems are available. **System A costs $30,000 and can be sold back to the vendor for $20,000 after five years. System B costs $25,000 and has no salvage value. Each would provide the same benefits. The company uses MARR = 20% for before-tax analysis. First, show that A is cheaper on a before-tax basis:**

Let B be the net present worth of benefits and noncapital costs.

$$P_{bt}^{(A)} = B + 30 + 20\beta^5 = \underline{B - 21.96 \text{ K\$}}$$

$$P_{bt}^{(B)} = \underline{B - 25 \text{ K\$}} \qquad \text{A is cheaper before taxes}$$

Next, consider the effects of depreciation. Assume $T = 40\%$, and MARR = 15% for after-tax analysis. Let the fastest allowable depreciation schedules be as follows:

End of year	Depreciation charge for A	Depreciation charge for B
0	0	$10,000
1	$2,000	$5,000
2	$2,000	$5,000
3	$2,000	$5,000
4	$2,000	0
5	$2,000	0

The depreciation schedule for A is a five-year straight-line schedule applied to the net investment; the salvage value is untaxed, because it is not depreciated. The depreciation schedule for B is more favorable: it includes the ability to declare $10,000 of the costs as expenses and to depreciate the remainder in a three-year straight-line schedule. Determine which system is cheaper after taxes.

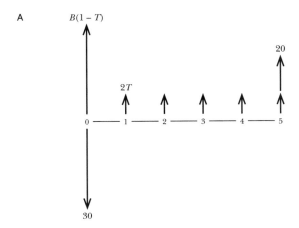

A

$$P_{at}^{(A)} = B(1 - T) - 30 + 2T(P/A\ 15\%,5) + 20\beta^5 = \underline{0.60B - 17.375 \text{ K\$}}$$

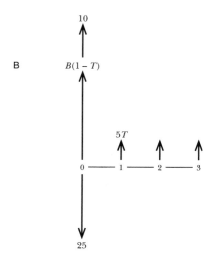

B

$$P_{\text{at}}^{(B)} = B(1 - T) + 10 - 25 + 5T(P/A\ 15\%,3) = \underline{0.60B - 10.434\ \text{K\$}}$$

System **B** has more than a $6900 advantage after taxes because of its more favorable depreciation schedule, although system **A** is intrinsically cheaper by more than $3000.

Depreciation has the effect of diminishing the attractiveness of long-term activities compared to short-term ones. Fast depreciation schedules encourage capital investment, and governments use depreciation rules as a tool to help adjust the general level of investment as compared to savings and consumption. Among competing investment alternatives, differences in their depreciation schedules can have a distorting effect; in Example E7, society as a whole loses $3000 so that a company can gain a $6900 tax advantage. The distortion is an unwanted side effect of the complexity and arbitrariness of depreciation rules and of the basic adversarial nature of a competitive economy.

In addition to depreciation, there are many incentives and disincentives that are enacted into income tax laws from time to time to accomplish specific economic purposes. These include such provisions as additional first-year depreciation and investment tax credits, which effectively accelerate depreciation for favored activities; depletion allowances, which effectively depreciate such holdings as oilfields or mines as resources are extracted; the taxation of capital gains at a separate rate from that of ordinary income; exclusion of certain kinds of income or on income from certain sources (interest on municipal bonds, for example, is not taxed in the United States); and a wide variety of adjustments to rules that regulate deductibility of expenses. These provisions attempt to fine-tune the economic behavior of businesses and individuals.

10.1.3 Tax-Free Interest, Tax-Deductible Interest

Until the 1990s, interest expenses were deductible from personal income in the United States. This greatly stimulated home ownership and consumer borrowing.

When consumer interest became no longer deductible, income taxes were thereby effectively increased for individuals who carried substantial consumer debt that could not be shifted to home mortgage debt. With some exceptions, interest expenses for business are fully deductible, and interest income is taxed as ordinary income. Exceptions include long-term debt obligations of local governments—tax-free municipal bonds. For the most part, engineering decisions are not greatly affected by tax treatment of interest expenses.

10.2 DEPRECIATION

In income tax accounting, investing B_0 dollars in a capital asset at time zero is treated as if the taxpayer spends a series of *depreciation charges* $\{D_t: t=1, 2,..,n\}$ instead. Each charge D_t represents a decrease from the asset's previous *book value* B_{t-1} to its new book value B_t:

$$B_t = B_{t-1} - D_t \qquad t = 1, 2,\ldots,n \qquad (10\text{-}1)$$

$$D_t = B_{t-1} - B_t$$

Depreciation charges are the expenses that decrement net income. Instead of being reduced by B_0 at time zero, the taxpayer's taxable income is reduced by $D_1, D_2, \ldots ,D_n$ at times $1, 2, \ldots ,n$. Income taxes are thus reduced by $TD_1, TD_2, \ldots ,TD_n$ at these times.

10.2.1 Depreciation Schedules

A *depreciation schedule* is a rule for determining $\{D_t\}$. There are two treatments of salvage value: recent methods depreciate the whole investment and ignore salvage value, while traditional methods depreciate the net investment $B_0 - S_n$, where S is the estimated salvage value at time n. For both whole-investment and net-investment depreciation schedules, the net proceeds from salvage or disposal generate positive or negative income or capital gains, taxed when they occur. In the case of net-investment depreciation, the amount taxed is the amount by which proceeds exceed S_n.

Precise timing of depreciation charges is of great importance in tax accounting. Formulas given here have time zero as the time the capital investment is made and the assets are put into service; the first depreciation charge occurs a year later. Tax authorities such as the IRS publish standard depreciation schedules or procedures in which timing is keyed to the start of the tax year. The IRS assumes that assets are put into service at midyear, so that the first depreciation charge occurs after six months; accordingly, the first depreciation charge in a standard schedule is halved from what it otherwise would be, and an additional half-year charge is added at the end. We will take this into account in all comparisons. However, in our basic formulas we will assume that the tax savings for an expensed (noncapital) expenditure are immediate, and that tax savings for capitalized expenses occur at the ends of periods $1, 2, \ldots ,$ where the periods are years unless otherwise specified.

A depreciation schedule can apply to an individual asset or to a *class* or group of assets lumped together for tax accounting purposes. Recent methods depreciate assets in *life classes,* where a class account contains items sharing the same depreciation schedule (and thus having similar estimated or assumed economic lives).

Depreciation schedules are *standard* or *negotiated*. Older standard methods include the *standard straight-line* (SL) method, the obsolete *sum-of-the-years'-digits* (SYD) method, and the *declining balance* (DB) method. SL and DB schedules underlie recent depreciation methods, both standard and negotiated.

A standard depreciation method is one published by the IRS or other tax authority and available for use by taxpayers. A negotiated depreciation method is one proposed by a taxpayer (generally a large corporation) and accepted by the tax authority. In the United States, the standard method is the current successor to the "Modified Accelerated Cost Recovery System" (MACRS) first published in 1986. The details of allowable schedules change somewhat from year to year but are based on DB and SL depreciation. The most widely used negotiated method is the *declining class account* (DCA) method, based on DB depreciation.

In all depreciation schedules the sum of depreciation charges equals B_0 for whole-investment depreciation or $B_0 - S_n$ for net-investment depreciation:

$$\sum_{t=1}^{n} D_t \;=\; B_0 \text{ or } B_0 - S_n \tag{10-2}$$

The final book value B_n is either 0 for whole-investment depreciation or S_n for net-investment depreciation.

All depreciation methods have a *life parameter* that measures the assumed economic life of an asset. The life parameter may be expressed in various ways, just as interest can be expressed as i or β. The life parameter of the standard MACRS method in the United States is the *recovery period n*. Table 10-2 shows allowable recovery periods as of 1990:

TABLE 10-2. Standard Recovery Periods

Standard Recovery Period (yr)	Assets for which allowed
3	Tooling, loading devices, taxis, racehorses
5	Copiers, computers, light motor vehicles, cargo containers, solar energy devices
7	Heavy trucks, pumps, generators, manufacturing equipment, office furniture, barns, railroad track
10	Casting molds, chemical reactors, refinery equipment
15	Sewage plants, ships, telephone lines, power switchgear
20	Power plants, sewer line, pipelines, long-lived equipment
27.5	Residential rental property
31.5	Nonresidential rental property

Although every depreciation schedule has a recovery period n, all methods except SL have greater depreciation charges in earlier periods than in later ones. A more meaningful measure of the speed of a depreciation schedule is its *average dwell time L*:

$$L = \frac{\sum\limits_{t=0}^{n} t\, D_t}{\sum\limits_{t=0}^{n} D_t} \tag{10-3}$$

L measures the average delay in the depreciation charges attributable to an asset.

**E8. A crane costs $10,000 to purchase and install. Of this, $3000 is immediately de-
ductible as noncapital expense; depreciation charges in the first through third
years are $4100, $2367.42, and $532.58. Determine the average dwell for this
schedule.**

$$L = \frac{0(3000) + 1(4100) + 2(2367.42) + 3(532.58)}{10,000} = \underline{\underline{1.043258 \text{ yr}}}$$

The average dwell can be used to give a rough approximation of the present worth
of depreciation charges. A depreciation schedule with a shorter dwell will almost
always have a greater worth than one with a longer dwell.

**E9. The purchaser of the abovementioned crane is in the 40% income-tax bracket and
uses MARR = 15% after taxes. If the purchaser could have expensed the crane,
the present worth of tax reductions from depreciation charges would have been
40% of $10,000, or $4000, so that the crane would effectively have cost $6000
after taxes. For the actual depreciation schedule, determine the present worth of
depreciation charges, the present worth of the tax reductions from them, and the
resultant effective after-tax cost of the crane. Also compute approximations to
these quantities using the average dwell.**

Actual

Present worth of depreciation charges at 15% interest:

$$3000 + 4100\beta + 2367.42\beta^2 + 532.58\beta^3 = \underline{\underline{\$8705.51}}$$

Present worth of tax reduction: $0.40(8705.51) \quad = \underline{\underline{\$3482.20}}$
Effective after-tax cost of crane: $10,000 - 3482.20 = \underline{\underline{\$6517.80}}$

Approximated from L = 1.043258 yr

Approximate present worth of charges: $\qquad 10,000\beta^L \qquad = \underline{\underline{\$8643.24}}$
Approximate present worth of tax reduction: $0.40(8643.24) \qquad = \underline{\underline{\$3457.30}}$
Approximate after-tax cost of crane: $\qquad 10,000 - 3457.30 = \underline{\underline{\$6542.70}}$

10.2.2 Straight-Line (SL) Depreciation

A straight-line depreciation schedule is defined in terms of its recovery period n.
There are n depreciation charges, each equal to $1/n$th of the initial depreciable
amount:

Whole-investment SL depreciation: $D_t = B_0/n$ $t = 1, 2, \ldots, n$ (10-4)

Net-investment SL depreciation: $D_t = (B_0 - S_n)/n$ $t = 1, 2, \ldots, n$ (10-5)

E10. At a cost of 15 K\$, a hosiery manufacturer installs a new workstation that will last five years and contribute 5 K\$ to operating profits each year. It will be replaced with a like workstation, at a net cost of 6 K\$; that is, there is a 9 K\$ salvage value. The replacement workstation will be sold for 9 K\$ at the end of year 10. Determine the workstation's contribution to taxable income for years 1 through 10 under (a) expensing (immediate depreciation), (b) whole-investment SL depreciation where the salvage values are income, (c) net-investment SL depreciation, and (d) whole-investment SL depreciation where the salvage value at year 5 is absorbed as a cost reduction for the second workstation.

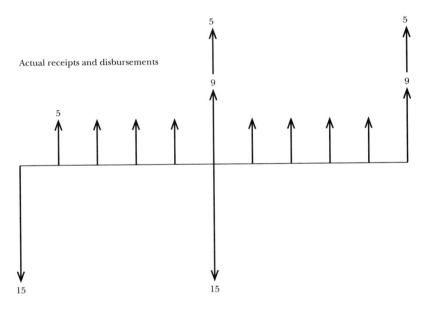

(a) Taxable-income contributions under expensing

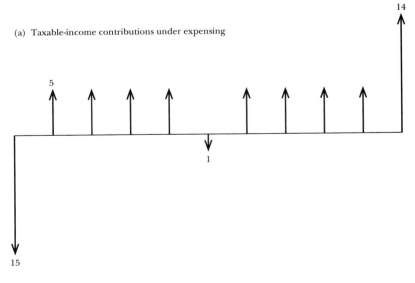

(b) Taxable income contributions under whole-investment SL depreciation where salvage values are income. $D_t = 15/5 = 3$ for $t = 1, \ldots, 10$

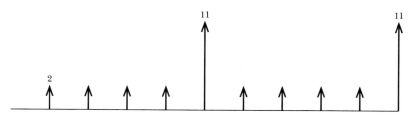

(c) Taxable income contributions under net-investment SL depreciation. $D_t = (15 - 9)/5 = 1.2$ for $t = 1, \ldots, 10$

(d) Taxable income contributions under whole-investment SL depreciation where salvage at year 5 is absorbed in replacement investment. $D_t = 15/5 = 3$ for $t = 1, \ldots, 5$. $D_t = 6/5 = 1.2$ for $t = 6, \ldots, 10$.

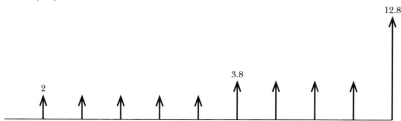

In each case the total taxable income over the 10-year period is 38 K$, but the three SL schedules differ from each other in their timing. The tax authority would prefer the net-investment version (c) because of its leveling effect on tax collections, but the taxpayer would prefer whole-investment deprecation. When there is replacement in kind, usual accounting practice is to treat salvage revenues as reductions in the cost of replacement, as in (d).

The average dwell for SL depreciation is

$$L = \frac{\left(\sum_{t=0}^{n} t D_t\right)}{\sum_{t=0}^{n} D_t} = \frac{(n + 1)}{2} \tag{10-6}$$

For example, in SL depreciation of $1000 for four years, the depreciation charges are $250 each year; the first $250 stays in the account one year, the next two years, and so on, so that the average dwell is 2.5 years: $[250(1) + 250(2) + 250(3) + 250(4)]/1000$.

10.2.3 Sum-of-Years'-Digits (SYD) Depreciation

The sum-of-years'-digits schedule has linearly decreasing depreciation charges and was one of the first accelerated depreciation methods adopted by the IRS (it has not been a standard method since 1981).

Given a recovery period n, define $s = n(n + 1)/2$, the sum of the digits 1 through n. The depreciation charges are the linearly decreasing fractions $n/s, (n - 1)/s, \ldots, 1/s$ of the initial depreciable amount, for times t = 1, 2, \ldots ,n:

Whole-investment SYD depreciation: $D_t = B_0(n - t + 1)/s$ (10-7)

Net-investment SYD depreciation: $D_t = (B_0 - S_n)(n - t + 1)/s$ (10-8)

The average dwell for SYD depreciation is

$$L = \frac{n + 2}{3}$$ (10-9)

For example, in SYD depreciation of $1000 for four years, the sum of years' digits is 10, and the depreciation charges are $D_1 = \$400$, $D_2 = \$300$, $D_3 = \$200$, and $D_4 = \$100$; the average dwell is two years.

10.2.4 Declining Balance (DB) Depreciation

Recall that SL depreciation charges are an equal-payment series, and SYD charges are a gradient series. Declining balance (DB) depreciation is the schedule that is a geometric series. Each DB depreciation charge is a fraction α of the previous book value:

DB depreciation, first k periods: $D_t = \alpha B_{t-1}$, $t = 1, 2, \ldots ,k$ (10-10)

where $k < n$ for a switched DB schedule
$k = n$ for a recovery-period DB schedule
$k = \infty$ for a perpetual DB schedule

and
$0 < \alpha < 1$,   the *depreciation factor*

The initial depreciable amount is B_0 for both whole-investment and net-investment DB depreciation. Since all standard depreciation schedules in the United States are referenced to a recovery period n that is related to the estimated life, α is defined in terms of n. Specifically, the depreciation factor α is usually set by law or negotiation as a multiplier times $1/n$, and the multiplier is commonly 1.5 or 2. Thus there is the "2DB" or "double declining balance" (DDB) method and the "1.5DB" or "one and one-half declining balance" method, respectively meaning DB depreciation where $\alpha = 2/n$ or $1.5/n$.

From Eq. 10-1 and 10-10, given B_0 as the initial book value, the first k book values are

$$B_t = B_0(1 - \alpha)^t \qquad t = 1, 2, \ldots ,k$$ (10-11)

and the first k depreciation charges are

$$D_t = B_0\alpha(1 - \alpha)^{t-1} \qquad t = 1, 2, \ldots, k \qquad (10\text{-}12)$$

There are six versions of DB depreciation to consider: *switched DB* $(k > n)$, *recovery-period DB* $(k = n)$ and *perpetual DB* $(k = \infty)$, each for whole-investment depreciation and for net-investment depreciation.

Switched DB depreciation involves a switch at time $k + 1$ to SL deprecation of the remaining undepreciated balance, which is $B_k - S_n$ for net-investment depreciation. Since there are $n - t + 1$ depreciation charges from periods t through n, the SL alternative depreciation charge at t would be $(B_t - S_n)/(n - t + 1)$. Until this charge exceeds the DB charge αB_t, it is more advantageous for the taxpayer to stay with DB depreciation. The taxpayer chooses k as the greatest t for which the DB charge remains greater than the alternative SL charge, and then switches for periods $k + 1$ to n to the SL charge $(B_k - S_n)/(n - t + 1)$.

For example, in switched 1.5DB depreciation of a $1000 asset with a recovery period of $n = 4$ years and a zero salvage value, the depreciation factor is $\alpha = 1.5/n = 0.375$, and the depreciation schedule unfolds as shown in Table 10-3.

Note that the switch at $t = k + 1$ is not to the original SL depreciation schedule, but to the one that would begin at $k + 1$ to depreciate $B_k - S_n$ dollars in the remaining $n - k$ periods.

Whole-investment switched DB is identical, but with $S_n = 0$. Net-investment DB, as described above, was standard in the United States until 1981; MACRS and its successors prescribe whole-investment switched DDB depreciation for property with recovery periods 10 years or less, with the switch (at the correct time) built into the prescribed amounts.

In the MACRS variation of DB depreciation, an adjustment is included for a half-year convention under which, unless otherwise permitted or required, an asset is assumed to have been placed in service not at the beginning of the tax year but at midyear. Accordingly, MACRS prescribes only half the ordinary defined first-year depreciation, and the SL alternative assumes an additional half-year of remaining life after time n, so that the SL alternative D_t is $B_{t-1}/(n - t + 1 + 0.5)$ for $t = 2, \ldots, n$; it is half that for $t = 1$, and it is B_n for $t = n + 1$.

E11. **A 1992 IRS publication prescribes depreciation charges, in percentages of B_0, as 33.33%, 44.44%, 14.81%, and 7.41% at times $t = 1, 2, 3, 4$ for an asset with a three-year recovery-period assumed by the half-year convention to have been placed in service at time 0.5. Including the previously described adjustments for**

TABLE 10-3. Switched 1.5DB Depreciation Example

t	1.5DB D_t: αB_{t-1}	SL Alternative D_t: $B_{t-1}/(n - t + 1)$	Chosen D_t	B_t
0				1000
1	375	250	375	625
2	234.38	208.33	234.38	390.62
3	146.48	195.31 (switch)	195.31	195.31
4	91.55	195.31	195.31	0

the half-year convention, prepare a table in the format of Table 10-3, and determine whether it verifies the prescribed charges, for a 100 K$ asset with a three-year recovery period.

$\alpha = 2(1/3) = 0.6667$, $n = 3$. For $t = 1$ only, D_t's are halved; for $t = 4$, $D_t = B_3$.

t	DDB D_t: αB_{t-1}	SL alternative D_t: $B_{t-1}/(n - t + 1 + 0.5)$	Chosen D_t	B_t
0				100
1	33.33	28.57	33.33	66.67
2	44.44	26.67	44.44	22.22
3	14.81	14.81	14.81	7.41
4	4.94	7.41	7.41	0

Yes, the prescribed charges are verified.

Recovery-period DB depreciation depreciates an asset for not more than n periods, where the last depreciation charge D_n is B_{n-1} for whole-investment depreciation, or $B_{n-1} - S_n$ for net-investment depreciation.

For example, in recovery-period 1.5DB net-investment depreciation of a three-year $1000 asset with a $150 salvage value, the depreciation factor is $\alpha = 1.5/3 = 0.5$, and the depreciation schedule unfolds as shown in Table 10-4.

Table 10-5 shows the case in which the net-investment DB schedule fully depreciates the asset before time n. It is for the same example as above, but with DDB rather than 1.5DB, so that $\alpha = 2/3$.

Note that there is an *implied salvage value* associated with recovery-period DB depreciation. If DB depreciation runs for n years without adjustment of the last charge, then Eq. 10-11 implies

$$B_n = B_0(1 - \alpha)^n = \text{implied salvage value at } n$$

TABLE 10-4. Recovery-Period 1.5DB Depreciation Example

t	1.5DB D_t: αB_{t-1}	Upper Limit on D_t: $B_{t-1} - 150$	D_t	B_t
0				1000
1	500	850	500	500
2	250	350	250	250
3	125	100	100	$150 = S_n$

TABLE 10-5. Recovery-Period DDB Depreciation Example

t	DDB D_t: αB_{t-1}	Upper Limit on D_t: $B_{t-1} - 150$	Chosen D_t	B_t
0				1000
1	666.67	850	666.67	333.33
2	222.22	183.33	183.33	150
3	100	0	0	$150 = S_n$

For example, a \$1000 three-year asset would have an implied salvage value of

$$1000(1 - \alpha)^3$$

For 1.5DB, with $\alpha = 1.5/3 = 0.5$, the implied salvage value is \$125, while for DDB, with $\alpha = 2/3$, it is \$37.04. Tables 10-4 and 10-5 illustrated salvage values greater than the implied salvage value, so that the final depreciative charges were less than those given by Eq. 10-11. If the salvage value is small, the final depreciation charge is greater than that given by Eq. 10-11. Table 10-6 illustrates this: let a \$1000 three-year asset with a salvage value of \$0 be depreciated on a DDB recovery-period schedule, so that $\alpha = 2/3$ and $S_n = 0$. The result is a "balloon" final depreciation charge.

The implied salvage value is used as a basis for choosing the DB depreciation factor in some negotiated schedules. For example, if the salvage value for a three-year \$1000 asset was $S_3 = \$150$, then the implied salvage value equals the estimated salvage value if

$$100(1 - \alpha)^3 = 150$$

This implies a depreciation factor $\alpha = 0.46867$ (so that the corresponding multiplier would be 3α, or about 1.4; "1.4DB" depreciation would come out about even for this example, as illustrated in Table 10-7, where $\alpha = 1.4/3$ and $S_n = 150$).

Perpetual DB depreciation ($k = \infty$) follows Eqs. 10-11 and 10-12 "forever" or until the salvage value or a negligible book value is reached. For example, at 12 years a three-year \$1000 asset has a 1.5DB depreciation charge of $D_{12} = 1000\alpha(1 - \alpha)^{11}$ where $\alpha = 1.5/3$, which would be about \$0.24, giving a book value $B_{12} = 1000(1 - \alpha)^{12}$, which is also about \$0.24. The net-investment version of perpetual DB depreciation stops at the salvage value in the obvious manner.

TABLE 10-6. Recovery-Period DDB Example with \$0 Salvage

t	DDB D_t: αB_{t-1}	Upper Limit on D_t: $B_t - S_n$	Last Charge $D_n = B_{n-1} - S_n$	Chosen D_t	B_t
0					1000
1	666.67	1000		666.67	333.33
2	222.22	333.33		222.22	111.11
3	74.07	111.11	111.11	111.11	111.11

TABLE 10-7. Recovery-Period 1.4DB Example

t	1.4DB D_t: αB_{t-1}	Upper Limit on D_t: $B_t - S_n$	Last Charge $D_n = B_{n-1} - S_n$	Chosen D_t	B_t
0					1000
1	466.67	850		466.67	533.33
2	247.89	383.33		248.89	284.44
3	132.74[a]	134.44	134.44	134.44	150 = S_n

[a]Would be exactly 134.44 if $\alpha = 0.48867$, giving "1.4060DB" depreciation.

E12. A \$1000 asset has an estimated $S_n = \$150$ salvage value at time $n = 3$ and is depreciated by perpetual net-investment 1.5DB depreciation ($\alpha = 1.5/3$). It was put in service at the start of the tax year. Determine the entire schedule.

t	1.5DB D_t: αB_{t-1}	Upper Limit on D_t: $B_{t-1} - S_n$	D_t	B_t
0				1000
1	500	850	500	500
2	250	350	250	250
3	125	100	100	$150 = S_n$

Modify the schedule for an estimated salvage value of $S_n = \$23$ instead of \$150.

3	125	227	125	125
4	62.50	120	62.50	62.50
5	31.25	39.50	31.25	31.25
6	15.63	8.25	8.25	$23 = S_n$

The whole-investment version of perpetual DB depreciation does not stop and is the basis for *declining class account* (DCA) depreciation, to be discussed in the next section.

Average dwell times for DB schedules are determined by applying Eq. 10-2, with two special considerations: There can be more than n terms (since not all versions of DB depreciation equate the estimated life with the recovery period), and the rule for determining D_t can switch at time $k + 1$.

The simplest case is the dwell for perpetual whole-investment DB depreciation. Since for whole-investment schedules the sum of charges is B_0, and since $D_t = B_0\alpha(1 - \alpha)^{t-1}$, the perpetual ($k = \infty$) DB dwell is

Perpetual whole-investment DB average dwell time:

$$L = \frac{\sum_{t=0}^{\infty} t D_t}{\sum_{t=0}^{\infty} D_t} = \alpha[1 + 2(1 - \alpha) + 3(1 - \alpha)^2 + ...] = \frac{1}{\alpha} \qquad (10\text{-}13)$$

For example, if a whole asset with an estimated life of 7 years is depreciated by perpetual DDB depreciation, so that $\alpha = 2/7$, the average dwell time is $7/2 = 3.5$ years.

When there is closure or switching at time $k + 1$, the dwell contribution of the portion of B_0 that follows the DB rule (Eq. 10-12) is

Dwell of DB-rule charges before closure or switching:

$$L = \frac{\sum_{t=0}^{k} t D_t}{\sum_{t=0}^{k} D_t} = \frac{1}{\alpha} - \frac{k(1 - \alpha)^k}{1 - (1 - \alpha)^k} \qquad (10\text{-}14)$$

Equation 10-14 gives the dwell of the first k charges, computed as $D_t = \alpha B_{t-1}$ for $t = 1, \ldots, k$. This is the average dwell of $B_0 - B_k$ dollars in the depreciation account. The remaining B_k dollars either dwell longer or have a dwell of exactly k, depending on whether there is switching or closure at k. For *switched* whole-investment DB depreciation, define L_{SL} as the average SL dwell, from Eq. 10-6, of the B_k dollars that are depreciated by the SL method starting at $k + 1$ (where n in Eq. 10-6 is the number of SL charges, and $t = 0$ represents actual time k). Also define L_{DB} as the average dwell of the first $B_0 - B_k$ dollars, from Eq. 10-14. Then the average dwell for the entire switched whole-investment DB schedule is the amount-weighted average of the DB and SL dwells:

$$L = \frac{(B_0 - B_k)L_{DB} + B_k(L_{SL} + k)}{B_0} \tag{10-15}$$

E13. In the depreciation schedule shown in Table 10-3, there was DB depreciation of a $B_0 = 1000$ asset for the first $k = 2$ yr at $\alpha = 0.375$, leaving a book value of $B_2 = 390.62$. Then the remaining 392.62 was depreciated for 2 years by SL. Determine the average dwell from Eq. 10-15 and from first principles.

From Eq. 10-15 (L_{DB} from Eq. 10-14, L_{SL} from Eq. 10-6):

$$L_{DB} = \frac{1}{\alpha} - \frac{2(1-\alpha)^2}{1-(1-\alpha)^2} = 1.385$$

$$L_{SL} = \frac{2+1}{2} = 1.5$$

$$L = \frac{(1000 - 390.62)L_{DB} + 390.62(L_{SL} + 2)}{1000} = \underline{\underline{2.2109 \text{ yr}}}$$

From first principles ($1D_1 + 2D_2 + 3D_3 + 4D_4$):

$$L = \frac{1(375) + 2(234.38) + 3(195.31) + 4(195.31)}{1000} = \underline{\underline{2.2109 \text{ yr}}}$$

10.2.5 Declining Class Account (DCA) Depreciation

Equipment such as railroad track, pipeline, smelting plant, assembly lines, switchgear, power lines, and chemical processing plant is awkward to depreciate as individual items, because the items are married together. In an oil refinery, for example, you do see identifiable pieces of equipment—furnaces, distillation towers, pumps—but the most costly "item" is the network of pipes that interconnects everything. The piping is like a stocking that eventually becomes mostly darn; parts of it are various ages, some much younger than the age of the plant.

By the 1940s, the IRS had enough power to curb the practice of claiming noncapital expense status for practically every expenditure that did not add a recognizable new item to the equipment inventory. The general rule that repairs are noncapital expenses but replacements are capital expenditures was increasingly enforced. A typical ruling was that if you replace the bundle of tubes in a shell-and-tube heat exchanger, the new bundle is depreciable, but if you replace all but one tube in a bundle, you have incurred a noncapital repair expense.

When large companies found themselves keeping track of tens of thousands of individual depreciation accounts, requiring tens of dollars of accounting effort per year per account, with each account representing only hundreds of dollars of investment, some of them took action. By the end of the 1950s *class account* depreciation schedules had been negotiated for most of the largest stationary industrial equipment complexes in the United States.

The most commonly used of these negotiated class-account schedules is the *declining class account* (DCA) schedule, which is based on whole-investment perpetual DB depreciation. We will describe the beginning-of-year version, in which assets are treated mathematically as if they were placed in service (commissioned) at the beginning of the tax year, and a correction will be made to account for the fact that the average commissioning time is at midyear.

DCA depreciation is very simple: All depreciable equipment having an estimated economic life in a given range is added to the appropriate n-life DCA class account when put into service, where n is a typical life for items in the n-life class. The account begins the tth tax year with a book value B_{t-1}, builds up to $B_{t-1} + V_t$ during the year, where V_t is the sum of all capital expenditures during the year in the n-life class, and is decremented by a depreciation charge $D_t = \alpha(B_{t-1} + V_t)$ at the end of the year.

Declining class account (DCA) depreciation:

$$D_t = \alpha(B_{t-1} + V_t) \tag{10-16}$$

$$B_t = B_{t-1} + V_t - D_t \tag{10-17}$$

Any disposals of capital equipment are taxed as income or capital gains, according to relevant tax law, without affecting the class accounts.

E14. **In its 1991 tax year, a factory added \$312,444.96 of capital investments to its five-year declining class account, for which $\alpha = 0.375$ is the depreciation fraction. If the account started with a balance of \$6,111,257.88, what was the year-end depreciation charge and 1991 book value?**

$$D_{1991} = \alpha(B_{1990} + V_{1991}) = 0.357(6,111,247.88 + 312,444.96) = \underline{\$2,293,261.91}$$

$$B_{1991} = B_{1990} + V_{1991} - D_{1991} = \underline{\$4,130,440.93}$$

Note that a class account with a single item in it at time zero, with no additions ($V_t = 0$ for $t = 1, 2,...$), follows Eqs. 10-11 and 10-12 forever. Thus, for any particular item in the account, its depreciation follows a *perpetual whole-investment DB schedule.* Hence an individual item's exact depreciation schedule could be reconstructed from its initial cost, date put in service, and class membership.

E15. **The factory in Example E14 has undergone a tax audit, and a \$3200.16 access platform that was built during tax year 1988 has been found to have wrongly been expensed; it should have been added to this account. The factory's amended tax returns will show removal of a \$3200.16 expense for 1988. They must also show additional depreciation charges for 1989, 1990, and 1991. Determine these, and determine the corrected 1991 book value of the five-year declining class account.**

This asset's contribution to the DCA account:

t	$D_t = \alpha B_{t-1}$	B_t
1988		3200.16
1989	1142.46	2057.70
1990	734.60	1323.10
1991	472.35	850.75

The additional depreciation charges are as shown in the D_t column. The 1991 book value should be corrected to $4,130,440.93 + 850.75 = \underline{\$4,131,291.68}$

Since DCA depreciation is perpetual whole-investment DB depreciation for every item in a declining class account, the average dwell is the same as that given by Eq. 10-13.

DCA average dwell time:

$$L = \frac{1}{\alpha} \tag{10-18}$$

Recall from Eq. 10-6 that the average dwell time for SL depreciation, under the beginning-of-year convention, is $(n + 1)/2$. That is, with SL depreciation, the tax reductions due to a capital expenditure are triggered by depreciation charges an average of $(n + 1)/2$ years later than the beginning of the year in which they occurred.

By equating dwell times in Eqs. 10-6 and 10-18, we can obtain expressions to determine the depreciation factor α that gives a DCA schedule that depreciates assets just as fast as a given SL schedule with recovery period n, and vice versa.

α for DCA with same dwell as SL with given n:

$$\alpha = \frac{2}{n + 1} \tag{10-19}$$

n for SL with same dwell as DCA with given α:

$$n = \frac{2 - \alpha}{\alpha} = \frac{2}{\alpha - 1} \tag{10-20}$$

E16. Determine the appropriate α for DCA depreciation of assets in the five-year class, if the alternative is SL depreciation.

$$\alpha = \frac{2}{n + 1} = \frac{2}{5 + 1} = \underline{\underline{0.3333}}$$

Note that Eqs. 10-19 and 10-20 do not give equivalent DCA and SL schedules in the true sense; rather, they give schedules that have the same average dwell times. As will be seen in Section 10.2.7, the present worth of tax effects of a DCA schedule is slightly greater than that of the same-dwell SL schedule.

To accommodate the half-year convention, DCA schedules can be adjusted either by halving first-year depreciation charges, so that Eq. 10-16 is replaced by

DCA adjustment to half-year convention:

$$D_t = \alpha(B_{t-1} + 0.5V_t) \tag{10-16a}$$

or by adjusting α. Here we will adjust α, so as to preserve the simplicity of the dwell relationships in Eqs. 10-18, 10-19, 10-20.

An appropriate α for use with DCA depreciation under the beginning-of-year convention (Eqs. 10-16 and 10-17, not 10-16a and 10-17) is α such that the DCA schedules have the same dwell as standard schedules. It is recognized that in both the DCA and standard schedules the first charge occurs an average of six months after commissioning.

Table 10-8 lists the average dwell times (from start of tax year, not commissioning time) of the standard MACRS depreciation procedures published by the IRS in 1992 for equipment in various life classes from three years to 20 years, and it also lists the parameters of the DCA or perpetual DB schedule that has the same average dwell time.

E17. A $10,000 asset that your company has acquired is a "computer" under the classification system of Table 10-2. The IRS provides a standard depreciation schedule applicable to such equipment. However, your company actually uses DCA depreciation and has established five accounts, having depreciation fractions α of 0.10, 0.20, 0.30, 0.35, and 0.5. You are allowed to depreciate assets in the fastest (greatest α) DCA account whose dwell is no briefer than that of the currently published standard method. Assuming the 1992 MACRS rules are in effect, which DCA account can you use?

Table 10-2 gives $n = 5$ for computers. Table 10-6 shows that a DCA account with the same dwell would have $\alpha = 0.3574$. The fastest allowable account is the one that has $\alpha = \underline{0.35}$.

The DB multiplier column in Table 10-8 shows that the 1992 MACRS schedules have similar dwell times to those of 1.5DB and DDB (perpetual) schedules. Note that

TABLE 10-8. 1992 Standard Dwells and DCA Parameters

n Life Class (yr)	L Standard 1992 MACRS Average Dwell Time (yr)	$\alpha = 1/L$ DB or DCA Depreciation Fraction for Same Dwell	$x = 2L/(n + 1)$ DB multiplier giving same dwell and α
3	1.963	0.5094	1.528
5	2.798	0.3574	1.787
7	3.620	0.2762	1.934
10	4.844	0.2064	2.064
15	7.803	0.1282	1.922
20	10.166	0.0984	1.967

the multiplier gradually increases with estimated life, except that it is greater for $n = 7$ and especially $n = 10$ than the general trend, indicating a slight inconsistency in the standard schedules in favor of assets with these estimated lives.

Let us briefly consider the question of how a tax authority could derive a consistent set of standard depreciation schedules. A reasonable basis is SL depreciation. Figure 10-2 compares the average dwells of the 1992 MACRS schedules with those of SL depreciation for the same n. The two curves would almost coincide, with less than 5% error, if the SL dwell times were multiplied by 0.94. This means, within 5% error, that in 1992 the IRS's standard depreciation schedules had dwell times that could be characterized by the following expression:

Dwell times (within 5%) of 1992 MACRS standard schedules:

$$L_{standard} = \frac{0.94(n + 1)}{2} \qquad \text{for} \quad n = 3, 4, 7, 10, 15, 20 \qquad (10\text{-}21)$$

Thus the speed-of-depreciation policy of a tax authority can be described, with little error, in terms of just two things: (1) how it requires or allows estimated lives to be determined, and (2) the ratio of allowed depreciation dwell time to that of ordinary straight-line depreciation. The estimated life scale in Figure 10-2 shows the approximate estimated lives for equipment that the IRS had assigned to the various life classes of $n = 3, 4, 7, 10, 15,$ and 20.

The DCA schedule having a given dwell time has almost the same tax effects as those of any other method likely to be encountered in practice. This will be seen in detail in Section 10.2.7. In particular, methods likely to be chosen by a taxpayer or published or standard by a

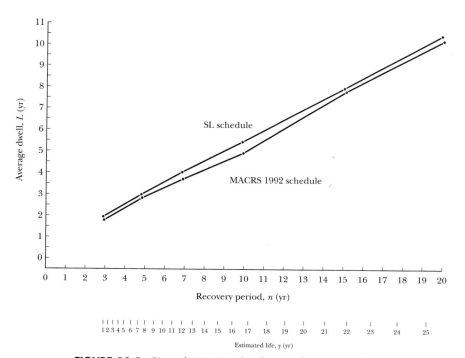

FIGURE 10-2. SL and MACRS dwell times for various lives.

TABLE 10-9. Accuracy of Simulating Standard Schedules by DCA

n, Life Class, (yr)	(n + 1)/3, Average SL Dwell (yr)	L, 94% of SL Dwell (yr)	α = 1/L, Depreciation Fraction Implied by L	Depreciation Fraction Implied by 1992 MACRS	Percentage Error in α Compared to 1992 MACRS
3	2	1.88	0.5319	0.5094	+4.4%
5	3	2.82	0.3546	0.3574	−0.8%
7	4	3.76	0.2660	0.2762	−3.7%
10	5	4.70	0.2128	0.2064	+3.1%
15	8	7.52	0.1330	0.1282	+3.7%
20	10.5	9.87	0.1013	0.0984	+2.9%

tax authority tend to have the DCA *shape* (that of a decreasing geometric series), so the DCA curve with the same "*size*" (dwell) can do a good job of representing any practical depreciation curve.

Table 10-9 illustrates simulation of 1992 schedules with DCA schedules having 94% of SL dwell times:

10.2.6 Expensing as Depreciation

"Computers are a great expense but a lousy investment," business executives agree. Businesses tend to rely on the tax relief from depreciation charges as sources of equipment replacement funding, or to use depreciation charges as a basis for budgeting for replacement. It is galling to hold—or sell—obsolete equipment that hasn't paid for itself and has a greater book value than its true worth.

Crying over sunk costs aside, it is always true that, given a choice, it is better to treat an expenditure as a noncapital expense than as a capital investment. Tax relief now is better than tax relief later.

Engineers should be aware of certain strategies in wide use to maximize the noncapital portions of expenditures.

1. *Small expenditures are expensed.* Many companies or their accounting firms have obtained agreement that any expenditure not exceeding a given limit is to be expensed. The limits acceptable to tax authorities vary by industry, but limits of $500 and even $750 had become common in heavy industry by 1990. The IRS audits hundreds of cases each year in which a taxpayer is accused of "piecemealing"— breaking up an obviously coherent capital expenditure into expensable pieces.
2. *Any large project has portions justifiably treated as expenses.* Without engaging in piecemealing, one can reclassify as expenses any activities such as site cleanup, repairs of inactive equipment that will become part of the project, and the like, that can be justified (perhaps tenuously) as being needed even if the project is not implemented. Such expenses must be treated in the cost accounting system as independent of the project.
3. *Repairs are expenses.* Especially when equipment is waiting to go back into service, it is cheaper, for example, to replace the impeller of a large pump than to repair and reinstall it. But since repair allows expensing, repair may be better after taxes than replacement.

4. *Life estimation is a ritual.* In the United States, the IRS currently publishes recovery periods (see Table 10-2) that are just enough shorter than average economic lives so that few taxpayers will beg exceptions except for robotics, graphics, and other kinds of rapidly obsolescent equipment whose quality will increase while prices drop. Let y denote the estimated life of a piece of equipment. The approximate empirical relationship

$$n = 2.7e^{0.0783y}$$

(where e = 2.71828... is the natural logarithm base) gives recovery periods or life classes n in terms of estimated lives; for example, an estimated life of $y = 8$ yr corresponds to a recovery period of $n = 5$ yr approximately. But the life classification system is very coarse: Nothing gets depreciated for less than 3 years if depreciated, nor for 4, 6, 8, or 9 years. Because the system is based on descriptions (not on life estimation procedures), there can be great advantages in conscious management of wording in catalogs, purchase orders, and cost accounts. For example, part of a process controller (say one that controls pressure in a tank) may be a computer. Described as a whole, the system may be in the 10-year class, but separate treatment may justify the computer portion's being in the 3-year class. In an amusing abuse of this strategy, a professional sports team tried to classify a scoreboard as a computer; this $30,000 computer just happened to have a $350,000 monitor.

5. *Cashing in is disadvantageous.* In the taxing of income or capital gains, money is not taxed except when it changes hands. Example E18 in Section 10.2.7 will show the tax advantages of incorporating salvageable capital assets into their successors, reducing the costs of the replacement assets rather than selling the old assets. Net-investment depreciation, which amounts to being taxed in advance on the salvage value, is a particularly disadvantageous form of cashing in; but at the end of the asset's life the taxpayer is almost forced to sell the asset rather than use it further, because the proceeds from selling are not taxed, although any further income from the assets would be taxed.

10.2.7 Present Worth of Depreciation Charge Schedules

In this section we will establish the present worth of various depreciation schedules, introduce the concept of *efficiency* of a depreciation schedule, and show that engineers can ignore depreciation accounting details and can represent depreciation effects in after-tax analysis using only life class and depreciation efficiency.

The worth of an *expense* of amount F is the expense itself. The worth of its tax relief is TF, where T is the marginal income tax rate. If the expense occurs at time zero and creates something of value that can be disposed of at a gain of S_n dollars at time n (S_n will be income, not capital gain), the present worth contribution to the taxable income is $-(F - S_n\beta^n)$, and the present worth of its tax relief is $T(F - S_n\beta^n)$. Its entire after-tax effect has a present worth of $-(1 - T)(F - S_n\beta^n)$.

Let B_0 represent a capital investment amount at time zero, and let S_n represent its salvage value at time n. The present worth of a *whole-investment SL* depreciation schedule (Eq. 10-4) is easily computed via the "pain" factor, since there are n equal depreciation charges of B_0/n dollars each.

Present worth of whole-investment SL depreciation charges:

$$P\{D_d\} = (B_0/n)(P/A\ i,n) = (B_0/n)(1 - \beta^n)/i \qquad (10\text{-}22)$$

Under whole-investment depreciation the salvage value S_n is income or capital gain. The investment's present worth contribution to after-tax income (that is, the negative of the investment's after-tax cost) is $-B_0 + TP\{D_d\} + TS_n\beta^n$, where TS_n is replaced by T_cS_n if there is a separate tax rate T_c for capital gains.

The present worth of a *net-investment SL* depreciation schedule (Eq. 10-5) has the salvage value taxed throughout the schedule, although it is not received until the end.

Present worth of net-investment SL depreciation charges:

$$P\{D_d\} = \frac{B_0 - S_n}{n}(P/A\ i,n) = (B_0 - S_n/n)\left(\frac{1 - \beta^n}{i}\right) \qquad (10\text{-}23)$$

The investment's present worth contribution to after-tax income is $-B_0 + TP\{D_d\} + S_n\beta^n$.

E18. At $i = 15\%$ and $T = 0.40$, a project has an after-tax present worth for net non-capital items of \$96,401.50. (That is, considering everything except capital, $P_{at} = 96{,}401.50$.) There is a capital investment of $B_0 = \$86{,}000$ in a machine at time zero, depreciable by a straight-line method with $n = 7$; at time 7, the machine will be replaced with an identical one. No monetary inflation will occur. The second machine will cost the same amount as the first, and each will have a \$17,000 salvage value. First determine $P\{D_d\}$ and the present worth contribution to after-tax income for a single machine under both whole-investment and net-investment SL depreciation. Then determine the after-tax present worth of the entire project (net noncapital items and two machines) under four cases: whole-investment and net-investment SL depreciation, with and without absorbing the salvage value of the first machine into the cost of the second.

Whole-investment depreciation of a single machine:

$B_0 = 86{,}000$; $n = 7$; $i = 15\%$; $(P/A\ i,n) = (1 - \beta^7)/i$, where $\beta = 1/(1 + i)$

$P\{D_d\} = (86{,}000/7)(1 - \beta^7)/i = \underline{\$51{,}113.73}$ \qquad from Eq. 10-22

After-tax present worth contribution $-B_0 + TP\{D_d\} + TS_n\beta^n$, with $T = 0.40$ and $S_n = 17{,}000$: $\underline{-\$62{,}998.14}$

Net-investment depreciation of a single-machine:

$P\{D_d\} = (86{,}000 - 17{,}000)(1 - \beta^7)/i7 = \underline{\$41{,}009.85}$ \qquad from Eq. 10-23

After-tax present worth contribution $-B_0 + TP\{D_d\} + S_n\beta^n$: $\underline{-\$63{,}205.13}$

Note that whole-investment depreciation is more favorable.

Whole-investment depreciation of a single machine:

Noncapital returns are worth \$96,401.50. Each machine contributes $-\$62998.14$ when installed.

$$P_{at} = 96{,}401.50 - 62{,}998.14 - 62{,}998.14\beta^7 = \underline{\$9720.02}$$

If the first machine's salvage value is absorbed into the cost of the second machine, the first machine has no $TS_n\beta^n$ term in its after-tax worth, and the second machine has an investment of only $69,000.

$P\{D_d\}$ remains $51,113.73 for the first machine, and with $S_7 = 0$ its after-tax contribution becomes $-86,000 + TP\{D_d\} = -\$65,554.51$. $P\{D_d\}$ becomes $41,009.85 for the second machine, and with its salvage value its after-tax contribution, as of time 7, becomes $-69,000 + 0.40(41,009.85) + 0.40(17,000\beta^7) = -\$50,039.69$.

$$P_{at} = 96,401.50 - 65,554.51 - 50,039.69\beta^7 = \underline{\$12,035.22}$$

Note that using salvage value to reduce investment in a replacement is a favorable strategy; with whole-investment depreciation it added over $2300 of after-tax present worth.

Entire project with net-investment depreciation:

$$P_{at} = 96,401.50 - 63,205.13 - 63,205.13\beta^7 = \$9435.22$$

If the first machine's salvage value is absorbed into the cost of the second machine, the net investment is the entire $86,000, so that $P\{D_d\} = \$51,113.73$ for the first machine. Its after-tax contribution has no salvage term and becomes $-86,000 + TP\{D_d\} = -\$65,554.41$. The second machine's first cost is reduced by the $17,000 salvage value of the first machine, and its *net* cost also takes into account its own salvage value; thus $52,000 is depreciated, given $P\{D_d\} = \$30,905.98$ for the second machine as of time 7. The second machine has a salvage value of $17,000 and a first cost of $69,000, so at time 7 the after-tax worth of its contribution is $-69,000 + TP\{D_d\} + 17,000\beta^7 = -\$50,246.68$.

$$P_{at} = 96,401.50 - 65,555.51 - 50,246.68\beta^7 = \underline{\$11,957.40}$$

Absorbing the first machine's salvage value again saves money, adding over $2500 to present worth. Cost absorption treats the first machine the same as does whole-investment depreciation and hence diminishes the disadvantage of net-investment depreciation.

The present worth of a *whole-investment SYD* depreciation schedule (Eq. 10-7) is the present worth of a linear gradient series, because the first charge is $B_0 n/s$ where $s = n(n + 2)/2$, and the charges decrease by B_0/s each time. Setting $A_1 = B_0 n/s$ and $G = -B_0/s$ in the linear gradient present worth formula (Eq. 2-17), we obtain a formula which simplifies to

Present worth of whole-investment SYD depreciation charges:

$$P\{D_d\} = (B_0/si)(n - (P/A\ i,n)) \tag{10-24}$$

The investment's present worth contribution to after-tax income is $-B_0 + TP\{D_d\} + TS_n\beta^n$, where TS_n is replaced by T_cS_n if there is a separate tax rate T_i for capital gains.

The present worth of a *net-investment SYD* depreciation schedule (Eq. 10-8) is

Present worth of net-investment SYD depreciation charges:

$$P\{D_d\} = \frac{B_0 - S_n}{si}[n - (P/A\ i,n)] \tag{10-25}$$

and the negative of the after-tax cost is $-B_0 + TP\{D_d\} + S_n\beta^n$.

E19. A depreciation schedule approved by a tax authority is as follows:

t, Time After Commissioning (yr)	D_t/B_0, Relative Depreciation Charge
0.5	0.20
1.5	0.32
2.5	0.192
3.5	0.1152
4.5	0.1152
5.5	0.0576
	1.0000

For both SL and SYD depreciation, derive a schedule with charges at $t = 1, 2,$ ..., 5 (not 0.5, 1.5, etc.) having the least n that gives at least the same dwell times as that of the approved schedule. List their sequence of relative depreciation charges D_t/B_0 for $t = 1, 2, \ldots, 5$, and compare the present worths of the approved, the SL, and the SYD depreciation schedules (per dollar of B_0) at $i = 15\%$.

Average dwell time of the approved schedule:

$$0.5(0.20) + 1.5(0.32) + 2.5(0.192) + 3.5(0.1152) + 4.5(0.1152) +$$
$$5.5(0.0576) = \underline{2.2984\ yr}$$

SL schedule: $n \geq 2L - 1$ (from Eq. 10-6) implies $n \geq 3.5968$. Set $\underline{n = 4}$. $D_t/B_0 = 0.25$, $t = 1,...,4$. *SYD schedule:* $n \geq 3L - 2$ (from Eq. 10-9) implies $n \geq 4.8952$. Set $\underline{n = 5}$. $\{D_d\} = \{5/15, 4/15,...,1/15\}$.

t	D_t/B_0 for SL	D_t/B_0 for SYD
1	0.25	5/15
2	0.25	4/15
3	0.25	3/15
4	0.25	2/15
5		1/15

From Eq. 10-22 for SL:
$$P\{D_d\}^{SL} = (1/4)(P/A\ 15\%, 4) = 0.7137446$$

From Eq. 10-24 for SYD:
$$P\{D_d\}^{SYD} = (1/si)[5 - (P/A\ i,5)]\ \text{where}\ s = 15$$
$$P = 0.7323755$$

For the approved schedule: $P\{D_d\} = 0.20\beta^{0.5} + 0.32\beta^{1.5} + 0.192\beta^{2.5} + 0.1152\beta^{3.5} + 0.1152\beta^{4.5} + 0.0576\beta^{5.5} = \underline{0.7401194}$.

Neither SL nor SYD can equal the approved schedule's present worth, both because the integer n requirement makes them unable to achieve equal dwell time, and because their distribution is not as left-skewed as that of the approved schedule.

To derive the present worth of various DB schedules, we first note that from Eq. 10-12 the *present worth of the first k DB depreciation charges* is

$$P\{D_i: \ t{=}1,...,k\} = B_0\alpha\sum_{t=1}^{k}(1-\alpha)^{t-1}\beta^t$$

$$= B_0\alpha\beta\frac{1-(1-\alpha)^k\beta^k}{1-(1-\alpha)\beta} \tag{10-26}$$

For example, for $B_0 = \$1000$ and $\alpha = 0.2$, the first $k = 3$ DB depreciation charges are $\$200$, $\$160$, and $\$128$. The present worth of these first three charges at $i = 15\%$ is $200\beta + 160\beta^2 + 128\beta^3 = \$379.06$, and Eq. 10-26 gives the same result.

By setting $k = \infty$ in Eq. 10-26, we immediately have the *present worth of a perpetual DB* schedule:

$$P\{D_i: \ t{=}1,...,\infty\} = B_0\alpha\beta\frac{1}{1-(1-\alpha)\beta} \tag{10-27}$$

This formula also gives the present worth of a DCA schedule.

To determine the present worth of a *switched DB* depreciation schedule, first determine k (from Section 10.2.4, the optimal k is the greatest t for which $\alpha B_t > (B_t - S_n)/[n - (t + 1)]$. Then determine the present worth of the first k charges from Eq. 10-26; this is $P\{D_i: \ t = 1,...,k\}$. Finally, from Eq. 10-22 or 10-23, determine the present worth of the SL depreciation of the underpreciated amount of $B_k - S_n$ (which becomes B_0 in Eq. 10-22 or $B_0 - S_n$ in Eq. 10-23) for the remaining number of periods $n - k$ (which becomes n in Eq. 10-22 or 10-23); this is the worth of $\{D_i: \ t = k+1,...,n\}$ as of time k; call it $P_k\{D_i: \ t = k+1,...,n\}$. Thus the *present worth of the entire switched DB depreciation schedule* is

$$P\{D_d\} = P\{D_i: \ t = 1,...,k\} + \beta^k P_k\{D_i: \ t = k+1,...,n\} \tag{10-28}$$

An alternative procedure, or course, is to generate the entire schedule, multiply each D_t by β^t, and sum the results.

To determine the present worth of a *recovery-period DB* schedule, first determine $P\{D_i: \ t = 1,...,n\}$ by setting $k = n$ in Eq. 10-26. This is the present worth if the actual salvage equal value S_n equals the implied salvage value $B_0(1 - \alpha)^n$. Then adjust the result for the discrepancy in salvage value. If the asset is fully depreciated before time n, the actual charge for the last one or more periods may be zero; conversely, there can be a balloon charge at time n. In either case, let m denote any period for which the actual charge Δ_m does not equal the computed charge D_m from Eq. 10-12. To adjust the present worth add

$$\sum_m (\Delta_m - D_m)\beta^m \qquad m \in \{t: D_t \neq \Delta_t\}$$

to the present worth. That is, add the sum of adjustments, where each adjustment is the difference between the actual and computed depreciation charge, multiplied by its discount factor.

E20. A $10,000 asset is to be depreciated for $n = 12$ years according to a recovery-period DB schedule with $\alpha = 0.20$. Determine the implied salvage value. Then determine the present worth of the depreciation schedule at $i = 15\%$ for (a) whole-investment depreciation, (b) net-investment depreciation with a salvage value of $500, and (c) net-investment depreciation with a salvage value of $1000.

Implied salvage value:

$$B_n = B_0(1 - \alpha)^n = 10,000(1 - 0.20)^{12} = \underline{\$687.19}$$

(a) Whole-investment depreciation

From Eq. 10-26, with $\beta = 1/1.15$ and $k = n = 12$:

$$P\{D_t: \ t = 1,...,12\} = 10,000\alpha\beta\frac{1 - (1 - \alpha)^{12}\beta^{12}}{1 - (1 - \alpha)\beta} = \underline{\$5640.89}$$

From Eq. 10-12, the computed charge at n is

$$D_{12} = B_0\alpha(1 - \alpha)^{11} = \underline{\$171.80}$$

The last charge is B_{n-1} for whole-investment depreciation:

$$\Delta_{12} = B_{n-1} = B_0(1 - \alpha)^{n-1} = 10,000(1 - 0.20)^{11} = \underline{\$858.99}$$

The adjustment to be added is $(\Delta_{12} - D_{12})\beta^{12} = (858.99 - 171.80)\beta^{12} = \underline{\$128.44}$

Thus the whole-investment DB present worth is

$$P = 5640.89 + 128.44 = \underline{\$5769.33}$$

(b) Net-investment depreciation $S_{12} - \$500$:

The last charge is $\Delta_{12} = B_{n-1} = 858.99 - 500 = \underline{\$358.99}$
The adjustment to be added is $(\Delta_{12} - D_{12})\beta^{12} = (358.99 - 171.80)\beta^{12} = \underline{\$34.99}$
Thus the net-investment DB present worth is

$$P = 5640.89 + 34.99 = \underline{\$5675.88}$$

(c) Net-investment depreciation with $S_{12} = \$1000$:

The asset will be depreciated to a book value of $S_{12} = \$1000$. From Eq. 10-11 determine the number of periods to reach $B_t = 1000$.

$$1000 = 10,000(1 - \alpha)^t \quad \text{implies} \quad t = (\ln 0.1)/\ln(1 - \alpha) = \underline{10.31 \text{ yr}}$$

Thus the depreciation charges will be $\Delta_t = D_t$ according to Eq. 10-12 for the first 10 periods, Δ_{11} will be smaller than D_{11}, and D_{12} will be zero.

$$B_{10} = 10,000(1 - \alpha)^{10} = \$1073.74$$

$$\Delta_{11} = B_{10} - S_{12} = \$73.74 \quad \text{but} \quad D_{11} = 10,000\alpha(1 - \alpha)^{10} = \$214.75$$

$$\Delta_{12} = 0 \quad \text{but} \quad D_{12} = \$171.80$$

$$P = 5640.89 + (\Delta_{11} - D_{11})\beta^{11} + (\Delta_{12} - D_{12})\beta^{12}$$
$$= 5640.89 + (-141.01)\beta^{11} + (-171.80)\beta^{12} = \underline{\$5578.47}$$

The present worth of depreciation charges attributable to an asset of cost B_0 put into a declining class account (DCA) is the same as if it were individually depreciated in a perpetual DB schedule. Equation 10-27 applies and is repeated here.

Present worth of DCA depreciation:

$$P\{D_i: \ t = 1,...,\infty\} = B_0\alpha\beta\frac{1}{1 - (1 - \alpha)\beta} \tag{10-27}$$

In the 1980s the IRS began publishing standard schedules that used the half-year convention, by which the first depreciation charge is halved to recognize that the typical asset commissioned during a tax year is in service only six months by the time the first depreciation charge Δ_1 triggers a tax relief amount $T\Delta_1$.

For a separate asset, the first depreciation charge in DB depreciation under the half-year convention is $D_1 = 0.5\alpha B_0$ so that the book value becomes $B_1 = B_0(1 - 0.5\alpha)$. Then $D_2 = \alpha B_1 = B_1\alpha(1 - 0.5\alpha)$, so that $B_2 = B_1 - D_2 = B_0(1 - 0.5\alpha) - B_0\alpha(1 - 0.5\alpha) = B_0(1 - 0.5\alpha)(1 - \alpha)$, and so forth. An asset's individual contribution within a declining class account (DCA) follows the same trajectory, where the overall depreciation charges are those given by Eq. 10-16a in Section 10.2.5. Let us denote perpetual DB and DCA schedules under the half-year convention as HDB schedules. The depreciation charges are given by the appropriate modification of Eq. 10-12.

Depreciation charges for HDB (half-year convention) schedules:

$$D_1 = 0.5\alpha B_0$$

$$D_t = B_0\alpha(1 - 0.5\alpha)(1 - \alpha)^{t-2} \quad \text{for} \quad t = 2,... \tag{10-29}$$

The book values are (Eq. 10-11 modified)

Book values for HDB (half-year convention) schedules:

$$B_t = B_0(1 - 0.5\alpha)(1 - \alpha)^{t-1} \qquad t = 1,... \qquad (10\text{-}30)$$

The *average dwell time* from $t = 0$ for HDB schedules is

$$L = 0.5 + \frac{1}{\alpha} \qquad (10\text{-}31)$$

The present worth of the HDB schedule is the present worth of the first charge plus the present worth of the remaining charges; these are a perpetual schedule delayed one year and depreciating $B_0(1 - 0.5\alpha)$ instead of B_0. If the present worth from Eq. 10-27 (ordinary full-year convention) is P, then the HDB present worth is thus $B_0[0.5\alpha\beta + (1 - 0.5\alpha)P]$. With P expanded from Eq. 10-27 and the result simplified, the HDB present worth formula is

Present-worth of HDB schedule:

$$P\{D_t\colon\ t = 1,...,\infty\} = B_0\alpha\beta\left(0.5 + \frac{(1 - 0.5\alpha)\beta}{1 - (1 - \alpha)\beta}\right) \qquad (10\text{-}32)$$

E21. A $1000 asset is depreciated by a perpetual DB schedule (or in a DCA schedule) with $\alpha = 0.80$. Let the interest rate be $i = 20\%$. Prepare a numerical schedule giving the first eight charges, book values, and present worths of charges and use the results to verify Eqs. 10-29, 10-30, and 10-32.

Each charge is $\alpha = 80\%$ of the previous book value, except that the first charge is 40% of the original book value $B_0 = \$1000$. Each book value is the previous book value less the current charge. The present worth contribution of each charge D_t is $\beta^t D_t$, where $\beta = 1/1.20$. Thus the schedule is

t	D_t	B_t	$P(D_t)$
0		1000	
1	400	600	333.33
2	480	120	333.33
3	96	24	55.56
4	19.20	4.80	9.26
5	3.84	0.96	1.54
6	0.768	0.192	0.26
7	0.1536	0.0384	0.04
8	0.03072	0.00768	0.01

Rounded present worth of first eight charges: <u>733.33</u>

To verify Eq. 10-29, for example, the charge at time 4 given by Eq. 10-29 is $B_0\alpha(1 - 0.5\alpha)(1 - \alpha)^2 = \underline{19.20}$, the same as in the above schedule.

To verify Eq. 10-30, for example, the book value at time 7 given by Eq. 10-30 is $B_0(1 - 0.5\alpha)(1 - \alpha)^6 = \underline{0.0384}$, the same as in the above schedule.

To verify Eq. 10-32, the present worth given by Eq. 10-32 is

$$B_0 \alpha \beta \left[0.5 + \frac{(1 - 0.5\alpha)\beta}{1 - (1 - \alpha)\beta} \right] = 733.3\overline{3},$$

which to the nearest cent equals the rounded present worth of the first eight charges.

Treatment of nondepreciable capital such as land is to define a *capital gain* $S_n - B_0$ that occurs upon disposal at time n. The capital gain is taxed at a capital gains tax rate T_c that may be lower than T, especially for long-term capital gains. The "depreciation schedule" is $D_t = B_0$, and the dwell time is $L = n$. The present worth of the "depreciation schedule" is $B_0 \beta^n$. This is smaller than that of any other schedule; to make up for this, T_c for long-term capital gains has historically been about 60% of T, although it was equal to T in the 1980s and early 1990s.

10.2.8 Depreciation Efficiency

Only rarely in an economic study would it be necessary to perform depreciation accounting computations. Every expenditure is subject to a specific treatment that determines the speed and shape of its depreciation schedule. For every treatment, it is possible to determine in advance its tax effect and to determine at any interest rate the treatment's *depreciation schedule efficiency* Ω, which is a single number that expresses the entire effects of an asset's depreciation schedule on the after-tax present worth of any project that includes acquiring the asset.

Recall definitions from previous sections: n, the recovery period or life class in years; l, the estimated life in years, from which n can be inferred when not otherwise determined; α, the depreciation fraction for DB or DCA schedules; L, the average dwell time of a depreciation schedule, in years from one year before time 1; B_0, the initial cost; S_n, the estimated salvage value at n; T, the marginal income tax rate; T_c, the capital gains tax rate if different from T.

To these definitions we now add

$$\begin{array}{ll} \lambda & \text{taxation lag, year} \\ \Omega & \text{depreciation schedule efficiency} \\ I_{\text{nat}} & \text{net after-tax investment} \end{array}$$

The *taxation lag* λ is the average time from an expenditure to the tax relief that recognizes it, or from a receipt to the tax payment that recognizes it. In the United States, there is a mixture of annual and quarterly taxation; $\lambda = 0.5$ for depreciation charges under standard MACRS schedules; $\lambda = 0.125$ for receipts and salvage values with quarterly taxation. In practice, many analysts use $\lambda = 0$ for all computations, which is consistent with the end-of-period convention that ignores timing within a period. It should be noted that the loopholes and delays built into reporting and collection procedures effectively add more time to the taxation lag; for example, a taxpayer may pay quarterly taxes one month after the end of a quarter without penalty, and some underreporting is allowed, for which a correction may be made later without penalty. We provide λ in formulas for schedule efficiency and net investment, which the analyst may use or ignore, as appropriate to the enterprise's analysis procedures.

Depreciation schedules defined in this book and elsewhere in the literature have charges $\{D_d\}$ occurring at times $t = 1, 2,...,$ so that formulas for $P\{D_d\}$ assume a lag of one year. We therefore include a factor $\beta^{\lambda-1}$ in efficiency definitions to recognize this fact.

The *depreciation schedule efficiency* Ω is defined as the present worth of the depreciation schedule divided by the whole (not net) initial cost B_0. Its ideal value, with continuous taxation ($\lambda = 1$) and with expensing (immediate depreciation) is $\Omega = 1$. It depends on the interest rate and measures the effective proportion of the whole investment that is recognized by the depreciation schedule. It expresses the schedule itself and is independent of T and T_c. It does not express the treatment of salvage value and has the same definition for whole-investment and net-investment schedules.

Depreciation schedule efficiency:

$$\Omega = P\{D_d\}\beta^{\lambda-1}/B_0 \qquad (10\text{-}33)$$

Noncapital expenses effectively have $\Omega = \beta^{\lambda}$.

The *net after-tax investment* I_{nat} is the effective net after-tax cost of an asset. Recall that the taxpayer disburses B_0 at time zero, then receives tax relief whose worth is $TP\{D_d\}$ as of one year before D_1 and thus has worth $TP\{D_d\}\beta^{\lambda-1}$ at time zero, and finally receives a salvage value S_n whose present worth is $(1 - T\beta^{\lambda})S_n\beta^n$ if taxed (it is taxed if a whole-investment depreciation schedule is used) or is $S_n\beta^n$ if not taxed (for net-investment depreciation). Thus the effective present cost of the expenditure, measured as the net after-tax investment, is

Net after-tax investment:

$$I_{\text{nat}} = B_0 - TP\{D_d\}\beta^{\lambda-1} - P_{\text{at}}\{\text{salvage}\} \qquad (10\text{-}34)$$

$$= B_0 - B_0 T\Omega - P_{\text{at}}\{\text{salvage}\}$$

where $P_{\text{at}}\{\text{salvage}\}$ is

$$P_{\text{at}}\{\text{salvage}\} = \begin{cases} (1 - T\beta^{\lambda})S_n\beta^n & \text{if taxed} \\ S_n\beta^n & \text{if untaxed} \end{cases}$$

Table 10-10 summarizes the depreciation schedule efficiencies and net after-tax investments for all the commonly used treatments of expenditures.

TABLE 10-10. Available Tax Treatments of Expenditures

Treatment of Expenditure B_0 Having Salvage S_n	Depreciation Schedule Efficiency, Ω	Net After-tax Investment, I_{nat}
Nondeductible (e.g., fines)	0	$B_0 - (1 - T\beta^{\lambda})S_n\beta^n$
Nondepreciable capital (e.g., land)	$\beta^{n+\lambda-1}$	$B_0 - B_0 T\Omega - (1 - T_c\beta^{\lambda})S_n\beta^n$
Noncapital expense	β^{λ}	$B_0 - B_0 T\Omega - (1 - T\beta^{\lambda})S_n\beta^n$
MACRS 1992, n-classes, 3, 5, 7, 10, 15, 20	Tabulated	$B_0 - B_0 T\Omega - (1 - T\beta^{\lambda})S_n\beta^n$
Arbitrary whole-investment schedule $\{D_d\}$	$P\{D_d\}\beta^{\lambda-1}/B_0$	$B_0 - B_0 T\Omega - (1 - T\beta^{\lambda})S_n\beta^n$
Arbitrary net-investment schedule $\{D_d\}$	$P\{D_d\}\beta^{\lambda-1}/B_0$	$B_0 - (1 - T\beta\lambda)S_n\beta^n$

TABLE 10-11. Efficiencies of MACRS 1992 Depreciation Schedules

MACRS 1992				Ω			
Life Class, n	i = 1%	i = 5%	i = 10%	i = 15%	i = 20%	i = 25%	i = 30%
n = 3	0.9856	0.9320	0.8728	0.8211	0.7754	0.7349	0.6986
n = 5	0.9775	0.8962	0.8110	0.7401	0.6804	0.6296	0.5859
n = 7	0.9696	0.8630	0.7566	0.6723	0.6043	0.5485	0.5021
n = 10	0.9581	0.8172	0.6861	0.5890	0.5151	0.4573	0.4112
n = 15	0.9305	0.7157	0.5425	0.4309	0.3552	0.3014	0.2616
n = 20	0.9099	0.6505	0.4640	0.3550	0.2861	0.2395	0.2061

For each life class n, the MACRS 1992 schedules prescribe $\{D_t: t = 1,...,n+1\}/B_0$. At a given interest rate i, with $\beta = 1/(1 + i)$, the charges have a present worth $P\{D_t\}$ at $t = 0$. The asset is commissioned at $t = 0.5$ on the average, so the present worth at commissioning time is $P\{D_t\}\beta^{-0.5}$. The efficiency given in this table is the present worth per dollar of cost B_0, or $\Omega = P\{D_t\}\beta^{-0.5}/B_0$.

Table 10-11 lists the depreciation efficiency for the MACRS 1992 schedules pre-scribed by the IRS. These are subject to change, but Table 10-11 can be recomputed with each change and used for all investments subject to the standard schedules. These depreciation efficiencies also apply approximately to investments whose de-tailed treatment is a matter of negotiated agreement between taxpayer and tax author-ity, because they express the highest level of depreciation efficiency the tax authority is likely to approve.

E22. A taxpayer who uses MARR of $i = 15\%$ and pays 40% income taxes spends $1000 building a mold from which aluminum castings could be prepared. It will have no salvage value. Under MACRS 1992 rules, determine the life class, the depreciation efficiency, the net after-tax investment, and the after-tax present worth of the project of building the mold if it generates after-tax revenues hav-ing a present worth of $2500 before taxes (as will be seen in the next section, the returns will have an after-tax present worth of $(1 - T\beta^\lambda)2500$ where $T = 0.40$ and $\lambda = 0.5$).

Life class: From Table 10-2, $n = \underline{10 \text{ years}}$ for casting molds.

Depreciation efficiency: From Table 10-11, $\Omega = \underline{0.5890}$.

Net after-tax investment: From Table 10-10 with no salvage, $T = 0.40$, $B_0 = 1000$,

$I_{nat} = 1000 - 1000(0.40)\Omega = \underline{764.40}$.

Present worth of project: $P_{at} = -764.40 + (1 - T\beta^{0.5})2500 = \underline{\$803.10}$.

E23. A chemical reprocessor proposes to use the HDB (half-year convention) declin-ing class account method to depreciate plant assets that would fall in the MACRS 10-year life class, whose depreciation schedule has a dwell time of $L = 4.845$ years. Each year the entire class book value would go from B_{t-1} to $B_t - B_{t-1} + V_t - D_t$, where V_t is the total value of new assets added during the year and D_t is determined as $D_t = \alpha B_{t-1} + 0.50V_t$ (Eq. 10-16a). The company's tax consultants feel the tax authority will approve the method if its dwell time is at least as long as that of a MACRS 10-year schedule and if its depreciation efficiency at 10% interest is no greater than that of a MACRS 10-year schedule. Would $\alpha = 0.21774$ meet both of the supposed approval criteria?

Dwell time of the HDB schedule at $\alpha = 0.21774$ from Eq. 10-31:

$$L = 0.5 + 1/\alpha = \underline{5.0926 \text{ yr}} \qquad \text{more than the MACRS dwell of } 4.845 \text{ yr}$$

Present worth of the HDB schedule from Eq. 10-32, with $B_0 = 1$, $\beta = 1/1.10$:

$$P\{D_i: t = 1,...,\infty\} = B_0 \alpha \beta \left[0.5 + \frac{(1 - 0.5\alpha)\beta}{1 - (1 - \alpha)\beta} \right] = \underline{0.65413}$$

Efficiency of the HDB schedule from Eq. 10-33 with $\lambda = 0.5$:

$$\Omega = P\{D_d\}\beta^{\lambda-1}/B_0 = 0.65413\beta^{-0.5} = \underline{0.6861}$$

This is equal to the MACRS efficiency from Table 10-11 for $n = 10$ and $i = 10\%$. Yes, both criteria are met.

10.3 AFTER-TAX ANALYSIS

After-tax analysis consists merely of including all taxes and incentives in an economic analysis. Since all taxes except income taxes are normally included anyway, income taxes are the only new consideration in going from before-tax to after-tax analysis.

We saw in Sections 10.1.1 and 10.1.2 that straight income taxation, without special consideration for capital, would make any cash flow set have, after taxes, the same rates of return as it had before taxes. The taxing authority would merely constitute a decision-neutral silent partner. But with depreciation, which consists of allowing the silent partner an interest-free delay in paying its share of capital expenditures, long-term investments are significantly penalized in comparison with short-term investments, and before-tax analysis gives wrong answers.

Although depreciation accounting procedures are complicated, the use of depreciation efficiencies simplifies after-tax analysis. Given an after-tax interest rate, every capital expenditure has a net after-tax investment amount I_{nat} that follows from its cost, its salvage amount and time, and the efficiency of the depreciation schedule applicable to it. In the following section, we will reduce after-tax analysis to a fixed formula and illustrate after-tax analysis in a variety of contexts, with emphasis on situations in which before-tax analysis would be inadequate.

10.3.1 The General After-Tax Present Worth Formula

Consider the problem of determining the after-tax present worth of a set of before-tax cash flows expressed in then-current dollars. The interest rate i is assumed to be the market interest rate appropriate for after-tax analysis.

Of the *negative* cash flows in the set, each one has a depreciation status and is subject to one of the treatments in Table 10-10. The present worth at i of the cost, the tax relief from depreciation charges, and the salvage value and any taxes on it are computed as the net after-tax investment I_{nat}. If parts of what conceptually is viewed as a single investment are treated differently, such as being expensed or depreciated on a distinct schedule, there is a distinct I_{nat} for each part. If an investment or negative cash flow occurs at some other time than time zero, its I_{nat} is computed on its own time scale; for instance, its salvage occurs n years after its commissioning, not at time n. I_{nat} represents the net after-tax worth of cost as of commissioning time, so its actual contribution to present worth of the overall cash-flow set is the negative of $I_{nat}\beta^t$, where t is its time of commissioning.

Allowing for the possibility of more than one negative cash flow in the set, let the mth one's $I_{nat}\beta^t$ be denoted $I^{(m)}$, the mth *equivalent cost*.

Each *positive* cash flow that is a salvage value is already incorporated in one of the equivalent costs. Of the remaining positive cash flows, we assume all are taxable at rate T and are subject to taxation delay λ (not necessarily that same delay as was used in determing depreciation effects). The positive cash flows $\{A_t\}$ occur at times $\{t\}$.

With these definitions, the general *after-tax present worth* formula is

General after-tax present worth formula:

$$P_{at} = -\sum_m I^{(m)} + (1 - T\beta^\lambda)\sum_t A_t\beta^t \tag{10-36}$$

E24. **A project being considered by an enterprise with an after-tax MARR of $i = 15\%$ requires a 10 K\$ investment of which 1 K\$ can be expensed ($\Omega = \beta^{0.5}$), 3 K\$ can be depreciated on a MACRS 5-year schedule ($\Omega = 0.7401$), and the remaining 6 K\$ will be depreciated on a MACRS 10-year schedule ($\Omega = 0.5890$). There are no salvage values. The net returns are 7 K\$ for year 1, 4 K\$ for year 2, and 3 K\$ for year 3. $T = 40\%$. Determine the after-tax present worth assuming $\lambda = 0.5$ yr for the returns.**

$\beta = 1/1.15$

$I^{(1)} = 1(1 - T\beta^{0.5}) = 0.626998$

$I^{(2)} = 3[1 - T(0.7401)] = 2.111880$

$I^{(3)} = 6[1 - T(0.5890)] = 4.586400$

$$P_{at} = -(I^{(1)} + I^{(2)}) + I^{(3)} + (1 - T\beta^{0.5})(7\beta + 4\beta^2 + 3\beta^3) = \underline{-0.37558 \text{ K\$}}$$

This is not a good project. *Note:* Its before-tax rate of return is about 22.59%

E25. **In the project of Example E23, since the returns continue only for three years and there are no salvage values, the depreciation schedules seem too long. Assume that the situation is like that of police cars run three shifts per day, where what is normally long-lived equipment is quickly used up. If the enterprise can apply the special depreciation schedule $\{D_t\} = (3, 3, 4)$ for the 10 K\$ investment, will the project be desirable?**

$$P\{D_t\} = 3\beta + 3\beta^2 + 4\beta^3 = 7.5071916 \text{ K\$}$$

$$\Omega = P\{D_t\}\beta^{\lambda-1}/B_0 \quad \text{where } \lambda = 0.50, \ B_0 = 10 \text{ K\$} = 0.8050566$$

$$I_{nat} = B_0(1 - T\Omega) = 6.77977$$

$$P_{at} = -6.77977 + (1 - T\beta^{0.5})(7\beta + 4\beta^2 + 3\beta^3) = \underline{0.16993 \text{ K\$}}$$

The special depreciation schedule makes the project desirable.

E26. **With equal benefits and operating costs, a rolling mill has a choice of purchasing $5000 machines that last eight years and would be depreciated on the MACRS $n = 5$ schedule, or $3300 machines that lasted four years and would be depreciated on the MACRS $n = 3$ schedule. Based on before-tax and after-tax analysis of a typical ordinary-course-of-business project, the rolling-mill management has concluded its MARR is $i = 25\%$ before taxes and is $i = 15\%$ after taxes. Determine the proper choice if the mill pays 40% income taxes and there are no salvage values.**

Basis: Eight years with one machine in service.

Alternative **A** (the $5000 machine), with $B_0 = 5000$, $T = 0.40$, $i = 15\%$:

$$I_{nat} = B_0(1 - T\Omega)$$

where for a MACRS 5-year schedule

$$\Omega = 0.7401$$

$$= \$3519.80$$

$$P_{at}{}^{(A)} = \underline{-3519.80} + P_{at}\{\text{benefits}\}$$

Alternative **B** (two successive $3300 machines):

$$I_{nat} = 3300(1 - T\Omega)$$

where for a MACRS 3-year schedule

$$\Omega = 08211$$

$$= \$2216.148 \qquad \text{valid for machine 1 and later for machine 2}$$

$$I^{(1)} = 2216.148 \qquad I^{(2)} = 2216.148\beta^4 = 1267.090$$

$$P_{at}{}^{(B)} = (2216.148 + 1267.090) + P_{at}\{\text{benefits}\}$$

$$= \underline{3483.24} + P_{at}\{\text{benefits}\}$$

Alternative **B** is best.

When benefits from both alternatives are equal in a repair-or-replace problem, the alternative having the lower effective cost I_{nat} is best.

E27. **A farmer can fix a worn-out fence for $15,000 or replace it for $14,000. Either way, the fence will provide the same benefits and last seven years. With $\beta = 0.85$,**

$T = 40\%$, and $\Omega = 0.72$ for fence depreciation (or $\beta^{0.5}$ of expensing), which is better?

If the fence is repaired, the effective cost is $I_{nat}^{(repair)} = 15,000(1 - T\beta^{0.5}) = \$9468.27$. If the fence is replaced, the effective cost is $I_{nat}^{(repair)} = 14.000[1 - T(0.72)] = \$9968$. Thus, although repair is $1000 more expensive before taxes, repair is about $500 better than replacement when taxes and depreciation are considered.

10.3.2 Survey of Significant Tax Effects on Decisions

As compared to the idealized decision-making environment in business and engineering as modeled by before-tax analysis, taxation adds *bias, risk,* and *complexity.*

The main bias, expressed mostly through depreciation regulations, is against long-lived capital investments. This bias has been examined at length in this chapter. From time to time, special incentives are introduced into tax law to influence decisions in directions desired by government; for example, some States in the United States offer low or zero State income tax rates to induce industries to locate there, and tax breaks have been offered through tax laws administered by the IRS to encourage investment in energy conservation, pollution control, and other activities.

Reaction to these biases is, at the individual economic decision-making level, to base decisions on after-tax analysis rather than before-tax analysis, as this chapter has shown how to do. But in actual practice many routine decisions are made on a before-tax basis. Are wrong decisions being made?

There is an attempt in the exercises at the end of this chapter to compare before-tax and after-tax analysis in a variety of situations, so as to establish a feel for the conditions under which tax effects are significant. To a certain extent, the proper setting of distinct MARRs for before-tax and after-tax analysis protects the analyst against wrong decisions. As a general rule, tax considerations will rarely override raw economic truth; the alternative that generates the most wealth the fastest will usually be chosen on either a before-tax or after-tax basis.

At a smaller scale than that of go/no-go decisions on large projects, taxes have significant bias effects. Many of these were discussed in Sections 10.1 and 10.1.2, and in the list of strategies in Section 10.2.6.

Not covered in this chapter are the effects of income taxation on risk. With the government as a silent partner, the taxpayer must engage in a greater volume of economic activity to earn a given take-home return. If the taxpayer in the $T = 40\%$ bracket would have chosen the safest 60% of profitable opportunities without taxation, under taxation he must choose 100% of them if he is to get the same after-tax profit.

Finally, there are the effects of complexity. Small businesses may avoid an entire line of endeavor for lack of tax know-how. Enterprises of all sizes find that tax-law complexity causes extra accounting effort and turns managerial attention away from the technological "real business" of the enterprise toward the artificial activities of playing the tax game.

The complexity of tax regulations engenders dishonesty, or at least causes examination of ethical questions. Many engineers are uncomfortable with the strategies listed in Section 10.2.6, which encourage a cynical view of government. Tax complexity creates an added risk: risk that a tax audit or unfavorable ruling will create a sudden, unexpected financial obligation.

Whenever a before-tax decision and an after-tax decision disagree, there is a societal effect. Consider, for example, a choice between alternatives A and B in which B is chosen although A would be better before taxes:

$$P_{at}^{(A)} < P_{at}^{(B)} \qquad \text{although} \qquad P_{bt}^{(A)} > P_{bt}^{(B)}$$

Now recall that the before-tax present worths measure wealth created by the projects, whereas the after-tax present worths measure that portion of wealth retained by the taxpayer. Thus society as a whole loses wealth.

Loss to society when B is chosen:

$$P_{bt}^{(A)} - P_{bt}^{(B)}$$

If the bias is intentional, to correct the effects of economic externalities, society may gain from the decision. An *externality* (see Chapter 7) is a cost, such as the harm to the public from pollution, that is not considered by a decision maker. The loss to society becomes

$$P_{bt}^{(A)} - E_A - (P_{bt}^{(B)} - E_B)$$

where E_A and E_B are the present worths of externalities associated with alternatives A and B. If E_A is much greater than E_B, society gains from the bias. This is the idea behind some tax provisions such as pollution taxes and energy-conservation incentives.

Perhaps the greatest effect of income taxation on society is the sheer waste represented by millions of man-hours of accounting effort that creates no wealth but is a necessary added expense to each taxpayer and each tax authority in the playing of the tax game.

10.3.3 After-Tax Analysis by Spreadsheet

When computations are performed by spreadsheet (or term-by-term using any computation tool), a straightforward practical approach to after-tax analysis is simply to incorporate depreciation charges and after-tax returns into the cash-flow diagram, as in Figure 10-1 at the beginning of the chapter.

According to the end-of-year (eoy) timing convention, it is usual to consider the taxation lag to be $\lambda = 0$ years rather than 0.5 years; depreciation charges $\{D_1, D_2, \ldots\}$ and their resulting tax decrements are considered to occur at times $\{1, 2, \ldots\}$. This is consistent with estimated before-tax returns' being considered to occur at times $\{1, 2, \ldots\}$ if they represent profits actually received throughout each year, or if the asset is considered to be commissioned at midyear.

The basic method for determining after-tax cash flows is that positive before-tax cash flows are multiplied by $1 - T$, where T is the tax rate; negative cash flows are as is, but there is also a delayed set of positive tax decrements for each negative cash flow; and the decrements are the depreciation charges multiplied by T.

The spreadsheet approach with the eoy convention is simple: Let there be a row $\mathbf{R_{bt}}$ of before-tax cash flows $\{A_t\}$ at $t = 0, 1, 2, \ldots$. This includes the negative cash flows that represent capital investments; assume for simplicity in this discussion that there is only one negative cash flow, B_0, which occurs at time zero. Let there be a row $\mathbf{R_{df}}$ of

TABLE 10-12. Depreciation Fraction for 1992 Standard MACRS Depreciation D_t/B_0

Life class, n	$t = 1$	$t = 2$	$t = 3$	$t = 4$	$t = 5$	$t = 6$	$t = 7$	$t = 8$	$t = 9$	...	$t = n+1$
$n = 3$	0.3333	0.4444	0.1481	0.0742							
$n = 5$	0.2	0.32	0.192	0.1152	0.1152	0.0576					
$n = 7$	0.1429	0.2449	0.1749	0.1249	0.0892	0.0892	0.0892	0.0448			
$n = 10$	0.1	0.18	0.144	0.1152	0.0922	0.0737	0.0655	0.0655	0.0655	...	0.0329
$n = 15$	0.05	0.095	0.0855	0.0770	0.0693	0.0623	0.0590	0.0590	0.0590	...	0.0299
$n = 20$	0.0375	0.0722	0.0668	0.0618	0.0571	0.0528	0.0489	0.0452	0.0446	...	0.0255

depreciation fractions; those for 1992 standard depreciation schedules are given in Table 10-12. Let there be a row **D** of depreciation charges computed by multiplying each element of $\mathbf{R_{df}}$ by B_0.

Let the row $\mathbf{A_{at}}$ of after-tax cash flows be determined by summing three things: the *after-tax returns,* which are the positive elements $\mathbf{R^+}$ of $\mathbf{R_{bt}}$ multiplied by $1 - T$; the (negative) *investments,* which are the negative elements $\mathbf{R^-}$ of $\mathbf{R_{bt}}$; and the *tax decrements* $\mathbf{D} \times T$, which are the depreciation charges multiplied by the tax rate.

After-tax cash flows:

$$\mathbf{A_{at}} = \mathbf{R^+} \times (1 - T) + \mathbf{R^-} + \mathbf{D} \times T \tag{10-37}$$

Let there be a row of discount factors $\mathbf{B} = \{1, \beta, \beta^2,...\}$ for $t = 0, 1, 2,...$, where $\beta = 1/(1 + i)$; the "present-worth" function of a spreadsheet program implicitly prepares this row.

The after-tax present worth is just the sum of the elements of the row obtained by multiplying each element of the after-tax-cash-flow row $\mathbf{A_{at}}$ by the corresponding element of **B**.

After-tax present worth:

$$P_{at} = \Sigma\mathbf{A_{at}} \cdot \mathbf{B} \tag{10-38}$$

E28. As illustrated in Figure 10-1, a $1000 investment yields before-tax returns of {300, 240, 225, 200, 180, 150, 130} dollars at times $t = 1, \ldots, 7$ yr. The investment is subject to 1992 standard MACRS depreciation at life class 5 years. Using the eoy convention, determine by spreadsheet the after-tax present worth if the owner uses an after-tax MARR of $i = 9\%$ and is taxed at a rate $T = 40\%$.

Let columns represent years $t = 0, 1, 2, \ldots, 7$. The before-tax cash flows are $\mathbf{R_{bt}} = \{A_t: t = 0,...,7\} = \{-1000, 300, 240, 225, 200, 180, 150, 130\}$. The after-tax returns, given $T = 0.40$, are $\mathbf{R^+} \times (1 - T) = \{0, 180, 144, 135, 120, 108, 90, 78\}$. The depreciation fractions from Table 10-12 at life class 5 (with no depreciation at times 0 and 7) are $\mathbf{R_{df}} = \{D_t/B_0: t = 0,...,7\} = \{0, 0.2, 0.32, 0.192, 0.1152, 0.1152, 0.0576, 0\}$. The depreciation charges are $\mathbf{D} = \mathbf{R_{df}} \times B_0$, and the tax decrements due to deprecation are $\mathbf{D} \times T = \{0, 80, 128, 76.80, 46.08, 46.08, 23.04,$

0}. The after-tax cash flows are the sum of the after-tax returns, the investment, and the tax decrements from depreciation:

Times	0	1	2	3	4	5	6	7
After-tax returns	0	180	144	135	120	108	90	78
Investments	−1000	0	0	0	0	0	0	0
Tax decrements	0	80	128	76.80	46.08	46.08	23.04	0
A_{at}	−1000	260	272	211.80	166.08	154.08	113.04	78
Discount factors	1	β^2	β^3	β^4	β^5	β^6	β^7	

Finally, the present worth is the sum of the products of the last two rows:

$$P_{at} = \Sigma A_{at} \cdot \mathbf{B} = \underline{\underline{-\$41.12}}$$

10.4 EXERCISES

1. Most citizens have a general knowledge of tax law and ethics. Consider each of the following scenarios and characterize the taxpayer's actions as *ethical, abusive* (something that may be viewed as unfair from the tax authority's standpoint), or *illegal*. (Of course, there cannot be full agreement on some answers.)

   (a) A car dealer's lot is partly in El Segundo County and partly in Manhattan County. The two counties levy ad valorem property taxes on the inventory on hand, as counted by a county inspector on a specific day. El Segundo counts inventory on May 1 and Manhattan counts inventory on May 15. The dealer crowds as many cars as possible on the Manhattan side on May 1 and on the El Segundo side on May 15.

   (b) A dentist fixes a plumber's teeth, and the plumber fixes the dentist's plumbing. Neither charges the other any money, nor reports the services received as income subject to income taxes.

   (c) A broker sets up a business whose sole purpose is to act as a clearinghouse to arrange barters between strangers to trade services of equal value without a taxable exchange of money.

   (d) Income tax law allows a standard deduction if the taxpayer does not elect to itemize deductions. Mary and Jack have $12,000 of itemized deductions in a typical year, including $9000 of deductible interest on the mortgage loan on their residence. They refinance their mortgage according to a deduction-bunching scheme, whereby payments in odd-numbered years include about double the usual amount of interest, and payments in even-numbered years include no interest. Thus in even-numbered years they take the standard deduction, which for them is $5000, and in odd-numbered years they have about $21,000 of itemized deduction. The deduction-bunching scheme thus reduces their two-year total taxable income from $26,000 to $24,000.

   (e) A waitress quits a job at a restaurant where strict records are kept and takes a similar job at a restaurant where there is no way to audit her income from tips. Her intent is to report only a fraction of her income to the tax authority.

(f) An engineer outfits an automobile with an engine that burns natural gas. Unlike gasoline or diesel fuel, natural gas does not carry excise taxes earmarked for financing installation and maintenance of streets and highways, but the engineer drives the automobile on them.

2. Finster Products will have a taxable income of $90,000 this year if it rejects the opportunities for short-term projects A and B. A will add $20,000 to taxable income and B will add $8000. Assume income-tax rates are those given by Table 10-1, except that the company must also pay 2% State income tax. In analyzing design choices within the new projects, what marginal tax rate is appropriate?

3. Gelid Yoghurt Inc. offers franchise licenses under which it effectively "taxes" its franchise owners continuously. The home office pays 70% of every bill immediately, and immediately takes 70% of daily operating profit. Income taxes and depreciation accounting are handled by the home office. Thus one owner decided to invest $2000 in an icemaker, and the investment earned $500 extra per year for six years; the owner spent $600 of his own money and received $150 extra per year. In negotiating with a prospective owner, the Gelid franchise saleswoman describes the icemaker project and argues, "If you spent $600 *on your own* to undertake a project with the same rate of return as the icemaker project, you'd earn the same $150 per year." She concludes, "Our services cost you nothing." Offer a rebuttal: Is there a concrete way in which the owner is worse off owning a franchised store than if he fully owned an equally successful independent store?

4. In Example E5, a comparison was made between (A) expensing and (B) whole-investment straight-line depreciation of an investment (ignoring taxation lags). At $i = 15\%$, expensing was about $4300 better than depreciation. Repeat the comparison at $i = 20\%$. Does the higher interest rate magnify the comparison? If taxation lags had been included in the analysis as in Section 10.2.8, would the conclusion (that expensing is better than depreciating) be significantly affected? (Answer without recalculating.)

5. In Example E5, alternative C, the after-tax present worth of a project was found to be 0.27586 K$ at 15% interest when the net investment was depreciated. In Example E6 the rate of return for C was claimed to be 15.18%. Verify this.

6. Land is a nondepreciable asset. In the United States, land is neither expensed nor depreciated, but its cost is recognized upon disposal, as if it were depreciated by a whole-investment schedule that has one depreciation charge, at time n. To Example E5, add a fourth depreciation treatment (D), in which the 50 K$ investment is for land, which is purchased at time zero and is sold, at a loss, for 20 K$ at time 6. Write P_{at} in terms of an equivalent depreciation charge of 50 K$ at time 6, along with treatment of the 20 K$ equivalent salvage value at the same time as ordinary income. In accepted practice, the situation is viewed a different way: A *capital gain* is defined as the difference between disposal revenue and original cost and is taxed at a rate T_c that may or may not be the same as the rate T on ordinary income. Rewrite P_{at} with no depreciation charge but with a capital gain taxed at rate T_c at time n (the taxpayer expends 50 K$ at time zero, receives 20 K$ at time 6, and receives tax relief for the negative capital gain at time 6).

Show that the two expressions are equal if $T_c = T$. Then with $T_c = T = 0.40$, determine the after-tax present worth of the project under this treatment. Compare the result to the other treatments.

7. It can be shown that $B_0\beta^L$ is a lower limit on $P\{D_t/B_0\}$. By what percentage does it underestimate the present worth of the four-year SL depreciation of $B_0 = \$1000$ if $i = 15\%$?

8. A depreciation schedule has charges $(3, 2, 1)$ at times $(1, 2, 3)$.
   (a) Determine its average dwell time.
   (b) Determine the present worth of the schedule of depreciation charges at $i = 15\%$.
   (c) If nothing were known about a depreciation schedule except its average dwell time, how could the present worth of the schedule be approximated? Give a formula, state a rationale for it, and test its accuracy (for $n = 3$, $i = 15\%$) by applying it to the schedule given in this exercise.

9. For straight-line depreciation of $2000 in five years, determine the depreciation charges $\{D_t: t = 1,...,5\}$, the average dwell time L, the present worth of the charges at 15% interest, and the approximate present worth based on β^L (as if the whole $2000 was charged at time L).

10. Show (demonstrate or prove) that β^L provides a lower limit on the present worth of a depreciation schedule. Let B_0 be the amount depreciated; the assertion is

$$\beta^L \le P\{D_t\}/B_0$$

11. An obsolescent candy puller that can still make 40 pounds of taffy per hour can be sold for $3000, which happens to equal the present worth of its pretax net earnings if kept instead of sold. Should it be sold or kept? Answer the question assuming a marginal income tax rate T and a capital gains tax rate T_c for three cases: (a) the disposal is taxable as income; (b) the disposal causes a capital gain of $3000, which is taxed at $T_c < T$; (c) the disposal is not taxable (as would be the case if the taffy puller had been depreciated on a net-investment schedule with a $3000 estimated salvage value).

12. Determine the depreciation charges for SYD depreciation of $4000 for six years, and determine the average dwell time.

13. Determine the depreciation charges for SYD depreciation of $4812.44 for five years, and determine the average dwell time.

14. If $1000 could be depreciated in either of the following alternative ways, how do their average dwell times compare, and which has the greater present worth of depreciation charges at $i = 15\%$ interest?

   Alternative 1: Whole-investment SL, $n = 5$
   Alternative 2: Whole-investment SYD, $n = 7$

15. A $14,445 asset is depreciated on a DB schedule at $\alpha = 0.20$. Determine the first three charges D_1, D_2, D_3. Determine the remaining book value B_{10} after 10 charges.

16. For a perpetual DB schedule at α, given B_0, derive from Eq. 10-11 a formula for how long it would take for the book value to become negligible (half a cent when B_0 is in dollars). Apply the result to a $1000 asset with $\alpha = 0.20$.

17. Table 10-3 illustrates switched 1.5DB depreciation on a net investment where the salvage value is zero. Revise the table for a salvage value of $200. Show that if the DB schedule were not ignored after the switch to SL, the DB schedule could give a candidate charge greater than $B_{t-1} - S_n$, which is not allowed.

18. Determine the average dwell time of the switched DB schedule given in Table 10-3, and compare the result to the average dwell time for perpetual DB depreciation.

19. Prepare a depreciation table like Table 10-3 except with DDB instead of 1.5 DB depreciation.

20. Example E11 illustrates the MACRS version of switched DDB depreciation, with the half-year convention. Prepare a table for the same example, except with a five-year recovery period rather than three.

21. A $1000 asset has an estimated salvage value of $150 at time $n = 3$ and is depreciated by perpetual net-investment DDB depreciation ($\alpha = 2/3$). It was put in service at the start of the tax year. Determine the entire schedule.

22. An asset has a three-year recovery period. Show that its depreciation by either a whole-investment SL schedule or a 1.5DB schedule would have the same average dwell time.

23. A company had $1,523,447 in its nine-year DCA depreciation account at the end of the previous tax year. The negotiated depreciation factor is $2/9$. This year the company added a net of $23,004 of nine-year-class capital expenditures. Determine the new balance, which is kept and reported in integer dollars.

24. The Garcia-Robles Shipyard uses DCA depreciation and has 15,000 capital items in its 10-year life class. The depreciation factor is that for 1.75DB. Under its accounting procedures, disposals are taxed as income and removed from the account (a common variation of DCA rules). This year the account started at $16,449,837.42. New capital expenditures were $1,155,501.10, and capital disposals were $312,598.00.
    (a) Determine the new balance.
    (b) The tax authority was presumably willing to allow disposals to stay on the books. Would it have been advantageous for the shipyard not to have agreed to revise the accounts for capital disposals?

25. Regardless of an enterprise's actual depreciation system, the simple DCA model represents the system's behavior conveniently for decision purposes. Big Pop Stores has a capital budgeting "rule of thumb" by which there is an attempt to replace equipment at a rate just sufficient to keep the total book value constant. It has been determined that the average dwell of all capital items in the Big Pop depreciation accounts is 6.14 years. The accounts currently total $631,400,000. What budget for the coming year's capital expenditures is inferred by the rule of thumb?

26. A country-music band in the $T = 40\%$ income tax bracket has purchased a new sound system. The old fully depreciated system can be sold for $8500, taxable as income. Alternatively, it can be kept as a spare, and it is considered to be worth $6000 in that role for its sentimental value and its contribution in providing peace of mind until the new system can be fully trusted. The owners, who are the band

members, tell their accountant that although they do value keeping the old system for these reasons, it probably will not save or earn any actual money. Should it be kept?

27. The standard MACRS three-year depreciation schedule has four depreciation charges, (33.33, 44.44, 14.81, and 7.42) to depreciate $100. The present worth of this schedule at 15% interest is $76.57, and the average dwell is 1.96 years (both measured according to the start-of-year convention, that is, as of one year before the first charge). At the same interest rate, compare the following schedules with this one as to present worth of their depreciation charges.

    (a) SL with integer n giving approximately the same dwell.
    (b) SYD with integer n giving approximately the same dwell.
    (c) DB or DCA with same dwell.
    (d) 1.5DB or 1.5DCA with integer n giving approximately the same dwell.

28. Verify the answer to Example E20(a) by generating a depreciation table showing each charge, computed from the previous balance by Eq. 10-10 to the nearest cent. Determine the present worth of the depreciation schedule to the nearest cent by multiplying each charge by β^t and summing the results.

29. Verify the answer to Example E20(c) by first computing the present worth of the first 10 charges and then adding the present worth of the $73.74 charge at time 11.

30. A $1000 asset has an estimated salvage value of $300 at time 4 and has whole-investment depreciation charges of (428.57, 285.71, 142.86, 142.86) at $t = 1, \ldots,$ 4. With annual taxation, determine at 15% interest its depreciation schedule efficiency and at $T = 40\%$ its net after-tax investment.

31. A $1000 asset has an estimated salvage value of $3000 at time 4 and has net-investment depreciation charges of (300, 200, 100, 100) at $t = 1, \ldots, 4$. With annual taxation, determine at 15% interest its depreciation schedule efficiency and at $T = 40\%$ its net after-tax investment.

32. For a $1000 asset in the $n = 10$-yr life class, the MACRS 1992 schedule provides for DDB depreciation with $\alpha = 2/n = 0.20$, except that there is a halved first-year charge and a switch to straight-line depreciation charges of $D_t = B_{t-1}/(n - t + 1.5)$ at the first t for which this charge would exceed αB_{t-1}. The exact schedule turns out to be this:

t	D_t	B_t
0		1000
1	100	900
2	180	720
3	144	576
4	115.20	460.80
5	92.16	368.64
6	73.73	294.91
7	65.54	229.37 294.91/4.5 > 0.20(294.91)
8	65.54	163.83
9	65.54	98.29
10	65.54	32.75
11	32.75	0

For a taxpayer who uses $i = 15\%$, assuming no salvage value, determine $P\{D_t\}$ and Ω. Does Ω agree with the relevant entry in Table 10-11?

33. Consider the following project (discussed in Examples E23 and E24):

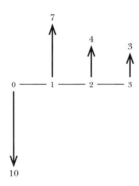

Let the after-tax MARR be $i = 15\%$, let the income tax rate be $T = 40\%$, and let the capital investment's depreciation treatments be broken down as follows:

Amount:	2	4	4
n	0	5	10
Ω	$\beta^{0.5}$	0.7401	0.5890

Determine the after-tax present worth of the project.

34. Exitprizes, Inc. uses an after-tax MARR of $i_{at} = 15\%$ and expects annual inflation. It assumes a half-year taxation lag in after-tax analysis and is subject to 42% income tax. A warehouse expansion project is estimated to bring benefits of $50,000 per year, expressed in indexed dollars, for 10 years, and zero salvage value. Its first cost is estimated as $200,000, of which $55,000 can be expensed and the remainder would be depreciated on a MACRS 10-year schedule.

    (a) Determine the after-tax present worth of the project.
    (b) The after-tax rate of return of the project is 19.77%. Determine the before-tax rate of return.
    (c) Assuming that this project is typical, determine an appropriate before-tax MARR i_{at} that Exitprizes, Inc. could use in performing before-tax analysis on projects that do not differ significantly from this one in their tax treatment.

35. For the Exitprizes, Inc. warehouse expansion project of Exercise 34, assume that an alternative version of the project is available, under which more of the project can be expensed than formerly, due to making repairs that effectively increase the warehouse capacity. The first cost would be $220,000, of which $160,000 could be expensed.

    (a) Determine the after-tax present worth of the alternative project.
    (b) Determine the after-tax rate of return of the alternative project. Choose among 20%, 22% ($\Omega = 0.4903$), 24% ($\Omega = 0.4678$), and 25%.

36. A process heater (furnace) at the Oilchem plant can be repaired or replaced. The benefits and operating costs under either alternative will be equal. Oilchem uses a

20% interest rate for after-tax analysis under a 48% taxation rate, assumes a half-year tax lag, and ignores salvage values. Under the repair option, the capital investment is $25,500 and the expensed portion of first cost is $155,000; the capital investment will be depreciated under a MACRS 15-year schedule. Under the replacement option, the capital investment is $170,000, which will be depreciated under a MACRS 15-year schedule; there is no expensed portion.

(a) Determine the after-tax present cost (the net after-tax investment) for the repair option.

(b) Determine the after-tax present cost (the net after-tax investment) for the replacement option.

(c) Which option is better after taxes, and which option would have been seen as better if before-tax analysis had been performed?

37. Scott Trucking Company has $640,000 of equipment on hand, which is being depreciated on a schedule whose depreciation efficiency at the company's 15% after-tax interest rate is 0.785. The company is subject to 40% income tax, and it ignores taxation lag ($\lambda = 0$). If the company were organized differently, so that its sideline of buying and selling equipment were considered its main business, and all equipment could have been expensed ("depreciation" with 100% depreciation efficiency), how much better off would the company be?

38. Determine the depreciation efficiency of an HDB depreciation schedule with a depreciation factor of 0.20 at an interest rate of 15%. Determine the net after-tax investment for a $100,000 piece of equipment depreciated this way by an enterprise that pays 40% income taxes.

WAVES in the gym circa 1947. It may not be actual diving, but at least it's exercise.

DESIGN EXERCISES

Engineering economy is one of the engineering sciences used in design, which is the central activity in the practice of engineering. Engineering economy provides the value system by which to evaluate and compare design alternatives. In the steps in engineering economic decision making reprinted here from Section 1.1 at the beginning of the book, note that only steps 6 and 7 are well covered by the examples and exercises in the first 10 chapters of this book.

Steps in Engineering Economic Decision Making

0. Recognize the need for an economic decision.
1. Formulate the decision problem. What are we trying to decide, what is given, and what is out of the question?.
2. Establish criteria for estimating and evaluating consequences.
3. Generate alternatives.
4. Establish technical understanding of alternatives.
5. Estimate consequences of alternatives and quantify the consequences economically. Estimate costs and benefits.
6. Select the preferred alternative.
7. Perform sensitivity analysis; return to step 6 if necessary; prepare to obtain ratifications and seek approvals.
8. Document and communicate the decision and its justification; advocate or implement the decision.

There is a gap between solving small illustrative exercises and evaluating real design alternatives. To apply engineering economy effectively, an engineer should learn to recognize which techniques are appropriate to a given situation, where and how to retrieve or generate data, how to avoid wasting time on issues that do not matter or on accuracy that is not needed, and how to communicate well both in seeking information and in reporting results.

The design exercises in this chapter are intended to help bridge the gap. Each requires applying material from various parts of the book, along with engineering judgment, to obtain and support a recommendation, in a situation more complex and less artificial than in small illustrative exercises. Depending on the instructor's requirements for depth of analysis and quality of documentation, each design exercise can require anywhere from 3 or 4 hours of student time to 10 or 12 hours. They are suitable for either individual or group work.

This chapter has three sections. In Section 11.1 we review the information-gathering activities necessary for applying engineering economy to real situations. In Section 11.2 we review the documents and reports first that define, organize, and describe a problem, and later that communicate results and recommendations. In Section 11.3 we present the situation and requirement for several design exercises with a discussion (not a solution) for each.

11.1 INFORMATION GATHERING AND ESTIMATION

There is an *exploratory phase* in every application of engineering economy, whether the decision is as large as that of building a plant or as small as selecting an impeller for a centrifugal pump. In the exploratory phase you are simply trying to find out as much as possible about the problem, what really matters, what alternatives are available, and so forth. After this familiarization, you should try to produce a problem statement (see Section 11.2.3) to focus precisely on the core of the problem. A formal Problem Statement carries you through steps 0 and 1 of the steps in engineering economic decision making reprinted above.

With the problem well described, the next step is to decide what matters (step 2: "establish criteria for estimating and evaluating consequences"). Is worth more important, or is efficiency the key (Section 4.6)? Does liquidity matter (Section 4.2.1)? Is there a MARR (Sections 5.1.4 and 6.2)? What is the planning horizon, and what costs are truly relevant (Section 5.1.3)? Might the decision hinge on risk (Chapters 8 and 9)? On taxes (Section 5.2.4.3 and Chapter 10)?

The next steps are to generate alternatives and to establish technical understanding of each. After these comes step 5: "estimate consequences of alternatives and quantify the consequences economically"—that is, to *estimate costs and benefits.*

In the real world, an engineer often performs and documents all the steps from 0 through 8, while in illustrative exercises a student usually performs only step 6 or step 7. The earlier steps are performed by the author of the exercise, and documentation (step 8) is required from the student only to a minimal extent.

One of the aims of the design exercises in this chapter is to provide students with the opportunity to reconsider or second-guess the issues that would already be settled in a small illustrative exercise—formulation, criteria, alternatives, costs, benefits—and thus gain some experience otherwise unavailable. We can meet this aim only to a limited extent, because specific technical issues dominate. A second aim of the design exercises is to provide students with the opportunity to prepare technical documentation that communicates decisions and their justification. This second aim is less dependent on specific technology, and the design exercises can provide significant experience in important parts of engineering economy documentation. To prepare for this, the next section reviews executive summaries, problem statements, and economic analysis documentation.

11.2 ENGINEERING ECONOMY REPORTS AND DOCUMENTS

A legend variously told at Bethlehem Steel, Crouse-Hinds, and many other places concerns a young engineer under extreme pressure to complete a cost estimate so that a bid could be submitted. The deadline loomed up, and on the last day, in desperation, the engineer typed "$438,259.08" in the center of a page of bond paper, bound the page neatly in a blue report folder, and ceremoniously handed the folder to his boss.

The documentation that must accompany the result of an engineering economic analysis ranges from nothing to a full-fledged technical report, depending mainly on how important the decisions are that rest on the analysis and who must approve them.

Engineering economic decisions can be *routine, direct,* or *formal.* Documentation can be required for the decision *process,* allowing review of how the decision was made or participation in making it, and for the decision *results,* allowing communication of the choice or recommendation.

Routine decisions are decisions directly implied by standard reference materials. The decision generator is the same person or group as the decision user, so the decision results are documented indirectly, often as values entered into drawings, specifications, or purchase orders. The decision process is documented in the designer's design notes, implicitly or explicitly. For example, if PD-1 is a commonly used policy document that says to replace an electric motor's armature when either its age reaches five years or its current leakage reaches 0.04 amperes, then the result of the replacement decision might be documented only in the form of a purchase requisition to buy the replacement armature and a work order to install it, and the decision process might be documented in the maintenance record for the motor. This might be all that is needed for this routine decision, because it would be straightforward to check what decision was made, and how.

Direct decisions are decisions where the person who performs steps 5 and 6 of the decision-making process is the person who has the authority to make the decision, or whose decision recommendations are normally accepted without detailed review by higher authority. Documentation of direct decisions is by making the designer's notes clear and well organized, so that, upon demand, the equivalent of a formal report could be generated from them.

E1. **Sun, a piping designer, trying to route a 10-in. cooling-water line to and from a condenser in a tight place, asks Lee, the engineer, if she would approve using 8-in. pipe instead. Lee makes some calculations and approves the change; it causes a corresponding change in specifications for the pump that moves the cooling water through the line, and for its electric-motor driver, and for its electrical energy consumption. List the relevant engineering economic decisions, who made them, and how they would normally be documented.**

First, there was a decision that 10 in. is the best diameter for pipe that carries cooling water at a given rate. Lee probably looked up the appropriate size in a design manual, its recommendations having been computed in advance by its author. This was a *routine* decision, documented in standard reference materials.

When Sun raised the downsizing question, based on a perception that, because of the physical space limits, the cost of doing the job with 10-in pipe would be much greater than with 8-in. pipe, Lee was faced with a *direct* decision. Lee had to repeat the calculations behind the standard recommendations in the manual for this special case. Assuming she had authority to specify the pipe size, the pump, and the driver, the *results* of her analysis would be documented indirectly in the relevant specifications. The *process* of her analysis would be documented in her project file. Her supervisor could expect to see, upon request, how she computed the extra cost, if any, for a larger pump and driver, and the extra electrical energy expense, and how she compared these to the construction savings achieved by allowing the smaller pipe size.

Formal decisions are decisions for which the person or group who generates the decision is not the same person or group who uses the decision. Formal documentation is required.

11.2.1 Formal Documentation of Engineering Economic Analysis

Technical documents that include formal reporting of an engineering economic analysis include design project reports, proposals, feasibility study reports, requests for proposal (RFPs), and capital appropriation requests.

The generic structure of all such technical documents is as shown in Table 11.1.

11.2.2 Executive Summary

The executive summary of a technical report is the full report in miniature. It is the only part of the report that a "busy executive" would need to read in order to understand the recommendations at an appropriate level of detail, except that the executive summary may refer to important charts, graphs, or tables in the body of the report.

Table 11-2 gives an example of an executive summary for a technical report.

TABLE 11-1. Generic Structure of Technical Documents
. . . .

Executive Summary
Background
Alternatives
Statement of Problem
Technical Issues
  (chemical, civil, communications, electrical, environmental, information, legal, mechanical, medical, physical, statistical, structural, systems)
Economic Analysis
  Cost estimate
  Benefit or savings estimate
  Evaluation of alternatives
  Conclusions

TABLE 11-2. Example of an Executive Summary

We, the Infinite Transform Group, were given detailed cost estimates and limited benefits valuations for four mutually exclusive long-term projects to renovate and upgrade the voice/video/data/graphics communication system at West Point and were asked to provide a recommendation for choice of one of them, supported by a detailed economic analysis at 12% interest through year 2017.

The proposals are Zerop, Mixop, Bigop, and Newop. Their estimated cost schedules are given in tables 1 to 4, page ___. Zerop is a series of minimal bottleneck removals, delaying fiber optics investments as long as possible. Mixop introduces fiber optics in several phases. Bigop and Newop make a complete move to fiber optics in 1996, with Bigop installing interim optics gear to delay replacement of the existing telephone switch.

We accepted cost data as given, except to remove sunk engineering costs and to speculate on effects of rapid technological advances. All alternatives were assumed to provide the same basic benefits of providing communication, with disputed differences: Col. Hefalump provided estimates of extra benefits due to temporary large overcapacities; the Livery Committee advocated using half these benefits, while also adding penalties of $10,000 per year against Mixop while it kept the campus torn up and $20,000 against it while it provided mixed service. Maj. Zaster also suggested a $50,000 penalty against Newop for having less capacity in year 2017 than the other alternatives.

Results are summarized below (in K$):

			Present Worth at 12% of		
				Benefits and	
		Monetary	Overcapacity	Penalties	Overall
	Major	Costs, Savings,	Benefits	per Livery	per Livery
Alternative	Expenditures	and Salvage	per Hefalump	and Zaster	and Zaster
Zerop	1572 thru '07	−625	90	53	−572
Mixop	1621 thru '12	−580	68	−47	−627
Bigop	572 thru '96; 800 at '05	−620	125	75	−545
Newop	1262 thru '96	−795	180	77	−718

Although Mixop is cheapest, Bigop is our clear recommendation. The most comprehensive attempt at benefit estimation is that of the Livery Committee, whose valuations favor Bigop. Modifying these valuations to agree with Hefalump and Zaster only widens the Bigop advantage.

The main thing about an executive summary is that it is usually the *only part of the report read by a busy executive.* Completeness is the key. Brevity is also important; generally the executive summary should be no more than about 10% of the report body and should be held to 1 or 2 pages for a 10- or 20-page report.

The Executive Summary *does not* do these things:

· Does not echo the given data.
· Does not review background information in detail.
· Does not review standard methodology.
· Does not waste words or contain redundant information.
· Does not give a full audit trail for complex calculations or logical arguments.
· Does not sacrifice clarity for brevity—it is not meant to be as severely limited as an abstract.

The Executive Summary *does* do these things:

- Constitutes an *entire report in miniature*, including:
  - Problem Statement (explicit or implicit)
  - Facts
  - Assumptions
  - Discussion
  - Results, Conclusions, Recommendations
  - Contains all bottom-line details.
- Contains selected graphics that summarize facts, results, conclusions—that is, it has copies of the most important summary graphics in the report, if they are essential or very useful to the reader. Usually only one chart or graph is included; main tables or charts in the body of the report may sparingly be mentioned.
- Focuses on the *problem* instead of the *process*—that is, even if the report is largely about what was done to solve the problem, the Executive Summary is mostly about the problem itself.

11.2.3 Problem Statement

A problem statement is a concise statement of a problem to be solved or of objectives to be accomplished. It should identify who the authors are, what their starting point is, what they set out to do, what alternatives were available, and what conditions and limitations defined the scope of their work.

The problem statement is almost the only part of a good report that focuses as much on the authors as on the problem, because its main purpose is to identify what its authors set out to do.

E2. In the executive summary illustrated in Table 11-2, identify a problem statement, if present, or assemble one from various parts of the executive summary. Then show how the problem statement succeeds or fails to meet the requirements listed above.

The first paragraph of the illustrated executive summary is the problem statement. Let it be broken up into numbered lines as follows:

(0)	We, the Infinite Transform Group, were	(1)
(1)	given detailed cost estimates and limited	(2)
(2)	benefits valuations for four mutually	(3)
(3)	exclusive long-term projects to renovate	(4)
(4)	and upgrade the voice/video/data/graphics	(5)
(5)	communication system at West Point	(6)
(6)	and were asked to provide a recommendation	(7)
(7)	for choice of one of them, supported	(8)
(8)	by a detailed economic analysis at 10%	(9)
(9)	interest through year 2017.	(10)

The statement identifies who the authors are (0–0.9), tells what their starting point was (0.9–2.5), identifies alternatives (2.5–6), states what the authors were asked to do (6–7.8), and gives conditions and limitations on the scope of their work (7.8–10). Thus it succeeds in meeting the requirements for a problem statement.

In the scenario of this exercise, the U. S. Military Academy at West Point was faced with choosing a way to renovate and upgrade its campus communication system. But this was *not* the problem to be defined in the problem statement, because this was the problem faced by the "client," not by the report authors. The report authors faced a much narrower problem; they were brought in to complete an economic analysis where the most important part of the analysis—estimation of costs and benefits—had already been done.

When students submitted reports for the illustrated design exercise, the poorer attempts at a problem statement exhibited these common flaws:

1. Failure to specify what was given, so that the reader could not easily tell whether the authors were to perform the cost estimate and benefit valuations or whether they were receiving these from the client.
2. Failure to specify the alternatives, so that the reader could not easily tell whether the authors were to generate alternatives or whether they were to limit alternatives to those provided by the client.
3. Failure to define the main goal exactly, as in the erroneous goal "to choose the alternative," which suggests that the authors were the decision makers.

Every part of a good report serves at least one purpose. One purpose of a problem statement is to serve as a sort of contract. If the client is unhappy with the completeness of the analysis or report, the authors should be able to point to the problem statement and show that the disputed items were not within the scope. The main purpose of a well written problem statement is to specify clearly what the authors were to do and what they were not to do.

11.2.4 Economic Analysis Documentation

Many technical reports contain an economic analysis section in which the choice among the main design alternatives is explained. A four-part structure is recommended. It is assumed that alternatives have already been described.

The first part is a *cost estimate* for each alternative. The split between costs and benefits is the "user-provider" split explained in Chapter 7. Assuming that an alternative involves an investment, its cost estimate documents the anticipated costs to implement and operate the facilities or equipment required by the alternative.

There are two main approaches to the cost estimate: the *synthetic* approach and the *analogue* approach; usually both are used. A synthetic (or "detailed") cost estimate creates a taxonomy of all the materials, labor, and effort of every kind needed to implement, supply, operate, and maintain the facilities or equipment, and the estimated cost, for each time period, is the sum of all these costs, plus a *contingency cost*, often 10%, to account for the inevitable neglect of some needed elements. It is better practice to provide only one contingency cost than to overestimate every item.

The analogue approach involves comparing the alternative to a previous one with known costs, correcting for differences. The "six-tenths rule" in Section 5.1.3.4.2 is an example of such a correction.

As an example of the synthetic and analogue approaches to cost estimation, a paving contractor made a synthetic estimate of $46,000 for the job of paving a parking lot. But this worked out to 15% less on a cost-per-square-foot basis than the actual costs of two recent jobs. Inspecting the analogy in detail, he saw that the two recent jobs included subsoil preparation and traffic control costs that this job would not require. Making the corrections to the analogous costs, he found the synthetic estimate still $2000 below the analogous costs; he added $2000 to his contingency cost estimate and finally submitted a cost estimate of $48,000.

The next part of an economic analysis is a *benefit estimate* for each alternative. This is often an estimate of cost savings that the alternative will provide relative to an ongoing operation. If so, similar estimation techniques to those of cost estimation are applicable.

After costs and benefits have been separately documented for all alternatives, the documentation for *evaluation of alternatives* is straightforward. Economic assumptions, particularly those of MARR, economic lives, planning horizons, tax treatments, and risk, are stated, and engineering economy calculations are performed and reported. Sensitivity analysis calculations are also performed and reported. Finally, an economic analysis documents conclusions in the form of definite *recommendations* or selections.

11.3 DESIGN EXERCISES

The following Design Exercises are presented to give students practice in evaluating more realistic sets of design alternatives than are available in small illustrative exercises and to give students practice in documenting economic analyses.

11.3.1 Dialysis Manufacturing Capacity Expansion

SITUATION:

The Kennedy European Company (KE) owns a five-year license to manufacture and market the Belgian Home Dialysis Machine, a specialty machine whose demand is expected to level off at 50 machines per year. The current demand is 30 machines per year, and KE has the capacity to produce at that rate.

Each year, while the demand is below the 50 level, KE engineers assume that the demand can either increase by 10 or stay level. The demand is autocorrelated; if it increases by 10 in one year, it has a 40% probability of increasing again; otherwise it has a 20% probability of increasing. There was an increase in the year just ended.

KE would like to increase capacity in pace with demand, but there is always the possibility of increasing too rapidly or too slowly, or too late, considering the short five-year horizon and the fact that manufacturing capacity for the dialysis machine will have no salvage value. At any (integer year) time, the capacity can be increased to a level that is 10 machines per year greater, at a one-time cost of $180,000. The annual operating profit is $10,000 per machine sold. The number of machines sold is the minimum of demand and capacity.

By the eoy convention, when the expansion decision is made at the end of one year, the increase in capacity, the cost of the increase, and the increase in demand, if any, are all treated as if they occurred at the end of the next year. The real discount factor is 1/1.06, and all amounts are in indexed dollars.

REQUIREMENT:

Recommend a comprehensive capacity expansion plan. That is, determine a rule that for each year and each set of current demands and current capacities recommends whether or not to expand.

DISCUSSION:

Whether or not mentioned in the instructor's reporting requirements, the report should make the solution method clear, should give expected present worths, and should include some sensitivity analysis. If an intuitively simple rule of thumb can be stated that describes the entire capacity expansion plan for this case (even though a similar rule might not apply in all similar cases), it should be reported.

11.3.2 Antenna Construction Project

SITUATION:

Prim Cable Company (PCC) provides cable TV service to eight communities in Minnesota. The company has ordered a dish antenna assembly for use in a ground receiving station. Revenues from the station, less operating costs, will be $160,000 monthly when the station is completed, or $140,000 monthly when the station is completed except for this antenna.

Atlantis Science and Technology (AST) is the contractor selected to construct, deliver, and install the dish antenna assembly. The AST project to perform this work consists of five subprojects or tasks. Task 1 takes an expected four months and can begin at go-ahead. Task 2 takes an expected six months and can begin when Task 1 is completed. Task 5 takes an expected two months and can begin when Task 1 is completed. Task 3 takes an expected three months and can begin at go-ahead. Task 4 takes an expected five months and can begin when Task 3 and Task 5 are both completed. When all tasks are completed, the project is completed, and PCC can begin using the antenna.

The station except for the antenna is scheduled by PCC to be complete 10 months after go-ahead. PCC knows it will lose money if it completes the station before AST installs the antenna, so the appropriate penalty has been built into the antenna contract to have the effect of reimbursing losses to PCC caused by AST delay. The AST engineer believes that PCC may not finish at the scheduled time, and specifically believes there is a 29% chance of a 1-month PCC delay, a 9% chance of a 2-month PCC delay, and a 3% chance of a 3-month PCC delay.

The AST engineer estimates that Task 2 can be speeded up ("crashed") by one month at an additional cost of $5000, and that Task 4 can similarly be crashed for $4000. The MARR for either PCC or AST is unknown.

500   CHAPTER 11   DESIGN EXERCISES

The AST engineer has decided to run 34 Monte Carlo experiments to estimate project duration. For this, 34 sets of variates of task durations have already been prepared:

1	2	3	4	5		1	2	3	4	5
4	6	3	5	2		4	6	3	5	2
4	7	3	4	2		4	6	3	5	3
4	6	5	7	2		4	6	4	3	2
3	5	3	5	2		4	6	2	4	2
4	6	7	8	2		4	6	3	5	2
4	6	2	4	2		5	6	3	5	2
5	6	2	3	2		4	6	2	4	2
4	6	3	5	2		4	7	2	4	2
3	6	3	5	2		4	6	3	5	2
4	6	4	5	3		5	5	6	8	2
4	6	3	5	2		4	6	3	5	3
3	7	4	6	2		5	5	3	5	2
4	6	6	9	2		4	6	2	5	2
4	6	3	5	2		4	5	2	3	2
5	6	3	6	2		4	6	4	4	2
3	6	2	4	2		4	6	2	3	2
4	6	3	4	2		4	5	3	5	2

The same variates, with 1 subtracted as appropriate, will be used to estimate the project duration when tasks are crashed.

The following (0, 1) uniform random variates have been generated to aid in simulating PCC delays:

.0374	.1128	.5840	.3710	.9364	.8900	.3749	.3973	.4999
.1829	.0276	.8367	.5937	.3746	.9734	.3726	.2207	.7379
.2525	.4254	.6063	.6872	.2014	.7006	.6108	.2085	.8092
.1108	.7042	.5002	.0031	.9834	.3996	.4408	.6182	.9401

REQUIREMENT:

As the AST engineer, determine whether it is worthwhile to speed up either or both of Tasks 2 and 4. Also determine the impact of the penalty clause on AST.

DISCUSSION:

If inflation, interest rate, or the distinction between indexed and current amounts is judged important, make and report appropriate assumptions. The approach, each step of the method, intermediate results, and interesting incidental quantities would be reported whether or not mentioned in the instructor's reporting requirements. In project scheduling situations, one incidental quantity that is usually considered important to estimate is the probability of a given task's being "critical"; in each experiment there is at least one longest path that determines the project duration, and any activity on one of these "critical paths" is a "critical activity"—one that, in this experiment, was critical in the sense that if it had been delayed, the whole project would have been delayed.

11.3.3 Communication System Upgrading

SITUATION:

The United States Military Academy at West Point has a need to renovate and upgrade its communication system, including its telephone system, computer data network, and cable TV network. Funding must be sought. Most of the major needs through the year 2017 are already documented and accepted by higher authority, so the choice is largely a matter of meeting the established needs in the most economical manner; however, most categories of benefits, even purely esthetic ones, can weigh into the analysis to discriminate among alternatives, so that cost is not the only criterion.

Two years ago (assume now is 1 January 1992), a state-of-the-art telephone switch, having good voice but no data capabilities, was acquired. It is an owned switch, as opposed to a leased one. Another "sunk" investment is an extensive system of underground guideways carrying telephone cable (copper wire pairs), coaxial cables for data, and other coaxial cables for TV. Extensive engineering design work has already been completed for replacing major cable arteries with much higher capacity fiber optics lines that would replace existing copper pairs and coaxial cables in the backbone, and for installing multiplexer gear (allowing the switch to process light signals) that would protect the existing investment in the telephone switch, but not for the associated fiber optics data converters that would be required either at every terminal or at the file servers for groups of terminals. These fiber optic data converters would be required to make the network completely fiber optic. The actual total cost of this work was $9400 in indexed dollars, equivalent to $10,200 in 1992 dollars.

The basic need is to provide data transfer capacities that would gradually grow to 20 times the current load, allowing remote graphics applications, distributed super computing and voice/video/data/graphics integration.

PROPOSALS:

Competing teams of communications engineers have generated four specific project proposals, nicknamed "Zerop" (1), "Mixop" (2), "Bigop" (3), and "Newop" (4).

There is a "future demand profile" (not available to you) that expresses the official forecast of what information systems capabilities will be needed when and where. All four proposals meet or exceed this profile at all times from now to the year 2017, and at each major expenditure point for each proposal it barely meets the profile (none of the proposals goes to its next phase before the previous phase becomes inadequate).

Proposal 1 ("Zerop") is based on bottleneck removal and represents an effort to get the most out of existing wiring in buildings and guideways, going to fiber optics technology only when demand outstrips capacity. Voice, data, and TV would remain separate systems until 2000. Fiber optics would be added in two phases, in 2000 and 2007.

Proposal 2 ("Mixop") does not carry bottleneck removal to the hilt, but brings in fiber optics for data transmission in 1996. Later it brings in fiber optics for part of the telephone system, and it does not reach full voice/data graphics integration until 2012. In most years it involves inconvenience due to uneven service, with some users still connected to an older system and unable (or inconveniently able) to communicate with devices in the newer system. This alternative also involves the greatest amount of excavation over the years.

Proposal 3 ("Bigop") carries bottleneck removal to 1996 and then makes a complete move to fiber optics. The existing telephone switch is not replaced but fitted with multiplexer and optics-translation gear and finally is replaced in 2005.

Proposal 4 ("Newop") is similar to "Bigop" except that the switch is replaced with one of optic design in 1996 (the interim upgrading step is skipped).

CONDITIONS:

All costs and benefits are cited in 1992 dollars.

A 10% real annual interest rate is used for discounted cash flow computations.

Operations and maintenance costs are similar for all systems, except that the optical switch draws less electrical power and is estimated to save $1000 per year in electrical costs compared to the existing switch.

Salvage value of the existing telephone switch was $240,000 on 1 January 1992 and is decreasing at a rate of 18% per year. Multiplexer gear has no net salvage value. Because the price of copper is expected to fluctuate widely and to decrease (in 1992 dollars) over the long term, any differences among alternatives in the schedule of copper recovery will be neglected.

The cash-flow diagrams in Figure 11-1 summarize the estimated cash flows for the alternatives.

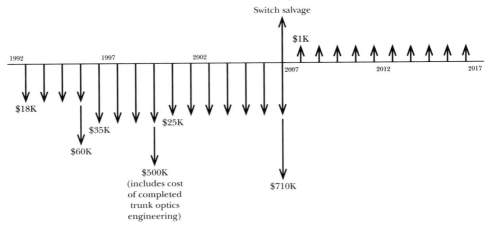

FIGURE 11-1a. Alternative 1, "Zerop."

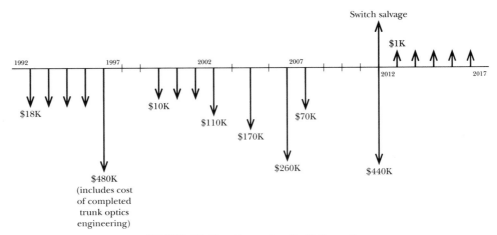

FIGURE 11-1b. Alternative 2, "Mixop."

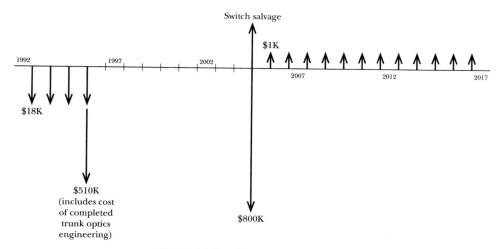

FIGURE 11-1c. Alternative 3, "Bigop."

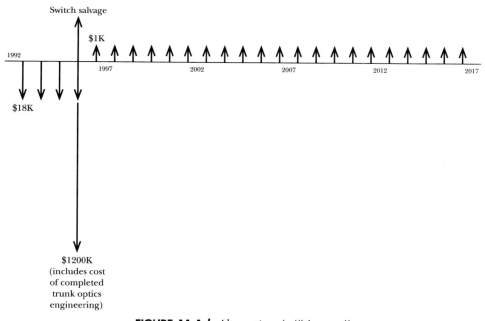

FIGURE 11-1d. Alternative 4, "Newop."

REQUIREMENTS:

Prepare a report that provides definite, well-supported recommendations.

The data that have been given reflect the service-provider's viewpoint, emphasizing costs. Analyze the situation from this viewpoint, but also separately take into account other considerations as follows:

1. From the user's viewpoint, the alternatives do not have equal benefits. Colonel Hefalump has estimated that the large overcapacities provided by some of the

alternatives will be highly beneficial to users, bringing prestige and research opportunities to West Point in the years immediately following major capacity increases. Specifically:

For the alternative	The capacity increases at the beginning of year	Will bring extra benefits worth (at that time, in 1992 dollars)
1 (Zerop)	2000	100K$
1 (Zerop)	2007	160K$
2 (Mixop)	1996	100K$
2 (Mixop)	2012	100K$
3 (Bigop)	1996	115K$
3 (Bigop)	2005	200K$
4 (Newop)	1996	240K$

2. General Livery is concerned about users and others as well. He agrees generally with Colonel Hefalump's views, except that he feels the "real" overcapacity benefits are half what Colonel Hefalump has estimated. He also advocates two additional refinements of the analysis:

a. Alternative 2 (Mixop) will keep various parts of the campus torn up almost constantly from 1999 to 2008. A committee that General Livery chaired debated this point and finally suggested a penalty of $10,000 per year for the torn-up years (that is, the ends of years 1999 through 2008).

b. When the committee's report reached the Goldcoats, the noted computer genius Private Bath pointed out that the Mixop alternative also would give mixed service during those years. On the basis that extra Goldcoats consulting effort would be required in the amount of about 0.4 man-years per year to deal with complexities of mixed service, and that users would also be inconvenienced to a similar extent, Private Bath suggested an additional penalty of $20,000 per torn-up year. General Livery's committee revised their report accordingly.

3. Major Zaster, in reviewing the data, has pointed out that alternative 4 (Newop), being based on 1996 technology, will probably end the study period having significantly less capacity on 1 January 2017 than the other alternatives. This overcapacity deficit is one that in Colonel Hefalump's analysis would be worth $50,000 at that time.

You are to conduct your analysis from the point of view of an analyst working for the Superintendent, USMA. Your guidance is that the Superintendent desires to see a complete economic analysis, to include what impact the conflicts in benefits may have on his final decision. However, he wants a single, well-thought-out recommendation as to which alternative to pursue.

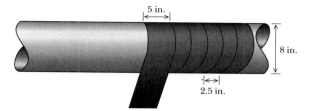

FIGURE 11-2. Pipe wrapping.

11.3.4 Pipe Wrapping Operation Optimization

SITUATION:

IMEX Industries is a Louisiana firm that installs underground pipelines for municipalities, utilities, and process plants. To protect against corrosion, steel pipe is always wrapped with various materials. One machine in particular applies plastic wrapping to pipe as shown in Figure 11.2. It handles two pipe sizes; let us focus on 8-in. pipe, which is pipe whose outside diameter is 8 in. A random length of 8-in. pipe, about 20 ft long, is mounted on an axle and rotated past a fixed taping head, which releases 5-in.-wide tape that adheres to the outside of the pipe at an angle such that each revolution advances the pipe 2.5 in.; this puts a double layer of tape on the pipe in an overlapping spiral.

The speed of the wrapping machine is adjustable by installing gears with the proper ratio. Operators have tended to use a speed slow enough so that the tape hardly ever breaks. The speed of taping is measured as v ft/min, which is the rate at which tape is fed out of the taping head. Considering that it takes $8\pi/12$ ft of tape to wrap $2.5/12$ lineal feet of pipe, a 20-ft length of pipe takes $201.0619298/v$ minutes to wrap.

T is the expected time in minutes until the tape breaks, and a study of its relationship to v gave the empirical equation $T = (80/v)^5$. Each time the tape breaks, the operator must spend 3.1 min fixing it.

The setup time for each length of pipe is 0.2 min. The machine runs 2280 hr/yr, including downtime for setup and repair, which is just enough to meet demand and utilize its operator the same number of hours. The cost of the operator including fringe benefits is \$28.50/hr for 2000 hr/yr, and 50% more than that for overtime hours. The taping speed currently being used is $v = 20$ ft/min.

The demand will not increase. If the production rate is increased, overtime costs will be decreased, but the operator will not be paid for less than 2000 hr/yr.

IMEX uses a 20% market interest rate and anticipates 3.5% annual inflation in labor and other costs. The wrapping machine will be retired in 5 yr. Meanwhile, it would be possible to invest \$8000 to improve the machine so that its tape-breaking equation would improve to $T = (100/v)^5$.

REQUIREMENT:

Determine the best taping speed for the machine, assuming that the changeover cost to install gears for a new speed is \$750. Determine whether it would be profitable to invest in improving the machine.

DISCUSSION:

Whether or not mentioned in the instructor's reporting requirements, there are several intermediate and incidental quantities that need to be reported. For example, any user of the result would want to know what the demand is assumed to be, and what speed the improved machine would run at if the improvement was recommended. Do not fail to make clear what quantity is being minimized or maximized.

11.3.5 Rubber Press Replacement

SITUATION:

Having purchased the Worth Rubber Plant in Dallas, Texas, Chung Jae Yop is faced with a need to keep up the plant's productive capacity. There are four 10-ton/day presses of various ages. There is an approximate aging model that gives the operating cost per ton as a function of age:

$$C = 5.4071e^{0.035t}$$

where C is the operating cost of a press in indexed dollars per ton and t is the age of the press in years. Mr. Chung uses the continuous timing convention and considers MARR to be $r = \ln 1.1$ as a real nominal continuous interest rate.

To produce 10 ton/day per press, the current daily operating costs of the four presses are about $70, $90, $140, and $175, respectively. There are 260 operating days per year. A press can be replaced for $120,000, but the replacement costs are expected to increase 1% faster than inflation.

REQUIREMENT:

Recommend what should be done immediately, if anything, and what the replacement policy should be in the future. If the policy calls for replacing more than one press in any one year, it is of interest to know the cost of delaying replacements so that the capital requirements are spread out.

DISCUSSION:

The fact that Mr. Chung uses the continuous timing convention means that the solution will be better communicated in this form. It is acceptable to use the eoy convention in the analysis; if the continuous convention is used, it is acceptable to deal with time only to the nearest year. Whether or not mentioned in the instructor's reporting requirements, there are several incidental quantities that should be reported and sensitivity analyses that should be performed.

11.3.6 Capital Budgeting for Tooling-Cost Reductions

(Note: This exercise concerns a fictional situation. Some of the data would be classified if it were true or realistic.)

SITUATION:

SIGSAT: The Sigsat ("signature saturation") System, based on research completed in 1991 at Ft. Bliss, UTEP, and White Sands, will allow air defense commanders to manage their radar and command-and-control signature flexibly. Each battalion would emplace up to 24 "sigsat" units—8 expensive "saturants" and 16 cheaper "satyrs"—over a wider area. Each sigsat unit is a phony radar installation. The saturants can simulate heavy communications radio traffic as well; both kinds of unit can simulate typical air defense radar activities, including target search, lock-on, tracking, fire control (linked ingeniously with units actually controlling fire, so that an enemy target could not distinguish which site is actually controlling the missile on its way), jamming and other electronic countermeasures (ECM), and even some electronic counter-countermeasures (ECCM). In conjunction with the Sigsat System is the issue of redundant genuine systems. (Under research is a proposed upgrade kit that would convert saturant units to genuine installations.)

A sigsat control net intermittently ties the sigsat units together and coordinates their activities. This "signet" is the most expensive component of the Sigsat System.

Prototype field tests were a joy to behold, at least for the Army participants. The Air Force ducks would detect several systems, tens of kilometers apart, all locked onto them, and would be unable to sort out who was real and who phony, even when missiles were approaching. In several days they fired on 35 ground targets, "taking out" 20 of them, of which 13 were cheap satyr units (a generator, two antennas, and less than 500 kg of electronics), 5 were saturants, and only 2 were real. The most beautiful thing about the system (and the main motivator for early development funding) is its ability to make the whole battlefield electronic environment so dirty that even the opposer's navigation radars don't work right, while the control net gear that removes most of the phony signals keeps the corrected environment clean enough for friendly units to function.

PROCUREMENT: The Sigsat System received a boost and a speedup when Senator Sam Nunn (D, GA) insisted that the contract be awarded to the same contractors who supplied the real systems—an unselfish gesture, seeing that this locked out a major Georgia firm.

The current situation is this: Servomech of Inglewood, CA, has been awarded the contract for three systems: 32 *signal emulators*, 14 *net brains*, and 61 *dual antenna systems*. They are to deliver over the next 12 years. Your supervisor at Servomech has assigned you to conduct an economic analysis on a set of proposed cost-savings projects associated with these manufacturing efforts.

DATA: You have been given the following cost data (all in current dollars) by the project manager:

1. An opportunity for reducing tooling costs for the dual antenna system requires that $40K be expended immediately and $17K be expended one year from now. This will result in a base savings of $50K at the end of year 3 and a savings of 28% less each year through the end of year 10.

    Two possible modifications of this cost-savings project exist. The first would require an additional $4.5K to be spent at the end of this year and would result in an increased savings of $1K per year for years 4 through 10.

    The alternative modification would require an additional $6K immediately and an added $4.5K at the end of the year, resulting in a $4K per year additional savings at the end of each year for years 4 through 10.

2. A second savings project under consideration involves the prime mover that the signal emulators will be installed upon. If the company performs a baseline modification of the M1008 (5/4 ton) pickup truck, at costs of $20K now and at the end of

each of two more years, savings of $28K each year for years 4 through 7 and $25K each year for years 8 through 12 will be realized.

An alternative modification to the chassis of the prime mover requires the same expenditures as above, but also requires an investment in year 3 of $11.5K. The savings are $30K each year for years 4 through 7 and $27K each year for years 8 through 12.

A third alternative exists that requires $33K immediately and $20K in each of years 1 and 2. It would yield savings of $30K each year from year 4 through year 12.

3. An experimental superconducting microcomputer can be purchased to control the net brains. It would require an immediate investment of $30K and an additional cost at the end of the year of $44K. If this microcomputer is installed, your experts estimate that the savings to the project will result in $50K at the end of year 2, $30K at the end of year 3, $18K for year 4, $20K in year 5, $21K in year 6, and $28.75K in each of years 7 through 11.

The project manager is very excited about the possibility of including this technology in the project. He also tells you that there are two possible software modifications for this microcomputer. The first modification requires an initial $40K investment and $50K at the end of the year. The savings will improve over the basic microcomputer project by $20K at the end of year 3, $5K per year for the next three years and $3.25K per year for the last five years of the project.

The second software modification requires $55K to be invested immediately, and $61K to be spent at the end of the year. This will result in an additional savings of $25K (over the base microcomputer project) at the end of year 3, $20K at the end of year 4, $15K in year 5, and $10K in year 6.

RESOURCES: Servomech has allocated $35K per year in plowback capital for cost-cutting projects. Because the Sigsat System contract is firm, you have been told by the finance division that you can borrow up to $25K per year to invest in additional cost-cutting projects. This money will be available to Servomech at an interest rate of 12.5%.

You have gone back to the finance division and requested additional capital based on "back of envelope" calculations (that show these cost-cutting projects to be good). The finance division has stated that you can have an additional $30K per year from Servomech's chemical division if the cost-savings projects justify the transfer of funds. The chemical division is currently earning 20% MARR on an i basis (consider this division as a lender at $i = 20\%$).

REQUIREMENTS:

1. Recommend the best feasible set of savings projects, and justify the recommendations clearly and completely. Obviously it is of great interest to know whether the capital restrictions severely limit the capacity to undertake cost-savings projects, and what additional amounts of capital would allow a more desirable cost-savings program.

2. Unfortunately, no one has estimated the costs and benefits of *delayed* cost-savings opportunities. Since the benefits are tied to the schedule of the overall Sigsat program, Servomech cannot simply wait a year to take advantage of an opportunity. However, as a rule of thumb we can postulate that a negative cash flow can be delayed a year with these consequences:

(a) The hurry-up associated with the delay will cause a 30% increase in the amount of both the delayed investment and any other investment already scheduled (thus instead of spending $20K in each of years 0 and 1, you could spend $52K in year 1).

(b) The delay itself means that any savings anticipated for year M will be zero if the investment scheduled for year $M - 1$ is delayed. Also, savings for a year will be reduced 50% if an investment scheduled two years earlier is delayed to one year earlier.

Ignore the possibility of delaying only part of a year's expenditures in a cost-saving project. A project can be delayed for additional years under the same rules for each year of delay. Report which delays, if any, would appear attractive under the above rules of thumb, assuming no further extra amounts of capital are available.

3. For easy interpretation of results and recommendations, the final result should be reported in a tabular form showing capital requirements and profitability of not only the recommended solution but of reasonable variations from it.

11.3.7 Mon Bijou Flood Control[1]

SITUATION:

You are assigned to the Miami District of the U. S. Army Corps of Engineers as a project analyst in the Engineering Design Section. Your District has received a request by the Department of Public Works, U. S. Virgin Islands, for assistance in reducing flooding in the Mon Bijou area. This area is a residential suburb of the city of Christiansted and is subject to frequent and severe flooding.

Your section has conducted an extensive study to investigate flooding and related problems in the Mon Bijou area. It was found that feasible means for reducing these problems do exist. Now your team is to recommend the most appropriate course of action from an engineering economic standpoint.

The Mon Bijou and Glynn residential areas are located in the upper part of the Salt River watershed about 5 miles west of the city of Christiansted, St. Croix. A tributary to the Salt River, Canaan Gut, originates on the south slopes of the northern coastal mountain range of St. Croix. Canaan Gut drains the southern slopes of Blue Mountain and Mount Eagle before entering the Mon Bijou area at the base of the mountains. It travels through the Mon Bijou and Glynn areas before joining with another tributary to form the Salt River just below Glynn. The total drainage area of Canaan Gut is 2.5 square miles, of which only 0.87 square miles lie above the Mon Bijou area. However, due to heavy rainfall generated by the mountains and the steep slopes, flood flows are substantial, with a 100-year flood flow of over 3200 cubic feet per second (cfs) where Canaan Gut enters Mon Bijou. This, combined with severe encroachment of the flood plain of the normally dry stream, has resulted in 96 homes' being subject to flooding by a 100-year event. This would result in over $1.7 million in damages and related flood losses. Even a two-year event produces over $340,000 in damages. Total average annual damages are estimated at $442,150. During the period 1986–1991, three major floods caused widespread damage in the area.

To address these flood problems, the design engineer team has developed several

---

[1] Adapted from a design exercise written by Richard A. Paradiso, Jr. Used by permission.

plans to reduce flooding and has compiled information regarding their overall economic, environmental, social, and other impacts. These plans are detailed as follows:

A. Flood plain evacuation.
B. Construction of new culvert through upper portion of Mon Bijou.
C. Channel modification through the upper portion only.
D. Channel diversion around the developed areas.

The flood plain evacuation plan (Plan A) would remove all structures within the 20-year flood plain. This involves 35 houses in Mon Bijou and five houses in the Glynn area. Implementation of this plan would require the purchase of the land and improvements from the then-current owners. Relocation assistance would be provided to the occupants in accordance with the provisions of Public Law 91-646. When the structures are empty, all salvageable equipment would be removed and the structures demolished. The area would be cleaned and replanted as necessary to provide an acceptable appearance. Annual savings would be realized beginning in 1996.

The culvert enlargement plan (Plan B) actually would involve the construction of a new culvert adjacent to the existing culvert. The existing culvert would be left in place. This plan would include a diversion channel and levee to intercept flow from Little Fountain Gut and direct it to Canaan Gut. Also included would be two new concrete bridges with paved approaches, a debris basin, a gabion-lined approach channel, a 10 × 15-ft reinforced concrete box culvert 512 ft long with stilling basin, and a gabion-lined exit channel. A construction easement would be needed to install the box culvert, and areas of the open channel, levee, and debris basin would have to be acquired. No relocation of houses or other structures would be required under this plan, even though minor utility and street work would be required. Annual maintenance costs estimated at $40,000 per year beginning in 1996 would also be required to remove debris from the debris basin, maintain the gabion lining, and maintain the levee and access areas. It should be noted that this plan involves a high velocity (>20 ft/s) culvert. Therefore, the debris basin is very important to the proper functioning of the works. Annual savings would be realized beginning in 1997.

The open channel plan (Plan C) involves the reestablishment of an open channel through the upper Mon Bijou area. A channel would be excavated. A diversion plan for Little Fountain Gut would be included to direct the flow to the new channel. Plan C would require the removal of six houses along the new channel right-of-way. These would be acquired, the occupants relocated, and the structures removed to permit construction of the channel. The main channel would be trapezoidal with a bottom width of 20 ft and side slopes of one vertical to two horizontal. The sides and bottom would be grassed to prevent erosion. Seven steel drop structures would be provided to reduce velocities in the new channel reach. Each structure would lower the channel grade about 6 ft. The total length of the new channel would be about 1800 ft. Two new bridges would be required to span the new channel. One local street would be barricaded. Annual savings would be realized beginning in 1996.

Plan D involves the construction of a 6500-ft-long bypass channel around the northern side of Mon Bijou and Glynn. This channel would begin at the roadway upstream of the Mon Bijou area and travel through the undeveloped areas in an easterly direction. A levee on the southern side of the new channel would divert runoff into the new channel. The new channel and levee would also intercept water draining from Little Fountain Gut. This diversion channel would follow the natural ground slope through the existing dam, which would be removed. It would then rejoin the Canaan Gut channel at the headwaters of the Salt River just downstream of Glynn. The diversion channel would be trapezoidal with a bottom width of 75 ft and a side slope of 3 horizontal to 1 vertical. Channel depth would vary with topography but generally range from 8 to 12 ft. To control flow velocities in the channel, a series of 34 gabion-lined drop structures would be placed along the channel. Each would lower the water 3 to 4 ft. The main channel would be grass lined between the drop structures. Two new bridges would be required, as well as the removal of at least three houses in the lower portion of Glynn. Annual savings would be realized beginning in 1996.

CONDITIONS:

All costs and benefits are cited in 1991 dollars. A 20-yr horizon is to be used, with "now" considered to be the end of year 1991.

A 10% real annual interest rate is used for discounted cash flow computations.

The do-nothing alternative would result in the estimated $442,150 annual damages for the 20-yr analysis period.

The cash-flow diagrams in Figure 11-3 summarize all costs but not benefits for each of the plans.

Compared to the do-nothing alternative, annual savings of each plan are the estimated $442,150 per year starting in the years mentioned above in each plan. They are not shown in Figure 11-3.

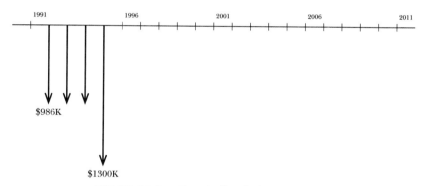

FIGURE 11-3a. Plan A: flood plain evacuation.

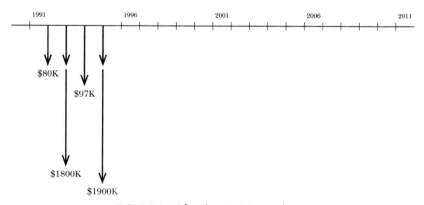

FIGURE 11-3b. Plan B: New culvert.

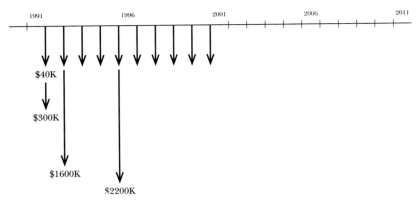

FIGURE 11-3c. Plan C: Channel modification.

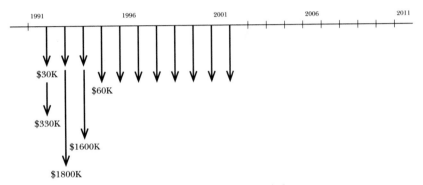

FIGURE 11-3d. Plan D: Channel diversion.

REQUIREMENTS:

Prepare a report that provides definite, well-supported recommendations.

The data that have been given reflect the service-provider's viewpoint, emphasizing costs. Analyze the situation from this viewpoint. Additionally, your analysis should take into account the following considerations:

1. From the Islander's viewpoint, the plans do not have equal benefits. Colonel Largedam (construction division chief) has estimated that the negation of flood risk and the freeing of accessible undeveloped land provided by some of the plans will be highly beneficial to the township, bringing additional tax revenues each year beginning in the year immediately following major development. Specifically:

For the Plan	The increased tax revenues beginning in year	Will bring extra benefits worth (at that time, in 1991 dollars)
B (new culvert)	2005	40K$
C (channel modification)	2003	34K$
D (channel diversion)	2006	20K$

2. Lt. Col. Brick, head of Project Review, is concerned about future development as well. He agrees generally with Colonel Largedam's views, except that he feels the

"real" benefits are twice what Colonel Largedam has estimated. He also advocates two additional refinements of the analysis:

(a) Plans C and D will keep various tourist areas of the island torn up almost constantly from 1992 to 2000 and 2002, respectively. A committee that LTC Brick chaired debated this point and finally suggested a penalty of $9000 per year for the torn-up years.

(b) When the committee's report reached the Value Engineering Section, the Director, Lt. Col. Mortar, pointed out that the negotiations for the purchase of 40 homes in Plan A would likely result in some sort of court action whereby one or more of the homeowners would probably file a class action in an attempt to stop the project (actually in an effort to increase the amount for settlement payments). Lt. Col. Mortar suggested an additional penalty of $20,000 in legal fees per year for the years 1992–1994. Lt. Col. Brick's committee revised their report accordingly.

3. Maj. Clearwater of the Environmental Protection Branch, in reviewing the data, has pointed out that Plan D calls for construction of a bypass channel directly through the breeding grounds of the Red Chested Water Frog. This species of frog is only found in certain areas of the U. S. Virgin Islands and is protected. Adoption of this plan will necessitate a relocation effort of the frogs. Maj. Clearwater estimated that this will cost $60,000 and that the frogs will be relocated in 1993.

You are to conduct your analysis from the point of view of an analyst working for the Commander of the Miami District. Your guidance is that the Commander desires to see a complete economic analysis, to include what impact the differences in estimated benefits may have on his final decision. However, he wants a single, well-thought-out recommendation as to which plan to pursue.

DISCUSSION:

The report should make all assumptions clear, particularly those that are not explicitly given above.

11.3.8 Capital Budgeting for CDP Corporation[1]

SITUATION:

You are the newly appointed Chief Financial Officer (CFO) of the CDP Corporation, a relatively small manufacturer of speakers for component and cabinet stereos. The firm manufactures both stand-alone speakers (sold under both the CDP label and under the label of major retail organizations) and individual speaker assemblies (for installation in cabinet stereos). The Chief Executive Officer (CEO) of the firm has long been interested in expanding the firm, but the inability of your predecessor to collect and interpret evaluations of prospective investments has made that expansion impossible. He was fired yesterday afternoon, and you were advised of your promotion from your previous position as executive vice-president of corporate philanthropy when you arrived at work yesterday morning.

The corporation's annual shareholders' meeting is scheduled within two weeks. The CEO insists that she will announce a detailed set of expansion plans during the

[1]Adapted from a design exercise written by James D. Renbarger. Used by permission.

meeting, and your sole task until then is to provide her with both recommendations and the analysis behind them. There is not nearly enough time for you to ask division chiefs within the corporation for input beyond that which they have already provided. Much of the problem encountered by your predecessor was caused by his inability to enforce a required format for the submission of data by division chiefs; your major difficulty will be interpreting and comparing the different types of information that they have provided. The firm currently has $750,000 that could be committed to expansion plans. The CEO would like to be able to announce a "million-dollar" plan, however, and will allow borrowing up to $400,000 if there are projects that warrant it. The only requirement that she has imposed is that at least one project must come from the speaker subdivision—speakers, after all, are the company's signature product.

The only data that you have to work with are in the three Division Reports listed below. You have already determined that all projects were evaluated on a current-dollar basis, that the company has in the past earned a rate of return of approximately 12% on its investments, and that the company can expect to pay an effective interest rate of 17.5% on any money that is borrowed. You may assume that no project requires an investment of funds in excess of the initial requirement identified for each.

MARKETING DIVISION REPORT: The chief of the marketing division has evaluated a number of projects designed to increase CDP's market share west of the Mississippi River. The marketing division chief's background is as a government project analyst; he has finally recognized the importance of using interest rates other than 10% in evaluations, but has yet to report data in anything other than benefit/cost ratios. All of these projects are independent.

Project	Required Investment	Benefit/Cost Ratio, Determined at $i =$					
		10%	13%	16%	19%	22%	25%
M-1	$100K	1.87	1.68	1.52	1.38	1.27	1.17
M-2	$170K	1.10	0.99	0.89	0.81	0.75	0.69
M-3	$235K	1.70	1.53	1.39	1.26	1.16	1.06
M-4	$320K	1.20	1.08	0.98	0.89	0.81	0.75
M-5	$350K	1.59	1.43	1.29	1.18	1.08	0.99
M-6	$400K	1.40	1.26	1.14	1.04	0.95	0.87

ENGINEERING DIVISION REPORT: The chief of the engineering division had focused his effort exclusively on a proposed upgrade of the computer system used by product engineers. The system under consideration consists of both the basic workstation (project "X") and a number of independent (and optional) hardware enhancements. The enhancements are incompatible with existing corporation equipment.

Project	Required Investment	ROR	Net Present Worth (K$), at $i =$					
			10%	13%	16%	19%	22%	25%
			(Basic Workstation)					
X	$225K	.208	95.1	62.9	35.6	12.3	−7.8	−25.3
			(Optional Enhancements)					
X-1	$75K	.367	85.0	69.0	55.3	43.6	33.6	24.9
X-2	$100K	.132	12.0	0.8	−8.8	−17.0	−24.0	−30.1
X-3	$90K	.208	38.0	25.2	14.2	4.9	−3.1	−10.1

MANUFACTURING DIVISION REPORT: The chief of the manufacturing division has asked a number of his subdivision chiefs to suggest investment proposals for their particular areas.

Cabinet Subdivision:

CDP Corporation currently subcontracts for both our wood and our plastic speaker enclosures. The cabinetry subdivision chief has suggested a number of equipment purchases that could allow us the flexibility to manufacture some or all of our cabinets. All of these projects are independent.

Project	Required Investment	Net Present Value Index, Determined at $i =$					
		10%	*13%*	*16%*	*19%*	*22%*	*25%*
C-1	$65K	0.34	0.19	0.07	−0.04	−0.13	−0.21
C-2	$175K	0.09	0.06	0.03	0.01	−0.02	−0.04
C-3	$200K	0.20	0.70	−0.05	−0.14	−0.23	−0.30
C-4	$225K	0.29	0.15	0.03	−0.08	−0.17	−0.24
C-5	$445K	0.17	0.08	0.00	−0.07	−0.13	−0.19
C-6	$590K	0.26	0.17	0.08	0.00	−0.06	−0.12

Electronics Subdivision:

The electronics assembly line is the only part of the CDP Corporation operation that seems to cause significant worker dissatisfaction. The electronics subdivision chief has recommended a number of projects that can increase the number and variety of tasks performed by employees while, concurrently, allowing more worker conversation and interaction. All of these projects are independent.

Project	Required Investment	Net Present Value (K$), Determined at $i =$					
		10%	*13%*	*16%*	*19%*	*22%*	*25%*
E-1	$75K	69.2	51.4	36.6	24.2	13.6	4.7
E-2	$150K	63.6	35.6	12.4	−7.0	−23.4	−37.2
E-3	$210K	147.8	102.0	64.0	32.1	5.2	−17.6
E-4	$285K	169.0	110.3	61.5	20.7	−13.7	−42.8
E-5	$330K	172.1	105.3	49.9	3.7	−35.2	−68.1
E-6	$425K	82.5	12.0	−46.4	−95.0	−116.3	−132.2

Speaker Subdivision:

Speaker production is the heart of CDP Corporation. To remain competitive, new and innovative speaker designs must constantly be tested and fielded. A number of independent design proposals have been forwarded by the chief of the speaker subdivision, who is a particularly difficult person to work with. His knowledge of the CEO's insistence on including at least one proposal from his division, in fact, led him to believe that he could get away with providing far less information than that provided by the other chiefs.

Project	Required Investment	ROR
S-1	$80K	.219
S-2	$95K	.330
S-3	$185K	.185
S-4	$300K	.122
S-5	$350K	.201

REQUIREMENT:

Prepare a report that recommends a specific course of action.

11.3.9 Heavy Equipment Options[1]

SITUATION:

The New Orleans District of the U. S. Army Corps of Engineers, within the last year, received a request by the Louisiana Department of Public Works for environmental control assistance in an important residential area. This area is a residential suburb of the city of Hammond, and it has been subject to frequent and severe flooding for many years. The feasibility study conducted by the New Orleans District concluded that means for reducing the flooding exist, and a subsequent study recommended the course of action outlined below. You are the Chief Financial Officer (CFO) of World-wide Construction, Inc., and your firm has been awarded the contract for procuring and delivering fill materials during the construction and initial maintenance phases of the project. Because of extensive commitments elsewhere in the United States, your firm does not currently have enough heavy equipment to complete the task. Your assignment is to determine the most economical means for the company to fulfill its obligations.

The residential areas of concern are located in the upper part of a watershed about five miles west of the city of Hammond. Eighty-seven homes have been subjected to repeated flooding, and total average annual damages in this area have been estimated at $842,150. Floods occurred in the area during the last six years, causing widespread damage.

To address these flood problems, the engineer design team developed several alternative plans. The plan that was eventually selected involves the construction of a long bypass channel around the affected residential areas. This channel will begin at the roadway upstream of the area and will travel through an undeveloped area in an easterly direction. A levee on the southern side will divert runoff into the new channel. This diversion channel will require several drop structures in order to control the speed of runoff through the channel and will be lined with grass between those structures. Two new bridges will be required for the channel, as will the removal of at least five houses in the area. Savings from damage control will be realized beginning in 1994.

Although the channel excavation will provide much of the material required for levee construction, the soil around Hammond is too sandy for exclusive use. Your contract calls for you to procure and deliver additional soil with a higher clay content. Specifically, your firm is to deliver 320,000 cubic yards per year both this year and

---

[1]Adapted from a design exercise written by James D. Renbarger. Used by permission.

next, and then 185,000 cubic yards per year for the following six years. You have already purchased the rights to the required amount of material (to be extracted from a pit already in operation in another part of the state), and you have subcontracted the equipment required to excavate and load the material. Your sole remaining task is to identify how to transport the material to the construction site.

TRANSPORT OPTIONS:

You have narrowed your vehicle choice to the Mark Transporter and the Kenwood Hauler, and you are considering both leases and outright purchases of each vehicle.

Mark Transporter T-5:

Capacity: 5 cubic yards

Current purchase price: $51,050

Two-year lease option: $1350 per month; last month's lease due at delivery; purchase option at the end of lease for projected fair market retail value of $36,500 (current dollars). Sum of total monthly payments for two-year lease = $32,400. Lessee responsible for all maintenance and upkeep costs.

Estimated operation and maintenance costs: $2300 per year for the first three years; increasing by $300 per year every year thereafter.

Kenwood Hauler H-85:

Capacity: 8.5 cubic yards

Current purchase price: $73,400

Two-year lease option: $1700 per month; last month's lease due at delivery; purchase option at the end of the lease for projected fair market value of $55,000 (current dollars). Sum of total monthly payments for two-year lease = $40,800. Lessee responsible for all maintenance and upkeep costs.

Estimated Operation and Maintenance Costs: $3000 for the first year; increasing by a real rate of 10% per year every year thereafter.

Purchase/Lease Options:

The prices that you have been quoted are dependent on using each truck exclusively, and you have already considered and eliminated the possibility of combining smaller numbers of the different trucks. Regardless of the truck that you choose, the following three purchase/lease options exist:

Option 1: Purchase all the trucks required for the initial two-year period, sell the trucks not required for the last six years as soon as they are no longer needed, and sell the rest of the trucks when the contract expires.

Option 2: Lease all the trucks required for the initial two-year period, invoke the purchase option at the end of the two years for enough trucks to fulfill your remaining obligations, and sell the trucks that you purchased when the contract expires.

Option 3: Purchase (now) all the trucks that you will need for the last six years of the project, and sell them at the end of the eight-year period. Lease any additional trucks that you will need for the first two years.

CONDITIONS:

All cost figures, unless obvious from the context or otherwise identified, are in constant 1991 dollars. Contractual agreements, such as leases, are expressed in current dollars unless they specifically contain inflation-linked escalation clauses. The anticipated general inflation rate over the next 10 years is 4.5% per year.

A 7.5% real annual interest rate is used by your firm for discounted cash-flow calculations.

The distance between sites and the loading capacity of your excavation equipment will limit each truck to, on average, six round trips per day of operation.

You may estimate the fair market retail value for trucks that are older than two years old by applying a real rate of decline of 10% per year to the fair market retail value of two-year-old trucks. You expect to pay the full retail value if you are purchasing trucks, but expect to receive only 80% of that amount if you are selling trucks.

The Chief Executive Officer (CEO) has indicated a strong desire to continue the firm's past relationship with the manufacturer of the Mark Transporter, but he has also committed to a series of cost-cutting moves within the company that suggest to you that he finds the economic consequences of decisions to be the most important at the current time. You also know that he believes that cost differences of 5% or less, given the natural uncertainty of the many estimates that are required in evaluations such as the one that you are conducting, are usually not sufficient to override significant nonmonetary concerns.

You may *not* approximate your annual lease payments by simply summing your monthly payments. The requirement to pay your last month's lease at time of delivery does not reduce your total number of lease payments, but does shift the timing of them.

If you choose, at any point, to purchase vehicles, you will pay for them with cash from corporate funds.

REQUIREMENT:

Prepare a report that makes and justifies a specific recommendation.

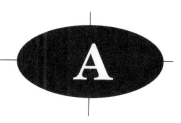

ANSWERS TO EVEN EXERCISES

CHAPTER 1

2. (a) The alternative criterion discriminates against furnaces that are much cheaper but slightly less fuel-efficient or that are very efficient but slightly more expensive than the budget allows.
   (b) Students, teachers, administrators, maintenance workers, food-service workers, government (public health, cost), and even donors of sensitive art or equipment.

4. $0.59

6. It is worthwhile to continue; abandonment is $6 million worse than continuing.

8. $44,000/yr

10. (a) Primo ($1456.85/mo compared to $1679.05/mo for Uggle) (b) $3.04 per gallon (c) Primo is cheaper for any number of operating hours per month.

12. Changed elements of the balance sheet ($000):

Total Current Assets	Total Assets	Total Current Liabilities	Total Liabilities	Total Owner Equity	Retained Earnings
6,280	10,730	2,696	5,516	5,214	2,544

14. Changed elements of the balance sheet ($000):

Provision for bad debt	150	Short-term notes payable	780
Total current assets	6,230	Total current liabilities	2,740
Plant and equipment	6,210	Total liabilities	5,560
Depreciation	2,270	Retained earnings	2,480
Total fixed assets	4,480	Total owner equity	5,150
		Total liabilities and	
Total assets	10,710	owner equity	10,710

16. 63.8%

18. (a) Operating margin of profit is 5.40%. Net profit ratio is 11.95%. Interest coverage is 3.27. (b) $1,248,500, a 17.86% increase

20. 10.8%; $597,000 per year

CHAPTER 2

2. (a) $592.08 (b) $350.56 (c) $821.57 (d) $910.95

4. 0.8165% (monthly)

6. 0.5-year: 10.25% (0.8165% monthly); 1-year: 10% (0.7974%)

8. 18 months

10. $310.58

12. 4.254 years

14. $797.19

16. Before: $5014.95; After: $5914.95. $1618.48

18. $568.43

20. 9%

22.

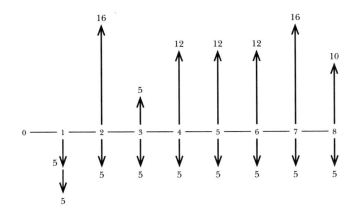

24.

$$F_m = \sum_{t=0}^{n} A_t \beta^{t-m}$$

At $m = 0$,

$$F_0 = \sum_{t=0}^{n} A_t \beta^t \equiv \underline{\underline{P}}$$

26.

$$P = \sum_{t=0}^{n} A_t \beta^t$$

where $\beta = 1/(1 + i)$. For $i = 0$, $\beta = 1$, so $\beta^t = 1$ for all t. Thus,

$$P = \sum_{t=0}^{n} A_t$$

28.

$$F_m = \sum_{t=0}^{n} A_t \beta^{t-m}$$

where $\beta = 1/(1 + i)$. For $i = 0$, $\beta = 1$, so $\beta^{t-m} = 1$ for all $t - m$. Thus,

$$F_m = \sum_{t=0}^{n} A_t$$

30.

$$\sum_{t=0}^{n} A_t \beta^{t-m} = \sum_{t-0}^{n} A_t \beta^{t-m'}$$

$$\beta^{-m} \sum_{t=0}^{n} A_t \beta^t = \beta^{-m'} \sum_{t=0}^{n} A_t \beta^t$$

$$\beta^{-m} P = \beta^{-m'} P$$

Now since $i > 0$ and m and m' are distinct, certainly β^{-m} and $\beta^{-m'}$ are distinct. [Recall $\beta = 1/(1 + i)$, and only for $\beta = 1$ or $i = 0$ would β raised to two distinct powers give the same result.] Thus, for the equation to hold, we must have $P = 0$. This means that if a cash-flow set has zero worth at any time, it has zero worth at all times.

32.

i	β	F_1
5%	1/1.05	0.35476
10%	1/1.10	0.31818
15%	1/1.15	-0.01087
20%	1/1.20	-0.33333
25%	1/1.25	-0.65000

34. $F_0 = -5 + 4\beta + 2\beta^2 = 0$

$F_2 = -5(1 + i)^2 + 4(1 + i) + 2 = 0$

36.

i	β	P
0.05	1/1.05	0.9229
0.10	1/1.10	−0.2479
0.15	1/1.15	−0.8639

Rate of return $\cong 9\%$

38.

40. $2009.09

42. $X = \$643.10$

44. $5503.54

46.

$$
\begin{array}{r}
1 + x + x^2 + \cdots \\
1 - x\,\overline{)\,1} \\
\underline{1 - x} \\
x \\
\underline{x - x^2} \\
x^2 \\
x^2 - x^3 \quad \text{etc.}
\end{array}
$$

48.

$$P = C\beta^n + c\beta^2 n + C\beta^3 n + \cdots$$

This is an infinite geometric sum $C(x + x^2 + x^3 + \cdots)$ where $x = \beta^n$.

$$
\begin{aligned}
P &= C[\beta^n + (\beta^n)^2 + (\beta^n)^3 + \cdots] \\
&= C\beta^n[1 + \beta^n + (\beta^n)^2 + \cdots] \\
&= C\beta^n \frac{1}{1 - \beta^n}
\end{aligned}
$$

in terms of β. In terms of i, substituting $1/(1 + i)$ for β and simplifying:

$$P = C\frac{1}{1/\beta^n - 1} = \frac{C}{(1 + i)^n - 1}$$

50. The precursor to Eq. 2-28 says $1 + 2x + 3x^2 + \cdots = 1/(1-x)^2$. Let $x = 1 - \alpha$.

$$L = \frac{\alpha}{2} + \alpha\left(1 - \frac{\alpha}{2}\right)[2 + 3x + 4x^2 + \cdots]$$

$$= \frac{\alpha}{2} + \alpha\left(1 - \frac{\alpha}{2}\right)\frac{1}{x}[2x + 3x^2 + 4x^3 + \cdots]$$

$$= \frac{\alpha}{2} + \alpha\left(1 - \frac{\alpha}{2}\right)\frac{1}{x}[1 + 2x + 3x^2 + 4x^3 + \cdots) - 1]$$

$$= \frac{\alpha}{2} + \alpha\left(1 - \frac{\alpha}{2}\right)\frac{1}{x}\left[\frac{1}{(1-x)^2} - 1\right]$$

$$= \frac{\alpha}{2} + \alpha\left(1 - \frac{\alpha}{2}\right)\frac{1}{1-\alpha}\left[\frac{1 - \alpha^2}{\alpha^2}\right]$$

$$= \frac{\alpha}{2} + \left(1 - \frac{\alpha}{2}\right)\frac{1 + \alpha}{\alpha}$$

$$= \frac{\alpha}{2} + \frac{\left(1 - \frac{\alpha}{2}\right)}{\alpha} + 1 - \frac{\alpha}{2}$$

$$= \left(1 - \frac{\alpha}{2}\right)/\alpha$$

52.

Day	A^- Payments	A^+ Advances	$I = iB_{\text{old}}$ Interest	$B = B_{\text{old}} + A^+ - A^- + I$ Balance
0	—	—	—	24,101.44
1	174,231.15	100,441.27	7.23	−49,681.21
2	101,475.16	129,388.40	−14.90	−21,782.87
3	118,031.22	101,276.99	−6.53	−38,543.63

54.

Interval t	Interest iB_{t-1}	Payment A_t	Balance $B_t = B_{t-1} + iB_{t-1} - A_t$
0	—	$-P$	P
1	iP	iP	$P + iP - iP = P$
2	iP	iP	$P + iP - iP = P$
$\vdots$	$\vdots$	$\vdots$	$\vdots$
n	iP	iP	P

The balance is always P, so does not depend on n.

56. 3 months; $A_3 = \$222.91$

58. Up about \$5.56; down about \$4.65

60. 20%

62. 40.154

64. \$222.23

66. $10

68. $325 per year

70. $3717.65

72. $595.91

74. (a) 18 keystrokes (b) Speeds of 4 keystrokes per second (0.25 seconds per keystroke) can be achieved with hours of practice, but 0.6 seconds per keystroke is fast enough.

76. 25%

78. (a) 12.950555% (b) 12.6825% (c) 19.25186%

80. 11.33287% continuous; 11.33462% daily

82. *Time in*

Months	Interest	Payment	Balance
0	—	−61,000	61,000
0.32	194.54	−40,000	101,194.54
0.38	60.43	−15,000	116,254.97
0.42	46.28	196,000	−79,698.75
0.91	−389.53	−196,000	115,911.72
1.30	450.68	−10,000	126,362.40
2.21	1149.38	74,211.15	53,300.63
3.01	425.98	53,726.61	0

84. Yes; a savings of $661,392.82

86. (a) It is worth $13,567.65. (b) $7623.16

88. Using Taylor series expansions:

$$\beta^{-\tau} = (1 + i) \quad = 1 + \tau i + \frac{\tau(\tau - 1)}{2!} i^2 + \frac{\tau(\tau - 1)(\tau - 2)}{3!} i^3 + \cdots$$

$$\beta^{\tau} = (1 + i)^{-\tau} = 1 - \tau i + \frac{\tau(\tau - 1)}{2!} i^2 - \frac{\tau(\tau - 1)(\tau - 2)}{3!} i^3 + \cdots$$

The sum of the two series is

$$\beta^{-\tau} + \beta^{\tau} = 2 + \frac{2\tau(\tau - 1)}{2!} i^2 + \text{terms of order } i^4$$

Hence $\beta^{-\tau} + \beta^{\tau} > 2$.

90. $62.93 absolute error (underestimate); −6.7%

92. In this case, the end-of-year convention does not cause a wrong decision.

94. No; present worth of prepaid plan is $1200, whereas worth of current plan is −$1136.51.

96.

$$P = \frac{A_1}{i} + \frac{G}{i^2} - \beta^n \left[\frac{A_1}{i} + \frac{nG}{i} + \frac{G}{i^2} \right]$$

Let $L = A_1/(G)$, so $A_1 = -LG$.

Let P_L denote P when $n = L$; let P_{L+1} denote P when $n = L + 1$.

$$P_L = \frac{-LG}{i} + \frac{G}{i^2} - \beta^L \left[\frac{-LG}{i} + \frac{LG}{i} + \frac{G}{i^2} \right] = \frac{-LG}{i} + \frac{G}{i^2} - \frac{\beta^L G}{i^2}$$

$$P_{L+1} = \frac{-LG}{i} + \frac{G}{i^2} - \beta^{L+1} \left[\frac{-LG}{i} + \frac{(L+1)G}{i} + \frac{G}{i^2} \right] =$$

$$\frac{-LG}{i} + \frac{G}{i^2} - \beta^{L+1} \left[\frac{G}{i} + \frac{G}{i^2} \right]$$

$$P_{L+1} - P_L = -\beta^L \left[\frac{\beta G}{i} + \frac{\beta G}{i^2} - \frac{G}{i^2} \right] = -\beta^L G \left[\frac{\beta}{i} + \frac{\beta}{i^2} - \frac{1}{i^2} \right]$$

The quantity in brackets is zero, so $P_{L+1} - P_L = 0$. To verify this, invoke

$$\frac{1}{i} = \frac{\beta}{1 - \beta} \quad \text{and} \quad \frac{1}{i^2} = \frac{\beta^2}{(1 - \beta)^2}$$

and simplify.

98. $86,053.17

100. (a) $1,833,333.33 (b) $1,322,748.21

102. P becomes $2,842,243.34.

104. $1696.85

106. $11,738.09

108. 20%

110. "Equivalent to," "surrogate banker," "indistinguishable from"

112. If Ahmad lost $35.71 now, he would make an extra $35.71 credit-card charge to cover the loss, and in 12 months this charge would increase his owed balance by $35.71(1.01)^{12} = \$40.24$ over what it would otherwise be.

With acceptance of the opportunity, Ahmad would charge the piano on his credit card, so that in 12 months his owed balance would be increased by $1500(1.01)^{12} = \$1690.24$ over what it would otherwise be. He would sell the piano, use the proceeds to pay off $1650 of the balance, leaving it $1690.24 - 1650 = \$40.24$ over what it would otherwise be.

114. (a)

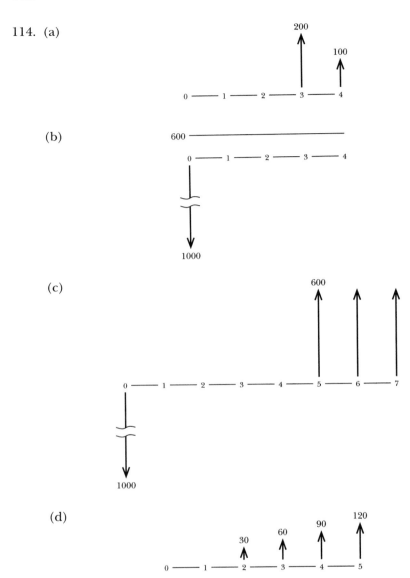

116. $3896.93

CHAPTER 3

2. Long-term lenders are hurt worst.

4. Expected CPI: 391.92

6. Actual inflation was 6.9252%, not 7%.

8. (a) 5.9028% (b) greatest j: 1974 to 1982; least j: 1982 to 1990.

10. 3.4843%

12. No, 29.6148%

14. Use $i = 13.6238\%$

16. (a) 13.9285% (b) $800

18. Cost of 1 is $5307.08; cost of 2 is $5558.74. Choose 1.

20. (a) Yes, it is worth about $922. (b) 10.57692% (c) 1.89282 K$ (d) $\{-6, -1.04, -1.0816, 14.623232\}$ at times $\{0, 1, 2, 3\}$, giving the same answer: 1.89282 K$ (e) 2.60301 K$

22. Applying inflation at 6%, the current-dollar amounts are (see Example E8 for data):

$$9075(1.06) \ = \$9{,}619.50 \text{ at time } 1$$
$$9075(1.06)^2 = \$10{,}196.67 \text{ at time } 2$$
$$9075(1.06)^3 = \$10{,}808.47 \text{ at time } 3$$

At $i = 15\%$ the present worth is

$$P = 9{,}619.50\left(\frac{1}{1.15}\right) + 10{,}196.67\left(\frac{1}{1.15}\right)^2 + 10{,}808.47\left(\frac{1}{1.15}\right)^3$$

$$= \underline{\$23{,}181.67}$$

as in the solution to Example E8.

24. New worth: $24,913.07

26. (a) 12.27% (b) $g = 3\%$; $v = -5.5\%$ (c) 12.27%

28. $38,373.56

30. (a) $v = -0.072308896$ (b) $1378.58 million

32. $2681.69

CHAPTER 4

2. Given

$$P = -I + \bar{A}\left(\frac{1 - \beta n}{r}\right) + S\beta^n$$

$I > 0$, $S > 0$, $0 < \beta < 1$, $n > 0$, $r > 0$. Recall

$$\beta = e^{-r}$$

$$\frac{dP}{dr} = \frac{\bar{A}}{r} - \bar{A}\frac{d}{dr}\left(\frac{e^{-rn}}{r}\right) + S\frac{de^{-rn}}{dr}$$

$$= \bar{A}\left(-\frac{1}{r^2} + \frac{rne^{-rn}}{r^2} + \frac{e^{-rn}}{r^2}\right) - Sne^{-rn}$$

Define $M = -1 + rne^{-rn} + e^{-rn}$. Since $r^2 > 0$, dP/dr is negative if $M < 0$. But $M < 0$ if $(1 + rn)e^{-rn} < 1$. But

$$(1 + rn)e^{-rn} = \frac{1 + rn}{e^{rn}} = \frac{1 + rn}{1 + rn + \cdots} < 1 \qquad \text{Q.E.D.}$$

4.

$$P = -I + A\left(\frac{1 - \beta^n}{i}\right) + S\beta^n = -I + \frac{A}{i} - \frac{A\beta^n}{i} + S\beta^n$$

$$\frac{dP}{dn} = 0 \Rightarrow \left(-\frac{A}{i} + S\right)\frac{d\beta^n}{dn} = 0 \Rightarrow S = \frac{A}{i} \quad \text{or} \quad \frac{d\beta^n}{dn} = 0$$

$$\frac{d\beta^n}{dn} = (\ln\beta)\beta^n < 0$$

because $\ln\beta < 0$, $\beta^n > 0$.

$$S > \frac{A}{i} \Rightarrow \frac{dP}{dn} < 0 \text{ sell early}$$

$$S < \frac{A}{i} \Rightarrow \frac{dP}{dn} > 0 \text{ sell late}$$

6. For a pure investment project, every $A_t \geq 0$ in

$$P = -I + \sum_{t=1}^{n} A_t\beta^t$$

$$\frac{dP}{d\beta} = \sum_{t=1}^{n} t\beta^{t-1}A_t \underline{\underline{\geq 0}} \qquad \text{since} \qquad t \geq 0, \; \beta^{t-1} \geq 0, \; A_t \geq 0$$

Every term of $dP/d\beta$ is nonnegative. To show that $dP/d\beta \geq 0$ implies $dP/di \leq 0$ is simple; thus $dP/d\beta \geq 0 \Rightarrow (dP/d\beta)(d\beta/di) \geq 0 \Rightarrow dP/di \leq 0$.

$$\beta = \frac{1}{1 + i}$$

$$\frac{d\beta}{di} = \frac{-1}{(1 + i)^2} < 0$$

8. Recall the definition of the present worth of $\{A_t\}$:

$$P\{A_t\} = \sum_{t=0}^{n} A_t\beta^t$$

If $\beta = 1/(1 + i^*)$ where i^* is the rate of return, then by definition $P\{A_t\} = 0$.

The opposite-signed cash-flow set $\{-A_t\}$ at the same β has worth

$$P\{-A_t\} = -P\{A_t\} = -0 = \underline{\underline{0}}$$

Thus i^* is the rate of return for $\{-A_t\}$.

At an exchange rate ϕ the cash-flow set expressed in an alternative monetary unit is $\{\phi A_d\}$.

$$P\{\phi A_d\} = \phi P\{A_d\} = \phi \times 0 = \underline{\underline{0}}$$

Thus i^* is the rate of return for $\{\phi A_d\}$.

10. 38.455%; 40%. The returns after 10 years are not greatly important in determining the approximate desirability.

12. If building codes were to begin requiring solar-energy retention walls, the supply of discarded glass bottles would quickly be depleted, and the required glass containers would cost money.

   The main reason butane is cheap is that a tax is added to the cost of gasoline to pay for roadways. Large-scale use of butane as automobile fuel would be taxed, making it cost essentially the same as gasoline.

   High-sugar agricultural waste, usable as livestock feed or not, is in limited supply. Any significant replacement of gasoline would require new supplies of ethanol, and growing high-sugar crops to make ethanol would certainly be more costly than pumping petroleum from the ground.

14. (b) It is an investment project if P decreases with i. Investigate near its RORs.
   (c) At 10%, the protagonist could borrow $11,518.05 from the surrogate banker to be repaid by the first 9 years of returns. Investing $5000, the protagonist could then deposit the remaining $6518.05. By year 10 it would grow to $16,906.14, or not enough to cover the disposal. The protagonist loses money at 10% interest ($P = -\$421.73$).

   At 20%, the protagonist could borrow $8061.93 on the returns, invest $8061.93 - \$5000 = \$3061.93$, and let it grow to $18,958.68 by time 10, where it more than covers the $18,000 net expenditure. The protagonist makes money at 20% interest ($P = \$154.83$).

   At 30%, the protagonist could borrow $6038.00 on the returns, invest $1038.00, and let it grow to $14,309.75, insufficient to cover the $18,000 net expenditure. The protagonist loses money at 30% interest ($P = -\$267.68$).

   Note: Many alternative surrogate-banker transaction schemes can be devised, all equally valid.
   (d) Assume the protagonist starts with $5000 and invests it in the project. Then, if a $2000 scaled-down version were implemented at time 1, there would be $4000 to invest at time 2, $6000 at time 3, $8000 at time 4, and so forth. Any interruption would mean that future "disposal and cleanup" obligations already incurred could not be met, and the kiting would collapse.

16. $P = -1000 + 3300\beta - 3630\beta^2 + 1331\beta^3$

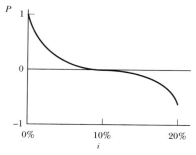

18. (a) 0.54826 years (b) \$37,583.56 (c) 1.133037024 years; the deficit starts at time $2 + k = 3.133037024$ yr. (d) \$500,107.60

20. From Eq. 4-9, with i replaced by i^* ("reinvestment rate is equal to the ROR"):

$$\sum_{t=0}^{n} A_t^+ (1 + i^*)^{n-t} = \sum_{t=0}^{n} A_t^- (1 + i')^{n-t} \qquad (1)$$

But if i^* is the ROR, it is by definition the rate at which present worth is zero; the present worth is the present worth of the positive cash flows minus that of the negative cash flows:

$$\sum_{t=0}^{n} A_t^+ \left(\frac{1}{1 + i^*} \right)^t - \sum_{t=0}^{n} A_t^- \left(\frac{1}{1 + i^*} \right)^t = 0$$

Multiplying both sides by $(1 + i^*)^n$:

$$\sum_{t=0}^{n} A_t^+ (1 + i^*)^{n-t} - \sum_{t=0}^{n} A_t^- (1 + i^*)^{n-t} = 0 \qquad (2)$$

Equations 1 and 2 are identical for $i' = i^*$, which proves the assertion.

22. (a) Rate of return: 12.31884%   (b) Rate of return: 16.8966%

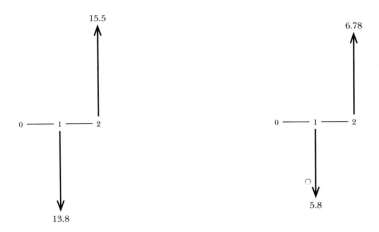

24. \$343,716.22

26. ROR: 11.7%; undesirable

28. The 11% alternative is more profitable.

30. 13%

32. This proposition is untrue and can easily be disproved by demonstrating a counterexample. Clearly the following two projects are investment projects:

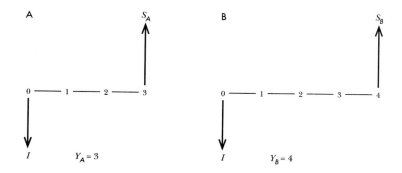

The proposition says, at some interest rate i, the fact that $Y_A < Y_B$ implies $P_A > P_B$. But we can easily set S_B much greater than S_A so that, at any finite i, $P_B > P_A$, thus disproving the proposition.

34. (a) Plan **X** has greater worth. (b) Neither plan necessarily has the greater worth.

36. Part 1: The cash-flow diagram and present-worth formula are:

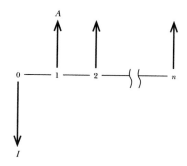

$$P = -I + A\left(\frac{1 - \beta^n}{i}\right)$$

$$= -I + A(P/A \ i,n)$$

$B/C = 1$ implies

$$\frac{A(P/A \ i_1,n)}{I} = 1$$

(*Remark:* i_1 is the rate of return, since the above implies $P = 0$.)

If A increases to a new value A_2, and the rate of return becomes i_2, then from the present-worth formula

$$0 = -I + A_2(P/A \ i_2,n)$$

$$A_2 = \frac{I}{(P/A \ i_2,n)}$$

The new B/C is the present worth of returns at i_1 divided by I:

$$B/C = \frac{A_2(P/A\ i_1,n)}{I} = \frac{I}{(P/A\ i_2,n)} \frac{(P/A\ i_1,n)}{I} = \frac{(P/A\ i_1,n)}{(P/A\ i_2,n)}$$

as asserted.

Part 2: For a Figure 4-1c profile:

$$\text{NPVI} = B/C - 1$$

For the same i_1 to i_2 increase as here:

$$B/C = \frac{(P/A\ i_1,n)}{(P/A\ i_2,n)}$$

38. (a) For $i = 0.08$, $n = 20$: $385,451.79. For $i = 0.12$, $n = 10$: $52,017.84. For $i = 0.15$, $n = 5$: $-$131,827.59 (b) 19.4257947%; 15.09841448%; 0%

40. (a) $X = 162.75$; $Y = 1100$ (b) Yes. Payback time indicates duration of illiquidity. ROR indicates rate at which the returns recover the investment, but greater returns offset greater times to keep the rate the same while the time spans vary.

42. RORs: (a) 10% (b) 10.858625% (c) 18.015%. Yes, the ROR indicates quickness of returns here.

44. (a) The "small" project has the greatest ROR, and thus is the most time-efficient. (b) "Small": 21.4%; "medium": 10.7%; "large": 7.2%. The "small" project has the greatest NPVI, and thus is the most capital-efficient.

CHAPTER 5

2. (a) A has the greater MARR. (b) Projects in plant B generally have a greater economic life.

4. $n = 3.938 \Rightarrow$ 4-yr horizon

6. It appears that the truck will not actually be sold, and of course it will not be necessary to spend $18,000 on a truck if one is available for $16,000. The proper salvage value is $16,000; the project has, as one of its consequences, the avoidance of a $16,000 cost at time 2.

8. (a) 18.429% (c) -0.04584 (d) a_0

10. (a) The infinite-horizon declining series has present worth

$$P = \sum_{t=1}^{\infty} a_0(1 + g)^t \beta^t = \sum_{t=1}^{\infty} a_0 \alpha^t = a_0 \frac{\alpha}{1 - \alpha} = a_0/s$$

where $\alpha = (1 + g)/(1 + i)$ and $s = (1 + i)/(1 + g) - 1$.

From Table 3-1 of Chapter 3, note $s = (i - g)/(1 + g)$, so that P can be expressed as

$$P = a_0/s = \frac{a_0(1 + g)}{i - g} = \frac{A_1}{i - g}$$

The finite equal-payment series that the engineers are asked to use should have the same present worth. Its present worth is

$$P = A_1\left(\frac{1 - \beta^n}{i}\right)$$

Equating $P = P$,

$$\frac{A_1}{i - g} = A_1\left(\frac{1 - \beta^n}{i}\right)$$

$$i = (i - g)(1 - \beta^n)$$

$$\beta^n = 1 - \frac{i}{i - g} = \frac{-g}{i - g}$$

$$n = \frac{\ln\left(\frac{-g}{i - g}\right)}{\ln \beta} = \frac{\ln\left(\frac{-g}{i - g}\right)}{-\ln(1 + i)} \qquad \underline{\text{the formula}}$$

(b) $n = 4.086 \Rightarrow 4$ yr (c) \$6815.21

14. $P_{\text{abandon}} = \$45,000$; $P_{\text{continue}} = \$43,000$; continue

16. The best size is #6.

18. (a) $P^{(B-A)}$ increases with i, so B − A is not an investment project. (From 25% to 30%, $P^{(B-A)}$ does decrease with i, but it does not decrease throughout the 10% to 30% range.)

(b) $P^{(A)} = \$1222.22$; $P^{(B)} = \$1336.84$; B − A is attractive.

20. B. Most likely, the reactor itself was somewhat overdesigned, and its overcapacity became a free good that could be exploited by relatively inexpensive upgrades of surrounding equipment. These upgrades would be more efficient than the original project, because most of the cost of providing increased yield was already sunk.

22. \$0.60/ton

24. A and B both have the disadvantage of treating the proposal's benefits as an increase in annual production, whereas for there to be an increase in production the demand would need to rise; a demand increase is not a consequence of this proposal. A and B also both have the disadvantage of requiring inquiry into widget selling prices and other data not related to the proposal's arena. C properly assumes that the annual production will remain the same, and it demands only data directly related to the proposal's arena; the proposal is to reduce manufacturing costs, and C is the best basis because it is the one that evaluates the reduction in manufacturing costs. *Note:* If a specific increase in demand were independently estimated, C would remain the best basis.

26.
1. "general and admin. cost"   fixed
2. "direct labor cost"   variable
3. "general and admin. cost"   fixed
4. "marketing cost"   fixed
5. "general and admin. cost"   fixed
6. "direct material cost"   variable
7. "direct material cost"   variable
8. "overhead cost"   fixed and variable
   (indirect labor,
   indirect material,
   fixed overhead)
9. "indirect labor"   variable
10. "general and admin. cost"   fixed

28.

No. of Boxing Machines	No. of Wrapping Machines	Boxing Capacity	Wrapping Capacity	Combined Capacity	Cost	Cost per Capacity
$\frac{3}{4}$	4	1050	1060	1050	$46,000	43.8
$\frac{4}{4}$	4	1400	1060	1060	$56,000	52.8
$\frac{4}{4}$	5	1400	1325	1325	$60,000	45.3
$\frac{4}{4}$	6	1400	1590	1400	$64,000	45.7

The two balances marked are more efficient than the suggested alternative.

30. Marginal (38%)

32. Choose 4-in. thickness. Any greater thicknesses are incrementally unprofitable. The results for the various thicknesses are:

Thickness, X (in.)	$P^{(X)}$	Thickness, X (in.)	$P^{(X)}$	
1	2125.91	7	3106.82	
2	3645.93	8	2239.14	
3	4474.41	9	1314.85	greatest
4	4701.71	10	344.65	thickness
5	4494.83	11	−637.45	profitable
6	3892.88			

most profitable → 4

34. (a) MC has a conservative conservation policy; PS's is liberal. (b) Yes; the project is attractive for PS, not attractive to MC. (c) MC

36. (a) $2304 (b) $v \geq 2.304$ $/unit; at the minimum v it is just barely profitable to do database work with the new DBMS. (c) $w = 2.88$ $/unit; the monthly benefit of the new DBMS is *greater* than if the idle time were used elsewhere.

38. (a) B is more attractive at lower interest rates. At extremely high interest rates, neither is attractive, but B is better. The claim is refuted. (b) Yes

40. (c) 9.54539%

42. $288,169.59

44. $438.69

46. The cheaper alternatives are (a) bag, (b) vial, and (c) bag.
    (d) $P^{(\text{bags-vials})} = 0 \Rightarrow d = 14.124456\%$ (e) They both cost $4.3165 per year.
    (f) Yes

48. (a) Buta (b) Buta (c) Obtain a Buta tire now and replace it with an Acme tire.

50. Where L is the present worth of revenues from selling the land,

τ	0	1	2	3
$P^{(\tau)}$	L	$40 + L$	$52.56 + L$	$46.67 + L$

52. $P^{(\tau)} = P_x^{(\tau)} + \beta P_y^{(n-\tau)}$ and $P^{(\tau+1)} = P_x^{(\tau+1)} + \beta^{\tau+1} P_y^{(n-\tau+1)}$

$P^{(\tau+1)} - P^{(\tau)}$ will contain the "x" terms for one more "x" return and the changes and shift in salvage value, as in Eq. 5-15:

$$X_{\tau+1}\beta^{\tau+1} + S(\tau + 1)\beta^{\tau+1} - S(\tau)\beta^{\tau}$$

$P^{(\tau+1)} - P^{(\tau)}$ will also "y" terms. $P_y^{(n-\tau)}$ loses its final term and is delay-shifted, so its worth at time τ becomes (when the switchover is at $\tau + 1$)

$$\beta(P_y^{(n-\tau)} - Y_{(n-\tau)}\beta^{(n-\tau)})$$

Hence

$$P^{(\tau+1)} - P^{(\tau)} = X_{\tau+1}\beta^{\tau+1} + S(\tau + 1)\beta^{\tau+1}$$
$$- S(\tau)\beta^{\tau} - \beta^{\tau}[-\beta P_y^{(n-\tau)} + Y_{n-\tau}\beta^{n-\tau} + P_y^{(n-\tau)}]$$
$$P^{(\tau+1)} - P^{(\tau)} = X_{\tau+1}\beta^{\tau+1} + S(\tau + 1)\beta^{\tau+1}$$
$$- S(\tau)\beta^{\tau} - \beta^{\tau}(1 - \beta)P_y^{(n-\tau)} - \beta^{\tau}Y_{n-\tau}\beta^{n-\tau}$$

Now the criterion is $0 \geq P^{(\tau+1)} - P^{(\tau)}$. Divide by β^{τ}.

$$\boxed{0 \geq X_{\tau+1}\beta + S(\tau + 1)\beta - S(\tau) - (1 - \beta)P_y^{(n-\tau)} - Y_{n-\tau}\beta^{n-\tau}}$$

54. (a) From Eq. 5-16 the differential criterion is for h to be the smallest τ for which

$$0 \geq R\beta + s_0\gamma^{\tau+1}\beta - s_0\gamma^{\tau}$$
$$0 \geq R\beta - s_0\gamma^{\tau}(1 - \gamma\beta) \qquad (1)$$
$$\gamma^{\tau} \geq \frac{\beta R/s_0}{1 - \gamma\beta}$$
$$\tau \geq \frac{\ln\left(\dfrac{\beta R/s_0}{1 - \gamma\beta}\right)}{\ln \gamma} = \underline{\underline{h}} \qquad (2)$$

(c) 69.66, or 70, months

60. A simple Basic-language program to determine the replacement age that minimizes $-A^{(\tau)}$ can be written as follows:

10	D = 0.12	D is d
20	B = 1/(1 + D)	B is β
30	FOR T = 1 TO 10	T is τ
40	P = 4	P is $-P_1^{(\tau)}$
50	FOR Y = 1 TO T	Y is θ
60	P = P + 81.5*(8 − 0.6*Y)^(−1.8)*B^Y	
70	NEXT Y	
80	A = P*D/(1 − B^T)	A is $-A^{(\tau)}$
90	PRINT T, P, A	
100	NEXT T	

The results of running the program:

τ	$-P_1^{(\tau)}$	$-A^{(\tau)}$	
1	5.983	6.701	
2	8.045	4.760	
3	10.218	4.254	
4	12.549	4.132	$\tau = 4$ is optimal
5	15.102	4.189	
6	17.970	4.371	
7	21.304	4.668	
⋮			

62. Results from the output of a simple computer program with $d = 0.06$ and $I = 10000$:

τ	$A^{(\tau)}$	W_τ	
⋮	⋮	⋮	
5	3329.19	4213.59	
6	3455.98	3834.37	
7	3501.06	3489.27	$A^{(\tau)} > W_\tau$ for $\tau = 7$
8	3499.87	3175.24	
⋮			

64. If Blatzworth has MARR of less than 9% in real-interest terms, the delay is attractive; otherwise it is better to act immediately.

66. Here is a program written in the Basic language; the names of variables may not be obvious. D represents d; B represents β; N represents n; T1, T2, and T3 represent τ_0, $\tau_0 + \tau_1$, and $\tau_0 + \tau_1 + \tau_2$, that is, the start times of the three challengers; I1, I2, and I3 represent $I(\tau_0)$, $I(\tau_0 + \tau_1)$, and $I(\tau_0 + \tau_1 + \tau_2)$; PI represents the discounted total investment; R1, R2, and R3 represent $R_1(\tau_1)$, $R_2(\tau_2)$, and $R_3(\tau_3)$ where $\tau_3 = n$, and these are each initialized to zero and summed in a loop in which TH represents the age θ; R represents the discounted total of returns; P represents the present worth in Eq. 5-29; AP represents $(A/P\ d,n)$; A represents the annual worth of the sequence of coverage of the entire horizon, which (or P) is the quantity to be optimized. Following the program listing is a run, in which it

is found by exhaustive trials that 3, 13, 19 is the optimal set of replacement times, yielding an annual worth of $452.69.

```
list
10 REM E51
20 D=.1
30 B=1/(1+D)
40 N=22
50 INPUT T1,T2,T3
60 REM investments
70 REM actual
80 I1=2000+7000*(.85)^T1
90 I2=2000+7000*(.85)^T2
100 I3=2000+7000*(.85)^T3
110 REM discounted total
120 PI=I1*B^T1+I2*B^T2+I3*B^T3
130 REM returns
140 R1=0
150 FOR TH=1 TO T2-T1
160 R1=R1+(2000-100*TH)*B^TH
170 NEXT TH
180 R2=0
190 FOR TH=1 TO T3-T2
200 R2=R2+(2000-100*TH)*B^TH
210 NEXT TH
220 R3=0
230 FOR TH=1 TO N-T3
240 R3=R3+(2000-100*TH)*B^TH
250 NEXT TH
260 REM discounted total
270 R=R1*B^T1+R2*B^T2+R3*B^T3
280 REM overall present worth
290 P=-PI+R
300 AP = D/(1-B^N)
305 A=P*AP
310 REM coverage includes from 0 to n
320 PRINT P,,A
330 GOTO 50
Ok
run
? 3,9,15
 3603.681                      410.8378
? 3,9,16
 3644.679                      415.5119
? 3,9,17
 3646.465                      415.7154
? 3,9,18
 3615.428                      412.177
? 3,10,18
 3823.167                      435.8603
```

```
? 3,10,17
 3836.218                              437.3483
? 3,10,16
 3814.65                               434.8893
? 3,11,17
 3934.377                              448.5388
? 3,11,18
 3939.311                              449.1014
? 3,11,19
 3913.57                               446.1667
? 4,11,19
 3819.013                              435.3868
? 4,12,19
 3908.131                              445.5467
? 4,13,20
 3910.794                              445.8502
? 3,12,20
 3934.162                              448.5143
? 3,12,19
 3970.824                              452.6941
? 3,12,20
 3934.162                              448.5143
?   3,13,20
 3944.521                              449.6953
? 3,13,19
 3966.32                               452.1806
?
Break in 50
Ok
rem 3,12,19 seems to be optimal for horizon n=22
```

68.

t	A_t	
⋮	⋮	
5	642.47	
6	684.75	
7	703.18	Purchase the machine at time $\underline{\underline{7}}$.
8	688.22	
⋮	⋮	

CHAPTER 6

2. $P^{(A)} = \$935.28$; $P^{(B)} = \$777.19$. The point is verified; the shorter horizon at Plant B causes rejection of a project accepted at Plant A.

4. Maximize $26x_1 + 30x_2 + 100x_3 + 60x_4$
   subject to $30x_1 + 40x_2 + 90x_3 + 50x_4 \leq 100$
   and $x_j \in \{0,1\}$ for $j = 1, \ldots, 4$

6. (a) The projects in decreasing NPVI order are (4, 3, 1, 2). Choose 4 and 3. (b) 4, 3 and 1; 4, 3, and 2 would be better.

8. (a) A, B, and C; yes (b) B, C, and D; no

10. Scenario A: $7840; scenario B: $12,490.18; Yes.

12. (a) BC (b) AC (c) CA (d) 1. ROR; 2. MARR; 3. MARR; 4. ROR

14. (a) AB (b) efficiency

16. (a) 18% interest: level 1; 20% interest: level 1; 22% interest: level 1; 24% interest: No level should be proposed. (b) Level 1 for 14% MARR (c) 16.67%

18. (a) The largest version that earns at MARR or greater over smaller versions will be submitted for each opportunity. (b) 16% (c) 16%; first increment

20. 3%

22. (a) A: 33.3%; B: 50%; C: 60%; A − B: 42.857% (b) 65% (c) Leveraged C: $15,000; unleveraged C: $16,666.67 (d) Yes (e) $13,333.33 (f) $P_L^{(AC)} = \$18,333.33$ (g) AC leveraged

24. (a) BC yields $30,200 (b) Yes

26. 72%

CHAPTER 7

2. (a) A: option 2; B: option 1. The overall proportion of recycled paper is 49.5%. The extra cost is $270/day. (b) A: option 1; B: option 2. The overall proportion of recycled paper is 56.4%. The total daily extra operating costs are $210/day. The total fees paid are $220/day. (c) Yes (d) A is better off by $45/day. B is better off by $5/day. The Wood Authority is better off by $10/day. The public is better off, since more recycling is done.

4. Owners have the special status in decision making in capitalistic societies. The public has the special status in decision making in socialistic or communist societies (and in public-sector decision making in any society).

6. (a) No (b) $100,000

8. 0.625 ideals/stogie. The loss to the stogie industry is 3.75 million ideals per year. The loss to society due to tax inefficiency is 0.75 million ideals per year.

10. After inflation worth: −$4,864,012.76, undesirable. Before inflation worth: −$30,340,742.05, very undesirable.

12. (a) Current dollars

14. (a)

Alternative	$P = B - C$	B/C
A	−$1,150,000	0.952
B	−$6,490,000	0.834
C	−$5,550,000	0.895

(b) The do-nothing alternative is best. Alternative **A** is closest to being attractive.
(c)

Alternative	$P = B - C$	B/C
A	$6,846,000	1.348
B	$3,900,000	1.115
C	$9,902,000	1.220

(d) **C** has greatest worth: $B - C \cong \$9.9$ million. **A** is most efficient: $B - C \cong \$1.35$ million. (e) **A**

16. (a) $M > 1.055$ (b) There is no range of M for which **C** is more efficient.

18. (a) Program **2** (b) Action 1 is least appropriate.

20. The list of bills in decreasing B/C order is (7, 4, 6, 3, 1, 2, 5).

22. (a) Program **1** is more cost effective. (b) Choose do-nothing.

24. (a) Using nonmonetary/monetary B/C split, the second program gives more particulate-count reduction per dollar. (b) A value of harm

26. (a) It is neither a benefit nor a cost, because it is a transfer payment. (b) Harder (c) Yes (d) Regional: 15; national: 1.5

CHAPTER 8

2. 10 years

4. $v \leq 0.001059759 \cong 1\%$

6. (a) The price of electrical energy must be > 0.039 $/kW-hr. (b) The number of operating hours per year must be < 1955 hr/yr. (c) $0.14/yr

8. (a) $390 decrease (b) $342.71 decrease (c) The interplay between n and A is nonlinear.

12. There is no discrepancy because P is linear in T.

14. No, since $E(P) = -\$7000$

16. (a) $E(P) = \$358.68$ (b) 100%

18. (a) $E(P) = \$119.54466$ million (b) $E(t) = 3.666\overline{6}$; $P = \$116.8$ million (c) $137.26233

20. (a) Yes; $3.7 is outside the three-σ range. (b) No; $2 is inside the three-$\sigma$ range.

22. Expected worth: 158.30; minimum worth: 77.8

24. **A**

26. $E(P) = -23.266568$

28. $58.82; $-$10.00; 0.008474576

30. (a) Yes, it is worth $243.20188. (b) No; worth is -5056.63. (c) 6.91286 years

32.

Month	Expected Balance	Expected Interest	Expected Payment
0	0	—	−1000
1	1000	9.58	340.42
2	669.16	6.41	339.74
3	335.83	3.22	339.06
ending	0.01 (roundoff error)		

34. $121,968.43

38. $728,790.05

CHAPTER 9

2. $6985.55

4. $9624.88

6. $21,400

8. $98,064.35

10. $853.62

12. 9 or 10 years. If the warehouse earns $\bar{A}$ per year, it would expect to earn a total present worth of about $4.354\bar{A}$ in the first 7 years and $0.734\bar{A}$ afterward. If it lasts exactly 9 years, it would earn about $0.12\bar{A}$ less; if 10 years, about $0.12\bar{A}$ more.

14. If there were no delay loss, the patent would earn royalties having a present worth of $319,213.73 (under the continuous timing convention). But there is a $40,000/yr continuous delay loss for t years, where t is exponentially distributed with mean two years. The loss has, for fixed t, a present worth of $40,000(1 - e^{15r})/r$. From Eq. 9-19, its expected worth is determined by letting r go to $r + 1/\theta$. The result is $67,182.97, so the expected worth of royalties is the difference, which is about $252,000.

16. Discounting the first three years' cash flows at r and later ones at $r + 1/17$, the result is about $1162, which is about $1088 more than before.

18. Gamma life, $k = 5$, $\theta = 2.1$ year. $E(P) \Rightarrow \$3,730,000$.

20. 12, 10, 15

22. Starting with $z_0 = 10$, we get

25	20	11	14	13	24	31	18	1	28	19	22	21	0	7	26
9	4	27	30	29	8	15	2	17	12	3	6	5	16	23	10

24. (a) u^2 (b) In thousands of dollars: 215.6, −0.6, 151.3, 224.2, 184.2, . . .

26. $93,748.61 and $29.931.37

28. Experiment: a full day's operation. Run: a set of experiments.

30. (a) Approximately −$951.85 (b) Approximately $163.29

32. (a) $\{\pi_4, \ldots, \pi_7\} = \{0.1488, 0.1612, 0.0690, 0.6210\}$ (b) $\{t_4, \ldots, t_7\} = \{2,5,1,4\}$
    (c) $\{P_2, \ldots, P_7\} = \{-7.686, -18.818, 3.443, 4.004, 13.173, 8.059\}$ (d) 2.174

34. (a) 1 (b) 0.1276 (c) 0.475

36. Always try to sell; expected present worth is $1.606 million.

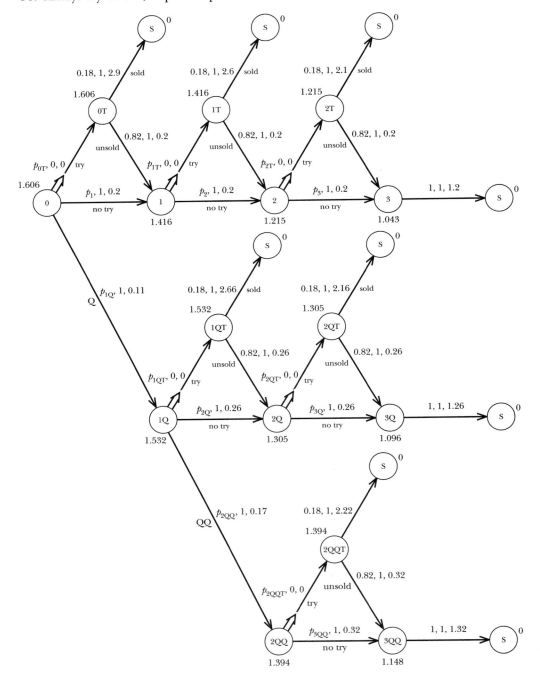

38. $V_1 = 181.6912$ (and $V_2 = 172.3618$)

40. $262.40

42. $V = (22{,}399.91 \ 16{,}481.41 \ 9194.98 \ 0)$

CHAPTER 10

2. 42%

4. Yes, the higher rate magnifies the comparison. No, taxation lags do not significantly affect the answer.

6. $P_{at} = -50 + T50\beta^6 + (1 - T)15(P/A \ 15\%,6) + (1 - T)20\beta^6;$
   $P_{at} = -50 + (1 - T)15(P/A \ 15\%,6) + 20\beta^6 - T_c(-30)\beta^6;$
   $-2.10517 \ K\$ \cong -2 \ K\$$

8. (a) $10/6 = 1.6667$ (b) $4.7785 \ K\$ \cong 5 \ K\$$

   (c) $P(D_t) \cong \beta^L \sum_t D_t$

12. $\{D_t\} = \{1142.86, 952.38, 761.90, 571.43, 380.95, 190.48\}; \ L = 2.6667$ yr

14. Equal dwell times; $P\{D_t^{(1)}\} = \$670.43; \ P\{D_t^{(2)}\} = \$676.09$

16. $t = \ln(0.005/B_0)/\ln(1 - \alpha); \ 54.7$ yr

18. Switched DB schedule: 2.2109 years; perpetual DB: 2.6667 years

20.

t	$D_t^{DDB} = \alpha B_{t-1}$	SL Alternative D_t: $(B_{t-1} - S_n)/(n - t + 1 + 0.5)$	Chosen D_t	B_t
0				100.00
1	20.00	18.18	20.00	80.00
2	32.00	17.78	32.00	48.00
3	19.20	13.71	19.20	28.80
4	11.52	11.52	11.52	17.28
5	6.91	11.52	11.52	5.76
6	2.30	5.76	5.76	0

22. $L = 2$ yr

24. (a) $14,266,510.93 (b) Yes, with a worth of $54,704.65

26. Yes; $P_{at} = \$900$

28. Present worth: $5769.33

t	$D_t = \alpha B_{t-1}$	B_t
0		10,000
1	2000	8,000
2	1600	6,400
3	1280	5,120
4	1024	4,096

5	819.20	3,276.80
6	655.36	2,621.44
7	524.29	2,097.15
8	419.43	1,677.72
9	335.54	1,342.18
10	268.44	1,073.74
11	214.75	858.99
12	858.99 (not 171.80)	0

30. $\Omega = 0.819643$; $I_{nat} = \$569.23$

32. $P\{D_j\} = \$549.2405$; $\Omega = 0.588995$; agrees

34. (a) $31,760 (b) 25.0% (market rate; real rate of return is 21.4%) (c) 25%, or less if the project is considered typical of a good investment rather than an ordinary-course-of-business project.

36. (a) Approximately $108,230, made up of about $21,150 for the $25,500 depreciated portion and about $87,080 for the $155,000 expensed portion (b) About $141,020 (c) Repair is better, by the difference in the two above answers. But on a before-tax basis, replacement is better by $10,500.

38. $\Omega \cong 0.5728$ using Eq. 10-32

INDEX